Beginning VB.NET 2nd Edition

D0144485

Matthew Reynolds
Richard Blair
Jonathan Crossland
Thearon Willis

Wrox Press Ltd. ®

Reprinted: February 2003

Published by Wrox Press Ltd,
Arden House, 1102 Warwick Road, Acocks Green,
Birmingham, B27 6BH, UK
Printed in the United States
ISBN 1-86100-761-2

Trademark Acknowledgments

Wrox has endeavored to provide trademark information about all the companies and products mentioned in this book by the appropriate use of capitals. However, Wrox cannot guarantee the accuracy of this information.

Credits

Authors
Matthew Reynolds
Richard Blair
Jonathan Crossland
Thearon Willis

Technical Reviewers
Panangipally Anand
Alice Backer
Billy Cravens
Robin Dewson
Damien Foggon
Zach Greenvoss
Scott Hanselman
Hope Hatfield
Sunil Kumar
Pramod Kumar Singh
Ron Landers
Wendy Lanning
Dianna Leech
Dale Onyon
Troy Proudfoot
Daniel Read
Scott Robertson
Rita Ruban
Sean M Schade
Larry Schoeneman
David Schultz
Andrew Stopford
David M Williams
Carvin Wilson
Warren Wiltsie

Additional Material
David Schultz

Technical Architect
Kate Hall

Commissioning Editor
Paul Jeffcoat

Technical Editors
David Barnes
Victoria Blackburn
Mike Foster
Gareth Oakley

Managing Editors
Sarah Drew
Louay Fatoohi

Author Agents
Sarah Bowers
Avril Corbin
Laura Jones

Project Managers
Beth Sacks
Rob Hesketh
Christianne Bailey

Production Coordinator
Sarah Hall

Production Assistants
Abbie Forletta
Neil Lote

Cover
Natalie O'Donnell

Index
Martin Brooks

Proof Reader
Chris Smith

About the Authors

Matthew Reynolds

After working with Wrox Press on a number of projects since 1999, Matthew is now an in-house author for Wrox Press writing about and working with virtually all aspects of Microsoft .NET. He's also a regular contributor to Wrox's ASPToday and C#Today, and Web Services Architect. He lives and works in North London and can be reached on matthewr@wrox.com.

For Fanjeev Sarin.

Thanks very much to the following for their support and assistance in writing this book: Len, Edward, Darren, Alex, Jo, Tim, Clare, Martin, Niahm, Tom, Ollie, Amir, Gretchen, Ben, Brandon, Denise, Rob, Waggy, Mark, Elaine, James, Zoe, Faye, and Sarah. And, also thanks to my new friends at Wrox, who include Charlotte, Laura, Karli, Dom S, Dom L, Ian, Kate, Joy, Pete, Helen, Vickie, John, Dave, Adam, Craig, Jake, Julian, and Paul.

Richard Blair

Richard is Web Application Architect specializing in Microsoft Web Technologies, focusing on emerging technology and its impact on business and development. Key areas that he has helped clients evaluate include: streamlining the electronic business process, expanding access to vital information, and creating usable systems. He now works as a Senior Consultant for SEI-Information Technology. Besides his consulting work, he has also co-authored *Professional ASP XML, Beginning Visual Basic .NET*, and *Professional VB.NET*, all published by Wrox Press Ltd.

Richard has a dual concentration bachelor's degree from the University of Michigan in English Literature and Theatre, so not only is he a Web Architect, he could play one on TV.

Richard welcomes questions and comments at richblair@hotmail.com.

I am grateful for the love and support of my family (Kathy, Graehme, Thomas) and my furry housemates (Grover, Squeakie, and Fidget). I would also like to thank all the wonderful people at Wrox Press who have allowed me to finally justify my degree in Literature.

Jonathan Crossland

Jonathan Crossland is co-author of *Professional Windows DNA, Professional VB.NET*, and *Beginning VB.NET*. He is currently working at Yokogawa Electric Corporation in the UK, where he is happily involved with the creation of software for the Batch manufacturing industry. Jonathan has been working in and out of various software technologies for eight years now, and spends most of his time in C# and ASP.NET. Jonathan also works with VB, VB.NET, and web technologies such as JavaScript, DHTML, XML, ASP, and of course, writing Web Services.

I would like to thank all at Wrox Press for giving me the opportunity to share my knowledge with so many. I would also like to thank my wife and my son (who is currently learning his first language) who both have provided me with so much support.

Thearon Willis

Thearon began his career in computers in 1980 as a computer operator. During the fall of 1980 he took a course in BASIC programming using the Radio Shack TSR-80 computer and has been hooked on programming ever since.

After learning the BASIC language, Thearon moved on to learn COBOL and began writing programs to help automate some of his daily tasks as a computer operator. Advancing his career, Thearon became an Operations Analyst and learned several other languages to assist in his job.

In 1989, Thearon moved into Systems Programming and started programming in S370 assembler language. He coded batch programs in assembler language and then moved on to code CICS programs. The Help Desk and Network Operations used these batch and on-line programs to perform some of their daily tasks, such as monitoring CICS printers and polling sales. During this time, he started working with relational databases on the mainframe and immediately saw the benefits that relational databases provided.

Between the years of 1988 and 1993, Thearon learned several more programming languages, which include QBASIC, Pascal and C++. Thearon decided that he enjoyed programming so much that he switched his career path and became a developer full time.

The first application that Thearon worked on was written in assembler language and included over 70 assembler programs. To help automate some of the tasks that were performed by the department that used this application, he wrote several programs in Visual Basic. One of these programs read and processed data from message queues that were populated from the mainframe and performed automated balancing.

Thearon first began working with Visual Basic in version 3.0. After version 4 was released he switched his career from the mainframe to client-server development. He still enjoys working with relational databases and uses SQL Server as the backend to all of his applications that store and retrieve data.

Thearon currently works as a senior consultant and develops intranet applications using ASP, DHTML, XML, JavaScript, VBScript, VB COM components, and SQL Server. He lives with his wife Margie and daughter Stephanie in the Raleigh, North Carolina area.

As always, I want to thank my wife Margie for her for the patience she has shown while I write one book after another. I would also like to thank my daughter Stephanie for her patience. Without their support, none of this would be possible.

Table of Contents

Table of Contents

Table of Contents

Table of Contents

Introduction

Visual Basic .NET is Microsoft's latest version of the highly popular Visual Basic, a product based on the easy-to-learn BASIC language. Visual Basic .NET's strengths lie in its ease of use and the speed at which you can put together your own applications for the Windows operating system.

In the past, Visual Basic has been used largely to create applications with a rich user interface including buttons, lists, and drop-down boxes. In this book, we will show you how to incorporate all of these things into your applications, and we will also show you where we think the *future* of programming for Windows will be.

With the introduction of Microsoft's .NET Framework, there has never been a more exciting time to learn Visual Basic. For the first time, Visual Basic programmers have access to full object-orientation in their programs, a powerful technique for handling errors that arise, and the ability to incorporate programs that exist on the Internet into their applications. Exciting times indeed!

This book will give you a thorough grounding in the basics of programming using Visual Basic .NET; from there the world is your oyster.

Who Is This Book For?

This book is designed to teach you how to write useful programs in Visual Basic .NET as quickly and easily as possible.

There are two kinds of beginners for whom this book is ideal:

❑   You're **a beginner to programming** and you've chosen Visual Basic .NET as the place to start. That's a great choice! Visual Basic .NET is not only easy to learn, it's fun to use and very powerful.

❑   You can program in another language but you're a **beginner to .NET programming**. Again, you've made a great choice! Whether you've come from Fortran or VB6, you'll find that this book quickly gets you up to speed on what you need to know to get the best from Visual Basic .NET.

What Does This Book Cover?

Visual Basic .NET offers a great deal of functionality, in both tools and language. No book could ever cover Visual Basic .NET in its entirety – you'd need a library of books. What this book aims to do is to get you started as quickly and easily as possible. It shows you the roadmap, so to speak, of what there is and where to go. Once we've taught you the basics of creating working applications (creating the windows and boxes, how your code should handle unexpected events, what object-oriented programming is and how to use it in your applications, etc.) we'll show you some of areas you might want to try your hand at next:

❑ Chapters 15 and 16 provide a taster of programming with databases and so cover Access, SQL Server, and ADO.NET

❑ Chapter 17 discusses how to use web forms to create your own ASP.NET applications for the Web

❑ Chapter 18 provides a brief introduction to XML; a powerful tool for integrating your applications with others – regardless of the language they were written in

❑ Chapter 19 introduces you to web services, a technology whereby functionality offered on the Internet can be accessed by your applications and seamlessly integrated into them

What Do I Need to Run Visual Basic .NET?

Apart from a willingness to learn, all you'll need for the first 14 chapters are a PC running Windows 2000, XP, or NT4 Server, Internet Explorer, and of course:

❑ Microsoft Visual Studio .NET

   or

❑ Microsoft Visual Basic .NET Standard Edition

As the later chapters cover more advanced subject areas, you will need further software to get the best out of them:

❑ Chapter 15 requires Microsoft Access 2000.

❑ For Chapter 16, you will need to have access to SQL Server 7 or SQL Server 2000.

   If you don't have the full version of SQL Server 2000, you can use MSDE (Microsoft Data Engine) instead. MSDE is a cut-down version of SQL Server. A version compatible with SQL Server 7 is available with Office 2000 Professional and Premium editions, and a version compatible with SQL Server 2000 is available with Office XP. The big difference between MSDE and the full version of SQL Server is that MSDE does not have a user interface – the good news is that this difference has no impact on the exercises in Chapter 16.

❑ Chapters 17 and 19 rely on ASP.NET technology so you will need IIS 5 (which comes with Windows 2000 and Windows XP).

Don't worry if you don't have these products already and want to wait a while before you purchase them. You should still find that you get a *lot* out of this book.

Conventions

We've used a number of different styles of text and layout in this book to help differentiate between the different kinds of information. Here are examples of the styles we used and an explanation of what they mean.

1. Each step has a number.

2. Follow the steps through.

3. Then read *How It Works* to find out what's going on.

> **These boxes hold important, not-to-be forgotten, mission-critical details that are directly relevant to the surrounding text.**

Background information, asides, and references appear in text like this.

Bullets appear indented, with each new bullet marked as follows:

❑ **Important words** are in a bold type font

❑ Words that appear on the screen, or in menus like the File or Window, are in a similar font to the one you would see on a Windows desktop

❑ Keys that you press on the keyboard like *Ctrl* and *Enter*, are in italics

Code has several styles. If it's a word that we're talking about in the text – for example, when discussing a For ... Next loop, it's in this font. If it's a block of code that can be typed as a program and run, then it's also in a gray box:

```
Private Sub btnAdd_Click(ByVal sender As System.Object, _
          ByVal e As System.EventArgs) Handles btnAdd.Click

    Dim n As Integer
    n = 27

    MessageBox.Show(n)

End Sub
```

Sometimes we'll see code in a mixture of styles, like this:

```
Private Sub btnAdd_Click(ByVal sender As System.Object, _
          ByVal e As System.EventArgs) Handles btnAdd.Click

    Dim n As Integer
    n = 27
```

```
n = n + 2

MessageBox.Show(n)

End Sub
```

In cases like this, the code with a white background is code we are already familiar with; the line highlighted in gray is a new addition to the code since we last looked at it.

Customer Support

We always value hearing from our readers, and we want to know what you think about this book: what you liked, what you didn't like, and what you think we can do better next time. You can send us your comments, either by returning the reply card in the back of the book, or by e-mail to feedback@wrox.com. Please be sure to mention the book title in your message.

How to Download the Sample Code for the Book

When you visit the Wrox site, http://www.wrox.com/, simply locate the title through our Search facility or by using one of the title lists. Click on Download in the Code column, or on Download Code on the book's detail page.

The files that are available for download from our site have been archived using WinZip. When you have saved the attachments to a folder on your hard drive, you need to extract the files using a de-compression program such as WinZip or PKUnzip. When you extract the files, the code is usually extracted into chapter folders. When you start the extraction process, ensure your software (WinZip, PKUnzip, etc.) is set to use folder names.

Errata

We've made every effort to make sure that there are no errors in the text or in the code. However, no one is perfect and mistakes do occur. If you find an error in one of our books, like a spelling mistake or a faulty piece of code, we would be very grateful for feedback. By sending in errata, you may save another reader hours of frustration, and of course, you will be helping us provide even higher quality information. Simply e-mail the information to support@wrox.com; your information will be checked and if correct, posted to the errata page for that title, or used in subsequent editions of the book.

To find errata on the web site, go to http://www.wrox.com/, and simply locate the title through our Advanced Search or title list. Click on the Book Errata link, which is below the cover graphic on the book's detail page.

E-mail Support

If you wish to directly query a problem in the book with an expert who knows the book in detail then e-mail support@wrox.com, with the title of the book and the last four numbers of the ISBN in the subject field of the e-mail. A typical e-mail should include the following things:

❑ The **title of the book, last four digits of the ISBN (7312)**, and **page number** of the problem in the Subject field

❑ Your **name**, **contact information**, and the **problem** in the body of the message

We *won't* send you junk mail. We need the details to save your time and ours. When you send an e-mail message, it will go through the following chain of support:

❑ Customer Support – Your message is delivered to our customer support staff, who are the first people to read it. They have files on most frequently asked questions and will answer anything general about the book or the web site immediately.

❑ Editorial – Deeper queries are forwarded to the technical editor responsible for that book. They have experience with the programming language or particular product, and are able to answer detailed technical questions on the subject.

❑ The Authors – Finally, in the unlikely event that the editor cannot answer your problem, they will forward the request to the author. We do try to protect the author from any distractions to their writing; however, we are quite happy to forward specific requests to them. All Wrox authors help with the support on their books. They will e-mail the customer and the editor with their response, and again all readers should benefit.

The Wrox Support process can only offer support to issues that are directly pertinent to the content of our published title. Support for questions that fall outside the scope of normal book support, is provided via the community lists of our http://p2p.wrox.com/ forum.

p2p.wrox.com

For author and peer discussion, join the P2P mailing lists. Our unique system provides **programmer to programmer™** contact on mailing lists, forums, and newsgroups, all in addition to our one-to-one e-mail support system. If you post a query to P2P, you can be confident that it is being examined by the many Wrox authors and other industry experts who are present on our mailing lists. At p2p.wrox.com you will find a number of different lists that will help you, not only while you read this book, but also as you develop your own applications. Particularly appropriate to this book are the beginning_vb and vb_dotnet lists.

To subscribe to a mailing list just follow these steps:

1. Go to http://p2p.wrox.com/.

2. Choose the appropriate category from the left menu bar.

3. Click on the mailing list you wish to join.

4. Follow the instructions to subscribe and fill in your e-mail address and password.

5. Reply to the confirmation e-mail you receive.

6. Use the subscription manager to join more lists and set your e-mail preferences.

Why This System Offers the Best Support

You can choose to join the mailing lists or you can receive them as a weekly digest. If you don't have the time, or facility, to receive the mailing list, then you can search our online archives. Junk and spam mails are deleted, and your own e-mail address is protected by the unique Lyris system. Queries about joining or leaving lists, and any other general queries about lists, should be sent to listsupport@p2p.wrox.com.

NING VB.NET 2ND EDITION BEGINNING VB.NET 2ND ED
NING VB.NET 2ND EDITION BEGINNING VB.NET 2ND ED
NING VB.NET 2ND EDITION BEGINNING VB.NET 2ND ED
NING VB.NET 2ND EDITION BEGINNING VB.NET 2ND ED
NING VB.NET 2ND EDITION BEGINNING VB.NET 2ND ED
NING VB.NET 2ND EDITION BEGINNING VB.NET 2ND ED
NING VB.NET 2ND EDITION BEGINNING VB.NET 2ND ED
NING VB.NET 2ND EDITION BEGINNING VB.NET 2ND ED
NING VB.NET 2ND EDITION BEGINNING VB.NET 2ND ED
NING VB.NET 2ND EDITION BEGINNING VB.NET 2ND ED
NING VB.NET 2ND EDITION BEGINNING VB.NET 2ND ED
NING VB.NET 2ND EDITION BEGINNING VB.NET 2ND ED
NING VB.NET 2ND EDITION BEGINNING VB.NET 2ND ED
NING VB.NET 2ND EDITION BEGINNING VB.NET 2ND ED
NING VB.NET 2ND EDITION BEGINNING VB.NET 2ND ED
NING VB.NET 2ND EDITION BEGINNING VB.NET 2ND ED
NING VB.NET 2ND EDITION BEGINNING VB.NET 2ND ED
NING VB.NET 2ND EDITION BEGINNING VB.NET 2ND ED
NING VB.NET 2ND EDITION BEGINNING VB.NET 2ND ED
NING VB.NET 2ND EDITION BEGINNING VB.NET 2ND ED
NING VB.NET 2ND EDITION BEGINNING VB.NET 2ND ED
NING VB.NET 2ND EDITION BEGINNING VB.NET 2ND ED
NING VB.NET 2ND EDITION BEGINNING VB.NET 2ND ED
NING VB.NET 2ND EDITION BEGINNING VB.NET 2ND ED
NING VB.NET 2ND EDITION BEGINNING VB.NET 2ND ED
NING VB.NET 2ND EDITION BEGINNING VB.NET 2ND ED
NING VB.NET 2ND EDITION BEGINNING VB.NET 2ND ED
NING VB.NET 2ND EDITION BEGINNING VB.NET 2ND ED
NING VB.NET 2ND EDITION BEGINNING VB.NET 2ND ED
NING VB.NET 2ND EDITION BEGINNING VB.NET 2ND ED
NING VB.NET 2ND EDITION BEGINNING VB.NET 2ND ED
NING VB.NET 2ND EDITION BEGINNING VB.NET 2ND ED
NING VB.NET 2ND EDITION BEGINNING VB.NET 2ND ED

Welcome to Visual Basic .NET

The goal of this book is to help you come up to speed with the Visual Basic .NET language even if you have never programmed anything before. We will start slowly, and build on what we learn. So take a deep breath, let it out slowly, and tell yourself you can do this. No sweat! No kidding!

Programming a computer is a lot like teaching a child to tie their shoes. Until you find the correct way of giving the instructions, not much gets accomplished. Visual Basic .NET is a language in which you can tell your computer how to do things. But like a child, the computer will only understand if you explain things very clearly. If you have never programmed before, this sounds like an arduous task, and sometimes it is. However, Visual Basic .NET gives you a simple language to explain some very complex things. Although it never hurts to have an understanding of what is happening at the lowest levels, Visual Basic .NET frees the programmer from having to deal with the mundane complexities of writing Windows programs. You are free to concentrate on solving problems.

Visual Basic .NET helps you create solutions that run on the Microsoft Windows operating system. Chances are, if you are looking at this book, you have already felt the need or the desire to create such programs. Even if you have never written a computer program before, as you progress through the Try It Outs in this book, you will become familiar with the various aspects of the Visual Basic .NET language, as well as its foundation in Microsoft's .NET Framework. You will find that it is not nearly as difficult as you have been imagining. Before you know it, you will be feeling quite comfortable creating a variety of different types of programs with Visual Basic .NET. As the name implies, Visual Basic .NET can be used to create applications for use over the Internet. However, as when learning any new technology, you have to walk before you can run, so we will start out focusing on Windows applications, before extending our boundaries.

Windows Versus DOS Programming

A Windows program is quite a bit different from its ancient relative, the MS-DOS program. A DOS program follows a relatively strict path from beginning to end. Although this does necessarily limit the functionality of the program, it also limits the road the user has to take to get to it. A DOS program is like walking down a hallway; to get to the end you have to walk down the hallway, passing any obstacles that you may encounter. A DOS program would only let you open certain doors along your stroll.

Windows on the other hand, opened up the world of **event-driven programming**. Events in this context include, for example, clicking on a button, resizing a window, or changing an entry in a textbox. The code that you write responds to these events. To go back to the hallway analogy: in a Windows program to get to the end of the hall, you just click on the end of the hall. The hallway can be ignored. If you get to the end and realize that is not where you wanted to be, you can just set off for the new destination without returning to your starting point. The program reacts to your movements and takes the necessary actions to complete your desired tasks. Visual Basic .NET simplifies the process of writing the code to handle each event by allowing the programmer to write code only for those events that mean something in the context of the program. All other events are ignored. For example, Windows distinguishes clicks from double-clicks, which means that if you only want your program to react to a single click, you need only write code for this single click; you do not have to write code to handle both single and double-click events.

You have probably already begun to suspect that the hallway analogy is grossly over-simplified. The main idea here is that in the DOS world, the user reacts to the program, and in the Windows world, the program reacts to the user.

Another big advantage in a Windows program is the **abstraction** of the hardware. What this means is that Windows takes care of communicating with the hardware for you. You do not need to know the inner workings of every laser printer on the market, just to create output. You do not need to study the schematics for graphics cards to write your game. Windows wraps up this functionality by providing generic routines that communicate with the drivers written by the manufacturers of hardware. This is probably the main reason why Windows has been so successful. The generic routines are referred to as the **Windows API** (**Application Programming Interface**).

A Brief History of Visual Basic

Before Visual Basic 1.0 was introduced to the world in 1991, developers had to be well versed in C++ programming, as well as the rudimentary building blocks (Windows API) of the Windows system itself. This complexity meant that only the dedicated and properly trained were capable of turning out software that could run on Windows. Visual Basic changed all of that, and it has been estimated that there are now as many lines of production code written in Visual Basic as in any other language.

Visual Basic changed the face of Windows programming by removing the complex burden of writing code for the **user interface** (**UI**). By allowing programmers to *draw* their own UI, it freed them to concentrate on the business problems they were trying to solve. Once the UI is drawn, the programmer can then add code to react to events.

Visual Basic has also been extensible from the very beginning. Third-party vendors quickly saw the market for reusable modules to aid developers. These modules, or controls, were original referred to as **VBXs** (named after their file extension). If you didn't like the way a button behaved you could either buy or create your own. However, these controls had to be written in C or C++. Database access utilities were some of the first controls available.

When Microsoft introduced Visual Basic 3.0, the programming world changed again. Now you could build database applications directly accessible to users (so called **front-end applications**) completely with Visual Basic. There was no need to rely on third-party controls. Microsoft accomplished this task with the introduction of the **Data Access Objects** (**DAO**), which allowed programmers to manipulate data with the same ease as manipulating the user interface.

Versions 4.0 and 5.0 extended the capabilities of version 3.0 in order to allow developers to target the new Windows 95 platform. Crucially they also made it easier for developers to write code, which could then be manipulated in order to be used by other language developers. Version 6.0 gave us a new way to access databases with the integration of **ActiveX Data Objects** (**ADO**). ADO was developed by Microsoft to aid web developers using Active Server Pages to access databases. With all of the improvements to Visual Basic over the years, it ensured its dominant place in the programming world. It helps developers write robust and maintainable applications in record time.

With the release of Visual Basic .NET, many of the restrictions that used to exist have been obliterated. In the past, Visual Basic has been criticized and maligned as a "toy" language, as it did not provide all of the features of more sophisticated languages such as C++ and Java. Now, Microsoft has removed these restrictions and made Visual Basic .NET a very powerful development tool. Visual Basic .NET has become a great choice for programmers of all levels.

Installing Visual Basic .NET

You may own Visual Basic .NET:

❑ As part of **Visual Studio .NET**, a suite of tools and languages that also includes **C#** (pronounced C-sharp) and **Visual C++ .NET**

❑ Standard Edition, which includes a cut down set of the tools and languages available with Visual Studio .NET

Both enable you to create your own applications for the Windows platform. The installation procedure is straightforward and easy to do. In fact, the Visual Basic .NET Install is smart enough to figure out exactly what your computer requires in order to make it work.

The descriptions that follow are based on installing Visual Studio .NET. However, all of Visual Studio .NET's languages use the same screens and windows (and hence look very similar), so you won't be seeing much that you would not see anyway.

Try It Out – Installing Visual Basic .NET

1. The Visual Basic .NET CD has an auto-run feature, but if the Setup screen does not appear after inserting the CD, then you will have to run `setup.exe` from the root directory of the CD. To do this, go to your Windows **Start** menu (usually found right at the bottom of your screen) and select **Run**. Then type d:\setup.exe into the **Open** box, where d is the drive letter of your CD drive. After the setup program initializes you will see the following screen:

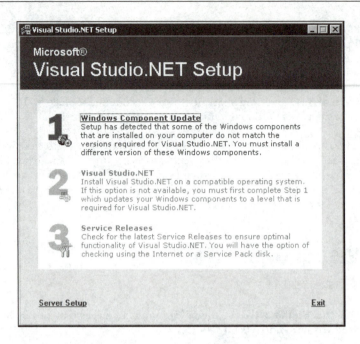

2. This dialog box shows the order in which the installation takes place. In order to function properly, Visual Basic .NET requires that several components and updates be installed on your machine. Step 1 is the Windows component update, so click on the **Windows Component Update** link; you will then be prompted to insert the Component Update CD that came with your Visual Studio .NET disks.

3. The installation program will then examine your system to see exactly which components have to be installed. Depending on the current state of your machine, this list could include any of the following items:

❑ Windows NT 4.0 Service Pack 6.0a

❑ Windows 2000 Service Pack 2

❑ Windows Installer 2.0

❑ Windows Management Infrastructure

❑ FrontPage 2000 Web Extensions

❑ FrontPage 2000 Server Extensions

❑ Setup Runtime Files

❑ Internet Explorer 6.0 and Internet Tools

❑ Microsoft Data Access Components 2.7

❑ .NET Framework

If you don't know what some of those things are, don't worry about it. They are just Windows components that Visual Studio .NET or Visual Basic .NET requires.

4. There may be numerous reboots of your computer as the system components are updated. However, Microsoft has added a nifty automatic login feature to minimize the time required to watch the installation if your computer requires a password to login:

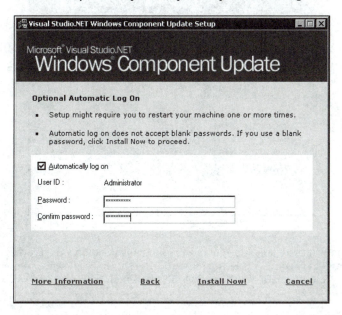

As you can see, this feature is optional. If you choose not to use it, you will be prompted to login after every reboot. This feature could provide a possible security breach, as the person who is actually logged in does not have to be sat at the computer (so you may want to avoid using this option in a busy office, for example), but it can reduce the boredom of watching installation progress screens.

5. Click on Install Now! and the component update will begin. Completed items will have a check mark and the component currently being installed will be identified by a red arrow:

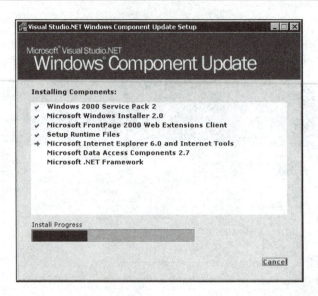

> Depending on what components you already have installed on your machine, your list of components that require updating may be different. For reference, these are the options on a fresh install of Windows 2000 Professional, with no other software.

6. After the Windows Component Update has finished, you will be returned to the Setup screen once more. You will now be able to install Visual Studio .NET, so click on Visual Studio.NET:

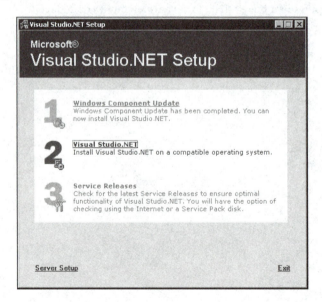

If at some point you wish to develop Web applications on this same machine, you will need to have Internet Information Services (IIS) and FrontPage Extensions installed. These are installed by default on Windows 2000 Server however, when installing on Windows 2000 Professional you may encounter the following screen:

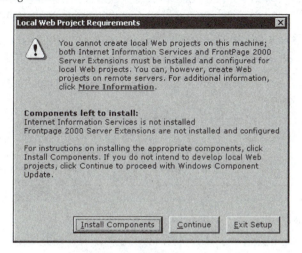

Selecting Install Components will guide you through the process of getting IIS and FrontPage 2000 Server Extensions installed. You will then be able to continue installing Visual Basic .NET.

> **If you choose Continue, you will not be able to develop local Web applications (such as those discussed in Chapters 17 and 19) and will require access to a Web server.**

7. As with most installations you will be presented with an option list of components to install. You can just install the features that you need. For example, if your drive space is limited and you have no immediate need for Visual C++ .NET, you can exclude it from the installation. You will also be given the chance to select the location of items (although the defaults should suffice unless your particular machine has special requirements). Any options not chosen at the initial setup can always be added later as your needs or interests change.

There are three sections of information given for each feature:

❑ The Feature properties section outlines where the required files will be installed and how much space will be needed to do this

❑ The Feature description box gives you an outline of what each feature is and does

❑ Finally, the Space Allocation section illustrates how the space on your hard drive will be affected by the installation as a whole

When you are running Visual Basic .NET, a lot of information is swapped from the disk to memory and back again. Therefore, it is important to have some free space on your disk. There is no exact rule for determining how much free space you will need, but if you use your machine for development as well as other tasks, anything less than 100MB free should be considered a full disk.

8. Visual Studio .NET includes a large set of documentation files, the settings for which are displayed under MSDN Documentation. The documentation can be set to run from the CD, or installed directly on to your hard disk. You can set the install location as Path (install to your hard disk) or Run from source (to have the documentation remain on the CD), via the Feature properties box. Each piece of the documentation can be configured in this manner.

The default is for the documentation to remain on the CD. Only the indexes are copied to your hard drive to aid in searches. This means that you will have to have the CDs available in order to access the documentation. You are free to install some or all of MSDN onto your hard drive. The following table lists the approximate sizes of each of the document sets by their installed location:

	Hard Disk Space Required	
	Docs on CD	Docs on Hard Drive
Visual Basic Documentation	0.02 MB	5.93 MB
Visual C# Documentation	0.01 MB	1.48 MB
Visual C++ Documentation	0.04 MB	22.84 MB
.NET Framework Documentation	0.02 MB	39.70 MB
Platform SDK Documentation	0.31 MB	137.21 MB
Additional MSDN Documentation	0.17 MB	467.99 MB
Visual Studio Tools Documentation	0.05 MB	11.22 MB
Visual Studio Documentation	0.03 MB	9.90 MB
Knowledge Base Articles	0.14 MB	114.30 MB

As you can see there is quite an impact on your free disk space if you install all of the documentation!

9. Once you have chosen all of the features you want, click on Install Now! Installation will begin and you can sit back and relax for a bit. The setup time varies depending on how many features you chose to install. As a reference, the installation process took over an hour on a 650 MHz laptop computer with 256MB RAM, a 12GB hard drive, and running Windows 2000 Server. Keep in mind that this included all of Visual Studio .NET and all of the documentation.

10. When installation is completed, you will see the following:

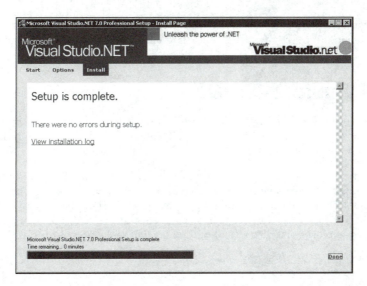

Here you will see any problems that Setup encountered along the way. You are also given the chance to look at the **installation log**. This log provides a list of all actions taken during the installation process. Unless your installation reported errors, the installation log can safely be ignored. The Visual Studio .NET setup is nearly complete. Click on Done to move on to the final step.

11. We are returned to the initial setup screen again and the third choice is now available:

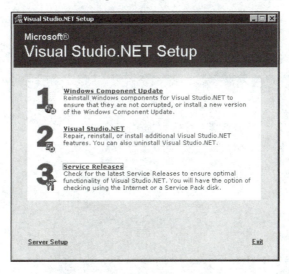

It is a good idea to select Service Releases to check for updates. Microsoft has done a good job of making software updates available through the Internet. These updates can include anything from additional documentation, to bug fixes. You will be given the choice to install any updates via a Service Pack CD or the Internet. Obviously, the Internet option requires an active connection. Since updates can be quite large, a fast connection is highly recommended.

Once you have performed the update process, Visual Basic .NET is ready to use. Now the real fun can begin! So get comfortable, relax, and let's enter the world of Visual Basic .NET.

The Visual Basic .NET IDE

You don't actually need the Visual Basic .NET product to write applications in the Visual Basic .NET language. The actual ability to run Visual Basic .NET code is included with the .NET Framework. You could actually just write all of your Visual Basic .NET using a text editor such as Notepad.

However, by far the easiest way to write in Visual Basic .NET is by using the Visual Studio.NET **Integrated Development Environment**, also known as the **IDE**. This is what you actually see when working with Visual Basic .NET – the windows, boxes, etc. The IDE provides a wealth of features that are unavailable in ordinary text editors – such as code checking, visual representations of the finished application, and an explorer that displays all of the files that make up your project.

Let's look at the Visual Basic .NET IDE now!

The Profile Setup Page

An IDE is a way of bringing together a suite of tools that make developing software a lot easier. Let's fire up Visual Basic .NET and see what we've got. If you used the default installation, go to your Windows Start menu and then Programs | Microsoft Visual Studio.NET 7.0 | Microsoft Visual Studio.NET 7.0. A splash screen will briefly appear and then you should find yourself presented with the Start screen's My Profile tab:

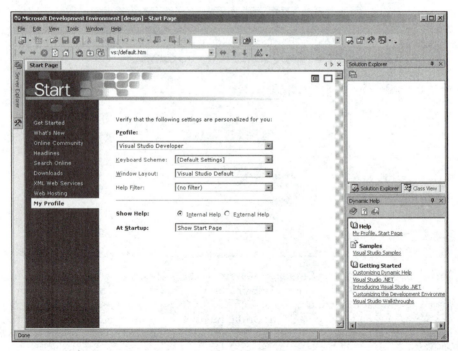

This screen allows us to do some basic configuration of the IDE so that it serves us better. Since this IDE serves all the Visual Studio .NET languages, there are some settings to tailor it to our particular development interests.

Try It Out – Setting Up Our Profile

1. We are learning how to program using Visual Basic .NET, so select Visual Basic Developer from the drop-down box. The IDE will now rearrange itself (it actually looks similar to the Visual Basic 6 IDE).

2. You will also notice that the Keyboard Scheme and Window Layout options have changed to show: Visual Basic 6. If you are at all familiar with earlier versions of Visual Basic, then this should make you feel right at home. The Window Layout options rearrange the windows in the IDE to look similar to previous versions of other Microsoft development tools. How you lay out your windows in the future will be a matter of preference, but for now let's use the Visual Basic 6 option.

3. The Help Filter drop-down box also allows the help system to focus better on what you will find most useful. Set the Help Filter to Visual Basic.

4. The Show Help radio buttons allow us to select where help topics are displayed – Internal Help shows topics within the IDE window (the same window where you see the Start Page), whereas the External Help option opens topics in a separate window. This choice between Help displayed within the IDE or in a separate window is a matter of personal preference. However, until you are comfortable manipulating the various windows of the IDE, the external option might prove more useful, as the IDE remains constant while Help is open. You may receive a message that the change will not take effect until the next time you start Visual Studio .NET.

5. The At Startup pull-down permits you to define what you see whenever you first start Visual Studio .NET. The options here are:

Option	Description
Show Start Page	Shows the Start Page (with its Get Started tab selected)
Load last loaded Solution	Opens last used solution
Show Open Project dialog box	Allows opening of a previously created project
Show New Project dialog box	Allows creation of a new project
Show Empty environment	Opens only the IDE

> **Note here that a *project* is a group of forms and code files that work together to create your application and these files are usually compiled into a single file. Sometimes when we create very complex applications, we need to group more than one project together in a *solution*. By default, however, each new project starts in its own separate solution.**

6. Once you have configured your profile to your liking, select Get Started from the vertical menu bar to the left to begin using Visual Basic .NET.

The Get Started Page

By now, you may be a bit anxious to start writing some code. First, let's take a brief look at the Get Started tab and see what is there. Assuming that you have been following along while setting up Visual Studio .NET, your screen should now look something like this:

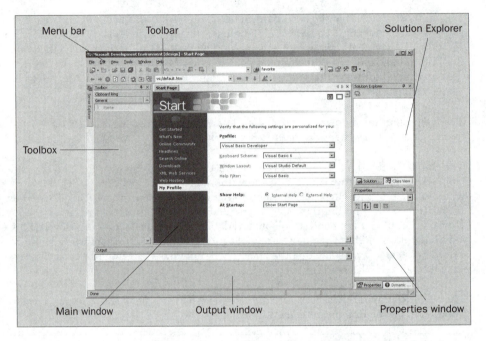

Let's begin our exploration of the Visual Basic .NET IDE by looking at the toolbar and menu, which as you'll learn are not really that different from toolbars and menus you'll have seen in other Microsoft software such as Word, Excel, and PowerPoint.

The Menu

Visual Studio .NET's menu is dynamic, meaning that items will be added or removed depending on what you are trying to do. While we are still looking at the Get Started page, the menu bar will only consist of the File, Edit, View, Tools, Window, and Help menus. However, when you start working on a project, the full Visual Studio .NET menu appears as:

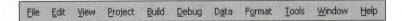

At this point, there is no need to cover each menu topic in great detail. You will become familiar with each as you progress through the book. Here is a quick rundown of what activities each menu item pertains to:

File

It seems every Windows program has a File menu. It has become the standard where you should find, if nothing else, a way to exit the application. In this case, you can also find ways of opening and closing single files and whole projects.

Edit

The Edit menu provides access to the items you would expect: Undo, Redo, Cut, Copy, Paste, and Delete.

View

The View menu provides quick access to the windows that make up the IDE, such as the Solution Explorer, Properties window, Output window, Toolbox, etc.

Project

The Project menu allows you to add various extra files to your application.

Build

The Build menu becomes important when you have completed your application and want to be able to run it without the use of the Visual Basic .NET environment (perhaps running it directly from your Windows Start menu as you would any other application such as Word or Access).

Debug

The Debug menu allows you to start and stop running your application within the Visual Basic .NET IDE. It also gives you access to the Visual Studio .NET **debugger**. The debugger allows you to step through your code while it is running to see how it is behaving.

Data

The Data menu helps you use information that comes from a database. It only appears when you are working with the visual part of your application (the [Design] tab will be the active one in the main window), not when you are writing code. Chapters 15 and 16 will introduce you to working with databases.

Format

The Format menu also only appears when you are working with the visual part of your application. Items on the Format menu allow you to manipulate how the windows you create will appear to the users of your application.

Tools

The Tools menu has commands to configure the Visual Studio .NET IDE, as well as links to other external tools that may have been installed.

Window

The Window menu has become standard for any application that allows more than one window to be open at a time, such as Word or Excel. The commands on this menu allow you to change the physical layout of the windows in the IDE.

Help

The Help menu provides access to the Visual Studio .NET documentation. There are many different ways to access this information (for example, via the help contents, an index, or a search). The Help menu also has options that connect to the Microsoft Web site to obtain updates or report problems.

The Toolbars

There are many toolbars available within the IDE, including Formatting, Image Editor, and Text Editor, which you can add to and remove from the IDE via the View | Toolbars menu option. Each one provides quick access to often-used commands, preventing you from having to navigate through a series of menu options. For example, the leftmost icon on the toolbar shown below (New Project) is available from the menu by navigating to File | New | Project.

The default toolbar (called Standard) appears at the top of the IDE as:

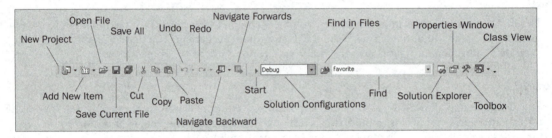

The toolbar is segmented into groups of related options, which are separated by a vertical bar.

The first five icons provide access to the commonly used project and file manipulation options available through the File and Project menus, such as opening and saving files.

The next group of icons is for editing (Cut, Copy, and Paste).

The third group of icons is for editing and navigation. The navigation buttons replicate functionality found in the View menu and allow us to cycle through the tabs at the top of the main window.

The fourth group of icons provides the ability to start your application running (via the blue triangle) and to specify **build configurations**. There are times when you want certain parts of your code only to appear in a **debug version**, a bit like a rough draft version of your application. For example, you may have code in your application that is only useful for tracking down problems in the application. When it is time to release your application to the world, you will want to exclude this code by setting the Solution Configurations settings to Release. You can also access the functionality offered by this group via the Build and Debug menus.

The next section allows you to locate parts of your code quickly. The simplest way to search is to type some text into the Find textbox and hit *Enter*. If the text is found, it will be highlighted in the central window. The Find in Files option allows you to specify more sophisticated searches, including matching the case of the text, looking in specific files or projects, and replacing the found text with new text. The search functionality can also be accessed via the Edit | Find and Replace menu option.

The next group of icons provides quick links back to the Solution Explorer, Properties window, Toolbox, and Class View. If any of these windows are closed, clicking the appropriate icon will bring it back into view.

> **If you forget what a particular icon does, you can hover your mouse pointer over it so that a tooltip appears displaying the name of the toolbar option.**

We could continue to look at each of the other windows directly from the Start Page. But, as you can see they're all empty at this stage, and therefore not too revealing. The best way to look at the capabilities of the IDE is to use it while writing some code.

Creating a Simple Application

To finish our exploration of the Visual Basic .NET IDE we need to create a project, so that the windows labeled in the earlier diagram actually have some interesting content for us to look at. We're now going to create a very simple application called HelloUser that will allow us to enter a person's name and will display a greeting to that person in a message box.

Try It Out – Creating a HelloUser Project

1. Click on the New Project button on the Start Page.

2. The New Project dialog box will open. Make sure you have Visual Basic Projects selected in the Project Types tree-view box to the left. Next, select Windows Application in the Templates box on the right. If you need to save this project to a location other than the default, be sure to enter it into the Location box. Finally, type HelloUser in the Name text box and click on the OK button:

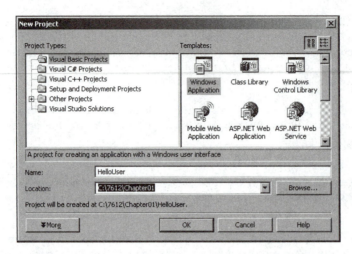

3. Visual Basic .NET will then create an empty Windows application for us. So far, our HelloUser program consists of one blank window called a **Windows Form** (or sometimes just a **form**), with the default name of Form1.vb:

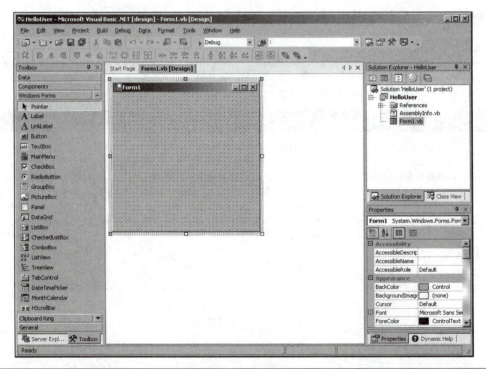

Whenever Visual Studio .NET creates a new file, either as part of the project creation process, or when you create a new file, it will use a name that describes what it is (in this case, a form) followed by a number.

Windows in the Visual Studio .NET IDE

At this point, you can see that the various windows in the IDE are beginning to show their purposes, and we will take a brief look at them now before we come back to the *Try It Out*. Note that if any of these windows are not visible on your screen, you can use the View menu to select and show them. Also if you do not like the location of any particular window you can move it by clicking on its title bar (the blue bar at the top) and dragging it to a new location. The windows in the IDE can **float** (stand out on their own) or be **dockable** (as they appear above).

Server Explorer

The Server Explorer gives you management access to the servers on your network. Here you can create database connections, and view the services provided by the available servers.

Toolbox

The Toolbox contains reusable components that can be inserted into your application. These can range from buttons to data connectors to customized controls either purchased or developed yourself.

Design Window

The Design window is where a lot of the action takes place. This is where you will draw your user interface and write your code. This window is sometimes referred to as the **Designer**.

Solution Explorer

The Solution Explorer window contains a hierarchical view of your solution. A solution can contain many projects while a project contains code and code references that solve a particular problem.

Class View

The Class View window (shown as a tab with the Solution Explorer) gives you a tree view of the classes in your program and shows the properties and methods that each contains. A **class** is code file that groups data and the functions that manipulate it together into one unit. A **property** is data, and a **method** is a function or subroutine.

Properties

The Properties window shows what properties the selected object makes available. Although you can set these properties in your code, sometimes it is much easier to set them while you are designing your application. You will notice that the File Name property has the value Form1.vb. This is the physical file name for the form's code and layout information.

Task List

The Task List window highlights any errors encountered when you try to run your code. Clicking on the item in this window will take you to the line of code containing the error.

Output

When you run your code the progress made in reading it (or **compiling** it) is registered via messages posted in the Output window.

Dynamic Help

The Dynamic Help window displays a list of help topics that relate to whatever in the IDE has focus. If you click on the form in the Design Window and then open Dynamic Help, you will see a list of help topics relating to forms.

Try It Out – Creating a HelloUser Project – Continued

1. Let's change the name of our form to something more indicative of what our application is. Click on Form1.vb in the Solution Explorer window. Then, in the Properties window, change the File Name property from Form1.vb to HelloUser.vb and hit *Enter*: When changing properties you must either hit *Enter* or click off the property for it to take effect.

2. Notice that the form's file name has also been updated in the Solution Explorer to read HelloUser.vb:

3. Now click on the form displayed in the main window; the Properties window will change to display the form's **Form properties** (instead of the **File properties**, which we have just been looking at). You will notice that the Properties window is dramatically different. The difference is the result of two different views of the same file. When the form name is highlighted in the Solution Explorer window, the physical file properties of the form are displayed. When the form in the Design View is highlighted, the visual properties and logical properties of the form are displayed.

The Properties window allows us to easily set a control's properties. Remember properties are a particular object's set of internal data. Properties usually describe appearance or behavior. In the screenshot, you can see that properties are grouped together in categories – Accessibility, Appearance, and Behavior are the ones shown in here:

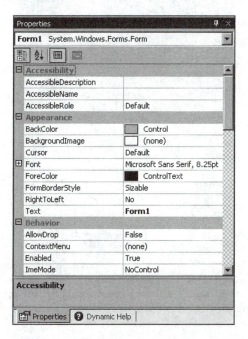

You can see that under the Appearance category are such properties as BackColor (the form's background color), Font (the typeface used for text on the form), and Text (the form's caption displayed in the title bar). These are all examples of properties that describe the form's appearance.

One property, FormBorderStyle, tells Windows how to draw the form. In this case, the window is resizable, meaning that when the form is displayed, the user can change its size (like most application windows).

4. Right now, the title of our form (displayed in the bar at the top) is Form1. This isn't very descriptive, so let's change it to reflect the purpose of this application. Locate the Text property in the Appearance section of the Properties window and change its value to Hello from Visual Basic .NET and hit *Enter*. Notice that the form's title has been updated to reflect the change:

If you have trouble finding properties, click the little AZ button on the toolbar towards the top of the Properties window. This changes the property listing from being ordered by category to being ordered by name:

5. We are now finished. Click on the Start button on the Visual Studio .NET toolbar (the blue triangle) to run the application. As you work through the book, whenever we say "run the project" or "start the project", just click on the Start button. An empty window with the title Hello from Visual Basic .NET is displayed:

> **Notice how the grid pattern of dots has now disappeared. These are displayed at design time to help us place controls such as boxes, labels, and radio buttons onto our form. They're not needed (or even particularly desirable) at run time, so they're not shown.**

OK, that was simple, but our little application isn't doing much at the moment. Let's make it a little more interactive. To do this we are going to add some controls – a label, textbox, and two buttons to the form. This will let us see how the toolbox makes adding functionality quite simple. You may be wondering at this point when we will actually look at some code. Soon! The great thing about Visual Basic .NET is that you can develop a fair amount of your application *without* writing any code. Sure, the code is still there, behind the scenes, but as we'll see, Visual Basic .NET writes a lot of it for us.

The Toolbox

The Toolbox is accessed via the View | Toolbox menu option, the Toolbox icon on the Standard menu bar, or by pressing *Ctrl + Alt + X*.

The Toolbox contains a tabbed view of the various controls and components that can be placed onto your form. Controls such as textboxes, buttons, radio buttons, and drop-down boxes can be selected and then *drawn* onto your form. For the HelloUser application, we will only be using the controls on the Windows Forms tab:

Here we can see a listing of standard .NET controls for Windows forms. The down arrow button to the right of the Clipboard Ring tab title actually scrolls the Windows Forms control list down as there are too many to fit in otherwise. The up arrow button on the Windows Forms tab scrolls the list up. Note that the order in which your controls appear may be different.

Controls can be added to your forms in any order, so it does not matter if we add the label control after the textbox or the buttons before the label.

Try It Out – Adding Controls to the HelloUser Application

1. Stop the project if it's still running, as we now want to add some controls to our form. The simplest way to do this is to click on the X button in the top right corner of the form. Alternatively, you can click on the blue square in the Visual Studio .NET IDE (which displays the text **Stop Debugging** if you hover over it with your mouse pointer).

2. Let's add a **Label** control to the form. Click on **Label** in the Toolbox to select it. Move the cursor over the form's Designer. You'll notice that the cursor looks like a crosshair with a little floating letter A beneath it. Click and hold the mouse button where you want the top left corner of the label and drag the mouse to where you want the bottom right. (Placing controls can also be accomplished by double-clicking on the required control in the Toolbox.)

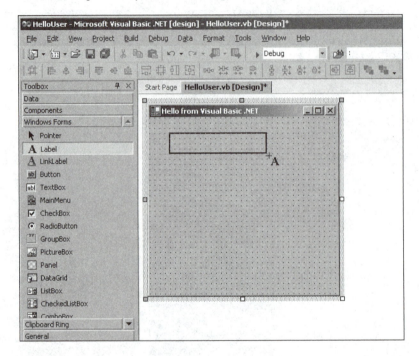

3. If the **Label** control you have just drawn is not in the your desired location, or is too big or too small, that is not really a problem. Once the control is on the form you can resize it or move it around. The image opposite shows what the control looks like after you place it on the form. To move it, click on the gray dotted border and drag it to the desired location. To resize it, click and drag on one of the white box "handles" and stretch the control in the needed direction. The corner handles resize both the horizontal and vertical dimension at the same time:

4. After drawing a control on the form, we should at least configure its name and the text that it will display. You'll see that the Properties window to the right of the Designer has changed to **Label1**, telling you that you're currently examining the properties for it. In the Properties window, set our new label's **Text** property to **Enter Your Name:** and its **(Name)** property to **lblName**:

5. Now, directly beneath the label, we want to add a textbox, so that we can enter a name. We're going to repeat the procedure we followed for adding the label, but this time make sure you select the **TextBox** from the toolbar. Once you have dragged-and-dropped (or double-clicked) the control into the appropriate position, use the Properties window to set its **Name** property to **txtName** and clear the **Text** property so that the textbox now appears to be blank.

Notice how, out of the eight sizing handles surrounding the control, only two are shown in white. By default, the TextBox control cannot be made any taller than the absolute height necessary to contain the font that it will use to draw the text.

6. In the bottom left corner of the form, add a **Button** control in exactly the same manner as you added the label and textbox. Set its **Name** property to **OK**, and its **Text** property to **&OK**.

> **The ampersand (&) is used in the Text property of buttons to create a keyboard shortcut (known as a *hot key*). The letter with the & sign placed in front of it will become underlined to signal to users that they can select that button by pressing the *Alt-letter* key combination, instead of using the mouse (on some configurations the underline doesn't appear to the user until they press ALT). In this particular instance, pressing *Alt+O* would be the same as clicking directly on the O̲K button. There is no need to write code to accomplish this.**

7. Now add a second **Button** control to the bottom right corner of the form and set the **Name** property to **btnExit** and the **Text** property to **E&xit**. Your form should look similar to this:

Modified Hungarian Notation

You may have noticed that the names given to the controls look a little funny. Each name is prefixed with a shorthand identifier describing the type of control it is. This makes it much easier to understand what type of control we are working with when we are looking through code. For example, say we had a control called simply Name, without a prefix of lbl or txt, we would not know whether we were working with a textbox that accepted a name or a label that displayed a name. Imagine if, in the previous *Try It Out*, we had named our label Name1 and our textbox Name2 – we'd very quickly become confused. How about if we left our application for a month or two, and then came back to it to make some changes?

When working with other developers, it is very important to keep the coding style consistent. One of the most commonly used styles used for controls within application development in many languages is **Modified Hungarian notation**. The notion of prefixing control names to identify their use was brought forth by Dr. Charles Simonyi. He worked for the Xerox Palo Alto Research Center (XPARC), before joining Microsoft. He came up with short prefix mnemonics that allowed programmers to easily identify the type of information a variable might contain. Since Dr. Simonyi is Hungarian, and the prefixes make the names look a little foreign, the name Hungarian Notation stuck. Since the original notation was used in C/C++ development, the notation for Visual Basic .NET is termed Modified. Here is a table of some of the commonly used prefixes that we shall be using in this book:

Control	Prefix
Button	btn
ComboBox	cbo
CheckBox	chk
Label	lbl
ListBox	lst
MainMenu	mnu
RadioButton	rdb
PictureBox	pic
TextBox	txt

Hungarian Notation can be a real time-saver when looking at code someone else wrote, or at code that you have written months past. However, by far the most important thing is to be consistent in your naming. When you start coding, pick a convention for your naming. It is recommended that you use the *de facto* standard Modified-Hungarian for Visual Basic .NET, but it is not required. Once you pick a convention, stick to it. When modifying someone else's code, use theirs. There is very little code that is ever written, put into production and then forgotten. A standard naming convention followed throughout a project will save countless hours when the application is maintained.

Now let's get back to the application. It is now time to write some actual code.

The Code Editor

Now that we have the HelloUser form defined, we have to add some code to actually make it do something interesting. We have already seen how easy it is to add controls to a form. Providing the functionality behind those on-screen elements is not much more difficult. To add the code for a control, just double-click on it. This will open the code editor in the main window:

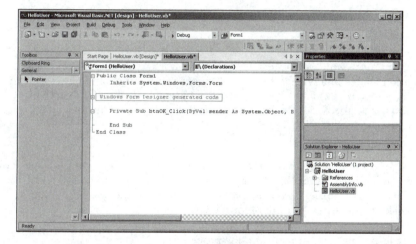

Notice that an additional tab has been created in the main window. Now we have the Design tab and the code tab. We drew the controls on the Design tab, and we write code on the code tab. One thing to note here is that we have not created a separate file for the code. The visual definition and the code behind it both exist in the same file: HelloUser.vb. This is actually the reason why building applications with Visual Basic .NET is so slick and easy. Using the Design view you can visually lay out your application, and then using the Code view add just the bits of code to implement your desired functionality.

You will also notice that there are two pull-downs at the top of the window. These provide shortcuts to the various parts of our code. If you pull down the one on the left, Form1 (HelloUser), you will see a list of all of the objects within our application. If you pull down the one on the right, (Declarations), you will see a list of all of the defined functions or subroutines. If this particular form had a lot of code behind it, these pull-downs would make navigating to the desired area very quick – jumping to the selected area. However, since all of the code fits in the window, there are not a lot of places to get lost.

Now let's look at the code in the window. The code in Visual Studio .NET is set up into **regions** designated by the plus (+) and minus (-) buttons along the left side. These regions can be collapsed and expanded in order to simplify what you are looking at. If you expand the region labeled `Windows Form Designer generated code`, you will see a lot of code that Visual Basic .NET has automatically generated for us, which takes care of defining each of the controls on the form and how the form itself should behave. We do not have to worry about the code in this region, so collapse the `Windows Form Designer generated code` region once more and let's just concentrate on the code we have to write ourselves.

Try It Out – Adding Code to the HelloUser Project

1. To begin adding the necessary code, click on the Design tab to show the form again. Then double-click on the OK button. The code window will reopen with the following code. This is the shell of button's `Click` event and is the place where we enter code that we want to be run when we click on the button. This code is known as an **event handler**, and sometimes is also referred to as an **event procedure**:

```
Private Sub OK_Click(ByVal sender As SystemObject, ByVal e As _
          System.EventArgs) Handles OK_Click


End Sub
```

> **Due to the typographic constraints in publishing, it is not possible to put the Sub declaration on one line. Visual Basic .NET allows you to break up lines of code by using the underscore character (_) to signify a line continuation. The space before the underscore is required. Any whitespace preceding the code on the following line is ignored.**

`Sub` is an example of a **keyword**. In programming terms, a keyword is a special word that is used to tell Visual Basic .NET to do something special. In this case, it tells Visual Basic .NET that this is a procedure. Anything that we type between the lines `Private Sub` and `End Sub` will make up the event procedure for the OK button.

2. Now add the highlighted code into the procedure:

```
Private Sub OK_Click(ByVal sender As SystemObject, ByVal e As _
          System.EventArgs) Handles OK_Click
    'Display a message box greeting the user
    MessageBox.Show("Hello, " & txtName.Text & _
                "! Welcome to Visual Basic .NET.", _
                "HelloUser Message")
End Sub
```

Throughout this book, you'll be presented with code that you should enter into your program if you're following along. Usually, we'll make it pretty obvious where you put the code, but as we go we'll explain anything that looks out of the ordinary.

3. After you have added the code, go back to the Design tab, and double-click on the Exit button. Add the highlighted code to the `ExitButton_Click` event procedure.

```
Private Sub ExitButton_Click(ByVal sender As SystemObject, ByVal e As _
          System.EventArgs) Handles ExitButton_Click
    'End the program
    Me.Dispose()
End Sub
```

You may be wondering what Me is. Me refers to the form. Just like the pronoun, *me*, it is just a shorthand for referring to oneself.

4. Now that the code is finished, the moment of truth has arrived and we can see our creation. First though, save your work by using File | Save from the menu, or by clicking the disk icon on the toolbar.

5. Now click on the Start button on the toolbar. You will notice a lot of activity in the Output window at the bottom of your screen. Providing you haven't made any mistakes in entering the code, this information just lets you know what files are being loaded to run your application.

It's at this point that Visual Studio .NET will **compile** the code. Compiling is the activity of taking the Visual Basic .NET source code that you've written and translating it into a form that the computer understands. After the compilation is complete, Visual Studio .NET will **run** (also known as **execute**) the program and we'll be able to see the results.

If Visual Basic .NET encountered any errors, they will be displayed as tasks in the Task List window. Double-clicking on a task will transport you to the offending line of code. We will learn more about how to debug the errors in our code in Chapter 11.

6. When the application loads you will see the main form. Enter a name and click on OK (or press the *Alt+O* key combination):

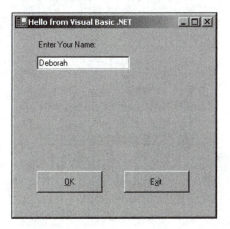

7. A window known as a message box appears, welcoming the person whose name was entered in the textbox to Visual Basic .NET – in this case Deborah:

8. After you close the message box by clicking on its OK button, click on the Exit button on our form. The application will close and you will be brought back to the Visual Basic .NET IDE.

That completes our first Visual Basic .NET application. Well done! Before we move on to the next chapter, let's take a quick look at the Visual Studio .NET Help system.

Using the Help System

The **Help system** included with Visual Basic .NET is an improvement over Help systems in previous versions. As you begin to learn Visual Basic .NET, you will probably become very familiar with the Help system. However, it is worthwhile to give you an overview, just to help speed your searches for information.

The Help menu appears as:

As you can see this menu contains many more entries than the typical Windows application. The main reason for this is the vastness of the documentation. Few people could keep it all in their heads – but luckily, that's not a problem, as we can always quickly and easily refer to the Help system. Think of it as a safety net for your brain.

One really fantastic new feature is Dynamic Help. If you turn this option on (by selecting Dynamic Help from the Help menu), a window will display a list of relevant topics for whatever you may be working on. If you followed the default installation and have not rearranged the IDE, the Dynamic Help is displayed as a tab behind Properties.

Let's say for example, that we are working with a textbox (perhaps the textbox in the HelloUser application) and want to find out some information; we just select the textbox on our form and we can see all the help topics that pertain to textboxes:

The other help commands in the Help menu (Contents, Index, and Search), function just as they would in any other Windows application.

The domain of help topics to search and display is defined by the profile that we defined at installation. However, the Edit Filters... menu option allows you to further focus what types of documentation to include in the search:

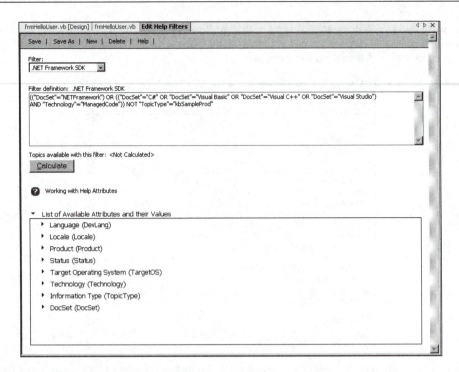

The filter is a logical statement that either includes or excludes documentation, based on some predefined types. The statement is in the upper text area; the document attributes and values are listed below. Although the filter equation can be edited directly, selecting attributes from the list automatically updates the statement. You can then save your changes to the current filter name, or use **Save As** to create a new one based on the existing equation.

Summary

Hopefully, you are beginning to see that developing basic applications with Visual Basic .NET is not that difficult. We have taken a look at the IDE and how it can help you put together good software quickly. The Toolbox allows you to add controls quickly and easily to your programs. The Properties window makes configuring those controls a snap, while the Solution Explorer gives us a bird's eye view of the files that make up our project. We even wrote a little code.

Questions

At this point, we have not covered much about Visual Basic .NET, the language. So these exercises won't be too difficult.

1. What Modified-Hungarian prefix should you use for a combo box? A label? A textbox?

2. (*This assumes you set the Help Filter to Visual Basic and Related.*) Open the Help System and search for MessageBox. Notice how many topics are returned. Change the Help Filter option on the My Profile screen, to No Filter. Repeat the search for MessageBox. Did the Help System return more or fewer topics?

3. When creating a button, how would you make the button respond to a keyboard hot key?

> **The answers for these questions and those at the end of all the other chapters can be found in Appendix B.**

Writing Software

If you're reading this book, it's safe to assume that you have an interest in writing software using Visual Basic .NET. In the next three chapters, we're going to look at the fundamentals behind the process of writing software and start putting together some exciting programs of our own.

In this chapter we'll be looking at:

❑   Algorithms

❑   Variables

❑   Different data types including integers, floating-point numbers, strings, and dates

❑   Scope

❑   Debugging applications

❑   Learning more about how computers store data in memory

Information and Data

What's the difference between information and data? Well, **information** describes facts and can be presented or found in any format, whether that format is optimized for humans or for computers. For example, if we send four people out to survey cars at a particular intersection, at the end of the process we'll end up with four handwritten tallies of the number of cars that went past.

Data is used to describe information that has been collated, ordered, and formatted in such a way that it can be directly used by a piece of computer software. The information we have (several notebooks full of handwritten scribbles) cannot be directly used by a piece of software. Rather, someone has to work with it to convert it into data, for example, the scribbles can be transferred to an Excel spreadsheet that can be directly used by a piece of software designed to analyze the results.

Algorithms

The computer industry is commonly regarded as one that changes at an incredible speed. Most professionals find themselves in a position of constant retraining and re-education to keep their skills sharp and up to date. However, some aspects of computing haven't really changed since they were first invented and perhaps won't change within our lifetimes.

The process and discipline of software development is a good example of an aspect of computer technology whose essential nature hasn't changed since the beginning and I personally can't see it changing for the next fifty years.

For software to work, you have to have some information to work with. The software then takes this information and manipulates it into another form. For example, software may take your customer database stored as ones and zeros on your computer's disk and make it available for you to read on your computer's monitor. The on-board computer in your car constantly examines environmental and performance information and continually adjusts the fuel mix to make the car run more efficiently. Your telephone service provider records the calls you make and generates bills based on this information so that they can get paid.

The base underpinning all software is the **algorithm**. Before you can write software to solve a problem, you have to first break it down into a step-by-step description of *how* the problem is going to be solved.

An algorithm is independent of programming language and so, if you like, you can describe it to yourself either as a spoken language, or with diagrams, or with whatever helps you visualize the problem.

Let's imagine we work for a telephone company and we've identified the need to produce bills based on calls that our customers make. Here's an algorithm that describes a possible solution:

- ❑ On the first day of the month, we need to produce a bill for each customer we have.
- ❑ For each customer, we have a list of calls that the customer has made over the previous month.
- ❑ We know the length of time of each call, and the time of day that the call was made. Based on this information, we can determine the cost of each call.
- ❑ For each bill, we total up the cost of each call.
- ❑ If a customer spends more than a preset limit, we give them a 10% discount.
- ❑ We have to apply sales tax to each bill.
- ❑ After we have the final bill, we need to print it.

Those seven points describe, fairly completely, an algorithm for a piece of software that generates bills for a telephone company. At the end of the day, it doesn't matter if we build this solution in C++, Visual Basic .NET, C#, Java, or whatever – the basic algorithms of the software will never change. (However, it's important to realize that each of those seven parts of the algorithm way well be made up of algorithms of their own.)

The good news for a newcomer to programming like you is that algorithms are usually very easy to construct. I'm sure that there's nothing in the above algorithm that you don't understand. Algorithms always follow common-sense reasoning, although you may find yourself in a position where you have to code algorithms that contain complex mathematical or scientific reasoning. It may not seem like common sense to you, but it will to someone else! The bad news is that the process of turning the algorithm into code can be arduous, but we'll worry about that later.

As a programmer, learning how to construct algorithms is the most important skill you will ever obtain. One thing I'll be trying to stress to you as we work through the chapters in this book is that you're not looking to become a "Visual Basic .NET programmer"; you're looking to become a "programmer".

All good programmers respect the fact that the preferred language of the programmer is largely irrelevant. Different languages are good at doing different things. C++ gives the developer a lot of control over the way a program works, at the expense that it's harder to write software in C++ than it is in Visual Basic .NET. Likewise, building the user interface for desktop applications is far easier to do in Visual Basic .NET than it is in C++. (Some of these problems do go away when using Managed C++ with .NET, so this statement is less true today than it was a few years ago.) What you need to learn to do as a programmer is adapt to different languages to achieve solutions to a problems in the best possible way. Although when you begin programming you'll be "hooked" on one language, remember that different languages are focused towards developing different kinds of solutions. At some point in the future, you may have to take your basic skills as an algorithm designer and coder to a new language.

As a beginner in the world of programming, the first language you use will be Visual Basic .NET. Luckily, you're coming into programming at a very interesting stage. (As you'll learn in Chapter 5, Microsoft is looking to change the landscape of software development forever.) Use this time to build on your algorithmic skills. I and the other authors of this book will be presenting you with some very exciting and interesting software, but remember to look "beneath" the code to find the algorithms!

Amir's Law

How do we know what a programming language is? In one way, we can regard a programming language as anything capable of making a decision. Computers are very good at making decisions, but they have to be fairly basic, for example: "Is four greater than three?" or "Is the car blue?"

If you have a complicated decision that you have to make, the process of making that decision has to be broken down into simple parts that the computer can understand. Coming back to our discussion on algorithms, you'll use algorithms to determine how to break down a complicated decision into simpler ones.

A good example of a problem that's hard for a computer to solve is recognizing peoples' faces. You can't just say to a computer, "Is this a picture of Dave?" Instead, you have to break the question down into a series of simpler questions that the computer can understand.

The decisions that you ask computers to make will have one of two possible answers: "yes" and "no". We also refer to these possibilities as "true" and "false" and also as "1" and "0".

You might be looking at this as a limitation, and you're right so far as the intelligence of human beings goes, but it's not a limitation when it comes to building software. In software terms, you cannot make a decision based on the question, "How much bigger is 10 compared to 4?" Instead, you have to make a decision based on the question, "Is 10 bigger than 4?" The difference is subtle, yet important – the first question does not yield an answer of "yes" or "no", whereas the second question does.

Of course, a computer is more than capable of answering the first question, but this is actually done through an **operation**, in other words, you have to actually subtract 4 from 10 to use the result in some other part of your algorithm.

A couple of years ago, I was working with a friend of mine called Amir. We were chatting over our morning coffee about some new whizzy piece of software that had intrigued us and, as part of this discussion, we tried to imagine how the developers would have put the software together.

At one point in the conversation, Amir turned to me and said, "It's all methods and variables." The more I thought about this seemingly casual statement, the more I came to realize that this sums up the essential nature of software engineering and I came to think of it as "Amir's Law". No matter how complicated this piece of software was, it was built up of methods and variables, just like the software that runs my cell phone, the software that powered the moon landing, the software that lets me write this document. All and any software is built up of methods and variables – the subject of this chapter.

Why is Amir's Law important? Well, remember that you're trying to become a "programmer", not a "Visual Basic .NET programmer", not a "Java programmer" – just a "programmer". Understanding that all software, no matter how flashy or whizzy, is just made up of methods and variables is key.

Variables

So what is a variable? Well, a **variable** is something that you store a value in as you work through your algorithm. You can then make a decision based on that value (for example, "Is it equal to 7?", "Is it more than 4?") or you can perform operations on that value to change it into something else (for example, "Add 2 to the value", "Multiply it by 6", etc.).

Let's not get bogged down in code for a moment, let's look at another algorithm:

- ❑ Create a variable called "n" and store in it the value "27"

- ❑ Add 1 to the variable called "n" and store it

- ❑ Display the value of variable "n" to the user

In this algorithm, we're creating a variable called "n" and storing in it the value "27". What this means is that there's a part of the computer's memory that is being used by the program to store the value "27". That piece of memory will keep storing that value until we either change it or tell the program we don't need it any more.

In the second bullet point, we're performing an "add operation". We're taking "n" and adding 1 to its value. After we've performed this operation, the piece of memory given over to storing "n" will now contain the value "28".

In the final bullet point, we want to tell the user what the value of "n" is. So, we read the current value from memory and write out to the screen.

Again, there's nothing about the algorithm there that you can't understand. It's just common sense! However, the Visual Basic .NET code looks a little more cryptic.

Try It Out – Working with Variables

1. Create a new project in Visual Studio .NET by selecting File | New | Project from the menu. When asked, select Windows Application from the right-hand pane and enter the project name as Variables:

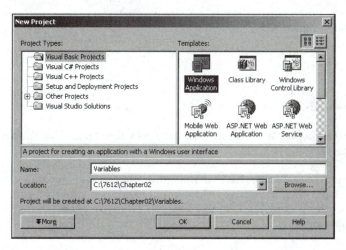

2. Make Form1 a little smaller and add a Button control from the Toolbox to it. Set the button's Text property to Add 1 to n and its Name property to btnAdd:

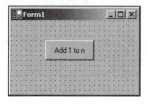

3. Double-click on the button to bring up the btnAdd_Click event handler. Add the following code to it:

```
Private Sub btnAdd_Click(ByVal sender As System.Object, _
        ByVal e As System.EventArgs) Handles btnAdd.Click

    Dim n As Integer
    n = 27

    n = n + 1

    MessageBox.Show("Value of n + 1 = " & n, "Variables")

End Sub
```

45

4. Run the project, click on the Add 1 to n button, and you'll see something like this:

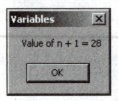

How It Works

The program starts at the top and works its way down, one line at a time, to the bottom. The first line defines a new variable, called n:

```
Dim n As Integer
```

Dim is a keyword. A **keyword** is a word that has a special meaning in Visual Basic .NET that is used for things such as commands. Dim tells VB that what follows is a variable definition.

> *Its curious name harks back to the original versions of BASIC and is short for "dimension", as in "make some space for".*

The As Integer tells Visual Basic .NET what kind of value we want to store in the variable. This is known as the **data type**. We don't need to worry about data types until a bit later on. For now, all you need to know is that this is used to tell Visual Basic .NET that we expect to store an integer (whole number) value in the variable.

The next line sets the value of n:

```
n = 27
```

...or, in other words, "make n become equal to the value 27."

The next statement is a bit of a conceptual leap, but simply adds one to n:

```
n = n + 1
```

What this line actually means is "make n become equal to the current value of n plus 1."

The final line displays a message box with the text Value of n + 1 = and the current value of n. We've also set the title of the message box to Variables to match the project name:

```
MessageBox.Show("Value of n + 1 = " & n, "Variables")
```

Comments and Whitespace

When writing software code, you must be constantly aware of that fact that you or someone else may have to change that code in the future. Therefore, you should be sensitive to the fact that someone will be looking at your code some day, so you must try to make it as easy to understand as possible.

Comments

Comments are ignored by the Visual Basic .NET compiler, which means you can write whatever you like in them, be it English, C#, PERL, Farsi, whatever. What they're supposed to do is help the developer reading the code understand what each part of the code is supposed to be doing.

> *All languages support comments, not just Visual Basic .NET. If you're looking at C# code, for example, you'll find comments start with a double-forward-slash (//).*

What's a good way of knowing when you need a comment? Well, it's different for different situations, but a good rule of thumb is to think about the algorithm. Our program in the previous *Try It Out* had this algorithm:

❑   Define a value for n

❑   Add 1 to the value of n

❑   Display the new value of n to the user

Let's see how we can add some comments to the code from the last example to match the steps in the algorithm:

```
    ' define a value for n...
    Dim n As Integer
    n = 27

    ' add 1 to the value of n...
n = n + 1

    ' display the new value of n to the user...
    MessageBox.Show("Value of n + 1 = " & n, "Variables")
```

In Visual Basic .NET, we begin our comments with an apostrophe (') and then anything *on the same line* following that apostrophe is our comment. We can also add comments on to a line that already has code, like this:

```
    n = n + 1    ' add 1 to the value of n...
```

This works just as well, as only comments (and not code) follow the apostrophe.

Notice that the comments in the above code more or less match the algorithm. A good technique for adding comments is to write a few words explaining the stage of the algorithm that's being expressed as software code.

Comments are primarily used to make the code easier to understand either to a new developer who's never seen your code before, or to you when you haven't visited your code for a while. The purpose of a comment is to point out something that might not be immediately obvious, or to summarize code to enable the reader to understand what's going on without having to pore over each and every line.

You'll find that programmers have their own foibles about how to write comments. I always write mine in lower case and end with an ellipsis (. . .). There's no particular reason for this, I just find it esthetically pleasing. If you work for a larger software company, or your manager/mentor is hot on coding standards they'll dictate what formats your comments should take and where you should and should not add comments to the code.

Whitespace

Another important aspect of writing readable code is to leave lots of **whitespace**. You'll notice in my last example, I've left a blank line before each comment. This implies to anyone reading the code that each block is a unit of work, which it is.

We'll be coming back to the idea of whitespace in the next chapter when we discuss controlling the flow through our programs using special code blocks, but you'll find that the use of whitespace varies between developers. For now, just try to remember not to be afraid to space out your code – it'll greatly improve the readability of your programs, especially as you come to write long chunks of code.

> **The compiler ignores both whitespace and comments, so there are no performance differences between code with lots of whitespace and comments, and code with none. So don't be afraid to increase your code's readability by judicious use of both.**

Data Types

When we use variables, it's a good idea to know ahead of time the things that we want to store in them. So far in this chapter, we've seen a variable that holds an integer number.

When we define a variable, we want to tell it the type of data that should be stored in it. As you might have guessed, this is known as the **data type** and all meaningful programming languages have a vast array of different types to choose from.

The data type of a variable has a great impact on how the computer will run your code. In this section, we'll take a deeper look at how variables work and how they might impact the performance of your program.

Working with Numbers

When we work with numbers in Visual Basic .NET, we'll be working with two kinds of numbers: **integers** and **floating-point numbers**. Both have very specific uses.

Integer numbers are, usually, not much use for math type calculations, for example calculating how much money you have left on your mortgage or calculating how long it would take to fill a swimming pool with water. For these kinds of calculations, you're more likely to use floating-point variables for the simple reason that it's possible to represent decimal numbers using these, whereas you can't with integer variables (which can only hold whole numbers).

Oddly, you'll find that in your day-to-day activities, you're far more likely to use integer variables than floating-point variables. Most of the software that you write will use numbers to keep track of what's going on, rather than for performing calculations.

For example, imagine you write a program that displays customer details on the screen. Let's also say that you have 100 customers in your database. When the program starts you'll display the first customer on the screen. You also need to keep track of which customer is being displayed, so that when the user says, "Next, please", you'll actually know which one is next.

As a computer is more comfortable working with numbers than with anything else, what you'll usually find is that each customer has been given a unique number. This unique number will, in virtually all cases, be an integer number. What this means is that each of your customers will have a unique integer number between 1 and 100 assigned to them. (You can choose any number range you want. For example, I might want to start at 48 and make all of my customers' IDs a factor of 6, so I'd have 48, 54, 60, 66, 72 and so on.) In your program, you'll also have a variable that stores the ID of the customer that you're currently looking at. When the user asks to see the next customer, we add one to that ID ("increment by one") and display the new customer.

You'll see how this kind of thing works as we move on to more advanced topics, but for now rest assured that we're more likely to use integer numbers than floating-points.

Let's take a look now at some common operations.

Common Integer Math Operations

Let's create a new project for our math operations.

Try It Out – Common Integer Math

1. Create a new project in Visual Studio .NET by selecting File | New | Project from the menu. When asked, select Windows Application from the right-hand pane and enter the project name as IntegerMath:

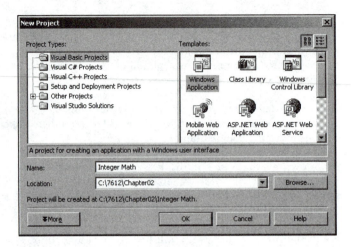

2. Using the Toolbox, add a new **Button** control to the **Form1** as before. Set its **Name** property to **btnIntMath** and its **Text** property to **Math Test**. Double-click it and add this code to the new `Click` event handler that will be created:

```
Private Sub btnIntMath_Click(ByVal sender As System.Object, _
          ByVal e As System.EventArgs) Handles btnIntMath.Click
```

```
    ' define n...
    Dim n As Integer

    ' try adding numbers...
    n = 16
    n = n + 8
    MessageBox.Show("Addition test..." & n, "Integer Math")

    ' try subtracting numbers...
    n = 24
    n = n - 2
    MessageBox.Show("Subtraction test..." & n, "Integer Math")

    ' try multiplying numbers...
    n = 6
    n = n * 10
    MessageBox.Show("Multiplication test..." & n, "Integer Math")

    ' try dividing numbers...
    n = 12
    n = n / 6
    MessageBox.Show("Division test..." & n, "Integer Math")

    End Sub
```

3. Run the project. You'll be able to click through to four message boxes:

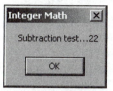

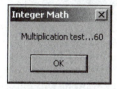

How It Works

Hopefully, none of the code we've seen should be too baffling.

We've already seen the addition operator before. Here it is again:

```
' try adding numbers...
n = 16
n = n + 8
```

So, all we're saying is this:

❑ Let n be equal to the value 16

❑ Then, let n be equal to the current value of n (which is 16) plus 8

As we can see from the message box we get a result of 24, which is correct.

The subtraction operator is a minus (–) sign. Here it is in action:

```
' try subtracting numbers...
n = 24
n = n - 2
```

Again, same deal as before:

❑ Let n be equal to the value 24

❑ Let n be equal to the current value of n (which is 24) minus 2

The multiplication operator is an asterisk (*). Here it is in action:

```
' try multiplying numbers...
n = 6
n = n * 10
```

Finally, the division operator is a forward slash (/). Here it is in action:

```
' try dividing numbers...
n = 12
n = n / 6
```

Integer Math Shorthand

There is a way of performing the same operations without having to write as much code. This is using **shorthand operators** (or **assignment operators**) and although they look a little less logical than their more verbose counterparts, you'll soon learn to love them.

Try It Out – Using Shorthand Operators

1. Go back to Visual Studio .NET and open Form1.vb again. Change the highlighted lines:

```
Private Sub btnIntMath_Click(ByVal sender As System.Object, _
        ByVal e As System.EventArgs) Handles btnIntMath.Click

    ' define n...
    Dim n As Integer

    ' try adding numbers...
    n = 16
    n += 8
    MessageBox.Show("Addition test..." & n, "Integer Math")

    ' try subtracting numbers...
    n = 24
    n -= 2
    MessageBox.Show("Subtraction test..." & n, "Integer Math")

    ' try multiplying numbers...
    n = 6
    n *= 10
    MessageBox.Show("Multiplication test..." & n, "Integer Math")

    ' try dividing numbers...
    n = 12
    n /= 6
    MessageBox.Show("Division test..." & n, "Integer Math")

    End Sub
```

2. Run the project. You'll get the same results as in the previous *Try It Out*.

How It Works

As you can see, in order to use the shorthand version we just rearrange the code and drop one of the ns. Here's the old version:

```
n = n + 8
```

...and here's the new version:

```
n += 8
```

As I said, there's nothing much to the use of shorthand operators. Simply learn to recognize them when they come up and learn to use them in your own code!

The Problem with Integer Math

The main problem with integer math is that you can't do anything that involves a decimal part. For example, you can't do this:

```
' try multiplying numbers...
n = 6
n = n * 10.23
```

...or rather, you can actually run that code but you won't get the result you were expecting. Because n has been defined as a variable designed to accept an integer only, the result is rounded up or down to the nearest integer. In this case, although the actual answer is 61.38, n will be set to the value 61. If the answer was 61.73, n would be set to 62.

Likewise, a similar problem occurs with division. Here's another piece of code:

```
' try dividing numbers...
n = 12
n = n / 7
```

This time the answer is 1.71. However, because the result has to be rounded up in order that it can be stored in n, we end up with n being set equal to 2.

As you can imagine, if we were trying to write programs that actually calculated some form of value, we'd be in big trouble, as every step in the calculation would be subject to rounding errors.

In the next section, we'll look at how we can do these kinds of operation with floating-point numbers.

Floating-Point Math

So, we know that integers are no good for mathematical calculations because most calculations of these types involve a decimal component of some description. Later in this chapter, we'll see how to use floating-point numbers to calculate the area of a circle, but for now we'll just introduce the concepts.

Try It Out – Floating Point Math

1. Create a new Windows Application project in Visual Studio .NET called Floating-Pt Math. As before, place a button on the form, setting its Name to btnFloatMath and its Text to Double Test:

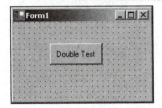

2. Double-click on btnFloatMath and add the following code:

```
Private Sub btnFloatMath_Click(ByVal sender As System.Object, _
            ByVal e As System.EventArgs) Handles btnFloatMath.Click

    ' define n...
    Dim n As Double

    ' try multiplying numbers...
    n = 45.34
    n *= 4.333
    MessageBox.Show("Multiplication test..." & n, "Floating Points")

    ' try dividing numbers...
    n = 12
    n /= 7
    MessageBox.Show("Division test..." & n, "Floating Points")

End Sub
```

3. Run the project and you'll see this:

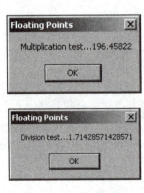

4. Be sure to save this project, we'll be returning to it later in the chapter.

How It Works

Perhaps the most important change in this code is the way we're defining n:

```
Dim n As Double
```

Rather than saying As Integer at the end, we're saying As Double. This tells Visual Basic .NET that we want to create a variable that holds a **double-precision floating-point number**, rather than an integer number. This means that any operation performed on n will be a floating-point operation, rather than an integer operation.

However, there's no difference in how either of these operations are performed. Here, we set n to be a decimal number and then multiply it by another decimal number:

```
' try multiplying numbers...
n = 45.34
n *= 4.333
```

When we run this, we get a result of 196.45822, which as you can see has a decimal component and therefore we can use this in calculations.

Of course, floating-point numbers don't have to have an explicit decimal component:

```
' try dividing numbers...
n = 12
n /= 7
```

This result still yields a floating-point result because n has been set up to hold such a result. We can see this by our result of 1.71, which is the same result we were looking for back when we were examining integer math.

Other States

Floating-point numbers can also hold a number of other states. Specifically, these are:

❑ NaN – which means "not a number"

❑ Positive infinity

❑ Negative infinity

We won't show how to get all of the results here, but the mathematicians among you will recognize that .NET will cater for their advanced math needs.

Single-Precision Floating-Point Numbers

We've been saying "double-precision floating-point" up until now. In .NET, there are two main ways to represent floating-point numbers depending on your needs.

Because in certain cases the decimal components of floating-point numbers can zoom off to infinity (pi being a particularly obvious example), there has to be some limit at which the computer will stop keeping track of the decimal component. These are usually related to the size of the variable, which is a subject we discuss in much more detail towards the end of the chapter. There are also limits on how large the non-decimal component can be.

A double-precision floating-point number can hold any value between -1.7×10^{308} and $+1.7 \times 10^{308}$ to a great level of accuracy. On the other hand, a **single-precision floating-point number** can only hold between -3.4×10^{38} and $+3.4 \times 10^{38}$. Again, still a pretty huge number, but this holds decimal components to a lesser degree of accuracy – the benefit being that single-precision floating point numbers require less memory.

> **You should avoid using double-precision numbers unless you actually require more accuracy than the single-precision allows. This is especially important in very large applications where using double-precision numbers for variables that only require single-precision numbers could slow up your program significantly.**

The calculations you're trying to perform will dictate which type of floating-point number you wish to use. If you want to use a single-precision number, use `As Single` rather than `As Double`, like this:

```
Dim n As Single
```

Working with Strings

A **string** is simply a collection of characters and we use double quotes to mark its beginning and end. We've seen how to use strings in order to display the results of our simple programs on the screen. Strings are commonly used for exactly this function – telling the user what happened and what needs to happen next. Another common use is storing a piece of text for later use in an algorithm. We'll see lots of strings throughout the rest of the book.

So far, we've used strings like this:

```
MessageBox.Show("Multiplication test..." & n, "Floating Points")
```

Both `"Multiplication test..."` and `"Floating Points"` are strings; we can easily tell because of the double quotes (`"`). However, what about n? Well, what's actually happening here is that the value contained within n is being converted to a string value that can be displayed on the screen. (This is a pretty advanced topic that we cover later in the chapter, but for now concentrate on the fact that a conversion is taking place.) For example, if n represents the value `27`, to display it on the screen it has to be converted into a string two-characters in length.

Let's look at some of the things we can do with strings.

Try It Out – Using Strings

1. Create a new Windows Application using the File | New | Project menu option. Call it Strings.

2. Using the Toolbox, draw a button called btnStrings on the form and set its Text property to Using Strings. Double-click it and then add this code:

```
Private Sub btnStrings_Click(ByVal sender As System.Object, _
        ByVal e As System.EventArgs) Handles btnStrings.Click
```

```
      ' define a string...
      Dim s As String
      s = "Hello, world!"

      ' display the result...
      MessageBox.Show(s, "Strings")

End Sub
```

3. Run the project. You'll see this:

How It Works

We can define a variable that holds a string using a similar notation to that used with the number variables, but this time using As String:

```
      ' define a string...
      Dim s As String
```

We can also set that string to have a value, again as we did before:

```
      s = "Hello, world!"
```

We need to use double quotes around the string value to **delimit** the string, meaning to mark where the string begins and where the string ends. This is an important point, because these double quotes tell Visual Basic .NET compiler not to compile the text that is contained within the string. If we didn't include the quotes, Visual Basic .NET would treat the value to be stored in the variable as part of the program's code, and this would cause all kinds of problems.

With the value "Hello, world!" stored in a string variable called s, we can pass that variable to the message box whose job it is to then extract the value from the variable and display it.

So, you can see that strings can be defined and used in the same way as the numeric values you saw before. Now let's look at how to perform operations on strings.

Concatenation

Concatenation means linking something together in a chain or series. If we have two strings that we join together, one after the other, we say they are concatenated. You can think of concatenation as addition for strings.

Try It Out – Concatenation

1. Open Form1.vb again, delete the old code and add this new code:

```
Private Sub btnStrings_Click(ByVal sender As System.Object, _
          ByVal e As System.EventArgs) Handles btnStrings.Click

    ' define a string...
    Dim s1 As String
    s1 = "Hello"

    ' define another string...
    Dim s2 As String
    s2 = ", world!"

    ' define a final string and concatenate...
    Dim s As String
    s = s1 & s2

    ' display the result...
    MessageBox.Show(s, "Strings")

End Sub
```

2. Run the project. You'll see the same results as before:

How It Works

In this *Try It Out* we have two strings s1 and s2:

```
    ' define a string...
    Dim s1 As String
    s1 = "Hello"

    ' define another string...
    Dim s2 As String
    s2 = ", world!"
```

After this we're free to define a third string (s) and we use the & operator to concatenate the two previous strings together:

```
    ' define a final string and concatenate...
    Dim s As String
    s = s1 & s2
```

What we're saying here is "let s be equal to the current value of s1 followed by the current value of s2".

By the time we call `MessageBox.Show`, s will be equal to `"Hello, world!"`, hence we get the same value as before.

Using the Concatenation Operator Inline

You don't have to define variables in order to use the concatenation operator. You can use it on the fly, as we'll show next.

Try It Out – Inline Concatenation

1. Open Form1.vb once more and remove the existing code, replacing it with this:

```
Private Sub btnStrings_Click(ByVal sender As System.Object, _
            ByVal e As System.EventArgs) Handles btnStrings.Click

        ' define a variable...
        Dim n As Integer
        n = 26

        ' display the result...
        MessageBox.Show("The value of n is: " & n, "Strings")

End Sub
```

2. Run the code. You'll see this:

How It Works

We've already seen the concatenation operator being used like this in previous examples. What this is actually doing is converting the value stored in n to a string so that it can be displayed on the screen.

Let's look at this line:

```
MessageBox.Show("The value of n is: " & n, "Strings")
```

The portion that reads, `"The value of n is: "` is actually a string, but we don't have to define it as a string variable. Visual Basic .NET calls this a **string literal**, meaning that it's a literal value contained in the code that doesn't change. When we use the concatenation operator on this string together with n, n is converted into a string and tacked onto the end of `"The value of n is: "`. The result is that we get one string passed to `MessageBox.Show` that contains both the base text and the current value of n.

More String Operations

There are plenty more things that we can do with strings! Let's take a look at some of them now.

The first thing we'll do is look at a property of the string that can be used to return its length.

Try It Out – Returning the Length of a String

1. Using the designer for Form1, add a TextBox control called txtString to the form, clear its Text property, and change the Text property of the button to Length. Rearrange the controls so that they look like this:

2. Double-click on the button control to open its Click event handler. Replace whatever code is there with this:

```
Private Sub btnStrings_Click(ByVal sender As System.Object, _
            ByVal e As System.EventArgs) Handles btnStrings.Click

    ' get the text from the text box...
    Dim myString As String
    myString = txtString.Text

    ' display the length of the string...
    MessageBox.Show(myString.Length & " character(s)")

End Sub
```

3. Run the project and enter some text into the textbox.

4. Click the Length button and you'll see this:

How It Works

The first thing we do in the event handler is extract the text from the textbox and store it in a variable called myString:

```
Private Sub btnStrings_Click(ByVal sender As System.Object, _
            ByVal e As System.EventArgs) Handles btnStrings.Click

    ' get the text from the text box...
    Dim myString As String
    myString = txtString.Text
```

Once we have the string, we can use the Length property to get hold of an integer value that represents the number of characters in it. Remember, as far as a computer is concerned, characters include things like spaces and other punctuation marks:

```
    ' display the length of the string...
    MessageBox.Show(myString.Length & " character(s)")

End Sub
```

That's it. Easy!

Substrings

A very common way to manipulate strings in a program is to use either a set of characters that appears at the start, a set that appears at the end or a set that appears somewhere in between. These are known as **substrings**.

What we'll do in this *Try It Out* is build on our previous application and get it to display the first three, last three, and middle three characters:

Try It Out – Working with Substrings

1. If the Strings program is running, close it.

2. Change the Text property of the button to Split. Then, using the code editor for Form1.vb, change the code as follows:

```
Private Sub btnStrings_Click(ByVal sender As System.Object, _
            ByVal e As System.EventArgs) Handles btnStrings.Click

    ' get the text from the text box...
    Dim myString As String
    myString = txtString.Text

    ' display the first three characters...
    MessageBox.Show(myString.Substring(0, 3))

    ' display the last three characters...
    MessageBox.Show(myString.Substring(myString.Length - 3))
```

```
   ' display the middle three characters...
   MessageBox.Show(myString.Substring(3, 3))
```

End Sub

3. Run the project. Enter a string that is nine characters in length:

4. Press the Split button and you'll see three message boxes one after another:

5. Make sure you save this project somewhere safe.

How It Works

The Substring method lets us grab a set of characters from any position in the string. The method can be used in one of two ways. The first way is to give it a starting point and a number of characters to grab. In the first instance, we're telling it to start at character 0 and grab 3 characters:

```
   ' display the first three characters...
   MessageBox.Show(myString.Substring(0, 3))
```

In the second instance, we're only providing one parameter. This tells the Substring to start at the given position and grab everything right up to the end. In this case, we're using Substring in combination with Length, so effectively we're saying, "Grab everything from three characters in from the right of the string to the end."

```
' display the last three characters...
MessageBox.Show(myString.Substring(myString.Length - 3))
```

Finally, we're using the first form of the method again to start three characters in from the start and grab three characters:

```
' display the middle three characters...
MessageBox.Show(myString.Substring(3, 3))
```

Formatting Strings

Often when working with numbers you'll come across situations where you need to alter the way that they are displayed as a string.

Here's an example. This is a screenshot taken from our program that showed how the division operator worked:

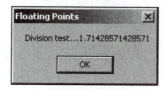

In this case, we don't really need to see fourteen decimal places – two or three would be fine! What we need to do is format the string so that we see everything to the left of the decimal point, but only three digits to the right.

Try It Out – Formatting Strings

1. Open up the Floating-Pt Math project that you saved previously in this chapter.

2. Open the code editor for Form1 and make the following changes:

```
Private Sub btnFloatMath_Click(ByVal sender As System.Object, _
        ByVal e As System.EventArgs) Handles btnFloatMath.Click

    ' define n...
    Dim n As Double

    ' try dividing numbers...
    n = 12
    n /= 7

    ' display it without formatting:
    MessageBox.Show("Without formatting: " & n)

    ' create a new, formatted string...
    Dim s As String
    s = String.Format("{0:n3}", n)

    ' display the new string...
    MessageBox.Show("With formatting: " & s)

End Sub
```

Notice that in addition to the new code at the end, we've removed the multiplication code immediately after n *is defined as a* `Double`.

3. Run the project. The first message box will look like this:

4. When you click OK, the second message box will be displayed and it will look like this:

How It Works

The magic here is all in the call to `String.Format`. This is a powerful method that allows formatting of numbers. The key is all in the first parameter as this defines the format the final string will take:

```
s = String.Format("{0:n3}", n)
```

You'll notice that we've passed `String.Format` two parameters. As we just mentioned, the first `"{0:n3}"` is the format that we want. The second parameter n is the value that we want to format.

The 0 in the format tells `String.Format` to work with the **zeroth data parameter**, which is just a cute way of saying "the second parameter", or n. What follows the colon is how we want n to be formatted. We've said n3, which means: floating-point number, three decimal places. We could have said n2 for: floating-point number, two decimal places.

There are a lot of different options related to string formatting, but in this chapter, we're only going to look at this and two others.

Localized Formatting

When building .NET applications, it's important to realize that the user may be familiar with cultural conventions that are uncommon to you. A classic example of this is if you live in the United States, you'll be used to seeing the decimal separator as a period (.). However, if you live in France the decimal separator is actually a comma (,).

Windows can deal with a lot of these problems for us based on the **locale** settings of the computer. At this stage, if you use the .NET Framework in the correct way, by and large you'll never need to worry about this problem.

Here's an example – if I use a formatting string of n3 again, I'm telling .NET that I want to format the number with thousands separators and also that I want the number displayed to three decimal places, like this:

Now, if I tell my computer that I want to use French locale settings, if I run the *same code* (I make no changes whatsoever to the application itself), I'll see this:

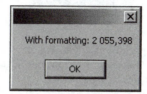

What's happened here is that in France, the thousands separator is a space not a comma. Likewise, the decimal separator is a comma not a period. By using String.Format appropriately, I can write one application that works properly regardless of how the user has configured the locale settings on the computer.

Replacing Substrings

Another common string manipulation is replacing occurrences of one string with another. To demonstrate this, we'll build an application that replaces the string "Hello" with the string "Goodbye".

Try It Out – Replacing Substrings

1. Open up the Strings program you were working with before.

2. In Form1, change the Text property of btnStrings to Replace and change the code in its Click event handler to this:

```
Private Sub btnStrings_Click(ByVal sender As System.Object, _
            ByVal e As System.EventArgs) Handles btnStrings.Click

    ' get the text from the text box...
    Dim myString As String
    myString = txtString.Text

    ' replace the string...
    Dim newString As String
    newString = myString.Replace("Hello", "Goodbye")

    ' display the new string...
    MessageBox.Show(newString)

End Sub
```

3. Run the project and enter Hello world! into the text box:

4. Click the button. You should see this:

How It Works

`Replace` works by taking the substring to look *for* as the first parameter and the new substring to replace it *with* whenever it finds it as the second parameter. Once the replacing has been done, a new string is returned that we can display in the usual way.

```
newString = myString.Replace("Hello", "Goodbye")
```

You're not limited to a single search and replace with this code. If you enter Hello twice into the textbox and click the button, you'll notice two Goodbyes. However, case is important – if you enter hello, it will not be replaced.

Using Dates

Another really common data type that you'll often use is `Date`. This data type holds, not surprisingly, a date value.

Try It Out – Displaying the Current Date

1. Create a new Windows Application project called Date Demo.

2. In the usual way, use the Toolbox to draw a new button control on the form. Call it btnDate and set its Text property to Show Date.

3. Double-click on the button to bring up its `Click` event handler and add this code:

```
Private Sub btnDate_Click(ByVal sender As System.Object, _
          ByVal e As System.EventArgs) Handles btnDate.Click

    ' get the current date and time...
    Dim theDate As Date
    theDate = Date.Now()

    ' display it...
    MessageBox.Show(theDate, "Date Demo")

End Sub
```

4. Run the project and click the button. You should see something like this depending on the locale settings on your machine:

How It Works

The Date data type can be used to hold a value that represents any date and time. After creating the variable, we initialized it to the current date and time using Date.Now:

```
' get the current date and time...
Dim theDate As Date
theDate = Date.Now()
```

In reality, Date data types aren't any different from other data types – although we can do more with them. In the next couple of sections, we'll look at ways in which we can manipulate dates and also control how they are displayed on the screen.

Formatting Date Strings

We've already seen one way in which dates can be formatted. By default, if we just pass a Date variable to MessageBox.Show, we'll see the date and time displayed, like this:

You can also see that, because my machine is in the UK, the date is being shown in dd/mm/yyyy format and that the time is being shown using the 24-hour clock. This is another example of how the computer's locale setting affects the formatting of different data types.

For example, if I set my computer to US locale, we get this:

Although we can control the date format to the nth degree, it's best to rely on .NET to properly ascertain how the user wants strings to look and automatically display them in their preferred format. In the next *Try It Out*, we'll look at four very useful methods that allow us to format dates.

Try It Out – Formatting Dates

1. If the Date Demo program is running, close it.

2. Using the code editor for Form1, find the Click event handler for the button and change the code to this:

```
Private Sub btnDate_Click(ByVal sender As System.Object, _
        ByVal e As System.EventArgs) Handles btnDate.Click

    ' get the current date and time...
    Dim theDate As Date
    theDate = Date.Now()

    ' display the date...
    MessageBox.Show(theDate.ToLongDateString, "Date Demo")
    MessageBox.Show(theDate.ToShortDateString, "Date Demo")

    ' display the time...
    MessageBox.Show(theDate.ToLongTimeString, "Date Demo")
    MessageBox.Show(theDate.ToShortTimeString, "Date Demo")

End Sub
```

3. Run the project. You'll be able to click through four message boxes similar to these:

How It Works

What we're seeing is the four basic ways that we can display date and time in Windows applications, namely long date, short date, long time, and short time.

I'm sure you can see that the names of each of the methods are self explanatory!

```
' display the date...
MessageBox.Show(theDate.ToLongDateString, "Date Demo")
MessageBox.Show(theDate.ToShortDateString, "Date Demo")

' display the time...
MessageBox.Show(theDate.ToLongTimeString, "Date Demo")
MessageBox.Show(theDate.ToShortTimeString, "Date Demo")
```

Extracting Date Properties

When we have a variable of type Date, there are a number of properties that we can call to learn more about the date; let's look at them.

Try It Out – Extracting Date Properties

1. If the Date Demo project is running, close it.

2. Using the code editor, make these changes to the Click handler in Form1:

```
Private Sub btnDate_Click(ByVal sender As System.Object, _
        ByVal e As System.EventArgs) Handles btnDate.Click

    ' get the current date and time...
    Dim theDate As Date
    theDate = Date.Now()

    ' display the date/time details...
    MessageBox.Show("Month: " & theDate.Month, "Date Demo")
    MessageBox.Show("Day: " & theDate.Day, "Date Demo")
    MessageBox.Show("Year: " & theDate.Year, "Date Demo")
    MessageBox.Show("Hour: " & theDate.Hour, "Date Demo")
    MessageBox.Show("Minute: " & theDate.Minute, "Date Demo")
    MessageBox.Show("Second: " & theDate.Second, "Date Demo")
    MessageBox.Show("Day of week: " & theDate.DayOfWeek, "Date Demo")
    MessageBox.Show("Day of year: " & theDate.DayOfYear, "Date Demo")

End Sub
```

3. Run the project. If you click the button, you'll see a set of fairly self-explanatory message boxes.

How It Works

Again, there's nothing here that's rocket science. If you want to know the hour, use the Hour property. To get at the year, use Year, and so on.

Date Constants

In our previous *Try It Out*, you'll notice that when we called `DayOfWeek` we were actually given an integer value:

The date that we're working with, May 31st 2002, is a Friday and we've been told that Friday is 5. From that we can assume that Monday is 1 and, although it's not immediately obvious, Sunday is 0. As the first day of the week is Sunday in the United States, we start counting from Sunday. However, there is a possibility that we're working on a computer whose locale setting starts the calendar on a Monday, in which case `DayOfWeek` would return 6. Complicated? Perhaps, but just remember that you can't guarantee that what you think is "Day 1" is always going to be Monday. Likewise, what's Wednesday in English is Mittwoch in German.

If we need to know the name of the day or the month in our application, a better approach is to get .NET to get the name for us, again from the particular locale settings of the computer.

Try It Out – Getting the Names of the Weekday and the Month

1. If the **Date Demo** project is running, close it.

2. Using the code editor, make these changes to the `Click` event handler:

```
Private Sub btnDate_Click(ByVal sender As System.Object, _
            ByVal e As System.EventArgs) Handles btnDate.Click

    ' get the current date and time...
    Dim theDate As Date
    theDate = Date.Now()

    ' display the weekday name...
    Dim s As String
    s = theDate.ToString("dddd")
    MessageBox.Show("Weekday name: " & s, "Date Demo")

    ' display the month name...
    s = theDate.ToString("MMMM")
    MessageBox.Show("Month name: " & s, "Date Demo")

End Sub
```

3. Run the project and click the button. You will see this message box and if you click **OK**, you'll see the other one:

How It Works

When we used our `ToLongDateString` method and its siblings, we were basically allowing .NET to go away and look in the locale settings for the computer for the date format the user preferred. In this example, we're using the `ToString` method but supplying our own format string.

```
' display the weekday name...
Dim s As String
s = theDate.ToString("dddd")
MessageBox.Show("Weekday name: " & s, "Date Demo")

' display the month name...
s = theDate.ToString("MMMM")
MessageBox.Show("Month name: " & s, "Date Demo")
```

Usually, it's best practice not to use `ToString` to format dates because you should rely on the built-in formats, but here we're using the `"dddd"` string to get the weekday name and `"MMMM"` to get the month name. (The case is important here – `"mmmm"` won't work.)

To show this works, if I set my computer to use Italian locale settings, this is what I get:

Defining Date Literals

We know that if we want to use a string literal in our code, we can do this:

```
Dim s As String
s = "Woofie"
```

Date literals work in more or less the same way. However, we use sharp signs (#) to delimit the start and end of the number.

Try It Out – Defining Date Literals

1. If the Date Demo project is running, close it.

2. Using the code editor, make this change to the Click event handler:

```
Private Sub btnDate_Click(ByVal sender As System.Object, _
            ByVal e As System.EventArgs) Handles btnDate.Click

    ' define a date...
    Dim theDate As Date
    theDate = #4/27/1978 3:00:00 AM#

    ' display the date...
    MessageBox.Show(theDate.ToLongDateString & " " & _
        theDate.ToLongTimeString, "Date Demo")

End Sub
```

3. Run the project and click the button. You should see this:

How It Works

When defining a date literal, it *must* be defined in mm/dd/yyyy format, regardless of the actual locale settings of the computer. You may or may not see an error if you try and define the date in the format dd/mm/yyyy. This is becuase you could put in a date in the format of dd/mm/yyyy (for example 06/07/2002) that is also a valid date in the required mm/dd/yyyy format. This requirement is to reduce ambiguity: does 6/7/2002 mean July 6th or June 7th?

> **In fact, this is a general truth of programming as a whole – there's no such thing as dialects when writing software. It's usually best to conform to North American standards. As you'll see through the rest of this book, this includes variables and method names, for example GetColor rather than GetColour.**

It's also worth noting that you don't have to supply both a date *and* a time – you can supply one, the other, or both.

Manipulating Dates

One thing that's always been pretty tricky for programmers to do is manipulate dates. We all remember New Year's Eve 1999, waiting to see if computers could deal with tipping into a new century. Also, dealing with leap years has always been a bit of a problem.

The next turn of the century that also features a leap year will be 2399 to 2400. In this section, we'll take a look at how we can use some of the methods available on the Date data type to adjust the date around that particular leap year.

Try It Out – Manipulating Dates

1. If the Date Demo program is running, close it.

2. Using the code editor, find the Click event handler and make this change:

```
Private Sub btnDate_Click(ByVal sender As System.Object, _
          ByVal e As System.EventArgs) Handles btnDate.Click

      ' start off in 2400...
      Dim theDate As Date, changedDate As Date
theDate = #2/28/2400#

      ' add a day...
      changedDate = theDate.AddDays(1)
      MessageBox.Show(changedDate.ToLongDateString, "Date Demo")

      ' add some months...
      changedDate = theDate.AddMonths(6)
      MessageBox.Show(changedDate.ToLongDateString, "Date Demo")

      ' subtract a year...
      changedDate = theDate.AddYears(-1)
      MessageBox.Show(changedDate.ToLongDateString, "Date Demo")

End Sub
```

3. Run the project and click the button. You'll see these three message boxes, one after another:

How It Works

`Date` supports a number of methods for manipulating dates. Here are three of them:

```
' add a day...
changedDate = theDate.AddDays(1)
MessageBox.Show(changedDate.ToLongDateString, "Date Demo")

' add some months...
changedDate = theDate.AddMonths(6)
MessageBox.Show(changedDate.ToLongDateString, "Date Demo")

' subtract a year...
changedDate = theDate.AddYears(-1)
MessageBox.Show(changedDate.ToLongDateString, "Date Demo")
```

It's worth noting that when you supply a negative number to an `Add` method when working with `Date` variables, the effect is subtraction. (As we've seen by going from 2400 back to 2399.)

The other important `Add` methods are: `AddHours`, `AddMinutes`, `AddSeconds`, and `AddMilliseconds`.

Boolean

So far we've seen the `Integer`, `Double`, `Float`, `String`, and `Date` data types. The other one we need to look at is `Boolean` and, once we've done that, we've seen all of the simple data types that we're ever likely to use in our programs.

A **Boolean** variable can be either `True` or `False`. It can never be anything else, and is indicative of the binary nature of a computer, in that we're only ever dealing with 1s and 0s.

Boolean values are really important when it's time for your programs to start making decisions, which is something we look at later on in this chapter and in much more detail in Chapter 3. But, it's worth taking a look at Booleans now.

Try It Out – Using Booleans

1. Create a new Windows Application project called Boolean Demo.

2. As usual, draw a button onto the form called `btnBoolean`. Double-click it to create a new `Click` event handler and add this code:

```
Private Sub btnBoolean_Click(ByVal sender As System.Object, _
         ByVal e As System.EventArgs) Handles btnBoolean.Click

    ' define a boolean...
    Dim myFirstBoolean As Boolean
    myFirstBoolean = True

    ' define another boolean...
    Dim mySecondBoolean As Boolean
    mySecondBoolean = False

    ' display the value...
    MessageBox.Show("First: " & myFirstBoolean, "Boolean Demo")
    MessageBox.Show("Second: " & mySecondBoolean, "Boolean Demo")

End Sub
```

3. Run the project and click the button. You'll see two message boxes, one after the other:

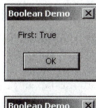

How It Works

To define a Boolean value, just put `As Boolean` onto the end of the `Dim` statement:

```
    ' define a boolean...
    Dim myFirstBoolean As Boolean
```

Once that's done, we can either assign the value `True` or the value `False`:

```
    myFirstBoolean = True
```

You cannot assign other values to a Boolean, although if you try to, Visual Basic .NET will attempt to convert the value. For example, if you supply an integer of 0, it will be converted to False, as False is represented internally within .NET by 0. Likewise, if you try and supply an integer with the value 27 this is "not zero", hence "not false", and hence deemed to be "true".

That's really all there is to Booleans. They prove themselves to be much more useful when it's time to start making decisions in our programs.

Let's now complete our discussion of variables in this chapter by looking at how we store them in our computer.

Storing Variables

The most limited resource on your computer is typically its memory. It is important that we try to get the most out of the available memory. Whenever we create a variable, we are using a piece of memory so we must strive to use as few variables as possible and use the variables that we do have in the most efficient manner.

Today, absolute optimization of variables is not something we need to go into a deep level of detail about for two reasons. Firstly, computers have far more memory these days, so the days when programmers tried to cram payroll systems into 32KB of memory are long gone. Secondly, the compilers themselves have a great deal of intelligence built in to help generate the most optimized code possible.

Binary

Computers use **binary** to represent everything. That means that whatever you want a computer to store, it must be expressed as a binary pattern of ones and zeros. Take a simple integer, 27. In binary code, this number is actually 11011, each digit referring to a power of two. The following diagram shows how we represent 27 in the more familiar base-10 format, and then in binary:

10^7	10^6	10^5	10^4	10^3	10^2	10^1	10^0
10,000,000	1,000,000	100,000	10,000	1,000	100	10	1
0	0	0	0	0	0	2	7

In base-10, each digit represents a power of ten. To find what number the "pattern of base-10 digits" represents, we multiply the relevant number by the power of ten that the digit represents and add the results.

$$2 \times 10 + 7 \times 1 = 27$$

2^7	2^6	2^5	2^4	2^3	2^2	2^1	2^0
128	64	32	16	8	4	2	1
0	0	0	1	1	0	1	1

In base-2, or binary, each digit represents a power of two. To find what number the "pattern of binary digits" represents, we multiply the relevant number by the power of two that the digit represents and add the results.

$$1 \times 16 + 1 \times 8 + 1 \times 2 + 1 + 1 = 27$$

Although this may appear to be a bit obscure, look what's happening. In base-10, the decimal system that we're all familiar with, each digit fits into a "slot". This slot represents a power of ten – the first representing ten to the power zero, the second ten to the power one, and so on. If we want to know what number the pattern represents, we take each slot in turn, multiply it by the value it represents and add the results.

The same applies to binary – it's just that we're not familiar with dealing with base-2. To convert the number back to base-10, we take the digit in each slot in turn and multiply it by the number that the slot represents. Add all of the results together and we get the number.

Bits and Bytes

In computer terms, a slot is called a **bit** and the reason why I've drawn eight slots/bits on the diagram is that eight bits is a **byte**. A byte is the unit of measurement that we use when talking about computer memory.

A **kilobyte**, or **KB** is 1,024 bytes. We use 1,024 rather than 1,000 because 1,024 is the 10th power of 2, so as far as the computer is concerned it's a "round number". Computers don't tend to think of things in terms of 10s like we do, so 1,024 is more natural to a computer than 1,000.

Likewise, a **megabyte** is 1,024 kilobytes, or 1,048,576 bytes. Again, that's another round number because this is the 20th power of 2.

Continuing the theme, we have a **gigabyte**, which is 1,024 megabytes, or 1,073,741,824 bytes. (Again, think 2 to the power of 30 and you're on the right lines.)

Finally, we have a **terabyte**, which is 2 to the 40th power and a **petabyte**, which is 2 to the 50th power.

So what's the point of all this? Well, it's worth having an understanding how computers store variables so you can better design your programs. Let's imagine that your computer has 256MB of memory. That's 262,144KB or 268,435,456 bytes or (multiply by eight) 2,147,483,648 bits. As we write our software, we have to make the best possible use of this available memory.

Representing Values

Most recent computers are 32-bit, which means that they're optimized for dealing with integer values that are 32-bits in length. The number we just saw in our example was an 8-bit number. With an 8-bit number, the largest value we can store is:

```
1x128 + 1x64 + 1x32 + 1x16 + 1x8 + 1x4 + 1x2 + 1x1 = 255
```

A 32-bit number can represent any value between 0 and 4,294,967,296. Now, we know that if we define a variable like this:

```
Dim n As Integer
```

…we want to store an integer number. In response to this, .NET will allocate a 32-bit block of memory in which we can store any number between 0 and 4,294,967,296. Also, remember we only have a finite amount of memory and on our 256MB computer we can only store a maximum of 67,108,864 long numbers. Sounds like a lot, but remember that memory is for sharing. You shouldn't write software that deliberately tries to use as much memory as possible. Be frugal!

We also defined variables that were double-precision floating-point numbers, like this:

```
Dim d As Double
```

Now to represent a double-precision floating point number, we need 64-bits of memory. That means we can only store a maximum of 33,554,432 double-precision floating-point numbers.

> **Single-precision floating-point numbers take up 32-bits of memory, in other words half that of a double-precision number and the same as an integer value.**

If we do define an integer, whether we store 1, 3,249 or 2,239,482,342 we're always using exactly the same amount of memory, 32-bits. The size of the number has no bearing on the amount of memory required to store it. This might seem incredibly wasteful, but the computer relies on numbers of the same type taking the same amount of storage. Without this, it would be unable to work at a decent speed.

Let's look at how we define a string:

```
Dim s As String
s = "Hello, world!"
```

Unlike integers and doubles, strings do not have a fixed length. Each character in the string takes up two bytes, or 16-bits. So, to represent this 13-character string, we need 13 bytes, or 104 bits. That means that our computer is only able to store a little over two million strings of that length. Obviously, if the string is twice as long we can hold half as many, and so on.

A common mistake that new programmers make is not taking into consideration the impact the data type has on storage. If we have a variable that's supposed to hold a string, and we try to hold a numeric value in it, like this:

```
Dim s As String
s = "65536"
```

...we're using 5 bytes (or 40-bit) to store it. That's less efficient than storing the value in an integer type. In order to store this numerical value in a string, each character in the string has to be converted into a numerical representation. This is done according to something called **Unicode**, which is a standard way of defining the way computers store characters. Each character has a unique number between 0 and 65,535 and it's this value that is stored in each byte allocated to the string.

Here are the Unicode codes for each character in the string:

❑   "6" – ASCII code 54, binary 0000000000110110

❑   "5" – ASCII code 53, binary 0000000000110101

❑   "5" – ASCII code 53, binary 0000000000110101

❑   "3" – ASCII code 51, binary 0000000000110011

❑   "6" – ASCII code 54, binary 0000000000110110

Each character requires 16 bits, so to store a 5-digit number in a string requires 80 bits – 5 16 bit numbers.

What we should do is this:

```
Dim s As Integer
s = 65536
```

This stores the value as a single number binary pattern. An Integer uses 32 bits, so the binary representation will be 00000000000000010000000000000000, far smaller than the space needed to store it as a string.

Converting Values

Although strings seem very natural to us, they're very unnatural to a computer. A computer eventually wants to take two numbers and perform some simple mathematical operation on them. However, a computer can perform such a vast number of these simple operations each second that we, as humans, get the results we want.

Let's imagine that a computer wants to add 1 to the value 27. We already know that that we can represent 27 in binary as 11011. This diagram shows what happens:

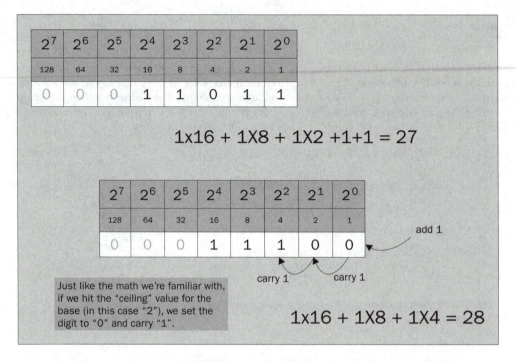

$$1x16 + 1X8 + 1X2 +1+1 = 27$$

$$1x16 + 1X8 + 1X4 = 28$$

As you can see, binary math is no different from decimal (base-10) math. If we try to add one to the first bit, it won't fit, so we revert it to zero and carry the one to the next bit. The same happens, and we carry the one to the third bit. At this point, we've finished and if we reckon up the value we get 28, as intended.

Any value that you have in your program ultimately has to be converted down to simple numbers in order for the computer to do anything with them. In order to make the program run more efficiently, you have to keep the number of conversions to a minimum.

Here's an example:

```
Dim n As String
n = "27"
n = n + 1
MessageBox.Show(n)
```

Let's look at what's happening:

❑   We create a string variable called n.

❑   We assign the value "27" to that string. This uses four bytes of memory.

❑   To add one to the value, the computer has to convert "27" to an internal, hidden integer variable that contains the value 27. This uses an additional four bytes of memory, taking the total to six. However, more importantly, this conversion takes time!

❏ When the string is converted to an integer, 1 is added to it.

❏ The new value then has to be converted back into a string.

❏ The string containing the new value is displayed on the screen.

In order to write an efficient program, we don't want to be constantly converting variables between different types. We want only to perform the conversion when it's absolutely necessary.

Here's some more code that has the same effect:

```
Dim n As Integer
n = 27
n = n + 1
MessageBox.Show(n)
```

❏ We create an integer variable called n.

❏ We assign the value 27 to the variable.

❏ We add 1 to the variable.

❏ We convert the variable to a string and display it on the screen.

In this case, we only have to do one conversion, and it's a logical one. `MessageBox.Show` works in terms of strings and characters so that's what it's most comfortable with.

What we have done is cut the conversions from two (string to integer, integer to string) down to one. This will make our program run more efficiently. Again, it's a small improvement, but imagine this improvement occurring hundreds of thousands of times each minute – we'll get an improvement in the performance of the system as a whole.

> **The point that I hope I've managed to put across to you, is that it is absolutely vital you work with the correct data type for your needs. In simple applications like the ones we've created in this chapter, a performance penalty is not really noticeable. However, as you come to write more complex, sophisticated applications you'll really want to be optimizing your code by using the right data type.**

Methods

Now that you know in principle what a variable is, and how to make decisions, we can move on to looking at what a method is.

A **method** is a self-contained block of code that "does something". They are *essential* for two reasons. Firstly, they break a program up and make it more understandable. Secondly, they promote code *reuse* – a topic we'll be spending most of our time on throughout the rest of this book.

As you know, when we write code we start with a high-level algorithm and keep refining the detail of that algorithm until we get the software code that expresses all of the algorithms up to and including the high-level one. A method describes a "line" in one of those algorithms, for example open a file, display text on screen, print a document, and so on.

Knowing how to break a program up into methods is something that comes with experience and, to add to the frustration, it's far easier to understand why you need to use methods when you're working on far more complex programs than the ones we've seen so far. In the rest of this section, I'll endeavor to show you how and why to use methods.

Why Use Methods?

In day-to-day use, we need to pass information to a method for it to produce the expected results. This might be a single integer value, a set of string values, or a combination of both. These are known as **input values**. However, some methods don't take input values, so having input values is not a requirement of a method. The method will use these input values and a combination of environmental information (for instance, facts about the current state of the program that the method knows about) to do something useful.

We say that when we give a method information, we **pass** it data. We also describe that data as **parameters**. Finally, when we want to use a method, we **call** it.

> To summarize, we "call a method, passing in data through parameters".

The reason for using methods is to promote this idea of code reuse. The principle behind using a method makes sense if you consider the program from a fairly high level. If we have an understanding of all the algorithms involved in a program, we can find commonality. If we need to do the same thing more than once, we should wrap it up into a method that we can reuse.

Imagine you have a program that comprises a number of algorithms. Some of those algorithms call for the area of a circle to be calculated. Because *some* of those algorithms need to know how to calculate the area of a circle, it's a good candidate for a method. We write some code that knows how to find the area of a circle given its radius, encapsulate it ("wrap it up") into a method, which we can reuse when we're coding the other algorithms. This means that we don't have to keep writing code that does the same thing – we do it once and reuse it as often as possible.

It might be the case that one algorithm always needs to work out the area of a circle with 100 for its radius, and another always needs to work out one with a radius of 200. By building the method in such a way that it takes the radius as a parameter, we can use the method from wherever we want.

> With Visual Basic .NET, we can define a method using the `Sub` keyword or using the `Function` keyword. `Sub` is used when the method doesn't return a value and is short for *subroutine*. `Function` is used when the method does return a value and we'll see this used in a little while.

Methods that You've Already Seen

The good news is that you've already been using methods. Consider this code that we wrote at the beginning of this chapter:

```
Private Sub btnAdd_Click(ByVal sender As System.Object, _
        ByVal e As System.EventArgs) Handles btnAdd.Click

    Dim n As Integer
    n = 27

    n = n + 1

    MessageBox.Show("Value of n + 1 = " & n, "Variables")

End Sub
```

That code is a method – it's a self-contained block of code that does something. In this case, it adds 1 to the value of n, and displays the result in a message box.

This method is a subroutine, so it is started with the Sub keyword and ended with the End Sub statement. Anything between these two statements is the code assigned to the method.

Let's take a look at how we define the method:

```
Private Sub btnAdd_Click(ByVal sender As System.Object, _
        ByVal e As System.EventArgs) Handles btnAdd.Click
```

❑ First of all, we have the word Private. For now, we can ignore this, but it's something we'll learn more about in Chapter 4.

❑ Secondly, we have the keyword Sub. This is how we tell Visual Basic .NET that we want to define a subroutine.

❑ Thirdly, we have btnAdd_Click. This is the name of the subroutine.

❑ Fourthly, we have ByVal sender As System.Object, ByVal e As System.EventArgs. This tells Visual Basic .NET that the method takes two parameters – one called sender and one called e. We'll talk about this more later.

❑ Finally, we have Handles btnAdd.Click. This tells Visual Basic .NET that this method should be called whenever the Click event on the control btnAdd is fired.

Let's take a look at how we can build a method that displays a message box, and call the same method from three separate buttons.

Try It Out – Using Methods

1. Create a new Windows Application project called Three Buttons.

2. Use the Toolbox to draw three buttons on the form, like this:

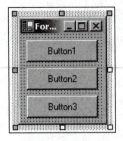

3. Double-click on the top button (`Button1`). This will create a new `Click` event handler. Add the highlighted code:

```
Private Sub Button1_Click(ByVal sender As System.Object, _
        ByVal e As System.EventArgs) Handles Button1.Click
```

```
    ' call our new method...
    SayHello()
```

```
End Sub
```

```
Sub SayHello()
    ' display a message box...
    MessageBox.Show("Hello, world!", "Three Buttons")
```

```
End Sub
```

4. Run the project and you'll see the form with three buttons appear. Click the topmost button and you'll see this:

How It Works

As we know now, when we double-click on a button control in the designer, a new method is automatically created for us:

```
Private Sub Button1_Click(ByVal sender As System.Object, _
        ByVal e As System.EventArgs) Handles Button1.Click


...


End Sub
```

The `Handles Button1.Click` statement at the end tell Visual Basic .NET that this method should automatically be called when the `Click` event on the button is fired. As part of this, Visual Basic .NET provides two parameters, which we don't have to worry about for now.

Outside of this method, we've defined a new method:

```
Sub SayHello()

    ' display a message box...
    MessageBox.Show("Hello, world!", "Three Buttons")

End Sub
```

Our new method is called `SayHello`. Anything that appears between the two highlighted lines is part of the method and when that method is called, the code will be executed. In this case, we've asked it to display a message box.

So, when the button is clicked we know that Visual Basic .NET will call the `Button1_Click` method. We then call our `SayHello` method. The upshot of all this is that when the button is clicked, the message box is displayed:

```
Private Sub Button1_Click(ByVal sender As System.Object, _
        ByVal e As System.EventArgs) Handles Button1.Click

    ' call our new method...
    SayHello()

End Sub
```

That should make the general premise behind methods a little clearer, but why did we need to break the code to display the message box into a separate method?

Try It Out – Reusing the Method

1. If the project is running, close it.

2. Now double-click on the second button. Add this code to the new event handler:

```
Private Sub Button2_Click(ByVal sender As System.Object, _
        ByVal e As System.EventArgs) Handles Button2.Click

    ' call our method...
    SayHello()

End Sub
```

3. Flip back to the design view and double-click on the third button. Add this code:

```
Private Sub Button3_Click(ByVal sender As System.Object, _
        ByVal e As System.EventArgs) Handles Button3.Click
```

```
' call our method...
SayHello()

End Sub
```

4. Now run the project and you'll notice that each of the buttons bring up the same message box.

5. Stop the project from running and find the `SayHello` method definition. Change the text to be displayed, like this:

```
Sub SayHello()

    ' display a message box...
    MessageBox.Show("I have changed!", "Three Buttons")

End Sub
```

6. Run the project again and you'll notice that the text displayed on the message boxes has changed:

How It Works

Each of the event handlers calls the same `SayHello()` method:

```
Private Sub Button1_Click(ByVal sender As System.Object, _
            ByVal e As System.EventArgs) Handles Button1.Click

    ' call our new method...
    SayHello()

End Sub

Private Sub Button2_Click(ByVal sender As System.Object, _
            ByVal e As System.EventArgs) Handles Button2.Click

    ' call our method...
    SayHello()

End Sub

Private Sub Button3_Click(ByVal sender As System.Object, _
            ByVal e As System.EventArgs) Handles Button3.Click
```

```
' call our method...
SayHello()

End Sub
```

You'll also notice that the `Handles` keyword on each of the methods ties the method to a different control – `Button1`, `Button2`, or `Button3`.

What's really important (and clever!) here is that when we change the way that `SayHello` works, the effect we see on each different button is the same. This is a really important programming concept. We can centralize code in our application so that when we change it in once place, the effect is felt throughout the application. Likewise, this saves us from having to enter the same or very similar code repeatedly.

Building a Method

In this section, we'll build a method that's capable of returning a value. Specifically, we'll build a method that can return the area of a circle given its radius. We can do this with the following algorithm:

❑ Square the radius

❑ Multiply it by pi

Try It Out – Building a Method

1. To try out this exercise, we can reuse the **Three Buttons** project we used before.

2. Add this code to define a new method (a **function**, as it returns a value):

```
' CalculateAreaFromRadius - find the area of a circle...
Function CalculateAreaFromRadius(ByVal radius As Double) As Double

    ' square the radius...
    Dim radiusSquared As Double
    radiusSquared = radius * radius

    ' multiply it by pi...
    Dim result As Double
    result = radiusSquared * Math.PI

    ' return the result...
    Return result

End Function
```

3. Now delete the existing code from the `Button1_Click` event handler, and add this code:

```
Private Sub Button1_Click(ByVal sender As System.Object, _
        ByVal e As System.EventArgs) Handles Button1.Click

    ' calculate the area of a circle with radius 100...
```

```
      Dim area As Double
      area = CalculateAreaFromRadius(100)

      ' print the results...
      MessageBox.Show(area, "Area")

End Sub
```

4. Run the project and click on Button1. You'll see something this:

How It Works

First of all, we built a separate method called `CalculateAreaFromRadius`. We did this by using the `Function ... End Function` block.

```
Function CalculateAreaFromRadius(ByVal radius As Double) As Double
   ...
End Function
```

Anything between `Function` and `End Function` is the "body" of the method and will only be executed when the method is called.

The `ByVal radius As Double` portion defines a parameter for the method. (You can ignore the `ByVal` for now. It means **by value**. As you become more experienced, you may want to pass in parameters **by reference** using `ByRef`. This is an advanced technique, and is beyond the scope of this book. In this case, we're telling it that we want to pass a parameter into the method called `radius`. In effect, this statement creates a variable called `radius`, just as if we had of done this:

```
Dim radius As Double
```

In fact, there's a little more. The variable will be automatically set to the value passed through as a parameter, so if we pass `200` through as the value of the parameter, what we're effectively doing is this:

```
Dim radius As Double = 200
```

...or, if we pass `999` as the value of the parameter, we'd have this:

```
Dim radius As Double = 999
```

The `As Double` sitting at the end of the method tells Visual Basic .NET that this method will return a double-precision, floating-point number back to whoever called it:

```
Function CalculateAreaFromRadius(ByVal radius As Double) As Double
```

Now we can look at the method proper. First off, we know that to find the area of a circle we have this algorithm:

❑   Get a number that represents the radius of a circle

❑   Square the number

❑   Multiply it by pi (π)

And that's precisely what we've done:

```
' square the radius...
Dim radiusSquared As Double
radiusSquared = radius * radius

' multiply it by pi...
Dim result As Double
result = radiusSquared * Math.PI
```

The `Math.PI` in the code above is a constant defined in Visual Basic .NET that defines the value of pi (π) for us. After the last line, we need to return the result back to whoever called the method. This is done with this statement:

```
' return the result...
Return result
```

The code we added in `Button1_Click` calls the method and tells the user the results:

```
' calculate the area of a circle with radius 100...
Dim area As Double
area = CalculateAreaFromRadius(100)

' print the results...
MessageBox.Show(area, "Area")
```

The first thing to do is define a variable called `area` that will contain the area of the circle. We set this variable to whatever value `CalculateAreaFromRadius` returns. Using parentheses at the end of a method name is how we send the parameters. In this case, we're passing just one parameter and we're always passing the value `100`.

After we call the method, we wait for the method to finish calculating the area. This area is returned from the method (the `Return result` line defined within `CalculateAreaFromRadius`) and stored in the variable `area`. We can then display this on the screen in the usual way.

Choosing Method Names

The .NET Framework has a few standards for how things should be named. This helps developers move between languages – a topic we talk about more in Chapter 5.

Whenever you create a method, you should use **Pascal casing**. This is a format where the first letter in each word in the method is uppercase but nothing else is, for example:

- ❑ CalculateAreaFromRadius
- ❑ OpenXmlFile
- ❑ GetEnvironmentValue

You'll notice that when an acronym is used (in this case, XML), it *isn't* written in uppercase. This is to alleviate confusion for developers who may or may not know how something should be capitalized.

Parameters are always written in something called **camel casing**. (If you've ever seen Java, you'll be familiar with this.) To get camel casing, we do the same as Pascal casing but we don't capitalize the very first letter:

- ❑ myAccount
- ❑ customerDetails
- ❑ updateDnsRecord

Again, acronyms are not treated as a special case and so appear as a mix of upper and lowercase letters, just like in Pascal casing.

> The name camel casing comes from the fact that the identifier has a hump in the middle, for example, `camelCasing`. Pascal casing comes from the fact that the convention was invented for use with the programming language Pascal.

In Chapter 5, we'll see that .NET isn't tied to a particular language. As some languages are case sensitive and others are not, it's important that we define standards to make life easier for programmers who may be coming from different languages.

Case sensitive means that the position of uppercase and lowercase letters are important. If Visual Basic .NET was case sensitive, MYACCOUNT would not be the same as myAccount. However, Visual Basic .NET is *not* a case-sensitive language, meaning that for all intents and purposes we can do whatever we like with respect to capitalization, in other words MYACCOUNT would be the same as mYacCounT.

Note that languages such as Java, C#, and C++ are case sensitive.

Scope

Right back when we first introduced the concept of methods, we described them as self-contained. This has an important effect on the way that variables are used and defined in methods.

Imagine we have these two methods, both of which define a variable called myName:

```
Sub DisplayStephsName()

    ' define a name...
    Dim myName As String
    myName = "Stephanie Leonard"

    ' show a message box...
    MessageBox.Show(myName)

End Sub

Sub DisplayHowardsName()

    ' define a name...
    Dim myName As String
    myName = "Howard Schultz"

    ' show a message box...
    MessageBox.Show(myName)

End Sub
```

Even though both of these methods use a variable with the same name, the "self containedness" feature of methods means that this is perfectly practicable and the variable names won't affect each other. Let's try it out.

Try It Out – Scope

1. Create a new **Windows Application** project called **Scope Demo**.

2. Add a button to the form called btnScope and double-click it. Add the highlighted code to the Click event handler:

```
Private Sub btnScope_Click(ByVal sender As System.Object, _
          ByVal e As System.EventArgs) Handles btnScope.Click

    ' run a method...
    DisplayHowardsName()

End Sub

Sub DisplayStephsName()

    ' define a name...
    Dim myName As String
    myName = "Stephanie Leonard"
```

```
    ' show a message box...
    MessageBox.Show(myName, "Scope Demo")
End Sub


Sub DisplayHowardsName()

    ' define a name...
    Dim myName As String
    myName = "Howard Schultz"

    ' show a message box...
    MessageBox.Show(myName, "Scope Demo")

End Sub
```

3. Run the project and you'll see this message box when you click on the button:

How It Works

What I'm trying to illustrate here is that even though we've used the same variable name in two separate places, the program still works as intended:

```
Sub DisplayStephsName()

    ' define a name...
    Dim myName As String
    myName = "Stephanie Leonard"

    ' show a message box...
    MessageBox.Show(myName, "Scope Demo")

End Sub

Sub DisplayHowardsName()

    ' define a name...
    Dim myName As String
    myName = "Howard Schultz"

    ' show a message box...
    MessageBox.Show(myName, "Scope Demo")

End Sub
```

When a method starts running, the variables that are defined within that method (in other words, between Sub and End Sub, or between Function and End Function) are given what's known as **local scope**. The **scope** defines which parts of the program can see the variable and **local** specifically means "within the method".

The myName variable technically doesn't exist until the method starts running. At this point, .NET and Windows allocate a member to the variable so that it can be used in the code. Firstly, we set the value and then we display the message box. Therefore, in this case as we're calling DisplayHowardsName, the variable is created the moment the method is called, we run the code in the method that alters the newly created version of myName, and when the method has finished, the variable is deleted.

Debugging Your Programs

Even the best developers make mistakes when they're writing code. In this section, we'll look at how you can spot those mistakes and how to fix them.

There are broadly two kinds of mistakes a developer can make:

❑ **Compile errors** – these are errors that occur when you're actually typing code into Visual Studio .NET. These are analogous to the spelling mistakes you might make when using Microsoft Word, and are often referred to as syntax errors.

❑ **Run-time errors**– these are errors that occur because something is wrong with your reasoning about how the program should work.

In this section, we'll look at compile errors. We'll look at run-time errors and how to deal with them in Chapter 11.

Compile Errors

Whenever you type code in Visual Studio .NET, it automatically compiles the code, looking for errors. This means that any compilation errors you make will actually show up as you're writing the code, much like spelling and grammar errors appear in Microsoft Word as you're typing.

Let's take a look now at how you can spot a compile error.

Try It Out – Looking for Compilation Errors

1. The most common kind of error is one caused by typing mistakes, or where we've got the wrong name for something. In the Scope Demo project, change the line in Form1.vb that reads DisplayHowardsName() to DisplayHoward(), like this:

```
Private Sub btnScope_Click(ByVal sender As System.Object, _
        ByVal e As System.EventArgs) Handles btnScope.Click
    ' run a method...
    DisplayHoward()
End Sub
```

2. After you make the change, Visual Basic .NET will mark the error with a wavy line:

```
' run a function...
DisplayHoward()
```

3. There are two ways you can see what's wrong with the line. If you've just got one error, you can float the mouse over the wavy line. You'll see a tool tip that "explains" the error:

```
' run a function...
DisplayHoward()
```
The name 'DisplayHoward' is not declared.

4. Alternatively, you can display the Task List window, which is at the bottom of the screen by default . This gives a list of things that need to be done, and in this case fixing the error is something that needs to be done. Using the Task List window is the best bet if you have a lot of wavy lines appearing. This window gives a description of the error, and if you double-click on the entry, you'll be shown where in the Visual Basic .NET code the error is.

To see the Task List, select View | Other Windows | Task List from the menu:

!	☑	Description	File	Line
		Click here to add a new task		
!	✎	Name 'DisplayHoward' is not declared.	C:\7612\Chapter02\Scope Demo\Form1.vb	82

Task List - 1 Build Error task shown (filtered)

☑ Task List | 🗏 Output

How It Works

As we work through the book, you'll come to understand what these error messages mean and how to resolve them. For now, however, if you do see a blue wavy line, be sure to double-check that the code you have *exactly* matches the code as written in this book.

Computers are extremely fussy about code and even the most innocuous-looking problem can cause these kinds of error.

Summary

In this chapter, we introduced the concept of writing software not just for Visual Basic .NET but also for all programming languages. We started by introducing the concept of an algorithm – the underpinnings of all computer software. We then introduced the concept of variables, and looked closely at the most commonly used data types: Integer, Double, String, Date, and Boolean. We saw how we could use these data types to perform operations such as mathematical operations, concatenation of strings, returning the length of a string, splitting text into substrings, retrieving the current date, and extracting date properties. We then looked at how variables are stored in the computer.

After this, we looked at methods – what they are, why we need them, how to create them, and how the variables we declare within our methods have local scope within that method and do not apply outside of it. We also described the difference between a function and a subroutine.

Finally, we briefly discussed how to detect compilation errors in your programs.

Questions

1. What is camel casing?

2. Which are we more likely to use – variables that store integer values or variables that store decimal values?

3. How do you define a variable that contains character data?

4. Write a line of code that multiplies n by 64, using the shorthand operator.

5. What is an algorithm?

Controlling the Flow

In the last chapter, we discussed algorithms and their role in programming. In this chapter, we're going to look at how we can control the flow through our algorithms so that we can make decisions like, "If X is the case, go and do A, otherwise do B". This ability to make decisions is known as **branching**. We'll also see how we can repeat a section of code (a process known as **looping**) a specified number of times, or while a certain condition applies.

Specifically, we'll discuss:

- ❑ The If statement
- ❑ Select Case
- ❑ For loops
- ❑ Do loops

Making Decisions

Algorithms often include decisions. In fact, it's this decision-making ability that makes computers do what they do so well.

When we're writing code we make two kinds of decisions. The first kind is used to find out what part of an algorithm we're currently working on or to cope with problems. For example, imagine you have a list of ten people and need to write a piece of code to send an e-mail to each of them in turn. To do this, after sending the e-mail to each person, we ask ourselves the question, "Have we finished?" If so, we quit the algorithm; otherwise we get the next person in the list. Alternatively, we might need to open a file and have to ask, "Does the file exist?" in which case we have to deal with both eventualities.

The second kind of decision is used to perform a different part of the algorithm depending on one or more facts. Imagine, when we're going through our list of ten people, that we want to send an e-mail to those who own a computer, but we'll telephone those who don't. As we look at each person in turn, we use the fact that they do or don't own a computer, to choose what to do.

Both of these kinds of decision are made in the same way, and it doesn't matter whether you have more of the first kind, more of the second kind or whatever. (You may, in practical use, discover that the first kind is more common.) Let's take a look now at how to make a decision using the `If` statement.

The If Statement

The simplest way to make a decision in a Visual Basic .NET program is to use the `If...Then` statement. Let's look at an example.

Try It Out – A Simple If...Then Statement

1. Create a Windows Application project called Simple If. Add a button called btnIf to the default form. Double-click on btnIf and add the following code:

```
Private Sub btnIf_Click(ByVal sender As System.Object, _
        ByVal e As System.EventArgs) Handles btnIf.Click

    ' define a value for n...
    Dim n As Integer
    n = 27

    ' here's where we make a decision,
    ' and tell the user what happened...
    If n = 27 Then
        MessageBox.Show("'n' is, indeed, 27!")
    End If

End Sub
```

2. Now run the project. You'll see this:

How It Works

After defining n and giving it the value 27, we use an `If...Then` statement to determine what we should do next. In this case, we say, "If n is equal to 27...":

```
    ' here's where we make a decision,
    ' and tell the user what happened...
    If n = 27 Then
        MessageBox.Show("'n' is, indeed, 27!")
    End If
```

What then follows is a code block. This block contains code that will only be executed if *n equals 27*. We end the code block with End If. Anything between If and End If will only be called if the expression we're testing for is "true".

So, as we walk through the code we get to the If statement and it's true, so we drop into the code block that runs if the expression is true and the text is displayed in a message box.

> *Notice that the code within the If...End If block is automatically indented for us. This is to increase readability, so that you can tell what code will run in the event of the case being true. I also like to add some whitespace before the If...Then statement and after the End If statement to further enhance readability.*

In the case of simple If blocks like the one above, you may also come across them being written on one line, without an End If statement, like this:

```
If n = 27 Then MessageBox.Show("'n' is, indeed, 27!")
```

This works equally well – although we are limited to only one line of code within the If statement.

So now we know what happens if our condition is true. But what happens if we fail the test and the result is "false"? Let's find out in the next *Try It Out*.

Try It Out – Failing the Test

1. Make the following changes to the **SimpleIf** program:

```
Private Sub btnIf_Click(ByVal sender As System.Object, _
        ByVal e As System.EventArgs) Handles btnIf.Click

    ' define a value for n...
    Dim n As Integer
    n = 27

    ' here's where we make a decision,
    ' and tell the user what happened...
    If n = 1000 Then
        MessageBox.Show("'n' is, indeed, 1000!")
    End If

End Sub
```

2. Run the code.

How It Works

OK, so we saw nothing, but why not?

In this case the question, "Is n equal to 1000?" comes out as false. Our code block will only execute if the statement is true, so it's skipped. If the statement had been true, the line between the If and End If lines would have executed as before. However, in this instance the statement was false, so the next line to be executed was the first line directly following the End If line (which is the end of the sub). In effect, the true code block is skipped.

The Else Statement

Well that's all well and good, but what do we do if we want to run one piece of code if the condition is true, and another piece if the condition is false? We use the Else statement. Let's expand on our previous *Try It Out* to see how it works.

Try It Out – The Else Statement

1. Change the SimpleIf program so that it looks like this:

```
Private Sub btnIf_Click(ByVal sender As System.Object, _
        ByVal e As System.EventArgs) Handles btnIf.Click

    ' define a value for n...
    Dim n As Integer
    n = 27

    ' here's where we make a decision,
    ' and tell the user what happened...
    If n = 1000 Then
        MessageBox.Show("'n' is, indeed, 1000!")
    Else
        MessageBox.Show("'n' is not 1000!")
    End If

End Sub
```

2. Run the code and you'll see this:

How It Works

The code following the Else statement will be run if the condition in the If statement is not met. In this case the value of n is 27, but the condition being tested for is n = 1000, so the code after the Else statement is run:

```
    Else
        MessageBox.Show("'n' is not 1000!")
    End If
```

Allowing Multiple Alternatives with ElseIf

If we want to test for more than one condition, we need to make use of the `ElseIf` statement. Let's take our SimpleIf program as an example as see how we can test for the value of n being 27 and 1000.

Try It Out – The ElseIf Statement

1. Change the SimpleIf program so that it looks like this:

```
Private Sub btnIf_Click(ByVal sender As System.Object, _
            ByVal e As System.EventArgs) Handles btnIf.Click

    ' define a value for n...
    Dim n As Integer
    n = 27

    ' here's where we make a decision,
    ' and tell the user what happened...
    If n = 1000 Then
        MessageBox.Show("'n' is, indeed, 1000!")
    ElseIf n = 27 Then
        MessageBox.Show("'n' is 27!")
    Else
        MessageBox.Show("'n' is neither 1000 nor 27!")
    End If

End Sub
```

2. Run the code and you'll see this:

How It Works

As you can see, this time the code in the `ElseIf` statement was run as n meets the condition n = 27. Note that we can still include the `Else` statement at the end to catch instances where n is neither 27 nor 1000, but something else entirely:

```
ElseIf n = 27 Then
    MessageBox.Show("'n' is 27!")
Else
    MessageBox.Show("'n' is neither 1000 nor 27!")
End If
```

We can continue adding as many **ElseIf** statements as we need to test for conditions. However, you should bear in mind that each **ElseIf** statement will be executed as Visual Basic .NET attempts to discover if the condition is true or not. This will slow up your program if you have a lot of conditions to be tested. If this is the case, you should try to put the statements in the order they are most likely to be executed, commonest at the top. Alternatively, you should use a **Select Case** block, which we will be looking at later in the chapter.

Nested If Statements

It's possible to nest an `If` statement inside another. For example:

```
If n = 3 Then
    MessageBox.Show("n = 3")

    If x = 6 Then
        MessageBox.Show("x = 6")
    End If

End If
```

There's no real limit to how far you can nest your `If` statements. However, the more levels of nesting you have, the harder you'll find to follow what's happening in your code. So, try to keep nesting of `If` statements to a minimum if you can.

Single-Line If Statement

The single-line form is typically used for short, simple tests, and saves space in the text editor. However, it doesn't provide the structure and flexibility of the multi-line form and is usually harder to read:

```
If n = 3 Then MessageBox.Show("n = 3") Else MessageBox.Show("n  is not 3")
```

Please note that we do not need an `End If` at the end of a single-line `If...Then` statement.

Multiple statements can also be executed within a single line `If...Then` statement. All statements must be on the same line and must be separated by colons, as in the following example:

```
If n = 3 Then MessageBox.Show("n = 3") : n = n + 1 : Total += n
```

Comparison Operators

OK, so we know how to check if a particular variable is equal to some value and execute code if this is the case. In fact, `If` is far more flexible than this. We can ask questions such as these, all of which have a true/false answer.

❑ Is n greater than 49?

❑ Is n less than 49?

❑ Is n greater than or equal to 49?

❑ Is n less than or equal to 49?

❑ Is name not equal to Ben?

When working with string values, most of the time we'll use the "equal to" or "not equal to" operators. When working with numeric values (both integer and floating-point), we can use all of these arithmetic operators.

Using "Not Equal To"

As we haven't seen it yet, let's test out the "not equal to" operator with strings.

Try It Out – Using "Not Equal To"

1. Create a new Windows Application project called If Demo.

2. When the Form Designer for Form1 appears, add a textbox control and a button control. Set the Name property of the textbox control to txtName and its Text property to Ben. Set the Name property of the button control to btnCheck and its Text property to Check. Your form should look like this:

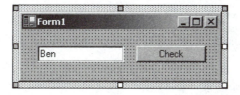

3. Double-click on the button control to create its Click event handler. Add this code:

```
Private Sub btnCheck_Click(ByVal sender As System.Object, _
          ByVal e As System.EventArgs) Handles btnCheck.Click

    ' get the name from the text box...
    Dim name As String
    name = txtName.Text

    ' is the name Gretchen?
    If name <> "Gretchen" Then
        MessageBox.Show("The name is *not* Gretchen.", "If Demo")
    End If

End Sub
```

4. Run the project and click on the Check button. You should see this:

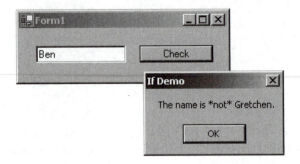

How It Works

The "not equal to" operator looks like this: <>

When the button is clicked, the first thing we do is retrieve the name from the textbox by looking up its Text property:

```
' get the name from the text box...
Dim name As String
name = txtName.Text
```

After we have the name, we use an If statement. This time, however, we use the "not equal to" operator rather than the "equal to" operator. Also notice that we are comparing two string values.

```
' is the name Gretchen?
If name <> "Gretchen" Then
    MessageBox.Show("The name is *not* Gretchen.", "If Demo")
End If
```

As we know, the code between Then and End If will only get executed if the answer to the question asked in the If statement is True. You'll probably find this a bit of a heady principle, because the question we're asking is, "Is name not equal to Gretchen?" to which the answer is "Yes, the name is *not* equal to Gretchen." As the answer to this question is yes, or True, the code is run and the message box is displayed.

However, if you enter Gretchen into the textbox and click on **Check**, nothing will happen because the answer to the question is "No, the name *is* equal to Gretchen," therefore we have a no, or False, answer.

> If you try this, be sure to enter **Gretchen** with an uppercase **G** and with the rest of the letters in lowercase, otherwise the application won't work properly. We'll see why later.

An alternative way of checking that something does not equal something is to use the Not keyword. Our condition in the If statement could have been written:

```
If Not name = "Gretchen" Then
```

Using the Numeric Operators

So now we know how to use the "equal to" and "not equal to" operators, let's quickly take a look at the other four comparison operators we can use. These are all fairly basic, so we'll go through this quite fast.

Try It Out – Using "Less Than"

1. If the project is running, close it. Open the Form Designer for Form1 and change the Name property of the textbox control to txtValue. Also, change the Text property to 10.

2. Now replace the existing Click event handler code with this code:

```
Private Sub btnCheck_Click(ByVal sender As System.Object, _
          ByVal e As System.EventArgs) Handles btnCheck.Click

    ' get the number from the text box...
    Dim n As Integer
    Try
        n = txtValue.Text
    Catch
    End Try

    ' is n less than 27?
    If n < 27 Then
        MessageBox.Show("Is 'n' less than 27?  Yes!", "If Demo")
    Else
        MessageBox.Show("Is 'n' less than 27?  No!", "If Demo")
    End If

End Sub
```

3. Run the project. Enter a number into the textbox and you should be told whether it is less than or greater than 27:

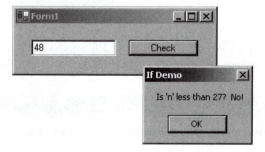

How It Works

The first thing we do in this case is to get the value back from the textbox. However, there is a slight wrinkle. As this is a textbox, the end users are free to enter anything they like into this and so, if a series of characters that cannot be converted into an integer are entered, the program will crash. I've used an **exception handler** to make sure that we always get a value back. If the user enters something invalid, n will remain set as 0, otherwise it will be whatever is entered:

```
' get the number from the text box...
Dim n As Integer
Try
    n = txtValue.Text
Catch
End Try
```

We introduce exception handlers properly in Chapter 11. For now, you can safely ignore it!

The "less than" operator looks like this: <

Here, we test to see if the number entered was less than 27 and if so we say so in a message box, otherwise we say not:

```
' is n less than to 27?
If n < 27 Then
    MessageBox.Show("Is 'n' less than 27?  Yes!", "If Demo")
Else
    MessageBox.Show("Is 'n' less than 27?  No!", "If Demo")
End If
```

Here's something interesting though. If you actually enter **27** into the textbox and click the button, you'll see this:

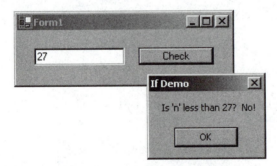

The If statement has said "No" and it's right. n is actually equal to 27 and the cutoff point for this operator is anything up to *but not including* the value itself. We can get around this problem with a different operator.

Try It Out – The "Less Than or Equal To" Operator

1. Change the If statement in the btnCheck_Click event handler as shown here:

```
Private Sub btnCheck_Click(ByVal sender As System.Object, _
        ByVal e As System.EventArgs) Handles btnCheck.Click

    ' get the number from the text box...
    Dim n As Integer
    Try
        n = txtValue.Text
```

```
        Catch
        End Try

           ' is n less than or equal to 27?
           If n <= 27 Then
               MessageBox.Show("Is 'n' less than or equal to 27?  Yes!", _
                               "If Demo")
           Else
               MessageBox.Show("Is 'n' less than or equal to 27?  No!", _
                               "If Demo")
           End If

        End Sub
```

2. Now run the project and enter 27 into the textbox. Click on the **Check** button and you should see this:

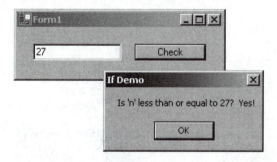

How It Works

The "less than or equal to" operator looks like this: <=

In this situation, we're extending the possible range of values up to include the value we're checking itself. So, in this case when we enter 27 we get the answer, "Yes, n is less than *or equal to* 27." This type of operator is known as an **inclusive operator**.

The final two operators look really similar to this, so let's look at them now.

Try It Out – "Greater Than" and "Greater Than or Equal To"

1. Once more, open the Click event handler. Change the first If statement and add this second one:

```
Private Sub btnCheck_Click(ByVal sender As System.Object, _
        ByVal e As System.EventArgs) Handles btnCheck.Click

    ' get the number from the text box...
    Dim n As Integer
    Try
        n = txtValue.Text
    Catch
    End Try
```

```
' check n...
If n > 27 Then
    MessageBox.Show("Is 'n' greater than 27?  Yes!", _
                    "If Demo")
Else
    MessageBox.Show("Is 'n' greater than 27?  No!", _
                    "If Demo")
End If
If n >= 27 Then
    MessageBox.Show("Is 'n' greater than or equal to 27?  Yes!", _
                    "If Demo")
Else
    MessageBox.Show("Is 'n' greater than or equal to 27?  No!", _
                    "If Demo")
End If
```

```
End Sub
```

2. Run the program. This time you'll see two message boxes, one after the other when you click on **Check**:

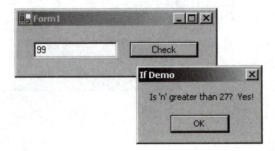

How It Works

The "greater than" and "greater than or equal to" operators are basically the opposite of their "less than" counterparts. This time, we're asking, "Is n greater than 27?" and, "Is n greater than or equal to 27?" The results speak for themselves.

The And and Or Operators

What happens when we need our `If` statement to test more than one condition? For example, if we want to make sure that "n is less than 27 *and* greater than 10"? Or, how about checking that "name is `'Zoe'` or `'Faye'`?"

We can combine operators used with an `If` statement with the `And` and `Or` operators. Let's take a look at this now.

Try It Out – Using the Or Operator

1. Open the Form Designer for **Form1**. Change the **Name** property of the textbox to **txtName1** and set its **Text** property to **Zoe**.

2. Make the form slightly larger and add another textbox control. Set its **Name** property to txtName2 and its **Text** property to **Faye**. It should look like this:

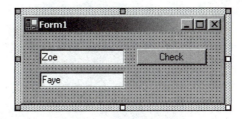

3. Change btnCheck's Click event handler to match this:

```
Private Sub btnCheck_Click(ByVal sender As System.Object, _
        ByVal e As System.EventArgs) Handles btnCheck.Click

    ' get the names...
    Dim name1 As String, name2 As String
    name1 = txtName1.Text
    name2 = txtName2.Text

    ' is one of them Zoe?
    If name1 = "Zoe" Or name2 = "Zoe" Then
        MessageBox.Show("One of the names is Zoe.", "If Demo")
    Else
        MessageBox.Show("Neither of the names are Zoe.", "If Demo")
    End If

End Sub
```

4. Run the project. Click the button and you should see this:

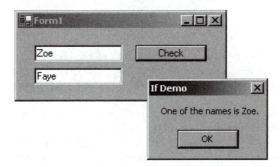

5. Click on **OK** to dismiss the message box and flip the names around so that the top one (txtName1) is **Faye** and the bottom one (txtName2) is **Zoe**. Click the button again:

109

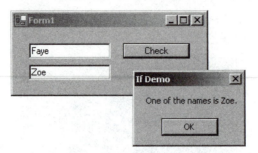

6. Now, click on OK to dismiss the message box again and this time change the names so that neither of them is **Zoe**. Click the button and you should see this:

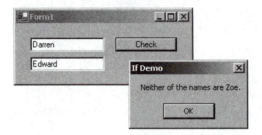

How It Works

The `Or` operator is a great way of building `If` statements that compare two different values in a single hit.

In our `Click` event handler, the first thing we do is retrieve both names and store them in variables `name1` and `name2`:

```
' get the names...
Dim name1 As String, name2 As String
name1 = txtName1.Text
name2 = txtName2.Text
```

You'll notice that we've defined two variables on the same line. This is perfectly legitimate coding practice, although it can sometimes make the code look congested. The variables are separated with commas and notice that it's still important to use `As` to tell Visual Basic .NET what data type each of the variables is.

Once we have both names, we use the `Or` operator to combine two separate `If` statements. The question we're asking here is, "Is `name1` equal to `Zoe` or is `name2` equal to `Zoe`?" The answer to this question (providing that one of the textboxes contains the name **Zoe**) is, "Yes, either `name1` is equal to `Zoe` or `name2` is equal to `Zoe`." Again, it's a yes/no or `True`/`False` answer, even though the question is seemingly more complex:

```
' is one of them Zoe?
If name1 = "Zoe" Or name2 = "Zoe" Then
    MessageBox.Show("One of the names is Zoe.", "If Demo")
Else
```

```
        MessageBox.Show("Neither of the names are Zoe.", "If Demo")
    End If
```

Using the And Operator

The And operator is conceptually similar to Or, except that both parts of the equation need to be satisfied.

Try It Out – Using the And Operator

1. Make this change to the btnCheck_Click event handler:

```
Private Sub btnCheck_Click(ByVal sender As System.Object, _
        ByVal e As System.EventArgs) Handles btnCheck.Click

    ' get the names...
    Dim name1 As String, name2 As String
    name1 = txtName1.Text
    name2 = txtName2.Text

    ' are both of them Zoe?
    If name1 = "Zoe" And name2 = "Zoe" Then
        MessageBox.Show("Both names are Zoe.", "If Demo")
    Else
        MessageBox.Show("One of the names is not Zoe.", "If Demo")
    End If

End Sub
```

2. Run the program. Click on the button and you should see this:

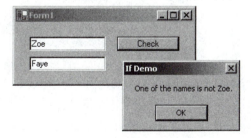

3. However, if you change both names so that they are both **Zoe** and click the button, you'll see this:

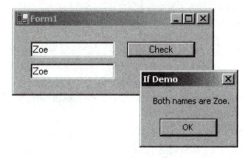

How It Works

After we've retrieved both names from the textboxes, we compare them. In this case, we're asking the question, "Is name1 equal to `Zoe` *and* is name2 equal to `Zoe`?" In this case, both parts of the `If` statement must be satisfied in order for the **Both names are Zoe** message box to be displayed:

```
' are both of them Zoe?
If name1 = "Zoe" And name2 = "Zoe" Then
    MessageBox.Show("Both names are Zoe.", "If Demo")
Else
    MessageBox.Show("One of the names is not Zoe.", "If Demo")
End If
```

More on And and Or

We've only seen `And` and `Or` used with strings. But, they can be used with numeric values, like this:

```
If a = 2 And b = 2.3 Then
    MessageBox.Show("Hello!")
End If
```

...or...

```
If a = 2 Or b = 2.3 Then
    MessageBox.Show("Hello, again!")
End If
```

Also, in Visual Basic, there's no realistic limit to the number of `And` operators or `Or` operators that you can include on a statement. It's perfectly possible to do this:

```
If a = 1 And b = 2 And c = 3 And d = 4 And e = 5 And f = 6 And g = 7 And _
    h = 1 And i = 2 And j = 3 And k = 4 And l = 5 And m = 6 And n = 7 And _
    o = 1 And p = 2 And q = 3 And r = 4 And s = 5 And t = 6 And u = 7 And _
    v = 1 And w = 2 And x = 3 And y = 4 And z = 5 Then
    MessageBox.Show("That's quite an If statement!")
End If
```

Although quite why you'd want to do that is beyond me!

Finally, it's possible to use parentheses to group together operators and look for a value within a range. For example, say we want to check for the value of n being between 12 and 20 exclusive or between 22 and 25 exclusive. We can use the following `If...Then` statement:

```
If (n > 12 And n < 20) Or (n > 22 And n < 25) Then
```

There are many other combinations of operators, far more than we have room to go into here. Rest assured, if you want to check for a condition, there is a combination to suit your needs.

String Comparison

When working with strings and `If` statements, we often run into the problem of **case sensitivity**.

A computer treats the characters `"A"` and `"a"` as completely separate entities, despite the fact that naturally we consider them to be very similar. This is known as case sensitivity – meaning that the case of the letters *does* matter when comparing strings.

For example, if we run the following code, the message box would be *not* displayed.

```
Dim name As String
name = "Winston"
If name = "WINSTON" Then
    MessageBox.Show("Aha! You are Winston.")
End If
```

Because `WINSTON` is not strictly speaking the same as `Winston` due to the case being different, this `If` statement will return, "No, `name` does not equal `WINSTON`."

However, in a lot of cases we don't actually care about the case, so we have to find a way of comparing strings and ignoring the case of the characters. Let's look at how we can do that.

Try It Out – Case-Insensitive String Comparisons

1. Open the Form Designer for **Form1** and delete the second textbox.

2. Change the **Name** property of the first textbox to **txtName** and the **Text** property to **Winston**.

3. Double-click on the button to open its `Click` event handler. Add this code:

```
Private Sub btnCheck_Click(ByVal sender As System.Object, _
         ByVal ex As System.EventArgs) Handles btnCheck.Click

    ' get the name...
    Dim name As String
    name = txtName.Text

    ' compare the name...
    If String.Compare(name, "WINSTON", True) = 0 Then
        MessageBox.Show("Hello, Winston!", "If Demo")
    End If

End Sub
```

4. Run the project and click the button. You should see this:

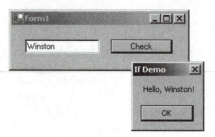

5. Now, dismiss the message box and enter the name as wINsTON, or some other combination of case and click the button. You should see this:

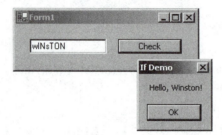

6. However, if you enter a name that isn't Winston, the message box will not be displayed when you click the button.

How It Works

Once we get the name back from the textbox, we have to use a function to compare the two values rather than using the basic "equal to" operator. In this instance, we're using the Compare method on System.String and giving it the two strings we want to compare. The first string is the value stored in name (which is the value entered into the textbox), with the second string being "WINSTON". The last parameter that we supply is True, which tells Compare to perform a case-insensitive match, in other words it should ignore the differences in case. If we had supplied False for this parameter, the comparison would have been case sensitive, in which case we would have been no better off than using the vanilla "equal to" operator:

```
' compare the name...
If String.Compare(name, "WINSTON", True) = 0 Then
    MessageBox.Show("Hello, Winston!", "If Demo")
End If
```

String.Compare returns a fairly curious result. It actually returns an integer, rather than a True or False value. This is because String.Compare can be used to determine *how* two strings are different rather than just a straightforward, "Yes, they are" or, "No, they're not". If the method returns 0, the strings match. If the method returns a value that is not 0, the strings do not match.

> *String.Compare returns an indication of how different two strings are in order to help in building sorting algorithms (which is off topic for this chapter).*

Select Case

On occasion, you will need to make a set of similar decisions like this:

- ❑ Is the customer called Darren? If so... do this.

- ❑ Is the customer called Stephanie? If so... do this.

- ❑ Is the customer called Cathy? If so... do this.

- ❑ Is the customer called Zoe? If so... do this.

- ❑ Is the customer called Edward? If so... do this.

You can, obviously do this with a set of If...Then statements. In fact, it would look a little like this:

```
If Customer.Name = "Darren" Then
    (do something)
ElseIf Customer.Name = "Stephanie" Then
    (do something)
ElseIf Customer.Name = "Cathy" Then
    (do something)
ElseIf Customer.Name = "Zoe" Then
    (do something)
ElseIf Customer.Name = "Edward" Then
    (do something)
End If
```

What happens if you decide you want to check Customer.FirstName instead of Customer.Name? You'd have to change every If statement, which is a pain.

Also, if Customer.Name turns out to be "Edward", you still have to go through the other four If statements, which is very inefficient.

However, there is a better way!

Try It Out – Using Select Case

1. Create a new Windows Application project. Call it Select Demo.

2. From the Toolbox, add a ListBox control to the form that appears and resize it so that it takes up the entire form.

3. Change the Name property of the listbox to lstData, and set its IntegralHeight property to False.

4. We also want to make sure that the textbox itself stretches with the form, so set its Anchor property to Top, Bottom, Left, Right. Your form should now look something like this:

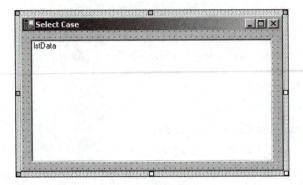

> By default, when most controls are created they are glued at their top-left position, which means that if the form is resized they remain in the same location and remain the same size. Here the control is stuck to the relative right and bottom positions as well, so the listbox will grow or shrink to fill the space between the fixed positions. To try out this anchoring feature, select the form itself and resize it. All of the controls will follow the size of the form.

5. With the lstData selected in the Form Designer, look at the Properties window and select the Items property. Click the ellipsis button (...) to the right of the property and in the String Collection Editor that appears, add these five names on separate lines:

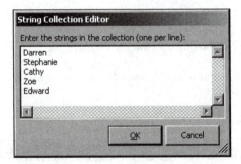

6. Click **OK** to save changes, and the names will now be added to your listbox. Now double-click on lstData to create a new `SelectedIndexChanged` event handler and add this code:

```
Private Sub lstData_SelectedIndexChanged(ByVal sender As _
        System.Object, ByVal e As System.EventArgs) _
        Handles lstData.SelectedIndexChanged

    ' what did we choose?
    Dim name As String
    name = lstData.Items(lstData.SelectedIndex)

    ' use a select case to do something...
    Dim favoriteColor As String
```

```
    Select Case name

        Case "Darren"
            favoriteColor = "Madras Yellow"

        Case "Stephanie"
            favoriteColor = "Starck Purple"

        Case "Cathy"
            favoriteColor = "Morning Mist"
        Case "Zoe"
            favoriteColor = "Evil Black"

        Case "Edward"
            favoriteColor = "Meeting Room Gray"

    End Select

    ' display a message box...
    MessageBox.Show(name & "'s favorite color is " & favoriteColor, _
                    "Select Demo")

End Sub
```

7. Run the project. Whenever you click on one of the names, a message box should appear:

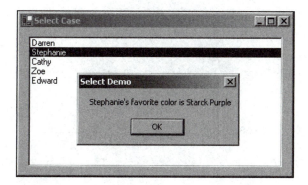

How It Works

The first thing we need to do in the `SelectedIndexChanged` handler is work out what name was selected. We do this by finding the item in the list that matches the current value of the `SelectedIndex` property:

```
' what did we choose?
Dim name As String
name = lstData.Items(lstData.SelectedIndex)
```

Once we have that, we start a `Select Case...End Select` block. To do this, we need to supply the variable that we're matching against – in this case, we're using the name that was selected in the list.

Inside the `Select Case...End Select` block, we define separate `Case` statements for each condition to be checked against. In this example, we have five and each one is set to respond to a different name. If a match can be found, Visual Basic .NET executes the code immediately following the relevant `Case` statement.

For example, if you clicked on **Darren**, the message box would display Madras Yellow as his favorite color, because Visual Basic .NET would execute the line, `favoriteColor = "Madras Yellow"`. Clicking on **Zoe** would display Evil Black as her favorite color, as Visual Basic .NET would execute `favoriteColor = "Evil Black"`:

```
' use a select case to do something...
Dim favoriteColor As String

Select Case name

    Case "Darren"
        favoriteColor = "Madras Yellow"

    Case "Stephanie"
        favoriteColor = "Starck Purple"

    Case "Cathy"
        favoriteColor = "Morning Mist"

    Case "Zoe"
        favoriteColor = "Evil Black"

    Case "Edward"
        favoriteColor = "Meeting Room Gray"

End Select
```

After the `Select Case...End Select` block, we display a message:

```
MessageBox.Show(name & "'s favorite color is " & favoriteColor, _
            "Select Demo")
```

So how do we get out of a `Select Case...End Select` block? Well, as we're processing code that's beneath a `Case` statement, if we meet another `Case` statement Visual Basic .NET jumps out of the block and down to the line immediately following the block. Here's an illustration:

❑   The user clicks **Stephanie**. The `SelectedIndexChanged` event is fired and we store `"Stephanie"` in name.

❑   We reach the `Select Case` statement. This is set to compare the value in name with one of the five supplied names.

❑   Visual Basic .NET finds a `Case` statement that satisfies the request and immediately moves down to:

```
favoriteColor = "Starck Purple"
```

❑ Visual Basic .NET moves to the next line. This is another `Case` statement, and seeing that we're already in one, we move to the first line after the `Select Case...End Select` block and display the message box.

`Select Case` is a very powerful and easy-to-use technique for making a choice from a number of possible options. However, you do need to understand that we leave the block as soon as another `Case` statement is reached.

Case-Insensitive Select Case

Just like `If`, `Select Case` is case sensitive; let's just prove it to ourselves in the next *Try It Out*.

Try It Out – Case-Sensitive Select Case

1. Open the Form Designer for Form1. Locate the Items property for the listbox and open the String Collection Editor again.

2. Change all of the names so that they appear all in uppercase letters:

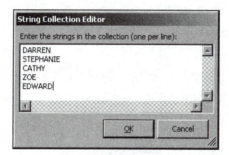

3. Click OK to save your changes and run the project. You'll notice that whenever you click on a name, the message box doesn't specify a favorite color:

How It Works

`Select Case` performs a case-sensitive match, just like `If`. This means that if we provide the name CATHY or EDWARD to the statement, there won't be a corresponding `Case` statement because we're trying to say:

```
If "CATHY" = "Cathy"
```

...or...

```
If "EDWARD" = "Edward"
```

Earlier in the chapter, we took a look at how we can use the `String.Compare` method to perform case-insensitive comparisons with `If` statements. With `Select Case`, we can't use this method, so if we want to be insensitive towards case, we need to employ a different technique.

Try It Out – Case-Insensitive Select Case

1. Open the code editor for **Form1** and make these changes to the event handler for `SelectedIndexChanged`. Pay special attention to the `Case` statements – the name that we're trying to match *must* be supplied in all lower case letters:

```
Private Sub lstData_SelectedIndexChanged(ByVal sender As _
        System.Object, ByVal e As System.EventArgs) _
        Handles lstData.SelectedIndexChanged

    ' what did we choose?
    Dim name As String
    name = lstData.Items(lstData.SelectedIndex)

    ' use a select case to do something...
    Dim favoriteColor As String

    Select Case name.ToLower

        Case "darren"
            favoriteColor = "Madras Yellow"

        Case "stephanie"
            favoriteColor = "Starck Purple"

        Case "cathy"
            favoriteColor = "Morning Mist"

        Case "zoe"
            favoriteColor = "Evil Black"

        Case "edward"
            favoriteColor = "Meeting Room Gray"

    End Select

    ' display a message box...
    MessageBox.Show(name & "'s favorite color is " & favoriteColor, _
                "Select Demo")
End Sub
```

2. Run the project and try again. This time you should see that the message box does now include the favorite color of the person you click on:

How It Works

To make the selection case insensitive, we have to convert the `name` that we are given into all lowercase letters. This is done using the `ToLower` method:

```
Select Case name.ToLower
```

This means that whatever string we're given (whether it's `"DARREN"` or `"dARrEN"`) we always convert it to all lowercase (`"darren"`). However, when we do this we have to make sure that we're comparing like with like, which is why we had to convert the values we're checking against in the `Case` statements to all lowercase too. Therefore, if we are given `"DARREN"`, we convert this to `"darren"`, and then try to find the `Case` that matches `"darren"`:

```
Case "darren"
    favoriteColor = "Madras Yellow"

Case "stephanie"
    favoriteColor = "Starck Purple"

Case "cathy"
    favoriteColor = "Morning Mist"

Case "zoe"
    favoriteColor = "Evil Black"

Case "edward"
    favoriteColor = "Meeting Room Gray"

End Select
```

Finally, once we have the favorite color, we display a message box as usual.

> *As an aside, we could have done the opposite of this and converted all the names to uppercase and used* `name.ToUpper` *instead of* `name.ToLower`.

Multiple Selections

We're not limited to matching one value inside a `Select Case...End Select` block. We can also match multiple items. In the next *Try It Out*, we'll change the application so that we report the sex of whoever we click on.

Try It Out – Multiple Selections

1. Open the code editor for **Form1** and change the code in the `SelectedIndexChanged` handler to this:

```
Private Sub lstData_SelectedIndexChanged(ByVal sender As _
            System.Object, ByVal e As System.EventArgs) Handles _
            lstData.SelectedIndexChanged

    ' what did we choose?
    Dim name As String
    name = lstData.Items(lstData.SelectedIndex)

    ' use a select case to do something...
    Select Case name.ToLower

        Case "darren", "edward"
            MessageBox.Show("Male", "Select Demo")

        Case "stephanie", "cathy", "zoe"
            MessageBox.Show("Female", "Select Demo")

    End Select

End Sub
```

Note that we've removed the line that declared `favoriteColor` *and the one that displayed the favorite color message box.*

2. Run the project and click on one of the names. You should see this:

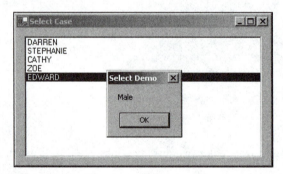

How It Works

You'll notice that the code we use to get back the name and initialize the Select Case block remains the same.

However, on each Case statement we can provide a list of possible values separated with commas. In the first one, we look for darren *or* edward. If either of these matches, we run the code under the Case statement as usual:

```
        Case "darren", "edward"
            MessageBox.Show("Male", "Select Demo")
```

In the second one, we look for stephanie *or* cathy *or* zoe. If any of these three match, we again run the code under the Case statement as usual:

```
Case "stephanie", "cathy", "zoe"
    MessageBox.Show("Female", "Select Demo")
```

It's important to realize that these are all "or" matches. We're saying "one *or* the other", not "one *and* the other".

The Case Else Statement

So what happens if none of the Case statements that we've included is matched? We saw this before when demonstrating the case-sensitive nature of Select Case.

Try It Out – Case Else

1. In the lstData_SelectedIndexChanged event handler, add this code:

```
Private Sub lstData_SelectedIndexChanged(ByVal sender As _
System.Object, ByVal e As System.EventArgs) Handles _
        lstData.SelectedIndexChanged

    ' what did we choose?
    Dim name As String
    name = lstData.Items(lstData.SelectedIndex)

    ' use a select case to do something...
    Select Case name.ToLower

        Case "darren", "edward"
            MessageBox.Show("Male", "Select Demo")

        Case "stephanie", "cathy", "zoe"
            MessageBox.Show("Female", "Select Demo")

        Case Else
            MessageBox.Show("I don't know the sex of this person.", _
                            "Select Demo")

    End Select

End Sub
```

2. Before running the project, use the String Collection Editor to add a new name to the list:

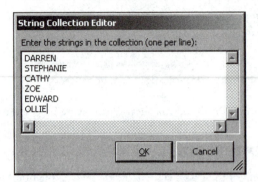

3. Click OK to save your changes and run the project. Click on Ollie and you should see this:

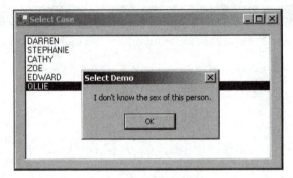

How It Works

The `Case Else` statement will be used if none of the other supplied `Case` statements match what we're looking for. As there isn't a `Case "ollie"` defined within the block, we default to using whatever is underneath the `Case Else` statement. In this instance, we display a message box indicating that we do not know the sex of the person who's been selected.

Different Data Types with Select Case

In this chapter, we've exclusively looked at using `Select Case` with variables of type `String`. However, you can use `Select Case` with all of the basic data types in Visual Basic .NET such as `Integer`, `Double`, and `Boolean`.

In day-to-day work, the most common types of `Select Case` will be based on `String` and `Integer` data types. However, as a general rule, if a data type can be used in an `If` statement with the equals (=) operator, it will work with `Select Case`.

Loops

When writing computer software, you often find situations where you need to perform the same task a number of times in order to get the effect you want. For example, you might need to create a telephone bill for *all* of your customers, or read in *ten* files from your computer's disk.

To accomplish this, we use a **loop**, and in this section, we'll take a look at the two main types of loop available in Visual Basic .NET. These are:

❑ **For loops** – these loops occur a certain number of times, for example exactly ten times

❑ **Do loops** – these loops keep running until a certain condition is reached, for example until it's 3 o'clock in the afternoon

Loops are hard to conceptualize, but very easy to understand once you look at them. Let's move on now and start building some loops.

The For...Next Loop

The simplest loop to understand is the For...Next loop.

Try It Out – Building a For...Next Loop

1. Create a new Windows Application project called Loops.

2. Add a listbox and a button control to the form that appears.

3. Change the Name property of the listbox to lstData. Also, set its IntegralHeight property to False and its Anchor property to Top, Bottom, Left, Right. This enables us to resize the form at run-time and still be able to easily to view everything within our listbox.

4. Change the Name property of the button to btnGo. Also, set its Text property to Go and change its Anchor property to Top, Right. Your form should now look something like this:

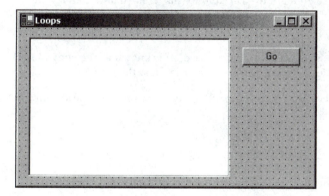

5. Double-click on the Go button to create its Click event handler. Add this code:

```
Private Sub btnGo_Click(ByVal sender As System.Object, _
        ByVal e As System.EventArgs) Handles btnGo.Click

    ' loop...
    Dim n As Integer
```

```
For n = 1 To 5

    ' add the item to the list...
    lstData.Items.Add("I'm item " & n & " in the list!")
Next
```

```
End Sub
```

6. Run the project and click the Go button. You should see this:

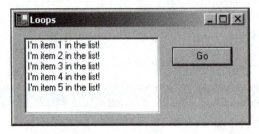

How It Works

The first thing we've done inside the `Click` event handler is to define a variable:

```
' loop...
Dim n As Integer
```

The second thing we do is start the loop by using the `For` keyword. This tells Visual Basic .NET that we want to create a loop. Everything that follows the `For` keyword is used to define how the loop should act. In this case, we're giving it the variable we just created and then telling it to count *from* 1 *to* 5:

```
For n = 1 To 5
```

The variable that we give the loop (in this case, n) is known as the **control variable**. When we first enter the loop, Visual Basic .NET sets the control variable to the initial count value – in this case 1.

After the loop has started, Visual Basic .NET moves to the first line within the `For` loop, in this case the line that adds a string to the listbox:

```
' add the item to the list...
lstData.Items.Add("I'm item " & n & " in the list!")
```

This time, this line of code will add I'm item 1 in the list! to the listbox.

Visual Basic .NET then hits the `Next` statement, and that's where things start to get interesting:

```
Next
```

When the `Next` statement is executed, Visual Basic .NET increments the control variable by one. The first time `Next` is executed, 1 changes to 2. Providing that the value of the control variable is less than or equal to the "stop" value (in this case, 5), Visual Basic .NET moves back to the first line after the `For` statement, in this case:

```
' add the item to the list...
lstData.Items.Add("I'm item " & n & " in the list!")
```

This time, this line of code will add I'm item 2 in the list! to the listbox.

Again, after this line is executed, we run the Next statement again. The value of n is now incremented from 2 to 3 and, because 3 is less than or equal to 5, we move back up to the line that adds the item to the list. This happens until n is incremented from 5 to 6. As 6 is greater than the stop value for the loop, the loop stops.

> When we're talking about loops, we tend to use the term *iteration*. An iteration describes one movement from the **For** statement to the **Next** statement. In our loop, we have *five* iterations.

Step

We don't have to start our loop at 1 – we can pick any value we like. We also don't have to increment the control value by 1 on each iteration – again, we can increment by any value we like.

Try It Out – Using Step

1. Make the following changes to the code in the Click event handler for btnGo:

```
Private Sub btnGo_Click(ByVal sender As System.Object, _
        ByVal e As System.EventArgs) Handles btnGo.Click

    ' loop...
    Dim n As Integer
    For n = 4 To 62 Step 7

        ' add the item to the list...
        lstData.Items.Add(n)

    Next

End Sub
```

2. Run the project and click the Go button. You should see this:

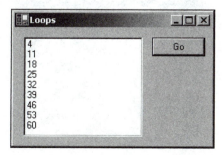

How It Works

The magic in this example all happens with this statement:

```
For n = 4 To 62 Step 7
```

Instead of using 1 as the start value, we're using 4. This means that on the first iteration of the loop, n is set to 4, and we can see this by the fact that the first item added to the list is indeed 4.

Also, we've used the Step value to tell the loop to increment the control value by 7 on each iteration rather than by the default 1. This is why, by the time we start running the second iteration of the loop, n is set to 11 and not 5.

One last thing to note here is that although we gave For a stop value of 62, the loop has actually stopped at 60. This is because the stop value is a *maximum*. After the ninth iteration, n is actually 67, which is more than 62 and so the loop stops.

Looping Backwards

By using a Step value that's less than 0, we can make the loop go backwards rather than forwards.

Try It Out – Looping Backwards

1. Change the Click event handler for btnGo to this:

```
Private Sub btnGo_Click(ByVal sender As System.Object, _
        ByVal e As System.EventArgs) Handles btnGo.Click

    ' loop...
    Dim n As Integer
    For n = 10 To 1 Step -1

        ' add the item to the list...
        lstData.Items.Add(n)
    Next

End Sub
```

2. Run the project and click the Go button. You should see this:

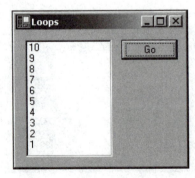

How It Works

For regards the supplied Step value literally. If we use a negative number, like -1, For will try to add -1 to the current control value. Adding a negative number has the effect of subtracting the number, so n goes from its start value of 10 to its new value of 9 and so on until the stop value is reached.

The For Each...Next Loop

In practical, day-to-day work, it's unlikely that you'll use For...Next loops in the way that we've illustrated here. Because of way the .NET Framework typically works, you'll usually use a derivative of the For...Next loop called for For Each...Next loop.

In the algorithms we design, whenever a loop is necessary, we'll have a set of things to work through and usually this set will be expressed as an **array**. For example, we might want to look through all of the files in a folder, looking for ones that are over a particular size. When we ask the .NET Framework for a list of files, we'll be given back an array of objects, each object in that array describing a single file.

In the next *Try It Out*, we'll change our Loops application so that it returns a list of subfolders contained in the root folder on our computer.

Try It Out – Looping Through Folders

1. Go to the top of the code for Form1.vb and add this namespace import declaration:

```
Imports System.IO

Public Class Form1
    Inherits System.Windows.Forms.Form
```

2. Change the Click event handler for btnGo to this:

```
Private Sub btnGo_Click(ByVal sender As System.Object, _
        ByVal e As System.EventArgs) Handles btnGo.Click

    ' get a list of subfolders...
    Dim subfolders() As DirectoryInfo
    subfolders = New DirectoryInfo("c:\").GetDirectories

    ' loop...
    Dim subfolder As DirectoryInfo
    For Each subfolder In subfolders

        ' add the item to the list...
        lstData.Items.Add(subfolder.FullName)

    Next

End Sub
```

3. Run the project and click the Go button. You should see something like this:

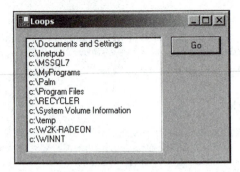

Obviously, these are the folders in the root of my C: *drive on my computer. It's highly likely you'll see different results!*

How It Works

`DirectoryInfo` is a class in the .NET Framework that allows us to learn more about the folders on the local computer and on computers on the network. In order to use the `DirectoryInfo` class in our code, we must add a **namespace import declaration** (as `DirectoryInfo` is actually found in `System.IO` and its full "name" is `System.IO.DirectoryInfo`):

```
Imports System.IO
```

In this case, we use it to return an array of `System.IO.DirectoryInfo` objects, each one representing one folder in the root of the computer's C: drive:

```
' get a list of subfolders...
Dim subfolders() As DirectoryInfo
subfolders = New DirectoryInfo("c:\").GetDirectories
```

Now that we have an array, we need a control variable for the loop. This control variable must by of the same type as the items in the array itself. As we've created an array of `DirectoryInfo` objects, our control variable is also a `DirectoryInfo` object:

```
Dim subfolder As DirectoryInfo
```

The principle with a `For Each...Next` loop is that for each iteration we'll be given the "thing" that we're supposed to be working with. We need to provide a source of "things" (in this case, our array of `DirectoryInfo` objects) and a control variable into which the current "thing" can be put:

```
For Each subfolder In subfolders
```

What this means is that on the first iteration, `subfolder` will be set equal to the first item in the `subfolders` array (in my case, `"c:\Documents and Settings"`). We then add that item to the listbox:

```
' add the item to the list...
lstData.Items.Add(subfolder.FullName)
```

As with normal `For...Next` loops, for every iteration of the loop we're given a `DirectoryInfo` object and we use the `FullName` property of this object to get the path of the folder, which we then add to the list.

The Do...Loop Loops

The other kind of loop we can use is one that keeps happening until a certain condition is met. These are known as `Do...Loop` loops and there are a number of variations.

The first one we'll introduce is the `Do Until...Loop`. This kind of loop keeps going until something happens. For this exercise, we're going to use the random number generator that's built into the .NET Framework, and as we haven't seen this yet, I'll introduce it using a `For...Next` loop before we look at `Do Until...Loop`.

1. Open the code editor for **Form1** and make the following changes to the `Click` event handler for `btnGo`:

```
Private Sub btnGo_Click(ByVal sender As System.Object, _
        ByVal e As System.EventArgs) Handles btnGo.Click

    ' create a random number generator...
    Dim random As New Random()

    ' loop...
    Dim n As Integer
    For n = 1 To 10

        ' add the item...
        lstData.Items.Add(random.Next(25))

    Next

End Sub
```

2. Run the project and click the **Go** button. You'll see something like this:

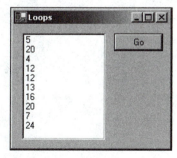

How It Works

To use the random number generator, we first need to create an instance of one:

```
' create a random number generator...
Dim random As New Random()
```

Once we have that, we can simply call the `Next` method of `Random` to get hold of random numbers. In this case, we've passed 25 as a parameter to `Next`, meaning that any number returned should be between 0 and 24 inclusive – as the number we supply must be one larger than the biggest number we ever want to get as the bounds that we ask for are non-inclusive. We do this in a loop so that we end up with a set of ten numbers rather than just one:

```
For n = 1 To 10

    ' add the item...
    lstData.Items.Add(random.Next(25))

Next
```

The Do Until...Loop

Now that you know how the random number generator works, let's create a loop that will keep generating random numbers *until* it produces the number 10. When we get the number 10, we'll stop the loop.

Try It Out – Do Until...Loop

1. In the `btnGo_Click` event handler, make these changes to the code:

```
Private Sub btnGo_Click(ByVal sender As System.Object, _
        ByVal e As System.EventArgs) Handles btnGo.Click

    ' clear the list...
    lstData.Items.Clear()

    ' create a random number generator...
    Dim random As New Random()

    ' loop...
    Dim randomNumber As Integer = 0
    Do Until randomNumber = 10

        ' get a random number...
        randomNumber = random.Next(25)

        ' add the item...
        lstData.Items.Add(randomNumber)

    Loop

End Sub
```

2. Run the project and click the **Go** button. You'll see something like this:

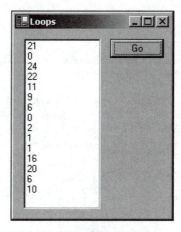

3. Keep clicking the **Go** button. You'll see that the number of elements in the list is different each time it is pressed.

How It Works

A `Do Until...Loop` will keep running the loop until the given condition is met. When we use this loop, there isn't a control variable *per se*, rather we have to keep track of the current position of the loop ourselves – let's see how we do this.

We begin by clearing the listbox (which is full of data from the previous *Try It Out*) and initializing the random number generator:

```
' clear the list...
lstData.Items.Clear()

' create a random number generator...
Dim random As New Random()
```

We then create our equivalent of a control variable:

```
' loop...
Dim randomNumber As Integer = 0
```

Next, we set up the loop and tell it that we want to keep running the loop until `randomNumber` is equal to `10`:

```
Do Until randomNumber = 10
```

With each iteration of the loop, we ask the random number generator for a new number between `0` and `24` and store it in `randomNumber`. We also add the number that we got to the list:

```
' get a random number...
randomNumber = random.Next(25)
```

```
' add the item...
lstData.Items.Add(randomNumber)
```

The magic happens when we get to the `Loop` statement. At this point, Visual Basic .NET returns not to the first line within the loop, but instead to the `Do Until` line.

When execution returns to `Do Until`, the expression is evaluated. Provided it returns `False`, the execution pointer will move to the first line within the loop. However, if `randomNumber` is `10`, the expression will return `True` and instead of moving to the first line within the loop, we continue at the first line immediately after `Loop`. In effect, the loop is stopped.

Do While...Loop

The conceptual opposite of a `Do Until...Loop` is a `Do While...Loop`. This kind of loop keeps iterating *while* a particular condition is `True`. Let's see it in action.

Try It Out – Do While...Loop

1. Make this change to `btnGo_Click`:

```
Private Sub btnGo_Click(ByVal sender As System.Object, _
        ByVal e As System.EventArgs) Handles btnGo.Click

    ' clear the list...
    lstData.Items.Clear()

    ' create a random number generator...
    Dim random As New Random()

    ' loop...
    Dim randomNumber As Integer = 0
    Do While randomNumber < 15

        ' get a random number...
        randomNumber = random.Next(25)

        ' add the item...
        lstData.Items.Add(randomNumber)

    Loop

End Sub
```

2. Run the project and click the Go button. You'll see something like this:

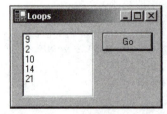

3. If you keep pressing the Go button, you'll notice that the loop will keep going until the random number generator produces a number greater than or equal to 15.

How It Works

A Do While...Loop will keep running so long as the given expression remains True. As soon as the expression becomes False, the loop will quit.

When we come to start the loop, we check to make sure that randomNumber is less than 15. If it is, the expression returns True and we can run the code within the loop:

```
Do While randomNumber < 15

    ' get a random number...
    randomNumber = random.Next(25)

    ' add the item...
    lstData.Items.Add(randomNumber)

Loop
```

Again, when we get to the Loop statement Visual Basic .NET moves back up to the Do While statement. When it gets there, it evaluates the expression again. If it's True, we run the code inside the loop once more. If it's False (because randomNumber is greater than or equal to 15), we continue with the first line after Loop, effectively quitting the loop.

Acceptable Expressions for a Do...Loop

You might be wondering what kind of expressions we can use with the two variations of Do...Loop. Well, the answer is, "If you can use it with an If statement, you can use it with a Do...Loop."

For example, we can write this:

```
Do While n > 10 And n < 100
```

...or...

```
Do Until (n > 10 And n < 100) Or b = True
```

...or...

```
Do While String.Compare(stringA, stringB) > 0
```

In short – it's a pretty powerful loop!

Other Versions of the Do...Loop

It's possible to put the Until *expression* or While *expression* statements after Loop rather than after Do as we have seen. Consider these two loops:

```
Do While n < 3
    n += 1
Loop
```

...and...

```
Do
    n += 1
Loop While n < 3
```

At first glance it looks like the `While n < 3` has just been moved around. You might think that these two loops were equivalent – but there's a subtle difference.

Suppose the value of n is greater than 3 (4 say) as these two `Do` loops start. The first loop will not run at all. However, the second loop will run *once*. When the `Loop While n < 3` line is executed, the loop will be exited. This happens despite the condition saying that n must be less than 3.

Now consider these two `Do Until` loops:

```
Do Until n = 3
    n += 1
Loop
```

...and...

```
Do
    n += 1
Loop Until n = 3
```

Again, although at first glance it looks like these two loops are equivalent, they're not and behave slightly differently. Let's say that n is 3 this time. The first loop isn't going to run, as n already meets the exit condition for this loop. However, the second loop will run *once*. Then when we execute `Loop Until n = 3` the first time, n is now 4. So we go back to the start of the loop again and increment n to 5, and so on. In fact, this is an example of an infinite loop (something we'll discuss further later in this chapter) and will not stop.

> When you use `Loop While` or `Loop Until`, you are saying that, no matter what, you want the loop to execute at least once.
>
> In general, I find it's best to stick with `Do While` and `Do Until`, rather than use `Loop While` and `Loop Until`.

You may also come across a variation of `Do While...Loop` called the `While...End While`. This convention is a throwback to previous versions of VB, but old-school developers may still use it with .NET code, so it's important that you can recognize it. These two are equivalent, but you should use the first one.

```
Do While n < 3
    n += 1
Loop
```

...and...

```
While n < 3
    n += 1
End While
```

Nested Loops

On occasion, you might find yourself in a situation where you need to start a loop even though you're already working through another loop. This is known as **nesting**, and is similar in theory to the nesting that we saw when we looked at `If` statements.

In this *Try It Out*, we'll see how we can create and run through a loop, even though we're already working through one.

Try It Out – Nested Loops

1. Change the code from our last Try It Out to this:

```
Private Sub btnGo_Click(ByVal sender As System.Object, _
        ByVal e As System.EventArgs) Handles btnGo.Click

    ' clear the list...
    lstData.Items.Clear()

    ' loop1...
    Dim n As Integer
    Dim m As Integer
    For n = 1 To 2

        ' loop2...
        For m = 1 To 3
            lstData.Items.Add(n & ", " & m)
        Next

    Next

End Sub
```

2. Run the program and click the Go button. You should see this:

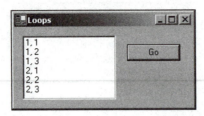

How It Works

This code is really quite simple. Our first loop iterates n from 1 to 2, and our second loop iterates m from 1 to 3. Within the second loop, we have a line of code to display the current values of n and m:

```
For n = 1 To 2

    ' loop2...
    For m = 1 To 3
        lstData.Items.Add(n & ", " & m)
    Next

Next
```

Each `For` statement must be paired with a `Next` statement, and each `Next` statement that we reach always "belongs" to the last created `For` statement. In this case, the first `Next` statement we reach is for the 1 To 3 loop, which results in m being incremented. When the value of m gets to be 4 we exit the loop.

After we've quit the second, inner loop, we hit another `Next` statement. This statement belongs to the first `For` statement, so n is set to 2 and we move back up to the first line within the first, outer loop – in this case, the other `For` statement. Once there, the loop starts once more.

Although in this *Try It Out* we've seen two `For...Next` loops nested together, you can nest `Do While` loops and even mix them, so you can have two `Do` loops nested inside a `For` loop and vice versa.

Quitting Early

Sometimes it might be the case that you don't want to see a loop through to its natural conclusion. For example, you might be looking through a list for something specific and, when you find it, there's no need to go through the remainder of the list.

In this exercise, we'll reprise our program that looked through folders on the local drive, but this time when we get to `c:\Program Files`, we'll display a message and quit.

Try It Out – Quitting a Loop Early

1. Find the `Click` event handler for `btnGo` and change the code to this:

```
Private Sub btnGo_Click(ByVal sender As System.Object, _
        ByVal e As System.EventArgs) Handles btnGo.Click

    ' get a list of subfolders...
```

```
Dim subfolders() As DirectoryInfo
subfolders = New DirectoryInfo("c:\").GetDirectories

' loop...
Dim subfolder As DirectoryInfo
For Each subfolder In subfolders

    ' add the item to the list...
    lstData.Items.Add(subfolder.FullName)

    ' have we got to c:\program files?
    If String.Compare(subfolder.FullName, _
        "c:\program files", True) = 0 Then

        ' tell the user...
        MessageBox.Show("Found it!", "Loops")

        ' quit the loop...
        Exit For

    End If

Next

End Sub
```

2. Run the program and click the Go button. You'll see something like this:

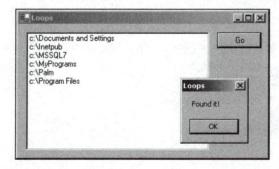

How It Works

This time, with each iteration we use the `String.Compare` method that we discussed earlier to check the name of the folder to see if it matches `c:\Program Files`:

```
    ' have we got to c:\program files?
    If String.Compare(subfolder.FullName, _
        "c:\program files", True) = 0 Then
```

If it does, the first thing we do is display a message box:

```
' tell the user...
MessageBox.Show("Found it!", "Loops")
```

After the user has clicked **OK** to dismiss the message box, we use the `Exit For` statement to quit the loop. In this instance, the loop is short-circuited and the Visual Basic .NET moves to the first line after the `Next` statement.

```
' quit the loop...
Exit For
```

Of course, if the name of the folder doesn't match the one we're looking for, we keep looping.

Using loops to find an item in a list is one of their most common uses. Once you've found the item you're looking for, using the `Exit For` statement to short-circuit the list is a very easy way to improve the performance of your application.

Imagine you have a list of a thousand items to look through. You find the item you're looking for on the tenth iteration. If you don't quit the loop after you've finished working with the item, you're effectively asking the computer to look through another 990 useless items. If, however, you do quit the loop early, you can move on and start running another part of the algorithm.

Quitting Do...Loops

As you might have guessed, we can quit a `Do...Loop` in more or less the same way.

Try It Out – Quitting a Do...Loop

1. Change the `Click` event handler for `btnGo` to this:

```
Private Sub btnGo_Click(ByVal sender As System.Object, _
        ByVal e As System.EventArgs) Handles btnGo.Click

    ' start looping...
    Dim n As Integer = 0
    Do While n < 10

        ' add n to the list...
        lstData.Items.Add(n)
        ' add one to n...
        n += 1

        ' do we need to quit?
        If n = 3 Then
            Exit Do
        End If

    Loop

End Sub
```

2. Run the project and click the **Go** button. You'll see this:

How It Works

In this case, because we're in a `Do...Loop`, we have to use `Exit Do` rather than `Exit For`. However, the principle is exactly the same. `Exit Do` will work with both `Do While...Loop` and `Do Until...Loop` loops.

Infinite Loops

When building loops you can create something called an **infinite loop**. What this means is a loop that, once started, will never finish. Consider this code:

```
Dim n As Integer = 0
Do
    n += 1
Loop Until n = 0
```

This loop will run *once*. Then when we execute `Loop Until n = 0` the first time, n is 1. So we go back to the start of the loop again and increment n to 2, and so on. What's important here is that it will never get to 0. The loop becomes infinite, and the program won't crash (at least not instantly), but it may well become unresponsive.

If you suspect a program has dropped into an infinite loop, you'll need to force the program to stop. With Windows 2000, this is pretty easy.

If Visual Studio .NET is running, flip over to it, and select Debug | Stop Debugging from the menu. This will immediately stop the program.

If Visual Studio .NET is not running, you'll need to use Task Manager. Press *Ctrl+Alt+Delete* and select Task Manager. Your program should show as Not Responding:

Select your program in Task Manager and click on **End Task**. Eventually this will pop up a dialog asking if you want to kill the program stone dead, so click **End Task** again on this new dialog.

In some extreme cases, the loop can take up so much processing power or other system resources that you won't be able to open Task Manager or flip over to Visual Studio. In these cases, you can persevere and try to use either of these methods; alternatively you can reset your computer and chalk it up to experience.

Visual Studio .NET automatically saves the program files before running the application, so you're unlikely to lose any of your program code should you have to reset. However, that may not be true of other applications, so it's a good idea to make sure that you don't have other programs open when running code. (And as you can see from the screenshot above, I have Outlook and Word open while coding, so clearly I don't listen to my own advice!)

In some cases, it's perfectly acceptable to create infinite loops deliberately. However, you must take care to ensure that you use the appropriate `Exit For` or `Exit Do` so that the program will end at some point.

Summary

In this chapter, we took a detailed look at the various ways that programs can make decisions and loop through code. We first of all detailed the alternative operators that can be used with `If` statements and examined how multiple operators could be combined by using the `And` and `Or` keywords. Additionally, we examined how case-insensitive string comparisons could be performed.

We then looked at `Select Case`, an efficient technique for choosing one outcome out of a group of possibilities.

Next we examined the concept of looping within a program and introduced the two main types of loops: For loops and Do loops. For loops iterate a given number of times, or the derivative For Each loop can be used to automatically loop through a list of items in an array. Do While loops iterate while a given condition remains True, whereas Do Until loops iterate until a given condition becomes True.

Questions

1. What are the six possible arithmetic operators that can be used with an If statement?

2. How do we do case-insensitive string comparisons?

3. What kind of loop is appropriate for iterating through items in an array?

4. How can we exit a loop early?

5. Why is a Select Case statement useful?

Building Objects

In the time you've been using computers you may well have heard the term **object-oriented**. You may also have heard that it's a scary subject and tricky to understand. In its early years it was, but today's modern tools and languages make object-orientation (or **OO**) a wonderfully easy-to-understand concept that brings massive benefits to software developers. This is mainly due to the fact that development tools like VB, C++, and of course Visual Basic .NET and C# have matured to a point where the tools make creating objects and software that uses them very easy indeed. With these tools, you'll have no problem understanding even the most advanced object-oriented concepts and using them to build exciting object-based applications.

In this chapter, we're going to be looking at object-orientation in great detail and building on the foundations of the last chapter to start producing some cool Visual Basic .NET applications.

What is an Object?

An object is almost anything you can think of. We work with physical objects all the time: televisions, cars, customers, reports, light bulbs – anything. In computer terms, an object is a *representation* of a thing that we want to manipulate in our application. The two, usefully, map exactly onto each other. So, if you have a physical car object sitting in your driveway and want to describe it in software terms you build a software car object that sits in your computer.

Likewise, if you need to write a piece of software that generates a bill for a customer, you may well have a "Bill" object and a "Customer" object. The Customer object represents the customer and may be capable of having a name, address, and also have the capability to generate the bill. The Bill object would represent an instance of a bill for a customer and would be able to impart the details of the bill and may also have the capability to print itself.

What's important here is the concept that the object has the intelligence to produce actions related to itself – the Customer object can generate the bill. In effect, if you have a Customer object you can simply say to it: "Produce a bill for me". The Customer object would then go away and do all the hard work related to creating the bill. Likewise, once you have a Bill object you can say to it: "Print yourself". What we have here is two examples of object **behavior**.

Objects are unbelievably useful because they turn software engineering into something conceptually similar to wooden building blocks. You arrange the blocks (the objects) in order to build something greater than the sum of the parts. The power of objects comes from the fact that, as someone using objects, you don't need to understand how they work behind the scenes. We're familiar with this with real-world objects too. When we use a mobile phone, we don't need to understand how it works inside. Even if you do understand how a mobile phone works inside – even if you made it yourself – it's still much easier to use the mobile phone's simple **interface**. The interface can also prevent you from accidentally doing something that breaks the phone. The same is true with computer objects – even if you build all the objects yourself, having the complicated workings hidden behind a simple interface can make your life much easier and safer.

Let's take another example. The way that object-orientation was first explained to me was by using a television metaphor. Look at the television sitting in your lounge. There are several things you know how to do with it, such as:

- ❑ Watch the image on the screen
- ❑ Change channel
- ❑ Change volume
- ❑ Switch it on or off
- ❑ Tune into stations
- ❑ Plug in a games console

What you don't have to do is understand how everything works to allow you to carry out these activities. If asked, I couldn't put together the components needed to make a modern television. I could, with a little research and patience, come up with something fairly basic, but nothing as complex as the one sitting in my lounge. However, I do understand how to use a television. I know how to change the channel, change the volume, switch it on and off, plug in a Nintendo Game Cube, and so on.

Objects in software engineering work in basically the same way. Once you have an object you can use it and ask it do things without having to understand how the internals of it actually work. This is phenomenally powerful, as we'll soon see.

Software objects typically have the following characteristics:

- ❑ **Identity** – User: "What are you?" TV: "I'm a TV."
- ❑ **State** – User: "What channel am I watching?" TV: "You're watching Channel 4."
- ❑ **Behavior** – User: "Please turn up the volume to 50%." Then, we can use the **state** again – User: "How loud is the volume?" TV: "50%."

Encapsulation

The core concept behind object-orientation is **encapsulation**. This is a big word, but it's very simple to understand. What this means is that the functionality is wrapped up in a self-contained manner and that you don't need to understand what it's actually doing when you ask it to do something.

If you remember back to Chapter 2, we built a function that calculated the area of the circle. Well, in that function we *encapsulated* the logic of calculating the area in such a way that anyone using the function could find the area without having to know how to physically perform the operation. This is the same concept but taken to the next level.

> **Objects are often referred to as** *black boxes*. **If you imagine software objects as small plastic boxes with buttons on the top and connectors on the side, with a basic understanding of what the box does, together with a general understanding of how boxes generally plug together, you can build up a complex system with them without ever having to have the capability of building a box independently.**

Methods and Properties

You interact with objects through methods and properties. These can be defined as:

- ❑ Methods are ways of instructing an object to do something
- ❑ Properties are things that describe features of an object

We've defined a method before as a self-contained block of code that "does something". This is true, but it is a rather simplistic definition. In fact the strict definition of a method applies only to OO, and is a way to manipulate an object – a way to instruct it to perform certain behaviors. In previous chapters we've created methods that instructed an object – in most cases a `Form` – to do something. When we create a `Form` in Visual Basic .NET, we are actually defining a new type of `Form` object.

So, if we need to turn on the TV, we need to find a *method* that does this because, as we just said, a method is something we get the object to do. When we **invoke** the method, the object itself is supposed to understand what to do in order to satisfy the request. To hammer the point home, we don't care what it actually does, we just say, "Switch on." It's down to the TV to switch relays to deliver power, boot up the circuitry, warm up the electron gun, and all the other things that I don't need to understand!

> **Invoke means the same as** *call*, **but is more OO-friendly. It reminds us that we are invoking a method** *on* **something, rather than just calling a chunk of code.**

On the other hand, if we need to change the channel we might **set** the channel *property*. If we want to tune into Channel 10, we set the channel property to the value 10. Again, the object is responsible for reacting to the request and we don't care about the technical hoops it has to go through in order to do that.

Events

We've already seen how in Visual Basic .NET we listen for events to determine when something has happened to a control on a form.

You can regard an event as something that an object does. In effect, someone using an object can listen for events, like a `Click` event on a button or a `PowerOn` event on a TV. When the event is received, the developer can take some action. Some old TVs take ages to warm up. In OO terms, there is the `SwitchOn` method that gets called on the TV object, when the TV has warmed up it raises a `PowerOn` event. We could then respond to this event by adjusting the volume to the required level.

An event might also be used when the performer of an action is not the only entity interested in the action having taken place. For example, when we have the TV on we might go and get a drink during a commercial break. But while we're in the kitchen, we keep our ears open for when the program starts again. Effectively we are listening for a `ProgramResume` event. We do not cause the program to resume, but we do want to know when it does.

Visibility

As we've said, to build decent objects we have to make them easy for developers to use. For example, internally it might be really important for our TV object to know what frequency the tuner needs, but does the person using the TV care? More importantly, do we actually want the developer to be able to change this frequency directly? What we're trying to do is make the object more "abstract".

Some parts of your object will be private, whereas other parts will be public. The public interface is what is available for others to use. The private part is what you expect the object itself to use internally. The logic for the object exists in the private part, and may include methods and properties that are important – but that won't get called from outside the object. For example, a TV object might have methods for `ConnectPower`, `WarmUp`, and so on. These would be private, and would all be called from the public `SwitchOn` method. Similarly, while there is a public `Channel` property there will probably be a private `Frequency` property. The TV could not work without knowing the signal frequency it was receiving, but the users are only interested in the channel.

That brings us to the end of all the basic OO concepts we need to talk about. We can now talk about how we build objects and then applications that use them.

Using Objects

Now that you understand the basics of object orientation, let's look at how we can use objects within an application.

What Is a Class?

A **class** is the definition of an object and is made up of the software code. This is effectively the circuitry inside the black box. If you want to build a software object, you have to understand how the internals work. We express those internals with Visual Basic .NET code. So, when the software developer using our object says, "Turn up the volume" we have to know how to instruct the amplifier to increase the output. (As an aside, remember that the amplifier is just another object. We don't necessarily need to know how it works inside. In OO programming, you will often find that one object is basically a load of other objects with some code to link them together – just as a TV is a load of standard components, and a bit of custom circuitry.)

When we want to use an object, we have to "instantiate an instance of the class". So, if we have 50 TV objects, we have 50 **instances** of the TV class. Each of those instances has been created by **instantiation**, which is a fancy term for creating. Typically, we "create classes" and "instantiate objects". The difference is used to reduce ambiguity. Creating a class is done at design time when you're building your software and involves writing the actual code. Instantiating objects is done at run time, when your program is being used.

A classic analogy is the cookie cutter. I can go out to my workshop and shape a piece of metal in the shape of a Christmas tree. I do this once and put the cutter in a drawer in my kitchen. Whenever I need to create Christmas tree cookies, I roll some dough (the computer's memory) and stamp out however many I need. In effect I'm instantiating cookies. I can reuse the cutter at a later date to create more cookies each the same as the ones before.

Once we've instantiated instances of the class to get the objects, we can manipulate the properties and methods defined on the class. For example, I can build a class once at design time that represents a television. However, I can instantiate two objects from that class – one to represent the TV in the lounge and one to represent the TV in the bedroom. Because both instances of the object share the same class, both instances have the same properties and methods. To turn on the TV I can call the SwitchOn method. To change the channel I can set the Channel property and so on.

Enough discussion! Let's get to work building some object-oriented code.

We've Already Been Using Objects!

You'll notice that some of the code samples we met in the last chapter included a line that looked something like this:

```
lstData.Items.Add(n)
```

That's a classic example of object orientation! lstData is, in fact, an object. Items is a property of the lstData object. The Items property is an object in its own right, and has an Add method. The period (.) tells Visual Basic .NET that the word to the right is a member of the word to the left. So Items is a member of lstData, and Add is a member of Items.

lstData is an instance of a class called System.Windows.Forms.ListBox (or just ListBox). This class is part of the **Framework**, which we'll talk about in a short while and then in plenty of detail in Chapter 5.

The ListBox class can display a list of items on screen, and let a user choose a particular one. Again, here's the concept of encapsulation. You as a user of ListBox don't need to know anything about technologies involved in displaying the list or listening for input. You may not have even *heard* of GDI+, stdin, keyboard drivers, display drivers, or anything else that goes into the complex action of displaying a list on screen, yet you still have the capability to do it.

The ListBox is an example of an object that we can see. Users can look at a program running and know that there is a ListBox involved. Most objects in OO programming are invisible, and represent something in memory.

Building Classes

You're now ready to start building classes. As you build your application, you'll be using both classes developed by others (in particular those in the Framework) and your own. When you design an algorithm, you'll discover certain objects described. We need to abstract these real-world objects into a software representation. Here's an example:

- ❏   Select a list of ten customers from the database
- ❏   Go through each customer and prepare a bill for each
- ❏   When each bill has been prepared, print it on a printer

For a pure object-oriented application (and with .NET we will end up using objects to represent everything) every real-world object will need a software object. For example:

- ❏   `Customer` – an object that represents a customer
- ❏   `Bill` – an object that represents a bill that is produced
- ❏   `Printer` – an object that represents a hardware printer that can be used to print the bill

Typically, when building an application, some of the classes you need will already be included in the Framework, others you will have to build yourself. In this case, although there's no specific `Printer` object, there are classes that deal with printing.

> **Although we don't talk about printing in this book, you can find the printing functionality in the `System.Drawing.Printing` namespace.**

When we write software in .NET, we are given a vast set of classes called the **Microsoft .NET Framework Classes**. These classes describe virtually everything about the computing environment that we're trying to write software for. Writing object-oriented software for .NET is simply an issue of using objects that fit our needs and creating new objects if required.

For example, there are objects in the Framework that provide printing functionality and database access functionality. As our algorithm calls for both kinds of functionality, we don't need to write our own. If we need to print something, we create an object that understands how to print, tell it what we want to print and then tell it to go print it out. Again, this is encapsulation– we don't care how to turn our document into PostScript commands and send it down the wire to the printer, the object knows how to do this for itself.

In some cases, there are some objects that we need to represent that do not exist in the Framework. In this example, we need a `Customer` object and a `Bill` object.

So now we know what the objects are that we need to satisfy our algorithm, and we also know that we can consume some directly from the Framework but have to build others.

Reusability

Perhaps the hardest aspect of object-oriented programming is coming to an understanding of how to divide up the responsibility for the work. One of the most beautiful aspects of object-orientation is **code reuse**. Imagine a company has a need for several different applications: one to display customer bills, one to register a new customer, and one to track customer complaints. Well, in each of those applications, we need to have a `Customer` object.

Let's simplify the issue and say that those three projects are not going to be undertaken simultaneously; we'll start by doing the first, and when finished, we'll move on to the second, and when we've finished that, we'll move on to the third. For each project do we want to build a new `Customer` class, or do we want to build the class once and reuse it in each of the other two projects?

Reuse is typically regarded as something that's universally good, although there is a tradeoff. Ideally, if you build a `Customer` class for one project, and another project you're working on calls for another `Customer` class, you should use the same one. However, it may well be the case that you can't just plug the class into another project for some reason. I say *for some reason* because there are no hard or fast rules when it comes to class design and reuse. It may also be the case that it's easier or more cost-effective to build simple classes for each project rather than trying to create one complex object that does everything. This might sound like it requires a degree in clairvoyance, but luckily it comes with experience! As you develop more and more applications, you'll gain a better understanding of how to design great, reusable objects.

Each object should be responsible for activities involving itself and no more. As we've only discussed two objects `Bill` and `Customer`, we'll look at those.

The activity of printing a bill for telephone charges follows this algorithm:

- ❏ For a given customer, find the call details for the last period
- ❏ Go through each call and work out the price of each one
- ❏ Aggregate the cost of each call into a total
- ❏ Apply tax charges
- ❏ Print out the bill – the customer's name, address, and bill summary on the first page, and then the bill details on subsequent pages

We've only got two places where we can code this algorithm: the `Bill` object or the `Customer` object, so which do we choose?

Well, the calls made are really a property of the `Customer`. Basically, we are using these details to create a `Bill`. Most of the functionality would be placed in the `Bill` object. A `Customer` is responsible for representing a customer, not representing a bill. When we create a Bill object, we would associate it with a particular customer. We could do that using a `Cust` property, like this:

```
myBill.Cust = myCustomer
```

The `Bill` object would then know that it was a `Bill` for a given customer (represented by the `myCustomer` object), and could use the customer's details when creating a bill. We might want to change some other properties of the `Bill`, such as where it will be mailed to, whether it should contain a warning because it is overdue, and so on. Finally, the Bill would have a Print method:

```
myBill.Print()
```

The `Bill` object would then **consume** (or use) a `Printer` object in order to print the bill.

In Chapter 10 of this book we'll take a look at more advanced object-oriented programming techniques, but for now this chapter will help you understand what's happening with objects under the hood.

Our First Object

Contrary to what we've said so far, we're not going to define an algorithm and then build objects to support it. For this rather academic example, I'm going to walk you through some of the features of a typical object, in this case, a car.

There are certain facts we might want to know about the object:

- ❑ What it looks like – for a car, this includes things like make, model, color, number of doors, and so on. These aspects of the car will rarely change during the object's lifetime.
- ❑ Its capabilities – horsepower, engine size, cylinder configuration, and so on.
- ❑ What it's doing – whether it's stationary, moving forward, or moving backwards, its speed and direction.
- ❑ Where it is – the GPS (Global Positioning System) coordinates of its current position. This is effectively its position relative to another object (the planet Earth). Likewise, controls on forms have coordinates that describe their location relative to the form.

We might also want to be able to control the object, for example:

- ❑ Tell it to accelerate
- ❑ Tell it to decelerate
- ❑ Tell it to turn left
- ❑ Tell it to turn right
- ❑ Tell it to straighten up
- ❑ Tell it to do a three-point-turn
- ❑ Tell it to stop completely

We mentioned the three concepts of identity, state, and behavior earlier in this chapter. We'll assume that the identity aspect is covered because we know what the class is, so the state and behavior are of interest here.

State

State describes facts about the object now. For example, a car's location and speed is part of its state. When designing objects, we need to think about what aspects of state we need to handle. It might not be useful to know a customer's speed, for example, but we might well want to know their current address.

State tends to be implemented as values inside an object. Some of these properties will be publicly available through **properties**, and some will be private. Also, some aspects of state might be publicly readable, but not changeable. For example cars have a speedo that is readable to anybody using the car. But you can't change the car's speed by playing with the speedo – you need to alter the car's **behavior** by braking or accelerating. We will see more about this particular example later.

Behavior

While a car might have a read-only speed property, it would have methods to accelerate and decelerate. When we call an object's method, we are telling our object to do something – so behavior is usually associated with methods. Properties can also be associated with behavior. When we set a property to a particular value, we can trigger behavior. Behavior is usually implemented as a set of VB.NET statements that do something. This will usually involve one or both of the following:

- ❑ Changing its own state. When we call the accelerate method on a car, it should get faster if it is capable of doing so.

- ❑ Somehow affecting the 'world' outside the object. This could be manipulating other objects in the application, displaying something to the user, saving something to a disk, or printing a document.

In this chapter, we won't build all of the properties and methods we've discussed. Instead, we'll build a handful of the more interesting ones.

Try It Out – Creating a New Project and the Car Class

1. We'll create a new project for this exercise, so start Visual Basic .NET and select File | New | Project from the menu.

2. When the New Project dialog appears, select the Visual Basic .NET Console Application template and enter the name of the project as Objects. Click OK to create the project:

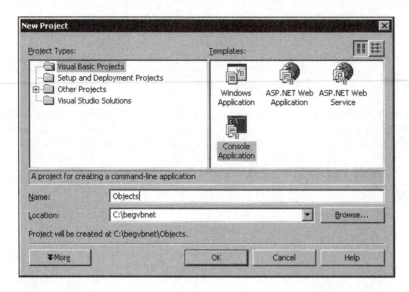

3. We now need to create a new class. This is done through the Solution Explorer, so right-click on the **Objects** project and select **Add | Add Class**. This will prompt you for a new class name, so enter **Car** and click **Open**:

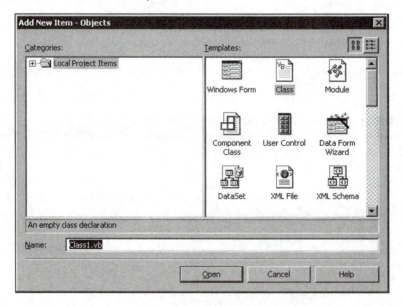

4. You'll notice that the new class and module have been added to the Solution Explorer and that the editor now shows the code listing for them, albeit empty:

5. That's all we have to do to create our new class. At the top of the code editor you'll notice something that looks like this:

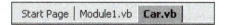

Each class and module is held within its own file and this tab provides a useful method for moving between open files. Alternatively, you can use the *Ctrl+Tab* key combination, or double-click on a file in the Solution Explorer to open it.

Storing State

As we know, state describes what the object understands about itself, so if you give a car object some state, for example "You are blue", what we're doing is giving the car object a fact: "The car I represent is blue".

So how do we actually manage state in our classes? Well, state is typically held in variables, and we define those variables within the class. We'll see how to do this in a moment.

Usually, the methods and properties you build will either affect or use the state in some way. Imagine we've built a property that changes the color of the car. When we set that property, the variable that's responsible for storing the state will be changed to reflect the new value that it has been given. When we retrieve (Get) that property, the variable that's responsible for storing the state will be read and the current value will be returned to the caller.

In a way, then, properties are behavior. Under the hood, a public property is two methods: a Get method and a Set method. A simple Get method for the Color property will contain code to tell the caller what color the car is. A simple Set method for the Color property will set a value that represents the car's color. In a real application, though, Color would probably mean something more than just remembering a value. In a driving game, the Set method of the Color property would need to change the color that car had on the screen, for example.

When a property has no behavior at all, we can cheat. In the next example we will create a Color 'property' by declaring a Color variable, and making it public. This can be a useful, very fast technique for adding properties. It does make them a bit less flexible, though.

Try It Out – Adding a Color Property

1. Open the `Car.vb` file and add this code:

```
Public Class Car

    Public Color As String

End Class
```

2. That's it! However, we do need a way of consuming the class so that we can see it working. Open `Module1.vb` and add this code:

```
Module Module1

    Sub Main()
        ' create a new car object...
        Dim myCar As Car
        myCar = New Car()

        ' set the Color property to "Red"...
        myCar.Color = "Red"

        ' show what the value of the property is...
        Console.WriteLine("My car is this color:")
        Console.WriteLine(myCar.Color)

        ' wait...
        Console.ReadLine()
    End Sub

End Module
```

3. Now run the project. A new window will appear that looks like this:

Press *Enter* to end the program.

How It Works

Defining the fake property is easy. The highlighted line:

```
Public Class Car

    Public Color As String
```

...tells the class that we want to create a variable called `Color` and that we want the property to hold a string of text characters. The use of the `Public` keyword when we declare the `Color` variable tells the class that the variable is accessible to people using the `Car` class, not only from within the class itself.

> **Variables defined in the location between the `Public Class` and `End Class` lines, but outside of a function definition are known as *member variables*.**

Using the object is a little trickier, and we do this from within `Module1.vb`. Firstly, we have to instantiate an instance of the class. With the following lines, we create a variable called `myCar` and tell it that it's going to exclusively hold objects created using the `Car` class:

```
Sub Main()

    ' create a new car object...
    Dim myCar As Car
```

When we define the variable, it doesn't have an object instance associated with it, you are simply identifying the type of object. It's a bit like telling the computer to give you a hook that you can hang a `Car` object on, and call the hook `myCar`. We haven't hung anything on it yet – to do that we have to create an instance of the object. This is done using the `New` keyword, like this:

```
    myCar = New Car()
```

So, what we're saying here is: "let `myCar` refer to a newly created object instantiated from the class `Car`". In other words, "create a new car, and hang it on the hook called `myCar`". We now have a `Car` object, and we can refer to it with the name `myCar`.

> **Note that in OO programming, the same object can be hanging on several different hooks at the same time – and therefore have several different names. This seems confusing, but in most cases it is a really intuitive way to work. Imagine how cool it would be if your keys could be on several hooks at the same time – they'd be so much easier to find!**

After we have an object instance, we can set its properties and call its methods. Here's how we set the `Color` property:

```
    ' set the Color property to "Red"...
    myCar.Color = "Red"
```

Once the property has been set, it can be retrieved again as many times as we want, or its value changed at a later point. We illustrated retrieval by passing the `WriteLine` method on the `Console` class:

```
    ' show what the value of the property is...
    Console.WriteLine("My car is this color:")
    Console.WriteLine(myCar.Color)
```

```
' wait...
Console.ReadLine()
```

The `Console.ReadLine` line means that the program does not end until we press *Enter*.

> **Console applications are a good way to test our in-memory objects because we don't need to worry about setting up a user interface. We can just display lines of text whenever we want. The objects we build will work just as well in a Windows Application, though.**

Even though this is not really a property, from the point of view of a developer using our class, it works just like one. In fact, 'real' properties are methods that *look* like variables to users of the class. Whether you use a method or a property really depends on what the users of your class will find easier. We'll start to see this in the next section.

Real Properties

Now that you've seen how to cheat, let's see how to do things properly. The property we've seen can be set to pretty much anything. As long as it's a `String`, it will be accepted. Also, setting the property doesn't do anything except change the object's internal state. Often we want to control what values a property can be set to, for example we might have a list of valid colors that a car can be. Alternatively, we might want to associate a change to a property with a particular action. For example, when we change a channel on the TV we want it to do a bit more than just change its mind about what channel it's displaying. We want the TV to show a different picture! Just changing the value of a variable won't help here.

The simplest reason to use real properties is that we want to prevent the user of the class from directly changing the value. We call this a **read-only** property. We've already mentioned that the car's speed is a good example. If we're doing 60 mph, we can't simply change the speed to a value we prefer. Rather, we want to use methods to control the speed (`Accelerate`, `Decelerate`) and keep a read-only property around called `Speed` that will report on the current speed of the vehicle.

This is a good example of how a class that models a real-world object should behave like that real-world object. We can read the speed of a car from the speedometer, but we cannot change (write) the speed of the car by physically moving the needle around the dial with our finger. We have to control the car in another fashion, which we do by using the throttle to signal the accelerate or decelerate methods.

What we need is a member variable that can only be seen or manipulated by the class itself. We can do this by using the `Private` keyword:

```
Public Color As String
Private _speed As Integer
```

Although we'll build this property in a little while, `_speed` is marked as `Private` and can therefore only be accessed by functions defined inside the class itself. Users of `Car` will not even be aware of its presence. Private members are camelCased rather than PascalCased, so that we can easily tell whether something is public or private when we use it. When a private variable maps directly to a public property, we prefix the variable name with an underscore (_).

Now we'll see how we can build a property that will give the user of the object read-only access to the car's speed.

1. To define a private variable, we use the `Private` instead of the `Public` keyword. Add this statement to `Car.vb`:

```
Public Class Car

    Public Color As String
    Private _speed As Integer

End Class
```

2. To report the speed, we need to build a read-only property. Add this code:

```
Public Class Car

    Public Color As String
    Private _speed As Integer

    ' Speed - read-only property to return the speed...
    ReadOnly Property Speed() As Integer
        Get
            Return _speed
        End Get
    End Property

End Class
```

3. Now, we'll build a method called `Accelerate` that will adjust the speed of the car by however many miles-per-hour we give it:

```
Public Class Car

    Public Color As String
    Private _speed As Integer

    ' Speed - read-only property to return the speed...
    ReadOnly Property Speed() As Integer
        Get
            Return _speed
        End Get
    End Property

    ' Accelerate - add mph to the speed...
    Sub Accelerate(ByVal accelerateBy As Integer)

        ' adjust the speed...
        _speed += accelerateBy
```

```
      End Sub

  End Class
```

4. To test the object we need to make some changes to `Module1.vb`. Open the file and add this code in the place of what we had previously:

```
Sub Main()

    ' create a new car object...
    Dim myCar As Car
    myCar = New Car()

    ' leave code for Color property here

    ' report the speed...
    Console.WriteLine("The car's speed is:")
    Console.WriteLine(myCar.Speed)

    ' accelerate...
    myCar.Accelerate(5)

    ' report the new speed...
    Console.WriteLine("The car's speed is now:")
    Console.WriteLine(myCar.Speed)

    ' wait...
    Console.ReadLine()

End Sub
```

5. Now run the project and you should see this:

How It Works

The first thing we did was to define a private member variable called _speed.

```
Private _speed As Integer
```

By default, when the object is created _speed will have a value of zero because this is the default value for the data type Integer.

We then defined a read-only property that would return the current speed:

```
' Speed - read-only property to return the speed...
ReadOnly Property Speed() As Integer
    Get
        Return _speed
    End Get
End Property
```

When we define properties, we can either set them to be read-only (through the ReadOnly keyword), write-only (through the WriteOnly keyword that we haven't seen yet) or both readable and writable by using neither. Reading a property is known as *getting* the value, whereas writing to a property is known as *setting* the value. The code between Get and End Get will be executed when the property is read. In this case, the only thing we're doing is returning the value currently stored in _speed.

We also created a method called Accelerate. As this method doesn't have to return a value, we use the Sub keyword:

```
' Accelerate - add mph to the speed...
Sub Accelerate(ByVal accelerateBy As Integer)

    ' adjust the speed...
    _speed += accelerateBy

End Sub
```

The method takes a single parameter, called accelerateBy that we'll use to tell the method how much to increase the speed by. You'll notice that the only action of the method is to adjust the internal member _speed. In real life the pressure on the accelerator along with factors such as wind speed and road surface will affect the speed. The speed will be an outcome of several factors – not something we can just change. We'd need some quite complex code to simulate this – here we are just keeping things simple, and showing how to use properties.

Accelerating a car is another example of encapsulation. To accelerate the car in a real-world implementation we'd need an actuator of some kind to further open throttle until the required speed was reached. We, as consumers of the object, don't care how this is done. All we do care about is how we tell the car to accelerate.

Consuming this new functionality is pretty simple. Firstly, we create the object:

```
' create a new car object...
Dim myCar As Car
myCar = New Car()
```

After the code for using the `Color` property, we write out the speed:

```
' report the speed...
Console.WriteLine("The car's speed is:")
Console.WriteLine(myCar.Speed)
```

Notice how we're using the read-only `Speed` property to get the current speed of the car. When the object is first created, the internal _speed member will be set to 0.

Now we can call `Accelerate` and use it to increase the speed of the car:

```
' accelerate...
myCar.Accelerate(5)
```

Finally, we write out the new speed:

```
' report the speed...
Console.WriteLine("The car's speed is now:")
Console.WriteLine(myCar.Speed)
```

Read/Write Properties

So, why would you need to use the `Property` keyword to define properties that were both readable and writable if you can achieve the same effect with a line like this?

```
Public Color As String
```

Well, if we manually build the property using the `Property` keyword, we can write code that is executed whenever the property is called. This is extremely powerful.

For example, the `Property` keyword allows us to provide validation for new values. Imagine we had a property called `NumberOfDoors`. We wouldn't want this to be set to nonsense values like 0 or 23453. Rather, we'd have some possible range. For modern cars, this is going to go from 2 to 5.

> **This is an important consideration for developers building objects. It's imperative that you make life as easy as possible for a developer to consume your object. The fact that you deal with problems like making sure a car can't have ten million doors is an important aspect of object design.**

Likewise, we might not have the information to hand when we are asked to return the property and might have to retrieve the value from somewhere or otherwise calculate it. We might have a property that describes the total number of orders a customer has ever made, or the total number of chew toys a dog has destroyed in his life. If we build this as a property, we can intercept the instruction to "get" the value and find the actual value we require on demand from some other data store, like a database or a web service. We'll see this covered in later chapters.

For now, let's deal with the number of doors problem.

Try It Out – Adding a NumberOfDoors Property

1. The first thing we need to do is build a private member that will hold the number of doors. We're going to define this property as having a default of 5. Add this code:

```
Public Color As String
Private _speed As Integer
Private _numberOfDoors As Integer = 5
```

2. Now we can build a property that will get and set the number of doors, providing that the number of doors we're asked to set to is always between 2 and 5. Add this code to Car.vb directly beneath the Accelerate method:

```
' NumberOfDoors - get/set the number of doors...
Property NumberOfDoors() As Integer

    ' called when the property is "got"...
    Get
        Return _numberOfDoors
    End Get

    ' called when the property is "set"...
    Set(ByVal Value As Integer)

        ' is the new value between two and five?
        If Value >= 2 And Value <= 5 Then
            _numberOfDoors = Value
        End If

    End Set

End Property
```

> In this chapter, we're going to ignore the problem of telling the developer if the user has provided an invalid value for a property. Ideally whenever this happens you need to *throw* something called an *exception*. The developer will be able to detect this exception and behave accordingly. (For example, if the user typed the number of doors as 9999 into a textbox, the program could display a message box telling the user that they have provided an invalid value for the number of doors since no car has that many doors.) Exception handling is quite an advanced topic, and we talk about it more in Chapter 11.

3. To test the property, we again need to change `Module1.vb`:

```
Sub Main()

    ' create a new car object...
    Dim myCar As Car
    myCar = New Car()

    ' leave existing code for Color and Speed properties here

    ' report the number of doors...
    Console.WriteLine("The number of doors is:")
    Console.WriteLine(myCar.NumberOfDoors)

    ' try changing the number of doors to 1000...
    myCar.NumberOfDoors = 1000

    ' report the number of doors...
    Console.WriteLine("The number of doors is:")
    Console.WriteLine(myCar.NumberOfDoors)

    ' now try changing the number of doors to 2...
    myCar.NumberOfDoors = 2

    ' report the number of doors...
    Console.WriteLine("The number of doors is:")
    Console.WriteLine(myCar.NumberOfDoors)

    ' wait...
    Console.ReadLine()

End Sub
```

4. Try running the project and you should see this:

How It Works

The first thing we did was define a private member variable called _numberOfDoors. We also assigned the value 5 to this variable.

```
Private _numberOfDoors As Integer = 5
```

The motivation behind setting a value at this point is simple: we want _numberOfDoors to always be between 2 and 5. When the object is created, the _numberOfDoors will be assigned a value of 5. Without this assignment, _numberOfDoors would have a default value of 0. This would be inconsistent with the understanding that the number of doors must always be between 2 and 5 so we guard against it.

Next comes the property itself. The Get portion is simple – just return the value held in _numberOfDoors – but the Set portion involves a check to ensure the new value is valid. The new value is passed in through a parameter called Value:

```
' NumberOfDoors - get/set the number of doors...
Property NumberOfDoors() As Integer

    ' called when the property is "got"...
    Get
        Return _numberOfDoors
    End Get

    ' called when the property is "set"...
    Set(ByVal Value As Integer)

        ' is the new value between two and five?
        If Value >= 2 And Value <= 5 Then
            _numberOfDoors = Value
        End If

    End Set

End Property
```

The test code we added to Module1.vb was not very complex. All we did was display the initial value of _numberOfDoors, and then try to change it to 1000. The validation code in the _numberOfDoors property won't change _numberOfDoors if an inconsistent number is used, so when we report the number of doors again we find it hasn't changed from 5. Lastly, we try setting it to 2, which is a valid value, and this time when we report the number of doors we get an output of 2.

> **Even though read-write properties and public variables seem to work the same way, they are very different. When your VB.NET code is compiled, the compiled code sees property calls as a call to a method. Always using properties instead of public variables makes your objects more flexible and extendable. Of course, using public variables is easier and quicker. You need to decide what is most important in each case.**

The IsMoving Method

When we're building objects we should always have the following question in the backs of our minds, "How can I make this object easier to use?" For example, if the consumer needs to know if the car is moving, what would be the easiest way to determine this?

One way would be to look at the Speed property. If this is zero, it can be assumed the car is stopped (although on most cars the speed is not reported when the car is moving in reverse. So, we'll assume we only have forward gears!) However, relying on the developer using the object to understand this relies on their having an understanding of whatever is being modeled. Common sense tells us that an object with a speed of "zero mph" is stationary, but should we assume anyone consuming the object shares our idea of common sense?

Instead, it's good practice to create methods that deal with these eventualities. One way we can solve this problem is by creating an IsMoving method.

Try It Out – Adding an IsMoving Method

1. All the IsMoving method needs in order to work is a simple test to look at the speed of the car and make a True or False determination as to whether it's moving. Add this code to Car.vb:

```
' IsMoving - is the car moving?
Public Function IsMoving() As Boolean

    ' is the car's speed zero?
    If Speed = 0 Then
        Return False
    Else
        Return True
    End If

End Function
```

2. To test this method, make these changes to Module1.vb:

```
Sub Main()

    ' create a new car object...
    Dim myCar As Car
    myCar = New Car()

    ' code for Color, Speed, and NumberOfDoors properties

    ' accelerate the car to 25mph...
    myCar.Accelerate(25)

    ' report whether or not the car is moving...
    If myCar.IsMoving = True Then
        Console.WriteLine("The car is moving.")
```

```
      Else
        Console.WriteLine("The car is not moving.")
      End If

      ' wait...
      Console.ReadLine()

  End Sub
```

3. Now try running the project. You should see the following:

How It Works

All we've done is created a simple method that examines the value of the Speed property and returns True if the speed is not zero, False if it is.

```
' IsMoving - is the car moving?
Public Function IsMoving() As Boolean

    ' is the car's speed zero?
    If Speed = 0 Then
        Return False
    Else
        Return True
    End If

End Function
```

Simple though this method is, it removes the conceptual leap required on the part of the consumer to understand whether or not the object is moving. There's no confusion as to whether or not the car is moving based on interpreting the value of one of more properties; one simple method returns a definitive answer.

Of course, before you go off building hundreds of methods for every eventuality, remember that paradoxically, the more methods and properties an object has, the harder it is to understand. Use care when designing the object and try to strike the right balance between too few and too many methods and properties.

You may be wondering why we used a method here when really this is a property. All we are doing is reporting the object's state – we are not affecting behavior. There is no really reason for not using a property here. However, using a method does remind users of the object that this value is calculated and is not a simple report of an internal variable. It also adds a bit of variety to our examples, and reminds us how easy it is to add a method!

Constructors

One of the most important aspects of object design is the concept of a **constructor**. This is a piece of initialization code that runs whenever an object is instantiated. It's extremely useful for occasions when you need the object to be set up in a particular way before you use it. For example, it can be used to set up default values just as we did for the number of doors earlier.

In this section, we'll take a look at a simple constructor. We'll see more advanced constructors in Chapter 10.

Try It Out – Creating a Constructor

1. For the sake of this discussion, we're going to remove the default value of 5 from the _numberOfDoors member. Make this change to Car.vb:

```
Public Class Car

    Public Color As String
    Private _speed As Integer
    Private _numberOfDoors As Integer
```

2. Now, add this method that will form the constructor. Any code within this method will be executed whenever a Car object is created:

```
Public Class Car

    Public Color As String
    Private _speed As Integer
    Private _numberOfDoors As Integer

    ' Constructor...
    Sub New()

        ' set the defaults:
        Color = "White"
        _speed = 0
        _numberOfDoors = 5

    End Sub
```

Setting the _speed to 0 here is actually redundant as it will have that value already (since all Integer variables are set to 0 when they start), but I've included it to make the example complete.

3. To test the action of the constructor, we're going to create a separate function that displays the car's details. Make these changes to `Module1.vb`:

```
Module Module1

    Sub Main()

        ' create a new car object...
        Dim myCar As Car
        myCar = New Car()

        ' display the details of the car...
        DisplayCarDetails(myCar)

        ' existing code for Color, Speed, NumberOfDoors, and IsMoving
        ' wait...
        Console.ReadLine()

    End Sub

    ' DisplayCarDetails - function that displays a car's details...
    Function DisplayCarDetails(ByVal myCar As Car)

        ' display the details of the car...
        Console.WriteLine("Color:" & myCar.Color)
        Console.WriteLine("Number of doors:" & myCar.NumberOfDoors)
        Console.WriteLine("Current speed:" & myCar.Speed)
        Console.WriteLine()

    End Function

End Module
```

4. Now try running the project and you should see this:

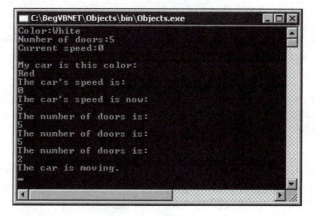

How It Works

The code in the constructor is called whenever an object is created. This is where we take the opportunity to set the values for the members:

```
' Constructor...
Sub New()

    ' set the defaults:
    Color = "White"
    _speed = 0
    _numberOfDoors = 5

End Sub
```

We see the results of the changes made to the properties when we run the project and see the details of the car displayed in the window.

A constructor must always be a subroutine (defined with the Sub keyword) and must always be called New.

When we come to test the object, we use a separate function called DisplayCarDetails. This is useful when we need to see the details of more than one Car object, which brings us nicely on to the next topic.

Inheritance

Although the subject of **inheritance** is quite an advanced object-oriented programming topic, it is really useful. In fact, the .NET Framework itself makes heavy use of it, and you have already created classes that inherit from another class – every Windows form that you write is a new class that inherits from a simple blank form (the starting point when we create a form). Let's take a look at what inheritance really means, and then return to how we use it.

Inheritance is used to create objects that have "everything another object had, but also some of their own bits and pieces". It's used to extend the functionality of objects, but doesn't require us to have an understanding as to how the internals of the object work. As I'm sure you understand, this is in line with our quest of building and using objects without having to understand how the original programmers put them together.

Inheritance enables us to, in effect, take another class and bolt on our own functionality, either by adding new methods and properties, or by replacing existing methods and properties. What we're trying to do is move from a general car class to more specific variations – for example, "sports car", "SUV", "van", and so on.

So, if we wanted to model a sports car it's likely that we'd want to have a default number of doors as 2 instead of 5, and we might also like to have properties and methods that help us understand the performance of the car, such as Weight and PowerToWeightRatio:

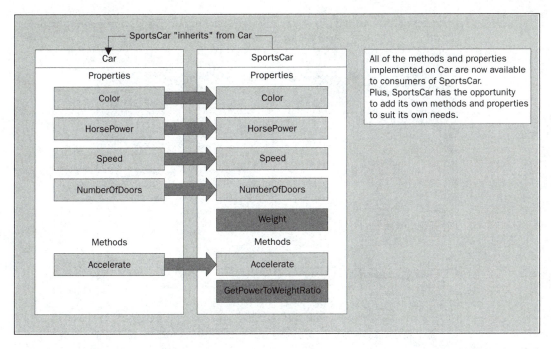

One thing that you need to understand about inheritance is the way that access to public and private members is controlled. Any public members, like `Color` are accessible to derived classes. However, private members, like `_speed` are not. This means that if `SportsCar` has to change the speed of the car, it has to do so through the properties and methods provided in `Car` itself.

Adding New Methods and Properties

Let's illustrate inheritance now by creating a new class called `SportsCar`, which inherits from `Car` and enables us to see the power to weight ratio of our sports car.

Try It Out – Inheriting from Car

1. For the purposes of this demonstration, we need to add an additional public variable to `Car` that represents the horsepower of the car. Of course, if we wanted to make it really robust we would use a property and ensure a sensible range of values. But here, simplicity, speed, and laziness wins out... open `Car.vb` and add this code:

```
Public Class Car

    Public Color As String
    Public HorsePower As Integer
    Private _speed As Integer
    Private _numberOfDoors As Integer
```

2. Now, create a new class in the usual way, by right-clicking on the **Car** project in the Solution Explorer and selecting **Add | Add Class**. Enter the name of the class as SportsCar, and click **Open**:

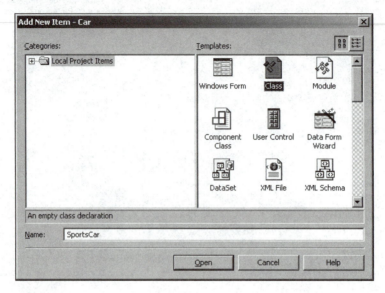

3. To tell SportsCar that it's inherited from Car, we need to use the Inherits keyword. Add this code to SportsCar.vb:

```
Public Class SportsCar
    Inherits Car

End Class
```

4. At this point, SportsCar now has all of the methods and properties that Car has. What we want to do now is add a new public variable called Weight:

```
Public Class SportsCar
    Inherits Car

    Public Weight As Integer

End Class
```

5. To test the new property, we need to make some changes to Module1.vb. Pay close attention to the fact that we need to create a SportsCar object, not a Car object in order to get at the Weight property:

```
Sub Main()
    ' existing code for normal Car object
```

```
    ' create a new SportsCar object...
    Dim mySportsCar As SportsCar
    mySportsCar = New SportsCar()

    ' set the horsepower and weight (kg)...
    mySportsCar.HorsePower = 240
    mySportsCar.Weight = 1085

    ' report the details...
    Console.WriteLine("Sports Car Horsepower:" & mySportsCar.HorsePower)
    Console.WriteLine("Sports Car Weight:" & mySportsCar.Weight)

    ' wait...
    Console.ReadLine()

End Sub
```

6. Try running the project and you'll see this:

```
C:\BegVBNET\Objects\bin\Objects.exe
Color:White
Number of doors:5
Current speed:0

My car is this color:
Red
The car's speed is:
0
The car's speed is now:
5
The number of doors is:
5
The number of doors is:
5
The number of doors is:
2
The car is moving.

Sports Car Horsepower:240
Sports Car Weight:1085
```

How It Works

The directive to inherit SportsCar from Car is done with the Inherits keyword:

```
Public Class SportsCar
    Inherits Car
```

At this point, the new SportsCar class contains all of the methods and properties in the Car class, but it cannot see or modify the private member variables. When we add our new property:

```
Public Weight As Integer
```

...we now have a new property that's only available when we create instances of SportsCar, and not available to those creating plain instances of Car. This is an important point to realize – if we don't create an instance of SportsCar, we'll get a compile error if we try to access the Weight property. Weight isn't, and never has been, a property of Car. This picture clarifies the situation:

173

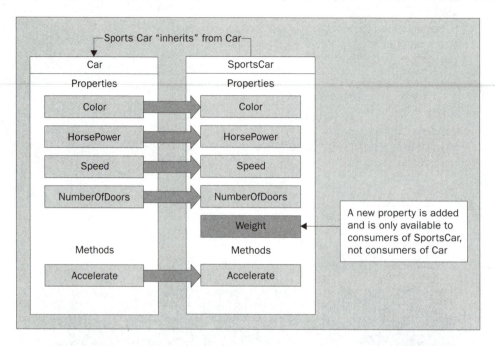

When we run the project, we do indeed instantiate a new instance of `SportsCar`. This lets us get and set the value for `Weight`.

Adding a GetPowerToWeightRatio Method

A `GetPowerToWeightRatio` method could be implemented as a read-only property (in which case we'd probably call it `PowerToWeightRatio` instead), but for this discussion we'll do it as a method.

Try It Out – Adding a GetPowerToWeightRatio Method

1. For this method, all we need to do is divide the horsepower by the weight. Add this code to `SportsCar.vb`:

```
Public Class SportsCar
    Inherits Car

    Public Weight As Integer

    ' GetPowerToWeightRatio - work out the power to weight...
    Function GetPowerToWeightRatio() As Double

        ' do the calculation...
        Return CType(HorsePower, Double) / CType(Weight, Double)

    End Function

End Class
```

2. To see the results, add this line to `Module1.vb`:

```
Sub Main()

    ' existing code for standard Car object

    ' create a new SportsCar object...
    Dim mySportsCar As SportsCar
    mySportsCar = New SportsCar()

    ' set the horsepower and weight (kg)...
    mySportsCar.HorsePower = 240
    mySportsCar.Weight = 1085

    ' report the details...
    Console.WriteLine("Horsepower:" & mySportsCar.HorsePower)
    Console.WriteLine("Weight:" & mySportsCar.Weight)
    Console.WriteLine("Power/weight:" & mySportsCar.GetPowerToWeightRatio)

    ' wait...
    Console.ReadLine()

End Sub
```

3. Run the project and you'll see something like this:

```
C:\BegVBNET\Objects\bin\Objects.exe                           _ □ X
Current speed:0
My car is this color:
Red
The car's speed is:
0
The car's speed is now:
5
The number of doors is:
5
The number of doors is:
5
The number of doors is:
2
The car is moving.

Sports Car Horsepower:240
Sports Car Weight:1085
Power/weight:0.221198156682028
```

How It Works

Again, all we've done is add a new method to the new class called `GetPowerToWeightRatio`. This method then becomes available to anyone working with an instance of `SportsCar`:

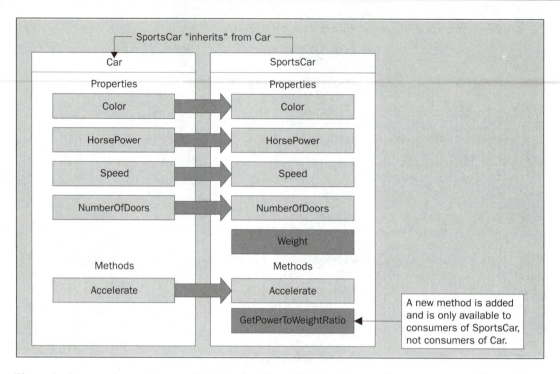

The only thing we have to be careful of is that if we divide an integer by an integer, we'll get an integer result, but what we actually want here is a floating-point number. We have to convert the integer `HorsePower` and `Weight` roperties to `Double` values in order to see the results:

```
Return CType(HorsePower, Double) / CType(Weight, Double)
```

Changing Defaults

As we mentioned at the beginning of this section, as well as adding new properties and methods, we might want to change the way an existing method or property works from that of the base class. In order to do this, we need to create our own implementation of the method or property.

Think back to our discussion on constructors. These are methods that are called whenever the object is created and let us get the object into a state where it can be used by a developer. In this constructor we set the default `_numberOfDoors` value to be 5. However, in a sports car this number should ideally be 2.

The class that we're inheriting from is known as the **base class** (which is `Car` in our example). If we want to replace an existing method or property with our own, we call that process **overriding**. In this next section, we'll learn how to override the base class's constructor.

1. To override the constructor, all we have to do is create our own constructor in the new `SportsCar` class. Add this code to `SportsCar`:

```
Public Class SportsCar
    Inherits Car

    Public Weight As Integer

    ' Constructor...
    Sub New ()

        ' change the defaults...
        Color = "Green"
        NumberOfDoors = 2

    End Sub

    ' GetPowerToWeightRatio - work out the power to weight...
    Function GetPowerToWeightRatio() As Double

        ' do the calculation...
        Return CType(HorsePower, Double) / CType(Weight, Double)

    End Function

End Class
```

2. To test the constructor, we need to display the details of a `SportsCar`. So we'll add a call to `DisplayCarDetails`, and pass in `mySportsCar`. Make this addition to `Module1.vb`:

```
Sub Main()

    ' existing code for manipulating a Car object

    ' create a new SportsCar object...
    Dim mySportsCar As SportsCar
    mySportsCar = New SportsCar()

    ' display the details of the sports car...
    DisplayCarDetails(mySportsCar)

    ' set the horsepower and weight (kg)...
    mySportsCar.HorsePower = 240
    mySportsCar.Weight = 1085

    ' existing code to write out SportsCar properties
End Sub
```

3. Now try running the project. You should see this:

```
C:\BegVBNET\Objects\bin\Objects.exe
Current speed:0

My car is this color:
Red
The car's speed is:
0
The car's speed is now:
5
The number of doors is:
5
The number of doors is:
5
The number of doors is:
2
The car is moving.


Color:White
Number of doors:5
Current speed:0

Sports Car Horsepower:240
Sports Car Weight:1085
Power/weight:0.221198156682028
```

How It Works

The new constructor that we added to `SportsCar` runs after the existing one in `Car`. .NET knows that it's supposed to run the code in the constructor of the base class before running the new constructor, so in effect it runs this code:

```
' Constructor...
Sub New()

    ' set the defaults:
    Color = "White"
    _speed = 0
    _numberOfDoors = 5

End Sub
```

... and then runs this code:

```
' Constructor...
Sub New()

    ' change the defaults...
    Color = "Green"
    NumberOfDoors = 2

End Sub
```

To summarize what happens:

❑   The constructor on the base class `Car` is called

❑   `Color` is set to `White`

❑   `_speed` is set to `0`

❑   `_numberOfDoors` is set to `5`

178

- ❑ The constructor on the new class `SportsCar` is called

- ❑ `Color` is set to `Green`

- ❑ `NumberOfDoors` is set to 2

Because we defined `_numberOfDoors` as a private member in `Car`, we cannot directly access it from inherited classes, just as we wouldn't be able to directly access it from a consumer of the class. Instead, we rely on being able to set an appropriate value through `NumberOfDoors`.

Polymorphism – Scary Word, Simple Concept

Another very common word to hear mentioned when talking about object-oriented programming is **polymorphism**. This is, perhaps, the scariest term but one of the easiest to understand!

Let's remind ourselves of the code for `DisplayCarDetails`:

```
' DisplayCarDetails - function that displays a car's details...
Function DisplayCarDetails(ByVal myCar As Car)

    ' display the details of the car...
    Console.WriteLine("Color:" & myCar.Color)
    Console.WriteLine("Number of doors:" & myCar.NumberOfDoors)
    Console.WriteLine("Current speed:" & myCar.Speed)
    Console.WriteLine()

End Function
```

Look at the first line – we're saying that the parameter we want to accept is a `Car` object. But, when we call the object, we're actually passing it a `SportsCar` object. Look at how we create the object and call `DisplayCarDetails`:

```
    ' create a new car object...
    Dim mySportsCar As SportsCar
    mySportsCar = New SportsCar()

    ' display the details of the car...
    DisplayCarDetails(mySportsCar)
```

How can it be that, if the function takes a `Car` object, we're allowed to pass it a `SportsCar` object?

Well, polymorphism (which comes from the Greek for "many forms") means that an object can be treated as if it were a different kind of object, providing common sense prevails. In this case, we can treat a `SportsCar` object like a `Car` object because `SportsCar` inherits from `Car`. This act of inheritance dictates that anything a `SportsCar` object can do must include everything that a `Car` object can do; therefore we can treat the two objects in the same way. If we need to call a method on `Car`, `SportsCar` must also implement the method.

This doesn't hold true the other way round. If we had a function defined like this:

```
Function DisplaySportsCarDetails(ByVal mySportsCar As SportsCar)
```

...we could not pass it a `Car` object. `Car` is not guaranteed to be able to do everything a `SportsCar` is, because the extra methods and properties we add on to `SportsCar` won't exist on `Car`. `SportsCar` is a more specific type of `Car`.

So, to summarize, when people talk about polymorphism, this is the action they are referring to – the principle that an object can behave as if it were another object without the developer having to go through too many hoops to make it happen.

Overriding More Methods

Although we've overridden `Car`'s constructor, for completeness we should look at how to override a normal method.

To override a method we need to have method in the base `Car` class. Since `Accelerate` shouldn't change depending on whether we have a sports car or a normal car and `IsMoving` was added for ease of use – and hence doesn't really count in this instance as it isn't a behavior of the object, let's add a new method called `CalculateAccelerationRate`. We'll assume on a normal car that this is a constant, and on a sports car we'll change it so that it takes the power to weight ratio into consideration.

Try It Out – Adding Another Method

1. Add this method below the `IsMoving` method in `Car.vb`:

```
' CalculateAccelerationRate - assume a constant for a normal car...
Function CalculateAccelerationRate() As Double

    ' if we assume a normal car goes from 0-60 in 14
    ' seconds, that's an average rate of 4.2 mph/s...
    Return 4.2

End Function
```

2. Now to test the method, change `Module1.vb` to read like this:

```
Sub Main()

    ' create a new car object...
    Dim myCar As Car
    myCar = New Car()

    ' report the details...
    Console.WriteLine("Acceleration rate:" & _
        myCar.CalculateAccelerationRate)

    ' display the details of the car...
    DisplayCarDetails(myCar)

    ' existing code...

End Sub
```

3. Run the project and you'll get the following (you may need to scroll up to see the top line):

```
C:\BegVBNET\Objects\bin\Objects.exe                                 _ □ ✕
Acceleration rate:4.2
Color:White
Number of doors:5
Current speed:0

My car is this color:
Red
The car's speed is:
0
The car's speed is now:
5
The number of doors is:
5
The number of doors is:
5
The number of doors is:
2
The car is moving.


Color:White
Number of doors:5
Current speed:0
Sports Car Horsepower:240
```

How It Works

OK, so we've built a method on `Car` as normal. This method always returns 4.2 for the acceleration rate.

Of course, our acceleration calculation algorithm is pure fantasy – no car is going to accelerate at the same rate irrespective of the gear, environment, current speed, etc.

Try It Out – Overriding the New Method

1. To override the method, we just have to provide a new implementation in `SportsCar`. However, there's one thing we need to do first. In order to override a method, we have to mark it as `Overridable`. To do this, open `Car.vb` again and add the `Overridable` keyword to the method:

```
' CalculateAccelerationRate - assume a constant for a normal car...
Overridable Function CalculateAccelerationRate() As Double

    ' if we assume a normal car goes from 0-60 in 14
    ' seconds, that's a rate of 4.2 mph/s...
    Return 4.2

End Function
```

2. Now, we can create a method with the same name in `SportsCar.vb`. In order to override the method, we must add the `Overrides` keyword to the front of the method:

```
' CalculateAccelerationRate - take the power/weight into
' consideration...
Overrides Function CalculateAccelerationRate() As Double
```

```
      ' we'll assume the same 4.2 value, but we'll multiply it
      ' by the power/weight ratio...
      Return 4.2 * GetPowerToWeightRatio()

End Function
```

> We didn't add the **Overrides** keyword when we overrode the constructor because,
> basically, we didn't need to! Visual Basic .NET handled this for us.

3. In order to test the method, we need to create a `SportsCar` object and set the power and
weight details. Find the part of `Module1.vb` where we instantiate the `SportsCar` object,
and make this change:

```
Sub Main()
    ' existing code for playing with a normal Car object

    ' create a new sports car object...
    Dim mySportsCar As SportsCar
    mySportsCar = New SportsCar()

    ' display the details of the sports car...
    DisplayCarDetails(mySportsCar)

    ' set the horsepower and weight (kg)...
    mySportsCar.HorsePower = 240
    mySportsCar.Weight = 1085

    ' report the details...
    Console.WriteLine("Acceleration rate:" & _
        mySportsCar.CalculateAccelerationRate)

    ' display the details of the sports car...
    DisplayCarDetails(mySportsCar)

    ' remaining code...

    ' wait...
    Console.ReadLine()

End Sub
```

4. Now if we run the project we'll get an adjusted acceleration rate:

```
C:\BegVBNET\Objects\bin\Objects.exe
My car is this color:
Red
The car's speed is:
0
The car's speed is now:
5
The number of doors is:
5
The number of doors is:
5
The number of doors is:
2
The car is moving.

Color:White
Number of doors:5
Current speed:0

Acceleration rate:0.929032258064516
Sports Car Horsepower:240
Sports Car Weight:1085
Power/weight:0.221198156682028
```

How It Works

Well, you can see that overriding the method lets us create our own implementation of an existing method on the object. Again, coming back to this concept of encapsulation, the object consumer doesn't have to know that anything is different about the object – they just call the method in the same way as they would for a normal `Car` object. This time, however, they get a different result rather than the constant value they always got on the normal `Car` object.

> When we override a method, it's quite different from overriding a constructor. When we override a constructor, the original constructor still gets called first. When we override a method, the original method only gets called if we specifically call it from inside the new method using `Base.MethodName`. For example we could invoke `Base.CalculateAccelerationRate` from `SportsCar.CalculateAccelerationRate` to return a value of 4.2.

Inheriting from Object

The final thing to look at with respect to inheritance is the fact if you create a class without using the `Inherits` clause, the class will automatically inherit from a class called `Object`. This object provides us with a few methods that we can guarantee will be supported by every object we ever have. Most of these methods are beyond the scope of this book. However, the two most useful methods at this level are:

❑   `ToString` – this method returns a string representation of the object. We can override this to provide a helpful string value for any object, for example we might want a person object to return that person's name. If we do not override it, it will return the name of the class name.

❑   `GetType` – this method returns a `Type` object that represents the data type of the object

Remember, we don't have to explicitly tell a class that it inherits from `Object`. This happens automatically.

The Framework Classes

Although we discuss the Framework in detail in the next chapter, let's take a look now at some aspects of the Framework's construction.

Namespaces

The .NET Framework is actually a vast collection of classes. There are around 3,500 classes in the Framework all told, so how are we as developers supposed to find the ones that we want?

The Framework is divided into a broad set of **namespaces** that group similar classes together. This limits the number of classes that you have to hunt through if you're looking for a specific piece of functionality.

These namespaces are also hierarchical in nature, meaning that a namespace can contain other namespaces that further group classes together. Each class must belong to exactly one namespace – it can't belong to multiple namespaces and it must belong to a namespace.

Most of the Framework classes are lumped together in a namespace called System, or namespaces that are also contained within System. For example:

❑   System.Data contains classes related to accessing data stored in a database

❑   System.Xml contains classes used to read and write XML documents

❑   System.Windows.Forms contains classes for drawing windows on the screen

❑   System.Net contains classes for communicating over a network

The fact that namespaces exist means that all of the objects we've been using actually have longer names than the one's we've used in our software code. Up until this point, we've been using a shorthand notation to refer to classes.

In fact, earlier when we said that everything has to derive from Object, that was a small lie. Because Object is contained within the System namespace, its full name is System.Object. Likewise, Console is actually shorthand for System.Console, meaning that this line:

```
Console.ReadLine()
```

…is actually the same as this line:

```
System.Console.ReadLine()
```

> This can get a little silly, especially when you end up with object names like
> **System.Web.Services.Description.ServiceDescription!**

.NET automatically creates a shorthand version of all the classes within System for us, so we don't have to type System. all the time. Later, we'll see how we can add shorthand references to other namespaces.

We've just said that every class must be in exactly one namespace, but what about the classes we've made so far? Well, our project has a default namespace and our new classes are placed into this namespace.

Try It Out – Finding the Name of the Current Namespace

1. To see the namespace that we're using, right-click on the Objects project in the Solution Explorer and select Properties.

2. The Root namespace entry in the Objects Property Pages window gives the name of the namespace that will be used for new classes:

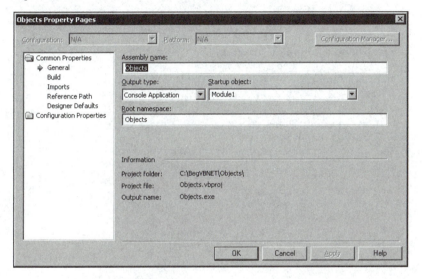

3. What this means is that our classes will have the text Objects. prefixed to them, like this:

❑ The Car class is actually called Objects.Car

❑ The SportsCar class is actually called Objects.SportsCar

> **As you may have guessed, .NET automatically creates a shorthand version of our classes too, so we can refer to SportsCar instead of having to type Objects.SportsCar.**

The motivation behind using namespaces is to make life easier for developers using your classes. Imagine that you give this project to another developer to use and they have already built their own class called Car. How do they tell the difference between their class and our class?

Well, ours will actually be called Objects.Car, whereas theirs will have a name like MyOwnProject.Car or YaddaYadda.Car. Namespaces remove the ambiguity of class names. Of course, we didn't choose a very good namespace because it doesn't really describe the classes that the namespace contains – we just chose a namespace that illustrated the purpose of the chapter.

185

The Imports Statement

OK so we know we don't need to prefix our classes with `Car.` or `System.` as .NET automatically creates a shorthand version, but how do we do this ourselves?

The answer is the `Imports` statement!

If you think back to the last chapter, you might remember this code from the top of a form:

```
Imports System.IO

Public Class Form1
    Inherits System.Windows.Forms.Form
```

as well as this code, behind a button on that form:

```
Private Sub btnGo_Click(ByVal sender As System.Object, _
            ByVal e As System.EventArgs) Handles btnGo.Click

    ' get a list of subfolders...
    Dim subfolders() As DirectoryInfo
    subfolders = New DirectoryInfo("c:\").GetDirectories

    ' loop...
    Dim subfolder As DirectoryInfo
    For Each subfolder In subfolders

        ' add the item to the list...
        lstData.Items.Add(subfolder.FullName)

    Next

End Sub
```

We used the `Imports System.IO` statement to import the `System.IO` namespace into our project. We needed to do this, as we wanted to use the `DirectoryInfo` class. As we stated in Chapter 3, the full name of this class is `System.IO.DirectoryInfo`, but because we had added a **namespace import declaration**, we could just write `DirectoryInfo` instead.

All `Imports` statements must be written right at the top of the code file you want to use them in, *before* any other code.

The only drawback happens if you import two namespaces that have an identically named class or child namespace and Visual Basic .NET can't tell what it is you're after (like our `Car.Car` and our friend's `MyOwnProject.Car`). If this happens you'll be informed by Visual Basic .NET that the name is ambiguous – in which case the quickest and easiest thing to do is to specify the full name that you're after.

Creating Our Own Namespace

Namespaces are defined by wrapping the `Class...End Class` definition in a `Namespace...End Namespace` definition. By default, classes created in Visual Basic .NET are automatically assigned to a **root namespace**. Visual Studio .NET automatically names this root namespace based on the project name.

1. Using the Solution Explorer, right-click on the project and select Properties. The Root namespace field in the Common Properties | General pane option tells us the name. In this case, the root namespace name is Objects; when you are finished viewing the namespace – click Cancel:

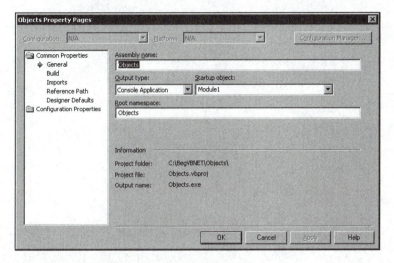

2. Visual Studio. NET's Object Browser is a useful tool that lets us see what classes we have available in our project. You can find it by selecting View | Other Windows | Object Browser from the menu. When the Object Browser is displayed, the first item is usually the project. You can drill down into it to find our Car class:

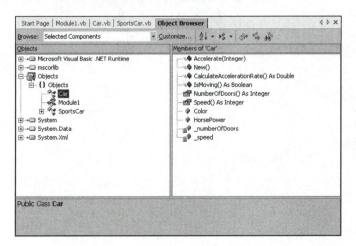

3. Note that you can also see the methods, properties, and member variables listed for the class. Pertinent to this discussion, however, is the namespace. This is immediately above the class and is indicated by the icon containing the open and closed brace symbols ({ }). As the namespace name is Objects, we can surmise that the full class name is Objects.Car.

4. It's often recommended that you build your namespaces such that the full names of the classes you develop are prefixed with the name of your company. So, if my company was called MyCodeWidgets, ideally I'd want my classes called `MyCodeWidgets.Car`. To do this, open the Properties window for the project again and change Root namespace from Car to MyCodeWidgets.

5. Look at the Object Browser again and notice how the namespace name has changed:

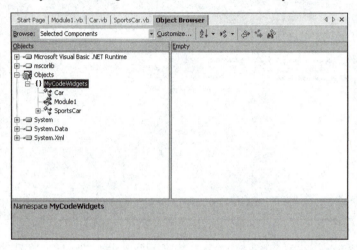

6. So, that's fine, but imagine now we have two projects both containing a class called `Car`. We need to use namespaces to separate the `Car` class in one project from the `Car` class in another. Open the code editor for `Car` and add `Namespace CarPerformance` before the class definition and `End Namespace` after it. (I've omitted most of the code for brevity.)

```
Namespace CarPerformance

    Public Class Car
        ...
    End Class

End Namespace
```

7. Now open the Object Browser again and you'll see this:

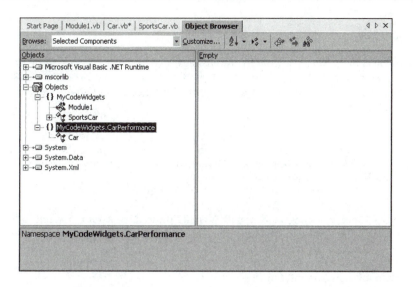

How It Works

What we've done is put `Car` inside a namespace called `CarPerformance`. As this namespace is contained within `MyCodeWidgets`, the full name of the class becomes `MyCodeWidgets.CarPerformance.Car`. If we put the classes of the other (imaginary) project into `CarDiagnostics`, it would be called `MyCodeWidgets.CarDiagnostics.Car`.

Notice how **Module1** still appears directly inside **MyCodeWidgets**. That's because we haven't wrapped the definition for `Module1` in a namespace as we did with `Car`. If you try this now you'll find the module will be shown as a sibling of `Car`, in other words they will both appear within the same namespace.

Inheritance in the Framework

As I said at the top of this section, inheritance is quite an advanced object-oriented topic. However, it's really important to include here because the Framework makes heavy use of inheritance.

One thing to understand about inheritance in .NET is that no class can inherit from more than one class. As everything must inherit from `System.Object` (as we just discussed) the upshot of this is that everything must inherit from exactly one class. (Well, all except `System.Object` itself, but that's the exception that proves the rule.)

When we say that each class must inherit from exactly one class, we mean that each class can only mention one class in its `Inherits` clause. The class that it's inheriting from can also inherit from another class. So, for example, we could create a class called `Porsche` that inherited from `SportsCar`. We could then say that it indirectly inherits from `Car`, but *directly* inherits from only one class – `SportsCar`. In fact, many classes *indirectly* inherit from lots of classes – but there is always a direct ancestry, where each class has exactly one parent.

Most of the classes that you will use in the Framework, or that have been used so far inherit some of their behavior from some other class.

Using MSDN

The **Microsoft Developers Network** (**MSDN**) publishes a very broad reference guide to all of the Microsoft published software development kits, including .NET, in the form of the **MSDN Library**. MSDN is available both on the Web at http://msdn.microsoft.com/ and an offline version is included with your Visual Studio .NET CDs.

> **While MSDN is a definitive guide, it's the job of us at Wrox to pitch the information in separate ways. The information on MSDN tends to be quite dry and reference-oriented, rather than solution-oriented.**

Today, the MSDN Library is integrated in with Visual Studio .NET so if you need to look up the methods or properties of a class, it's the best place to start. It's also so useful in your day-to-day programming activities that we're going to take a look at how it works here. You can also find the latest information at http://msdn.microsoft.com/ and a list of the most recent material at http://msdn.microsoft.com/recent.asp.

The theory behind MSDN is that you can select any keyword in your code, hit *F1*, and be presented with some documentation about the object. This often doesn't happen quite as well as it should, so let's take a look at one way to look up an object in the Library.

Try It Out – Looking up a Class in MSDN

1. We've used the `Console` class quite often with lines like these:

```
Console.WriteLine("Color:" & myCar.Color)
```

To look up a class in MSDN, we need to know its full name. We can often get away without using the full name, but this can lead to us accidentally looking at information about a different class with the same name. If you don't know what namespace `Console` belongs to, try assuming it belongs to `System`. Therefore, let's try the full name `System.Console`.

2. Select Help | Index from the Visual Studio .NET menu.

3. The Index pane will appear somewhere on the IDE. Select the Look for textbox, and enter the name of the class:

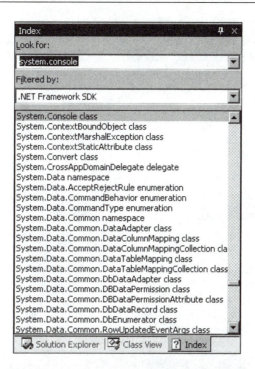

4. You'll notice that the first entry in the list is indeed the **System.Console class**. Double-click on it. Depending on your MSDN installation, the following may appear at the bottom of the screen:

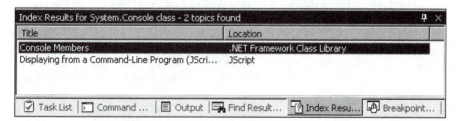

This gives us a choice of topics that match this index entry. Only one of the topics above is located in the .NET Framework Class Library, so double-click that one.

5. This will load a page that lists all of the properties, methods, and events of the Console class:

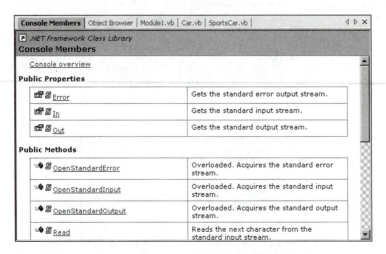

For now, though, this is too much detail for us. Click the link near the top that says
Console overview.

6. We are now at the Console Class overview page. Now let's see what all the different parts of the
page mean. When the page loads, the header displays the name of the topic and three buttons.

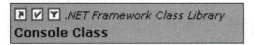

Yes, these three boxes at the top are buttons! The first one, "See Also", lets you see topics
related to the current topic. The second, Requirements tells you what platform the class is
dependent on. (For the most part, you can ignore this one.) The third, Language lets you
choose the language that example code should be displayed in. It may be a good idea to
choose Show All, because sometimes there are no examples in Visual Basic .NET, but the C#
example is still clear enough useful. If you prefer to keep non-Visual Basic .NET code hidden
then choose Visual Basic.

7. The next thing you'll be shown is which classes the class inherits from and the definition of
the object itself. A brief blurb about what the object does precedes this, for example:

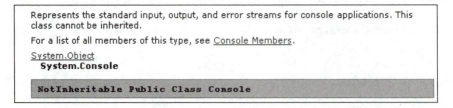

For a beginning developer, MSDN might contain overwhelming information. However, we
can see here that `Console` inherits from `Object` and we also have a link to see the Console
Members, which here refers to the methods and properties that the object supports.

The gray box is the object definition itself, and is in fact what we'd enter into Visual Studio .NET if we wanted to create the class ourselves. For now, we can ignore this.

8. Beneath the gray box is a discussion of what the class does. Usually this is your best bet if you've found a class and want to know more about it.

9. If you're lucky, you'll see some example code that shows how the class can be used in a typical situation. (Sometimes there won't be a Visual Basic .NET example and you may have to try to decipher a C# example.)

```
Public Shared Sub Main()
    Console.Write("Hola ")
    Console.WriteLine("Mundo!")
    Console.WriteLine("What is your name: ")
    Dim name As String = Console.ReadLine()
    Console.Write("Buenos Dias, ")
    Console.Write(name)
    Console.WriteLine("!")
End Sub 'Main
```

10. Down at the bottom you'll find a link back to the **Console Members** page that we've just come from. For other classes, of course, it will be a link to their members. Typically, next to each member on this page is a short description and you can click through to see more information and, perhaps, an example.

```
See Also
    Console Members | System Namespace
```

When you get to the point where you're writing your own programs rather than relying on examples from this book, you'll find MSDN most useful. It's the fastest way to remind yourself what methods and properties a class supports and how to actually use them in your own code.

Summary

In this chapter we took a look at how to start building our own objects. We kicked off by learning how to design an object in terms of the properties and methods that it should support and then built a class that represented a Car. We then started adding properties and methods to that class and using it from within our application.

Before moving on to the subject of inheritance we took a look at how an object can be given a constructor – or rather a block of code that's executed whenever an object is created. Our discussion of inheritance demonstrated a number of key aspects of object-oriented design, including polymorphism and overriding. Finally, we took another look at the Framework classes and also introduced MSDN.

Questions

1. What's the difference between a public and private member?

2. How do you decide if something should be a property or a method? Give an example.

3. What is a constructor? Why are they useful?

4. What class do all other classes in .NET inherit from?

5. What is overriding?

The Microsoft.NET Framework

The **Microsoft.NET Framework** has taken a considerable amount of time to go from concept to final product. In fact, its journey has only just begun because at the time of publication, with the exception of a few specialist partners (mainly government bodies and large US corporations) .NET has only begun to show its face on public Internet sites. With Visual Studio .NET and the .NET Framework being officially released both small and large companies are starting to take note and jump on board.

For those of us writing and editing this book, it's difficult to predict where .NET is going to be in 2003, or 2005, let alone 2010. In this chapter, we'll be attempting to outline what the .NET Framework is and why Microsoft dared to spend $2 billion on a single development project.

Microsoft's Reliance on Windows

In terms of the great corporations of the world, Microsoft is still a new kid on the block. OK, so it's a fabulously rich and successful one, but nonetheless the company has grown from nothing to a "corporate superpower" in a very short space of time.

What's perhaps more concerning is that although we can trace the origins of Microsoft back to the mid-70s, it's really the Windows family of operating systems that has brought the company great success. Based on Presentation Manager for OS/2, Windows has seen many incarnations from Windows/286 through to Windows XP, but the essential way that we use Windows and Windows applications hasn't changed in all that time. (Granted there have been many advances in the way the UI is constructed and the hardware that runs the platform, but we still use the version of Excel included with Office XP in roughly the same way that we used the first version.)

The scary thing to Microsoft and its investors is that the pace of technological change means that in 2011, we can't be sure that Windows is going to be as relevant as it is today. All it takes is one sea change in the way that we want to use computers and perhaps, just perhaps, the Windows platform will be rendered obsolete.

It's unfair to say that Microsoft has been extremely lucky over the past five or so years in the way that it reacted to the new opportunities afforded by the Internet. Yes, luck was involved, but don't underestimate the number of smart people working for that company! Once they discovered that companies like Netscape were making bucks with the Internet and identified the risk, they turned a gargantuan corporation on a dime and went after an unexplored market with teeth bared. So far their gamble has paid off, but with the announcement of .NET we get the impression that the strategists in Microsoft don't want to be scared like that again.

Luckily for Microsoft, the applications that drove the adoption of the Internet worked well on a desktop operating system. Microsoft managed to adapt the Windows platform to provide the two killer Internet applications (e-mail and the Web) to the end user with a minimum of hassle, securing the Windows platform for another few years. It also delivered a number of great tools for developers, like ASP and IIS, and improved existing tools like VB and SQL, all of which made it easier for developers to build advanced Internet applications.

MSN 1.0

When the Internet started to become popular, Microsoft was trying to push the original incarnation of MSN. Rather than the successful portal that it is today, MSN was originally a proprietary dialup service much like CompuServe. In the beginning, MSN didn't provide access to the rich world of the Internet that we know today – it was a closed system. Let's call the original MSN "MSN 1.0".

What MSN 1.0 did was provide an opportunity for innovative companies to steal a march on Microsoft, which was already seen as an unshakable behemoth thanks to the combination of Windows and Office.

Let's imagine an alternate 1995 where Microsoft sticks to its guns with MSN 1.0, rather than plotting the course that brings it to where it is today. Let's imagine that a large computer manufacturer, like Dell, identifies this burgeoning community of forward-thinking business leaders and geeks called the Internet. Let's also say that Dell has predicted that Microsoft's strategy is to usurp this community with MSN 1.0; in other words rather than cooperating with this community, Microsoft decide to crush it at all costs.

Now Dell needs to find a way to build this community. It predicts that home users and small businesses will love the Internet and so put together a very low cost PC. They need software to run on it and, luckily, predict that the Web and e-mail will be the killer applications of this new community. They find Linus Torvalds, who's been working on this thing called Linux since 1991 and they find Sun which is keen to start pushing Java as a programming language to anyone who will listen. Another business partner builds a competent, yet usable, suite of productivity applications for the platform using Java. Another business partner builds easy-to-use connectivity solutions that allow the computers to easily and cheaply connect to the Internet and other computers in the LAN.

Dell, Sun, and their select business partners start pushing this new computer to anyone and everyone. The concept is a success and, for the first time since 1981, the dominance of the IBM-compatible PC is reduced, and sales of Microsoft products plummet. This is all because Microsoft didn't move on a critical opportunity.

We all know that this didn't happen, but there's nothing outlandish or crazy about this idea. It *could* have happened, and that's what really scared Microsoft. It came very close to losing everything and .NET is its insurance against this happening again.

The .NET Vision

In order to understand .NET, you have to ignore the marketing hype from Microsoft and really think about what it's doing. At the time of writing (June 2002), Microsoft appears to be pushing .NET as a platform for building Web Services and large-scale enterprise systems. Although we cover Web Services in Chapter 19, it's a tiny, tiny part of what .NET is about and, in this author's opinion, misinformation!

In simple terms, .NET splits an operating systems platform, be it Windows, Linux, Mac, whatever, into two layers: a **programming layer** and an **execution layer**.

All computer platforms are trying to achieve roughly the same effect: to provide applications to the user. If I wanted to write a book I would have the choice of using Star Office on Linux, or Word on Windows. However, I'm using the computer in the same way, in other words the *application* remains the same irrespective of the platform.

It's commonly understood that the success of a platform is driven by its software support. Typically, the more high-quality software is available for a given platform, the larger the consumer adoption of that platform. The PC is the dominant platform because, back in the early-80s, that's what everyone was writing software for. That trend has continued today where we're writing applications that run on Windows targets for the Intel x86 type processors. The x86 processor harks back to the introduction of the Intel 8086 processor in 1979 and today we have the Intel Pentium 4 processor and competitors like AMD's Athlon and Duron.

OK, so without .NET, we're still reliant on Windows, and Windows is still reliant on Intel. Although the relationship between Microsoft and Intel is thought to be fairly symbiotic, it's fair to assume that the strategists at Microsoft, who are feeling (rightly) paranoid about the future, might also want to lessen the dependence on a single family of chips, too.

The Windows/Intel combination (sometimes known as Wintel) is what's known as the execution layer. It's the platform that takes the code and runs it – simple as that.

Although in its first incarnation .NET is targeted at the Windows platform, there's no reason why later versions of .NET can't be targeted at other platforms. There are already rumors of a Linux version of .NET. What this means is that a program written by a .NET developer on Windows could run *unchanged* on Linux. In fact, between the first draft of this chapter and the time it went into editing, Miguel de Icaza, a prominent member of the Linux development community, began trying to put together the Ximian Mono project (http://www.go-mono.com/). This project is currently developing an open-source version of a C# compiler, a runtime for the Common Language Infrastructure (CLI, also known as the Common Intermediate Language – CIL), a subset of the .NET classes, and other .NET goodies independent of Microsoft's involvement.

.NET is a programming layer. It's totally owned and controlled by Microsoft. By turning all of us into *.NET* programmers rather than *Windows* programmers, software is written as *.NET* software, not *Windows* software.

To see the significance of this, imagine that a new platform is launched and starts eating up market share like crazy. Imagine that, like the Internet, this new platform offers a revolutionary way of working and living that offers real advantages. With the .NET vision in place, all Microsoft has to do to gain a foothold on this platform is develop a version of .NET that works on it. All of the .NET software now runs on the new platform, lessening the chance that the new platform will usurp Microsoft's market share.

In short, while Microsoft is a good innovator, what it is great at doing is taking someone else's bright idea and bringing it to the next level.

This Sounds Like Java

Some of this does sound a lot like Java. In fact, Java's mantra of "write once, run anywhere" fits nicely into the .NET doctrine. However, .NET isn't a Java clone. Microsoft has a different approach.

To write in Java, developers were expected to learn a new language. This language was based on C++, and while C++ is a popular language, it's not *the most popular* language. In fact, the most popular language in terms of number of developers is Visual Basic and, obviously, Microsoft owns this. There are something like three million VB developers worldwide, but bear in mind that this number includes VB professionals and also people who tinker with macros in the various Office products.

Whereas Java is "one language, many platforms", .NET is "many languages, one platform… for now". Microsoft wants to remove the barrier to entry to .NET by making it accessible to anyone who's used pretty much any language. The two primary languages for .NET are Visual Basic .NET and C#, and Visual Studio .NET comes supplied with both of these. (Other languages are in various stages of development, so developers should have no problems developing .NET applications in any language they feel comfortable with. A list of .NET language vendors can be found at http://www.gotdotnet.com/resourcecenter/resource_center.aspx?classification=Language%20Vendors.) Although C# is not C++, C++ developers should be able to migrate to C# with about the same amount of relearning that a VB6 developer will have to do in order to move to Visual Basic .NET.

With Java, Sun attempted to build from the ground-up something so abstracted from the operating system that when you compare an application written natively in something like Visual C++ with a Java equivalent, it is fairly obvious that the Java version will run slower and not look as good in terms of user interface. In this author's opinion, Sun tried to take too big a bite out of the problem by straight away attempting to support everything, so that in the end it didn't support one single thing completely.

Microsoft's .NET strategy is more like a military campaign. Firstly, it'll use its understanding of the Windows platform to build .NET into something that will stand against a native C++ application. It'll also try to bolster the lackluster uptake of Pocket PC with the **Compact Framework**. After it's "won over the voters" on Windows, it may "invade" another platform, most likely Linux. This second stage will prove the concept that .NET applications can be ported from one platform to the next. After "invading and conquering Linux", it'll move to another platform. Microsoft has been attempting to shake Solaris from the top spot in the server market for a long time, so it's likely that it'll go there next, probably with (and this is conjecture) as-yet-unannounced server products like SQL Server .NET and Exchange .NET.

> **One thing to clarify here** – Microsoft has recently started rebadging existing server software like SQL Server 2000, Internet Security and Acceleration Server 2000, and Exchange 2000 as ".NET Enterprise Servers". Technically these are *not* .NET applications and are limited to the Windows platform. We'll have to wait for new, next-generation versions of these products to become available to enjoy the advantages afforded by .NET.

If .NET works in the real world, we can expect to see the technology spreading across all facets of the industry: to the desktop, to servers, to network appliances, to set-top boxes, to PDAs, to cellphones, and so on. In fact, Microsoft has already announced and delivered early versions of the Compact Framework designed for use with a Pocket PC.

Where Now?

Microsoft has bet its future on .NET. With developers writing software for the programming layer rather than an execution layer, it really doesn't matter whether Windows is the dominant platform in 2011 or Linux is, or whether something totally off the radar will be. If .NET works, we'll start calling ourselves .NET developers, rather than C# developers and Visual Basic .NET developers. Eventually, Microsoft hopes we'll simply call ourselves "developers".

In the remainder of this chapter, we're going to drill into the mechanics of .NET and take a detailed look at how the whole thing works.

Writing Software for Windows

To understand how .NET works, let's take a look at how we used to write software for Windows. The general principle is the same, only we have to do things in different ways to work with different technologies (COM, WIN32 API).

Any software that you write has to talk to various parts of the operating system in order to do its job. If you need a block of memory to store some data in, you talk to the memory manager. To read a file from disk, you use the disk subsystem. To request a file from the network, you use the network subsystem. To draw a window on the screen, you use the graphics subsystem, and so on.

Where this system breaks down so far as .NET is concerned is that there's no commonality between the ways you use the subsystems on different platforms, despite that fact that platforms tend to have things in common. For example, even if you're writing an application for Linux, you still may need to use the network, disk, and screen subsystems. However, because these subsystems have been developed by different organizations, the *way* you open a file using the Linux subsystem may be different from the way you do it on Windows. If you want to move code dependent on the subsystem implementation on one platform to another, you will probably have to rewrite portions of the code. You'll also have to test the code to make sure it still works as intended. (This process is called **porting**.)

Windows software communicates with the operating system and various subsystems using something called the **Windows 32-bit Application Programming Interface**, or **Win32 API**. Although object-orientation was around at the time, this API was designed to be an evolution of the original Windows API, which predates the massive adoption of object-oriented techniques that we've discussed in Chapter 4.

The API is not easy to port to other platforms, which is why (despite the fact that Linux has been around for ten years) there isn't a version of the Win32 API for Linux. There is a cut-down version of the Win32 API for the Mac, but this has never received much of an industry following.

The Win32 API provides all of the basic stuff, but now and again, Microsoft will extend the functionality of Windows with a new API. A classic example is the **Windows Internet API**, also known as the **WinInit API**. This API allows an application to download resources from a Web server, upload files to an FTP server, discover proxy settings, and so on. Again, it's not object-oriented, but it does work.

A large factor in the success of early versions of VB is that it took the tricky-to-understand Win32 API calls and packaged them in a way that could be easily understood. Using the native Win32 API, it takes about a hundred lines of code to draw a window on the screen. The same effect can be achieved in Visual Basic with a few gestures of the mouse. VB represents an abstraction layer on top of the Win32 API that makes it easier for developers to use.

A long-time frustration for C++ developers was that a lot of the things that were very easy to do in VB remained not so much hard as laborious in C++. Conversely, developers like C++ because it gives them an amazing amount of control over how a program works, but at the cost that their programs take longer to write. Microsoft introduced the Microsoft Foundation Classes (MFC) because of this overhead, which, along with the IDE of Visual Studio, brought the ease of Visual C++ development a little towards that of Visual Basic.

The .NET Framework Classes

Unlike the Win32 API, .NET is totally object-oriented. Anything you want to do in .NET, you're going to be doing with an object. If you want to open a file, you'll create an object that knows how to do this. If you want to draw a window on the screen, you'll create an object that knows how to do this. If you remember back to Chapter 4, this is called encapsulation; the functionality is encapsulated in an object and we don't really care how it's done behind the scenes.

There's still the concept of subsystems in .NET, but they are never accessed directly – instead they are abstracted away by the Framework classes. Either way, your .NET application will never talk directly to the subsystem (although you can do this if you really need or want to). Rather, you'll talk to objects that then talk to the subsystem. In the following diagram, the box marked `System.IO.File` is a class defined in the .NET Framework:

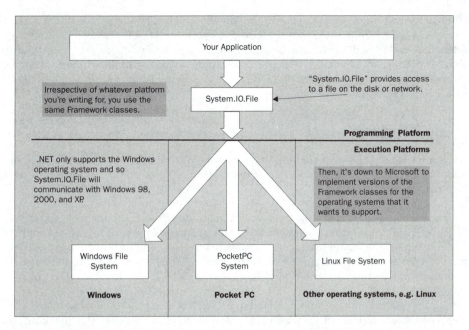

If we're talking to objects that talk to subsystems, do we really care what the subsystem looks like? Thankfully the answer is "no", and this is how Microsoft removes our reliance on Windows. If I know the name of a file, I use the same objects to open it whether I'm running on Windows XP, a Pocket PC or, once the required Framework is released, Linux. Likewise, if I need to display a window on the screen, I don't care if it's on Windows or a Mac.

The first release of the .NET Framework is actually a set of classes, called **base classes**, which can be used to create objects that manipulate virtually every aspect of the Windows platform. There are, at the time of writing, things that are not supported by .NET. This is because Microsoft needs to port everything from the old Win32 model to the new .NET model and some things are deemed more important than others. For example, the DirectX API is an API used by games and multi-media developers that makes it easy to build their kinds of application and is not natively supported on .NET. Given time, however, this API will be made available as Framework classes.

Microsoft has developed the first release of .NET so that the vast majority of the functionality is in place. Developers moving from the old Win32 approach have to retrain great swathes of their knowledge to move to .NET as some things are vastly different. Luckily for you, as a reader of this book you're likely to be a newcomer and so you won't have to go through the relearning process. You only have to learn it, not forget what you used to know!

The class library itself is vast. There are several thousand objects available to developers, although in your day-to-day development you'll only need to understand a handful of these to create some powerful applications.

The other wrinkle to this is that the classes are the same *irrespective of the language used*. So, if I'm writing a Visual Basic .NET application, I'll use the same object as I would from within a C# application. That object will have the same methods, properties, and events, meaning that there's very little difference in capabilities between the two languages.

At the time of writing, there's great debate going on about which language is better: Visual Basic .NET or C#. As is often the case in the computer industry, everyone has a favorite and will protect it with almost deadly force! In reality, and as a new programmer, you'll find there's virtually no difference so far as .NET is concerned. If you're building a .NET application, any of the supported languages should be equally capable because the power of .NET doesn't lie in the language – it lies in the Framework Classes, which were discussed in Chapter 4.

Executing Code

The class library is only half the equation. Once you've written code that talks to the classes, you still need to run it. This poses a tricky problem; to remove the reliance on the platform is to remove the reliance on the processor.

Whenever you write software for Windows, you're guaranteed that this code will run on an Intel x86 chip. With .NET, Microsoft doesn't want to make this guarantee. It might be that the dominant chip in 2006 is a Transmeta chip, or something we've never even seen. What we need to do is abstract .NET away from the processor in a similar fashion to the way we abstracted .NET from the underlying subsystem implementations.

If you wrote an application with VB6, you had to compile it into a set of x86 instructions before you could deploy it. These instructions are sometimes known as **machine code**. This machine code would then be installed and executed on any machine that supports x86 instructions. Well, that's a mild over-simplification because the application also needs to have Windows around in order to run, but you get the idea.

Programming languages are somewhere in-between the languages that you and I speak every day and the language that the computer itself understands. The language that a computer uses is machine code (sometimes called **machine instructions**). When we're using a PC with an Intel or competing processor, this language is more specifically known as **x86 machine instructions**.

If you write an application with Visual Basic .NET, you still have to compile the code. However, we don't compile the Visual Basic .NET code directly into x86 machine instructions as this would mean that the resulting program would only ever run on processors that support this language – in other words, the program would only run on Intel chips and their compatible competitors. Instead, the application is compiled into something called **Microsoft Intermediate Language**, or **MSIL**. This language isn't dependent on any processor and it's completely owned by Microsoft, and fits into what we've already talked about regarding its strategy to not be dependent on any execution platform.

MSIL code won't just run on any processor. To run the code, it has to be further compiled from MSIL code into the native code that the processor understands:

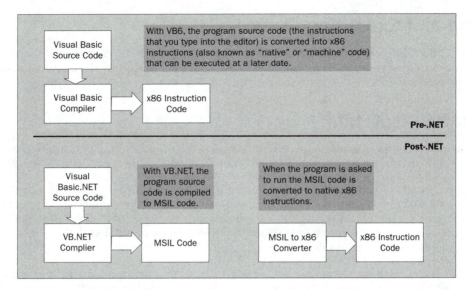

However, this approach also provides the industry with a subtle problem. In a world where .NET is extremely popular (some might say dominant), who is responsible for developing an MSIL-to-native compiler when a new processor is released? Is the new processor at the mercy of Microsoft's willingness to port .NET to the chip? Time, as they say, will tell!

Let's take a look at the thing that makes .NET work: the Common Language Runtime.

Common Language Runtime

The **Common Language Runtime** (**CLR**) is the heart of .NET. This is the thing that takes your .NET application, compiles it into native processor code, and runs it. It provides an extensive range of functionality for helping the applications run properly, so let's take a look at each one in turn.

- ❏ Loading and executing code
- ❏ Application isolation
- ❏ Memory management
- ❏ Security
- ❏ Exception handling
- ❏ Interoperation

Don't worry if you don't understand what all these are – we'll discuss all of them except for memory management now. Memory management is quite a complex subject, so we'll talk about it in Chapter 10.

Loading and Executing Code

This part of the CLR deals with pulling the MSIL code from the disk and running it. This is the part of the CLR we've already spoken about; it compiles the code from MSIL into the native language that the processor understands.

Application Isolation

One important premise of modern operating systems like Windows and Linux is that applications are **isolated** from one another. This is critically important from both security and stability standpoints.

Imagine you have a program on your PC that is badly written and crashes. Should this happen, you want only the badly behaved program to crash, as you don't want other applications or even the operating system itself to be affected. For example, if your e-mail program crashes, you don't want to lose any unsaved changes in your word processor. With proper application isolation, one application crashing should not cause others to crash.

In some instances, even on Windows 2000, a badly behaved program can do something so horrendous that the entire machine crashes. This is commonly known as a **Blue Screen of Death**, or **BSOD**, so called because your attractive Windows desktop is replaced with a stark blue screen with a smattering of white text "explaining" the problem. This problem should be alleviated in .NET, but it's unlikely to be completely solved.

The other aspect to application isolation is one of security. Imagine that you're writing a personal and sensitive e-mail. You don't want other applications running on your computer to be able to grab the contents of the e-mail and pass it on to someone else. Traditionally, applications running in an isolated model can't just take what they want. Instead, they have to ask if they can have something and, if they can, they are given it.

This level of application isolation is already available in Windows. .NET extends and enhances this functionality further improving it.

Security

One thing that .NET has a lot of powerful support for is the concept of code security. This is designed to give system administrators, users, and software developers a fine level of control over what a program can and can't do.

Imagine you have a program that scans your computer's hard disk looking for Word documents. You might think this is a pretty useful program if it's one that you run yourself in order to find documents that are missing. Now imagine that this program is delivered through e-mail, and automatically runs and e-mails copies of any "interesting" documents to someone else. You're less likely to find that useful.

This is the situation we find ourselves in today with old-school Windows development. Basically, to all intents and purposes Windows applications have unrestricted access over your computer and can do pretty much anything they want. That's why the Melissa and "I Love You" type viruses are possible – Windows doesn't understand the difference between a benign script file you write yourself, which looks through your address book and sends e-mails to everyone, and those written by someone else and delivered as viruses.

With .NET this situation will change because of the security features built into the CLR. Code requires "evidence" to run. This evidence can be policies set by you and your system administrator, as well as the origin of the code (for example, whether it came off your local machine, off a machine on your office network, or over the Internet).

Security is a very involved topic and it's not something we'll be covering in this book. However, you can find more information in *Professional VB.NET* published by Wrox (ISBN 1-86100-497-4).

Exception Handling

Exception handling is the concept of dealing with "exceptional happenings" when you're running code. Imagine you write a program that opens a file on disk. What if that file isn't there? Well, the fact that file isn't there is exceptional and we need to deal with it in some way. It could be that we crash, or we could display a window asking the user to supply a new file name. Either way, we have a fine level of control over what happens when an error does occur.

.NET provides a powerful exception handler that can "catch" exceptions when they occur and give your programs the opportunity to react and deal with the problem in some way. We will talk about exception handling more in Chapter 11, but for now we'll just introduce exception handling as something provided by the CLR to all applications.

Interoperation

As we mentioned before, the classes in the .NET Framework that are in the first release won't be complete insofar as there will be things that you can do with Windows that won't be implemented as a Framework class. For example, you might want to create an Excel spreadsheet or a Word document from your code. Office will not be available as a .NET implementation at the time of writing, so we need to use **interoperation** (or more commonly **interop**) functionality that allows .NET developers to call into old-school applications.

The Common Type System and Common Language Specification

One of the most important aspects of .NET that Microsoft has to get right is inter-language operation. Remember, Microsoft's motivation is to get *any* developer using *any* language using .NET, and in order for this to happen all languages have to be treated equally. Likewise, applications created in one language have to be understood by other languages. For example, if I create a class in Visual Basic .NET, a C# developer has to be able to use and extend that class. Alternatively, if I define a string in C#, I need to pass that to an object built in Visual Basic .NET, and have that object understand and manipulate the string successfully.

The **Common Type System** (CTS) allows software written in different languages to work together. Before .NET, the way that VB and C++ handled strings was done completely differently, meaning that each time you went from one to the other you had to go through a conversion process. With the Common Type System in place, Visual Basic .NET, C#, and other .NET languages use strings, integers, and so on, in the same way and therefore no conversion needs to take place.

In addition, the **Common Language Specification** (CLS) was introduced by Microsoft to make it easier for language developers to adapt their languages to make them compatible with .NET.

> **The Common Type System and Common Language Specifications are the foundation for this interoperation, but detailed discussion is unfortunately beyond the scope of this book.**

When talking to other .NET developers, it's likely you'll hear the term **managed code**. This simply describes code that runs inside the CLR. In other words, you get all of the advantages of the CLR such as the memory management and all of the language interoperability features we mentioned.

Code written in Visual Basic .NET and C# is automatically created as managed code. C++ code is *not* automatically created as managed code because C++ doesn't fit well into the memory management scheme implemented by the CLR. You can, if you're interested, turn on an option to create managed code from within C++, in which case we use the term **managed C++**.

Hand-in-hand with managed code is **managed data**. As you can probably guess, this is data managed by the CLR, although in nearly all cases this data is actually objects. Objects managed by the CLR can easily be passed between languages.

Summary

In this chapter, we introduced the Microsoft .NET Framework from the perspective of *why* Microsoft had chosen to radically change the way programs were written for Windows. We also saw that part of Microsoft's motivation for this was to move the dependence of developers from the execution platform (Windows, Linux, whatever) over to a new programming platform that it would always own.

After learning about why Microsoft developed .NET, we saw how writing for it isn't much different from writing for Windows previously. We still have a layer that we program against; it's just that now, rather than being flat like the Win32 API, it's a rich set of classes. We also discussed how these classes could be ported to other platforms, and how our applications could also transfer across.

Finally, we took a look at the some of the more technical aspects of the Framework, specifically the Common Language Runtime, or CLR.

Questions

1. What's the general premise behind .NET?

2. What's the similarity between .NET and Java?

3. What is the Framework Class Library?

4. What is interoperation?

5. How is application code compiled in .NET?

Working with Data Structures

In this chapter, we're going to see some ways in which we can work with complex sets of data.

We'll start by introducing the array, which is used to hold lists of similar data. For example, you may create an array of friends' names (and we'll do exactly that later in this chapter). We will then discuss how enumerations can be used to allow a previously defined set of values to be made available (preventing you from supplying an invalid value). Constants will be the next topic, and we'll see how they improve the maintainability of our code by replacing recurring literal values. We'll then move on to working with structures (which we'll discover are similar to classes), and then see how we can build powerful collection classes for working with, maintaining, and manipulating lists of complex data.

Arrays

A fairly common requirement when writing software is the ability to hold lists of similar or related data. We can provide this functionality by using an **array**. Arrays are just lists of data that have a single data type. For example, you might want to store a list of friends' ages in an integer array or their names in a string array.

In this section, we'll be taking a look at how to define, populate, and use arrays in our applications.

Defining and Using Arrays

When we define an array, we're actually creating a variable that has more than one dimension. For example, if we define a variable as a string, like this, we can only hold a single string value in it:

```
Dim s As String
```

However, with an array we create a kind of "multiplier effect" with a variable, so you can hold more than one value in a single variable. An array is defined by entering the size of the array after the variable name. So, if we wanted to define a string array of length 10, we'd do this:

```
Dim s(9) As String
```

> The reason why we use **(9)** instead of **(10)** to get an array of length 10 will be explained in detail later. For now it is simply because numbering in an array starts at zero, so one to us is zero in an array, two to us is one in an array, and so on.

Once we have an array, we can access individual elements in it by providing an index value between 0 and a maximum possible value – this maximum possible value happens to be one less than the total size of the array.

So, to set the element with index 2 in the array, we'd do this:

```
s(2) = "Disraeli"
```

To get that same element back again, we'd do this:

```
MessageBox.Show(s(2))
```

What's important is that other elements in the array are *unaffected* when you set their siblings. So, if we do this:

```
s(3) = "Winston"
```

...`s(2)` remains set to `"Disraeli"`.

Perhaps the easiest way to understand what an array looks like and how one works is to write some code that uses them.

Try It Out – Defining and Using a Simple Array

1. Using Visual Studio .NET, create a new **Windows Application** project. Call it **Array Demo**.

2. When the Designer for **Form1** appears, add a **ListBox** control to the form. Using the Properties window set its **Name** property to **lstFriends** and its **IntegralHeight** property to **False** (this tells the listbox not to resize, but to show partial items).

3. Now add a **Button** control to the form. In this case, set its **Name** property to **btnGo** and set its **Text** property to **Go**. Your form should now look something like this:

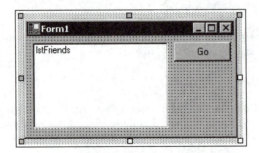

4. Double-click on the Go button. Add this code:

```
Private Sub btnGo_Click(ByVal sender As System.Object, _
        ByVal e As System.EventArgs) Handles btnGo.Click

    ' define an array to hold friends in...
    Dim friends(4) As String

    ' store the name of each friend...
    friends(0) = "Darren"
    friends(1) = "Edward"
    friends(2) = "Alex"
    friends(3) = "Charlotte"
    friends(4) = "Len"

    ' add Alex to the list...
    lstFriends.Items.Add(friends(2))

End Sub
```

5. Run the project. Click the Go button and you'll see this:

How It Works

When we define an array we have to specify both a data type and a size. In this case, we're specifying an array of type `String` and also defining an array size of 5:

```
Private Sub btnGo_Click(ByVal sender As System.Object, _
        ByVal e As System.EventArgs) Handles btnGo.Click

    ' define an array to hold friends in...
    Dim friends(4) As String
```

The way the size is defined is a little quirky. You have to specify a size one less than the final size you want. (We'll explain why in a minute.) So here we've used the line:

```
    Dim friends(4) As String
```

In this way, we end up with an array of size 5. Another way of expressing this is to say that we have an array comprising 5 **elements**.

Once this is done we'll have our array and we can access each item in the array by using an index. The index is given as a number in parentheses after the name of the array. Indexes start at zero and go up to one less than the number of items in the array. Here we set all five possible items in the array to the names:

```
' store the name of each friend...
friends(0) = "Darren"
friends(1) = "Edward"
friends(2) = "Alex"
friends(3) = "Charlotte"
friends(4) = "Len"
```

In a similar way to how we use an index to set the items in an array, we use an index to get items back out. In this case, we're asking for the item at position 2, which returns the third item in the array, namely Alex:

```
' add Alex to the list...
lstFriends.Items.Add(friends(2))

End Sub
```

The reason why the indexes and sizes seem skewed is because the indexes are **zero-based** and in typical human logic we tend to number things from 1. In our array definition, we specify the size of the array as the **upper-index bound**, or rather the highest possible index that the array will support. Likewise, when we put items into or retrieve items from an array, we have to adjust the position we want down by one to get the actual index – for example, the fifth index is actually at position 4, the first index is at position 0, and so on.

Using For Each...Next

One really common way that we work with arrays is by using a For Each...Next loop. We introduced these in Chapter 3, but we used them with collections returned from Framework classes. Let's look at how we use For Each...Next with an array.

Try It Out – Using For Each...Next with an Array

1. If the program is running, close it. Open the code editor for Form1 and change the btnGo_Click event procedure so that it now looks like this:

```
    ...

    friends(4) = "Len"

    ' go through each friend...
    Dim friendName As String
    For Each friendName In friends

        ' add each one to the list...
        lstFriends.Items.Add(friendName)

    Next

End Sub
```

2. Run the project and click Go. You'll see this:

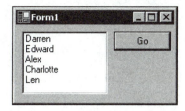

How It Works

Previously, we saw the `For Each...Next` loop iterate through a collection returned from the Framework. In this example, we've seen it used in an array. The principle is similar – we have to create a control variable that is of the same type as the array and give this to the loop when it starts. The internals behind the loop move through the array starting at element 0 until it reaches the last element. For each iteration, we can examine the value of the control variable and do something with it – in this case, we add the name to the list.

Also, notice that the items are added to the list in the same order that they appear in the array. That's because `For Each...Next` goes through from the first item to the last item as they are defined.

Passing Arrays as Parameters

It's extremely useful to be able to pass an array (which could be a list of values) to a function as a parameter. In this section, we'll look at how to do this.

Try It Out – Passing Arrays as Parameters

1. Open the code editor for Form1. Move the loop into a separate function, like this:

```
Private Sub btnGo_Click(ByVal sender As System.Object, _
        ByVal e As System.EventArgs) Handles btnGo.Click

    ' define an array to hold friends in...
    Dim friends(4) As String

    ' store the name of each friend...
    friends(0) = "Darren"
    friends(1) = "Edward"
    friends(2) = "Alex"
    friends(3) = "Charlotte"
    friends(4) = "Len"

End Sub
```

```
Sub AddFriendsToList(ByVal friends() As String)

    ' go through each friend...
    Dim friendName As String
    For Each friendName In friends

        ' add each one to the list...
        lstFriends.Items.Add(friendName)
```

215

```
      Next

End Sub
```

2. Now, change the code in `btnGo_Click` so that it reads as follows:

```
...

friends(4) = "Len"

' show the friends...
AddFriendsToList(friends)

End Sub
```

3. Run the project and click Go. You'll see the same results as before:

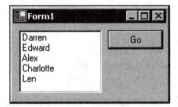

How It Works

The trick here is to tell the function that the parameter is expecting an array of type `String`. We do this by using empty parentheses, like this:

```
Sub AddFriendsToList(ByVal friends() As String)
```

If we specify an array but don't define a size (or upper bound value) we're telling VB that we don't know or care how big the array is. That means that we can pass an array of any size through to `AddFriendsToList`. Here, we're sending our original array:

```
    friends(4) = "Len"

    ' show the friends...
    AddFriendsToList(friends)
```

But, what happens if we define another array of a different size?

Try It Out – Adding More Friends

1. Open the code editor for Form1 and add this code to the `btnGo_Click` method:

```
...

friends(4) = "Len"

' store more friends...
Dim moreFriends(1) As String
moreFriends(0) = "Zoe"
moreFriends(1) = "Ollie"

' show the friends...
AddFriendsToList(friends)
AddFriendsToList(moreFriends)

End Sub
```

2. Run the project and click **Go**. You'll see this:

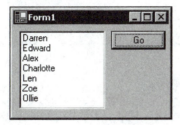

How It Works

What we've done here is proven that the array we pass as a parameter does not have to be of a fixed size. We've created a new array of size 2 and passed it through to the same `AddFriendsToList` function.

As you're writing code, you can tell whether a parameter is an array type by looking for empty parentheses in the IntelliSense popup, as illustrated below:

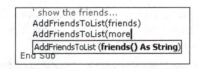

Not only are we informed that `friends` *is an array type, but we also see that the data type of the array is* `String`.

Sorting Arrays

It's sometimes useful to be able to take an array and sort it. In this section, we'll see how we can take an array and sort it alphabetically.

Try It Out – Sorting Arrays

1. Open the code editor for **Form1** and find the `AddFriendsToList` method. Add this code:

```
Sub AddFriendsToList(ByVal friends() As String)
```

```
    ' sort it...
    Array.Sort(friends)
```

```
    ' go through each friend...

    ...
```

2. Run the project and click Go. You'll see this:

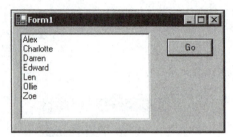

How It Works

All arrays are internally implemented in a class called `System.Array`. In this case, we want to use a shared method on that class called `Sort`, which takes a single parameter, namely the array you want to sort. Depending on the data type used by the array, the `Sort` method will then do as its name suggests and sort it for you. In our case, we have a string array so we get an alphanumeric sort.

> If we were to attempt to use this technique on an array containing integer or floating-point values, the array would be sorted in numeric order.

Going Backwards

`For Each...Next` will only go through an array in one direction. It starts at position 0 and loops through to the end of the array. If we want to go through an array backwards (from the length − 1 position to 0) we have to use a standard `For...Next` loop.

Try It Out – Going Backwards

1. In Form1 remove the second array definition and the second call to `AddFriendsToList` so you have what you had before:

```
Private Sub btnGo_Click(ByVal sender As System.Object, _
         ByVal e As System.EventArgs) Handles btnGo.Click
```

```
    ' define an array to hold friends in...
    Dim friends(4) As String
```

```
    ' store the name of each friend...
    friends(0) = "Darren"
```

```
    friends(1) = "Edward"
    friends(2) = "Alex"
    friends(3) = "Charlotte"
    friends(4) = "Len"

    ' show the friends...
    AddFriendsToList(friends)

End Sub
```

2. Alter `AddFriendsToList` so that it now looks like this:

```
Sub AddFriendsToList(ByVal friends() As String)

    ' sort it...
    Array.Sort(friends)

    ' how big is the array?
    Dim upperBound As Integer = friends.Length - 1

    ' go through each friend...
    Dim index As Integer
    For index = upperBound To 0 Step -1

        ' add each one to the list...
        lstFriends.Items.Add(friends(index))

    Next

End Sub
```

3. Run the project and click Go. You'll see the friends listed in reverse order. (The array is sorted, and the items are added to the list in reverse order, so we see them here in reverse order. Len was added first, then Edward, then Darren, and so on.)

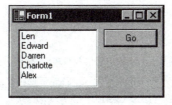

How It Works

When we're given an array in `AddFriendsToList`, we don't know how big it actually is. We can, however, use the `Length` property to find out how big it is. We subtract 1 from this number in order to get the upper bound – in other words the highest index value that the array supports:

```
    ' how big is the array?
    Dim upperBound As Integer = friends.Length - 1
```

Once we have that value, we can set up a `For...Next` loop that accesses each index in the array one at a time, and in reverse order:

```
' go through each friend...
Dim index As Integer
For index = upperBound To 0 Step -1

    ' add each one to the list...
    lstFriends.Items.Add(friends(index))
```

Being Random

We've seen how we can go through an array in one direction, and then back through it in another. Now let's look at how to go through the array in a random order.

Try It Out – Being Random

1. Make these changes to `AddFriendsToList`:

```
Sub AddFriendsToList(ByVal friends() As String)

    ' sort it...
    Array.Sort(friends)

    ' how big is the array?
    Dim upperBound As Integer = friends.Length

    ' create a randomizer...
    Dim random As New System.Random()

    ' count ten items...
    Dim n As Integer
    For n = 1 To 10

        ' which index?
        Dim index As Integer = random.Next(upperBound)
        lstFriends.Items.Add(index & ": " & friends(index))

    Next

End Sub
```

2. Run the project and click the Go button. You'll see something like this:

How It Works

The .NET random number generator (implemented in `System.Random`) can be used to create random numbers on demand. In this instance, for every iteration of the loop, we're asking the generator to give us a random number between 0 and `upperBound` – or the length of the array. The parameter passed to the `Random` class's `Next` method is *exclusive*, so we have to give it one more than the number we require:

```
Dim upperBound As Integer = friends.Length

' create a randomizer...
Dim random As New System.Random()

' count ten items...
Dim n As Integer
For n = 1 To 10

    ' which index?
    Dim index As Integer = random.Next(upperBound)
    lstFriends.Items.Add(index & ": " & friends(index))
```

UBound and LBound

We've shown how you can get the size of the array using the `Length` property of the array itself. However, there are two Visual Basic .NET keywords that can help us determine the bounds of an array.

`UBound` and `LBound` are Visual Basic .NET-specific keywords that return the highest possible index and the lowest possible index that the array supports.

Try It Out – UBound and LBound

1. Find the `AddFriendsToList` method and add this code:

```
Sub AddFriendsToList(ByVal friends() As String)

    ' upper and lower...
    MessageBox.Show("Upper bound: " & UBound(friends), "Array Demo")
    MessageBox.Show("Lower bound: " & LBound(friends), "Array Demo")

    ' sort it...
    Array.Sort(friends)

    ...
```

2. Run the project and click Go. You'll see this:

3. Click OK and you'll see this:

How It Works

UBound and LBound are throwbacks to earlier versions of VB, which is why those adventurous sorts among you won't find them in C# (or other .Net languages). In earlier versions, it was possible to set the lower bound of an array to something other than zero. This isn't possible in Visual Basic .NET, so LBound will always return 0.

Initializing Arrays with Values

It is possible to create an array in Visual Basic .NET and populate it in one line of code, rather than having to write specific lines to populate each item as we have here:

```
' store the name of each friend...
friends(0) = "Darren"
friends(1) = "Edward"
friends(2) = "Alex"
friends(3) = "Charlotte"
friends(4) = "Len"
```

Try It Out – Initializing Arrays with Values

1. Find the btnGo_Click event handler and make this change:

```
Private Sub btnGo_Click(ByVal sender As System.Object, _
         ByVal e As System.EventArgs) Handles btnGo.Click

    ' define an array to hold friends in...
    Dim friends() As String = {"Darren", "Edward", "Alex", _
        "Charlotte", "Len"}

    ' show the friends...
    AddFriendsToList(friends)

End Sub
```

2. Run the project. The program will behave just like it did before.

How It Works

The pair of braces { } allows us to set the values that should be held in an array directly. In this instance, we have five values to enter into the array, separated with commas.

Notice that when we do this, we don't specify an upper bound for the array – instead we use empty parentheses. Visual Basic .NET prefers to calculate the upper bound for us based on the values we supply.

This technique can be quite awkward to use when populating large arrays. If your program relies on populating large arrays, you might want to use the method we've illustrated earlier – specifying the position and value.

Enumerations

So far, the variables we've seen have had virtually no limitations on the kinds of data we can store in them. Technical limits not withstanding, if we have a variable defined `As Integer`, we can put any number we like in it. Same with `String` and `Double`. However, we have seen a variable that has only two possible values: Boolean variables can be either `True` or `False` and nothing else.

Often when writing code you want to limit the possible values that can be stored in a variable. For example, if you have a variable that stores the number of doors that a car has, do you really want to be able to store 163,234?

Enumerations allow us to build a new type of variable, based on one of these data types: `Integer`, `Long`, `Short`, or `Byte`. This variable can be set to one value of a set of possible values that you define, and ideally prevents you from supplying invalid values. It is used to provide clarity in the code, as it can describe a particular value. In this section, we'll take a look at how to build an application that looks at the time of day and, based on that, can record a *DayAction* of one of these possible values:

- ❏ Asleep
- ❏ Getting ready for work
- ❏ Traveling to work
- ❏ At work
- ❏ At lunch
- ❏ Traveling from work
- ❏ Relaxing with friends
- ❏ Getting ready for bed

Try It Out – Using Enumerations

1. Using Visual Studio .NET, create a new **Windows Application** project called **Enum Demo**.

2. Enumerations are typically defined as a member of the class that intends to use them (though this does not have to be the case). When the Designer for **Form1** opens, open the code editor for the form and add this to the top:

```
Public Class Form1
    Inherits System.Windows.Forms.Form
```

```
' enum...
Public Enum DayAction As Integer
    Asleep = 0
    GettingReadyForWork = 1
    TravelingToWork = 2
    AtWork = 3
    AtLunch = 4
    TravelingFromWork = 5
    RelaxingWithFriends = 6
    GettingReadyForBed = 7
End Enum
```

3. With an enumeration defined, we can create new member variables that use the enumeration as their data type. Add this member:

```
...

End Enum
```

```
' members...
Public CurrentState As DayAction
```

4. Flip back to the Designer for Form1. Change the Text property of Form1 to What's Len Doing? Now add a TrackBar control and a TextBox control to the form so that it looks like this:

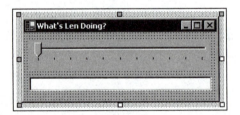

5. Using the Properties window, change the Name property of the track bar to trkHour. Set its Maximum property to 23 and its Minimum property to 0 (to cater for the twenty-four hour clock). In similar fashion, change the Name property of the textbox to txtState. Clear its Text property.

6. Double-click on the background of the form to create a new Load event handler. Add this code:

```
Private Sub Form1_Load(ByVal sender As System.Object, _
            ByVal e As System.EventArgs) Handles MyBase.Load
```

```
    ' set the hour to the current hour...
    Me.Hour = Date.Now.Hour
```

```
End Sub
```

7. Now, add this property below the code we added in Step 3:

```
' Hour property...
Public Property Hour() As Integer
    Get
        Return trkHour.Value
    End Get
    Set(ByVal Value As Integer)

        ' set the hour...
        trkHour.Value = Value

        ' set the text...
        Dim statusText As String
        statusText = "At " & Value & ":00, Len is "

        ' update the display...
        txtState.Text = statusText

    End Set
End Property
```

8. Flip over to the Designer again and double-click on the track bar. Add this code to the new `Scroll` event handler:

```
Private Sub trkHour_Scroll(ByVal sender As System.Object, _
            ByVal e As System.EventArgs) Handles trkHour.Scroll

    ' update the hour...
    Me.Hour = trkHour.Value

End Sub
```

9. Run the project. You'll be able to slide the track bar around and the text will update to reflect the hour you select:

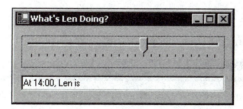

How It Works

In this application, the user will be able to use the track bar to choose the hour. We're then going to look at the hour and determine which one of the eight states Len is in at the given time.

In order to achieve this we've created a property called `Hour` that is set to the current hour when the application starts:

```
' set the hour to the current hour...
Me.Hour = Date.Now.Hour
```

225

We also set the same property when the thumb on the track bar is moved:

```
Private Sub trkHour_Scroll(ByVal sender As System.Object, _
        ByVal e As System.EventArgs) Handles trkHour.Scroll

    ' update the hour...
    Me.Hour = trkHour.Value

End Sub
```

When the Hour property is set, we form a string. At the moment, we haven't evaluated the Hour property to determine the state, but we'll do this next:

```
' Hour property...
Public Property Hour() As Integer
    Get
        Return trkHour.Value
    End Get
    Set(ByVal Value As Integer)

        ' set the hour...
        trkHour.Value = Value

        ' set the text...
        Dim statusText As String
        statusText = "At " & Value & ":00, Len is "

        ' update the display...
        txtState.Text = statusText

    End Set
End Property
```

Determining the State

Now we'll look at determining the state when the Hour property is set.

Try It Out – Determining State

1. Open the code editor for **Form1** and find the Hour property; add this code:

```
' Hour property...
Public Property Hour() As Integer
    Get
        Return trkHour.Value
    End Get
    Set(ByVal Value As Integer)

        ' set the hour...
        trkHour.Value = Value
```

```
          ' determine the state...
          Dim hour As Integer = Value
          If hour >= 6 And hour < 7 Then
              CurrentState = DayAction.TravelingToWork
          ElseIf hour >= 7 And hour < 8 Then
              CurrentState = DayAction.TravelingToWork
          ElseIf hour >= 8 And hour < 13 Then
              CurrentState = DayAction.AtWork
          ElseIf hour >= 13 And hour < 14 Then
              CurrentState = DayAction.AtLunch
          ElseIf hour >= 14 And hour < 17 Then
              CurrentState = DayAction.AtWork
          ElseIf hour >= 17 And hour < 18 Then
              CurrentState = DayAction.TravelingFromWork
          ElseIf hour >= 18 And hour < 22 Then
              CurrentState = DayAction.RelaxingWithFriends
          ElseIf hour >= 22 And hour < 23 Then
              CurrentState = DayAction.GettingReadyForBed
          Else
              CurrentState = DayAction.Asleep
          End If

          ' set the text...
          Dim statusText As String
          statusText = "At " & Value & ":00, Len is " & CurrentState

          ' update the display...
          txtState.Text = statusText

      End Set
  End Property
```

2. Run the project. You'll see something like this:

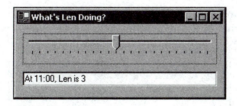

3. Here's a problem – the user doesn't know what 3 means. Close the project and find the
    following section of code within the Hour property:

```
          ' set the text...
          Dim statusText As String
          statusText = "At " & Value & ":00, Len is " & CurrentState
```

Change this so that it now reads:

```
' set the text...
Dim statusText As String
statusText = "At " & Value & ":00, Len is " & _
    CurrentState.ToString ()
```

4. Now run the project and you'll see something like this:

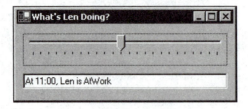

How It Works

As you typed the code in, you'll have noticed that whenever you tried to set a value against `CurrentState`, you were presented with a list of possibilities:

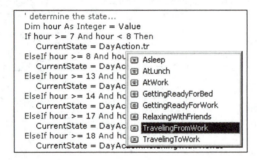

Visual Studio .NET knows that `CurrentState` is of type `DayAction`. It also knows that `DayAction` is an enumeration and that it defines eight possible values, each of which is displayed in the IntelliSense popup.

Fundamentally though, because `DayAction` is based on an integer, `CurrentState` is an integer value. That's why the first time we ran the project with the state determination code in place we saw an integer at the end of the status string:

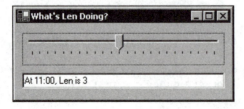

At 11 a.m., we know that Len is at work, or rather `CurrentState` equals `DayAction.AtWork`. We've defined this as 3, hence the reason why 3 is displayed at the end of the string.

What we've done in this *Try It Out* is tacked a call to the `ToString` method onto the end of the string. This results in a string representation of `DayAction` being used, rather than the integer representation, as illustrated in the case of `AtWork` below:

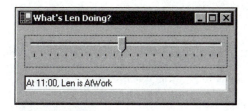

Enumerations are incredibly useful when you want to store one of a possible set of values in a variable. As you start to drill into more complex objects in the Framework you'll find that they are used all over the place!

Setting Invalid Values

One of the limitations of enumerations is that it is possible to store values against an enumeration that technically aren't one of the possible defined values. For example, if we change the Hour property so that rather than setting CurrentState to Asleep, we set it to 999:

```
ElseIf hour >= 22 And hour < 23 Then
    CurrentState = DayAction.GettingReadyForBed
Else
    CurrentState = 999
End If

' set the text...
Dim statusText As String
statusText = "At " & Value & ":00, Len is " & _
    CurrentState.ToString()

' update the display...
txtState.Text = statusText
```

If we build the project, you'll notice that Visual Basic .NET doesn't flag this as an error. Further, if we actually run the project, you'll notice this:

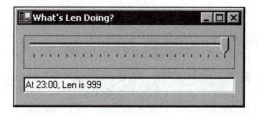

So, you can see that we can set a variable that references an enumeration to a value that is not defined in that enumeration and the application will still "work" (as long as the value is of the same type as the enumeration). If you build classes that use enumerations, you'll have to rely on the consumer of that class being well behaved. One technique to solve this problem would be to disallow invalid values in any properties that used the enumeration as their data type.

Constants

Another good programming practice that we need to look at is the constant. Imagine you have these two methods, each of which does something with a given file on the computer's disk. (Obviously, I'm omitting the code here that actually manipulates the file.)

```
Public Sub DoSomething()

    ' what's the filename?
    Dim filename As String = "c:\Wrox\Demo.txt"

    ' open the file...
    ...

End Sub

Public Sub DoSomethingElse()

    ' what's the filename?
    Dim myFilename As String = "c:\Wrox\Demo.txt"

    ' do something with the file...
    ...

End Sub
```

You'll notice that in the code we've defined a string literal giving the name of a file twice. This is poor programming practice because if both methods are indeed supposed to access the same file, should that filename change, this change has to be made in two separate places.

In this instance, both methods are next to each other and the program itself is small, but imagine that you have a massive program where a separate string literal pointing to the file is defined in ten, fifty, or even a thousand places. If you need to change the filename you'll have to change it many times. This is exactly the kind of thing that leads to serious problems when maintaining software code.

What we need to do instead is define the filename globally and then use that global definition of the filename in the code, rather than using a string literal. This is known as a **constant**. This is, in effect, a special kind of variable that cannot be changed when the program is running.

Try It Out – Using Constants

1. Using Visual Studio .NET, create a new Windows Application project and call it Constants Demo.

2. When the Designer for Form1 opens, add three buttons. Set the Name property of the first one to btnOne, the second to btnTwo, and the third to btnThree. Change the Text property of each to One, Two, and Three respectively:

3. Now, at the top of the class definition, add this code:

```
Public Class Form1
    Inherits System.Windows.Forms.Form

    ' consts...
    Public Const MyFilename As String = "c:\Wrox\Hello.txt"
```

4. Double-click on **One**. Add this code:

```
Private Sub btnOne_Click(ByVal sender As System.Object, _
        ByVal e As System.EventArgs) Handles btnOne.Click

    ' use a constant...
    MessageBox.Show("1: " & MyFilename, "Constants Demo")

    End Sub
```

5. Flip over to the Designer again and double-click on **Two**. Add this code:

```
Private Sub btnTwo_Click(ByVal sender As System.Object, _
        ByVal e As System.EventArgs) Handles btnTwo.Click

    ' use the constant again...
    MessageBox.Show("2: " & MyFilename, "Constants Demo")

End Sub
```

6. Finally, flip over to the Designer and double-click on **Three**. Add this code:

```
Private Sub btnThree_Click(ByVal sender As System.Object, _
        ByVal e As System.EventArgs) Handles btnThree.Click

    ' one more time...
    MessageBox.Show("3: " & MyFilename, "Constants Demo")

End Sub
```

7. Run the project and click **One**. You'll see this:

8. Likewise, you'll see the same filename if you click Two or Three:

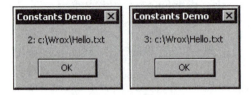

How It Works

A constant is actually a type of value that cannot be changed when the program is running. It's defined like a member is, but we add Const to the definition.

```
Public Class Form1
    Inherits System.Windows.Forms.Form

    ' consts...
    Public Const MyFilename As String = "c:\Wrox\Hello.txt"
```

You'll notice that it has a data type, just like a member, and that we have to give it a value when it's defined. (Which makes sense, as we can't change it later.) You should define constants as members of the class, in the following way. Constants are available throughout the class definition. They are also available to other classes as they are **shared** by default. (We'll talk more about what shared means in Chapter 10.)

When we want to use the constant, we refer to it just as we would a normal member:

```
Private Sub btnOne_Click(ByVal sender As System.Object, _
        ByVal e As System.EventArgs) Handles btnOne.Click

    ' use a constant...
    MessageBox.Show("1: " & MyFilename, "Constants Demo")

End Sub
```

Changing Constants

As I mentioned before, the appeal of a constant is that it allows you to change a value that's used throughout a piece of code by altering a single piece of code. Let's look at how this works.

Try It Out – Changing Constants

1. Let's change the value stored against MyFilename:

```
Public Class Form1
    Inherits System.Windows.Forms.Form

    ' consts...
    Public Const MyFilename As String = "c:\7612\Chapter06\Welcome.txt"
```

2. Run the project. When you click any of the buttons you'll see that the new value of `MyFilename` is used:

How It Works

This illustrates the power of constants – we can define a string literal value in a single location and then use that literal throughout the code. If the value of the literal has to change, we do it in one place and everything that used the old value automatically starts using the new value.

As a rule, constants should be used wherever you use a literal value more than once. However, this is a bit of overkill and developers tend to use constants whenever they need to store a reference to a resource that they use that might change at some point in the future. Filenames and instructions on how to connect to a database that an application needs are classic cases.

Different Constant Types

In this section, we've seen how to use a string constant, but we can use other types of variables as a constant. There are some rules – basically a constant must not be able to change, so you should not store an object in a constant.

Integers are a very common form of constant. They can be defined like this:

```
Public Const HoursAsleepPerDay As Integer = 8
```

Also, it's fairly common to see constants used with enumerations, like this:

```
Public Const LensTypicalState As DayAction = DayAction.Asleep
```

Structures

Back in Chapter 4, we introduced the concept of creating our own classes for use in our applications. Now we'll introduce **structures**.

Structures are very similar to classes, but have some subtle differences. As a rule of thumb, I would suggest that if you end up putting a lot of methods on a structure, it should probably be a class. It's also relatively tricky to convert from a structure to a class later on as the instantiation method is different, so choose once and choose wisely!

In terms of semantics, structures are known as **value types** and classes are known as **reference types**. This explains the difference in instantiation – you don't need to use the New keyword to instantiate an integer before you use it because it is a value type. Likewise, you do have to use the New keyword with a Form or other complex object because it is a reference type.

Also, you cannot inherit from a structure – another important consideration when choosing whether to use a class or a structure.

Let's now take a look at how we can build a structure.

Try It Out – Building a Structure

1. Using Visual Studio .NET, create a new Windows Application project. Call it Structure Demo.

2. When the project is created, use the Solution Explorer to add a new class called Customer.

3. When the code editor appears, add the following code:

```
Public Structure Customer

    ' members...
    Public FirstName As String
    Public LastName As String
    Public Email As String

End Structure
```

Note that you must ensure that you change **Class** to **Structure** on the first and last lines!

4. Open the Designer for Form1. Add four textboxes, four label controls, and a button. Using the Properties window, change these properties:

Control	Name	Property
First textbox	txtName	Text = *nothing*
Second textbox	txtFirstName	Text = *nothing*
Third textbox	txtLastName	Text = *nothing*
Fourth textbox	txtEmailName	Text = *nothing*
First label control	lblName	Text = Name:

Control	Name	Property
Second label control	lblFirstName	Text = First Name:
Third label control	lblLastName	Text = Last Name:
Fourth label control	lblEmailName	Text = E-mail:
Button	btnTest	Text = Test

Your form should now look something like this:

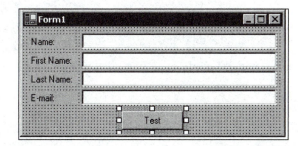

5. Double-click on the button to create a new `Click` event handler. Add this code:

```
Private Sub btnTest_Click(ByVal sender As System.Object, _
        ByVal e As System.EventArgs) Handles btnTest.Click

    ' create a new customer...
    Dim testCustomer As Customer
    testCustomer.FirstName = "Amir"
    testCustomer.LastName = "Aliabadi"
    testCustomer.Email = "amir@pretendcompany.com"

    ' display the customer...
    DisplayCustomer(testCustomer)

End Sub
```

6. Next, add this method:

```
' DisplayCustomer - show the customer...
Public Sub DisplayCustomer(ByVal customer As Customer)

    ' update the fields...
    txtFirstName.Text = customer.FirstName
    txtLastName.Text = customer.LastName
    txtEmailName.Text = customer.Email

End Sub
```

7. Run the project and click the Test button. You'll see this:

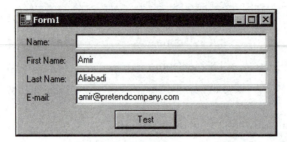

How It Works

A structure is conceptually very similar to a class.

The difference in definition is equally subtle: we use Structure...End Structure rather than Class...End Class.

```
Public Structure Customer

    ' members...
    Public FirstName As String
    Public LastName As String
    Public Email As String

End Structure
```

As you can see, structures can have public members just like classes can. They can also have private members, properties, and methods.

One important difference between structures and classes is that you don't have to create a structure with the New keyword before you can use it. In the Click handler code, you can see that we define a variable of type Customer, but we don't have to call New:

```
' create a new customer...
Dim testCustomer As Customer
testCustomer.FirstName = "Amir"
testCustomer.LastName = "Aliabadi"
testCustomer.Email = amir@pretendcompany.com
```

Adding Properties to Structures

As we've seen, structures and classes are very similar. We can add properties to a structure just as we can with a class.

Try It Out – Adding a Name Property

1. Open the code editor for Customer and add this code below the members declaration code we added earlier:

```
' Name property...
Public ReadOnly Property Name() As String
    Get
        Return FirstName & " " & LastName
    End Get
End Property
```

2. Now, open the code editor for Form1. Find the `DisplayCustomer` method and add this code:

```
' DisplayCustomer - show the customer...
Public Sub DisplayCustomer(ByVal customer As Customer)

    ' update the fields...
    txtName.Text = customer.Name
    txtFirstName.Text = customer.FirstName
    txtLastName.Text = customer.LastName
    txtEmail.Text = customer.Email

End Sub
```

3. Run the project and click the Test button. You'll see that the top textbox is now populated:

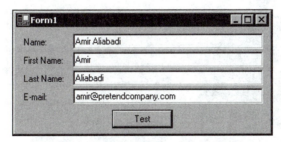

How It Works

As you can see here, we can add a property to a structure just as we can to a normal class.

Collections and Lists

One common construct you'll find used a lot in the Framework classes is the **collection**. These are conceptually similar to arrays, in other words they are a set of related information stored in a list of some sort, but they offer more flexibility to the developer using them.

For example, imagine we need to store a set of `Customer` structures. We could use an array, but in some cases, the array might not be so easy to use:

❏   If we need to add a new `Customer` to the array, we need to change the size of the array and insert the new item in the new last position in the array. (We'll talk more about how to change the size of an array later in this chapter.)

237

❑   If we need to remove a `Customer` from the array, we need to look at each item in the array in turn. When we find the one we want, we have to create another version of the array one element smaller than the original array and copy everything but the one we want to delete into the new array.

❑   If we need to replace a `Customer` in the array with another customer, we need to look at each item in turn until we find the one we want and then replace it manually.

The `System.Collections.ArrayList` provides a way for us to create an array that can be easily manipulated as we run our program. Let's look at using one of these now.

Try It Out – Using an ArrayList

1.   Using the Designer for **Form1**, rearrange the form and add a new **ListBox** control. Change the **Name** property of the listbox to **lstCustomers**. Change its **IntegralHeight** property to **False**. The form should now look something like this:

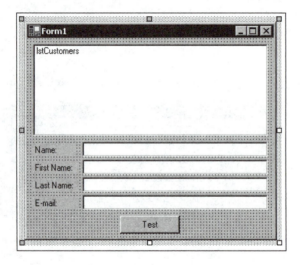

2.   Open the code editor for **Form1** and add this member to the top of the class definition:

```
Public Class Form1
    Inherits System.Windows.Forms.Form

    ' members...
    Private _customers As New ArrayList()
```

3.   Now, add this method to the `Form1` class:

```
' CreateCustomer - create a new customer...
Public Function CreateCustomer(ByVal firstName As String, _
    ByVal lastName As String, ByVal email As String) As Customer
```

```
' create the new customer...
Dim newCustomer As Customer
newCustomer.FirstName = firstName
newCustomer.LastName = lastName
newCustomer.Email = email

' add it to the list...
_customers.Add(newCustomer)

' add it to the view...
lstCustomers.Items.Add(newCustomer)

' return the customer...
Return newCustomer

End Function
```

4. Next, find the `btnTest_Click` method and make these changes to the code:

```
Private Sub btnTest_Click(ByVal sender As System.Object, _
       ByVal e As System.EventArgs) Handles btnTest.Click

    ' create some customers...
    CreateCustomer("Amir", "Aliabadi", "amir@pretendcompany.com")
    CreateCustomer("Gretchen", "Aliabadi", _
                "gretchen@pretendcompany.com")
    CreateCustomer("Ben", "Aliabadi", "ben@pretendcompany.com")

End Sub
```

5. Run the project and click the Test button. You'll see this:

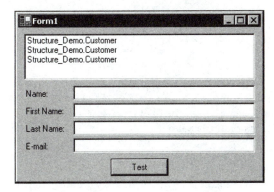

How It (Almost) Works

What I wanted to demonstrate here was that we're adding `Customer` structures to the list, but they are being displayed by the list as `Structure_Demo.Customer`. This is the full name of the class, so what we want to do is tweak `Customer` so that it can display something more meaningful. Once we've done that, we'll look at how `ArrayList` works.

239

Try It Out – Overriding ToString

1. Open the code editor for `Customer` and add this method to the structure, ensuring that it is below the member declarations:

```
' ToString...
Public Overrides Function ToString() As String
    Return Name & " (" & Email & ")"
End Function
```

2. Run the project and click **Test**. You'll see this:

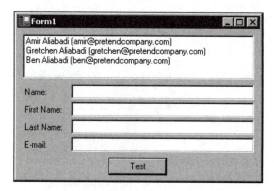

How It Works

Whenever a `Customer` structure is added to the list, the listbox calls the `ToString` method on the structure to get a string representation of that structure. With this code, we override the default functionality of `ToString` so that rather than returning the full name of the structure, we get some interesting text:

```
' ToString...
Public Overrides Function ToString() As String
    Return Name & " (" & Email & ")"
End Function
```

An `ArrayList` can be used to store a list of objects/structures of any type (in contrast to a regular array) – in fact, you can mix the types within an `ArrayList`, a topic we'll be talking about in a little while. What we've done is create a method called `CreateCustomer` that initializes a new `Customer` structure based on parameters that it is passed:

```
' CreateCustomer - create a new customer...
Public Function CreateCustomer(ByVal firstName As String, _
    ByVal lastName As String, ByVal email As String) As Customer

    ' create the new customer...
    Dim newCustomer As Customer
    newCustomer.FirstName = firstName
    newCustomer.LastName = lastName
    newCustomer.Email = email
```

Once the structure has been initialized, we add it to the `ArrayList` stored in `_customers`:

```
' add it to the list...
_customers.Add(newCustomer)
```

We also add it to the list itself, like this:

```
' add it to the view...
lstCustomers.Items.Add(newCustomer)
```

Finally, we can return the newly initialized `Customer` structure back to the caller:

```
' return the customer...
Return newCustomer

End Function
```

With `CreateCustomer` defined, we can just call it to add new members to the `ArrayList` and to the list control:

```
Private Sub btnTest_Click(ByVal sender As System.Object, _
        ByVal e As System.EventArgs) Handles btnTest.Click

    ' create some customers...
    CreateCustomer("Amir", "Aliabadi", "amir@pretendcompany.com")
    CreateCustomer("Gretchen", "Aliabadi", _
                   "gretchen@pretendcompany.com")
    CreateCustomer("Ben", "Aliabadi", "ben@pretendcompany.com")

End Sub
```

Deleting from an ArrayList

OK, so now we know the principle behind an `ArrayList`. Let's now use it to do something that's traditionally hard to do with arrays but is pretty easy to do with an `ArrayList`.

Try It Out – Deleting Customers

1. Using the Designer for **Form1**, add a new button. Change its **Name** property to **btnDelete** and its **Text** property to **Delete**:

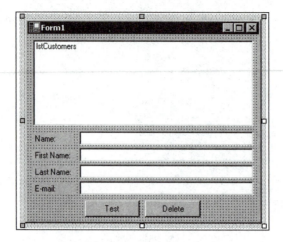

2. Double-click on the **Delete** button. Add this code:

```
Private Sub btnDelete_Click(ByVal sender As System.Object, _
    ByVal e As System.EventArgs) Handles btnDelete.Click

    ' what customer to we want to select?
    If SelectedCustomer.IsEmpty = False Then

        ' ask the user...
        If MessageBox.Show("Are you sure you want to delete " & _
            SelectedCustomer.Name & "?", "Structure Demo", _
            MessageBoxButtons.YesNo, MessageBoxIcon.Question) _
            = DialogResult.Yes Then

            ' store the customer that we want to delete...
            Dim deleteCustomer As Customer = SelectedCustomer

            ' remove it from the arraylist...
            _customers.Remove(deleteCustomer)
            ' remove it from the list view...
            lstCustomers.Items.Remove(deleteCustomer)

        End If

    Else
        MessageBox.Show("You must select a customer.", _
                    "Structure Demo")
    End If

End Sub
```

3. Next, add this property (below the section of code we added in Step 2):

```
Public ReadOnly Property SelectedCustomer() As Customer
    Get

        ' do we have a selection?
        If lstCustomers.SelectedIndex <> -1 Then

            ' return the selected customer...
            Return lstCustomers.Items(lstCustomers.SelectedIndex)

        End If

    End Get
End Property
```

> **Remember, adding the `ReadOnly` keyword to a property definition prevents the developer from being able to change the value contained in the property.**

4. Finally, open the code editor for `Customer` and add this method:

```
' IsEmpty - are we populated?
Public Function IsEmpty() As Boolean
    If FirstName = "" Then
        Return True
    Else
        Return False
    End If
End Function
```

5. Run the project and click the Test button. *Do not* select a customer and click Delete. You'll see this:

6. Now select a customer and click Delete. You'll see something like this:

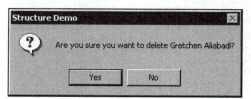

7. Click Yes and the person you selected will be removed from the list:

243

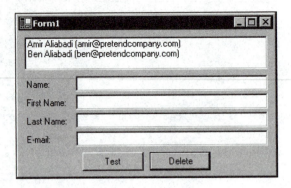

How It Works

The trick here is to build a property that will return the `Customer` structure that's selected in the list back to the caller on demand.

If no selection has been made in the list (or the list is empty) the `ListBox` control's `SelectedIndex` property will return −1. If we get a number other than this, an item has been selected and we can simply return this item back to the caller:

```
Public ReadOnly Property SelectedCustomer() As Customer
    Get

        ' do we have a selection?
        If lstCustomers.SelectedIndex <> -1 Then

            ' return the selected customer...
            Return lstCustomers.Items(lstCustomers.SelectedIndex)

        End If

    End Get
End Property
```

However, there is a problem. Due to the way structures work, the caller will be given a `Customer` structure that they can use regardless of whether or not one was actually selected. We need a way of determining whether or not a structure is empty, hence the `IsEmpty` method that we added to `Customer`:

```
' IsEmpty - are we populated?
Public Function IsEmpty() As Boolean
    If FirstName = "" Then
        Return True
    Else
        Return False
    End If
End Function
```

This method will return `True` if the `FirstName` member has not been populated or `False` if the member has been populated.

Inside the `Click` event for the `Delete` button, we can test to see if `SelectedCustomer` is empty, in other words whether or not a selection has been made:

```
' what customer to we want to select?
If SelectedCustomer.IsEmpty = False Then
```

If a selection has been made, we ask the user if they really want to go ahead with the deletion:

```
' ask the user...
If MessageBox.Show("Are you sure you want to delete " & _
    SelectedCustomer.Name & "?", "Structure Demo", _
    MessageBoxButtons.YesNo, MessageBoxIcon.Question) _
    = DialogResult.Yes Then
```

If the user does want to delete, we'll get a return value from `MessageBox.Show` equal to `DialogResult.Yes`. The `Remove` method of the `ArrayList` can then be used to remove the offending customer!

```
' remove it from the arraylist...
_customers.Remove(SelectedCustomer)
```

We also use a similar technique to remove the customer from the listbox as well:

```
' remove it from the list view...
lstCustomers.Items.Remove(SelectedCustomer)

        End If

    Else
        MessageBox.Show("You must select a customer.", _
                        "Structure Demo")
    End If

End Sub
```

Showing Items in the ArrayList

For completeness, let's add a quick piece of functionality to enhance the UI of our application.

Try It Out – Showing Details of the Selected Item

1. Using the Designer for Form1, double-click on the listbox. This will create a new `SelectedIndexChanged` event handler. Add this code:

```
Private Sub lstCustomers_SelectedIndexChanged(ByVal _
    sender As System.Object, ByVal e As System.EventArgs) _
    Handles lstCustomers.SelectedIndexChanged
    DisplayCustomer(SelectedCustomer)
End Sub
```

2. Run the project and click the `Test` button to populate the listbox. Now when you select items from the list they will appear in the fields at the bottom of the display:

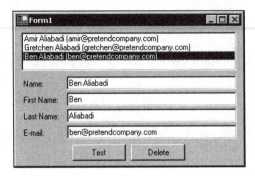

Collections

One thing that the .NET Framework uses all over the place is the **collection**. This is a way of easily creating *ad hoc* groups of similar or related items. If you take a look back at our `Structure Demo` code and peek into the `CreateCustomer` method, you'll notice that when adding items to the `ArrayList` and to the listbox, we use a method called `Add`:

```
' add it to the list...
_customers.Add(newCustomer)

' add it to the view...
lstCustomers.Items.Add(newCustomer)
```

Again, if we look at the code that deletes a customer, we use a method called `Remove` on both objects:

```
' remove it from the arraylist...
_customers.Remove(SelectedCustomer)

' remove it from the list view...
lstCustomers.Items.Remove(SelectedCustomer)
```

Microsoft is very keen to see developers use the collection paradigm whenever they need to work with a list of items. It's also keen to see collections work in the same way irrespective of what they actually hold – which is why we use `Add` to add an item and `Remove` to remove an item, even though we're using a `System.Collections.ArrayList` object in one case and a `System.Windows.Forms.ListBox.ObjectCollection` object in another. This is something that Microsoft has taken a great deal of care over when building the Framework. Consistency is good – it allows us to map an understanding of one thing and use that same understanding with a similar thing. When designing the classes for use in your application, you should take steps to follow the conventions that Microsoft has laid down. For example, if you have a collection class and want to create a method the removes an item, call it `Remove` not `Delete`. Developers using your class will have an intuitive understanding of what `Remove` does because they're familiar with it. On the other hand, developers would "double-take" `Delete` because this has a different connotation.

One of the problems with using an `ArrayList` is that the developer who has an array list cannot guarantee that every item in the list is of the same type. Note that `ArrayList` makes no guarantees about the type of object (when I say object, I mean "object or structure") that it has a hold of. For this reason, each time an item is extracted from the `ArrayList`, the type should be checked to minimize the chances of causing an error.

The solution is to create a **strongly-typed collection**. This is a separate class that contains only objects of a particular type. They're very easy to create and, according to .NET best-programming standards as defined by Microsoft, the best way to create one is to derive a new class from `System.Collections.CollectionBase`, and add two methods (`Add` and `Remove`) and one property (`Item`):

- ❑ `Add` – adds a new item to the collection
- ❑ `Remove` – removes an items from the collection
- ❑ `Item` – returns the item at the given index in the collection

Although we're going to be creating a strongly-typed collection class for holding *structures*, this technique works equally well for classes.

Creating CustomerCollection

Let's look at how we can create a `CustomerCollection` class that's designed to hold a collection of `Customer` structures.

Try It Out – Creating CustomerCollection

1. Using the Solution Explorer, create a new class called `CustomerCollection`. Set the class to inherit from `CollectionBase`, and add a method such that your code now looks like this:

```
Public Class CustomerCollection
    Inherits System.Collections.CollectionBase
    ' Add - add a customer...
    Public Sub Add(ByVal newCustomer As Customer)
        Me.List.Add(newCustomer)
    End Sub

End Class
```

2. Then, add this method:

```
' Remove - delete a customer...
Public Sub Remove(ByVal removeCustomer As Customer)
    Me.List.Remove(removeCustomer)
End Sub
```

3. Finally, open the code editor for `Form1` and find the definition for the `_customers` member. Change its type from `ArrayList` to `CustomerCollection`:

```
Public Class Form1
    Inherits System.Windows.Forms.Form
```

```
' members...
    Private _customers As New CustomerCollection()
```

4. Run the project. The application should work as it did before.

How It Works

The `System.Collections.CollectionBase` class contains a basic implementation of a collection that can hold any objects. In that respect it's very similar to an `ArrayList`. However, the advantage comes when we add our own methods to the class that inherits from `CollectionBase` as is the case with `CustomerCollection`.

Since we've provided a version of `Add` that only accepts a `Customer` structure, it's impossible to put anything into the array that isn't a `Customer`. Here's what IntelliSense looks like when we access the `Add` method in code:

You can see there that IntelliSense is telling us that the only thing we can pass through to `Add` is a `Structure_Demo.Customer` structure.

Internally, `CollectionBase` provides us with a protected property called `List` that we can use to store our items in. That's precisely what we use when we need to add or remove items from the list:

```
' Add - add a customer...
Public Sub Add(ByVal newCustomer As Customer)
    Me.List.Add(newCustomer)
End Sub

' Remove - delete a customer...
Public Sub Remove(ByVal removeCustomer As Customer)
    Me.List.Remove(removeCustomer)
End Sub
```

The reason why we're supposed to build collections like this is that it's a .NET best practice. As a newcomer to .NET programming, you may not appreciate just how useful this is – but trust me – it is! Whenever you need to use a collection of classes that you build yourself, this technique is the right way to go.

Adding an Item Property

Back when we introduced collections, we mentioned that we were supposed to add two methods and one property. We've seen the methods but not the property – let's look at it now.

Try It Out – Adding an Item Property

1. Open the code editor for `CustomerCollection` and add this code:

```
' Item - return a customer given an index...
Default Public Property Item(ByVal index As Integer) As Customer
    Get
        Return Me.List.Item(index)
    End Get
    Set(ByVal Value As Customer)
        Me.List.Item(index) = Value
    End Set
End Property
```

2. To prove that this works, open the code editor for **Form1**. Find the `SelectedCustomer` property and make this change:

```
' return the selected customer...
Return _customers(lstCustomers.SelectedIndex)
```

3. Run the project. Click the **Test** button and notice that when you select items in the list the details are shown in the fields as they were before.

How It Works

The `Item` property is actually very important as it gives the developer direct access to the data stored in the list, but maintains the strongly-typed nature of the collection.

If you look at the code again for `SelectedCustomer`, you'll notice that when we wanted to return the given item from within `_customers`, we didn't have to provide the property name of `Item`. Instead, `_customers` behaved as if it were an array:

```
' do we have a selection?
If lstCustomers.SelectedIndex <> -1 Then

    ' return the selected customer...
    Return _customers(lstCustomers.SelectedIndex)

End If
```

If we look at what IntelliSense told us when we entered that line, we saw this:

```
' return the selected customer...
Return _customers(lstcustome|
          Item (index As Integer) As Structure_Demo.Customer
End If
```

You can see that we're being told to enter the index of the item that we require and that we should expect to get a `Customer` structure back in return.

The reason why we don't have to specify the property name of `Item` is that we marked the property as default by using the `Default` keyword:

```
' Item - return a customer given an index...
Default Public Property Item(ByVal index As Integer) As Customer
```

```
      Get
           Return Me.List.Item(index)
      End Get
      Set(ByVal Value As Customer)
           Me.List.Item(index) = Value
      End Set
  End Property
```

A given class can only have a single default property, and that property must take a parameter of some kind. This parameter must be an index or search term of some description. The one we've used here provides an index to an element in an array. You can have multiple overloaded versions of the same property so you could provide an e-mail address rather than an index. This gives a great deal of flexibility.

What we have at this point is the following:

❑   A way of storing a list of `Customer` structures, and just `Customer` structures

❑   A way of adding new items to the collection on demand

❑   A way of removing existing items from the collection on demand

❑   A way of accessing members in the collection as if it were a normal array

Building Lookup Tables with Hashtable

So far, whenever we want to find something in an array or in a collection we have to provide an integer index representing the position of the item. It's quite common to end up needing a way of being able to look up an item in a collection when you have something other than an index. For example, we might want to find a `Customer` structure when we provide an e-mail address.

In this section we'll take a look at `System.Collections.Hashtable`. This is a special kind of collection that works on a "key-value" principle.

Each item in the collection is given a **key**. This key can be used at a later time to "unlock" the value. So, if I add Amir's `Customer` structure to the `Hashtable`, I'll be given a key that matches his e-mail address of `amir@pretendcompany.com`. If at a later time I come along with that key, I'll be able to find his record quickly. As we know, all .NET objects are derived from an object called `System.Object`. This object itself provides a method called `GetHashCode`. This method is used to return an integer value that uniquely identifies the object. So, if you create a class of your own and generate ten instances of that class, each call to `GetHashCode` will return a value that represents the object. More importantly, this value never changes for a given object, so if you call `GetHashCode` on an object called `MyObject`, you might get a value back of 27. On every subsequent call to `GetHashCode` on that object, you'll always get 27.

> **In the vast majority of cases, you'll never need to supply your own implementation of `GetHashCode`.**

Whenever you add an object to the `Hashtable`, it calls `GetHashCode` on the object to be added and uses this as the key. Likewise, whenever you want to retrieve an object from the `Hashtable`, it calls `GetHashCode` on the object to get a lookup key and matches that key against the ones it has in the list. When it finds it, it will return the related value to you.

Lookups from a Hashtable are very, very fast. Irrespective of whatever object you pass in, you're only ever matching on a relatively small integer ID.

An integer ID takes up four bytes of memory, so if you pass in a 100-character string (which is 200-bytes long), the lookup code only ever needs to compare four bytes, which makes everything run really quickly.

Try It Out – Using a Hashtable

1. Open the code editor for `CustomerCollection`. Add this member to the top of the class definition:

```
Public Class CustomerCollection
    Inherits System.Collections.CollectionBase

    ' members...
    Private _emailHashtable As New Hashtable()
```

2. Next, add this read-only property:

```
' EmailHashtable - return the e-mail hashtable...
Public ReadOnly Property EmailHashtable() As Hashtable
    Get
        Return _emailHashtable
    End Get
End Property
```

3. Now, make this change to the `Add` property:

```
' Add - add a customer...
Public Sub Add(ByVal newCustomer As Customer)

    Me.List.Add(newCustomer)
    ' add to the hashtable...
    EmailHashtable.Add(newCustomer.Email, newCustomer)

End Sub
```

4. Next, add this alternative, overloaded version of `Item` that allows us to find a customer by giving an e-mail address:

```
' Alternative version of Item. Finds customer from e-mail address...
Default Public ReadOnly Property Item(ByVal email As String) _
        As Customer
    Get
```

```
        Return EmailHashtable.Item(email)
      End Get
End Property
```

5. Open the Designer for Form1, shrink the txtEmail control, and add a new button. Set the Name property of the button to btnLookupEmail and the Text property to Lookup:

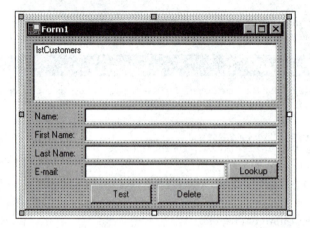

6. Double-click on the Lookup button and add this code:

```
Private Sub btnLookupEmail_Click(ByVal sender As System.Object, _
      ByVal e As System.EventArgs) Handles btnLookupEmail.Click
```

```
      ' what e-mail address do we want to find?
      Dim findEmail As String = txtEmailName.Text

      ' lookup and display the customer by email...
      Dim foundCustomer As Customer
      foundCustomer = _customers(findEmail)
      If foundCustomer.IsEmpty = False Then

          ' show the customer's name...
          MessageBox.Show("The name is: " & foundCustomer.Name, _
                      "Structure Demo")

      Else

          ' display an error...
          MessageBox.Show( _
            "There is no customer with the e-mail address " & _
            findEmail & ".", "Structure Demo")

      End If

End Sub
```

7. Run the project and click the **Test** button. If you enter an e-mail address that doesn't exist into the E-mail textbox and click **Lookup**, you'll see something like this:

8. However, if you do enter one that exists, for example, ben @pretendcompany.com, the name will be shown:

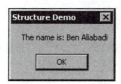

How It Works

What we've done is added a new member to the `CustomerCollection` class that can be used to hold a `Hashtable`:

```
' members...
Private _emailHashtable As New Hashtable()
```

Whenever we add a new `Customer` to the collection, we also add it to the `Hashtable`:

```
' Add - add a customer...
Public Sub Add(ByVal newCustomer As Customer)

    Me.List.Add(newCustomer)

    ' add to the hashtable...
    EmailHashtable.Add(newCustomer.Email, newCustomer)

End Sub
```

However, unlike the kinds of `Add` methods that we've seen earlier, this method takes two parameters. The first is the key – and we're using the e-mail address as the key. The key can be any object you like, but it must be unique. You cannot supply the same key twice. (If you do, an exception will be thrown.) The second parameter is the value that you want to link the key to, so whenever we give that key to the `Hashtable`, we'll get that object back.

The next trick was to create an overloaded version of the default `Item` property. This one, however, takes a string as its only parameter. This is what happens when we access it from code:

```
' lookup and display the customer by email...
Dim foundCustomer As Customer
foundCustomer = _customers(fin|
If foundCustomer.IsEmp  ▲ 2 of 2 ▼  Item (email As String) As Structure_Demo.Customer
```

This time we can provide either an index or an e-mail address. If we use an e-mail address we'll end up using the alternative version of `Item` and this defers to the `Item` property of the `Hashtable` object. This takes a key and returns the related item, providing the key can be found:

```
Default Public ReadOnly Property Item(ByVal email As String) _
        As Customer
    Get
        Return EmailHashtable.Item(email)
    End Get
End Property
```

So, at this point we have a collection class that not only enables us to look up items by index but also allows us to look up objects by e-mail address.

Cleaning up Remove, RemoveAt, and Clear

We fleetingly mentioned before that it isn't possible to use the same key twice in a `Hashtable`. Therefore, we have to take steps to ensure that what's in the `Hashtable` matches whatever is in the list itself.

Although we've implemented our own `Remove` method, `CollectionBase` also implements `RemoveAt` and `Clear` methods. Whereas `Remove` takes an object, `RemoveAt` takes an index. We need to provide new implementations of those that also adjust the `Hashtable`.

Try It Out – Cleaning up the List

1. Open the code editor for **Form1**. Find the `btnTest_Click` method and add this code to clear the two lists:

```
Private Sub btnTest_Click(ByVal sender As System.Object, _
        ByVal e As System.EventArgs) Handles btnTest.Click

    ' clear the lists...
    _customers.Clear()
    lstCustomers.Items.Clear()
    ' create some customers...
    CreateCustomer("Amir", "Aliabadi", "amir@pretendcompany.com")
    CreateCustomer("Gretchen", "Aliabadi", _
                "gretchen@pretendcompany.com")
    CreateCustomer("Ben", "Aliabadi", "ben@pretendcompany.com")

End Sub
```

2. To demonstrate this going wrong, run the project and click the **Test** button. When the list has loaded, click the **Test** button again. An exception will be thrown telling us that the item has been used already. (This illustrates my earlier point about how a `Hashtable` can only contain one instance of a particular key.)

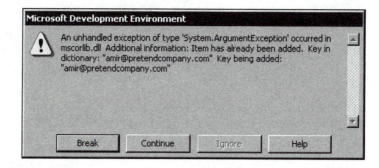

3. Click the **Continue** button. This will stop the debugging session.

4. Using the code editor, add this method to `CustomerCollection`:

```
' Clear - provide a new implementation of clear...
Public Shadows Sub Clear()

    ' get collectionbase to clear...
    MyBase.Clear()

    ' clear our hashtable...
    EmailHashtable.Clear()

End Sub
```

5. Next, make this change to `Remove`:

```
' Remove - delete a customer...
Public Sub Remove(ByVal removeCustomer As Customer)

    ' remove from our list...
    Me.List.Remove(removeCustomer)

    ' remove from the hashtable...
    EmailHashtable.Remove(removeCustomer.Email)

End Sub
```

6. Now, add this new version of `RemoveAt` to override the default functionality defined in `CollectionBase`:

```
' RemoveAt - remove an item by index...
Public Shadows Sub RemoveAt(ByVal index As Integer)
    Remove(Item(index))
End Sub
```

7. Run the project. Click **Test** to load the items and click **Test** again straight afterwards. This won't cause an exception to be thrown again.

How It Works

The exception isn't thrown the second time round because we are now making sure that the `Hashtable` and the internal list maintained by `CollectionBase` are properly synchronized. Specifically, whenever our `CustomerCollection` list is cleared using the `Clear` method, we make sure that the `Hashtable` is also cleared.

To clear the internal list maintained by `CollectionBase`, we ask the base class to use its own `Clear` implementation rather than trying to provide our own implementation. Straight after that, we call `Clear` on the `Hashtable`:

```
' Clear - provide a new implementation of clear...
Public Shadows Sub Clear()

    ' get collectionbase to clear...
    MyBase.Clear()

    ' clear our hashtable...
    EmailHashtable.Clear()

End Sub
```

You'll also find that when you delete items from the collection by using `Remove`, the corresponding entry is also removed from the `Hashtable`, because of the line added in Step 5 above.

The `Shadows` keyword indicates that this `Clear` procedure should be used instead of the `Clear` in the base class. Even though they do here, the arguments and the return type do not have to match those in the base class procedure.

Shadows and Overrides

We've used the `Shadows` keyword here to override a method. Remember in Chapter 4 we achieved something similar using `Overrides` – creating a new method that had the same name and arguments as a method in the base class. Let's briefly take a look at the difference between `Shadows` and `Overrides`.

In order to use `Overrides` on a method, the equivalent method in the base class must be specified as `Overridable`. If it is not, we are not allowed to override it using `Overrides`, however, we can use the `Shadows` keyword.

So why have two words? And if they do the same thing, why are we always allowed to use one, but only sometimes use the other? The reasons are quite obscure. In fact, you probably don't need to understand the distinction any more than we've already mentioned. However, here is an explanation of the distinction – if you're not interested, just skip onto the *Case Sensitivity* section.

In Chapter 4 we discussed polymorphism, and saw that an object of a particular class, or an object derived from it, could be passed to a method as a parameter. In that chapter we had `Car` objects, from which we derived the more specialized `SportsCar` objects. `Car` had a method called `CalculateAcceleration`, and declared that this method was `Overridable`. Then `SportsCar` had its own `CalculateAcceleration` method so did override it, using the `Overrides` keyword.

We could pass a `SportsCar` object into a method that expected a `Car` object because of polymorphism. If this method, which really expected a `Car` object, uses the `SportsCar` object's `CalculateAcceleration` method, the `SportsCar` version of the method will be called. You should be aware that the specialized class could behave differently from the base class. This is expected though, because the method is declared as `Overridable` giving you warning in advance.

Now let's consider where `Shadows` fits in. If `CalculateAcceleration` was not declared as `Overridable` in `Car`, you could rely on `CalculateAcceleration` always behaving the same in any class that derived from `Car`. What happens if a `SportsCar` class is added at a later date and you want it to have its own `CalculateAcceleration` method? In this case, you could declare the method in `SportsCar` with the `Shadows` keyword.

If a method takes `SportsCar` as a parameter, or has declared its own `SportsCar` object, then the `SportsCar` version will be used. But if a `SportsCar` object is passed to a method that expects a `Car` object, and that method will call `CalculateAcceleration`, the `Car` version will be used – there will be no surprises for the method that relies on having the function behave in the expected way.

This has implications for class design – should you make a method `Overridable` or not? It can be better to use `Overridable` as this avoids conflict with the base class's design and implementation. It also allows us to utilize polymorphism in a more common and familiar manner. There are no hard and fast rules here, but remember that even if a method is not `Overridable`, we still have the freedom to use `Shadows`.

Don't worry too much about the distinction. You probably won't come across the situation too often, and when you are actually facing the problem this description will seem much clearer than it does now!

Case Sensitivity

It's about this time that case sensitivity rears its ugly head again. If you run the project and click **Test**, you'll see something like this if you don't specify the e-mail address as lowercase characters:

What we need to do is get the collection to ignore case on the key. We'll do this by making sure that, whenever we save a key, we transform the e-mail address into all lowercase characters. Whenever we look up based on a key, we'll transform whatever we search for into lowercase characters too.

Try It Out – Case Sensitivity

1. Open the code editor for `CustomerCollection` and make this change to the `Add` method:

```
' Add - add a customer...
Public Sub Add(ByVal newCustomer As Customer)

    ' add to the list...
    Me.List.Add(newCustomer)
```

```
                  ' add to the hashtable...
                  Dim useEmail As String
                  useEmail = newCustomer.Email.ToLower
                  EmailHashtable.Add(useEmail, newCustomer)
```

```
        End Sub
```

2. Now, find the version of the `Item` property that takes an e-mail address and add this code:

```
Default Public ReadOnly Property Item(ByVal email As String) _
        As Customer
    Get

            ' use a lower case term...
            email = email.ToLower()
            Return EmailHashtable.Item(email)

        End Get
End Property
```

3. Next, find the `Remove` method and add this code:

```
' Remove - delete a customer...
Public Sub Remove(ByVal removeCustomer As Customer)

        ' remove from our list...
        Me.List.Remove(removeCustomer)

        ' remove from the hashtable...
        Dim useEmail As String
        useEmail = removeCustomer.Email.ToLower()
        EmailHashtable.Remove(useEmail)
```

```
        End Sub
```

4. Run the project and click **Test**. Now if you enter the e-mail address in a non-matching case the lookup will still work:

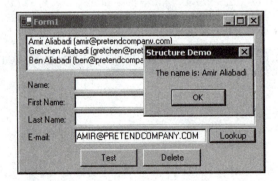

How It Works

Back in Chapter 3 we saw how we could do case-insensitive string comparisons using the `String.Compare` method. We can't use this technique here because the `Hashtable` is handling the comparison and, ideally, we don't want to produce our own version of the comparison code that `Hashtable` uses just to do a case-insensitive match.

What we can do is use the `ToLower` method available on strings. This creates a new string where all of the characters are transformed into the lower-case equivalent, so if we pass aMiR@pRETendCOMpany.COM we'll always get amir@pretendcompany.com out.

When we add an item to the collection, we get `ToLower` to convert the e-mail address stored in the `Customer` structure so that it is always in lower case:

```
Dim useEmail As String
useEmail = newCustomer.Email.ToLower()
EmailHashtable.Add(useEmail, newCustomer)
```

Likewise, when we actually do the lookup, we also turn whatever value is passed in as a parameter into all lowercase characters:

```
' use a lower case term...
email = email.ToLower()
Return EmailHashtable.Item(email)
```

Providing you're consistent with it, what this does is make uppercase characters "go away" – in other words you'll never end up with uppercase characters being stored in the key or being checked against the key.

> This technique for removing the problem of uppercase characters can be used for normal string comparisons, but **String.Compare** is more efficient.

That brings us to the end of our discussions on collections. At this point, you should know how to build your own custom collections for your classes and structures and how to use the `Hashtable` object to provide a little extra functionality.

Advanced Array Manipulation

At the beginning of this chapter we introduced the concept of arrays. We've left some of the more advanced discussions on arrays until later in the chapter, namely those involving adjusting the size of an array and multidimensional arrays.

If I had been writing a book on writing VB code five years ago, these topics would not have been left until the end of this chapter. Being able to manipulate the size of an array from code, and being able to store complex sets of data in an array is important, but with .NET it's far easier to achieve both of these using the collection functionality that the majority of this chapter discusses. These next two sections are included for completeness.

Dynamic Arrays

When we're using an array, if we want to change its size in order to add items, or clean up space when we remove items, we need to use the ReDim keyword to make it a **dynamic array**. This is short for, not surprisingly, **re-dimension**. We'll reuse the Array Demo project we used at the start of the chapter and tweak it so that we can add new friends to the array after the initial array has been created.

Try It Out – Using ReDim

1. Find and open the Array Demo project. Open the code editor for Form1 and replace the code in the AddFriendsToList method so that it looks like this:

```
Sub AddFriendsToList(ByVal friends() As String)
```

```
    ' add each friend...
    Dim friendName As String
    For Each friendName In friends

        ' add it...
        lstFriends.Items.Add("[" & friendName & "]")

    Next
```

```
End Sub
```

2. Run the project and click Go. You should see this:

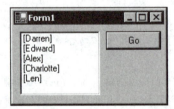

The reason why I've chosen to display each name enclosed in brackets will become apparent later.

3. Now, close the project and make this change to btnGo_Click.

```
Private Sub btnGo_Click(ByVal sender As System.Object, _
        ByVal e As System.EventArgs) Handles btnGo.Click
```

```
    ' define an array to hold friends in...
    Dim friends() As String = {"Darren", "Edward", "Alex", _
                               "Charlotte", "Len"}
```

```
    ' make friends bigger!
    ReDim friends(6)
    friends(5) = "Zoe"
    friends(6) = "Faye"
```

```
' show the friends...
AddFriendsToList(friends)

End Sub
```

4. Run the project and click **Go**. You'll see this:

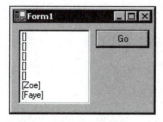

How It Works

After defining an array of length 5, we use the `ReDim` keyword to re-dimension to have an upper bound of 6, which as we know gives it a size of 7. After we do that, we have two new items in the array to play with – items 5 and 6:

```
' make friends bigger!
ReDim friends(6)
friends(5) = "Zoe"
friends(6) = "Faye"
```

Then, we can pass the resized array through to `AddFriendsToList`:

```
' show the friends...
AddFriendsToList(friends)
```

But, as you can see from the results, the values for the first five items have been lost. (This is why we wrapped brackets around the results – if the name stored in the array is blank we still see something appear in the list.) `ReDim` does indeed resize the array, but by default it will also *clear* the array.

We can solve this problem by using the `Preserve` keyword. When an array is re-dimensioned, by default all of the values in the array are cleared, losing the values we defined when we initialized the array in the first place.

Using Preserve

By including the `Preserve` keyword with the `ReDim` keyword, we can ask Visual Basic .NET not to clear the existing items. One thing to remember is that if you use `Preserve` to make an array smaller than it originally was, data will be lost from the eliminated elements.

Try It Out – Using Preserve

1. Open the code editor for **Form1** and find the `btnGo_Click` method. Add the `Preserve` keyword to the `ReDim` statement:

```
Private Sub btnGo_Click(ByVal sender As System.Object, _
            ByVal e As System.EventArgs) Handles btnGo.Click

    ' define an array to hold friends in...
    Dim friends() As String = {"Darren", "Edward", "Alex", _
                            "Charlotte", "Len"}

    ' make friends bigger!
    ReDim Preserve friends(6)
    friends(5) = "Zoe"
    friends(6) = "Faye"

    ' show the friends...
    AddFriendsToList(friends)

End Sub
```

2. Run the project and click **Go**. You should now find that the existing items in the array are preserved.

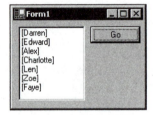

Multidimensional Arrays

Multidimensional arrays let you hold tables of data in an array. Except in some very specific cases, it would be unusual for you to have to use these instead of using a structure or class in combination with a collection or a standard array of some kind. We're going to illustrate them quickly here as there's a chance you'll come across them from time to time, especially when dealing with some pretty specific bits of computer science and some math operations.

Here's some data you might want to store:

Name	E-mail address	Sex
Darren	darren@pretendcompany.com	M
Edward	edward@pretendcompany.com	M
Alex	alex@pretendcompany.com	M
Charlotte	charlotte@pretendcompany.com	F
Len	len@pretendcompany.com	F
Zoe	zoe@pretendcompany.com	F
Faye	faye@pretendcompany.com	F

You can probably tell how we would store that information in a structure:

```
Public Structure Person

    Public Name As String
    Public Email As String
    Public Sex As String

End Structure
```

However, we can store that information in an array too. Again, I'm including this for completeness as you might find some older code that works in this way, but if I were giving you advice on how to do this, I'd suggest using a structure like Person and a collection.

Try It Out – Multidimensional Arrays

1. Open the code editor for Form1. Add this enumeration to the top of the class:

```
Public Class Form1
    Inherits System.Windows.Forms.Form

    ' enum...
    Public Enum PersonDataIndex As Integer
        Name = 0
        Email = 1
        Sex = 2
    End Enum
```

2. Now, make these changes to btnGo_Click:

```
Private Sub btnGo_Click(ByVal sender As System.Object, _
        ByVal e As System.EventArgs) Handles btnGo.Click

    ' define an array to hold friends in...
    Dim friends(2, 2) As String
    ' set the data...
    friends(0, PersonDataIndex.Name) = "Darren"
    friends(0, PersonDataIndex.Email) = "darren@pretendcompany.com"
    friends(0, PersonDataIndex.Sex) = "M"

    friends(1, PersonDataIndex.Name) = "Edward"
    friends(1, PersonDataIndex.Email) = "edward@pretendcompany.com"
    friends(1, PersonDataIndex.Sex) = "M"

    friends(2, PersonDataIndex.Name) = "Len"
    friends(2, PersonDataIndex.Email) = "len@pretendcompany.com"
    friends(2, PersonDataIndex.Sex) = "F"

    ' show the friends...
    AddFriendsToList(friends)

End Sub
```

3. Then, make these changes to `AddFriendsToList`:

```
Sub AddFriendsToList(ByVal friends(,) As String)

    ' add each friend...
    Dim row As Integer
    For row = 0 To UBound(friends, 1)

        ' we'll need a string...
        Dim buf As String = ""

        ' go through each part...
        Dim column As Integer
        For column = 0 To UBound(friends, 2)

            ' add it...
            buf &= friends(row, column) & ", "

        Next

        ' add the string...
        lstFriends.Items.Add(buf)

    Next

End Sub
```

4. Run the project and click **Go**. You'll see this:

How It Works

So far, when we've defined arrays, we've provided just a single dimension. We can, in theory, provide a number of dimensions that are only limited by the long data type, but in this exercise we've provided two:

```
Private Sub btnGo_Click(ByVal sender As System.Object, _
         ByVal e As System.EventArgs) Handles btnGo.Click

    ' define an array to hold friends in...
    Dim friends(2, 2) As String
```

This creates a "grid" that's three rows deep and three columns across.

We can then use a coordinate system to access each "cell" in that grid. We specify the row first, then the column, so here we're using the first ("zeroth") row and using the `PersonDataIndex` enumeration to enter data into each column for that row. (Using an enumeration in this way will make your life much easier if you end up having to work with multidimensional arrays.)

```
' set the data...
friends(0, PersonDataIndex.Name) = "Darren"
friends(0, PersonDataIndex.Email) = "darren@pretendcompany.com"
friends(0, PersonDataIndex.Sex) = "M"
```

After the first row, we can do the second:

```
friends(1, PersonDataIndex.Name) = "Edward"
friends(1, PersonDataIndex.Email) = "edward@pretendcompany.com"
friends(1, PersonDataIndex.Sex) = "M"
```

And then the third:

```
friends(2, PersonDataIndex.Name) = "Len"
friends(2, PersonDataIndex.Email) = "len@pretendcompany.com"
friends(2, PersonDataIndex.Sex) = "F"
```

Finally, we can pass the array over to `AddFriendsToList`:

```
' show the friends...
AddFriendsToList(friends)


End Sub
```

When we come to work with the list, we'll find the `For Each...Next` doesn't work so well. What we can do, though, is set up one `For...Next` loop that goes through each of the rows one at a time and for every iteration, goes through each of the columns one at a time:

```
Sub AddFriendsToList(ByVal friends(,) As String)

    ' add each friend...
    Dim row As Integer
    For row = 0 To UBound(friends, 1)
```

You can see that I've used an optional parameter on `UBound`. (`Length` will not return an appropriate value here, so we have to use `UBound`.) This specifies the dimension, and in this case, we want the first dimension, so we provide 1.

```
        ' we'll need a string...
        Dim buf As String = ""
```

As I mentioned, for each iteration of the `row` loop, we go through each of the items in the second dimension. In each iteration of this list, we tack the value stored in the cell onto the end of `buf`:

```
        ' go through each part...
        Dim column As Integer
        For column = 0 To UBound(friends, 2)

            ' add it...
            buf &= friends(row, column) & ", "

        Next
```

After we've gone through the columns, we can add the string to the list:

```
' add the string...
lstFriends.Items.Add(buf)

    Next

  End Sub
```

I'm sure you can see that working with multidimensional arrays is more complicated than working with structure collections in the way that we saw earlier in the chapter.

Summary

In this chapter, we saw some ways in which we could manage complex groups of data. We started off by looking at the concept of an array, or rather defining a special type of variable that's configured to hold a one-dimensional list of similar items rather than a single item.

We then took a look at the concepts behind enumerations and constants. Both these can be used to great effect in making more readable and manageable code. An enumeration lets you define human-readable, common sense titles to basic variable types. So rather than saying "mode=3", you can say "mode=MyModes.Menu". Constants allow us to globally define literal values and use them elsewhere in our code.

We then looked at the structure. This is a relative of the class that we've already met, and is well suited to storing lists of information. After taking a look at these we moved on to look at various types of collection, including the basic ArrayList and then saw how we could build our own powerful collection classes inherited from CollectionBase. Finally, we took a look at the Hashtable class and covered some of the less-commonly used array functionality.

Questions

1. What is an array?

2. What's the difference between a structure and a class?

3. What's the best way to build a collection?

4. What is an enumeration?

5. What is a Hashtable?

Building Windows Applications

When Microsoft first released Visual Basic, developers fell in love with it because it made building the user interface components of an application very simple. Instead of having to write thousands of lines of code to display windows – the very staple of a Windows application – developers could simply "draw" the window on the screen.

In Visual Basic, a window is known as a **form**. With .NET, this form design capability has been brought to all of the managed languages as **Windows Forms**. We've been using these forms over the course of the previous six chapters, but we haven't really given that much thought to them – focusing instead on the code that we've written inside them.

In this chapter, we'll look in detail at Windows Forms and show you how you can use Visual Basic .NET to put together fully featured Windows applications. In particular, we will look at:

- ❑ Adding features such as buttons, textboxes, and radio buttons
- ❑ Creating a simple toolbar and code buttons to respond to events
- ❑ Creating additional forms in a Windows Forms application
- ❑ Deployment of a Windows application

> Note that, on occasion, you'll hear developers refer to Windows Forms as WinForms.

Responding to Events

Building a user interface using Windows Forms is all about responding to **events** (such as Clicks), so programming for Windows is commonly known as **event-driven programming**. As you know, to build a form, we "paint" controls onto a blank window called the Designer using the mouse. Each of these controls is able to tell us when an event happens, for example if we run our program and click a button that's been painted onto a form, that button will say, "Hey, I've been clicked!" and give us an opportunity to run some code that we provide to respond to that event.

Button Events

A good way to illustrate the event "philosophy" is to wire up a button. An example would be the `Click` event that is **fired** whenever the button is clicked. We have more events than just the `Click` event, although, in day-to-day practice it's unlikely we'll use more than a handful of these.

1. Start Visual Studio .NET and select File | New | Project from the menu. Create a Windows Application project called Hello World 2 and click OK.

2. Scroll up the Properties window until you find the Text property for Form1. Change it to Hello, world! 2.0.

3. From the Toolbox, select the Button control, and then drag and drop a button onto the form. Change its Text property to Hello, world! and its Name property to btnSayHello:

4. Double-click on the button and add the following code:

```
Private Sub btnSayHello_Click(ByVal sender As System.Object, _
            ByVal e As System.EventArgs) Handles btnSayHello.Click

    ' say hello!
    MsgBox("Hello, world!")

End Sub
```

5. Drop down the left list at the top of the code window. You'll see this:

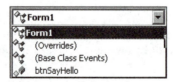

Notice that the last three items are indented slightly. This tells us that (Overrides), (Base Class Events), and btnSayHello are all related to Form1. btnSayHello is a **member** of Form1. As we add more members to the form, they will appear in this list.

6. Before we go on, let's take a quick look at the right list. Drop it down, and you'll see this:

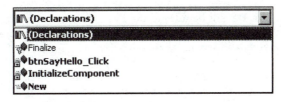

The contents of the right list change depending on the item selected from the left list. The right list lets us navigate through items related to whatever we've selected in the left. In this case, its main job is to show us the methods and properties that we've added to the class.

The (Declarations) entry takes us to the top of the class where we can change the definition of the class and add member variables.

The Finalize option is quite interesting – whenever an entry in the right list appears in faint (as opposed to **bold**) text, the method doesn't exist. However, selecting the object will make Visual Basic .NET create a definition for the function we selected. In this case, if we select Finalize, Visual Basic .NET will create a new method called Finalize and add it to the class.

You'll notice that Visual Basic .NET adds a little icon to the left of everything it displays in these lists. These can tell you what the item in the list actually is. A small purple square represents a method, a small blue square represents a member, four-books stacked together represents a library, and three squares joined together with lines represents a class.

Visual Studio may also decorate these icons with other icons to indicate the way they are defined. For example, next to Finalize you'll see a small key, which tells us the method is **protected**. The padlock icon tells us the item is **private**.

It's not really important to memorize all of these now, but Visual Basic .NET is fairly consistent with its representations, so if you do learn them over time they will help you understand what's going on.

7. Select btnSayHello from the left list. Now, drop down the right list again:

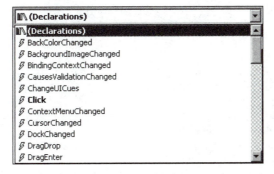

Since the left list is set to btnSayHello, now the right list exclusively shows items related to that control. In this case, we've got a huge list of events. One of those events, Click, is shown in bold because we've provided a definition for this. If you select Click, you'll be taken to the method in Form1 that provides an event handler for this method.

8. We'll now add another event handler to the button control. With **btnSayHello** still selected in the left list, select **MouseEnter** from the right list. A new event handler method will be created, and we need to add some code to it:

```
Private Sub btnSayHello_MouseEnter(ByVal sender As Object, _
        ByVal e As System.EventArgs) Handles btnSayHello.MouseEnter

    ' change the text...
    btnSayHello.Text = "The mouse is here!"

End Sub
```

The `MouseEnter` event will be fired whenever the mouse pointer "enters" the control, in other words crosses its boundary.

9. To complete this exercise, we'll need another event handler. Select **btnSayHello** from the left list and select **MouseLeave** from the right list. Again, a new event will be created, so add this code:

```
Private Sub btnSayHello_MouseLeave(ByVal sender As Object, _
        ByVal e As System.EventArgs) Handles btnSayHello.MouseLeave

    ' change the text...
    btnSayHello.Text = "The mouse has gone!"

End Sub
```

The `MouseLeave` event will be fired whenever the mouse pointer moves back outside of the control.

10. Run the project. Move the mouse over and away from the control and you'll see the text change:

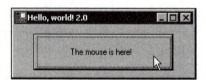

How It Works

Most of the controls that you use will have a dazzling array of events, although in day-to-day programming only a few of them will be consistently useful. For the button control, the most useful is usually the `Click` event.

Visual Basic .NET knows enough about the control to automatically create the default event handlers for us. This makes our life a lot easier and saves on typing!

When we created our `MouseEnter` event and added our custom code, here's what we had:

```
Private Sub btnSayHello_MouseEnter(ByVal sender As Object, _
        ByVal e As System.EventArgs) Handles btnSayHello.MouseEnter
```

```
    ' change the text...
    btnSayHello.Text = "The mouse is here!"

End Sub
```

You'll notice that at the end of the method definition is the `Handles` keyword. This ties the method definition into the `btnSayHello.MouseEnter` subroutine. When the button fires this event, our code will be executed.

Although previously we've only changed the button's `Text` property at design time using the Properties window, here you can see that we can change it at run time too.

> As a quick reminder here, **design time** is the term used to define the period of time that you're actually writing the program, in other words, working with the Designer or adding code. **Run time** is the term used to define the period of time when the program is running.

Likewise, the `MouseLeave` event works in a very similar way:

```
Private Sub btnSayHello_MouseLeave(ByVal sender As Object, _
        ByVal e As System.EventArgs) Handles btnSayHello.MouseLeave

    ' change the text...
    btnSayHello.Text = "The mouse has gone!"

End Sub
```

A Simple Application

.NET comes with a comprehensive set of controls that we can use in our projects. For the most part, we'll be able to build all of our applications using just these controls, but in Chapter 14 we look at how we can create our own.

For now, let's take a look at how we can use some of these controls to put together a basic application. In the following Try It Out we'll build a basic Windows application that lets the user enter a bunch of text into a form. We'll count the number of letters in the block of text that they enter, and the number of words.

Building the Form

The first job is to start a new project and build a form, so let's do that now.

Try It Out – Building the Form

1. Select File | New | Project from the Visual Basic .NET menu and create a new Windows Application project. Enter the project name as Word Counter and click OK.

2. Stretch the form until it looks like this and use the Properties window to change the form's Text property to Word Counter:

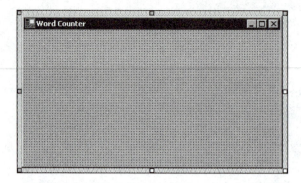

3. From the Toolbox, select the TextBox control and paint it onto the form. Now change the properties of the textbox as shown in the following table:

Property	Value
ScrollBars	Vertical
Text	*Leave blank*
Multiline	True
Name	txtWords

4. Note that when we changed the Multiline property, our six gray sizing handles around the control turned white. This means that we can now change the height of the textbox. Stretch it until it occupies a lot more of the form:

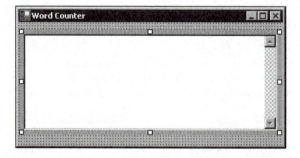

5. To tell the user what they should do with the form, we'll add a label. Select the Label control from the Toolbox, and drag and drop it just above the textbox. Change the Text property to Enter some text into this box...:

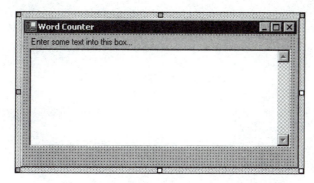

Strictly speaking, unless we're going to need to talk to the control from our Visual Basic .NET code, we don't need to change its Name property. With the textbox, we will need to use its properties and methods to make the application work. However, the label is just there for esthetics, so we don't need to change the name from Label1. (This depends on how fussy you are – some developers give every control a specific name, others only give controls that really need them a name.)

> It's worth noting that if you are going to refer to a control from Visual Basic .NET code, it's bad practice *not* to give it a name, in other words you should never end up with a line like **Button1.Text**. Developers should be able to work out what the control represents based on its name even if they've never seen your code before.

6. Our application is going to be capable of counting either the characters the user entered, or the number of words. In order to allow the user to select which they would prefer to use, we will use two radio buttons. Draw two RadioButton controls onto the form. We'll need to refer to the radio buttons from our Visual Basic .NET code, so change the following properties:

First radio button	
Property	**Value**
Name	radCountChars
Text	Chars
Checked	True

Second radio button	
Property	**Value**
Name	radCountWords
Text	Words

Your form should now look like this:

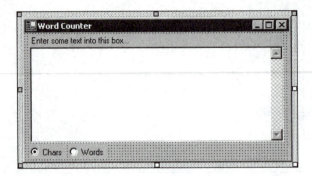

7. As the user types, we'll take the words that they enter and count up the words or characters as appropriate. We'll want to pass our results on to the user, so add two new Label controls like this:

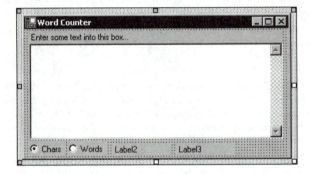

8. The first Label control (marked Label2) is just for esthetics, so change its Text property to The results are:. The second Label control will report the results, so we need to give it a name. Delete the value for its Text property (in other words make it blank) and enter the Name property as lblResults.

9. We also need a Button control that will pop up a message box displaying the results, so add a button control to the form. We don't strictly need this because the user can read the results on the form, but it illustrates a couple of important points. Change the Text property to Show Me! and the Name property to btnShowMe:

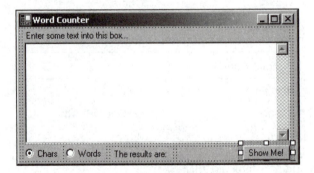

10. Finally, now that we have our form exactly how we want it, let's keep it that way. Make sure you select one of the controls and not the actual form, and then select Format | Lock Controls from the menu. This will set the Locked property of each of the controls to True and prevent them from accidentally being moved, resized, or deleted.

Counting Characters

With our form designed, let's build some event handlers to count the number of characters in a block of text that the user types.

Try It Out – Counting Characters

1. Since our application will be able to count both words and characters, we'll build separate methods for each. In this *Try It Out*, we'll write the code to count characters. Add this code to the bottom of Form1 just before the End Class statement:

```
' CountCharacters - count the characters in a block of text...
Public Function CountCharacters(ByVal text As String) As Integer

    ' return the number of characters...
    Return text.Length

End Function
```

2. Now we need to build an event handler for the textbox. Double-click on the textbox control and Visual Studio .NET will create a default handler for TextChanged. Add this code to it:

```
Private Sub txtWords_TextChanged(ByVal sender As System.Object, _
        ByVal e As System.EventArgs) Handles txtWords.TextChanged

    ' count the number of characters...
    Dim numChars As Integer = CountCharacters(txtWords.Text)

    ' report the results...
    lblResults.Text = numChars & " characters"

End Sub
```

3. Run the project. Enter some text into the textbox and you'll see something like this:

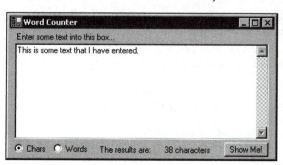

How It Works

Notice that whenever you type a character into the textbox, the label at the bottom of the form reports the current number of characters. That's because the `TextChanged` event is fired whenever, not surprisingly, the user changes the text in the box. This will happen when new text is entered, changes are made to existing text, and when old text is deleted. We're "listening" for this event and whenever we "hear" it (or rather receive it), we call `CountCharacters` and pass in the block of text. As the user types text into `txtWords`, the `Text` property will be updated to reflect the text that has been entered. We can get the value for this property (in other words the block of text), and pass it to `CountCharacters`:

```
' count the number of characters...
Dim numChars As Integer = CountCharacters(txtWords.Text)
```

In return, it will pass back an integer representing the number of characters:

```
' return the number of characters...
Return text.Length
```

Once we have the number of characters, we need to update the `lblResults` control:

```
' report the results...
lblResults.Text = numChars & " characters"
```

Counting Words

Although on the surface, building a Visual Basic .NET application is actually very easy, building an elegant solution to a problem requires a combination of thought, experience, and a bit of luck.

Take our application – when the **Words** radio button is checked, we want to count the number of words, whereas when **Chars** is checked we want to count the number of characters. This has three implications. Firstly, when we respond to the `TextChanged` event we need to call a different method that counts the words, rather than our existing method for counting characters. This isn't too difficult. Secondly, whenever we select a different radio button, we need to change the text in the results from "characters" to "words" or back again. In a similar way, whenever the **Show Me!** button is pressed, we need to take the same result, but rather than displaying it in the label control, we need to use a message box.

Let's now add some more event handlers and, when we've finished we'll examine the logic behind the technique we've used.

Try It Out – Counting Words

1. The first thing we want to do is add a method after `CountCharacters` that will count the number of words in a block of text:

```
' CountCharacters - count the characters in a block of text...
Public Function CountCharacters(ByVal text As String) As Integer

    ' return the number of characters...
    Return Text.Length
```

```
End Function
```

```
' CountWords - count the number of words in a block of text...
Public Function CountWords(ByVal text As String) As Integer

    ' is the text box empty?
    If txtWords.Text = "" Then Return 0

    ' split...
    Dim words() As String = text.Split(" ".ToCharArray())
    Return words.Length

End Function
```

2. Now, add this method:

```
' UpdateDisplay - update the display...
Public Function UpdateDisplay() As String

    ' what text do we want to use?
    Dim countText As String = txtWords.Text
    Dim resultText As String

    ' do we want to count words?
    If radCountWords.Checked = True Then

        ' count the words...
        Dim numWords As Integer = CountWords(countText)

        ' return the text...
        resultText = numWords & " words"

    Else

        ' count the chars...
        Dim numChars As Integer = CountCharacters(countText)

        ' return the text...
        resultText = numChars & " characters"

    End If

    ' update the display...
    lblResults.Text = resultText

End Function
```

This method will deal with the hassle of getting the text from the textbox and updating the display. It also understands whether it's supposed to find the number of words or number of characters by looking at the Checked property on the radCountWords radio button.

3. Now, instead of calling `CountCharacters` from within our `TextChanged` handler, we want to call `UpdateDisplay`. Make this change:

```
Private Sub txtWords_TextChanged(ByVal sender As System.Object, _
        ByVal e As System.EventArgs) Handles txtWords.TextChanged

    ' something's changed... update the display...
    UpdateDisplay()

End Sub
```

4. Finally, we want the display to alter when we change the radio button from **Chars** to **Words** and vice versa. To add the `CheckedChanged` event, select **radCountWords** from the left drop-down at the top of the code window and **CheckedChanged** from the right one:

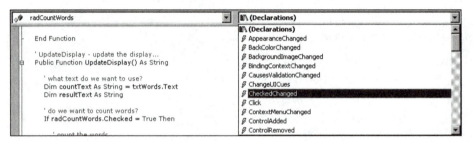

5. Add this code to the new event handler:

```
Private Sub radCountWords_CheckedChanged(ByVal sender As Object, _
        ByVal e As System.EventArgs) Handles radCountWords.CheckedChanged

        ' something's changed... update the display...
        UpdateDisplay()

End Sub
```

6. Repeat this step for `radCountChars`:

```
Private Sub radCountChars_CheckedChanged(ByVal sender As Object, _
        ByVal e As System.EventArgs) Handles radCountChars.CheckedChanged

        ' something's changed... update the display...
        UpdateDisplay()

End Sub
```

7. Run the project. Enter some text in the box and check **Words**. Notice how the display changes:

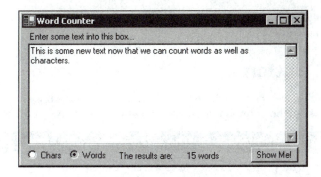

How It Works

Before we look at the technique we used to put the form together, we'll take a quick look at `CountWords`:

```
' CountWords - count the number of words in a block of text...
Public Function CountWords(ByVal text As String) As Integer

    ' is the text box empty?
    If txtWords.Text = "" Then Return 0

    ' split...
    Dim words() As String = text.Split(" ".ToCharArray())
    Return words.Length

End Function
```

We start by checking to see if the textbox is empty; if no text has been entered we immediately return a value of 0.

The `Split` method of the `String` class is used to take a string and turn it into an array of string objects. Here, the parameter we've passed it is equivalent to the "space" character and so we're effectively telling `Split` to break up the string based on a space. This means that `Split` will return to us an array containing each of the words in the string. We return the length of this array, in other words the number of words, back to the caller.

> Note that because this code uses a *single* space character to split the text into words, you'll get unexpected behavior if you separate your words with more than one space character or use the *Return* button to start a new line.

One of our golden rules of programming is that we never write more code than we absolutely have to. In particular, when you find yourself in a position where you're going to write the same piece of code twice, try to find a way that means you only have to write it once. In our example, we have to change the value displayed in `lblResults` from two different places. The most sensible way to do this is to split off the code that updates the label into a separate function. We can then easily set up the `TextChanged` and `CheckedChanged` event handlers to call this method. The upshot of this is that we only have to write the tricky "get the text, find the results, and display them" routine once. This technique also creates code that is easier to change in the future and easier to debug when a problem is found.

You'll find as you build applications that this technique of breaking out the code for an event handler is something you'll do quite often.

The Show Me! Button

To finish off this exercise, we need to wire up the **Show Me!** button. All we're going to do with this button is display a message box containing the same text that's displayed on `lblResults`.

Try It Out – Wiring up the Show Me! Button

1. From the code window for `Form1`, create a `Click` event handler for the button by selecting **btnShowMe** from the left drop-down list and then selecting **Click** from the right one. Then add this code:

```
Private Sub btnShowMe_Click(ByVal sender As System.Object, _
          ByVal e As System.EventArgs) Handles btnShowMe.Click

    ' display the text contained in the label...
    MessageBox.Show(lblResults.Text, "Word Counter")

End Sub
```

2. Run the project. If you type something into the textbox and click **Show Me!** the same value will be displayed in the message box as appears in the results label control.

How It Works

In this case, all we're doing is selecting the `Text` property from the label control and passing it to `MessageBox.Show`.

Complex Applications

Normal applications generally have a number of common elements. Among these are toolbars and status bars. Putting together an application that has these features is a fairly trivial task in Visual Basic .NET.

In this next section, we'll build an application that allows us to make changes to text entered into a textbox, such as changing its color, and making it all uppercase or lowercase.

The Project

Our first step on the road to building our application is to create a new project.

Try It Out – Creating the Text Editor Project

1. Create a new **Windows Application** project and call it **Text Editor**.

2. Most of the time, Form1 isn't a very appropriate name for a form as it's not very descriptive. Right-click on the form in the Solution Explorer, select **Rename**, and change its name to TextEditor.vb. Then press *Enter* to save the changes:

3. That's only half the battle – although we've renamed the form, we haven't actually renamed the class that contains the form's implementation. To do this, select the form in the Designer and change its **Name** property to TextEditor.

4. Select **View | Other Windows | Task List** from the menu to bring up the Task List window. It will display an error message saying that Form1 could not be found, which makes sense because we just renamed it:

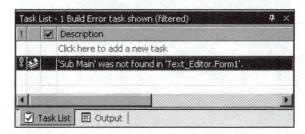

5. Double-click on the error message and you'll be prompted to select a new startup class. Select Text_Editor.TextEditor and click **OK**:

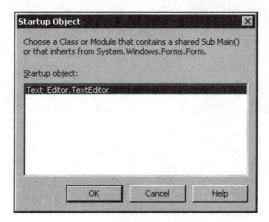

6. In the screenshots, I'm going to show the design window as quite small in order to save paper! You should explicitly set the size of the form by going to the Properties window of the form and setting the Size property to 600, 460.

Now let's move on and start building the fun part of the application.

The Status Bar

Perhaps the most boring part of our project is the **status bar**, so we'll tackle this first. This is a panel that sits at the bottom of an application window and tells the user what's going on.

Try It Out – Adding a Status Bar

1. Open the Designer for the TextEditor form, and select the StatusBar control from the Toolbox. Draw it anywhere on the form. You will find that it automatically glues itself to the bottom edge of the form and you'll only be able to change the height portion of its Size property. Make the Height property something sensible (in other words a little larger than the text). Set its Name property to statusBar and delete the value for the Text property. You'll get something like this:

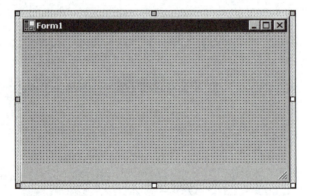

2. Open the code editor for the form and add the following code:

```
' StatusText - set the text on the status bar...
Public Property StatusText() As String
    Get
        Return statusBar.Text
    End Get
    Set(ByVal Value As String)
        statusBar.Text = Value
    End Set
End Property
```

There's no need to run the project at this point, so let's just talk about what we've done here.

How It Works

.NET has some neat features for making form design easier. One thing that was always laborious in previous versions of Visual Basic and Visual C++ was to create a form that would automatically adjust itself when the user changed its size.

In .NET, controls have the capability to **dock** themselves to edges of the form. By default, the status bar control sets itself to dock to the bottom of the form, but this can be changed to other areas of the form. So, when we resize the form, either at design time or at run time, the status bar stays where it's put.

So why have we built a `StatusText` property to get and set the text on the status bar? Well, this comes back to abstraction. Ideally, we want to make sure that anyone using this class doesn't have to worry about how we've implemented the status bar. We might want to replace the .NET-supplied status bar with another control, and if this happened anyone wanting to use our `TextEditor` class in their own applications (or a developer wanting to add more functionality to this application later on), would have to change their code to make sure it continued to work properly.

That's why we've defined this property as being `Public`. This means that anyone creating an instance of `TextEditor` in order to use its functionality in their own application can change the status bar if they want. If we didn't want them to be able to change the text themselves, relying instead on other methods and properties on the form to change the text on their behalf, we'd mark it as `Private`.

As we work through this example, we'll define things as `Public` and `Private`. From this you'll be able to infer what functionality a developer using our `TextEditor` class might have available.

The Toolbar

To make up for the fact that building the status bar was so dull, we'll add the toolbar in this next *Try It Out*.

Try It Out – Adding the Toolbar

1. Adding the toolbar is a similar deal to adding the status bar. Select the ToolBar control from the Toolbox and draw it anywhere on the form. It will automatically dock at the top of the form:

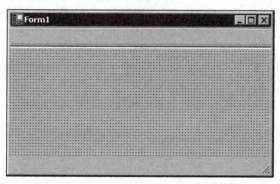

2. Note that the toolbar control doesn't display any sizing handles when it's selected. This is because the Framework controls the size and position of the toolbars itself, and doesn't expect you do to it! To see if it is selected, look in the Properties window to make sure that the list at the top does indeed refer to the toolbar. If it doesn't, click on the toolbar to make the selection.

285

3. Change the Name property of the toolbar to toolbar.

4. To add buttons to the toolbar, we'll use a built-in editor. Find the Buttons property, select it, and left-click on the ellipsis (...) to the right of (Collection).

5. We're going to add six buttons to the toolbar – Clear, Red, Blue, Uppercase, Lowercase, and About. Let's add the first one by clicking the Add button in the ToolBarButton Collection Editor.

6. The Collection Editor displays a properties palette much like the one that we're used to using. For each button, we need to change its text, give it an icon, give it a name, and provide some explanatory tooltip text. We'll add the icons in the next *Try It Out*, so just change these properties of ToolBarButton1:

Property	Value
Name	toolbarClear
Text	Clear
ToolTipText	Clear the text box

The Collection Editor should look like this:

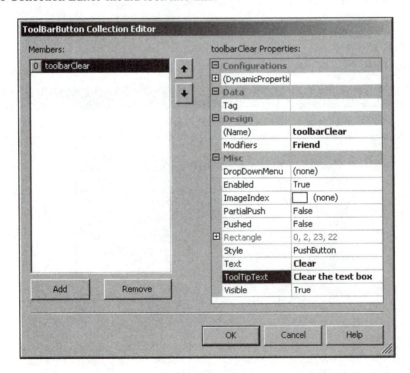

7. Click the Add button again to add the Red button. Set the following properties:

Property	Value
Name	toolbarRed
Text	Red
ToolTipText	Make the text red

8. Click the Add button again to add the Blue button. Set these properties:

Property	Value
Name	toolbarBlue
Text	Blue
ToolTipText	Make the text blue

9. Click the Add button again to add the Uppercase button. Set these properties:

Property	Value
Name	toolbarUppercase
Text	Uppercase
ToolTipText	Make the text uppercase

10. Click the Add button again to add the Lowercase button. Set these properties:

Property	Value
Name	toolbarLowercase
Text	Lowercase
ToolTipText	Make the text lowercase

11. Now we want to add a **separator** to make a space between the Lowercase button and the About button. Click Add and change the Style property to Separator. You don't need to change the name of the control, unless you particularly want to.

12. Click the Add button one last time to add the About button. Set these properties:

Property	Value
Name	toolbarHelpAbout
Text	About
ToolTipText	Display the About box

13. Finally, click the OK button to save the toolbar.

How It Works

Much like the status bar control, the toolbar control also docks to a particular position on the form. In this case, it docks itself to the top edge.

The seven controls (six buttons and one separator) that we added to the toolbar actually appear as full members of the `TextEditor` class, but it's unlikely in this application that we'll need to access them directly. Later, we'll see how we can respond to the `Click` event on the toolbar itself to determine when the button has been pressed.

The `ToolTipText` property enables .NET to display a tooltip above the button whenever the user hovers their mouse over it. We don't need to worry about actually creating or showing a tooltip – .NET does this for us.

At the moment our toolbar is looking pretty boring, so we'll add some images.

Adding Images to the Toolbar

Now that we have added our buttons to the toolbar, we need to add some images to demonstrate the purpose of each button.

Try It Out – Finding Toolbar Pictures in the .NET Framework Samples

1. The first thing you need to do is find the `Microsoft Visual Studio.NET` folder. This will usually be under `c:\Program Files\`, but you may have to dig around to find it if you changed the default installation location.

2. In the `Common7\Graphics\bitmaps` folder beneath it, you'll find numerous pictures that we can use in our toolbar.

3. In my project I shall be using `NEW.BMP` for the Clear button, `DIAMOND.BMP` for the Red and Blue buttons (with the color changed for the Blue button), `BLD.BMP` for the Uppercase button, `JST.BMP` for Lowercase button, and `HELP.BMP` for the About button, but you can use whatever you like. `DIAMOND.BMP` has been renamed to Red.bmp and Blue.bmp.

Browse the folders for the figures you want, and copy them over to a new `Figures` folder in your `Text Editor` project folder.

Icons can be created using Visual Studio .NET by simply right-clicking on a project, and selecting **Add | Add New Item**. Choose **Icon File** from the **Add New Item** window, and give the icon a meaningful name. Select Open, and you will be presented with an icon editor that can be used to create your own icons.

Try It Out – Adding the Toolbar Pictures

1. Now we need to add the toolbar pictures to the project. The first step in doing this is to create an image list that we can add the pictures to. Open the Form Designer and locate the ImageList control in the Toolbox. Add it to your form.

2. You'll notice that the image list doesn't appear on the form, but appears in a new region at the bottom of the designer. ImageList controls don't have a user interface at run time, and this region is where controls that don't have a UI appear:

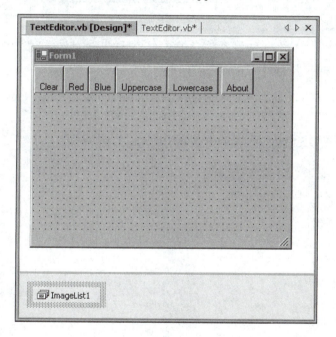

3. Change the Name property of the ImageList control to imglstToolbar.

4. Select its Images property. Again, you'll find an ellipsis button (...) next to (Collection). Click it.

5. Another Collection Editor window appears, but this time we're adding new images to the image list. Click Add.

6. The File Open dialog will appear. Browse to the correct folder using the Look in box:

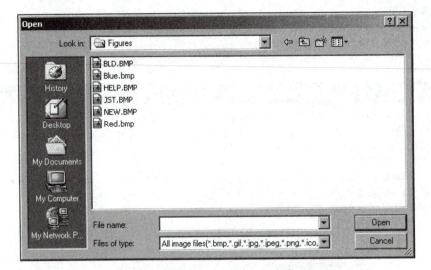

7. The folder should appear. Select NEW.BMP and click Open.

8. Go through the same process to add the images for the Red, Blue, Uppercase, Lowercase, and About buttons (in that order). Finally, click OK to dismiss the Collection Editor:

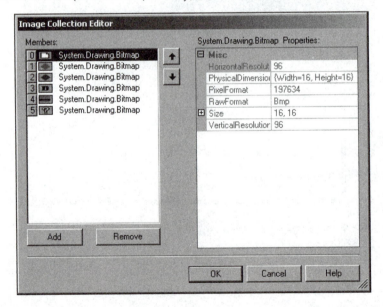

9. Select the Toolbar control and find its ImageList property. Select imglstToolbar from the list. This action ties the ImageList control to the toolbar. We can now point each button to an image in the image list.

10. Find the Buttons property and click the ellipsis button to open the Collection Editor.

11. toolbarClear should be selected. Drop down the ImageIndex property and select 0, which corresponds to the icon we've chosen for the Clear button:

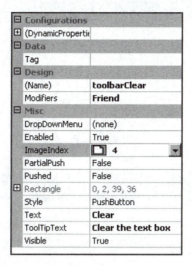

12. Repeat the process with the other buttons. When you've finished, you should have something like this:

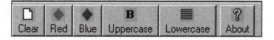

Finally, we can start working on the code!

Creating an Edit Box

The first thing we want to do is create a textbox that can be used to edit the text entered.

Try it Out – Creating an Edit Box

1. Open the Designer for `TextEditor` and draw a TextBox control into the center between the bottom of the toolbar and the top of the status bar.

2. Change these properties of the TextBox control:

Property	Value
ScrollBars	Vertical
Text	*Blank*
Multiline	True
Name	txtEdit

Your form should now look like this:

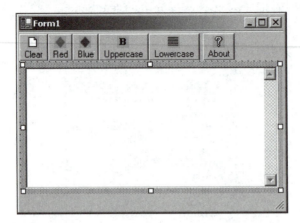

3. As we know, when the form changes size, the toolbar and status bar will stay "locked" in their position. To make sure that the textbox itself stretches with the form, set the Anchor property to Top, Bottom, Left, Right:

Clearing the Edit Box

In the following *Try It Out*, we're going to create a property called `EditText` that will get or set the text we're going to be editing. Then, clearing the edit box will simply be a matter of blanking out the `EditText` property.

Try It Out – Clearing txtEdit

1. Add this code to `TextEditor`:

```
' EditText - gets or sets the text that we're editing...
Public Property EditText() As String
    Get
         Return txtEdit.Text
    End Get
    Set(ByVal Value As String)
         txtEdit.Text = Value
    End Set
End Property
```

As previously when we created a property to abstract away the action of setting the status bar text, we've created this property to give developers using the `TextEditor` form the ability to get or set the text of the document irrespective of how we actually implement the editor.

2. We can now build `ClearEditBox`, the method that actually clears our textbox. Add the following code:

```
' ClearEditBox - empties txtEdit...
Public Sub ClearEditBox()
```

```
' reset the EditText property...
    EditText = ""

    ' reset the font color
    txtEdit.ForeColor = System.Drawing.Color.Black

    ' reset the status bar...
    StatusText = "Clear text box"

End Sub
```

3. Now select **txtEdit** from the left drop-down list and **TextChanged** from the right list at the top of the code editor. Add this code:

```
Private Sub txtEdit_TextChanged(ByVal sender As Object, _
        ByVal e As System.EventArgs) Handles txtEdit.TextChanged

    ' reset the status bar...
    StatusText = "Ready"

End Sub
```

How It Works

The first thing we want to do is clear out our textbox. In the next *Try It Out*, we'll see how we can call `ClearEditBox` from the toolbar.

```
' ClearEditBox - empties txtEdit...
Public Sub ClearEditBox()

    ' reset the EditText property...
    EditText = ""

    ' reset the font color
    txtEdit.ForeColor = System.Drawing.Color.Black

    ' reset the status bar...
    StatusText = "Clear text box"

End Sub
```

All this function does is set the `EditText` property to `" "`, set the `ForeColor` property of the textbox (which is the color of the actual text) to black, and place the text **Clear text box** in the status bar.

As we mentioned, `EditText` abstracts the action of getting and setting the text in the box away from our actual implementation. This will make it easier for another developer down the line to use our `TextEditor` form class in their own application:

```
' EditText - gets or sets the text that we're editing...
Public Property EditText() As String
    Get
```

```
            Return txtEdit.Text
        End Get
        Set(ByVal Value As String)
            txtEdit.Text = Value
        End Set
    End Property
```

As we type, the `TextChanged` event handler will be repeatedly called:

```
Private Sub txtEdit_TextChanged(ByVal sender As Object, _
        ByVal e As System.EventArgs) Handles txtEdit.TextChanged

    ' reset the status bar...
    StatusText = "Ready"

End Sub
```

Changing the status text at this point resets any message that might appear. For example, if the user has to type in a load of text and looks down to see Clear text box, they may be a little concerned. Setting it to Ready is a pretty standard way of saying "doing something", or "waiting". It doesn't mean anything specific.

Responding to Toolbars

The toolbar implementation in .NET is a little disappointing, since to make effective use of it we need to go through a number of hoops. When we look at building application menus in Chapter 9, you'll notice that menus are far easier to build.

Try It Out – Responding to Toolbar Clicks

1. In the code window, select **toolbarClear** from the left dropdown and then drop down the right list. You'll see this:

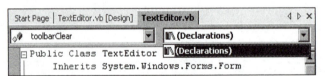

If we follow the convention that we have been used to, it's pretty logical to assume that the toolbar button control itself is capable of firing an event like `Click` that we could respond to. Unfortunately, this isn't the case and we actually have to respond to a `ButtonClick` event on the `ToolBar` control itself.

2. Select **toolbar** from the left dropdown, and then select **ButtonClick** from the right one. You'll see something like this:

```
Private Sub toolbar_ButtonClick(ByVal sender As System.Object, _
        ByVal e As System.Windows.Forms.ToolBarButtonClickEventArgs) _
        Handles toolbar.ButtonClick

End Sub
```

The second parameter passed to this event handler is a `ToolBarButtonClickEventArgs` object. This object contains a property that refers to the actual button that was clicked. In order to find out what button actually was clicked, we need to try to match it to one of the other controls.

3. Add the following code:

```
Private Sub toolbar_ButtonClick(ByVal sender As System.Object, _
        ByVal e As System.Windows.Forms.ToolBarButtonClickEventArgs) _
        Handles toolbar.ButtonClick

    ' do we want to empty the text box?
    If e.Button Is toolbarClear Then
        ClearEditBox()
    End If

End Sub
```

4. Now run the project. Type some text into our edit box, and click on any of the buttons except **Clear** – nothing will happen. Now click the **Clear** button. The box will become blank and the status bar will inform you that it has been cleared:

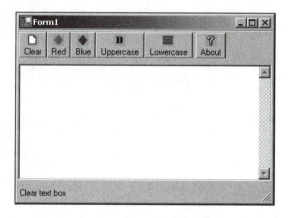

How It Works

The trick here is to use the `Is` operator. This operator allows matching of objects, so when we say:

```
    If e.Button Is toolbarClear Then
```

...we're actually saying, "Is the button passed through from the `ToolbarButtonClickEventArgs` object the same as the reference we already have in `toolbarClear`?"

When you click any button other than the **Clear** button, this isn't true. However, when you click the **Clear** button it is true and so we call the `ClearEditBox` method.

Coding the Red Button

Now let's add the code that will make our Red button turn any text we enter red.

Try It Out – Coding the Red Button

1. The first thing we have to do is create a function that will actually change the text red and update the status bar:

```
Public Sub RedText()

    ' make the text red...
    txtEdit.ForeColor = System.Drawing.Color.Red

    ' reset the status bar...
    StatusText = "The text is red"

End Sub
```

2. Next, change the `toolbar_ButtonClick` method to look like this:

```
Private Sub toolbar_ButtonClick(ByVal sender As Object, _
        ByVal e As System.Windows.Forms.ToolBarButtonClickEventArgs) _
        Handles toolbar.ButtonClick

    ' do we want to empty the text box?
    If e.Button Is toolbarClear Then
        ClearEditBox()
    End If

    ' do we want to make our text red?
    If e.Button Is toolbarRed Then
        RedText()
    End If

End Sub
```

3. Now run the project and enter some text. Click the Red button, and the text's color will change from black to red. Notice that if you carry on typing into the box, the new text will also be red:

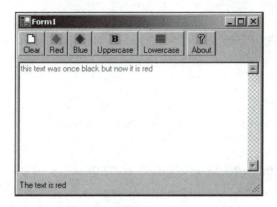

4. Click on **Clear**, to remove the text, and revert the color of the text back to black.

How It Works

This *Try It Out* was really quite simple. All we did was call the `RedText` function from our **Red** button. `RedText` used `System.Drawing.Color.Red` to set the `ForeColor` property of our textbox to red:

```
' make the text red...
txtEdit.ForeColor = System.Drawing.Color.Red
```

The `ForeColor` remains red until we set it to something else – so clicking the **Clear** button turns it back to black.

Coding the Blue Button

Let's see how we implement the **Blue** button. This Try It Out will be almost identical to the previous one.

Try It Out – Coding the Blue Button

1. Add the following `BlueText` function to the `TextEditor` form:

```
Public Sub BlueText()

    ' make the text blue...
    txtEdit.ForeColor = System.Drawing.Color.Blue

    ' reset the status bar...
    StatusText = "The text is blue"

End Sub
```

2. Now add this `If...Then` statement to `toolbar_ButtonClick`:

```
' do we want to make our text red?
If e.Button Is toolbarRed Then
    RedText()
End If
```

```
' do we want to make our text blue?
   If e.Button Is toolbarBlue Then
       BlueText()
   End If
```

```
End Sub
```

3. Run the project, and you'll see that the Blue button works in a similar fashion to the Red button, except it turns all our text blue.

Coding the Uppercase and Lowercase Buttons

The code for the Uppercase and Lowercase buttons is very similar, so let's look at them both now.

Try it Out – The Uppercase and Lowercase Buttons

1. Add the following functions to your TextEditor form:

```
Public Sub UppercaseText()

    ' make the text uppercase...
    EditText = EditText.ToUpper

    ' update the status bar...
    StatusText = "The text is all uppercase"

End Sub
```

```
Public Sub LowercaseText()

    ' make the text lowercase
    EditText = EditText.ToLower

    ' update the status bar...
    StatusText = "The text is all lowercase"

End Sub
```

2. Now add this code to toolbar_ButtonClick to connect our UppercaseText and LowercaseText methods to their respective buttons:

```
' do we want to make our text blue?
If e.Button Is toolbarBlue Then
    BlueText()
End If
```

```
' do we want to make our text uppercase?
If e.Button Is toolbarUppercase Then
    UppercaseText()
End If
```

```
        ' do we want to make our text lowercase?
        If e.Button Is toolbarLowercase Then
           LowercaseText()
        End If

     End Sub
```

3. Run the project and enter some text into the box in a mixture of lowercase and uppercase. Then click the **Uppercase** button to make it all uppercase:

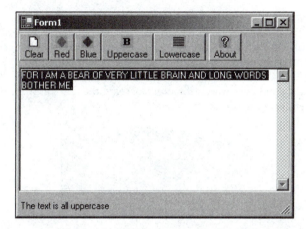

4. Click on the **Lowercase** button and all the text becomes lowercase:

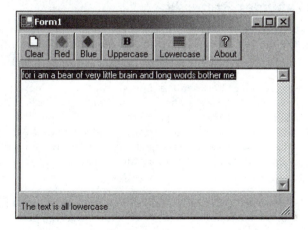

How It Works

The code in this *Try It Out* is very simple; we have seen it all before. If the user clicks on the **Uppercase** button we call `UppercaseText`, which uses the `ToUpper` method to convert all the text held in `EditText` to uppercase text:

```
' make the text uppercase...
EditText = EditText.ToUpper
```

Likewise, if the user clicks on the **Lowercase** button we call `LowercaseText`, which uses the `ToLower` method to convert all the text held in `EditText` to lowercase text:

```
' make the text lowercase
EditText = EditText.ToLower
```

Focus

However, there's a problem with our `Text Editor` project. When we change the case using the **Uppercase** and **Lowercase** buttons, the entire text in the box is highlighted. This happens because the **focus** has been set to the textbox control. The control that has focus is the control that is currently selected. For example, if you have two buttons on a screen, the code in the event handler for the button that has focus will be executed if you press *Return*:

If there are a number of textboxes on a form, any text you type will be entered into the textbox that currently has the focus.

Tab Keys and the TabIndex Property

We can move focus between controls at run time by pressing the *Tab* key. For example, if the user of the previous form pressed the *Tab* key, focus would jump to the **I don't** button. If the user pressed the *Tab* key again, focus would jump back to **I have focus**.

The order in which the focus moves between the controls on a form is not arbitrary. As you place controls on a form they are assigned a value for their `TabIndex` property. The first control to be placed on the form has a `TabIndex` of 0, the second 1, the third 2, and so on. This is the same order that the controls will have the focus as you *Tab* through them. If you have placed all your controls on the form, and are not happy with the resulting *Tab* order you can manually change it yourself, by using the Properties window to set the **TabIndex** properties of the controls.

> Note that although labels have a `TabIndex` property it is not possible to *Tab* to them at run time. Instead, the focus moves to the next control that can receive it, such as a textbox or button.

Visual Basic .NET has a very handy feature for displaying the tab order of your controls. Select **View | Tab Order** and your form will look something like this:

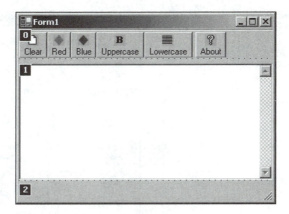

To remove the numbers, just select View | Tab Order once more.

> It is possible to assign shortcut keys to labels in a similar way to that in which shortcut keys can be assigned to menu items (see Chapter 9). With keyboard shortcuts on labels, pressing the shortcut key doesn't move the focus to the label, but it moves focus to the edit field (or other user input field) with a `TabIndex` one greater than the label's `TabIndex`.

Multiple Forms

All Windows applications have two types of windows – normal windows and dialog boxes. A normal window provides the main UI for an application. For example, if we use Word we use a normal window for editing our documents.

On occasion, the application will display a dialog box when we want to access a special feature. This type of window "hijacks" the application and forces us to use just that window. For example, when we select the Print option in Word, a dialog box appears, and from that point on we can't actually change the document – the only thing we can use is the Print dialog box itself. We call forms that do this **modal**.

We'll talk about dialog boxes in more detail in Chapter 8. For now, we'll look at adding additional forms to our application. The form that we will add will be a simple modal form.

Help About

Most applications have an About box that describes the application's name and copyright information. As we already have a toolbar button for this feature, let's wire it in now.

Try It Out – Adding an About Box

1. To add a new form to the project, we need to use the Solution Explorer. Right-click on the Text Editor project and select Add | Add Windows Form. Enter the name of the form as About and click Open to create the new form:

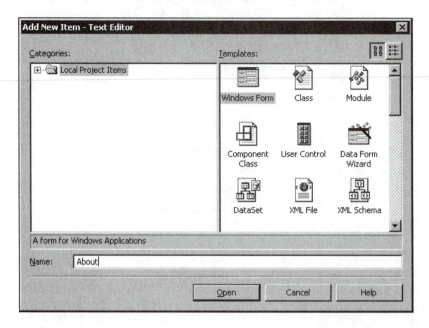

2. When the form's Designer appears, set its Text property to About Wrox Text Editor.

3. Dialog boxes and About boxes traditionally appear centered over the application window. Look for the StartPosition property and change this to CenterParent. This will make the About box start in the correct place.

4. Another tradition about modal windows is that they usually cannot be sized – although thanks to the fact that .NET makes it far easier to create resizable forms this tradition is likely to end. However, we want to make sure that our About box cannot be resized, so find the FormBorderStyle property and change it to FixedDialog.

5. Strangely, although we've told the form that it's a FixedDialog, it still has minimize and maximize buttons. Find the MinimizeBox and MaximizeBox properties and change them both to False.

6. Now we need to add two labels, a LinkLabel control (found in the Toolbox), and a button to the form. Here's what we'll end up with:

The properties of these controls are listed in the following table:

Control	Name	Properties
Label	Label1	Text = Wrox Text Editor; Font (Bold, Size = 10)
Label	lblVersion	Text = Version
LinkLabel	lnkWrox	Text = http://www.wrox.com
Button	btnOK	Text = OK; DialogResult = OK

7. To make the OK button the default button, select the form and change its AcceptButton property to btnOK. This means that when the user is looking at the dialog, if they press the *Enter* key, the dialog will be dismissed. (In effect, the `Click` event on the button is simulated.)

8. Double-click on the form background to create a handler for the form's Load event. Add this code:

```
Private Sub About_Load(ByVal sender As System.Object, _
        ByVal e As System.EventArgs) Handles MyBase.Load

    ' set the version number...
    lblVersion.Text &= " " & Environment.Version.ToString()

End Sub
```

9. Now, return to the form's Designer and double-click on the `LinkLabel` control. Add this code:

```
Private Sub lnkWrox_LinkClicked(ByVal sender As System.Object, _
        ByVal e As System.Windows.Forms.LinkLabelLinkClickedEventArgs) _
        Handles lnkWrox.LinkClicked

    ' run a Web browser and point it at wrox.com...
    System.Diagnostics.Process.Start("http://www.wrox.com/")

End Sub
```

10. We need to write a function that will display the About box, so add this to the `TextEditor` form:

```
' ShowAboutBox - display the about box...
Public Sub ShowAboutBox()
    Dim aboutBox As New About()
    aboutBox.ShowDialog(Me)
End Sub
```

11. Finally, we need to call `ShowAboutBox` from `toolbar_ButtonClick`:

```
' do we want to make our text lowercase?
If e.Button Is toolbarLowercase Then
    LowercaseText()
End If
```

```
' do we want to display the about box?
If e.Button Is toolbarHelpAbout Then
    ShowAboutBox()
End If
```

```
End Sub
```

12. Run the project and click on the About button. You should see this dialog and if you click the link Internet Explorer will start up and you'll be taken to http://www.wrox.com/:

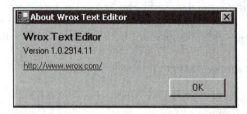

How It Works

Each form in our application has to have its own class, so to create a new form we need to get Visual Basic .NET to create a new class. We created a new class called About.

When the form starts, it will fire the Load event. We take this opportunity to write the version number to the lblVersion control:

```
Private Sub About_Load(ByVal sender As System.Object, _
        ByVal e As System.EventArgs) Handles MyBase.Load

    ' set the version number...
    lblVersion.Text &= " " & Environment.Version.ToString()

End Sub
```

The shared property Environment.Version provides access to the version number of the current application. **Version numbers** in .NET have four components. The major and minor version numbers in this case are 1 and 0, and can be set by the developer. The next two numbers (2914 and 11 in the screenshot above) are the build and revision numbers, and are generated by Visual Basic .NET automatically as we compile. The ToString method can be used to combine all four components of the version number into a string with the format: Major.Minor.Revision.Build.

The LinkLabel control is a general-purpose control that can be used in our applications for a variety of different reasons. In this case, we're using it to visit a URL. This is done through the shared System.Diagnostics.Process.Start method. What this does is ask Windows to run the supplied "program". Thanks to the way that web browsers integrate with Windows, when we try to run a URL as we are doing here, the default Web browser will open the URL for us:

```
Private Sub lnkWrox_LinkClicked(ByVal sender As System.Object, _
        ByVal e As System.Windows.Forms.LinkLabelLinkClickedEventArgs) _
        Handles lnkWrox.LinkClicked
```

```
' run a Web browser and point it at wrox.com...
System.Diagnostics.Process.Start("http://www.wrox.com/")

End Sub
```

To display another window, you have to create an instance of it. That's exactly what we've done in the `ShowAboutBox` method. Once we have an instance, we have to use the `ShowDialog` method to show it modally. We need to pass in a reference to the owner form (in this case, the `TextEditor` form):

```
' ShowAboutBox - display the about box...
Public Sub ShowAboutBox()
    Dim aboutBox As New About()
    aboutBox.ShowDialog(Me)
End Sub
```

To dismiss the dialog box, we rely on functionality built into the button control. When we drew the button onto the **About** form, we set its `DialogResult` property to `OK`. If the button is on a modal dialog this tells it that when it's pressed that modal dialog should be closed and the value in `DialogResult` (in this case, `OK`) should be passed back to the caller.

That brings us to the end of our discussion of the Wrox Text Editor application. Hopefully you should now see how easy it is to put together a Visual Basic .NET application that has all of the usual features you'd expect from a Windows application. Now lets look at how to deploy it.

Deploying the Wrox Text Editor

Our Wrox Text Editor works great on our development machine, but how do we get it to the end user? This is where deployment comes into play. For the deployment of Windows applications, Visual Studio .NET provides us with access to the Windows Installer, which provides the following functionality:

- ❑ Allows the user to select features they wish to install at the time of installation

- ❑ Allows applications to be completely uninstalled

- ❑ Allows the repair of files, should a file become corrupted

- ❑ Allows files to be copied to the destination machine, adding registry entries and creating desktop shortcuts

- ❑ If during an install a component fails to install, a rollback will occur and the system will be left in the state it started in

In the next *Try It Out* we will create a basic **Setup Project** that can be used to install our Wrox Text Editor to other machines in a professional manner.

Try It Out – Creating an Installer

1. We need to start by adding a new project to our solution. Right-click on **Solution 'Text Editor'** in the Solution Explorer and select **Add | Add New Project**. Then click on **Setup and Deployment Projects** to show the list of project templates.

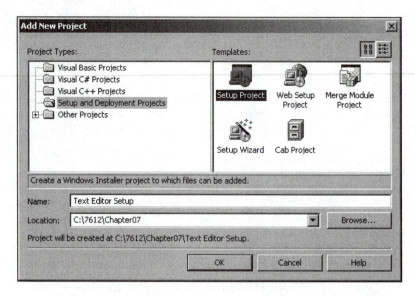

Select **Setup Project**, rename the project **Text Editor Setup**, and click the **OK** button.

Only Setup Project is available in Visual Basic Standard Edition, and this is the method we will use to create an Installer.

2. Click on the **Text Editor Setup** project in the Solution Explorer, then change the following information in the Properties window:

Property	Value
Author	Wrox Author Team
Description	Basic Text Editor
Manufacturer	Wrox Press
ManufacturerURL	http://www.wrox.com/
ProductName	Wrox Text Editor
Title	Wrox Text Editor

3. Click on the Text Editor Setup project in the Solution Explorer again. In the File System Editor select the Application Folder. Now go to the main menu bar and select the Action | Add | Project Output.

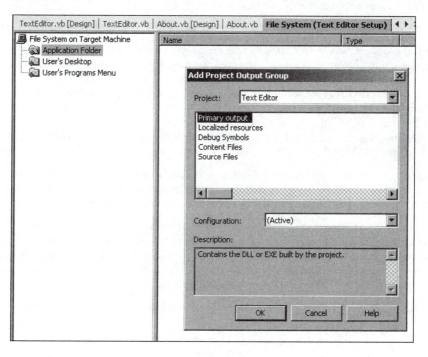

4. Ensure that Text Editor is displayed in the Project dropdown box. Next, select Primary output from the listbox and finally select (Active) for the configuration. Click the OK button to confirm these actions.

5. In the Solution Explorer right-click on Text Editor Setup and choose Build.

How It Works

Visual Studio makes it very easy for us to build an installation program that will help bundle our application for deployment. The first thing we did was add a new setup project to our solution. Several different types of setup templates are available:

❑ Setup Project – This was the template chosen, and is designed to create Installer Packages for Windows applications, hence is best suited for the task at hand.

❑ Web Setup Project – This template provides a convenient way to deploy a web site in a simple install package. It will not only encapsulate the web pages themselves, but also handles any issues with registration and configuration of the web site automatically. This is often used to allow an entire web site to be downloaded or for deployment to multiple web servers. We will not use this project in this chapter because we are deploying a Windows application.

❑ Merge Module Project – A Merge Module project creates an installer file for components that are to be used in multiple applications. This Merge Module can then be included in the Install Packages of each of the applications.

❑ Cab Project – used to create cabinet files. Cab files are used to compress single or multiple files together into a small distributable package. They are often used to distribute ActiveX controls from a web server to a web browser.

❑ Setup Wizard – This wizard provides a step-by-step walkthrough of the templates described above.

After choosing a Setup Project we changed various properties of the project relevant to our application, such as the name and author. These properties will be displayed when the text editor is being installed.

Next we told the installer that we wanted to add an application to the installer package. Here we chose several options:

❑ From the drop-down menu we chose which application we actually wanted to install – in this case it was the Text Editor.

❑ Next we chose what we want to install; in our case we only want the Primary output files. Other options include choosing debug symbols used for debugging, resources, the actual source code, or a help file for the user who is installing the application on the target machine.

❑ The default configuration (Active) will usually be sufficient. The other choices are Debug or Release. With Debug selected, the application is compiled along with additional information for the debugger to operate correctly. We use the Release configuration to install our applications on client's machines, as this doesn't include the debugger information, hence the application file is smaller and executes more quickly.

❑ Finally we built the Installation package and are ready to deploy it to our users.

Deploying the Installer

The Installation Package is treated like any other project in Visual Studio .NET. On the first screen when we chose the template we also selected where we wanted the project to exist. If we look in the Debug directory (this is my current configuration) it will contain all of the files needed to deploy the Wrox Text Editor. These files could be deployed in many ways:

❑   Burning them on a CD-ROM

❑   Placing them on a shared network

❑   Compressing them and emailing them

❑   Through a distribution product like SMS

The main point here is that the client machine needs access to all of the files in the directory (Debug or Release) in order to actually do the install.

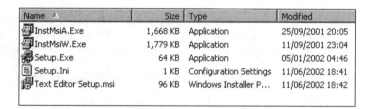

All that we need to deploy the solution are these files and a target computer with the .NET Framework installed. Double-clicking on Setup.exe will start the install process, and you will be greeted with the following screen.

The user simply follows the on-screen instructions to install the Wrox Text Editor.

We have covered the basic functionality here, but we have really only scratched the surface of how to deploy a Windows application. There are many other capabilities and options available within Visual Studio .NET that you can use to customize the way in which your application is deployed, to suit your needs and preferences.

Summary

In this chapter, we have discussed some of the more advanced features of Windows forms and the commonly used controls. We discussed the event-driven nature of Windows and looked at three events that can happen to a button (namely `Click`, `MouseEnter`, and `MouseLeave`).

We created a simple application that allowed us to enter some text and then choose between counting the number of characters or the number of words by using radio buttons.

We then turned our attention to building a more complex application that allowed us to edit text by changing its color or its case. This application showed how easy it was to build toolbars and status bars. We even added an About box to display the version number and a link to the Wrox web site.

Finally we built an Installation Package that makes our application look professional, and easy to deploy.

Questions

1. What event is fired when the mouse pointer crosses over a button's boundary to hover over it? What event is fired as it moves the other direction, away from the button?

2. How can we prevent our controls from being accidentally deleted or resized?

3. What should we consider when choosing names for controls?

4. What's special about the toolbar and status bar controls?

5. How can you add a separator to your toolbar?

Displaying Dialog Boxes

Visual Basic .NET provides several built-in dialogs that help you to provide a rich user interface in your front-end applications. These dialogs provide the common user interface that is seen in most Windows applications. They also provide many properties and methods that allow you to customize these dialogs to suit your needs while still maintaining the standard look.

In this chapter, we will cover the following dialogs:

- ❑ MessageBox
- ❑ Open
- ❑ Save
- ❑ Font
- ❑ Color
- ❑ Print

These dialogs help you to manage displaying messages to your users, opening and saving files, choosing fonts and colors, and printing documents. This chapter will explore these dialogs in depth and will show how you can use them in your Visual Basic .NET applications, to help you build a more professional looking application for your users.

The MessageBox Dialog

The **MessageBox dialog** will be one of the most often used dialogs for you as a developer. This dialog allows you to display custom messages to your users and accept their input regarding the choice that they have made. This dialog is very versatile – you can customize it by displaying a variety of icons with your messages and by choosing which buttons to display.

In our day-to-day operation of a computer, we have all seen message boxes that display one of the icons shown overleaf. In this section, we will show you how to create and display message boxes that use these icons:

When building a Windows application, there are times when we need to prompt the user for information or display a warning that something did not happen or something unexpected happened. For instance, suppose the user of your application has modified some data and is trying to close the application without saving the data. You could display a message box that carries an information or warning icon and an appropriate message – that they will lose all unsaved data. You could also provide OK and Cancel buttons to allow the user to continue or cancel the operation.

This is where the MessageBox dialog comes in as it allows us to quickly build custom dialogs that will prompt the user for a decision while displaying our custom message, a choice of icons, and a choice of buttons. All of this functionality also allows us to display a message box to inform users of validation errors, and to display formatted system errors that are trapped by error handling.

Before we jump into some code, let's take a look at the MessageBox class. The MessageBox class contains public and protected methods inherited from the Object class, and one **Shared** method called Show, which has to be called to display the MessageBox dialog. The title, message, icons, and buttons displayed are determined by the parameters passed to this method. The Shared keyword indicates that a field is not associated with any particular object or instance of the class – it is associated with the class itself. This may seem complicated, but actually using a MessageBox is very simple – as we will see.

Available Icons for MessageBox

The table below outlines the available icons that we can display in a MessageBox. Note that there are only four standard icons that can be displayed. The actual graphic displayed is a function of the operating system constants and (in the current implementations at least) there are four unique symbols with multiple field names assigned to them:

Icon	Field Name	Description
	IconAsterisk	Specifies that the message box displays an information icon
	IconInformation	Specifies that the message box displays an information icon
	IconError	Specifies that the message box displays an error icon
	IconHand	Specifies that the message box displays an error icon
	IconStop	Specifies that the message box displays an error icon

Icon	Field Name	Description
	IconExclamation	Specifies that the message box displays an exclamation icon
	IconWarning	Specifies that the message box displays an exclamation icon
	IconQuestion	Specifies that the message box displays a question mark icon
	None	Specifies the message box will not display any icon.

Available Buttons for MessageBox

There are several buttons that we can display in a message box, and the table below outlines them:

Field Name	Description
AbortRetryIgnore	Specifies that the message box displays Abort, Retry, and Ignore buttons
OK	Specifies that the message box displays an OK button
OKCancel	Specifies that the message box displays OK and Cancel buttons
RetryCancel	Specifies that the message box displays Retry and Cancel buttons
YesNo	Specifies that the message box displays Yes and No buttons
YesNoCancel	Specifies that the message box displays Yes, No, and Cancel buttons

Setting the Default Button

Along with displaying the appropriate buttons, we can instruct the message box to set a default button for us. This allows the user to read the message and just press the *Enter* key to specify the action for the default button. The table below outlines the available default button options:

Field Name	Description
Button1	Specifies that the first button in the message box should be the default button
Button2	Specifies that the second button in the message box should be the default button
Button3	Specifies that the third button in the message box should be the default button

The default button chosen is relative to the MessageBox buttons, from left to right. Therefore, if you have the Yes, No, and Cancel buttons displayed and choose the third button to be the default, Cancel will be the default button. Likewise, if you choose the third button to be the default and you only have OK and Cancel buttons, the first button becomes the default.

Miscellaneous Options

There are a couple of other options in the MessageBoxOptions enumeration that can be used with the message box and are shown in the table below:

Field Name	Description
DefaultDesktopOnly	Specifies that the message box be displayed on the active desktop
RightAlign	Specifies that the text in a message box will be right-aligned, as opposed to left-aligned, which is the default
RTLReading	Specifies that the text in a message box be displayed with the RTL (right-to-left) reading order; this only applies to languages that are read from right to left
ServiceNotification	Specifies that the message box be displayed on the active desktop. The caller is a Windows service notifying the user of an event.

The Show Method Syntax

We call the Show method to display the message box. The code example below displays the message box shown in the next figure. Notice that we have specified the text that is displayed in the message box as the first argument, followed by the text that is displayed in the title bar. Then we specify the buttons that should be displayed, followed by the type of icon that should be displayed alongside. Last, we specify the button that we want set as the default button – in this case button one.

To run this code, start a new Windows Application project, double-click on the form in the Designer to generate the Form1_Load event, and place the following code inside that sub:

```
MessageBox.Show("My Text", "My Caption", MessageBoxButtons.OKCancel, _
        MessageBoxIcon.Information, MessageBoxDefaultButton.Button1)
```

Now that we have seen the available icons, buttons, and default button fields, let's take a look at the `Show` method of the `MessageBox` class. The `Show` method can be specified in several ways, the more common syntaxes being shown below:

```
MessageBox.Show(text)

MessageBox.Show(text, caption)

MessageBox.Show(text, caption, MessageBoxButtons)

MessageBox.Show(text, caption, MessageBoxButtons, _
    MessageBoxIcon)

MessageBox.Show(text, caption, MessageBoxButtons, _
    MessageBoxIcon, MessageBoxDefaultButton)
```

In the examples above, *text* represents the message that will be displayed in the message box. This text can be static text (a literal string value) or can be supplied in the form of a string variable. This parameter is required.

caption represents either static text or a string variable that will be used to display text in the title bar of the message box. If this parameter is omitted then no text is displayed in the title bar.

MessageBoxButtons represents the `MessageBoxButtons` enumeration. This parameter allows you to specify which of the available buttons will be displayed in the `MessageBox` dialog.

MessageBoxIcon represents the `MessageBoxIcon` enumeration. This parameter allows you to specify which of the available icons will be displayed in the `MessageBox` dialog.

MessageBoxDefaultButton represents the `MessageBoxDefaultButton` enumeration. This parameter allows you to specify which of the buttons will be set as the default button in the `MessageBox` dialog.

DialogResult Values

All of the syntax examples above return a value from the `DialogResult` enumeration, which indicates which button in the `MessageBox` dialog was chosen. The table below shows the available members in the `DialogResult` enumeration:

Member Name	Description
Abort	The return value is `Abort`, which is the result of clicking the **Abort** button
Cancel	The return value is `Cancel`, which is the result of clicking the **Cancel** button
Ignore	The return value is `Ignore`, which is the result of clicking the **Ignore** button
No	The return value is `No`, which is the result of clicking the **No** button
None	Nothing is returned, which means the dialog continues running

Table continued on following page

Member Name	Description
OK	The return value is OK, which is the result of clicking the **OK** button
Retry	The return value is Retry, which is the result of clicking the **Retry** button
Yes	The return value is Yes, which is the result of clicking the **Yes** button

Example MessageBoxes

Because there are multiple buttons that can be displayed in a MessageBox dialog, there are multiple ways to display a dialog and check the results, which are described below. Of course, if we were only displaying one button, using the MessageBox for notification, we would not have to check the results at all and could use a very simple syntax.

Try It Out – A Single Button MessageBox

1. Create a new Windows Application project called SimpleMessageBox.

2. Next, we want to add a button control to the form that will open the MessageBox. Call this button btnShow, and set its text to Show.

3. The only code we have to add now is the code to actually show the MessageBox dialog. We want to add this code in the Click event for the btnShow button, so double-click on this button in the form designer.

4. Enter the following to the load event:

```
Private Sub btnShow_Click(ByVal sender As System.Object, _
                          ByVal e As System.EventArgs) Handles btnShow.Click
    MessageBox.Show("The print job has completed.", "Print Job Notification")
End Sub
```

5. Run the project. Execution of this code should produce the message box shown in the following figure:

How It Works

The MessageBox.Show method opens this simple dialog with the text and caption that we described:

```
MessageBox.Show("The print job has completed.", "Print Job Notification")
```

Notice that, in our sample code above, we did not specify an icon to be used, nor did we specify a button to be displayed. The **OK** button is the default button that gets displayed when you do not specify a specific button.

Let's take a look at an example that contains two buttons.

Try It Out – A Two Button MessageBox

1. Open the designer for the SimpleMessageBox again.

2. Go back to the form designer and add a textbox. Set its Name to txtResult, and clear the text field, so your form now looks like this:

3. In form1.vb, change the code in the `Click` event for the `btnShow` button to:

```
Private Sub btnShow_Click(ByVal sender As System.Object, _
                    ByVal e As System.EventArgs) Handles btnShow.Click
    If MessageBox.Show("Your Internet connection will be closed now.", _
        "DUN Notification", _
        MessageBoxButtons.OKCancel, _
        Nothing, _
        MessageBoxDefaultButton.Button1) = DialogResult.OK Then
        txtResult.Text = "OK Clicked"
        ' Hangup the dial-up connection...
        ' Call some method here...
    Else
        txtResult.Text = "Cancel Clicked"
        ' Do nothing or we could place code here to be executed
        ' When the user chose the Cancel button
    End If
End Sub
```

4. Run the project. Execution of this code would produce the message box shown in the following figure:

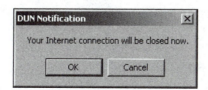

How It Works

The code uses the `Show` method of the `MessageBox` again, but this time it is in an `If` statement to see if the OK button was chosen by the user.

```
If MessageBox.Show("Your Internet connection will be closed now.", _
    "DUN Notification", _
    MessageBoxButtons.OKCancel, _
    Nothing, _
    MessageBoxDefaultButton.Button1) = DialogResult.OK Then
```

Notice that we have specified that the OK and Cancel buttons be displayed in the dialog and also that the OK button be the default button.

We did not want to display an icon so we have used the `Nothing` keyword. We have to specify something for the icon, as this is a required field when we want to set the default button parameter.

Also notice that we check the results returned from the `MessageBox` dialog using `DialogResult.OK`. We could just as easily have checked for `DialogResult.Cancel`, and written the if statement around this.

This is great if we only want to test the results of one or two buttons. But what happens when we want to test the results from a `MessageBox` dialog that contains three buttons?

Try It Out – A Three Button MessageBox

1. Once again, open the designer for the **SimpleMessageBox**.

2. Go to the form designer and change the code in the `Click` event for the `btnShow` button to:

```
Private Sub btnShow_Click(ByVal sender As System.Object, _
                          ByVal e As System.EventArgs) Handles btnShow.Click
    Dim intResult As Integer
    intResult = MessageBox.Show("The A drive is not ready." & _
        vbCrLf & vbCrLf & _
        "Please insert a diskette into the drive.", _
        "Device Not Ready", _
        MessageBoxButtons.AbortRetryIgnore, _
        MessageBoxIcon.Error, _
        MessageBoxDefaultButton.Button2)

        If intResult = DialogResult.Abort Then
        ' Do abort processing here...
        txtResult.Text = "Abort Clicked"
    ElseIf intResult = DialogResult.Retry Then
        ' Do retry processing here...
        txtResult.Text = "Retry Clicked"
    Else 'It has to be ignore
        ' Do ignore processing here...
        txtResult.Text = "Ignore Clicked"
    End If
End Sub
```

3. Run the project. The following `MessageBox` dialog displays an icon and three buttons, where the second button is the default:

How It Works

The `Show` method returns a `DialogResult`, which is an `Integer` value. What we need to do in a case where there are three buttons is to capture the `DialogResult` in an `Integer` variable and then test that variable.

In the sample code above, the first thing that we do is declare an `Integer` variable to capture the `DialogResult` returned from the `MessageBox` dialog. Then we set the variable equal to that `DialogResult`.

```
Dim intResult As Integer
intResult = MessageBox.Show("The A drive is not ready." & _
     vbCrLf & vbCrLf & _
     "Please insert a diskette into the drive.", _
     "Device Not Ready", _
     MessageBoxButtons.AbortRetryIgnore, _
     MessageBoxIcon.Error, _
     MessageBoxDefaultButton.Button2)
```

Notice that the message in the `Show` method syntax is broken up into two sections separated with the `vbCrLf` constant. This built-in constant provides a carriage return-line feed sequence, which allows us to break up our message and display it on separate lines.

Finally we test the value of the `intResult`, and act on it accordingly:

```
If intResult = DialogResult.Abort Then
    ' Do abort processing here...
    txtResult.Text = "Abort Clicked"
ElseIf intResult = DialogResult.Retry Then
    ' Do retry processing here...
    txtResult.Text = "Retry Clicked"
Else 'It has to be ignore
    ' Do ignore processing here...
    txtResult.Text = "Ignore Clicked"
End If
```

Here we write the name of the button selected to the textbox, to prove that the test actually works.

Now we have a general understanding of how the `MessageBox` dialog works and we have a point of reference for the syntax. To familiarize yourself further with the `MessageBox`, try altering the values of the `caption`, `text`, `MessageBoxButtons`, `MessageBoxIcon`, and `MessageBoxDefaultButton` in the previous examples.

We have now seen how to display the `MessageBox` dialog in several different ways and how to display several of the various icons, buttons, and default buttons. You should now know how to successfully display a `MessageBox` dialog in your own applications.

> **Be careful not to overuse the `MessageBox` dialog and display a message box for every little message. This can be a real annoyance to the user. You must use common sense and good judgment on when a `MessageBox` dialog is appropriate. You should only display a `MessageBox` dialog when you absolutely need to inform the user that some type of error has occurred or when you need to warn them of some type of possibly damaging action that they have requested. An example of the latter is shutting down the application without saving their work. You would want to prompt the user to let them know that, if they continue, they will lose all unsaved work, and give them an option to continue or cancel the action of shutting down the application.**

MsgBox

An alternative way of displaying message boxes to your users is to use the `MsgBox` function. This was used to display message boxes in previous versions of VB, and has been kept in the language, so you should be aware of this. The message boxes produced by using `MsgBox` appear identical to those written using `MessageBox` – although the code is slightly different.

The syntax to display a message box using `MsgBox` is as follows:

```
MsgBox (text, buttons, caption)
```

The `text` and `caption` parameters are the same as those for `MessageBox` – they display the message and the title respectively. The `buttons` parameter, however, is new. Here's a comparison of some of the available options, and their equivalents for `MessageBox`:

MsgBox option	MessageBox Equivalent
`MsgBoxStyle.AbortRetryIgnore`	`AbortRetryIgnore`
`MsgBoxStyle.OKCancel`	`OKCancel`
`MsgBoxStyle.OKOnly`	`OK`
`MsgBoxStyle.RetryCancel`	`RetryCancel`
`MsgBoxStyle.YesNo`	`YesNo`
`MsgBoxStyle.YesNoCancel`	`YesNoCancel`
`MsgBoxStyle.Critical`	`IconError`
`MsgBoxStyle.Exclamation`	`IconExclamation`

MsgBox option	MessageBox Equivalent
MsgBoxStyle.Information	IconInformation
MsgBoxStyle.Question	IconQuestion
MsgBoxStyle.DefaultButton1	DefaultButton1
MsgBoxStyle.DefaultButton2	DefaultButton2
MsgBoxStyle.DefaultButton3	DefaultButton3

So to display the Device Not Ready message box we saw earlier in the chapter:

...we'd write the following code:

```
MsgBox("The A drive is not ready." & _
    vbCrLf & vbCrLf & _
    "Please insert a diskette into the drive.", _
    MsgBoxStyle.AbortRetryIgnore + MsgBoxStyle.Critical _
    + MsgBoxStyle.DefaultButton2, "Device Not Ready")
```

The Open Dialog

Most Windows applications process data from files, so we need a mechanism to open and save files. The .NET Framework provides us with the OpenFileDialog and SaveFileDialog classes to do just that. In this section, we will take a look at the OpenFileDialog dialog box control, and in the next section we will look at the SaveFileDialog control.

When we use Windows applications, such as Microsoft Word or Paint, we see the same standard Open dialog. This does not happen by accident. There is a standard set of **Application Programming Interfaces** (**API**) available to every developer that allows us to provide this type of standard interface, however, using the API can be cumbersome and difficult for the beginner. Fortunately, most of this functionality is already built into the .NET Framework so we can use it as we develop with Visual Basic .NET.

The OpenFileDialog Control

We can use the OpenFileDialog as a .NET class – by declaring an instance of it in our code and modifying its properties in code – or as a control – by dragging an instance of it onto the form at design time. In either case, the resulting object will have the same methods, properties, and events.

❑ You can find the `OpenFileDialog` control in the Toolbox under the **Windows Forms** tab, from where we can drag and drop it onto our project. Then, all we need to do is set the properties and execute the appropriate method.

❑ To use `OpenFileDialog` as a class we declare our own objects, locally or globally, in order to use the dialog. Then we have control over the scope of the dialog and can declare an object for it when needed, use it, and destroy it thereby using fewer resources.

In this section, we will focus on using `OpenFileDialog` as a control. Once you have a better understanding of this dialog and feel comfortable using it, you can then expand your skills and use `OpenFileDialog` as a class by declaring your own objects for it.

We can use the `OpenFileDialog` by simply invoking its `ShowDialog` method, and this would produce results similar to this:

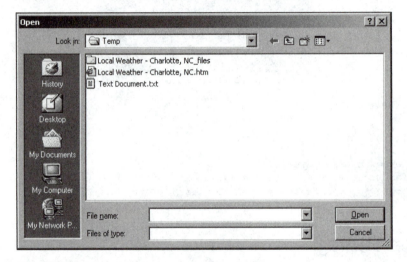

The Properties of OpenFileDialog

While the dialog shown above is the standard Open dialog in Windows, it provides no filtering. We see all file types listed in the window and we are unable to specify a file type for filtering because no filters exist. This is where the properties of `OpenFileDialog` come in. We are able to set some of the properties before the Open dialog is displayed, thereby customizing the dialog to our needs.

The table below lists some of the available properties for the `OpenFileDialog` control:

Property	Description
AddExtension	Indicates whether an extension is automatically added to a file name if the user omits the extension. This is mainly used in the `SaveFileDialog`, which we will see in the next section.
CheckFileExists	Indicates whether the dialog displays a warning if the user specifies a file name that does not exist.

Property	Description
CheckPathExists	Indicates whether the dialog displays a warning if the user specifies a path that does not exist.
DefaultExt	Indicates the default file name extension.
DereferenceLinks	Used with shortcuts. Indicates whether the dialog returns the location of the *file* referenced by the shortcut or whether it returns the location of the shortcut itself.
FileName	Indicates the file name of the selected file in the dialog box.
FileNames	Indicates the file names of all selected files in the dialog. This is a read-only property.
Filter	Indicates the current file name filter string, which determines the choices that appear in the Files of type combo box in the dialog.
FilterIndex	Indicates the index of the filter currently selected in the dialog box.
InitialDirectory	Indicates the initial directory displayed in the dialog.
MultiSelect	Indicates whether or not the dialog allows multiple files to be selected.
ReadOnlyChecked	Indicates whether or not the read-only checkbox is selected.
RestoreDirectory	Indicates whether or not the dialog restores the current directory before closing.
ShowHelp	Indicates whether the Help button is displayed in the dialog.
ShowReadOnly	Indicates whether the dialog contains a read-only checkbox.
Title	Indicates the title that is displayed in the title bar of the dialog.
ValidateNames	Indicates whether the dialog should only accept valid WIN32 file names.

As you can see from the list above, there are many properties that can be set before we call the ShowDialog method of the OpenFileDialog. Setting these properties allows us to customize the behavior of the dialog.

The Methods of OpenFileDialog

While there are many methods available in the OpenFileDialog, we will only be concentrating on the ShowDialog method in our examples. The list below contains some of the other available methods in the OpenFileDialog:

Method	Description
Dispose	Releases the resources used by the Open dialog.
OpenFile	Opens the file selected by the user with read-only permission. The file is specified by the FileName property.

Table continued on following page

Method	Description
Reset	Resets all properties of the Open dialog to their default values.
ShowDialog	Shows the dialog.

The ShowDialog Method

The ShowDialog method is straightforward as it accepts no parameters, so before calling the ShowDialog method you must set all of the properties that you want. After the dialog returns, you can query the properties to determine what file was selected, the directory, and the type of file selected. An example of the ShowDialog method is shown in the code fragment below:

```
OpenFileDialog1.ShowDialog()
```

The OpenFileDialog control returns a DialogResult of OK or Cancel, with OK corresponding to the **Open** or **Save** buttons on the dialog. This control does not actually open and read a file for you; it is merely a common interface that allows a user to locate and specify the file or files to be opened by the application. We need to query the OpenFileDialog properties that have been set by the control after the user clicks on the **Open** button, to determine what file or files should be opened.

The StreamReader Class

Visual Basic .NET provides a StreamReader class that allows us to read data from a file. So, we can get the file name or names from the OpenFileDialog control and then use those file names with the StreamReader class to process those files. Let's now take a look at the StreamReader class.

The StreamReader class is implemented from the System.IO namespace so you must add this namespace to your project before it can be used. The code fragment below shows how this is done. The Imports statement should be the very first line of code in your form class:

```
Imports System.IO
```

In order to use the StreamReader class, you must declare an object and set a reference to the StreamReader class as shown in the code fragment below. Notice that we have passed a string to the StreamReader class that contains the path and file name of the file that we want to read. Setting our object to the StreamReader class in this way causes the StreamReader to actually open the file for processing:

```
Dim objReader As StreamReader = New StreamReader("C:\Temp\MyFile.txt")
```

Once we have an object set to the StreamReader class, we are able to read from the file as shown in the next code fragment. This example reads the entire contents of the file into the String variable strData. We can also read one or more characters at a time, or read an entire line from the file. Those methods are shown in the table below:

```
strData = objReader.ReadToEnd()
```

Once you have read all of the data from the file, you need to close the file and remove your reference to the `StreamReader` class, as shown in the next code fragment:

```
objReader.Close()
objReader = Nothing
```

The Methods of the StreamReader Class

The table below shows some of the methods available in the `StreamReader` class:

Method	Description
Close	Closes the `StreamReader` and releases any resources associated with the reader.
DiscardBufferedData	Allows a `StreamReader` to discard its current data.
Peek	Returns the next available character without actually reading it from the input stream.
Read	Overloaded. Reads the next character or next set of characters from the input stream.
ReadBlock	Reads a maximum of count characters from the current stream and writes the data to buffer, beginning at index.
ReadLine	Reads a line of characters from the current stream and returns the data as a string.
ReadToEnd	Reads the stream from the current position to the end of the stream.

Using the OpenFileDialog Control

Now that we have had a look at the `OpenFileDialog` control and the `StreamReader` class, let's put this knowledge to use by coding a program that uses them both.

This program will use the `OpenFileDialog` control to display the Open File dialog. We will use the dialog to locate and select a text file, and then open the file and read its contents into a textbox on our form using the `StreamReader` class.

Try It Out – Working with OpenFileDialog

1. Create a new Windows Application project called Dialogs.

2. Let's give our form a new name. In the Solution Explorer, right-click on Form1.vb and choose Rename from the context menu. Then enter a new name of frmDialogs.vb. Set the properties of the form as shown in the table overleaf:

Property	Value
Size	456, 304
StartPosition	CenterScreen
Text	Dialogs

3. Since we are going to read the contents of a file into a textbox, we want to add a textbox to the form. We also want to add a button to the form so that we can invoke the Open File dialog at will. Add these two controls to the form and set their properties according to the table below:

Control	Name	Properties
Textbox	txtFile	Anchor = Top,Bottom,Left,Right; Location = 8,8; MultiLine = True; Size = 352, 264; Text = *nothing*
Button	btnOpen	Anchor = Top,Right; Location = 368, 8; Size = 75, 23; Text = Open

4. When you have finished placing the controls on your form, your form should look similar to the one below:

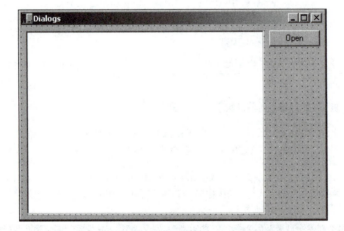

> The reason we anchored our controls in this example is so that, when we resize or maximize our form, the textbox is resized appropriately to the size of the form and the button stays in the upper right corner. You can test this at this point by running your project and resizing the form.

5. In the Toolbox, scroll down until you see the OpenFileDialog control and then drag it onto your form and drop it. The control will actually be added to the bottom on the workspace in the IDE.

At this point, we could click on the control in the workspace and then set the various properties for this control in the Properties window. However, we are going to accept the default name and properties for this control and set the various properties in code.

6. Because we are going to use the `StreamReader` class in our project, we need to import the `System.IO` namespace, so let's start there. Add the following code to your form class as the first line of code:

```
Imports System.IO
```

7. Next, let's declare a string variable that will contain a default path and file name. We will set this variable later in our code to the actual path and file name from the Open File dialog. You can create the file shown below or use an existing text file:

```
Public Class frmDialogs
    Inherits System.Windows.Forms.Form

    ' Declare variable...
    Private strFileName As String = "C:\Temp\Text Document.txt"
```

8. We now want to write some code in the `Click` event for the `btnOpen` button. So bring up the button's `Click` event procedure and add the following code:

```
Private Sub btnOpen_Click(ByVal sender As Object, _
        ByVal e As System.EventArgs) Handles btnOpen.Click
    ' Set the Open dialog properties...
    With OpenFileDialog1
        .Filter = "Text files (*.txt)|*.txt|All files (*.*)|*.*"
        .FilterIndex = 1
        .InitialDirectory = "C:\Temp\"
        .Title = "Demo Open File Dialog"
    End With

    ' Show the Open dialog and if the user clicks the OK button,
    ' load the file...
    If OpenFileDialog1.ShowDialog() = DialogResult.OK Then
        strFileName = OpenFileDialog1.FileName
        Dim objReader As StreamReader = New StreamReader(strFileName)
        txtFile.Text = objReader.ReadToEnd()
        objReader.Close()
        objReader = Nothing
    End If
End Sub
```

9. That's all there is to it. It's now time to test our code, so click on the **Start** button.

10. Once your form is displayed, click on the **Open** button to have the Open File dialog displayed, as shown in the following figure. The files you see will depend on the files in your `Temp` folder:

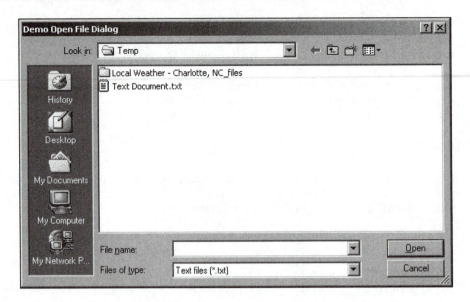

11. Notice the custom caption in the title bar of the dialog; we specified this in our code. Also notice that the dialog has opened in the Temp directory. If you click on the **Files of type** combo box, you will see two filters. Click on the second filter to see all of the files in the Temp directory.

12. Now locate a text file and click on that file. Then click on the **Open** button to have the file opened and the contents of that file placed in the textbox on the form, as shown here:

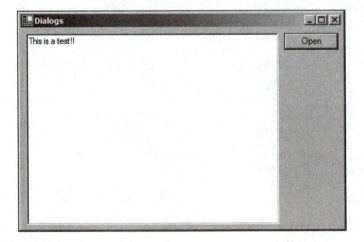

How It Works

Before displaying the Open File dialog, we needed to set some properties of `OpenFileDialog1` so that the dialog was customized for our application. We did this with a `With` statement. The `With` statement allows us to make repeated references to a single object without having to constantly specify the object name. We specify the object name once on the line with the `With` statement and then add all references to the properties of that object before the `End With` statement.

```
With OpenFileDialog1
```

The first property that we set was the `Filter` property. This property allows us to define the filters that are displayed in the **Files of type** combo box in the dialog. When we define a file extension filter, we specify the filter description followed by a vertical bar (|) followed by the file extension. When we want the `Filter` property to contain multiple file extensions, as shown in the code below, we separate each file filter with a vertical bar as we have done here:

```
.Filter = "Text files (*.txt)|*.txt|All files (*.*)|*.*"
```

The next property that we set was the `FilterIndex` property. This property determines which filter is shown in the **Files of type** combo box in the dialog. The default value for this property is 1, which is the first filter:

```
.FilterIndex = 1
```

Next, we set the `InitialDirectory` property. This is the directory that the Open File dialog will show when it opens:

```
.InitialDirectory = "C:\Temp\"
```

Finally, the last property that we want to set is the `Title` property. This is the caption that is displayed in the title bar of the dialog:

```
.Title = "Demo Open File Dialog"
```

Now we want to actually show the Open File dialog. Remember that the `ShowDialog` method returns a `DialogResult` value and, since there are only two possible results, we can compare the results from the `ShowDialog` method to the `DialogResult.OK` constant. If the user clicks on the **Open** button in the dialog, the `ShowDialog` method returns a value of `OK` and, if the user clicks on the **Cancel** button, the `ShowDialog` method returns `Cancel`:

```
If OpenFileDialog1.ShowDialog() = DialogResult.OK Then
```

Next, we want to retrieve the path and file name that the user has chosen. This is contained in the `FileName` property of the `OpenFileDialog` control. The next line of code sets this path and file name in our variable `strFileName`:

```
strFileName = OpenFileDialog1.FileName
```

In order to read the file, we need to declare an object as a `StreamReader` and pass it the file that we want opened. This next line of code is doing just that; we are passing it the `strFileName` variable that now contains the file that we chose in the Open File dialog:

```
Dim objReader As StreamReader = New StreamReader(strFileName)
```

This line of code reads the file to the end and places the results into the `Text` property of the `txtFile` textbox on our form:

```
txtFile.Text = objReader.ReadToEnd()
```

Finally, we want to close the file and then set the `StreamReader` object that we declared to `Nothing` to free up resources:

```
objReader.Close()
objReader = Nothing
```

This section has shown us that the `OpenFileDialog` control is very powerful, allowing us to provide standard interface for opening files that our users have become accustomed to. There are many properties in this control that we haven't touched and you should feel free to experiment on your own to see all of the possibilities that this dialog has to offer.

The Save Dialog

Now that we can open a file with the `OpenFileDialog` control, let's take a look at the `SaveFileDialog` control so that we can save a file. Again, the `SaveFileDialog` can be used as a control or a class. If you can master the `SaveFileDialog` as a control, you will not have any problems using `SaveFileDialog` as a class.

After we open a file, we may need to make some modifications to it and then need to save it. The `SaveFileDialog` control provides the same functionality as the `OpenFileDialog` control, except in reverse. It allows us to choose the location and file name where we want to save a file.

The Properties of SaveFileDialog

Let's look at some of the properties that are available in the `SaveFileDialog` control:

Property	Description
AddExtension	Indicates whether an extension is automatically added to a file name if the user omits the extension.
CheckFileExists	Indicates whether the dialog displays a warning if the user specifies a file name that does not exist. This is useful when you want the user to save a file to an existing name.

Property	Description
CheckPathExists	Indicates whether the dialog displays a warning if the user specifies a path that does not exist.
CreatePrompt	Indicates whether the dialog box prompts the user for permission to create a file if the user specifies a file that does not exist.
DefaultExt	Indicates the default file extension.
DereferenceLinks	Indicates whether the dialog returns the location of the *file* referenced by the shortcut, or whether it returns the location of the shortcut itself.
FileName	Indicates the file name of the selected file in the dialog box. This is a read-only property.
FileNames	Indicates the file names of all selected files in the dialog. This is a read-only property.
Filter	Indicates the current file name filter string, which determines the choices that appear in the Files of type combo box in the dialog.
FilterIndex	Indicates the index of the filter currently selected in the dialog box.
InitialDirectory	Indicates the initial directory displayed in the dialog.
OverWritePrompt	Indicates whether the dialog displays a warning if the user specifies a file name that already exists.
RestoreDirectory	Indicates whether or not the dialog restores the current directory before closing.
ShowHelp	Indicates whether the Help button is displayed in the dialog.
Title	Indicates the title that is displayed in the title bar of the dialog.
ValidateNames	Indicates whether the dialog should only accept valid WIN32 file names.

The Methods of SaveFileDialog

The SaveFileDialog control exposes the same methods as the OpenFileDialog exposes. If you want to review these methods, go back to *The Methods of OpenFileDialog* section. All of the examples will be using the ShowDialog method to show the Save File dialog.

The StreamWriter Class

Just as the OpenFileDialog control did not actually open and read a file, the SaveFileDialog control does not actually write to and close a file. For this we must rely on the StreamWriter class.

Visual Basic .NET provides a StreamWriter class that allows us to write data to a file. We get the file name from the SaveFileDialog control and give that file name to the StreamWriter class.

The `StreamWriter` class is also implemented from the `System.IO` namespace and so you must add this namespace to your project if you haven't already done so.

In order to use the `StreamWriter` class, you must declare an object and set a reference to the `StreamWriter` class as shown in the code fragment below. Notice that we have passed a string to the `StreamWriter` class, which contains the path and file name of the file that we want to write to, and also a Boolean value indicating whether or not the `StreamWriter` should append the contents to the file. If this value is `False`, the `StreamWriter` will completely replace the contents of the file. If this value is `True`, the `StreamWriter` will append the contents to the end of the file. Setting our object to the `StreamWriter` class in this way forces the `StreamWriter` to actually open the file for processing:

```
Dim objWriter As StreamWriter = _
            New StreamWriter("C:\Temp\MyFile.txt", False)
```

Once we have an object set to the `StreamWriter` class, we are able to write to the file as shown in the next code fragment. This example writes the entire contents of the string variable, `strData`, to the file referenced by the `objWriter` object:

```
objWriter.Write(strData)
```

Once you have written the data to the file, you need to close the file and remove your reference to the `StreamWriter` class, as shown in the next code fragment:

```
objWriter.Close()
objWriter = Nothing
```

The Methods of the StreamWriter Class

The table below shows some of the methods available in the `StreamWriter` class:

Method	Description
`Close`	Closes the `StreamWriter` and releases any resources associated with it.
`Flush`	Clears all buffers for the current writer and causes any buffered data to be written to the underlying device.
`Write`	Overloaded. Writes the given data type to a text stream.
`WriteLine`	Overloaded. Writes data followed by a line terminator as specified by the overloaded parameters.

Using the SaveFileDialog Control

To see how to include the `SaveFileDialog` control in our project, we will be using the **Dialogs** project from the last *Try It Out* as a starting point to build upon it. In this exercise, we want to save the contents of the textbox to a file.

We will use the `SaveFileDialog` control to display a Save File dialog that allows us to specify the location and name of the file. Then, using the `StreamWriter`, we will write the contents of the textbox on our form to the specified file.

Try It Out – Working with SaveFileDialog

1. Open the Dialogs project from the last *Try It Out.*

2. On the form, add another button from the Toolbox and set its properties as follows:

Property	Value
Name	btnSave
Anchor	TopRight
Location	368, 40
Size	75, 23
Text	Save

3. In the Toolbox, scroll down until you see the `SaveFileDialog` control and then drag and drop it onto your form. The control will be added to the bottom on the workspace in the IDE.

4. Double-click on the `btnSave` button to bring up its `Click` event and add the highlighted code:

```
Private Sub btnSave_Click(ByVal sender As Object, _
        ByVal e As System.EventArgs) Handles btnSave.Click

    ' Set the Save dialog properties...
    With SaveFileDialog1
        .DefaultExt = "txt"
        .FileName = strFileName
        .Filter = "Text files (*.txt)|*.txt|All files (*.*)|*.*"
        .FilterIndex = 1
        .InitialDirectory = "C:\Temp\"
        .OverwritePrompt = True
        .Title = "Demo Save File Dialog"
    End With

    ' Show the Save dialog and if the user clicks the Save button,
    ' load the file...
    If SaveFileDialog1.ShowDialog() = DialogResult.OK Then
        strFileName = SaveFileDialog1.FileName
        Dim objWriter As StreamWriter = _
            New StreamWriter(strFileName, False)
        objWriter.Write(txtFile.Text)
        objWriter.Close()
        objWriter = Nothing
    End If

End Sub
```

5. At this point, we are ready to test this code so run your project.

6. Let's start with a simple test. Type some text into the textbox on the form and then click on the Save button. Notice that the File name combo box already has a file name in it. This is the file name that was set in the `strFileName` variable when we declared it in the previous *Try It Out*:

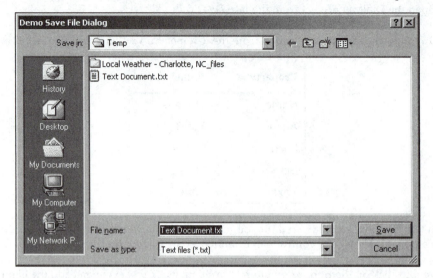

7. Enter another file name, but do not put a file extension on it. Then click the Save button and the file will be saved. To verify this, click the Open button on the form to invoke the Open File dialog. You will see your new file.

8. To test the `OverwritePrompt` property of the `SaveFileDialog` control, enter some more text in the textbox on the form and then click on the Save button. In the Save File dialog, choose an existing file name and then click on the Save button. You will be prompted to confirm replacement of the existing file. If you choose Yes, the file will be overwritten with the contents of the textbox by the `StreamWriter` object. If you choose No, you will be returned to the Save File dialog to enter another name:

> When the Open File or Save File dialogs are displayed, the context menu is fully functional and you can cut, copy, and paste files, as well as rename and delete them. There are other options in the context menu that vary depending on what software you have installed. For example, if you have WinZip installed, you will see the WinZip options on the context menu as well.

How It Works

Before displaying the Save File dialog, we need to set some properties in order to have the dialog customized to our application.

The first property that we set is the `DefaultExt` property. This property will automatically set the file extension if one has not been specified. For example, if you specify a file name of `NewFile` with no extension, the dialog will automatically add `.txt` to the file name when it returns, so that you end up with a file name of `NewFile.txt`.

```
.DefaultExt = "txt"
```

The `FileName` property is set to the same path and file name as was returned from the Open File dialog. This allows us to open a file, edit it, and then display the same file name when we show the Save File dialog. Of course, you can override this file name in the application's Save File dialog.

```
.FileName = strFileName
```

The next three properties are the same as in the `OpenFileDialog` control and set the file extension filters to be displayed in the **Save as type** combo box and set the initial filter. We also set the initial directory where the dialog shows the files:

```
.Filter = "Text files (*.txt)|*.txt|All files (*.*)|*.*"
.FilterIndex = 1
.InitialDirectory = "C:\Temp\"
```

The `OverwritePrompt` property accepts a Boolean value of `True` or `False`. When set to `True`, this property will prompt you with a `MessageBox` dialog if you choose an existing file name. If you select **Yes**, the existing file will be overwritten, and if you select **No**, you are returned to the Save File dialog to choose another file name. When the `OverwritePrompt` property is set to `False` the file will overwrite the existing files without asking for the user's permission.

```
.OverwritePrompt = True
```

The `Title` property sets the caption in the title bar of the Save File dialog:

```
.Title = "Demo Save File Dialog"
```

Now that we have the properties set, we want to show the dialog. The `ShowDialog` method `SaveFileDialog` control also returns a `DialogResult`, so we are able to use the `SaveFileDialog` control in an `If` statement and test the return value.

If the user clicks on the **Save** button in the Save File dialog, the dialog will return a `DialogResult` of `OK`. If the user clicks the **Cancel** button in the dialog, the dialog will return a `DialogResult` of `Cancel`. Here we test for `DialogResult.OK`:

```
    If SaveFileDialog1.ShowDialog() = DialogResult.OK Then
        strFileName = SaveFileDialog1.FileName
        Dim objWriter As StreamWriter = _
            New StreamWriter(strFileName, False)
        objWriter.Write(txtFile.Text)
        objWriter.Close()
        objWriter = Nothing
    End If
```

The first thing that we want to do here is to save the path and file name chosen by the user in our strFileName variable.

Then we declare an object for the StreamWriter class and pass it our string variable containing the path and file name. We also specify a value of False for the append parameter so that the StreamWriter will completely replace the contents of the file if it already exists, instead of appending the data to the end of the file.

Using the Write method of our StreamWriter object, we write the contents of the textbox on our form to the file. Notice that we have passed the textbox name and Text property as a parameter to the Write method.

Finally, we close the StreamWriter object and set it to Nothing to free up resources.

In this section, we have dealt with the SaveFileDialog control and the StreamWriter class. We have seen how the SaveFileDialog control provides a standard interface for the Save File dialog, while providing many properties that allow us to customize this dialog. At the same time, we have seen how the StreamWriter class can be used to write text to files, and either replace the contents of a file or create new files. The SaveFileDialog control and StreamWriter class will be very useful to you when writing applications that require file input and output.

The Font Dialog

Sometimes you may need to write an application that allows the user to choose the font that they want their data displayed in. Or perhaps you may want to see all available fonts installed on a particular system. This is where the FontDialog control comes in; it displays a list of all available fonts installed on your system in a standard dialog that your users have become accustomed to.

Like the OpenFileDialog and SaveFileDialog controls, the FontDialog class can be used as a control by dragging it onto a form, or as a class by declaring it in code.

The FontDialog control is really easy to use; we just set some properties, show the dialog, and then query the properties that we need. Let's take a look at the properties of FontDialog.

The Properties of FontDialog

The table below lists some of its available properties:

Property	Description
AllowScriptChange	Indicates whether the user can change the character set specified in the Script drop-down box to display a character set other than the one currently displayed.
Color	Indicates the selected font color.
Font	Indicates the selected font.
FontMustExist	Indicates whether the dialog box specifies an error condition if the user attempts to select a font or style that does not exist.
MaxSize	Indicates the maximum size (in points) a user can select.
MinSize	Indicates the minimum size (in points) a user can select.
ShowApply	Indicates whether the dialog contains an Apply button.
ShowColor	Indicates whether the dialog displays the color choice.
ShowEffects	Indicates whether the dialog contains controls that allow the user to specify strikethrough, underline, and text color options.
ShowHelp	Indicates whether the dialog displays a Help button.

The Methods of FontDialog

We will only be using one method (ShowDialog) of FontDialog in the forthcoming *Try It Out*. Other methods available include Reset, which allows you to reset all the properties to their default values.

Using the FontDialog Control

We can display the FontDialog control without setting any properties:

```
FontDialog1.ShowDialog()
```

The dialog looks like this:

339

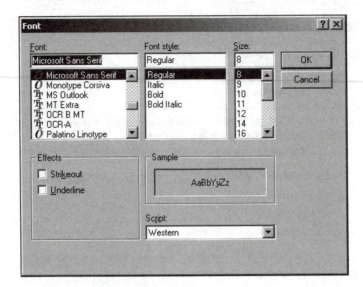

Notice that the Font dialog contains an **Effects** section that allows us to check the options for **Strikeout** and **Underline**. However, color selection of the font is not provided by default. If we want this, we must set the `ShowColor` property before calling the dialog:

```
FontDialog1.ShowColor = True
FontDialog1.ShowDialog()
```

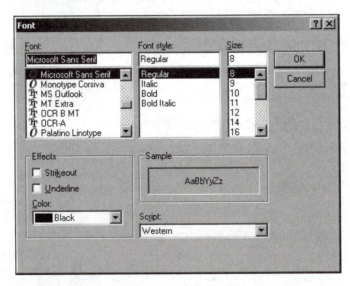

The `ShowDialog` method of this dialog, like all of the ones that we have examined thus far, returns a `DialogResult`. This will be either `DialogResult.OK` or `DialogResult.Cancel`.

Once the dialog returns, we can query the `Font` and `Color` properties to see what font and color the user has chosen. We can then apply these properties to a control on our form or store them to a variable for later use.

Now that we know what the Font dialog looks like and how to call it, let's put it to use in a *Try It Out*. We will use the program from the last two *Try It Outs*, open a file, and have the contents of the file read into the text box on the form. We will then use the `FontDialog` control to display the Font dialog, to allow us to select a font. We will then change the font in the textbox to the font that we have chosen.

Try It Out – Working with FontDialog

1. Open the Dialogs project again.

2. On the form add another button from the Toolbox and set its properties according to the values shown in this table:

Property	Value
Name	btnFont
Anchor	TopRight
Location	368, 72
Size	75, 23
Text	Font

3. We also need to add the FontDialog control to our project, so locate this control in the Toolbox and drag and drop it onto the form. It will be added to the workspace below the form and we will accept all default properties for this control.

4. We want to add code to the `Click` event of the `btnFont` button, so double-click on it and add the following code:

```
Public Sub btnFont_Click(ByVal sender As Object, _
        ByVal e As System.EventArgs) Handles btnFont.Click

    ' Set the FontDialog control properties...
    FontDialog1.ShowColor = True

    ' Show the Font dialog...
    If FontDialog1.ShowDialog() = DialogResult.OK Then
        ' If the OK button was clicked set the font
        ' in the text box on the form...
        txtFile.Font = FontDialog1.Font
        ' Set the color of the font in the text box on the form...
        txtFile.ForeColor = FontDialog1.Color
    End If

End Sub
```

5. Let's test our code. Click on the Start button. Once your form has been displayed, click on the Font button to display the Font dialog as shown here. Choose a new font and color and then click OK:

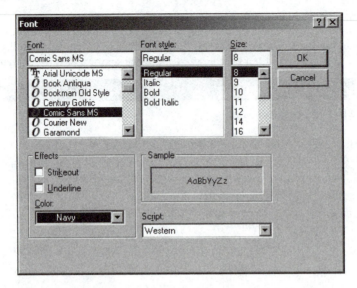

6. Now add some text in the textbox on your form. The text will appear with the new font and color that you have chosen.

7. This same font and color will also be applied to the text that is inserted from a file. To demonstrate this, click the Open button on the form and open a text file. The text from the file is displayed in the same font and color that you chose in the Font dialog:

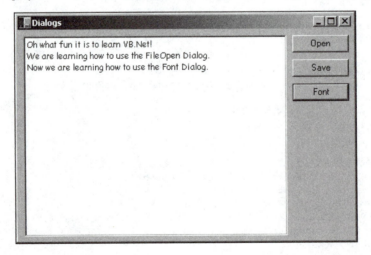

How It Works

We know that the Font dialog does not show a Color box by default, so we begin by setting the ShowColor property of the FontDialog control to True so that the Color box is displayed:

```
FontDialog1.ShowColor = True
```

Next, we actually show the Font dialog. Remember that the ShowDialog method of the FontDialog control returns a DialogResult, so we compare the return value from the FontDialog control to DialogResult.OK. If the button that the user clicked was OK, we execute the code within the If statement:

```
If FontDialog1.ShowDialog() = DialogResult.OK Then
    ' If the OK button was clicked set the font
    ' in the text box on the form...
    txtFile.Font = FontDialog1.Font
    ' Set the color of the font in the text box on the form...
    txtFile.ForeColor = FontDialog1.Color
End If
```

We set the Font property of the textbox (txtFile) equal to the Font property of the FontDialog control. This is the font that the user has chosen. Then we set the ForeColor property of the textbox equal to the Color property of the FontDialog control, as this will be the color that the user has chosen. Once these properties have been changed for the textbox, the existing text in the textbox will automatically be updated to reflect the new font and color. If the textbox does not contain any text, then any new text that is typed into the text box will be of the new font and color.

In this section, we have learned how to use the FontDialog control. We have seen how we can set the Font and Color properties of the FontDialog control, so that the Font dialog will display the current font and color in use by our textbox when we open it. We have also seen how to set the Font and ForeColor properties of the textbox using the Font and Color properties of the FontDialog control.

The Color Dialog

Sometimes we may need to allow the user to customize the colors on their form. This may be the color of the form itself, of a control, or of text in a textbox. Whatever the need, Visual Basic .NET provides the ColorDialog control. Once again, the ColorDialog control can also be used as a class – declared in code without dragging a control onto the forms designer.

The `ColorDialog` control allows the user to choose from 48 basic colors:

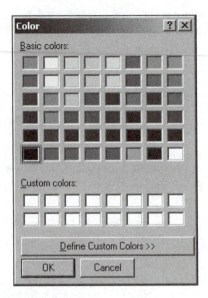

Notice that the users can also define their own custom colors, adding more flexibility to your applications. When the users click on the Define Custom Colors button in the Color dialog, they can adjust the color to suit their needs:

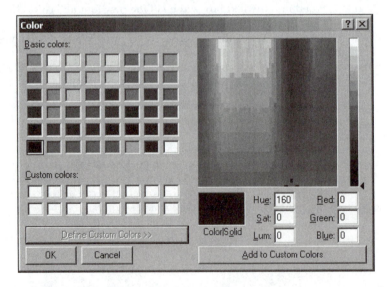

Having this opportunity for customization and flexibility in your applications gives them a more professional appearance, plus your users are happy because they are allowed to adjust their look.

The Properties of ColorDialog

Before we dive into some code, let's look at some of the available properties for `ColorDialog`:

Property	Description
AllowFullOpen	Indicates whether the user can use the dialog box to define custom colors.
AnyColor	Indicates whether the dialog displays all available colors in the set of basic colors.
Color	Indicates the color selected by the user.
CustomColors	Indicates the set of custom colors shown in the dialog box.
FullOpen	Indicates whether the controls used to create custom colors are visible when the dialog is opened.
ShowHelp	Indicates whether a **Help** button appears in the dialog.
SolidColorOnly	Indicates whether the dialog will restrict users to selecting solid colors only.

There aren't many properties that we need to worry about for this dialog, which makes it even simpler to use than the other dialogs that we have examined so far.

The Methods of ColorDialog

As with other dialogs, `ColorDialog` has a `Reset` method and a `ShowDialog` method.

Using the ColorDialog Control

All we need to do to display the Color dialog is to execute its `ShowDialog` method:

```
ColorDialog1.ShowDialog()
```

The `ColorDialog` control will return a `DialogResult` of `OK` or `Cancel`. Hence, we can use the statement above in an `If` statement and test for a `DialogResult` of `OK`, as we have done in the previous examples that we have coded.

To retrieve the color that the user has chosen, we simply set the `Color` property to a variable or any property of a control that supports colors, such as the `ForeColor` property of a textbox:

```
txtFile.ForeColor = ColorDialog1.Color
```

In the next *Try It Out*, we are going to continue using the same project and make the `ColorDialog` control display the Color dialog. Then we'll select a color. If the dialog returns a `DialogResult` of `OK`, we are going to change the color of the text on the buttons on the form.

Try It Out – Working with ColorDialog

1. Open the Dialogs project.

2. On the form, add another button from the Toolbox and set its properties according to the values shown:

Property	Value
Name	btnColor
Anchor	TopRight
Location	368, 104
Size	75, 23
Text	Color

3. Next, add a ColorDialog control to your project from the Toolbox. It will be added to the workspace below the form and we will accept all default properties for this control.

4. Double-click on btnColor to bring up its Click event procedure and add the following code:

```
Public Sub btnColor_Click(ByVal sender As Object, _
        ByVal e As System.EventArgs) Handles btnColor.Click

    ' Show the Color dialog...
    If ColorDialog1.ShowDialog() = DialogResult.OK Then
        ' Set the ForeColor property of all the controls on the form...
        btnOpen.ForeColor = ColorDialog1.Color
        btnSave.ForeColor = ColorDialog1.Color
        btnFont.ForeColor = ColorDialog1.Color
        btnColor.ForeColor = ColorDialog1.Color
    End If

End Sub
```

5. That's all the code we need to add, so let's test our changes to this project. Click on the Start button.

6. Once the form is displayed, click on the Color button to display the ColorDialog. Choose any color that you want, or create a custom color by clicking on the Define Custom Colors button. Once you have chosen a color, click the OK button in the Color dialog.

7. The color of the text in each of the buttons has now been changed to match the color that you chose (in black and white it's hard to tell in the next screenshot but, if you look closely, you'll see that the text on the buttons is now a different shade of gray):

8. Like the Font dialog, we do not have to set the `Color` property of the `ColorDialog` control before displaying the Color dialog again. It automatically remembers the color chosen and this will be the color that is selected when the dialog is displayed again. To test this, click on the Color button again and the color that you chose will be selected:

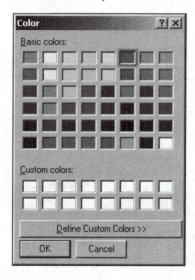

How It Works

This time, we did not want to set any properties of the `ColorDialog` control, so we jumped right in and displayed it in an `If` statement to check the `DialogResult` returned by the `ShowDialog` method of this dialog:

```
If ColorDialog1.ShowDialog() = DialogResult.OK Then
```

Within the `If` statement, we added the code necessary to change the text color of all of the buttons on the form. We did this by setting the `ForeColor` property of each button:

```
btnOpen.ForeColor = ColorDialog1.Color
btnSave.ForeColor = ColorDialog1.Color
btnFont.ForeColor = ColorDialog1.Color
btnColor.ForeColor = ColorDialog1.Color
```

In this section, we have looked at a very simple dialog that can make your applications more interesting. We have seen how simple it is to display and use the Color dialog. Even though we used the `ColorDialog` control, everything that you have learned will apply to the `ColorDialog` class, since the `ColorDialog` control is actually derived from that class.

The Print Dialog

Any application worth its salt will incorporate some kind of printing capabilities, whether it is basic printing or more sophisticated printing, such as allowing a user to print only selected text or a range of pages. In this last section of the chapter, we will explore basic printing. We will take a look at several classes that help us to print text from a file.

Visual Basic .NET provides the `PrintDialog` control. It does not actually do any printing but allows you to select the printer that you want to use, and set the printer properties such as page orientation and print quality. It also allows you to specify the print range. We will not be using this feature in our example, but it is worth noting that this functionality is available in `PrintDialog`.

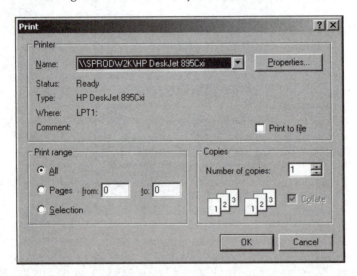

Like the previous dialogs that we have examined, the `PrintDialog` provides **OK** and **Cancel** buttons – thus its `ShowDialog` method will return a `DialogResult` of `OK` or `Cancel`. We can then use this in an `If` statement and test for the `DialogResult`.

The Properties of PrintDialog

Let's take a quick look at some of the properties provided in `PrintDialog`:

Property	Description
AllowPrintToFile	Indicates whether the Print to file checkbox is enabled.
AllowSelection	Indicates whether the Selection radio button is enabled.
AllowSomePages	Indicates whether the Pages radio button is enabled.
Document	Indicates the PrintDocument used to obtain the PrinterSettings.
PrinterSettings	Indicates the printer settings that the dialog box will be modifying.
PrintToFile	Indicates whether the Print to file checkbox is checked.
ShowHelp	Indicates whether the Help button is displayed.
ShowNetwork	Indicates whether the Network button is displayed.

The Methods of PrintDialog

Just like the other dialogs, `PrintDialog` exposes a `ShowDialog` method and a `Reset` method.

Using the PrintDialog Control

The only method that we will be using is the `ShowDialog` method, which will display the Print dialog. As we mentioned above, the `PrintDialog` control merely displays the Print dialog, it does not actually do any printing. The code fragment below shows how we display the Print dialog:

```
PrintDialog1.ShowDialog()
```

The PrintDocument Class

To perform the task of actually printing, we must rely on the `PrintDocument` class. This class requires the `System.Drawing.Printing` namespace, so we must include this namespace before attempting to define an object that uses the `PrintDocument` class.

The `PrintDocument` class will send output to the printer. You may be wondering where the `PrintDocument` gets its input. The answer to that question is the `StreamReader` class. (Remember this class from *The Open Dialog* section; we used this class to read text from a file.)

The Properties of the PrintDocument Class

Before we continue, let's take a look at some of the important properties of the `PrintDocument` class:

Property	Description
DefaultPageSettings	Indicates the default page settings for the document.
DocumentName	Indicates the document name that is displayed while printing the document. This is also the name that appears in the Print Status dialog and printer queue.
PrintController	Indicates the print controller that guides the printing process.
PrinterSettings	Indicates the printer that prints the document.

The Print Method of the PrintDocument Class

The `Print` method of the `PrintDocument` class prints the document to the printer specified in the `PrinterSettings` property.

When we call the `Print` method of the `PrintDocument` class, the `PrintPage` event is raised for each page as it prints. Therefore, we need to create a procedure for that event and add an event handler for it. The procedure that we create for the `PrintPage` event will do the actual reading of our text file using the `StreamReader` object that we define.

Now that we know a little bit about how printing works, let's look at how all this fits together in a *Try It Out*.

Again, we will be expanding on the previous *Try It Outs* and implementing printing into the same project. When we created this project in *The Open Dialog* section, we created a class-level variable that contained the path and name of the file that was opened. We will be using this variable in this *Try It Out*, so we will always print the last file opened or saved, as we also set this variable when we save a file.

Try It Out – Working with PrintDialog

1. Open the Dialogs project.

2. On the form, add another button from the Toolbox and set its properties according to the values shown:

Property	Value
Name	btnPrint
Anchor	TopRight
Location	368, 136
Size	75, 23
Text	Print

3. Now add a PrintDialog control to the project, dragging and dropping it from the Toolbox onto the form. It will be added to the workspace below the form and we will accept all default properties for this control.

4. The first thing that we want to add in our code is the required namespace for the `PrintDocument` class. Add this namespace to your code:

```
Imports System.IO
Imports System.Drawing.Printing
```

5. Next, we want to add a class-level object for the `StreamReader` class and an object for the font used for printing:

```
' Declare variable...
Private strFileName As String = "C:\Temp\Text Document.txt"
Private objStreamToPrint As StreamReader
Private objPrintFont As Font
```

6. Now add the following code to the `btnPrint_Click` event procedure:

```
Public Sub btnPrint_Click(ByVal sender As Object, )_
        ByVal e As System.EventArgs) Handles btnPrint.Click

    ' Declare an object for the PrintDocument class...
    Dim objPrintDocument As PrintDocument = New PrintDocument()

    ' Set the DocumentName property...
    objPrintDocument.DocumentName = "Text File Print Demo"

    ' Set the PrintDialog properties...
    PrintDialog1.AllowPrintToFile = False
    PrintDialog1.AllowSelection = False
    PrintDialog1.AllowSomePages = False

    ' Set the Document property to the objPrintDocument object...
    PrintDialog1.Document = objPrintDocument

    ' Show the Print dialog...
    If PrintDialog1.ShowDialog() = DialogResult.OK Then
        ' If the user clicked on the OK button then set the
        ' StreamReader object to the file name in the strFileName
        ' variable...
        objStreamToPrint = New StreamReader(strFileName)

        ' Set the print font...
        objPrintFont = New Font("Arial", 10)

        ' Add an event handler for the PrintPage event of the
        'objPrintDocument object...
        AddHandler objPrintDocument.PrintPage, _
                AddressOf objPrintDocument_PrintPage

        ' Set the PrinterSettings property of the objPrintDocument
        ' object to the PrinterSettings property returned from the
        ' PrintDialog control...
```

```
            objPrintDocument.PrinterSettings = PrintDialog1.PrinterSettings

            ' Print the text file...
            objPrintDocument.Print()

            ' Clean up...
            objStreamToPrint.Close()
            objStreamToPrint = Nothing
        End If

    End Sub
```

7. Remember that, when we call the `Print` method of the `PrintDocument` class, the
`PrintPage` event is raised. We need to create a procedure for this event, which will be
responsible for actually reading from the file and sending data to the printer. Since the
`objPrintDocument` object raises this event, we will name this procedure using this object
name, an underscore, and the event name. Enter the following code:

```
Private Sub objPrintDocument_PrintPage(ByVal sender As Object, _
        ByVal e As System.Drawing.Printing.PrintPageEventArgs)
    ' Declare variables...
    Dim sngLinesPerpage As Single = 0
    Dim sngVerticalPosition As Single = 0
    Dim intLineCount As Integer = 0
    Dim sngLeftMargin As Single = e.MarginBounds.Left
    Dim sngTopMargin As Single = e.MarginBounds.Top
    Dim strLine As String

    ' Work out the number of lines per page.
    ' Use the MarginBounds on the event to do this...
    sngLinesPerpage = _
        e.MarginBounds.Height / objPrintFont.GetHeight(e.Graphics)

    ' Now iterate through the file printing out each line.
    ' This assumes that a single line is not wider than the page
    ' width. Check intLineCount first so that we don't read a line
    ' that we won't print...
    strLine = objStreamToPrint.ReadLine()
    While (intLineCount < sngLinesPerpage And Not (strLine Is Nothing))
        ' Calculate the vertical position on the page...
        sngVerticalPosition = sngTopMargin + _
            (intLineCount * objPrintFont.GetHeight(e.Graphics))

        ' Pass a StringFormat to DrawString for the
        ' Print Preview control...
        e.Graphics.DrawString(strLine, objPrintFont, Brushes.Black, _
            sngLeftMargin, sngVerticalPosition, New StringFormat())

        ' Increment the line count...
        intLineCount = intLineCount + 1
```

```
        ' If the line count is less than the lines per page then
        ' read another line of text...
        If (intLineCount < sngLinesPerpage) Then
            strLine = objStreamToPrint.ReadLine()
        End If

    End While

    ' If we have more lines then print another page...
    If (strLine <> Nothing) Then
        e.HasMorePages = True
    Else
        e.HasMorePages = False
    End If

End Sub
```

8. We are now ready to test our code, so run the project.

9. Click on the Open button to open a file. This will cause the `strFileName` variable to be set with the path and file name that you just opened. Now click on the Print button to display the Print dialog:

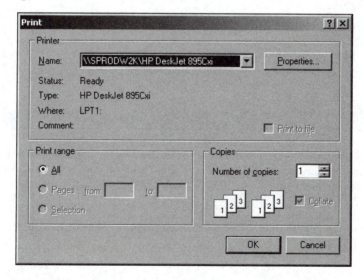

Notice that the Print to file checkbox is disabled as well as the Pages and Selection radio buttons. This is because we set the `AllowPrintToFile`, `AllSelection`, and `AllowSomePages` properties in the `PrintDialog` control to `False`.

If you have more than one printer installed, you can choose the name of the printer in the Name drop-down box. You can also click on the Properties button to set the way your document will be printed. For example, you can choose between landscape printing and portrait printing.

10. Click the OK button in the Print dialog to have the text file printed.

11. Now open the print queue for the printer that you have specified by clicking Start on the task bar at the bottom of your screen and then clicking on Settings. Next, select Printers from the menu. This will open the Printers window:

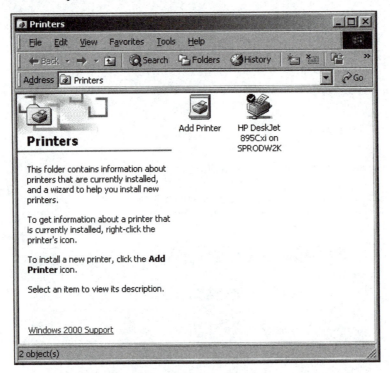

12. Choose your printer and either double-click on the icon, or right-click on the icon and select Open from the context menu. This will cause the print queue for the printer to open. In the print queue, click on the File menu and then Pause Printing. This will cause the printer to be paused.

> **You will need the appropriate permissions to pause the printer, such as being in the Administrators group.**

13. Next, click on the Print button again to print the file that you opened. Now click on the print queue to see the document waiting to be printed, as shown in the next screenshot. Notice the Document Name in the queue. This is the document name that we specified in the DocumentName property for the objPrintDocument object.

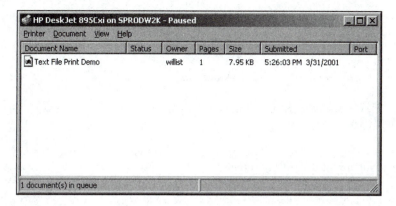

14. We have now finished testing. Click on the **File** menu in the print queue and then on the **Pause Printing** menu item to un-pause the printer and release the document for printing.

How It Works

We begin the `btnPrint` button's `Click` event procedure by declaring an object as a `PrintDocument`. We will use this object to perform the actual printing:

```
Dim objPrintDocument As PrintDocument = New PrintDocument()
```

Next, we set the `DocumentName` property for the `PrintDocument` object. This will be the name that we see when the document is printing and also the name that is shown in the printer queue:

```
objPrintDocument.DocumentName = "Text File Print Demo"
```

We then set some properties of the `PrintDialog` control. This will control the options on the Print dialog that is shown. Since we are only doing basic printing in this example, we want the **Print to file** checkbox to be disabled along with the **Pages** and **Selection** radio buttons. The next three lines of code do this by setting these properties to `False`:

```
PrintDialog1.AllowPrintToFile = False
PrintDialog1.AllowSelection = False
PrintDialog1.AllowSomePages = False
```

With the `PrintDialog`'s properties set, we are ready to set its `Document` property equal to the `PrintDocument` object:

```
PrintDialog1.Document = objPrintDocument
```

We are now ready to show the Print dialog so we execute the `ShowDialog` method of the `PrintDialog` control in an `If` statement, as shown in the code next. Notice that we are also checking the `DialogResult` returned from the `PrintDialog` control:

```
If PrintDialog1.ShowDialog() = DialogResult.OK Then
```

If the user clicks on the OK button in the Print dialog, then we actually want to execute the code for printing. The first thing that we do is to set the `objStreamToPrint` object to a new `StreamReader` class and pass it the `strFileName` variable:

```
objStreamToPrint = New StreamReader(strFileName)
```

Remember that this variable is set to the path and file name every time we open or save a file. This will be the file that we print.

Next, we want to set the `objPrintFont` object to a valid font and font size. We have chosen an `Arial` font here and a font size of `10` points, but you could have put in any font and size that you wanted:

```
objPrintFont = New Font("Arial", 10)
```

We now want to add an event handler for the `PrintPage` event. Since the `objPrintDocument` object raises this event, we specify this object and the event. We then specify the address of the `objPrintDocument_PrintPage` procedure:

```
AddHandler objPrintDocument.PrintPage, _
           AddressOf objPrintDocument_PrintPage
```

Next, we set the `PrinterSettings` property of the `objPrintDocument` object equal to the `PrinterSettings` property of the `PrintDialog` control. This will specify the printer used, page orientation, and print quality chosen by the user:

```
objPrintDocument.PrinterSettings = PrintDialog1.PrinterSettings
```

We then call the `Print` method of the `objPrintDocument` object. Calling this method will raise the `PrintPage` event and the code inside the `objPrintDocument_PrintPage` procedure will be executed:

```
objPrintDocument.Print()
```

Let's look at the `objPrintDocument_PrintPage` procedure. We need to add two parameters to this procedure – the first of which is the `sender`. Like every other procedure defined in this project, this argument is an `object` that lets us know what object called this procedure. The second parameter that we need to add is the `PrintPageEventArgs` object. The `PrintPage` event receives this argument and it contains data related to the `PrintPage` event, such as margin boundaries and page boundaries.

```
Private Sub objPrintDocument_PrintPage(ByVal sender As Object, _
           ByVal e As System.Drawing.Printing.PrintPageEventArgs)
```

The first thing that we want to do in this procedure is to declare some variables and set their default values. Notice that we are setting the values for the `sngLeftMargin` and `sngTopMargin` variables using the `PrintPageEventArgs` that were passed to this procedure:

```
Dim sngLinesPerpage As Single = 0
Dim sngVerticalPosition As Single = 0
Dim intLineCount As Integer = 0
Dim sngLeftMargin As Single = e.MarginBounds.Left
Dim sngTopMargin As Single = e.MarginBounds.Top
Dim strLine As String
```

Next, we want to determine the number of lines that will fit on one page. We do this using the `MarginBounds.Height` property of the `PrintPageEventArgs`. This property was set when we set the `PrinterSettings` property of the `objPrintDocument` to the `PrinterSettings` property of the `PrintDialog` control. We divide the `MarginBounds.Height` by the height of the font that was set in the `objPrintFont`:

```
sngLinesPerpage = _
        e.MarginBounds.Height / objPrintFont.GetHeight(e.Graphics)
```

Next, we read the first line from the text file and place the contents of that line in our `strLine` variable. Then we enter a loop to read and process all lines from the text file. We only want to process this loop while the `intLineCount` variable is less than the `sngLinesPerPage` variable and the `strLine` variable contains data to be printed:

```
strLine = objStreamToPrint.ReadLine()
While (intLineCount < sngLinesPerpage And Not (strLine Is Nothing))
```

Inside our `While` loop, we set the vertical position of the text to be printed. We calculate this position using the `sngTopMargin` variable and the `intLineCount` multiplied by the height of the printer font:

```
sngVerticalPosition = sngTopMargin + _
    (intLineCount * objPrintFont.GetHeight(e.Graphics))
```

Using the `DrawString` method of the `Graphics` class, we actually send a line of text to the printer. Here we pass the `strLine` variable (which contains a line of text to be printed), the font to be used when printing, the brush color to be used, the left margin, vertical position, and the format to be used:

```
e.Graphics.DrawString(strLine, objPrintFont, Brushes.Black, _
    sngLeftMargin, sngVerticalPosition, New StringFormat())
```

Next, we increment the line count on this page in the `intLineCount` variable:

```
intLineCount = intLineCount + 1
```

If the actual line count is less than the number of lines per page, we want to read another line from the text file to print. Then we go back to the beginning of our loop and process the next line of text:

```
If (intLineCount < sngLinesPerpage) Then
    strLine = objStreamToPrint.ReadLine()
End If

End While
```

357

Having completed our `While` loop, we then enter an `If` statement to test the value of `strLine`:

```
If (strLine <> Nothing) Then
    e.HasMorePages = True
Else
    e.HasMorePages = False
End If
```

If the `strLine` variable is not `Nothing`, then we have more printing to do so we set the `HasMorePages` property to `True`. This will cause the `PrintPage` event to be fired again, and we will continue to read the text file and print another page.

If `strLine` is `Nothing`, then we have no more printing to do so we set the `HasMorePages` property to `False`. This will cause the `Print` method of the `objPrintDocument` object to end processing and move on to the next line of code within the `btnPrint_Click` event procedure.

Since the printing has completed, we clean up by closing the text file that was used for printing and freeing up the resources used by the `objStreamToPrint` object:

```
objStreamToPrint.Close()
objStreamToPrint = Nothing
```

In this section, we have taken at look at basic printing and the steps necessary to print a text file. We used the `PrintDialog` control to allow us to choose the printer to use and the `PrintDocument` class to perform the actual printing. We also used the `StreamReader` class again to read the text file whose contents we printed.

Summary

This chapter has taken a look at some of the dialogs that are provided in Visual Basic .NET. We have examined the `MessageBox` dialog and `MsgBox` command, and the `OpenFileDialog`, `SaveFileDialog`, `FontDialog`, `ColorDialog`, and `PrintDialog` controls. Each of these dialogs will help you provide a common interface in your applications for their respective functions. They also hide a lot of the complexities required to perform their tasks, allowing you to concentrate on the logic needed to make your application functional and feature-rich.

While we used the controls from the Toolbox for all of these dialogs, except the `MessageBox` dialog and `MsgBox`, remember that these controls can also be treated as normal classes. This means that the classes that these dialogs use expose the same properties and methods, whether you are using a control or using the class. You can define your own objects and set them to these classes, and then use the objects to perform the tasks that we performed using the controls. This provides better control over the scope of the objects. For example, you could define an object, set it to the `OpenDialog` class, use it, and then destroy it all in the same procedure. This method only uses resources in the procedure that defines and uses the `OpenDialog` class, and reduces the size of your executable.

To summarize, you should now know how to:

- ❑ Use the `MessageBox` dialog to display messages
- ❑ Display icons and buttons in the `MessageBox` dialog
- ❑ Use the `OpenFileDialog` control and `StreamReader` class to open files
- ❑ Use the `SaveFileDialog` control and `StreamWriter` class to save files
- ❑ Use the `FontDialog` control to set the font and color of text in a textbox
- ❑ Use the `ColorDialog` control to set the color of the text on the buttons in your form
- ❑ Use the `PrintDialog` control and `PrintDocument` class to print from a text file

Questions

1. Write the code to display a message box with a message and caption of your choice, no icon, and OK and Cancel buttons. The Cancel button should be the default button.

2. How can you display the Open dialog with a default file name already displayed?

3. How can you change the color of the text displayed in a textbox using the Color dialog?

4. When you save a file using the `SaveFileDialog` control and the file already exists, you are prompted to replace it. If you choose Yes, does the file actually get overwritten?

5. The Font dialog has been displayed and you have chosen a font, clicked the OK button, and applied the font. When you display the Font dialog again, do you need to set the `Font` property to have the same font displayed as was previously selected?

Creating Menus

Menus are a part of every good application and provide not only an easy way to navigate within an application but also useful tools for working with that application. Take, for example, Visual Studio .NET. It provides menus for navigating the various windows that it displays and useful tools for making the job of development easier through menus and context menus (also called pop-up menus) for cutting, copying, and pasting code. It also provides menu items for searching through code.

This chapter takes a look at creating menus in your Visual Basic .NET applications. We will explore how to create and manage menus and how to create context menus and override the default context menus. Visual Studio .NET provides two menu controls in the toolbox and we will be exploring both of these.

So in this chapter, we will:

❑   Create menus

❑   Create submenus

❑   Create context menus

Overview

The **MainMenu** control in Visual Studio .NET provides several key features. First and foremost is that it provides a quick and easy way to add menus, menu items, and submenu items to your application. It also provides a built-in editor that allows you to add, edit, and delete menu items at the drop of a hat.

The menus that you create can contain access keys, shortcut keys, checkmarks, and radiochecks.

Access Keys

An **access key** (also known as an **accelerator key**) allows you to navigate the menus using the *Alt* key and a letter that is underlined in the menu item. Once the access key has been used the menu will appear on the screen and the user can navigate through them using the arrow keys or the mouse.

Shortcut Keys

Shortcut keys allow you to invoke the menu item without displaying the menus at all. For example, you usually use a control key and a letter such as *Ctrl+X* to cut text.

Check Marks and Radiochecks

Check marks are just that, either a checkmark symbol next to the menu item or, in the case of a **radiocheck**, a large dot next to the menu item. Both of these marks are indicators that the menu item is active. For example, if you click on the View menu in Visual Studio .NET and then click on the Toolbars menu item you will see a submenu that has many submenu items some of which have checkmarks. The submenu items that have checkmarks indicate the toolbars that are currently displayed. A radiocheck is more appropriate when you want to display a group of menu items and only want one menu item active at a time, just as we do with radio buttons.

What Do These Look Like?

The figure below shows many of the available features that you can incorporate into your menus. As you can see, this sample menu provides all of the features that we have just mentioned plus a separator. A **separator** provides a logical separation between groups of menu items.

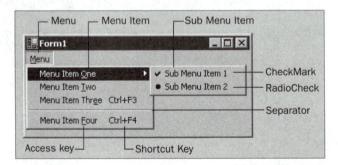

The figure shown above shows the menu the way it looks when the project is being run. The next figure shows how the menu looks in design mode.

The first thing that you'll notice when using the menu control is that it provides a method to allow you to quickly add another menu, menu item, or submenu item. Each time you add one of these, another blank text area is added.

The second thing that you may notice is the absence of the shortcut keys, since they are not displayed while in design mode.

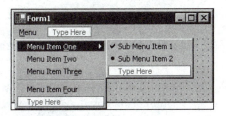

The Properties Window

While you are creating or editing a menu, the Properties window displays the available properties that can be set for the menu being edited as shown in the next figure, which shows the properties for the **Menu Item Four** menu item. Notice that the shortcut key has been set for this menu item although it is not displayed:

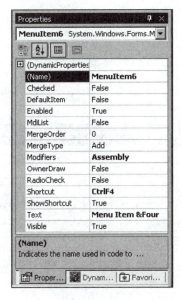

You can create as many menus, menu items, and submenu items as you need. You can even go as deep as you need to when creating submenu items by creating another submenu within a submenu.

> **Keep in mind though that if the menus are hard to navigate, or if it is hard to find the items your users are looking for, they will rapidly lose faith in your application.**

You should stick with the standard format for menus that you see in most Windows applications today. These are the menus that you see in Visual Studio .NET, Microsoft Word, or Microsoft Outlook for example. You always have a File menu and an Exit menu item in the File menu to exit from the application. If your application provides cut, copy, and paste functionality then you would place these menu items in the Edit menu and so on.

The MSDN library that was installed with Visual Sudio .NET contains a section on User Interface Design & Development. This section contains many topics that address the user interface and the Windows user interface. These should be explored for more details on Windows user-interface design-related topics.

The key is to make your menu look and feel like the menus in other Windows applications so the users can feel comfortable using your application. This way they do not feel like they have to learn the basics of Windows all over again. Granted, there will be menu items that are specific to your application but the key to incorporating them is to ensure they fall into a general menu category that the users are familiar with or to place them in your own menu category. You would then place this new menu in the appropriate place in the menu bar, generally in the middle.

Creating Menus

Let's move on now and see how easy it is to create menus in your applications. In the following *Try It Out* we are going to create a form that contains a menu bar, two toolbars, and two textboxes. The menu bar will contain three menus, File, Edit, and View, and a few menu items and submenu items. This will allow us to fully demonstrate the features of the menu controls.

We will be implementing code behind the menu items to demonstrate the menu and how to add code to your menu items, so let's get started.

Try It Out – Menus

1. Create a new Windows Application project called Menus and click the OK button to have the project created.

2. Set the properties of the form as outlined in the table below:

Property	Value
FormBorderStyle	FixedDialog
MaximizeBox	False
MinimizeBox	False
Size	300, 168
StartPosition	CenterScreen
Text	Menu Demo

3. Drag a MainMenu control from the toolbox and drop it on your form. It will be automatically positioned at the top of your form as shown in the next figure. The control will also be added to the bottom of the development environment just like the dialogs we discussed in Chapter 8. You can set the main properties of the `MainMenu` control there, but we will accept the default properties.

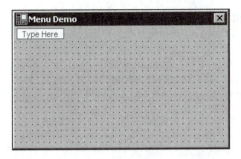

4. Enter the text &File in the box at the top of the form that says Type Here. This will become the File menu. Notice that the properties for this menu can be set in the Properties window. We will accept the default properties for this menu.

An ampersand (&) in the menu name provides an access key for the menu or menu item. Once you have entered the menu name, the letter that the ampersand appears before will become underlined. This will allow this menu item to be accessed using the *Alt* key and the letter that is underlined.

So for this menu, we will be able to access and expand the File menu by pressing the *Alt* key and the *F* key. We'll see this when we run our project later.

5. Notice that there is a box below and to the right of the menu that you just entered. This is only shown when the File menu is selected. This allows you to enter a new menu or a menu item. We want to enter a menu item of New, so type &New in the box below the File menu.

In the Properties window, change the Name property of this menu item to mnuFileNew.

6. We now want to enter a menu item separator. This is a line that separates the menu items, effectively grouping them together. In the box below the New menu item, enter a dash (-). Once you go to the next box, the dash will become a separator filling the entire width of the menu.

7. The next menu item that we want to add is the Exit menu item. In the box below the separator, enter the text E&xit. Set the Name property of this menu item to mnuFileExit in the Properties window:

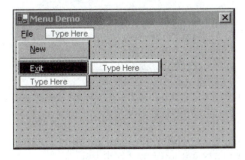

8. We now want to add an Edit menu so in the box to the right of the File menu enter the text &Edit. We'll accept all default properties for this menu.

9. The first menu item that we want to add here is the Undo menu item. Enter the text &Undo below the Edit menu. In the Properties window, enter a Name of mnuEditUndo and select CtrlZ in the ShortCut property drop-down list. This will assign a shortcut key for this menu item.

> Remember that you will not see shortcut keys in the menu items at design time. They are only visible at run time.

10. The next menu item that we want to add here is a menu item separator. In the box below the Undo menu item enter a dash (-) and accept all default properties.

11. In the next box down, enter the text Cu&t and set the Name property to mnuEditCut. Select CtrlX from the ShortCut drop-down list to assign the shortcut key for this menu item.

12. The next menu item that we want to add is Copy. Enter the text &Copy, set the Name property to mnuEditCopy, and assign a shortcut key of CtrlC in the ShortCut property.

13. As you probably guessed, the next menu item is Paste. Enter the text &Paste in the next box down, then set the Name property to mnuEditPaste, and assign a shortcut key of CtrlV in the ShortCut property.

14. We want to add another menu item separator so enter a dash (-) in the next box down and accept all default properties.

15. The final menu item in the Edit menu is Select All. Enter the text Select &All, set the Name property to mnuEditSelectAll, and assign a shortcut key of CtrlA in the ShortCut property. Your form should look like this:

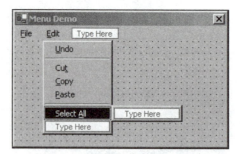

16. We have one final menu to add and that is the View menu. In the box next to the Edit menu enter &View and accept all default properties.

17. The one and only menu item under the View menu is Toolbars so enter the text &Toolbars and set the Name property to mnuViewToolbars.

18. We want to add two submenu items under the Toolbars menu item so in the box *next* to Toolbars enter the text &Main. Set the Name property to mnuViewToolbarsMain and set the Checked property to True. This will cause this submenu item to be checked as shown:

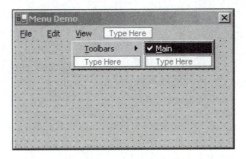

When we add a toolbar to this project, it will be displayed by default so this submenu item should be checked to indicate that the toolbar is displayed.

19. The next submenu item that we want to add is Formatting. Enter the text &Formatting in the box below Main and set the Name property to mnuViewToolbarsFormatting.

Instead of a normal checkmark being displayed for this submenu item as shown above, let's change the checkmark to a radiocheck to demonstrate how to set a radiocheck and see what it looks like in the menu. This will cause a radio button mark to appear when this item is checked. Set the RadioCheck property to True.

Since this toolbar will not be shown by default, we need to leave the Checked property set to False.

That's it for the menu so let's add the other controls that we need to this form.

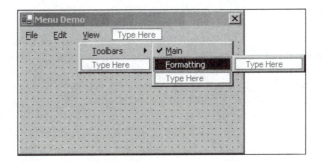

20. We need to add two toolbars to the form, so locate the ToolBar control in the toolbox and drag and drop it on your form. It will automatically align itself to the top of the form below the menu and fill the width of the form. Set its Name property to tbrMain:

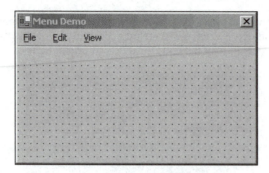

21. Now add a second toolbar to the form in the same manner. It will align itself under the first toolbar. Set the **Name** property to **tbrFormatting** and set the **Visible** property to **False**, as we don't want this toolbar shown by default.

22. In order to add images to the toolbars we need to add an **ImageList** control to the form. Locate the **ImageList** control in the toolbox and drag and drop it on your form. This control will appear at the bottom of the development environment and we will accept the default name for this control:

23. We now need to add some images to the **ImageList** control. The **Images** property of the **ImageList** control will contain a collection of images that will be placed on the toolbar buttons. Click on the ellipsis button (...) for this property to invoke the Image Collection Editor.

24. Click on the **Add** button to invoke the Open dialog. In the **Look In** combo box, navigate to the following folder: `C:\Program Files\Microsoft Visual Studio .NET\Common7\Graphics\bitmaps\Tlbr_W95`. (This assumes that Visual Studio .NET was installed in the default location. If you installed it in an alternative location, navigate to the `Tlbr_W95` folder where you installed Visual Studio .NET.)

25. Select the **New.bmp** image and click the **Open** button to have this image added to the **Members** list.

26. Click the **Add** button (Visual Studio will only allow you to add one at a time) again, and locate and select the images listed below to have them added to the **Members** list:

- ❑ `Undo.bmp`
- ❑ `Cut.bmp`
- ❑ `Copy.bmp`

- ❏   `Paste.bmp`
- ❏   `Lft.bmp`
- ❏   `Ctr.bmp`
- ❏   `Rt.bmp`
- ❏   `Jst.bmp`

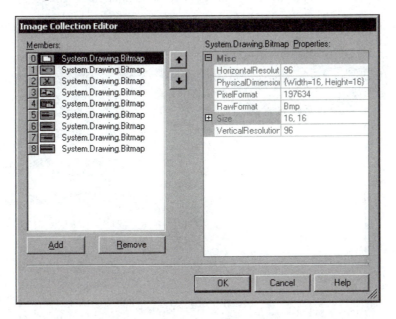

27. Click the **OK** button to close the Image Collection Editor. The images now contained in the `ImageList` control are available to any control on your form that supports images.

28. Click on the main toolbar, `tbrMain`, and in the Properties window change the **ButtonSize** property to **16,16**. This will make our buttons the same size as our images. You can set the **ButtonSize** property to any size that matches the images that you are using. Standard image sizes are 16x16 and 32x32 for toolbar buttons.

The **Appearance** property is set to **Normal** by default and provides raised buttons on the toolbar. Changing this property to **Flat** will cause the toolbar buttons to appear as flat buttons on the toolbar just as they appear in Visual Studio .NET.

You can choose **Normal** or **Flat**. However, if you choose **Flat**, ensure that you set the **Text** property of each button to nothing or your buttons will appear as large as possible, with the text in the **Text** property displayed below the button image.

29. Click on the **ImageList** property and select **ImageList1** from the drop-down list. This assigns the `ImageList1` control to our toolbar so we can access the images.

30. Click on the ellipsis button for the Buttons property. The Buttons property will also contain a collection of buttons and invokes the ToolBarButton Collection Editor.

The ToolBarButton Collection Editor is similar to the Image Collection Editor, though instead of a collection of images, this editor allows us to add a collection of buttons. The buttons that we define here though, will use the images that we defined in the Image Collection Editor.

31. Click the Add button to add the first button. The properties for the button will be shown in the Properties window as illustrated:

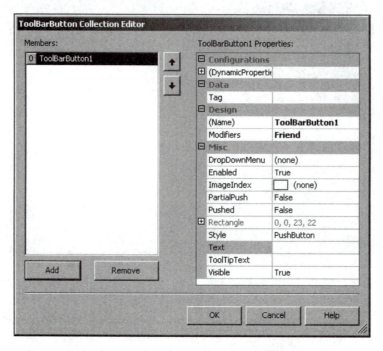

32. In the Properties window, set the following properties for this button:

Property	Value
Name	tbnNew
ImageIndex	0
Text	*nothing*
ToolTipText	New

33. Click the Add button again to add another button. Set the properties for this button as shown:

Property	Value
Style	Separator

34. Add five more buttons and set their properties as shown in the tables below:

Property	Value
Name	tbnCut
ImageIndex	2
Text	*nothing*
ToolTipText	Cut

Property	Value
Name	tbnCopy
ImageIndex	3
Text	*nothing*
ToolTipText	Copy

Property	Value
Name	tbnPaste
ImageIndex	4
Text	*nothing*
ToolTipText	Paste

Property	Value
Style	Separator

Property	Value
Name	tbnUndo
ImageIndex	1
Text	*nothing*
ToolTipText	Undo

35. Your completed collection should look like the one shown in the next figure:

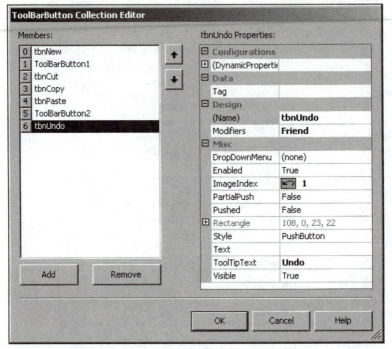

36. Click the OK button to close the ToolBarButton Collection Editor and you will see the buttons, with images, on the toolbar.

37. Now click on the second toolbar, `tbrFormatting`. In the Properties window set the ButtonSize property to 16, 16 and select ImageList1 as the ImageList property.

38. Click on the ellipsis in the Buttons property to once again invoke the ToolBarButton Collection Editor.

39. Add four buttons and set their ImageIndex properties to 5 through 8 respectively. We are not concerned with the other properties as this toolbar is for demonstration purposes only, we will not be using it. When done, click the OK button to close the ToolBarButton Collection Editor.

40. Add two text-boxes to the form and accept their default properties. Their location and size are not important but they should be wide enough to enter text in. Your completed form should now look similar to the one shown:

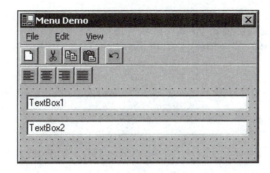

If you run your project at this point, you will see the menus, the main toolbar, and two textboxes. The formatting toolbar is not visible at this point because the Visible property was set to False.

Now that we have finally added all of our controls to the form, it's time to start writing some code to make these controls work. The first bit of functionality that we want to add here is to make the menus work. Once we have done that we will move on and add code to make the main toolbar work.

Try It Out – Coding the File Menu

1. Let's start by switching to the form class to view the code and adding a procedure for the New menu item. Click on the Class Name combo box and select mnuFileNew. Then in the Method Name combo box, select the Click event. The mnuFileNew_Click procedure will be added so add the following code to it:

```
Private Sub mnuFileNew_Click(ByVal sender As Object, ByVal e As _
                        System.EventArgs) Handles mnuFileNew.Click
    'Clear the textboxes
    TextBox1.Text = ""
    TextBox2.Text = ""
    'Set focus to the first textbox
    TextBox1.Focus()
End Sub
```

2. Now add the procedure for the Exit menu item by selecting mnuFileExit from the Class Name box and Click from the Method Name box:

```
Private Sub mnuFileExit_Click(ByVal sender As Object, ByVal e As _
                        System.EventArgs) Handles mnuFileExit.Click
    'Close the form and end
    Me.Close()
End Sub
```

How It Works

It is a good practice to prefix your menu items with the prefix of mnu. It is also good practice to specify not only the menu item name but also the menu that it belongs to as we have done here. This lets other developers quickly identify the menu item in code and know exactly what menu the menu item belongs to. This also becomes important when you have two menu items with the same name under different menus.

We want to add code to clear the textboxes on the form in the `mnuFileNew` procedure so we add the following code to it. All we are doing here is setting the `Text` property of the textboxes to an empty string. The next line of code will set focus to the first textbox by calling the `Focus` method of that textbox:

```
Private Sub mnuFileNew_Click(ByVal sender As Object, ByVal e As _
                        System.EventArgs) Handles mnuFileNew.Click
    'Clear the textboxes
    TextBox1.Text = ""
    TextBox2.Text = ""
    'Set focus to the first textbox
    TextBox1.Focus()
End Sub
```

Now when we click on the **New** menu item under the **File** menu, the textboxes on the form will be cleared of all text, and `TextBox1` will be ready to accept text.

When we click on the **Exit** menu item, we want the program to end. In the `mnuFileExit_Click` procedure we added the code shown below. The `Me` keyword refers to the class where the code is executing and in this case refers to the form class. The `Close` method closes the form, releases all resources, and ends the program:

```
Private Sub mnuFileExit_Click(ByVal sender As Object, ByVal e As _
                        System.EventArgs) Handles mnuFileExit.Click
    'Close the form and end
    Me.Close()
End Sub
```

That takes care of the code for the **File** menu so let's move on to the **Edit** menu and add the code for those menu items.

Try It Out – Coding the Edit Menu

1. The first menu item in the **Edit** menu is the **Undo** menu item. Add the following code to the `mnuEditUndo_Click` event:

```
Private Sub mnuEditUndo_Click(ByVal sender As Object, ByVal e As _
                        System.EventArgs) Handles mnuEditUndo.Click
    'Declare a TextBox object and set it to the ActiveControl
    Dim objTextBox As TextBox = Me.ActiveControl

    'Undo the last operation
    objTextBox.Undo ()
End Sub
```

2. Add a procedure for the `Click` event of the **Cut** menu item and add this code:

```
Private Sub mnuEditCut_Click(ByVal sender As Object, ByVal e As _
                        System.EventArgs) Handles mnuEditCut.Click
    'Declare a TextBox object and set it to the ActiveControl
```

```
        Dim objTextBox As TextBox = Me.ActiveControl

        'Copy the text to the clipboard and clear the field
        objTextBox.Cut()
    End Sub
```

3. The next menu item that we need to code is the **mnuEditCopy** menu item. Add the procedure for the `Click` event to your code:

```
Private Sub mnuEditCopy_Click(ByVal sender As Object, ByVal e As _
                    System.EventArgs) Handles mnuEditCopy.Click
    'Declare a TextBox object and set it to the ActiveControl
    Dim objTextBox As TextBox = Me.ActiveControl

    'Copy the text to the clipboard
    objTextBox.Copy()
End Sub
```

4. Add the procedure for the `Click` event to your code for the **mnuEditPaste** menu item. In this procedure add the following code:

```
Private Sub mnuEditPaste_Click(ByVal sender As Object, ByVal e As _
                    System.EventArgs) Handles mnuEditPaste.Click
    'Declare a TextBox object and set it to the ActiveControl
    Dim objTextBox As TextBox = Me.ActiveControl

    'Copy the data from the clipboard to the textbox
    objTextBox.Paste()
End Sub
```

5. The last menu item under the **Edit** menu is the **Select All** menu item. Add the procedure for the `Click` event of this menu item to your code:

```
Private Sub mnuEditSelectAll_Click(ByVal sender As Object, _
        ByVal e As System.EventArgs) Handles mnuEditSelectAll.Click
    'Declare a TextBox object and set it to the ActiveControl
    Dim objTextBox As TextBox = Me.ActiveControl

    'Select all text
    objTextBox.SelectAll()
End Sub
```

How It Works

We added the code for the **Edit** menu starting with the **Undo** item. Since we have two textboxes on our form, we need a way to determine which textbox we are dealing with or a generic way of handling an undo operation for both textboxes. We have opted to go with the latter and provide a generic way to handle both textboxes.

We do this by declaring a variable as a `TextBox` object and setting it to the active control using the `ActiveControl` property of the form, which retrieves the active control on the form. This is the control that has focus:

```
Private Sub mnuEditUndo_Click(ByVal sender As Object, ByVal e As _
                    System.EventArgs) Handles mnuEditUndo.Click
    'Declare a TextBox object and set it to the ActiveControl
    Dim objTextBox As TextBox = Me.ActiveControl
```

> It should be noted that the menu and toolbar are never set as the active control. This allows us to use the menus and toolbar buttons and always reference the active control.

Now that we have a reference to the active control on the form, we can invoke the `Undo` method as shown in the last line of code here. The `Undo` method is a method of the `TextBox` control and will undo the last operation in that textbox if it can be undone.

```
    'Undo the last operation
    objTextBox.Undo()
End Sub
```

> The **ActiveControl** property works fine in our small example since all we are dealing with is two textboxes. However, in a real-world application, you would need to test the active control to see if it supported the method that you were using (for example, **Undo**).

The next menu item under the Edit menu is Cut. The first thing that we do in this procedure is to again get a reference to the active control on the form and set it to the `TextBox` object that we declared.

Then we invoke the `Cut` method. This is a method of the `TextBox` control and will copy the selected text to the clipboard and then remove the selected text from the textbox:

```
Private Sub mnuEditCut_Click(ByVal sender As Object, ByVal e As _
                    System.EventArgs) Handles mnuEditCut.Click
    'Declare a TextBox object and set it to the ActiveControl
    Dim objTextBox As TextBox = Me.ActiveControl

    'Copy the text to the clipboard and clear the field
    objTextBox.Cut()
End Sub
```

Again, we declare a `TextBox` object and get a reference to the active control on the form for the Copy menu item. Then we invoke the `Copy` method to have the text in the active textbox copied to the clipboard:

```
Private Sub mnuEditCopy_Click(ByVal sender As Object, ByVal e As _
                    System.EventArgs) Handles mnuEditCopy.Click
    'Declare a TextBox object and set it to the ActiveControl
```

```
        Dim objTextBox As TextBox = Me.ActiveControl

        'Copy the text to the clipboard
        objTextBox.Copy()
    End Sub
```

For the `Click` event for the **Paste** menu item, the first thing that we do is to get a reference to the active control by setting it to our `TextBox` object that we have declared. Then we invoke the `Paste` method, which will paste the text contents of the clipboard into our textbox:

```
Private Sub mnuEditPaste_Click(ByVal sender As Object, ByVal e As _
                        System.EventArgs) Handles mnuEditPaste.Click
    'Declare a TextBox object and set it to the ActiveControl
    Dim objTextBox As TextBox = Me.ActiveControl

    'Copy the data from the clipboard to the textbox
    objTextBox.Paste()
End Sub
```

Lastly for the **Select All** item, we once again get a reference to the active control by setting it to the `TextBox` object that we declared. Then we invoke the `SelectAll` method, which will select all text in the textbox that is active:

```
Private Sub mnuEditSelectAll_Click(ByVal sender As Object, _
        ByVal e As System.EventArgs) Handles mnuEditSelectAll.Click
    'Declare a TextBox object and set it to the ActiveControl
    Dim objTextBox As TextBox = Me.ActiveControl

    'Select all text
    objTextBox.SelectAll()
End Sub
```

Having just added the code to make the **Edit** menu items functional, let's move on and make the menu items under the **View** menu functional. We will also add the code to make the toolbar buttons functional in this section.

Try It Out – Coding the View Menu and the Main Toolbar

1. Add the `mnuViewToolbarsMain_Click` event procedure to your code and then add the following:

```
Private Sub mnuViewToolbarsMain_Click(ByVal sender As Object, _
        ByVal e As System.EventArgs) Handles mnuViewToolbarsMain.Click
    'Toggle the View\Toolbars\Main menu item Checked property
    mnuViewToolbarsMain.Checked = Not mnuViewToolbarsMain.Checked

    'Toggle the visibility of the Main toobar
    tbrMain.Visible = Not tbrMain.Visible
End Sub
```

2. We need to add the same type of code that we just added above to the mnuViewToolbarsFormatting submenu item. So add the code shown below to its Click event procedure.

```
Private Sub mnuViewToolbarsFormatting_Click(ByVal sender As Object, _
        ByVal e As System.EventArgs) _
        Handles mnuViewToolbarsFormatting.Click
    'Toggle the View\Toolbars\Formatting menu item Checked property
    mnuViewToolbarsFormatting.Checked = Not _
    mnuViewToolbarsFormatting.Checked

    'Toggle the visibility of the Formatting toolbar
    tbrFormatting.Visible = Not tbrFormatting.Visible
End Sub
```

3. There's one last procedure that we need to add here and that is the procedure to implement the functionality for the main toolbar. Click on the **Class Name** combo box and select **tbrMain** and in the **Method Name** combo box select the **ButtonClick** event. This is the event that gets fired when a toolbar button is clicked:

```
Private Sub tbrMain_ButtonClick(ByVal sender As Object, ByVal e As _
        System.Windows.Forms.ToolBarButtonClickEventArgs) _
        Handles tbrMain.ButtonClick
    Select Case tbrMain.Buttons.IndexOf (e.Button)
        Case 0   'New
            'Call the corresponding menu item
            mnuFileNew_Click(Nothing, Nothing)
        Case 1   'Separator
        Case 2   'Cut
            'Call the corresponding menu item
            mnuEditCut_Click(Nothing, Nothing)
        Case 3   'Copy
            'Call the corresponding menu item
            mnuEditCopy_Click(Nothing, Nothing)
        Case 4   'Paste
            'Call the corresponding menu item
            mnuEditPaste_Click(Nothing, Nothing)
        Case 5   'Separator
        Case 6   'Undo
            'Call the corresponding menu item
            mnuEditUndo_Click(Nothing, Nothing)
    End Select
End Sub
```

4. It's now time to test our code! Click on the run toolbar button and when your form loads up, the only toolbar that you see is the main toolbar as shown:

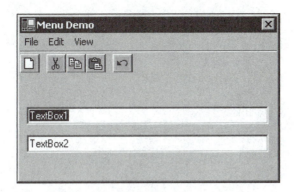

5. Notice that unlike most other applications, you do not immediately see the access keys. However, if you press the *Alt* key they will appear. Go ahead and press *Alt+E* to display the Edit menu. Notice that now we can see the shortcut keys that we did not see in design mode:

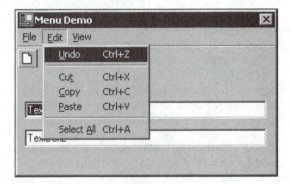

6. Click on the View menu and then click on the Toolbars menu item. Notice that the Main submenu item is checked and the main toolbar is visible. Go ahead and click on the Formatting submenu item. The formatting toolbar is now displayed along with the main toolbar.

7. If you click on the View menu again and then click on the Toolbars menu item you will see that both the Main and Formatting submenu items are checked. Notice the difference in the check marks. The Main submenu item uses a checkmark while the Formatting submenu item uses a radiocheck.

This was because we set the RadioCheck property to True for the Formatting submenu item. This demonstrates the different check marks that can be displayed in a menu.

The RadioCheck property has been used here for demonstration purposes. In a real world application, you would use this property for a group of menu items of which only one could be selected at a time.

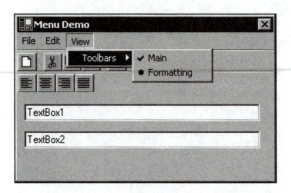

8. Let's now test the functionality of the **Edit** menu. Click in the first textbox and ensure that the text is not highlighted. Then click on the **Edit** menu and select the **Select All** menu item. Before selecting it though, take notice of the shortcut key for this menu item. Once you select the **Select All** menu item, the text in the textbox is highlighted.

   Now click in the second textbox and ensure the text is not highlighted. Press the shortcut keys *Ctrl+A* and the text in the second textbox will be highlighted. This demonstrates how the menu and shortcut keys work.

9. We now want to copy the text in the second textbox while the text is highlighted. Hover your mouse over the **Copy** icon on the toolbar to view the tool tip. Now either click on the **Copy** icon on the toolbar, or select the **Edit | Copy** menu item.

   Place your cursor in the first textbox at the end of the current text, ensuring that the text is not highlighted. Then either click on the **Paste** icon on the toolbar or click on the **Edit | Paste** menu item. The text TextBox2 is pasted in the first textbox behind the current text.

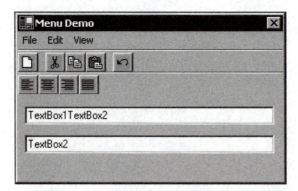

10. Now place your cursor in the second textbox between the letters t and B and either click on the **Paste** icon on the toolbar, or click on the **Edit | Paste** menu item. The text on the clipboard is now inserted between the letters where your cursor is:

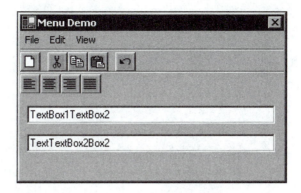

11. Click on the Undo icon on the toolbar, or click on the Edit | Undo menu item, or use the shortcut key of *Ctrl+Z* to undo the last operation in the textbox. The text in the second textbox is now restored to its previous state.

Place your cursor in the first textbox and perform an undo operation. Notice that the text in the first textbox is also restored to its previous state. If you perform an undo operation again, the text will be restored to the state before the undo and you will see the text TextBox1TextBox2 in the first textbox.

12. The last item on the Edit menu to test is the Cut menu item. Highlight the text in the first textbox by clicking on the Edit menu and selecting the Select All menu item. Then either click on the Cut icon on the toolbar or click on the Edit | Cut menu item. The text is copied to the clipboard and is then removed from the textbox.

Place your cursor in the second textbox and highlight the text there. Then paste the text in this textbox. The text that was there has been replaced with the text that was cut from the first textbox. This is how Windows cut, copy, and paste operations work and, as you can see, there was very little code required to implement this functionality in our program.

13. Now click on the File menu and choose the New menu item. The text in the textboxes is cleared. The only menu item left to test is the Exit menu item under the File menu. However, before we test that, we want to take a quick look at context menus.

Type some text in one of the textboxes. Now, right-click in that textbox and you will see a context menu pop up as seen in the next figure. Notice that this context menu appeared automatically; there was no code that you needed to add to have this done. This is a feature of the Windows operating system and Visual Studio .NET provides a way to override the default context menus, as we will see in the next section.

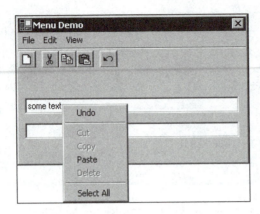

14. To test the last bit of functionality of our program, select the File | Exit menu item and your program will end.

How It Works

To begin with, we added the code to show and hide the toolbars on our form. The Main and Formatting submenu items are under the Toolbars menu item of the View menu. We added the procedures for these submenu items to our code just as we had done for the menu items above.

The first thing that we had to do was toggle the Checked property of the submenu item. We did this by setting the Checked property of the mnuViewToolbarsMain submenu item to not equal itself. Therefore, if the Checked property is set to True then this will cause it to be set to False and if it is set to False it will cause it to be set to True:

```
Private Sub mnuViewToolbarsMain_Click(ByVal sender As Object, _
        ByVal e As System.EventArgs) Handles mnuViewToolbarsMain.Click
    'Toggle the View\Toolbars\Main menu item Checked property
    mnuViewToolbarsMain.Checked = Not mnuViewToolbarsMain.Checked
```

The next line of code will toggle the visibility of the main toolbar by using the Visible property, which also contains a True or False value. We set the Visible property to not equal itself, and so toggle it between True and False:

```
    'Toggle the visibility of the Main toolbar
    tbrMain.Visible = Not tbrMain.Visible
End Sub
```

We then added the same type of code to the mnuViewToolbarsFormatting submenu item. The first line of code toggles the mnuViewToolbarsFormatting submenu item by checking it or unchecking it, and the second line of code toggles the visibility of the formatting toolbar.

Lastly, we added one further procedure that implemented the functionality for the main toolbar. When a toolbar button is clicked, the tbrMain_ButtonClick procedure is fired and the button that was clicked is passed in the ToolBarButtonClickEventArgs class. Remember that the buttons on the toolbar are a collection of buttons within the toolbar. The ToolBarButtonClickEventArgs class contains information about the button that was clicked in the Button property.

We can determine the exact button that was clicked by using a `Select Case` statement and assigning the index of the button that was clicked to the `IndexOf` method of the `Buttons` property of the toolbar. This will give us the exact index position of the button that was clicked. The `Button` property in the `ToolBarButtonClickEventArgs` class contains the index of the button in the `Buttons` collection that was clicked. This class is assigned to the parameter `e` in our procedure:

```
Private Sub tbrMain_ButtonClick(ByVal sender As Object, _
    ByVal e As System.Windows.Forms.ToolBarButtonClickEventArgs) _
    Handles tbrMain.ButtonClick
  Select Case tbrMain.Buttons.IndexOf (e.Button)
```

The first `Case` statement checks the index of the first button, which is the **New** button in the `Buttons` collection. The `Buttons` collection, like all other collections, is zero-based, meaning that the first button has an index of zero. If this was the button that was clicked, then we call the `mnuFileNew_Click` procedure passing it `Nothing` for the required arguments for that procedure. Since the `mnuFileNew_Click` procedure has two required arguments we need to pass something and the `Nothing` keyword works fine. The `mnuFileNew_Click` procedure contains all of the logic necessary to clear the textboxes on the form.

The next `Case` statement is here merely to document the collection of buttons for you. This is the separator button between the **New** button and the **Cut** button:

```
Case 0   'New
    'Call the corresponding menu item
    mnuFileNew_Click(Nothing, Nothing)
Case 1   'Separator
```

The next three buttons in the `Buttons` collection represent the **Cut**, **Copy**, and **Paste** buttons. We check the index of the button in a `Case` statement and then call the appropriate menu procedure that corresponds to the button clicked:

```
Case 2   'Cut
    'Call the corresponding menu item
    mnuEditCut_Click(Nothing, Nothing)
Case 3   'Copy
    'Call the corresponding menu item
    mnuEditCopy_Click(Nothing, Nothing)
Case 4   'Paste
    'Call the corresponding menu item
    mnuEditPaste_Click(Nothing, Nothing)
```

There is a separator button between the **Paste** button and the **Undo** button. We have listed it in the code merely to document it for you. The last `Case` statement in this code checks to see if the button that was clicked was the **Undo** button. If it is then we call the `mnuEditUndo_Click` procedure to perform an undo operation on the active textbox:

```
Case 5   'Separator
Case 6   'Undo
    'Call the corresponding menu item
```

```
                mnuEditUndo_Click(Nothing, Nothing)
        End Select
    End Sub
```

You can experiment with showing and hiding the toolbars by clicking the submenu items. Each time you click a submenu item, the corresponding toolbar will either be shown or hidden, and the check mark will either be shown or hidden.

Context Menus

Context menus are menus that pop up when a user clicks the right mouse button over a control or window. This provides the user with quick access to the most commonly used commands for the control that they are working with. As we just saw, the context menu that appeared provides us with a way to manage the text in a textbox.

Context menus are customized for the control that you are working with and in the more complex applications such as Visual Studio .NET or Microsoft Word, they provide quick access to the commands for the task that is being performed.

We saw that Windows provides a default context menu for the textbox that we were working with and, as we mentioned above, we can override the default context menu if our applications dictate that we do so. For example, suppose that you have an application where we want the user to be able to copy the text in a textbox, but not actually cut or paste text in that textbox. This would be an ideal situation to provide our own context menu to only allow the operations that we want.

Visual Studio .NET provides a **ContextMenu** control that we can place on our form and customize just as we did the MainMenu control. However, the main difference between the MainMenu control and the ContextMenu control is that we can only create one top-level menu with the ContextMenu control. We can still create submenu items with the ContextMenu if we need to.

Most controls in the toolbox have a ContextMenu property that can be set to the context menu that you define. Then when you right-click on that control, the context menu that you have defined will be displayed instead of the default context menu.

Some controls, such as the ComboBox and ListBox controls, do not have a default context menu. This is because they contain a list of items and not a single item like controls such as the textbox. They do, however, have a ContextMenu property that can be set to a context menu that you define.

Now that we know what context menus are, let's see how to create and use them in our Visual Basic .NET applications.

In the next *Try It Out*, we will be expanding the code in the previous one by adding a context menu to work with our textboxes. We will add one context menu and use it for both textboxes. You could, however, just as easily create two context menus, one for each textbox, and have the context menus perform different functions.

1. Open the Menus project if it is not already opened.

2. View the form in the designer and then click on the toolbox to locate the ContextMenu control. Drag and drop it onto your form. It will be added at the bottom of the development environment just as the MainMenu and ImageList controls were.

3. Click on the text that says Context Menu to have the first entry added. In the first text area, enter the text Undo. In the Properties window, set the Name property to cmuUndo and assign a shortcut key of CtrlZ in the ShortCut property.

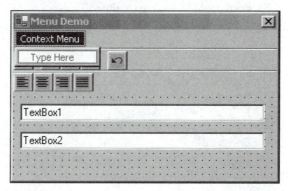

4. In the next text area, enter a dash (-) to create a separator bar between the menu items.

5. In the next few text areas enter the following menu items and set their properties accordingly.

Cut Menu Item	
Property	**Value**
Name	cmuCut
ShortCut	CtrlX
Text	Cut

Copy Menu Item	
Property	**Value**
Name	cmuCopy
ShortCut	CtrlC
Text	Copy

Paste Menu Item	
Property	**Value**
Name	cmuPaste
ShortCut	CtrlV
Text	Paste

Separator Menu Item	
Property	**Value**
Text	-

Select All Menu Item	
Property	**Value**
Name	cmuSelectAll
ShortCut	CtrlA
Text	Select All

6. When you are done, click on any part of the form and the context menu will disappear. (You can always make it reappear by clicking on the `ContextMenu` control at the bottom of the development environment.)

7. Click on the first textbox and in the Properties window select ContextMenu1 in the drop-down list for the **ContextMenu** property. Repeat the same action for the second textbox to assign a context menu in the **ContextMenu** property.

Let's test our context menu for look and feel. At this point, we haven't added any code to it but we can ensure it looks visually correct.

Run the application, then right-click in the first textbox and you will see the context menu that you have just added. The same context menu will appear if you also right-click in the second textbox:

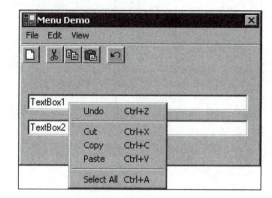

8. Now let's stop our program and switch to the code for our form so that we can add the code for the context menus. The first procedure that we want to add is that for the Undo context menu item. Bring up the `cmuUndo_Click` event procedure and add the following lines to it:

```
Private Sub cmuUndo_Click(ByVal sender As Object, ByVal e As _
                    System.EventArgs) Handles cmuUndo.Click
    'Call the corresponding menu item
    mnuEditUndo_Click(Nothing, Nothing)
End Sub
```

9. We now want to insert the procedure for the Cut context menu item. Bring up the `cmuCut_Click` event procedure and add the code to call the `mnuEditCut_Click` procedure as shown below:

```
Private Sub cmuCut_Click(ByVal sender As Object, ByVal e As _
                    System.EventArgs) Handles cmuCut.Click
    'Call the corresponding menu item
    mnuEditCut_Click(Nothing, Nothing)
End Sub
```

10. Insert the procedure for the Copy context menu item next (`cmuCopy_Click`). Add the code to call the `mnuEditCopy_Click` event as shown in the code below:

```
Private Sub cmuCopy_Click(ByVal sender As Object, ByVal e As _
                    System.EventArgs) Handles cmuCopy.Click
    'Call the corresponding menu item
    mnuEditCopy_Click(Nothing, Nothing)
End Sub
```

11. Insert the procedure for the Paste context menu item and add the code to call the `mnuEditPaste_Click` procedure as shown below:

```
Private Sub cmuPaste_Click(ByVal sender As Object, ByVal e As _
                    System.EventArgs) Handles cmuPaste.Click
    'Call the corresponding menu item
```

```
        mnuEditPaste_Click(Nothing, Nothing)
End Sub
```

12. The last procedure that we need to add (cmuSelectAll_Click) is for the **Select All** context menu item. Add the code to call the mnuEditSelectAll_Click procedure as shown below:

```
Private Sub cmuSelectAll_Click(ByVal sender As Object, ByVal e As _
                        System.EventArgs) Handles cmuSelectAll.Click
    'Call the corresponding menu item
    mnuEditSelectAll_Click(Nothing, Nothing)
End Sub
```

13. That's all the code that we need to add to implement our own context menu. Pretty simple huh? Let's run our project so we can see our context menu in action and test it.

You can test the context menu by clicking on each of the context menu items shown. They will perform the same functions as their counterparts in the toolbar and **Edit** menu.

Do you see the difference in our context menu from the one shown earlier (shown again in the next figure)? Our context menu shows the shortcut keys and we have left out the **Delete** context menu item:

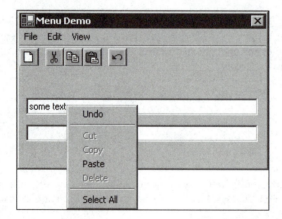

14. We need to add a procedure that can be called to toggle all of the **Edit** menu items, toolbar buttons, and context menu items from being enabled to disabled. They will be enabled and disabled based upon what should be available to the user. We'll call this procedure ToggleMenus, so add it to your code as shown below.

```
Private Sub ToggleMenus()

    'Declare a TextBox object and set it to the ActiveControl
    Dim objTextBox As TextBox = Me.ActiveControl

    'Toggle the Edit\Undo menu item
    mnuEditUndo.Enabled = objTextBox.CanUndo
```

```
    'Toggle the Undo context menu item
    cmuUndo.Enabled = objTextBox.CanUndo
    'Toggle the Undo toolbar button
    tbrMain.Buttons(6).Enabled = objTextBox.CanUndo

    'Toggle the Edit\Cut menu item
    mnuEditCut.Enabled = objTextBox.SelectionLength
    'Toggle the Cut context menu item
    cmuCut.Enabled = objTextBox.SelectionLength
    'Toggle the Cut toolbar button
    tbrMain.Buttons(2).Enabled = objTextBox.SelectionLength

    'Toggle the Edit\Copy menu item
    mnuEditCopy.Enabled = objTextBox.SelectionLength
    'Toggle the Copy context menu item
    cmuCopy.Enabled = objTextBox.SelectionLength
    'Toggle the Copy toolbar button
    tbrMain.Buttons(3).Enabled = objTextBox.SelectionLength

    'Toggle the Edit\Paste menu item
    mnuEditPaste.Enabled = _
        Clipboard.GetDataObject().GetDataPresent(DataFormats.Text)
    'Toggle the Paste context menu item
    cmuPaste.Enabled = _
        Clipboard.GetDataObject().GetDataPresent(DataFormats.Text)
    'Toggle the Paste toolbar button
    tbrMain.Buttons(4).Enabled = _
        Clipboard.GetDataObject().GetDataPresent(DataFormats.Text)
    'Toggle the Edit\Select All menu item
    mnuEditSelectAll.Enabled = objTextBox.SelectionLength < _
        objTextBox.Text.Length
    'Toggle the Select All context menu item
    cmuSelectAll.Enabled = objTextBox.SelectionLength < _
        objTextBox.Text.Length
End Sub
```

That's it! All of that code will toggle the Edit menu items, the context menu items, and the toolbar buttons. Now all we need is to figure out when and where to call this procedure.

15. Since we are only checking for the two textboxes on our form, we can call the ToggleMenu procedure when the user moves the mouse in a textbox. This way, we will toggle the Edit menu items and toolbar buttons when the user is in a textbox and the code will be applied against the textbox that we are in. To do this click on the Class Name combo box, select TextBox1, and in the Method Name combo box select the MouseMove event. This will insert an empty procedure into your code. All we need to do here is to call the ToggleMenus procedure as shown below:

```
Private Sub TextBox1_MouseMove(ByVal sender As Object, ByVal e As _
    System.Windows.Forms.MouseEventArgs) Handles TextBox1.MouseMove
    'Toggle the menu items and toolbar buttons
    ToggleMenus()
End Sub
```

16. Repeat this same process for the second textbox on the form. The code for this procedure is shown below:

```
Private Sub TextBox2_MouseMove(ByVal sender As Object, ByVal e As _
    System.Windows.Forms.MouseEventArgs) Handles TextBox2.MouseMove
    'Toggle the menu items and toolbar buttons
    ToggleMenus()
End Sub
```

17. Let's test our code again. Once the form has displayed, click in the first textbox and ensure the text is not selected. Then right-click the mouse to display our context menu. Now the context menu has the appropriate menu items enabled:

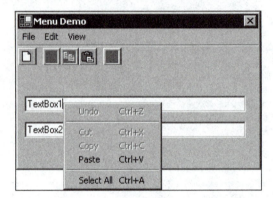

Notice also that the appropriate toolbar buttons are also enabled and disabled. If you click on the **Edit** menu, you will see that the appropriate menu items there are also enabled and disabled.

If you click on the **Select All** menu item or context menu item, you will see the toolbar buttons change as well as the menu items under the **Edit** menu and context menu.

How It Works

Notice that we are using a different prefix of cmu for our names here. This will distinguish this menu item as a context menu item.

Since we had already written all of the code that these context menu items needed, all we had to do was insert a call to the appropriate procedures. In the cmuUndo_Click procedure, we added the code shown below, which calls the mnuEditUndo_Click procedure. We pass the Nothing keyword as the required parameters to that procedure:

```
Private Sub cmuUndo_Click(ByVal sender As Object, ByVal e As _
                    System.EventArgs) Handles cmuUndo.Click
    'Call the corresponding menu item
    mnuEditUndo_Click(Nothing, Nothing)
End Sub
```

This was repeated for all the items on the **Edit** menu with the different Click procedures being called.

Besides having the shortcut keys shown, there's one other difference that stood out when we first tested our context menu. Our context menu had all of its items enabled. In order to enable and disable the appropriate menu items, we needed to perform some basic checks before the context menu was displayed.

The first thing that we had to do in the `ToggleMenus` procedure was declare an object and set it equal to the active `TextBox` control. We saw this in the last *Try It Out* and this object had all of the properties that the active textbox had:

```
Private Sub ToggleMenus()
    'Declare a TextBox object and set it to the ActiveControl
    Dim objTextBox As TextBox = Me.ActiveControl
```

The first **Edit** menu item is **Undo** so we started there. The `TextBox` control has a property called `CanUndo`, which returns a `True` or `False` value indicating whether or not the last operation performed in the textbox can be undone.

We'll use the `CanUndo` property to set the `Enabled` property of the **Edit** menu item. The `Enabled` property is set using a Boolean value, which works out great since the `CanUndo` property returns a Boolean value. The code below shows how we set the `Enabled` property of the **Undo** menu item.

We also want to toggle the `Enabled` property for the **Undo** context menu item and we use the `CanUndo` property for this too.

The toolbar also has an **Undo** button, and we want to enable or disable it also. Here we are specifying the main toolbar name, `tbrMain`, the `Buttons` collection, and the index of the item in the `Buttons` collection. Then we specify the `Enabled` property and set it to the `CanUndo` property of our `TextBox` object:

```
'Toggle the Edit\Undo menu item
mnuEditUndo.Enabled = objTextBox.CanUndo
'Toggle the Undo context menu item
cmuUndo.Enabled = objTextBox.CanUndo
'Toggle the Undo toolbar button
tbrMain.Buttons(6).Enabled = objTextBox.CanUndo
```

The next menu item in the **Edit** menu is the **Cut** menu item. This time we use the `SelectionLength` property of our `TextBox` object. `SelectionLength` returns the number of characters selected in a text box. We can use this number to act as `True` or `False` value because a value of `False` in Visual Basic .NET is 0 and a value of `True` is 1. Since the value of `False` is always evaluated first, any number other than 0 evaluates to `True`.

Therefore, if no text is selected, the `SelectionLength` property will return 0 and we will disable the **Cut** menu item, **Cut** context menu item, and **Cut** toolbar button. If no text is selected, we don't want to allow the user to perform this operation:

```
'Toggle the Edit\Cut menu item
mnuEditCut.Enabled = objTextBox.SelectionLength
'Toggle the Cut context menu item
cmuCut.Enabled = objTextBox.SelectionLength
'Toggle the Cut toolbar button
tbrMain.Buttons(2).Enabled = objTextBox.SelectionLength
```

The next menu item in the **Edit** menu is **Copy** menu item. Again, we use the SelectionLength property to determine if any text is selected in the textbox. If no text is selected, we do not want to allow the user to perform the copy operation and we disable the **Copy** menu items and toolbar button:

```
'Toggle the Edit\Copy menu item
mnuEditCopy.Enabled = objTextBox.SelectionLength
'Toggle the Copy context menu item
cmuCopy.Enabled = objTextBox.SelectionLength
'Toggle the Copy toolbar button
tbrMain.Buttons(3).Enabled = objTextBox.SelectionLength
```

The next menu item in the **Edit** menu is the **Paste** menu item. Setting the Enabled property of this menu item requires a little more work.

Using the Clipboard object, we invoke the GetDataObject method, which retrieves the data that is on the clipboard. Then using the GetDataPresent method, and passing it an argument of DataFormats.Text, we can determine if the data on the clipboard is text data.

The DataFormat class provides static clipboard data format names. The clipboard can contain text, images, and objects so we need a way to determine if the data on the clipboard is text and this is it.

The GetDataPresent method returns a Boolean value indicating whether the clipboard contains data in text format. Using this return value, we can set the Enabled property of the **Paste** menu item, context menu item, and the **Paste** toolbar button as shown in the code below:

```
'Toggle the Edit\Paste menu item
mnuEditPaste.Enabled = _
    Clipboard.GetDataObject().GetDataPresent(DataFormats.Text)
'Toggle the Paste context menu item
cmuPaste.Enabled = _
    Clipboard.GetDataObject().GetDataPresent(DataFormats.Text)
'Toggle the Paste toolbar button
tbrMain.Buttons(4).Enabled = _
    Clipboard.GetDataObject().GetDataPresent(DataFormats.Text)
```

You can view the MSDN Library that is installed with Visual Studio .NET to see more information about the Clipboard class and to view a complete list of its members.

The last **Edit** menu item is the **Select All** menu item. Again, we use the SelectionLength property to determine if any text has been selected. If all of the text has been selected, then we want to set the Enabled property to False, and set it to True at all other times. To do so we compare the length of the selected text to the length of the text in the textbox:

```
'Toggle the Edit\Select All menu item
mnuEditSellectAll.Enabled = objTextBox.SelectionLength < _
    objTextBox.Text.Length
'Toggle the Select All context menu item
cmuSellectAll.Enabled = objTextBox.SelectionLength < _
    objTextBox.Text.Length
End Sub
```

This concludes this *Try It Out,* and although we have added very little code we have gained a lot of functionality.

Summary

This chapter has taken a look at how to implement menus and context menus. We have also seen how to implement toolbars although that was not the focus of the chapter. Through practical hands-on exercises, you have seen how to create menus, menu items, and submenu items. You have also seen how to add access keys and shortcut keys to these menu items.

Since we used the Edit menu in the *Try It Outs* you have also seen how easy it is to implement basic editing techniques in your application using the Clipboard object and the properties of the TextBox control. You can see how easy it is to provide this functionality to your users – something users have come to expect in every good Windows application.

We have also explored how to create and implement context menus and to override the default context menus provided by Windows. Since we had already coded the procedure to implement cut, copy, and paste operations we simply reused these in our context menus.

To summarize, you should know how to:

❑ Add a MainMenu control to your form and add menus, menu items, and submenu items

❑ Customize the menu items with a checkmark or radiocheck

❑ Add access keys and shortcut keys to your menu items

❑ Add a ContextMenu control to your form and add menu items

❑ Use the properties of the TextBox control to toggle the Enabled property of menu items

Questions

1. How do you specify an access key for a menu item?

2. Can you specify any shortcut key that you want?

3. Can you specify checkmarks and radiochecks in a context menu?

4. Can you create submenu items in a context menu?

5. Can you create as many menu items as you want?

Advanced Object-Oriented Techniques

In Chapter 4, we looked at how we can build our own objects. Since then, we've mostly been using objects that already exist in the Framework to build our applications. In this chapter, we'll be taking a look at some more object-oriented software development techniques.

In the first half of this chapter, we will create our own classes. This will be a single-tier application like the others we have developed so far in this book. The idea of creating two-tier applications, as apposed to single-tier applications, will be introduced in Chapter 13.

We will then go on to talk about creating our own shared properties and methods. These are very useful when we want a method or property to apply to a class as a whole, rather than a specific instance of that class.

Finally, we will look at memory management in Visual Studio.NET and what we can do to clean up after our objects properly.

Building a Favorites Viewer

In the first half of this chapter, we're going to build a simple application that can display all of your Internet Explorer favorites and provides a button that you can click on to open up the URL in Internet Explorer. This will illustrate a key point regarding code reuse and illustrate some of the reasons why building code in an object-oriented fashion is so powerful.

Internet Shortcuts and Favorites

You're most likely familiar with the concepts of favorites in Internet Explorer. For example, here's my list of favorites:

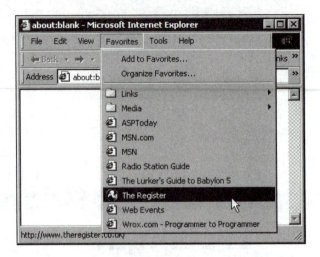

What you may not know is how Internet Explorer stores those favorites. In fact, the favorites list is available to all other applications – providing you know where to look.

Modern Windows 2000 and XP applications have the option of storing data in separate user folders within a folder called C:\Documents and Settings. Here you can see that my computer has only one user folder – **Administrator**.

> *Default User is a special folder that Windows uses whenever a new user logs onto the computer for the first time and All Users contains items that are available to all users irrespective of who they log in as.*

Depending on how the security of your computer is configured you may not be able to access this folder. Open the folder whose name matches the name that you supply when you log on. In the screenshots throughout this chapter, I've used **Administrator**. (If you consistently cannot open the folder, ask your system administrator to help you log in as a different user.) If you open this folder, you'll find another group of folders. You'll see something like the following screenshot (though it may look different depending upon how your login is configured):

You'll notice that, on my computer, some of these folders appear as faint icons, whereas others appear as normal folders. My computer is configured to show all folders, so you may find that on your machine the faint folders do not appear as these are normally hidden. This doesn't matter, because the one we're specifically looking for – Favorites – will appear whatever your system settings.

This **Administrator** folder is where Windows stores a lot of folders that are related to the operation of your computer, for example:

- ❑ Cookies – stores the cookies that are placed on the computer by Web sites that you visit

- ❑ Desktop – stores the folders and links that appear on your desktop

- ❑ Favorites – stores a list of Internet Explorer favorites

- ❑ My Documents – the default location for storing Microsoft Office and other application data

- ❑ Start Menu – stores a list of folders and links that appear when you press the Start button

It's the Favorites folder that we're interested in here, so open it up. You'll see something like this (obviously, this list will be different on your computer, as you'll have different favorites):

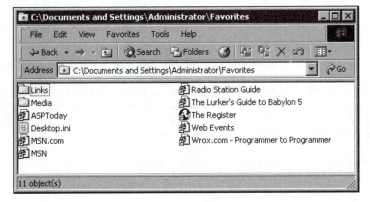

You'll notice that the links inside this folder relate to the links that appear in the Favorites menu in your browser. If you double-click on one of those links you'll see that Internet Explorer opens and navigates to the URL that the favorite points to.

We can be fairly confident at this stage that, if we have a folder of links that appear to be favorites, we can create an application that opens this folder and can do something with the links – namely iterate through each of them, add them to a list, find out what URL they belong to and provide a way to open that URL from our application. In our example, we're going to ignore the folders and just deal with the favorites that appear in the root **Favorites** folder.

Our final application will look like this:

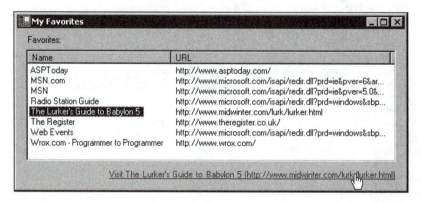

Using Classes

So far in this book we've built basic applications that do something, but most functionality that they provide has been coded into the applications' forms. Here, we're about to build some functionality that can load a list of favorites from the user's computer and provide a way to open Internet Explorer to show the URL. However, we will do it in a way that means we can use the *list of favorites* functionality elsewhere.

The best way to build this application is to create a set of classes that include:

❑ A class called `WebFavorite` that represents a single favorite, and has member variables such as `Name` and `Url`

❑ A class called `Favorites` that can scan the favorites list on the user's computer, creating a new `WebFavorite` object for each favorite

❑ A class called `WebFavoriteCollection` that contains a collection of `WebFavorite` objects

These three classes provide the **back-end** functionality of the application – in other words, all classes that do something but do not present the user with an interface. This isolates the code in the classes, and allows us to reuse the code from different parts of the application – **code reuse**. We'll also need a **front end** to our application, which, in our case, will be a Windows form with a couple of controls on it.

In the next few sections, we'll build our classes and Windows application, and come up with the application whose screenshot we saw above.

Creating the Windows Application Project

We'll start off by building the Windows Application project.

Try It Out – Creating Favorites Viewer

1. Open Visual Studio.NET and create a new Visual Basic Windows Application project called Favorites Viewer.

2. When the Form Designer for Form1 appears, add a ListView control and a LinkLabel control to it, like this:

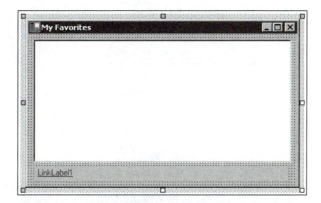

3. Select the ListView control and change these properties:

Property	Value
Name	lstFavorites
View	Details
Anchor	Top, Bottom, Left, Right

4. Select the LinkLabel control and change these properties:

Property	Value
Name	lnkUrl
TextAlign	MiddleRight
Anchor	Bottom, Left, Right

5. Select the lstFavorites control and select the Columns property in the Properties window. Click the ellipsis (...) button to display the ColumnHeader Collection Editor dialog.

6. Click the Add button. Set these properties on the new column header:

Property	Value
Name	hdrName
Text	Name
Width	250

7. Click the Add button again to add a second column. Set these properties on the new column header:

Property	Value
Name	hdrUrl
Text	URL
Width	250

8. Click OK to close the editor and you should see this:

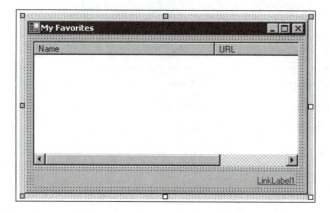

That's the basics of the form put together. Let's now look at how we can add the back-end classes.

Adding Classes

We learned in Chapter 4 how to add classes to a Visual Studio .NET project, so we will use this feature to create the back end of our application.

Try It Out – Adding Classes

1. Using the Solution Explorer, right-click on Favorites Viewer. Select Add | Add Class from the menu.

2. This will display the Add New Item dialog. Select Class from the Templates list and give the class a name of WebFavorite:

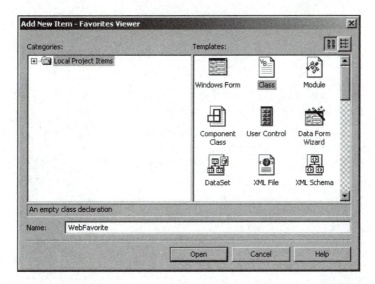

3. Click Open and the new class will be created.

How It Works

All we've done is create another class. For now, we need to turn our attention to actually putting some functionality into WebFavorite.

Building WebFavorite

Let's move on and start adding some methods and member variables to WebFavorite – the class that is used to instantiate objects that represent a single favorite.

Try It Out – Building WebFavorite

1. Using the Solution Explorer, open the code editor for WebFavorite by right-clicking on it and selecting View Code.

2. Add this namespace import declaration to the top of the code listing:

```
Imports System.IO

Public Class WebFavorite
End Class
```

3. Then, add these two members:

```
Public Class WebFavorite

    ' members...
    Public Name As String
    Public Url As String
```

401

```
End Class
```

4. Next, add this method:

```vb
' Load - open a .url file and populate ourselves...
Public Sub Load(ByVal fileInfo As FileInfo)

    ' firstly, set the name, but trim off the extension...
    Name = fileInfo.Name.Substring(0, _
        fileInfo.Name.Length - fileInfo.Extension.Length)

    ' open the file...
    Dim stream As New FileStream(fileInfo.FullName, FileMode.Open)
    Dim reader As New StreamReader(stream)

    ' go through each line...
    Do While True

        ' get a line...
        Dim buf As String = reader.ReadLine
        If buf Is Nothing Then Exit Do

        ' does the string start with "url="
        If buf.StartsWith("URL=") Then

            ' set the url...
            Url = buf.Substring(4)

            ' quit...
            Exit Do

        End If

    Loop

    ' close the file...
    reader.Close()
    stream.Close()

End Sub
```

5. Finally, add this method:

```vb
' Open - opens the favorite in IE...
Public Sub Open()
    System.Diagnostics.Process.Start(Url)
End Sub
```

Scanning Favorites

So that we can scan the favorites, we need to add a couple of new classes to the project. The first, `WebFavoriteCollection`, will be used to hold a collection of `WebFavorite` objects. The second, `Favorites` will physically scan the `Favorites` folder on the computer, create new `WebFavorite` objects and add them to the collection.

Try It Out – Scanning Favorites

1. Using the Solution Explorer, create a new class called `WebFavoriteCollection`. This class will be instantiated to an object that can hold a number of `WebFavorite` objects.

2. Add this code:

```
Public Class WebFavoriteCollection
    Inherits CollectionBase

    ' Add - add items to the collection...
    Public Sub Add(ByVal favorite As WebFavorite)
        List.Add(favorite)
    End Sub

    ' Remove - remove items from the collection...
    Public Sub Remove(ByVal index As Integer)
        If index >= 0 And index < Count Then
            List.Remove(index)
        End If
    End Sub

    ' Item - get items by index...
    Public ReadOnly Property Item(ByVal index As Integer) _
            As WebFavorite
        Get
            Return CType(List.Item(index), WebFavorite)
        End Get
    End Property
End Class
```

3. Create another new class called `Favorites`. This will be used to scan the favorites folder, and return a `WebFavoriteCollection` containing a `WebFavorite` object for each favorite in the folder.

4. Start off by adding this namespace declaration to the top of the code listing:

```
Imports System.IO

Public Class Favorites
End Class
```

5. Next, add this member:

```
Public Class Favorites

    ' members...
    Public FavoritesCollection As WebFavoriteCollection

End Class
```

6. We'll need a read-only property that can return the path to the user's `Favorites` folder. Add the following code within the `Favorites` class, below the code in the previous step and before the `End Class` statement:

```
' FavoritesFolder - returns the folder...
Public ReadOnly Property FavoritesFolder() As String
    Get
        Return _
        Environment.GetFolderPath(Environment.SpecialFolder.Favorites)
    End Get
End Property
```

7. Finally, we'll need a method that's capable of scanning through a folder looking for `.url` files. When it finds one, it will create a `WebFavorite` object and add it to the `Favorites` collection. We'll provide two versions of this method – one that automatically determines the path of the favorites by using the `FavoritesFolder` property and one that scans through a given folder. To do this add the following code to the `Favorites` class:

```
' ScanFavorites - look through the list of favorites...
Public Sub ScanFavorites()
    ScanFavorites(FavoritesFolder)
End Sub

Public Sub ScanFavorites(ByVal folderName As String)

    ' double-check... do we have a favorites list?
    If FavoritesCollection Is Nothing Then FavoritesCollection = New _
                    WebFavoriteCollection()

    ' get the folder...
    Dim scanFolder As New DirectoryInfo(folderName)

    ' look through each one...
    Dim favoriteFile As FileInfo
    For Each favoriteFile In scanFolder.GetFiles

        ' is it a .url file?
        If String.Compare(favoriteFile.Extension, ".url", True) = 0 Then

            ' create a new webfavorite...
            Dim favorite As New WebFavorite()
            favorite.Load(favoriteFile)
```

```
                        ' add it to the collection...
                        FavoritesCollection.Add(favorite)

                End If

        Next

End Sub
```

To make all of this work, we need to get the `Favorites Viewer` project to create an instance of a `Favorites` object, get it to scan the favorites, and add each one it finds to the list.

Try It Out – Creating an Instance of a Favorites Object

1. From the top-left drop-down list, select (**Overrides**). From the right-hand list, select **OnLoad**. Add this code:

```
Protected Overrides Sub OnLoad(ByVal e As System.EventArgs)

        ' create a favorites object...
        Dim favorites As New Favorites()
        favorites.ScanFavorites()

        ' go through each favorite...
        Dim favorite As WebFavorite
        For Each favorite In favorites.FavoritesCollection

                ' add it to the list...
                Dim item As New ListViewItem()
                item.Text = favorite.Name
                item.SubItems.Add(favorite.Url)
                lstFavorites.Items.Add(item)

        Next

End Sub
```

2. Run the project, and you should see something like this:

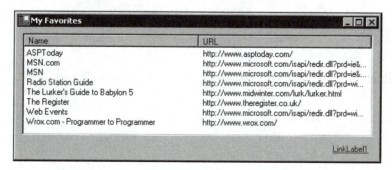

How It Works – WebFavoriteCollection

There's a lot to take in there, but a good starting point is the `WebFavoriteCollection` class. This illustrates an important best practice when working with lists of objects.

As we saw in Chapter 6, we can hold lists of objects in one of two ways – either by holding them in an array or by holding them in a collection.

When building classes that work with lists, best practice is to use a collection. We should build collections that are also tied into using whatever types we're supposed to be working with, so in this example we've built a `WebFavoriteCollection` class that exclusively holds a collection of `WebFavorite` objects.

We derived `WebFavoriteCollection` from `System.Collections.CollectionBase`. This provides the basic list that the collection will use:

```
Public Class WebFavoriteCollection
    Inherits CollectionBase
```

To fit in with the .NET Framework's way of doing things, we need to define three methods on a collection that we build. The `Add` method adds an item to the collection:

```
' Add - add items to the collection...
Public Sub Add(ByVal favorite As WebFavorite)
    List.Add(favorite)
End Sub
```

The `List` property is a protected member of `CollectionBase` that only code within classes inheriting from `CollectionBase` have access to. We access this property to add, remove, and find items in the list. You can see from the `Add` method here that we've specified that the item must be a `WebFavorite` object. This is why we're supposed to build collections using this technique – because we can only add objects of type `WebFavorite`, anyone who has hold of a `WebFavoriteCollection` object knows that it will only certain objects of type `WebFavorite`. This makes life much easier for them, because they will not get nasty surprises when they discover it contains something else, and therefore reduces the chance of errors.

The `Remove` method we have to build removes an item from the list:

```
' Remove - remove items from the collection...
Public Sub Remove(ByVal index As Integer)
    If index >= 0 And index < Count Then
        List.Remove(index)
    End If
End Sub
```

The `Item` method lets us get an item from the list when given a specific index:

```
' Item - get items by index...
Public ReadOnly Property Item(ByVal index As Integer) _
        As WebFavorite
    Get
        Return CType(List.Item(index), WebFavorite)
    End Get
End Property
```

How It Works – Favorites

So how do we populate this collection? Well, on the `Favorites` class we built a method called `ScanFavorites`. This takes a folder and examines it for files that end in `.url`. But, before we look at that we need to look at the `FavoritesFolder` property.

Since the location of the Favorites folder can change depending on the currently logged in user, we have to ask Windows where this folder actually is. To do this, we use the shared `GetFolderPath` method of the `System.Environment` class:

```
' FavoritesFolder - returns the folder...
Public ReadOnly Property FavoritesFolder() As String
    Get
        Return _
        Environment.GetFolderPath(Environment.SpecialFolder.Favorites)
    End Get
End Property
```

`GetFolderPath` can be used to return most of the special system folders available on the computer, including the location of the `My Documents` folder, the `Program Files` folder, and where Windows itself is installed. Look in the MSDN documentation under the `GetFolderPath` method of the `Environment` class for more information.

When the application asks us to load in the favorites from the disk, it will call `ScanFavorites`. The first version of this takes no parameters. It looks up the location of the user's `Favorites` folder and passes that to another version of the method:

```
' ScanFavorites - look through the list of favorites...
Public Sub ScanFavorites()
    ScanFavorites(FavoritesFolder)
End Sub
```

The first thing that this second version of the method does is check to ensure that the `Favorites` member contains a `WebFavoriteCollection` object. If it doesn't, it creates one.

```
Public Sub ScanFavorites(ByVal folderName As String)

    ' double-check... do we have a favorites list?
    If FavoritesCollection Is Nothing Then FavoritesCollection = New _
                WebFavoriteCollection()
```

The method then creates a `System.IO.DirectoryInfo` object that we can use to find the files:

```
    ' get the folder...
    Dim scanFolder As New DirectoryInfo(folderName)
```

Once we have that, we scan through each file in turn:

```
    ' look through each one...
    Dim favoriteFile As FileInfo
    For Each favoriteFile In scanFolder.GetFiles
```

Whenever we come across a file, we check to make sure that the file's extension is `.url`. We use `String.Compare` to perform a case-insensitive match for us here, so we'll detect files with an extension of `.url`:

```
' is it a .url file?
If String.Compare(favoriteFile.Extension, ".url", True) = 0 Then
```

If we find a file, we create a new `WebFavorite` object and call `Load`. We'll examine `Load` in a moment, but suffice it to say that this method opens the `.url` file and determines which URL the favorite actually points to:

```
' create a new webfavorite...
Dim favorite As New WebFavorite()
favorite.Load(favoriteFile)
```

After we have the new `WebFavorite` object, we add it to `FavoritesCollection`:

```
' add it to the collection...
FavoritesCollection.Add(favorite)

End If

Next

End Sub
```

How It Works – WebFavorite

The next thing we need to examine is how the `WebFavorite` object populates itself when the `Load` method is called. The first thing we do is set the `Name` variable.

We do this by taking the name of the file (for example `"The Register.url"`) and removing the extension. The `Substring` method of the string lets us do this, and here we're saying, "Take a substring, starting at the zeroth, or first, character, and continue for the complete length of the string minus the length of the `Extension` property." This, in effect, removes the `.url` from the end. Notice that the array of `Char` variables that make up a string is zero-based, just like all the arrays that we've seen so far.

```
' Load - open a .url file and populate ourselves...
Public Sub Load(ByVal fileInfo As FileInfo)

    ' firstly, set the name, but trim off the extension...
    Name = fileInfo.Name.Substring(0, _
        fileInfo.Name.Length - fileInfo.Extension.Length)
```

Once we have the name, we open the file and create a new `System.IO.StreamReader` object that lets us read data from the file line by line:

```
' open the file...
Dim stream As New FileStream(fileInfo.FullName, FileMode.Open)
Dim reader As New StreamReader(stream)
```

We then set up a loop and read a single line from the file per iteration. If this line comes back as blank, or `Nothing`, we quit the loop as this signals the end of the file:

```
' go through each line...
Do While True

    ' get a line...
    Dim buf As String = reader.ReadLine
    If buf Is Nothing Then Exit Do
```

When we have the line, we look to see if it starts with the text `URL=`. If it does, we use `Substring` again, but this time we create a string starting at the fourth index (fifth character) of the string all the way until the end. Once we have the URL, we also quit the loop because there's no need to continue looking through the file when we have the data we need:

```
    ' does the string start with "url="
    If buf.StartsWith("URL=") Then

        ' set the url...
        Url = buf.Substring(4)

        ' quit...
        Exit Do

    End If

Loop
```

After we've finished with the file, we close it and the `StreamReader`:

```
    ' close the file...
    reader.Close()
    stream.Close()

End Sub
```

So at this point we can create an instance of a `Favorites` object and ask it to scan through the favorites. We can also get a list of the favorites back. To finish off this discussion, this is what happens when the form is loaded.

How It Works – Form1

Firstly, we create a new `Favorites` object. Once we have the object, we ask it to scan the favorites by calling the `ScanFavorites` method. The effect here is that a new `WebFavoritesCollection` object will be created and filled, and will be accessible through the `FavoritesCollection` property:

```
Protected Overrides Sub OnLoad(ByVal e As System.EventArgs)

    ' create a favorites object...
    Dim favorites As New Favorites()
    favorites.ScanFavorites()
```

409

After `ScanFavorites` has finished, we take each favorite in turn and add it to the list:

```
' go through each favorite...
Dim favorite As WebFavorite
For Each favorite In favorites.FavoritesCollection

    ' add it to the list...
    Dim item As New ListViewItem()
    item.Text = favorite.Name
    item.SubItems.Add(favorite.Url)
    lstFavorites.Items.Add(item)

Next

End Sub
```

That's it! Now we can display a list of the favorites that the user has installed on their machine. However, we can't actually view favorites, so let's look at that now.

Viewing Favorites

We've already built a method on `WebFavorite` called `Open` that contains code to open the favorite and run it. What we need to do now is change our application so that when a favorite is selected from the list, the link label control at the bottom of the form is configured to report the name of the selected favorite and when this control is clicked, Internet Explorer will be opened to the URL of the favorite.

At the moment, when we add items to the list, we're creating, configuring, and adding `ListViewItem` objects. When an item is selected from the list, we can only find the currently selected `ListViewItem` object, and resolving this object to a `WebFavorite` that we can actually use is quite hard. What we want to do instead is create a new class derived from `ListViewItem`. We can easily add a property to this new class that references a `WebFavorite` object and by virtue of the fact that it's derived from `ListViewItem`, we can add it to the list without any problems.

Try It Out – Viewing Favorites

1. Using the Solution Explorer, add a new class to the `Favorite Viewer` project called `WebFavoriteListViewItem`.

2. Next, set the class to inherit from `System.Windows.Forms.ListViewItem`, like this:

```
Public Class WebFavoriteListViewItem
    Inherits ListViewItem

End Class
```

3. Finally, add this member and this new constructor to the class:

```
Public Class WebFavoriteListViewItem
    Inherits ListViewItem
```

```
    ' members...
    Public Favorite As WebFavorite

    ' Constructor...
    Public Sub New(ByVal newFavorite As WebFavorite)

        ' set the property...
        Favorite = newFavorite

        ' set the text...
        Text = Favorite.Name
        SubItems.Add(Favorite.Url)

    End Sub

End Class
```

4. Open the code editor for Form1. At the top of the class definition, add this member:

```
Public Class Form1
    Inherits System.Windows.Forms.Form

    ' members...
    Private _selectedFavorite As WebFavorite
```

5. Next, add this property:

```
' SelectedFavorite property...
Public Property SelectedFavorite() As WebFavorite
    Get
        Return _SelectedFavorite
    End Get
    Set(ByVal Value As WebFavorite)

        ' store the item...
        _SelectedFavorite = Value

        ' did we select anything?
        If Not _SelectedFavorite Is Nothing Then

            ' update the link label control...
            lnkUrl.Text = "Visit " & _SelectedFavorite.Name
            lnkUrl.Enabled = True

        Else

            ' disable the link...
            lnkUrl.Enabled = False

        End If

    End Set
End Property
```

6. From the left drop-down list of the code editor, select lstFavorites. From the right list, select Click. Add this code to the new event handler:

```
Private Sub lstFavorites_Click(ByVal sender As Object, _
        ByVal e As System.EventArgs) Handles lstFavorites.Click

    ' reset the selection...
    SelectedFavorite = Nothing

    ' go through each item looking for the selected one...
    Dim item As WebFavoriteListViewItem
    For Each item In lstFavorites.Items

        ' selected?
        If item.Selected = True Then

            ' store the selected item...
            SelectedFavorite = item.Favorite

            ' exit the loop...
            Exit For

        End If

    Next

End Sub
```

7. Next, find the OnLoad method. (Remember to select (Overrides) from the left drop-down at the top of the code editor, as we did previously.) Make this change to the method:

```
Protected Overrides Sub OnLoad(ByVal e As System.EventArgs)

    ' create a favorites object...
    Dim favorites As New Favorites()
    favorites.ScanFavorites()

    ' go through each favorite...
    Dim favorite As WebFavorite
    For Each favorite In favorites.FavoritesCollection

        ' add it to the list...
        Dim item As New WebFavoriteListViewItem(favorite)
        lstFavorites.Items.Add(item)

        ' if this is the first item, select it...
        If lstFavorites.Items.Count = 1 Then

            ' select it...
            item.Selected = True
            SelectedFavorite = favorite
```

```
        End If

    Next

End Sub
```

8. Finally, from the left drop-down list of the code editor select lnkUrl and from the right list select LinkClicked. Add this code to the new event handler:

```
Private Sub lnkUrl_LinkClicked(ByVal sender As System.Object, _
    ByVal e As System.Windows.Forms.LinkLabelLinkClickedEventArgs) _
    Handles lnkUrl.LinkClicked

    ' do we have a selection?
    If Not SelectedFavorite Is Nothing Then

        ' show it...
        SelectedFavorite.Open()

    End If

End Sub
```

9. Run the project. You should now see that when a URL is selected from the list, the link label control changes to reflect the name of the selected item. If you click on the link, Internet Explorer should open the URL:

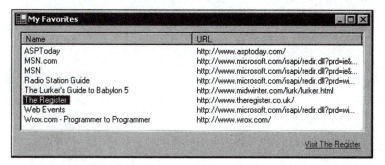

How It Works

The most important change here was altering the code so that WebFavoriteListViewItem objects were added to the list, rather than ListViewItem. If we hadn't done this, then when we asked the list for the selected item we would have got back the text ("MSN", "ASPToday", etc.) rather than a WebFavorite object. If we had only got back the text, we would have had to somehow find the related WebFavorite object from the list maintained by the Favorites object.

When we built WebFavoriteListViewItem, we provided a new constructor. This stored the favorite in the Favorite member, but also set the Text property of the item and added a new sub-item that the list used to display the URL of the link. Before we built the WebFavoriteListViewItem class, the functionality to add the link to the list was in the form's OnLoad event handler. We've moved it here to the constructor of the new class:

```
' Constructor...
Public Sub New(ByVal newFavorite As WebFavorite)

    ' set the property...
    Favorite = newFavorite

    ' set the text...
    Text = favorite.Name
    SubItems.Add(Favorite.Url)

End Sub
```

Our `SelectedFavorite` property was also quite important. This handled the updating of the link label control to report the currently selected favorite and also disabled the control if no item was selected:

```
' SelectedFavorite property...
Public Property SelectedFavorite() As WebFavorite
    Get
        Return _SelectedFavorite
    End Get
    Set(ByVal Value As WebFavorite)

        ' store the item...
        _SelectedFavorite = Value

        ' did we select anything?
        If Not _SelectedFavorite Is Nothing Then

            ' update the link label control...
            lnkUrl.Text = "Visit " & _selectedFavorite.Name
            lnkUrl.Enabled = True

        Else

            ' disable the link...
            lnkUrl.Enabled = False

        End If

    End Set
End Property
```

Finding the currently selected item from a list view control can be done in several ways. We can ask for the selected item using the `ListView.SelectedItems` property or we can iterate through each of the items in the list looking for one that has its `Selected` property set to `True`. We have selected the second option in this case:

```
Private Sub lstFavorites_Click(ByVal sender As Object, _
        ByVal e As System.EventArgs) Handles lstFavorites.Click

    ' reset the selection...
    SelectedFavorite = Nothing
```

```
' go through each item looking for the selected one...
Dim item As WebFavoriteListViewItem
For Each item In lstFavorites.Items

    ' selected?
    If item.Selected = True Then
```

Once we have it, we set the `SelectedFavorite` property and quit the loop. Remember, setting that property has the effect of updating the link label control:

```
        ' store the selected item...
        SelectedFavorite = item.Favorite

        ' exit the loop...
        Exit For

    End If

Next

End Sub
```

Finally, when the link label control is clicked, we check to make sure that we do have a `SelectedFavorite` and, if we do, call its `Open` method:

```
Private Sub lnkUrl_LinkClicked(ByVal sender As System.Object, _
    ByVal e As System.Windows.Forms.LinkLabelLinkClickedEventArgs) _
    Handles lnkUrl.LinkClicked

    ' do we have a selection?
    If Not SelectedFavorite Is Nothing Then

        ' show it...
        SelectedFavorite.Open()

    End If

End Sub
```

That brings us to the end of the discussion on building this simple favorite viewer application. We've seen some important aspects of object-oriented programming, including:

❑ Separating code into classes to promote reuse

❑ Inheritance

❑ Building specialized collections

An Alternative Favorite Viewer

OK, so we've been saying that building separate classes promotes reuse, but let's prove that. If code reuse is such a hot idea, we should be able to build another application that can use the functionality in the classes to find and open favorites but *without having to rewrite or change any of the code*.

In this case, we might have given a colleague the `Favorites`, `WebFavorite`, and `WebFavoriteCollection` classes, and that colleague should be able to build a new application that uses this functionality without having to understand the internals of how Internet shortcuts work or how Windows stores the user's favorites.

In this section, we'll build an application that displays a small icon on the system tray. Clicking on this icon will bring up a list of the user's favorites as a menu. Clicking on a favorite will then automatically open Internet Explorer to the URL.

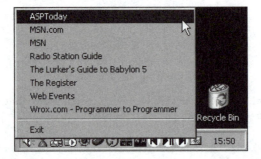

Another Application

To demonstrate this principle of reuse, we'll need to create a new Visual Basic.NET project.

Try It Out – Building Favorites Tray

1. Using Visual Studio, select File | New | Project from the menu and create a new Visual Basic.NET Windows Application project called Favorites Tray.

2. When the Designer for `Form1` appears, change the WindowState property to Minimized and change the ShowInTaskbar property to False. This will, effectively, prevent the form from being displayed.

3. Using the Toolbox, draw on a new NotifyIcon control. Set the Name property of the new control to icnNotify and set the Text property to Right-click me to view Favorites....

4. Next, open the code editor for `Form1`. Add the `_loadCalled` variable to the form:

```
Public Class Form1
    Inherits System.Windows.Forms.Form
    Private _loadCalled As Boolean = False
```

5. From the left drop-down list at the top of the code editor, select (**Overrides**) and from the right list select **OnVisibleChanged**. Add this code to the event handler:

```
Protected Overloads Overrides Sub OnVisibleChanged(ByVal _
            e As System.EventArgs)

    if _loadCalled = False Then
        Return
    End if
    ' if the user can see us, hide us...
    If Me.Visible = True Then Me.Visible = False

End Sub
```

6. We now need to design a new icon. (If we don't do this, the icon won't be displayed on the task bar and effectively our application won't do anything.) Using the Solution Explorer, right-click on the **Favorites Tray** icon and select **Add | Add New Item**. With **Local Project Items** selected in the **Categories** list, scroll down the **Templates** list and select **Icon File**. Enter the filename as **Tray.ico** and click **Open**:

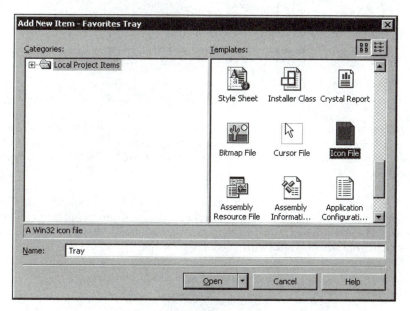

7. This will display Visual Studio .NET's Image Editor. You can use this to design new icons, new cursors, and new bitmap images for use in your applications. It's fairly intuitive to use, so I won't go through how you actually draw in much detail. In the toolbar, you'll find a list of tools that you can use to design the icon:

8. To bring up a palette of colors, select Image | Show Colors Window from the menu:

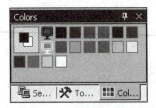

9. Before you start painting, you'll need to change the icon type. By default, Visual Studio.NET will create a 32x32 pixel icon, which is too large to fit on the tray. From the menu, select Image | New Image Type. Select 16x16, 256 colors and click OK:

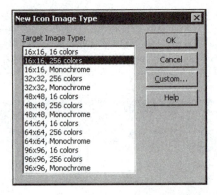

10. This will create a new sub-icon within the image file, but we need to delete the main 32x32 icon, otherwise things will get confusing. From the menu again, select Image | Current Icon Image Types | 32x32, 16 colors. Then, immediately select Image | Delete Image Type from the menu.

11. If you're feeling creative, you can design your own icon for this application. On the other hand, you can do what I've done, which is use a screen capture utility to take the favorites icon from Internet Explorer. My preferred utility is SnagIt (http://www.techsmith.com/), but a number of graphics programs offer this functionality.

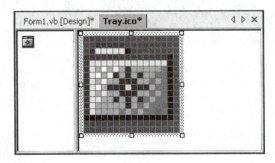

12. Save the icon by selecting File | Save from the menu.

13. Go back to the Form Designer and select the icnNotify control. Use the Icon property to load the icon into the control:

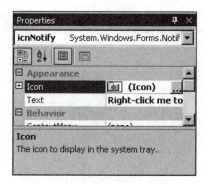

14. Try running the project now. You should discover that the tray icon will be added, but no window will appear.

15. Also, you'll notice that there appears to be no way to stop the program! Flip back to Visual Studio and select Debug | Stop Debugging from the menu.

16. When you do this, although the program will stop, the icon will remain in the tray. To get rid of it, float the mouse over it and it should disappear.

Windows only redraws the icons in the system tray when necessary, for example when the mouse is passed over it.

How It Works

Setting a form to appear minimized (WindowState = Minimized) and telling it not to appear in the taskbar (ShowInTaskbar = False) has the effect of creating a window that's hidden. We need a form to support the tray icon, but we don't need the form for any other reason. However, this is only half the battle because the form could appear in the *Alt+Tab* application switching list, unless we did this:

```
Protected Overloads Overrides Sub OnVisibleChanged(ByVal _
                e As System.EventArgs)

    ' if the user can see us, hide us...
    If Me.Visible = True Then Me.Visible = False

End Sub
```

This event handler is a brute force approach that says, "If the user can see me, hide me."

419

Displaying Favorites

Now, let's look at how we can display the favorites. The first thing we need to do is include the classes built in `Favorites Viewer` in this `Favorites Tray` solution. We can then use the `Favorites` object to get a list of favorites back and build a menu.

Try It Out – Displaying Favorites

1. In order to display favorites, we need to get hold of the classes defined in the `Favorites Viewer` project. To do this, we'll need to add the `Favorites`, `WebFavorite`, and `WebFavoriteCollection` classes to this solution.

Using the Solution Explorer, right-click on the **Favorites Tray** project and select **Add | Add Existing Item...** Click the **Browse** button and find the `Favorites` class. This will be in the `Favorites Viewer` project folder. After clicking **Open**, the class will appear in the **Solution Explorer**.

2. Repeat this for the other classes created in `Favorties Viewer`.

3. Now, create a new class in `Favorites Tray` by clicking on the project once more and selecting **Add | Add Class**. Call the new class `WebFavoriteMenuItem`. This new class is pretty similar to the `WebFavoriteListViewItem` that we added in `Favorites Viewer` before.

4. Set the new class to inherit from `System.Windows.Forms.MenuItem`:

```
Public Class WebFavoriteMenuItem
    Inherits MenuItem

End Class
```

5. Add this member and method:

```
Public Class WebFavoriteMenuItem
    Inherits MenuItem

    ' members...
    Public Favorite As WebFavorite

    ' Constructor...
    Public Sub New(ByVal newFavorite As WebFavorite)

        ' set the property...
        Favorite = newFavorite

        ' update the text...
        Text = Favorite.Name

    End Sub

End Class
```

6. Unlike `ListViewItem`, `MenuItem` objects can react to themselves being clicked by overloading the `OnClick` method. From the left drop-down list in the code editor, select (**Overrides**) and from the right drop-down list select **OnClick**. Add this code:

```
Protected Overrides Sub OnClick(ByVal e As System.EventArgs)

    ' open the favorite...
    If Not Favorite Is Nothing Then
        Favorite.Open()
    End If

End Sub
```

7. We need to do a similar trick to add an `Exit` option to our popup menu. Using the Solution Explorer, create a new class called `ExitMenuItem` in the `Favorites Tray` project. Add the following code:

```
Public Class ExitMenuItem
    Inherits MenuItem

    ' Constructor...
    Public Sub New()
        Text = "Exit"
    End Sub

    ' OnClick...
    Protected Overrides Sub OnClick(ByVal e As System.EventArgs)
        Application.Exit()
    End Sub

End Class
```

8. Finally, we're in a position where we can load the favorites and create a menu for use with the tray icon. Add this member:

```
Public Class Form1
    Inherits System.Windows.Forms.Form

    ' members...
    Public Favorites As New Favorites()
```

9. From the left drop-down list select (**Overrides**) and from the right drop-down list select **OnLoad**. Now add the following code:

```
Protected Overrides Sub OnLoad(ByVal e As System.EventArgs)

    ' load the favorites...
    Favorites.ScanFavorites()

    ' create a new context menu...
```

```
    Dim menu As New ContextMenu()

    ' go through each favorite...
    Dim favorite As WebFavorite
    For Each favorite In Favorites.FavoritesCollection

        ' create a menu item and add it to the menu...
        Dim item As New WebFavoriteMenuItem(favorite)
        menu.MenuItems.Add(item)

    Next

    ' add a separator...
    menu.MenuItems.Add("-")

    ' then, add an exit option...
    menu.MenuItems.Add(New ExitMenuItem())

    ' finally, tell the tray icon to use this menu...
    icnNotify.ContextMenu = menu

      ' Set load flag
        _loadCalled = True
        Me.Hide()
```

End Sub

10. Run the project and the icon should appear on the tray. Right-click on the icon and you'll be able to see a list of favorites. Clicking on one will open Internet Explorer, while clicking on **Exit** will close the application:

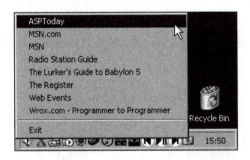

How It Works

One thing to note is because of the order of events we have to create a variable called `_loadCalled`. This variable will make sure that our favorites get loaded in the `OnLoad` method.

The `WebFavoriteMenuItem` is conceptually similar to the `WebFavoriteListViewItem` – in that we pass it a `WebFavorite` object and it configures itself. However, this class provides an `OnClick` method that we can overload. So, when the user selects the item from the menu, we can immediately open up the URL:

```
Protected Overrides Sub OnClick(ByVal e As System.EventArgs)

    ' open the favorite...
    If Not Favorite Is Nothing Then
        Favorite.Open()
    End If

End Sub
```

The `ExitMenuItem` does a similar thing. When this item is clicked, we call the shared `Application.Exit` method to quit the program:

```
' OnClick...
Protected Overrides Sub OnClick(ByVal e As System.EventArgs)
    Application.Exit()
End Sub
```

The important thing here is not the construction of the application itself, but rather the fact that we were able to reuse the functionality we built in a different project. This underlines the fundamental motive for reuse; it means you don't have to "reinvent the wheel" every time you want to do something.

The method of reuse we described here was to add the existing classes to our new project, hence making a second copy of them. This isn't efficient as it takes up double the amount of storage needed for the classes, however, the classes are small so the cost of memory is minimal, it did save us from having to create the classes from scratch, allowing us to reuse the existing code, and it was very easy to do.

An alternative way of reusing classes is to create them in a class library. This class library is a separate project that can be referenced by a number of different applications so only one copy of the code is required. This is discussed in Chapter 13.

Shared Properties and Methods

On occasion, you might find it useful to be able to access methods and properties that aren't tied to an instance of an object, but are still associated with a class.

Imagine you have a class that stores the username and password of a user for a computer program. You might have something that looks like this:

```
Public Class User

    ' members...
    Public Username As String
    Private _password As String

End Class
```

Now imagine that the password for a user has to be of a minimum length. You create a separate member to store the length and implement a property like this:

```
Public Class User

    ' members...
    Public Username As String
    Private _password As String
    Public MinPasswordLength As Integer = 6

    ' Password property
    Public Property Password As String
        Get
            Return _password
        End Get
        Set(Value As String)
            If Value.Length >= MinPasswordLength Then
                _password = Value
            End If
        End Set
    End Property

End Class
```

OK, so that seems fairly straightforward. But now imagine that you have five thousand user objects in memory. Each `MinPasswordLength`, takes up four bytes of memory, meaning that 20KB of memory is being used just to store the same value. Although 20KB of memory isn't a lot for modern computer systems, it's extremely inefficient and there is a better way.

Ideally, what we want to do is store the value for the minimum password length in memory against a specific class once and **share** that memory between all of the objects created from that class. Let's look at how we can do this now.

Try It Out – Using Shared Properties

1. Open Visual Studio.NET and create a new Visual Basic Windows Application project. Call it SharedDemo.

2. When the Designer for Form1 appears, paint on a listbox and a track bar control, like this:

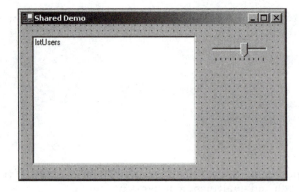

3. Set the Name property of the listbox to lstUsers.

4. Set the Name property of the track bar control to trkMinPasswordLength, and set the Value property to 6.

5. Using the Solution Explorer, create a new class named User. Add this code:

```
Public Class User

    ' members...
    Public Username As String
    Private _password As String
    Public Shared MinPasswordLength As Integer = 6

    ' Password property...
    Public Property Password() As String
        Get
            Return _password
        End Get
        Set(ByVal Value As String)
            If Value.Length >= MinPasswordLength Then
                _password = Value
            End If
        End Set
    End Property

End Class
```

6. Flip back to the Form Designer and double-click on the form background to create a new Load event handler. Add this code:

```
Private Sub Form1_Load(ByVal sender As System.Object, _
        ByVal e As System.EventArgs) Handles MyBase.Load

    Dim n As Integer
    For n = 1 To 100

        ' create a new user...
        Dim newUser As New User()
        newUser.Username = "Fred" & n
        newUser.Password = "password15"

        ' add it...
        _userList.Add(newUser)

    Next

    ' update the display...
    UpdateDisplay()

End Sub
```

7. You'll also need to add this member to `Form1.vb`:

```
Public Class Form1
    Inherits System.Windows.Forms.Form

    ' members...
    Private _userList As New ArrayList()
```

8. Next, add this method to the `Form1` class:

```
Private Sub UpdateDisplay()

    ' clear the list...
    lstUsers.Items.Clear()

    ' add them...
    Dim user As User
    For Each user In _userList
        lstUsers.Items.Add(user.Username & ", " & user.Password & _
                " (" & user.MinPasswordLength & ")")
    Next

End Sub
```

9. Flip back to the Form Designer and double-click on the track bar control to create a new `Scroll` event handler. Add this code:

```
Private Sub trackMinPasswordLength_Scroll(ByVal sender As _
        System.Object, ByVal e As System.EventArgs) _
        Handles trackMinPasswordLength.Scroll

    ' set the minimum password length...
    User.MinPasswordLength = trkMinPasswordLength.Value

    ' update the display...
    UpdateDisplay()

End Sub
```

10. Run the project. You should see this:

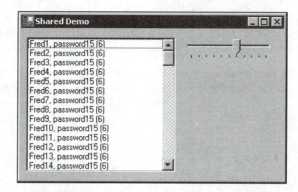

11. Slide the scroll bar, and the list should update itself and the number in parentheses should change:

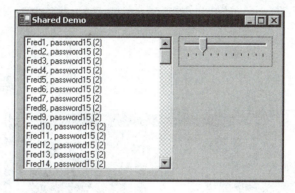

How It Works

To create a member variable, property, or method on an object that is shared, we used the Shared keyword.

```
Public Shared MinPasswordLength As Integer = 6
```

This tells VB.NET that the item should be available to all instances of the class.

Shared members can be accessed from within non-shared properties and methods as well as shared properties and methods. For example, here's the Password property that can access the shared MinPasswordLength member:

```
' Password property...
Public Property Password() As String
    Get
        Return _password
    End Get
    Set(ByVal Value As String)
        If Value.Length >= MinPasswordLength Then
            _password = Value
        End If
    End Set
End Property
```

427

What's important to realize here is that although the `Password` property and `_password` member "belong" to the particular instance of `User`, `MinPasswordLength` does not, therefore if it is changed the effect is felt throughout on all the object instances built from the class in question.

In the form, `UpdateDisplay` is used to populate the list. You can see that we can again access `MinPasswordLength` as if it were a normal, non-shared public member of the `User` object:

```
Private Sub UpdateDisplay()

    ' clear the list...
    lstUsers.Items.Clear()

    ' add them...
    Dim user As User
    For Each user In _userList
        lstUsers.Items.Add(user.Username & ", " & user.Password & _
                " (" & user.MinPasswordLength & ")")
    Next

End Sub
```

At this point, we have a listing of users that shows that the `MinPasswordLength` value of each is set to 6:

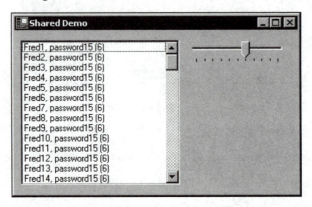

Things start to get interesting when we move the slider and change `MinPasswordLength`. As this is a shared member, we don't specifically *need* an instance of the class. Instead, we can set the property just by using the class name:

```
Private Sub trkMinPasswordLength_Scroll(ByVal sender As _
        System.Object, ByVal e As System.EventArgs) _
        Handles trkMinPasswordLength.Scroll

    ' set the minimum password length...
    User.MinPasswordLength = trkMinPasswordLength.Value

    ' update the display...
    UpdateDisplay()

End Sub
```

When building this method, you may have noticed that after you'd typed `User.`, Visual Studio.NET's IntelliSense popped up a list of members, including the `MinPasswordLength` property:

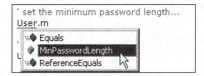

Shared members, properties, and methods can all be accessed through the class directly – you don't specifically need an instance of the class. (Actually, although you don't *need* one, if you have one you can use it, but it's not essential.)

When we change this member with code in the `Scroll` event handler, we update the display and this time you can see that the perceived value of `MinPasswordLength` has seemingly been changed for *all* instances of `User`, even though we only changed it in one place:

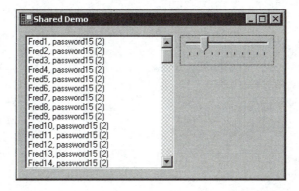

Shared Methods

Although we've seen how to make a public member variable shared, we haven't seen how to do this with a method. Let's look at an example of how to build a **shared method** that can create new instances of `User`. The main limitation with shared methods is that you can only access other shared methods and shared properties and methods.

> **This is a fairly artificial example of using a shared method as you could do the same job here with a customized constructor.**

Try It Out – Using a Shared Method

1. Open the code editor for `User`. Add this code to the `User` class:

```
' CreateUser - create a new user...
Public Shared Function CreateUser(ByVal username As String, _
            ByVal password As String) As User
```

```
    ' create a new user...
    Dim user As New User()
    user.Username = username
    user.Password = password

    ' return it...
    Return user

End Function
```

2. Open the code editor for `Form1` and find the `Load` event handler. Change the code so that it looks like this:

```
Private Sub Form1_Load(ByVal sender As System.Object, _
        ByVal e As System.EventArgs) Handles MyBase.Load

    Dim n As Integer
    For n = 1 To 100

        ' create a new user...
        Dim newUser As User
        newUser = User.CreateUser("Fred" & n, "password15")

        ' add it...
        _userList.Add(newUser)

    Next

    ' update the display...
    UpdateDisplay()

End Sub
```

3. You'll notice that as you type in the code, as soon as you type `User.`, IntelliSense offers `CreateUser` as an option:

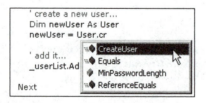

4. If you run the project, you'll get the same results as the previous example.

How It Works

The important thing to look at here is the fact that `CreateUser` appears in the IntelliSense list after you type the class name. This is because it is shared and you do not need a specific instance of a class to access it.

We created the method as a shared method by using the `Shared` keyword:

```
' CreateUser - create a new user...
Public Shared Function CreateUser(ByVal username As String, _
                ByVal password As String) As User
```

One thing to consider with shared methods – you can only access members of the class that are also shared. You cannot access non-shared methods because, simply, you don't know what instance of the class you're actually running on. Likewise, you cannot access Me from within a shared method for the same reason.

Memory Management

Object-orientation has an impact on how memory is used in an operating system. As we've already discussed, .NET is heavily object-oriented so it makes sense that .NET would have to optimize the way it uses memory to best suit the way objects are used.

Whenever you create an object, you're using memory. Most of the objects you use have **state**, which describes what an object "knows". The methods and properties that an object has will either affect or work with that state. For example, an object that describes a file on disk will have state that describes its name, its size, its folder, and so on. Some of the state will be publicly accessible through properties. For example, a property called `Size` will probably return the size of the file. Some state will be private to the object and is used to keep track of what the object has done or what it needs to do.

Objects use memory in two ways. Firstly, something needs to keep track of the objects that exist on the system in memory. This is usually a task shared between you as an application developer and the CLR. If you create an object, you'll have to hold a reference to it in your program's memory so that you know where it is when you need to use its methods and properties. The CLR also needs to keep track of the object to determine when you no longer need it.

Secondly, the CLR needs to allocate memory to the object so that the object can store its state. The more state an object has, the more memory it will need to use it.

The most expensive resource on a computer is the memory. I mean *expense* here in terms of what you get for your money. For $100, I can buy a 80GB hard disk, but for the same amount of money I can't buy 1GB of memory. Moreover, although I can, with relative ease, build a computer that supports thousands of gigabytes of storage, getting versions of Windows to use more than 4GB is a challenge. However, retrieving data from memory is thousands of times faster than retrieving it from disk so there's a tradeoff – if I need fast access, I have to store it in memory, but there isn't much memory around.

When building an application, you want to use as little memory as possible, so there's an implication that you want to have as few objects as possible and that those objects should have as little state as possible. The upside is that, today, computers have a lot more memory than they used to, so as developers we can be more relaxed about our use of memory than our predecessors writing code twenty years ago!

The CLR manages memory in several distinct ways. Firstly, it's responsible for creating objects at the request of the application. With a heavily object-oriented programming platform like .NET, this is going to happen all the time, so Microsoft has spent an awful lot of time on making sure that the CLR creates objects in the most efficient way. The CLR, for example, can create objects far faster than its COM predecessor.

Secondly, the CLR is responsible for cleaning up memory when it's no longer needed. In the developer community, the manner in which the CLR cleans up objects is one of the most controversial.

Imagine you're writing a routine that opens a file from disk and displays the contents on the screen. Well, with .NET we'll use, perhaps two Framework objects to open the file and read its contents – namely `System.IO.FileStream` and `System.IO.StreamReader`. However, after the contents have been read, do we need the objects anymore? Probably not, so what we want to do is delete the objects and make the memory the objects were using available for creating more objects.

Imagine now that we don't delete the objects. In this situation, the memory that the objects were using can't be used by anyone else. Now imagine that happening several thousand times. What happens is that the amount of memory that's being wasted keeps growing. In extreme circumstances, the computer will run out of memory, meaning that other applications won't ever be able to create any objects. This is a pretty catastrophic state of affairs.

We describe an object that is no longer needed but that holds onto memory as a **leak**. Memory leaks are one of the biggest causes of reliability problems on Windows, as when a program is no longer able to obtain memory, it will crash. There are plenty of system administrators out there who configure their servers to reboot on a daily or weekly basis just to reclaim memory that's no longer used.

With .NET, this *should* never happen or, at the very least, to leak memory you'd have to go to some pretty extreme steps. This is because of something called **garbage collection**. When an object is no longer being used, the **Garbage Collector** (**GC**) automatically removes the object from memory and makes the memory it was using available to other programs.

Garbage Collection

The Garbage Collector works by keeping track of how many parts of a program have a reference to an object. If it gets to the point where there are no open references to the object it is deleted.

To understand this, think back to our discussion of scope in Chapter 2. Imagine we create a method and at the top of that method define a variable with local scope. That variable is used to store an object (it doesn't matter what kind of object for this discussion). At this point, one part of the program "knows" about the object's existence – that is, the variable is holding a reference to the object. When we return from the method, the variable will go out of scope and therefore the variable will "forget" about the object's existence, in other words the only reference to the object is lost. At this point, nothing "knows" about the object and so it can be safely deleted.

For example:

```
Dim myObject As New MyObject
Console.WriteLine(myObject.GetType().FullName)
myObject = Nothing
```

In the above code snippet, we've created a new object from class `MyObject`, called a method on it, and then removed the reference to the object. In this case, when we create the object, the `myObject` variable is the only thing that holds a reference to it. In the last line, we set `myObject` to `Nothing`, hence removing the only reference to the object. The Garbage Collector is then free to remove the reference to the object.

The Garbage Collector does not run constantly. Instead, it runs periodically based on a complex algorithm that measures the amount of work the computer is doing and how many objects might need to be deleted. When the GC runs, it looks through the master list of all the objects the program has ever created and any that can be deleted are at this point.

In old school programming, programmers were responsible for deleting their own objects and had the freedom to say to an object, "You, now, clean yourself up and get out of memory." With .NET, this ability is gone; rather an object will be deleted at some *indeterminate* time in the future.

Exactly when this happens is non-deterministic, in other words as a developer you don't know when the Garbage Collector is going to run. This means that there is no immediate connection between the removal of the last reference to an object and the physical removal of that object from memory. This is known as **non-deterministic finalization**.

Finalize

When the object is removed from memory, the object itself has an opportunity to run some "finalize" code by way of the `Finalize` method. The Garbage Collector calls this method when the object is about to be removed from memory and can be used to implement any last minute clean-up operations that the object has to do.

Let's illustrate this now with a quick demo.

Try It Out – Exploring the Garbage Collector

1. Open Visual Studio.NET. Create a new Visual Basic Console Application (**not** a Windows Application) project and call it FinalizeDemo:

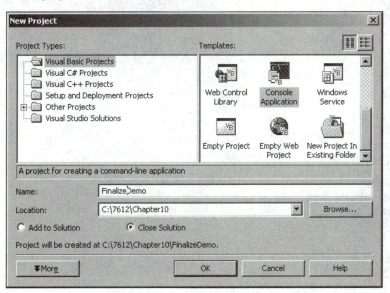

2. Using the Solution Explorer, right-click on the FinalizeDemo project and select Add | Add Class. Call the class MyObject.

3. When the code editor appears, enter this code:

```
Public Class MyObject

    ' Constructor - called when the object is started...
    Public Sub New()
        Console.WriteLine("Object " & GetHashCode() & " created.")
    End Sub

    ' Finalize - called when the object is removed from memory...
    Protected Overrides Sub Finalize()
        MyBase.Finalize()

        ' tell the user we've deleted...
        Console.WriteLine("Object " & GetHashCode() & " finalized.")

    End Sub

End Class
```

4. Open the code editor for `Module1` and add this code to `Main`:

```
Sub Main()

    ' create five objects and add them to a list...
    Dim n As Integer, list As New ArrayList()
    For n = 1 To 5
        list.Add(New MyObject())
    Next

    ' now delete the list, the objects now
    ' have no references...
    list.Clear()

    ' wait for the user to press return...
    Console.WriteLine("Press Return to collect the garbage...")
    Console.ReadLine()

    ' force a collect...
    GC.Collect()

    ' wait for the user to quit...
    Console.WriteLine("Press Return to quit...")
    Console.ReadLine()

End Sub
```

5. Run the project and you'll see this:

```
c:\temp\bin\FinalizeDemo.exe
Object 2 created.
Object 5 created.
Object 6 created.
Object 7 created.
Object 8 created.
Press Return to collect the garbage...
```

6. Press *Return* and you'll see this:

```
c:\temp\bin\FinalizeDemo.exe
Object 2 created.
Object 5 created.
Object 6 created.
Object 7 created.
Object 8 created.
Press Return to collect the garbage...

Press Return to quit...
Object 8 finalized.
Object 2 finalized.
Object 7 finalized.
Object 6 finalized.
Object 5 finalized.
```

If you wait for a long time rather than pressing *Return*, the Garbage Collector may run.

How It Works

What we've done in `MyObject` is created a class that has a constructor and a finalizer. In each case, we've used `Console.WriteLine` to report the status of the object to the user:

```
' Constructor - called when the object is started...
Public Sub New()
    Console.WriteLine("Object " & GetHashCode() & " created.")
End Sub

' Finalize - called when the object is removed from memory...
Protected Overrides Sub Finalize()
    MyBase.Finalize()

    ' tell the user we've deleted...
    Console.WriteLine("Object " & GetHashCode() & " finalized.")

End Sub
```

The `GetHashCode` method is guaranteed to be unique among objects of the same type. That means that if we call it from within `Console.WriteLine`, we can write out the ID of the object that's being constructed or finalized.

Inside `Module1`, we create five objects and add them to an array list. This means that each `MyObject` instance has one reference, and this reference is stored internally in the `ArrayList` object:

```
Sub Main()

    ' create ten objects and add them to a list...
    Dim n As Integer, list As New ArrayList()
```

```
For n = 1 To 5
    list.Add(New MyObject())
Next
```

Once we have the objects stored in the array list, we call `Clear`. This removes the references to the objects completely, meaning that they are now candidates for Garbage Collection:

```
' now delete the list, the objects now
' have no references...
list.Clear()

' wait for the user to press return...
Console.WriteLine("Press Return to collect the garbage...")
Console.ReadLine()
```

However, at this point, we see this:

We can see that five objects have been created, but none of them has been finalized because the output doesn't contain any `Object` *nn* `finalized` messages.

We can force the Garbage Collector to collect the objects. *You should never do this because it's very bad practice!* Garbage Collection is .NET's problem and you should leave it that way. However, I'm trying to show you what happens when garbage is collected, so we can get away with it here:

```
' force a collect...
GC.Collect()

' wait for the user to quit...
Console.WriteLine("Press Return to quit...")
Console.ReadLine()

End Sub
```

After `GC.Collect` has been called and the application is waiting again, we see this:

This is really interesting! The messages appear after the **Press Return to quit** message. Even though we called `GC.Collect`, the actual collection hasn't physically happened until later on in the code. Also, notice that the objects have been removed in a seemingly random order.

Remember, the `Finalize` method on the object is called just before the Garbage Collector removes it from memory. It's at this point that we display our message.

What this illustrates is that, even when you tell it to collect objects, there is no immediate link between removing the last reference to an object and `Finalize` being called. It happens some time in the future.

Releasing Resources

In some cases, objects that you build may need access to certain system and network resources, such as files and database connections. Using these resources requires a certain discipline to ensure that you don't inadvertently cause problems.

Here's an example – if you create a new file, write some data to it but forget to close it, no one else will be able to read data from that file. This is because you have an exclusive lock on the file; it doesn't make sense for someone to be able to read from a file when it's still being written to. You must take care to release system resources should you open them.

When an object has access to scarce system or network resources like this, it's important that the caller tells the object that it can release those resources as soon as they're no longer needed. For example, here's some code that creates a file:

```
' open a file...
Dim stream As System.IO.FileStream("c:\myfile.txt", _
            System.IO.FileMode.Create)

' do something with the file...
…

' close the file...
stream.Close
stream = Nothing
```

As soon as we've finished working with the file, we call `Close`. This tells .NET that the consumer is finished with the file and Windows can make it available for other people to use. This is known as "releasing the lock". When we clear the object reference by setting `stream = Nothing` in the next line, this is an entirely separate action from calling `Close`.

The `FileStream` object will release the lock on the file when its `Finalize` method is called. However, as we've just learned, the time period between the instance of the `FileStream` object becoming a candidate for Garbage Collection (which happens when `stream = Nothing`), and `Finalize` being called is non-deterministic. So, if we had not called `Close`, the file would have remained open for a period of time, which would have caused problems for anyone else who needed to get hold of the file.

Dispose

The Framework provides something called **disposing** as a standard way for users of objects to tell them to release their resources. The `FileStream` object is disposed by calling the `Close` method. Other objects are disposed by calling a method called `Dispose` method. In the vast majority of cases, these two are equivalent. The `Close` method exists because previous versions of Visual Basic used it and for compatibility (legacy) reasons some objects can still use it.

The best practice in .NET is to implement this `Dispose` method using a technique we're about to explore. In this *Try It Out*, we'll build an object that opens a file and writes to it, but that file will only be closed when it is disposed. This is a classic example of an object holding a reference to a system resource.

Try It Out – Implementing IDisposable and Dispose

1. Using `FinalizeDemo` again, add a new class called `MyFile`.

2. Add this namespace import directive to the top of the class:

```
Imports System.IO

Public Class MyFile
End Class
```

3. To build a `Dispose` method, we have to implement an **interface**. This topic is slightly beyond the scope of this book, but basically an interface is a collection of methods. By telling an object to implement an interface, that object enters into a contract with the interface to implement all of the methods on the interface. Add this code (`IDisposable` will be underlined in Visual Studio .NET until Step 7):

```
Imports System.IO

Public Class MyFile
    Implements IDisposable

End Class
```

4. Next, add these member variables to hold the file and a flag to indicate whether the object has been disposed:

```
Public Class MyFile
    Implements IDisposable

    ' members...
    Private _stream As FileStream
    Private _isDisposed As Boolean

End Class
```

5. Then, add this constructor to create or open the new file:

```
' Constructor...
Public Sub New(ByVal filename As String)

    ' create, or append to the file...
    _stream = New FileStream("c:\FinalizeDemo.txt", _
                FileMode.OpenOrCreate)

    ' tell the user...
    Console.WriteLine("Object " & GetHashCode() & " created.")
    Console.WriteLine("Using file: " & filename)

End Sub
```

6. Add this method to write to the file once it has been created:

```
' AddText - add some text to the file...
Public Function AddText(ByVal buf As String)

    ' have we been disposed?
    If _isDisposed = True Then
        Throw New ObjectDisposedException("I've been disposed!")
    End If

    ' write the time and the message...
    Dim writer As New StreamWriter(_stream)
    writer.WriteLine(Date.Now)
    writer.WriteLine(buf)
    writer.Close()

End Function
```

7. Next, add the `Dispose` method:

```
' Dispose - called when we need disposing...
Public Sub Dispose() Implements System.IDisposable.Dispose

    ' have we already been disposed?
    If _isDisposed = True Then Return

    ' clean up our resources...
    _stream.Close()
    _stream = Nothing

    ' flag us as being disposed...
    _isDisposed = True

    ' tell the GC not to collect us...
    GC.SuppressFinalize(Me)

    ' tell the user that we've been disposed...
    Console.WriteLine("Object " & GetHashCode() & " disposed.")

End Sub
```

8. Finally, add the `Finalize` method:

```
' Finalize - called when we're finalized...
Protected Overrides Sub Finalize()

    ' call dispose...
    Dispose()

    ' tell the user that we've been finalized...
    Console.WriteLine("Object " & GetHashCode() & " finalized.")

End Sub
```

9. Open the code editor for `Module1` and change the code in `Main` to match this:

```
Sub Main()

    ' create a file and write to it...
    Dim file As New MyFile("c:\FinalizeDemo.txt")
    file.AddText("Hello, world!")

    ' now, clear the reference to the object...
    file = Nothing

    ' wait for the user to press return...
    Console.WriteLine("Press Return to collect the garbage...")
    Console.ReadLine()

    ' force a collect...
    GC.Collect()

    ' wait for the user to quit...
    Console.WriteLine("Press Return to quit...")
    Console.ReadLine()

End Sub
```

10. Run the project and you should see this:

How It Works

This object is a classic example of an object that maintains a reference to a scarce system resource throughout its lifetime. When the object is created, we create a `System.IO.FileStream` object and store it in a member variable:

```
' Constructor...
Public Sub New(ByVal filename As String)

    ' create, or append to the file...
    _stream = New FileStream("c:\FinalizeDemo.txt", _
                FileMode.OpenOrCreate)

    ' tell the user...
    Console.WriteLine("Object " & GetHashCode() & " created.")
    Console.WriteLine("Using file: " & filename)

End Sub
```

However, in our `Module1` code we've done a bad thing! We've removed the reference to the object without having disposed of it:

```
Sub Main()

    ' create a file and write to it...
    Dim file As New MyFile("c:\FinalizeDemo.txt")
    file.AddText("Hello, world!")

    ' now, clear the reference to the object...
    file = Nothing
```

The upshot of this is that the reference to the `System.IO.FileStream` object remains in force and therefore no one else can gain access to the `c:\FinalizeDemo.txt` file. At some point, the Garbage Collector will call our `MyFile.Finalize` method, and then we call `Dispose`:

```
' Finalize - called when we're finalized...
Protected Overrides Sub Finalize()

    ' call dispose...
    Dispose()

    ' tell the user that we've been finalized...
    Console.WriteLine("Object " & GetHashCode() & " finalized.")

End Sub
```

Inside `Dispose`, we check to see if we have been disposed and if we are we return from the function. If not, we dispose of the `FileStream` object by calling its `Close` method:

```
' Dispose - called when we need disposing...
Public Sub Dispose() Implements System.IDisposable.Dispose

    ' have we already been disposed?
    If _isDisposed = True Then Return

    ' clean up our resources...
    _stream.Close()
    _stream = Nothing
```

We also set our _isDisposed member to True. This tells us later when we come to use other methods on the object whether we have been disposed:

```
' flag us as being disposed...
_isDisposed = True
```

Technically, after we've been disposed, there's no point in calling the Finalizer if it hasn't already been called (as it doesn't do anything), so we use GC.SuppressFinalize:

```
' tell the GC not to collect us...
GC.SuppressFinalize(Me)

' tell the user that we've been disposed...
Console.WriteLine("Object " & GetHashCode() & " disposed.")

End Sub
```

Nevertheless, all of this is an example of how *not* to do it. We can see from the screenshot that Dispose has been called some way into the future after we've actually finished with the file:

Let's amend Main so that we close the file the moment we no longer need it. This is the *right* way to do it.

Try It Out – Disposing of MyFile Properly

1. Open the code editor for Module1 and add this line:

```
Sub Main()

    ' create a file and write to it...
    Dim file As New MyFile("c:\FinalizeDemo.txt")
    file.AddText("Hello, world!")

    ' now, clear the reference to the object...
    file.Dispose()
    file = Nothing

    ' wait for the user to press return...
    Console.WriteLine("Press Return to collect the garbage...")
    Console.ReadLine()

    ' force a collect...
    GC.Collect()
```

```
        ' wait for the user to quit...
        Console.WriteLine("Press Return to quit...")
        Console.ReadLine()

    End Sub
```

2. Now run the project. `MyFile` will be disposed and the file will be closed at the earliest opportunity.

How It Works

The window shows us that the object has been disposed of at the proper time, in other words, before we ask the user to press *Return* for the first time. You can also see that there is no **Object 7 finalized** message here. That's because we called `SuppressFinalize` and therefore the Garbage Collector knows that it no longer needs to call `Finalize`.

This is a demonstration of the best practice in creating objects that can be properly disposed of by the user.

Just one more thing to point out – you can't just create a method called `Dispose`. You do have to add this to the class:

```
Public Class MyFile
    Implements IDisposable
```

This tells the Framework and anyone else who cares to look at that you do support a method called `Dispose` and (more importantly) that method is supposed to be used to dispose of the object.

AddText – What Was That Exception About?

In the `AddText` method, you may have been wondering about this piece of code:

```
        ' have we been disposed?
        If _isDisposed = True Then
            Throw New ObjectDisposedException("I've been disposed!")
        End If
```

In objects that support `Dispose`, it's important that each time before you try to access potentially disposed resources you check to make sure that they are still available. If they're not, you must use this code to throw an `ObjectDisposedException` exception. (You can find out more about **exceptions** in the next chapter. But, for now, remember that this is again another part of the best practice involved with `Dispose`.)

443

Defragmentation and Compaction

As the last part in its bag of tricks, the Garbage Collector is able to defragment and compact memory. In much the same way that your computer's hard disk needs periodic defragmentation to make it run more efficiently, so does memory. Imagine you create 10 small objects in memory, each about 1KB in size. Imagine that .NET allocates them all on top of each other so you end up taking up one 10KB piece of memory. (In reality, we don't usually care where objects exist in memory, so this discussion is a bit academic.)

Now imagine we want to create another object and this object is of medium size, say about 3KB. .NET will have to create this object at the end of the 10KB block. This means that we'll have allocated 13KB in total.

Now imagine that we delete every other small object, so now our 10KB block of memory has holes in it. Not much of a problem, but imagine we want to create another 3KB object. Although there's 5KB of space in the original block, we can't put it there because no gap is big enough. Instead, it has to go on the end, meaning our application is now taking up 16KB of memory.

What the Garbage Collector can do is defragment memory, which means that it removes the gaps when objects have been removed. The upshot of this is that your application uses space more efficiently, meaning that applications take up less memory.

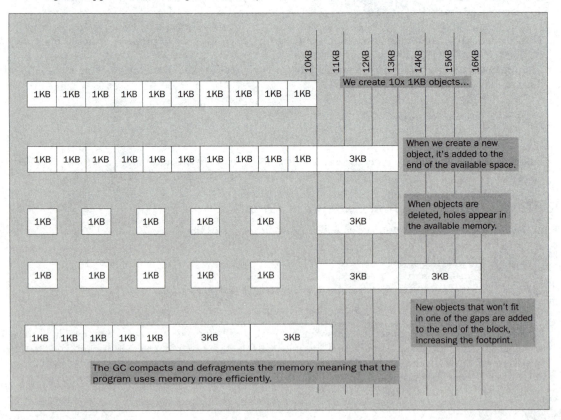

Although this may not seem like a big deal on a PC with 512MB of memory available, consider that .NET will eventually be running on much smaller devices where memory usage is a big deal, for example a cell phone with 256KB of memory in total. Besides, imagine making 3,000 5KB savings as we have in this example because then you've saved over 15MB of memory!

Summary

In this chapter, we took a look at some more valuable techniques that we are able to use to help us build object-oriented software. Initially, we examined the idea of reuse. Specifically, we looked at classes that would allow us to examine the Internet Explorer favorites stored on the user's computer. We consumed these classes from two applications – one standard desktop application and also as a mini-application that exists on the system tray.

We then examined the idea of shared members, properties, and methods. Sharing these kinds of items is a powerful way to make common functionality available to all classes in an application.

Finally, we examined how consumers of objects should ensure that scarce systems resources are freed whenever an object is deleted by the Garbage Collector using the `Dispose` and `Finalize` methods.

Questions

1. What's the advantage of using a class library?

2. In our `Favorites Tray` application, why did we create a new class that inherited from `System.Windows.Forms.MenuItem`?

3. Why do we create our own collections?

4. How much time usually elapses between an object no longer having references and the Garbage Collector cleaning it up?

5. What is the difference between `Dispose` and `Finalize`?

Debugging and Error Handling

Debugging is an essential part of any development project as it helps you find errors in your code and in your logic. Visual Studio .NET has a sophisticated debugger built right into the development environment. This debugger is the same for all languages that Visual Studio .NET supports. So once you have mastered debugging in one language, you can debug in any language that you can write in Visual Studio .NET.

In this chapter, we will take a look at some of the debugging features available in Visual Studio .NET and provide a walk through of debugging a program. We will examine how to set breakpoints in your code to stop execution at any given point, examine how to watch the value of a variable change, and how to control the number of times a loop can execute before stopping. All of these can help you determine just what is going on inside your code.

No matter how good your code is there are always going to be some unexpected circumstances that you have not thought of that will cause your code to fail. If you do not anticipate and handle errors, your users will see a default error message about an unhandled exception that is provided by the CLR (Common Language Runtime) . This is not a user-friendly message and usually doesn't clearly inform the user about what is going on or how to correct it.

This is where error handling comes in. Visual Studio .NET also provides common error handling functions that are used across all languages. These functions allow you to test some code and catch any errors that may occur. If an error does occur, you can write your own user-friendly message that informs the user of what happened and how to correct it. You also get to control execution of your code at this point and allow the user to try the operation again if it makes sense to do so. We will be taking a detailed look at the structured error-handling functions provided by Visual Studio .NET in this chapter. In particular, we will:

❑ Examine the major types of errors that you may encounter and how to correct them

❑ Examine and walk through debugging a program

❑ Examine and implement error handling in a program

Major Error Types

Error types can be broken down into three major categories: **syntax**, **execution**, and **logic**. This section will show you the important differences between these three types of errors and how to correct them.

Knowing what type of errors are possible and how to correct them will significantly speed up the development process. Of course, there are times when you just can't find the error on your own. Don't waste too much time trying to find errors in your code by yourself in these situations. Coming back to a nagging problem after a break can often help you crack it, otherwise ask a colleague to have a look at your code with you; two pairs of eyes are often better than one in these cases.

Syntax Errors

Syntax errors occur when the code you have written cannot be "understood" by the compiler because instructions are incomplete, supplied in unexpected order, or cannot be processed at all. An example of this would be declaring a variable of one name and misspelling this name in your code when you set or query the variable.

> **Syntax errors are the easiest type of errors to spot and fix.**

The development environment in Visual Studio .NET has a pretty sophisticated syntax-checking mechanism making it hard, but not impossible, to have syntax errors in your code. It provides instant syntax checking of variables and objects and will let you know immediately when you have a syntax error.

When you try to use a variable or object that you have not declared, the development environment will underline the variable or object name. This is your clue that a syntax error has occurred. If you hover your mouse over the syntax error, the development environment will display a tool tip informing you of the error:

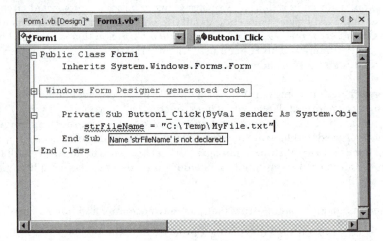

This all assumes that you have not changed the **Option Explicit** option in the project **Property Pages** dialog, which by default is turned on. This also assumes that you have not specified the `Option Explicit Off` statement in code, which overrides the **Option Explicit** option in the project **Property Pages** dialog.

The **Option Explicit** option or the statement `Object Explicit On` forces you to declare all variables before using them. This means that Visual Studio .NET can provide guidance such as that shown above, and also means that misspellings of variable names will be trapped by the compiler.

When this option or statement is turned off, all variables that are not explicitly declared are assumed to be of the `Object` data type. An `Object` data type can hold any type of value (for example, numeric or string) but it processes these values slower than the correct data type for the value being used. Therefore, it is good practice to always have the `Option Explicit` option turned on, which is the default.

If you want to turn this statement off in code, which overrides the option in the project's **Property Pages** dialog, then the `Option Explicit` statement must be the first statement in source code file. This statement will override the option in the project **Property Pages** dialog and will only apply to the code module (module or class) in which it is specified:

```
Option Explicit Off
```

The development environment also provides **IntelliSense** to assist in preventing syntax errors. IntelliSense provides a host of features such as providing a drop-down list of members for classes, structures, and namespaces as shown in the figure below. This allows you to choose the correct member for the class, structure, or namespace that you are working with:

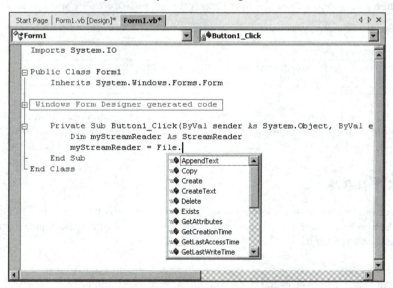

This provides two major benefits. First, you do not have to remember all of the available members for the class. You simply scroll through the list to find the member that you want to work with. To select the member in the list that you want to work with, you simply press the *Tab* key or *Enter* key, or double-click the member. Second, it helps to prevent syntax errors because we are less likely to misspell member names or try to use members that do not exist in the given class.

Another great feature of IntelliSense is that it provides a parameter list for the method that you are working with. IntelliSense will list the number, name, and type of the parameters required by the function. This is also a time saver, as you do not have to remember the required parameters for every class that you work with, or indeed search the product documentation for what you need:

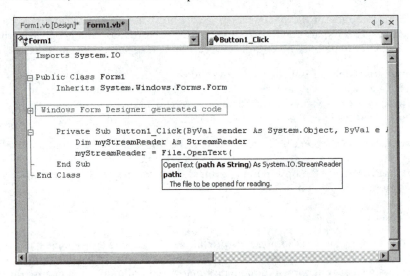

If the method is overloaded – that is, there are several methods with the same name but different parameters, then this popup will enable us to scroll through the different options, as shown here for the File.Open method:

```
File.Open(
▲1 of 3▼  Open (path As String, mode As System.IO.FileMode) As System.IO.FileStream
path: The file to open.
```

As you can see, there are plenty of built-in features in the development environment to prevent syntax errors. All you need to do is to be aware of these features and take advantage of them to help prevent syntax errors in your code.

Execution Errors

Execution errors (or **run-time errors**) are errors that occur while your program is executing. They are often caused because something outside of the application – such as a user, database, or hard disk – does not behave as expected.

Developers need to anticipate the possibility of execution errors, and build appropriate error-handling logic. Implementing the appropriate error handling will not prevent execution errors, but will allow you to handle them either by gracefully shutting down your application or bypassing the code that failed and giving the user the opportunity to perform that action again. We will cover error handling later in this chapter.

The best way to prevent execution errors is to try to anticipate the error before it occurs and to use error handling to trap and handle the error. You must also thoroughly test your code before deploying it.

Most execution errors can be found while you are testing your code in the development environment. This allows you to handle the errors and debug your code at the same time. You can then see what type of errors may occur and implement the appropriate error handling logic. We will cover debugging in the next section where we find and handle any execution errors that may crop up.

Logic Errors

Logic errors (or **semantic errors**) are errors that give unexpected or unwanted results, because we did not fully understand what the code we were writing did. Probably the most common logic error is an infinite loop:

```
Private Sub Button1_Click(ByVal sender As System.Object,
                          ByVal e As System.EventArgs) Handles Button1.Click
    Dim n As Integer
    Do While n < 10
        ' some logic here
    Loop
End Sub
```

If the code inside the loop will never set n to ten or above, then this loop will just keep going forever. This is a very simple example, but even experienced developers find themselves writing and executing loops where the exit condition can never be satisfied.

Logic errors can be the most difficult to find and troubleshoot, because it is very difficult to be sure that our program is completely free from logic errors.

Another type of logic error is when a comparison fails to give the result we expect. Say we did a comparison between a string variable set by our code from a database field or from text in a file, and the text entered by the user. We do not want the comparison to be case sensitive. We might write code like this:

```
If fileName = userInput.Text Then
    ...perform some logic
End If
```

However, if the fileName is set the Index.HTML and userInput.Text is set to index.html then the comparison will fail, causing our program to stop behaving in the way we want. One way to prevent this logic error is to convert both fields being compared to either uppercase or lowercase. This way, the results of the comparison would be True if the user entered the same text as was contained in the variable, even if the case was different.

The next code fragment shows how we can accomplish this:

```
If UCase(fileName) = UCase(userInput.Text) Then
    ...perform some logic
End If
```

The UCase statement accepts a string or character, and returns a string or character converted to all uppercase letters. This would make the comparison in the example above equal.

Since logic errors are the hardest errors to troubleshoot and can cause our applications to fail or give unexpected and unwanted results, we must ensure that we check our logic carefully as we code and try to plan for all possible errors that may be encountered by a user. As you become more experienced, you will encounter and learn from the common errors that your users make.

One of the best ways to identify and fix logic errors is to use the debugging features of Visual Studio .NET. Using these features we can find where loops execute too many times, or comparisons don't give the expected result. Let's take a look at these features now.

Debugging

Debugging code is part of life – even experienced developers will make mistakes and need to debug their code. Knowing how to efficiently debug your code can make the difference between enjoying your job as a developer and hating it.

In this section, we will take a look at some of the built-in debugging features in the Visual Studio .NET development environment. We will write a sample program and show you how to use the most common and useful debugging features available.

Before we get started talking about debugging features, let's write a sample program that we will use in our hands-on debugging exercises. This program will use the `OpenFileDialog` class to display the **Open File** dialog to allow us to choose a text file to open. We will then open and read the chosen text file line by line using the `StreamReader` class and place the contents into a textbox on the form. We will keep track of the number of lines read and also keep track of the current and previous file opened.

Try It Out – Creating a Sample Project to Debug

1. Create a new Windows Application project called Debugging and click the OK button to have the project created.

2. In the Solution Explorer window, change the form name from `Form1.vb` to `Debug.vb` and then set the form's properties as shown in the table below:

Property	Value
FormBorderStyle	FixedDialog
MaximizeBox	False
MinimizeBox	False
Size	408, 304
StartPosition	CenterScreen
Text	Debug Demo

3. Next, we want to add some basic controls to the form and set their properties. Using the table below, add these controls and set their properties:

Control	Name	Properties
TextBox	txtData	Location = 8, 8; Multiline = True; ScrollBars = Vertical; Size = 304, 192; Text = *blank*
Button	btnOpen	Location = 320, 8; Size = 75, 23; Text = Open
Button	btnClear	Location = 320, 40; Size = 75, 23; Text = Clear
Label	lblLines	Location = 8, 208; Size = 152, 16; Text = Number of lines read: 0
Label	lblLastFile	Location = 8, 232; Size = 296, 16; Text = Last file opened: None
Label	lblCurrentFile	Location = 8, 256; Size = 296, 16; Text = Current file opened: None

Your completed form should like this:

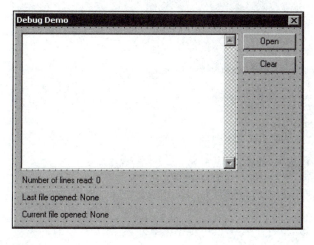

4. Add the following code to top of the Debug.vb source:

```
' Namespace for StreamReader...
Imports System.IO
```

and the following just below the Windows Forms Designer generated code region:

```vbnet
'Declare variables
Dim lastFileName As String = "None"

Public Sub btnOpen_Click(ByVal sender As System.Object, _
                         ByVal e As System.EventArgs) Handles btnOpen.Click
    ' Declare an object for the OpenFileDialog class...
    Dim myFileDialog As OpenFileDialog = New OpenFileDialog()

    ' Set the dialog properties...
    With myFileDialog
        .Filter = "Text files (*.txt)|*.txt|All files (*.*)|*.*"
        .FilterIndex = 1
        .InitialDirectory = "C:\Temp\"
        .Title = "Open File"
        .CheckFileExists = False
    End With

    ' Show the dialog...
    If myFileDialog.ShowDialog() = DialogResult.OK Then
        ' Process the file chosen...
        ProcessFile(myFileDialog.FileName)
        ' Display the last file opened...
        lblLastFile.Text = "Last file opened: " & lastFileName
        ' Display the current file opened...
        lblCurrentFile.Text = "Current file opened: " & _
                        myFileDialog.FileName
        ' Save the new file as the last file opened...
        lastFileName = myFileDialog.FileName
    End If

    ' Clean up...
    myFileDialog = Nothing
End Sub

Private Sub ProcessFile(ByVal fileName As String)
    ' Declare an object for the StreamReader class...
    Dim myReader As StreamReader

    ' Open the file...
    myReader = File.OpenText(fileName)

    ' Declare variables...
    Dim lineCounter As Integer = 0
    Dim currentLine As String, currentData As String

    ' Loop through the file counting the lines and loading the
    ' text box...
    Do
        currentLine = myReader.ReadLine
        lineCounter = lineCounter + 1
        currentData = currentData & currentLine & vbCrLf
```

```
        Loop While currentLine <> Nothing

        ' Load the text box...
        txtData.Text = currentData

        ' Display the number of lines read...
        lblLines.Text = "Number of lines read: " & _
                        lineCounter - 1

        ' Clean up...
        myReader.Close()
        myReader = Nothing
    End Sub

    Public Sub btnClear_Click(ByVal sender As System.Object,
                        ByVal e As System.EventArgs) Handles btnClear.Click
        ' Clear variables...
        lastFileName = ""

        ' Clear form fields...
        txtData.Text = ""

        ' Reset the labels...
        lblLines.Text = "Number of lines read: 0"
        lblLastFile.Text = "Last file opened: None"
        lblCurrentFile.Text = "Current file opened: None"
    End Sub
```

5. At this point, go ahead and save your project by clicking the Save All icon on the toolbar or by clicking on the File menu and choosing the Save All menu item.

How It Works

Most of this code is pretty familiar – the real purpose of it is to give us something to play with debugging. The most interesting section of this code is the Do...Loop in ProcessFile:

```
Do
    currentLine = myReader.ReadLine
    lineCounter = lineCounter + 1
    currentData = currentData & currentLine & vbCrLf
Loop While currentLine <> Nothing
```

The first line of code in this loop uses the StreamReader object myReader to read a line of text from the text file, and to set the variable currentLine to the data that has been read.

The next line of code increments the lineCounter variable to reflect the number of lines read.

The last line of code is concatenating the data read into the variable currentData. After each line of text that we concatenate to the currentData variable, we place a carriage return and line feed character using the built-in vbCrLf constant. This will cause the text in our text box to appear on separate lines instead of all on one line. We need to do this because when the StreamReader class reads a line of text it returns the line to us without the carriage return and line feed characters.

You should be familiar with most of the rest of code from Chapter 8.

Breakpoints

When trying to debug a large program you may find that you want to debug only a section of code. That is, you want your code to run up to a certain point and then stop. This is where **breakpoints** come in handy; they cause execution of your code to stop anywhere a breakpoint is defined. You can set breakpoints anywhere in your code and your code will run up to that point and stop.

> Note that execution of the code will stop *before* the line on which the breakpoint is set.

You can set breakpoints when you write your code and you can also set them at run time by switching to your code and setting the breakpoint at the desired location. You cannot set a breakpoint while your program is actually executing a section of code such as the code in a loop, but you can when the program is idle and waiting for user input.

When the development environment encounters a breakpoint, execution of your code halts and your program is considered to be in break mode. While your program is in break mode, a lot of debugging features are available. In fact, a lot of debugging features are only available to you while your program is in break mode. The following image shows what happens when executing code reaches a breakpoint:

We can set breakpoints by clicking the gray margin next to the line of code on which you want to set the breakpoint. When the breakpoint is set you will see a solid red circle in the gray margin, and the line will be highlighted in red. When you are done with a particular breakpoint, you can remove it by clicking on the solid red circle. We will see more of this in our exercise in just a moment.

Sometimes you'll want to debug code in a loop, such as one that reads data from a file. You know that the first *x* number of records are good, and it is time-consuming to step through all the code repetitively until you get to what you suspect is the bad record. A breakpoint can be set inside of the loop and you can set a hit counter on it. The code inside the loop will execute the number of times that you specified in the hit counter and then stop, and place you in break mode. This can be a real time saver and we will be taking a look at this in our next *Try It Out*.

We can also set a condition on a breakpoint, such as when a variable contains a certain value or when the value of a variable changes. We will also take a look at this in our *Try It Out*.

Before we begin, you should display the Debug toolbar in the development environment, as this will make it easier to quickly see and choose the debugging options that you want. You can do this in one of two ways. Either right-click on an empty space on the current toolbar and choose Debug in the context menu or click View | Toolbars | Debug from the menu.

Try It Out – A Simple Breakpoints Example

1. The first thing to do is set a breakpoint in the openText_Click method – on the If statement that displays the Open File dialog, to be precise. To set the breakpoint, click on the gray margin to the left of the line where the desired breakpoint should be:

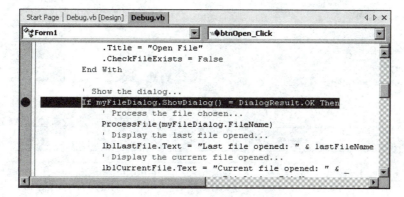

2. Now run the project.

3. In order to get to the code where the breakpoint is set we must click on the Open button on our form, so go ahead and click it. The code will be executed up to the breakpoint and the development environment window will receive focus making it the topmost window.

You should now see a yellow arrow on your breakpoint pointing to the line of code where execution has been paused and the entire line should be highlighted in yellow:

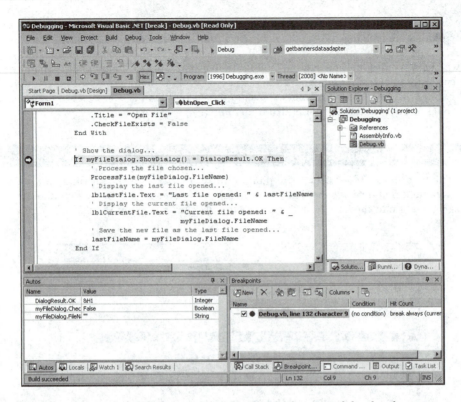

Also notice that there are a few new windows at the bottom of the development environment. What you see will vary depending on which windows you have specified to be shown – we can choose different ones using the tabs at the bottom.

Let's take a quick pause in the *Try It Out* to discuss some of the features of the IDE in debug mode. We'll carry on shortly.

The Breakpoints Window

We can display the Breakpoints window in the bottom-right of the IDE by clicking on the Breakpoints icon on the debug toolbar, or by clicking on the Debug | Windows | Breakpoints menu item:

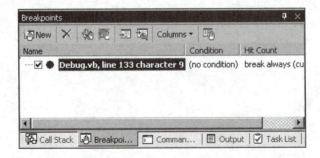

The Breakpoints window shows all of the breakpoints you have set, which in this case is only one. When a breakpoint is encountered, it will be highlighted as shown here.

In this window, we can set new breakpoints, delete existing breakpoints, and also change the properties of the breakpoints. We will see more of this later in the chapter.

Useful Icons on the Debug Toolbar

In this *Try It Out*, we want to step through our code line by line. On the Debug toolbar, there are three icons of particular interest to us:

There's one more really useful button that it's worth adding to the toolbar – Run To Cursor. Right-click on any empty area of the toolbar and choose Customize from the context menu. In the Customize dialog, click on the Commands tab, and then find and click on Debug in the Categories list. In the Commands list locate and click on Run To Cursor:

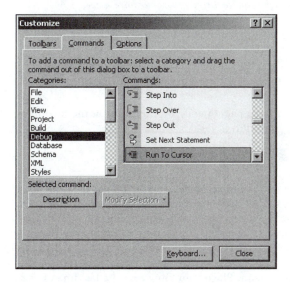

Drag this icon from the Commands list onto the debug toolbar, to form a group of icons as shown here:

The first of the icons is the Step Into icon. When we click this icon, we can step through our code line-by-line. This includes stepping into any functions or procedures that the code calls, and working through them line by line too.

The second of these icons is the Step Over icon. This works is a similar way to Step Into, but we pass straight over procedures and functions – they still execute, but all in one go. We then move straight on to the next line in the block of code that called the procedure.

The next of these icons is the **Step Out** icon. This icon allows us to jump to the end of the procedure or function that we are currently in, and move to the line of code *after* the line that called the procedure or function. This is handy when we step into a long procedure and want to get out. The rest of the code in the procedure still gets executed, but we don't need to step through it.

The last of the icons shown here is the **Run To Cursor** icon. We can place our cursor anywhere in the code following the current breakpoint where execution has been paused and then click this icon. The code between the current breakpoint and where the cursor is positioned will be executed, and execution will stop on the line of code where the cursor is located.

We're now ready to continue working through the *Try It Out*.

4. Since we are at our breakpoint now, let's click on the **Step Into** icon. The Open File dialog should be displayed and should be the window with focus. Select a text file that you worked with in Chapter 8 and then click the **Open** button in the **Open File** dialog.

If you didn't work through Chapter 8 then you need to create a text file, using something like Notepad, and save it in a suitable directory on your hard drive.

You should now be at the next line of code. This line of code calls the `ProcessFile` procedure and will process the file that you have selected:

```
ProcessFile(myFileDialog.FileName)
```

5. Click the **Step Into** icon again and you should be at the beginning of the `ProcessFile` procedure:

```
Private Sub ProcessFile(ByVal fileName As String)
```

Click the **Step Into** icon once more and you should be at the first line of executable code, which is `myReader = File.OpenText(fileName)`. Since we don't want to see any of this code at this time, we are going to step out of this procedure. This will place us back on the line that called `ProcessFile`. We do this by clicking on the **Step Out** icon. Notice that we are taken out of the `ProcessFile` procedure and back to where the call originated.

6. Let's test one more icon. Place your cursor on the last line of code in this procedure (the one shown below). Then click on the **Run To Cursor** icon. All of the code between the current line of code where execution is paused and the line of code where your cursor is will be executed, and the program will be paused again at the cursor.

```
myFileDialog = Nothing
```

7. We now want to continue processing as normal and have the rest of the code execute without interruption. If you hover your mouse over the **Start** icon on the toolbar, you will notice that the tool tip has been changed from **Start** to **Continue**. Click on this icon to let the rest of the code run.

You should now see your completed form as shown in the following figure. The labels of course will contain information that is relevant to the file that you opened:

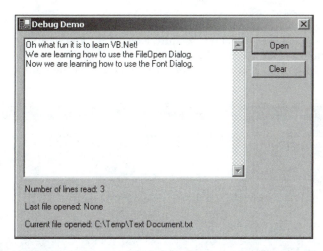

At this point, let's set another breakpoint in our code. This time we want to set a breakpoint in the `Do` loop of the `ProcessFile` procedure.

Try It Out – Using the Breakpoint's Hit Count

1. Click on the left margin next to this line of code to set the new breakpoint:

```
currentLine = myReader.ReadLine
```

2. In the Breakpoints window, click on this breakpoint and then click on the Properties icon on the Breakpoints window's toolbar. This will invoke the Breakpoint Properties dialog for this new breakpoint:

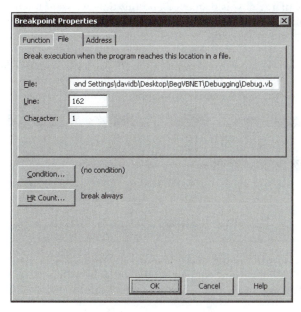

3. At the moment, this breakpoint will halt execution every time it's encountered. Let's change it to only break when the loop enters its third execution. We do this by clicking on the Hit Count button to invoke the **Breakpoint Hit Count** dialog. In the drop ndown in this dialog, select break when the hit count is equal to and then enter the number 3 in the textbox next to it as shown in the figure:

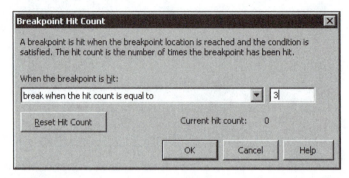

Click the OK button to close this dialog and then click the OK button to close the **Breakpoint Properties** dialog. Our program is still in run mode and just waiting for something to do.

4. At this point, let's click on the **Open** button on the form. By clicking on the **Open** button, we are again stopped at our first breakpoint.

5. This breakpoint is highlighted in the **Breakpoints** window and we no longer need it, so let's delete it. Click on the **Delete** icon in the **Breakpoints** window, and the breakpoint will be deleted. Our code is still paused at this point, so click on the **Continue** button on the **Debug** toolbar.

6. The **Open File** dialog now is displayed and this time we want to choose a different text file. Ensure that this file has at least three lines of text in it and then click the **Open** button to have the file opened and processed.

7. We are now stopped at our breakpoint in the `ProcessFile` procedure as the loop enters its third execution. Notice that the **Breakpoints** window shows the hit count criteria that we selected and also shows the current hit count:

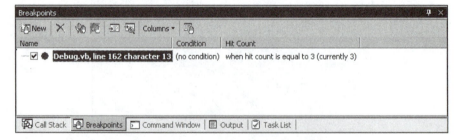

At this point it is worth noting that if you hover your mouse pointer over any of the variables in this procedure, the current contents of the variables will be displayed in a tool tip. This is a quick and handy way to see the contents of your variables while your code is paused.

This also works for properties of objects such as the textbox on the form. If you hover your mouse over the Text property of the txtData textbox, you will see the current contents of the textbox. Notice that the content of the Text property is from the previous file that you opened, as we have not set it to the contents of the current file we are reading yet.

8. Now let your code continue executing by clicking on the Continue button on the Debug toolbar.

This time let's modify the properties of the only breakpoint that we have left.

Try It Out – Changing Breakpoint Properties

1. In the Breakpoints window, click on the Properties icon to invoke the Breakpoint Properties dialog.

2. Click on the Hit Count button to invoke the Breakpoint Hit Count dialog. Notice the Reset Hit Count button. When you click this button you reset the hit counter for the next execution. Also, notice that this dialog displays the current hit count:

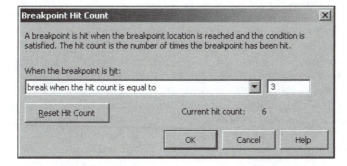

3. We want to change the hit count back to its original setting so select break always in the drop-down box and then click the OK button to close this dialog.

4. In the Breakpoints Properties dialog, we want to set a specific condition for this breakpoint so click on the Condition button to invoke the Breakpoint Condition dialog. Enter the condition as shown in the figure below. This will cause this breakpoint to only break when the variable lineCounter is equal to 3. Notice that we could also specify that the breakpoint would be activated when the value of a variable changes. Click the OK button to close the dialog and then click the OK button in the Breakpoint Properties dialog to close that dialog:

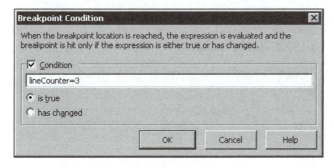

5. Now switch back to your form and open another file that has at least three lines of text. This can be the file that you just opened if you wish.

   Once the `lineCounter` variable is equal to 3, the breakpoint will be activated and the execution of the code will be paused at the line where the breakpoint is specified. Notice that this is actually our fourth time into the loop as the line of code that increments the `lineCounter` variable is the next line of code.

6. Finally, go ahead and let your code finish executing by clicking the Continue button on the Debug toolbar.

Command Window

The **Command window** (also known as the **Immediate window**) can be a very powerful ally when debugging our programs. It allows us to control the execution and outcome of our program by letting us query and set the values of variables. You can even write small amounts of code in the Command window to alter the outcome of your program such as closing objects or changing values. The Command window only allows you to enter code while your program is in break mode, but you can view the contents of the Command window at design time.

For instance, suppose you are debugging your program and query the value of a variable in your program. The results of that query are listed in the Command window. Once you stop executing your code, so long as you are in break mode, you can view the Command window and see the results of the commands that you executed, allowing you to make any adjustments to your code as necessary. Let's see how we can use the Command window while debugging. In the following Try It Out, we will use the Command window to query and set the value of various variables defined in our program. Once we are done, we will stop our program, and then display the Command window while we are in design mode.

Try It Out – Using the Command Window

1. If you previously stopped your program, start it back up again by clicking Start on the toolbar.

2. You should still have the breakpoint set. If not set it on this line of code:

```
currentLine = myReader.ReadLine
```

   and set it to break when `lineCounter = 3`.

3. Click on the Open button on your form and open a text file that has at least three lines of text in it.

4. Once the breakpoint has been activated, we are able to enter commands in the Command window. If you do not see the Command window at the bottom of the development environment, select Windows | Immediate from the Debug menu.

5. To query the value of variables in the Command window, you need to type a question mark followed by the variable name. Type `?currentData`, then press *Enter* to view the results:

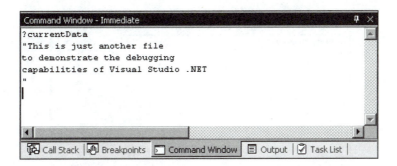

6. To change the value of a variable, you type the variable name followed by an equal sign (=) followed by the value that you want it to be, just as you would normally set your variables in code. Take note of the figure above. Since this is a string variable, the results are returned in a pair of quotation marks (" "). Thus if you want to change the value of this variable, you need to enclose the value in quotation marks as shown in the next figure.

Let's change the value of this variable to the phrase `"debugging can be easy"`. Once you type in the text, press *Enter* to have the value set:

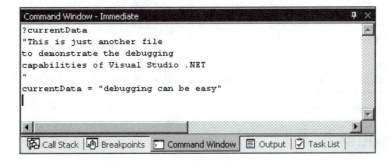

7. At this point, our code is still paused and we want to exit the loop in our code. Let's skip over the rest of the code in the loop and start with the next line of code following the `Loop While` statement. To do this, click on the yellow arrow on the breakpoint and hold down the left mouse button. Then drag the arrow to the line of code shown below and release the left mouse button. The yellow arrow should now be on this line of code:

```
txtData.Text = currentData
```

This method allows us to skip over code and not have it executed.

8. When we click on the Continue button, execution of our code will start from this point forward. Go ahead and click on the Continue button and let the rest of the code run. The textbox on your form should show the phrase that you entered in the Command window as shown in the next figure:

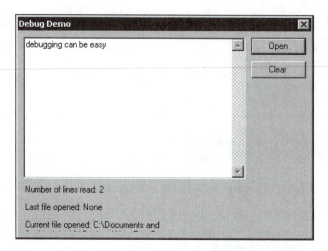

9. At this point, end the program by clicking on the **X** in the upper right-hand corner of the form.

10. From the Debug menu in the development environment, select Windows I Immediate to have the Command window displayed. Notice that you will see all of the commands that you executed. This is very handy when you are debugging code and need to see what values certain variables contained.

> You can clear the contents of the Command window by right-clicking in the window, and choosing **Clear All** from the context menu.

Watch Window

The **Watch window** provides a method for you to easily watch variables and expressions as the code is executing – this can be invaluable when you are trying to debug unwanted results in a variable. You can even change the values of variables in the Watch window. You can add as many variables and expressions as needed to debug your program. This provides a mechanism to quickly watch the values of your variables change without any intervention on your part, as was needed when we used the Command window.

You can only add and delete a **QuickWatch** variable or expression when your program is in break mode. Therefore, before you run your program, you need to set a breakpoint before the variable or expression that you want to watch. Once the breakpoint has been reached, you can add as many **Watch** variables or expressions as needed.

In the following *Try It Out*, we will add the lineCounter variable to the Watch window, and also add an expression using the lineCounter variable. This will allow us to observe this variable and expression as we step through our code.

Try It Out – Using the QuickWatch

1. If you have cleared the breakpoint that we have been using then you need to set it again on the following line of code in the `ProcessFile` procedure – but this time, do not set a condition:

```
currentLine = myReader.ReadLine
```

2. If you did not clear the breakpoint, we need to modify its condition. Bring up the Breakpoint Properties dialog for the breakpoint, using Debug | Windows | Breakpoints, highlight the desired breakpoint, and click the Properties icon. Next, click on the Condition button and in the Breakpoint Condition dialog remove all the text from the textbox. Click the OK button to close the dialog and then click OK to close the Breakpoint Properties dialog. This will cause this breakpoint to pause the program the first time that it is encountered.

We can add a QuickWatch variable or expression only while our program is paused. We can pause the program before the breakpoint is encountered, or we can wait until the breakpoint is encountered and the code is paused for us. Let's choose the latter. Click the Open button on the form and select a text file to open.

3. Once the breakpoint has been encountered, click the Debug menu and select QuickWatch to invoke the QuickWatch dialog. Notice that the Expression drop-down box is empty. We can enter a variable or expression at this point if we choose. However, in order to demonstrate another method, click on the Close button in the QuickWatch dialog.

4. Now back in your code window right-click on the `lineCounter` variable below the breakpoint, and select QuickWatch from the context menu. Notice that this variable has not only been added to the Expression drop-down box but has also been placed in the Current value grid in the dialog as shown in the figure. Click the Add Watch button to add this variable to the Watch window:

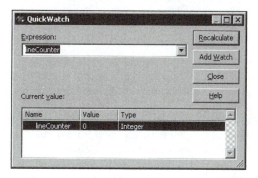

Note that if your computer displays the value as &H0, it means that Hex mode is switched on – and that values will display in hexadecimal. Click the Hex button on the Debug toolbar to toggle this setting.

5. While we have the QuickWatch dialog open, let's set an expression to be evaluated. Add the expression lineCounter = 1 in the Expression drop-down box. Then click the Add Watch button to have this expression added to the Watch window. Now close the QuickWatch dialog by clicking on the Close button.

6. If you do not see the Watch window at the bottom of the development environment, click on the on the Debug | Windows | Watch | Watch 1 menu item. You should now see a variable and an expression in the Watch window as shown in the figure below:

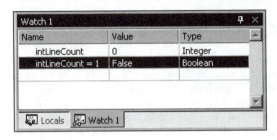

The second watch expression that we have added here returns a value of True when the lineCounter variable equals 1, so Visual Studio .NET has set the Type to Boolean.

7. We now want to step through our code line by line so that we can watch the value of the variable and expression change. Click on the Step Into icon on the Debug toolbar to step to the next line of code. Click once more to see the value of both the variable and expression in the Watch window change.

> As you step through the loop in your code, you will continue to see the value for the lineCounter variable change in the Watch window. When the value of the variable in the Watch window turns red, that value has just been changed. You can manually change the value anytime by entering a new value in the Value column in the Watch window.

8. When you are done click the Continue icon on the Debug toolbar to let your code finish executing.

Locals Window

The **Locals window** is very similar to the Watch window except that it shows all variables and objects for the current function or procedure executing. The Locals window also lets you change the value of a variable or object, and the same rules that apply to the Watch window apply here. That is: the program must be paused before a value can be changed. The text for a value that has just changed also turns red, making it easy to spot the variable or object that has just changed.

The Locals window is great if you want a quick glance at everything that is going on in a function or procedure but not very useful for watching the values of one or two variables or expressions. The reason for this is that the Locals window contains all variables and objects in a procedure or function. Therefore, if you have a lot of variables and objects, you will have to constantly scroll through the window to view the various variables and object. This is where Watch window comes in handy; it lets you watch just the variables that you need.

In this *Try It Out*, we will examine the contents of the Locals window in two different procedures. This will demonstrate how the contents of the Locals window change from one procedure to the next.

Try It Out – Using the Locals Window

1. To prepare for this exercise we need to have the same breakpoint set in the `ProcessFile` procedure that we have been working with. In addition, we want to set a breakpoint in the `btnOpen_Click` procedure at the following line of code:

```
With myFileDialog
```

2. Run your program by clicking on the Start icon on the Debug toolbar.

3. If you do not see the Locals window at the bottom of the development environment, click on the Debug | Windows | Locals menu item.

4. Notice that at this point, the Locals window contains no variables or objects. This is because we have not entered a procedure or function. Click on the Open button on the form and your breakpoint in the `btnOpen_Click` procedure will be encountered and execution will be paused.

5. Notice the various objects and their types listed in the Locals window. The first item in the list is Me, which is the form itself. If you expand this item, you will see all of the objects and controls associated with your form:

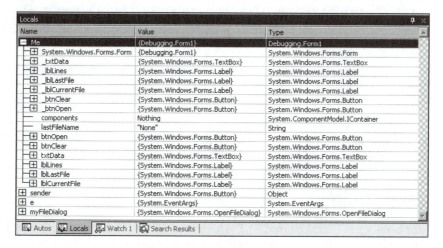

6. Now click on the Continue icon on the Debug toolbar and the Open File dialog will be displayed. Select a text file and click the Open button.

7. The next breakpoint that we encounter is in the `ProcessFile` procedure. Now take a look at the Locals windows and you will see different objects and variables. The one constant item in both procedures is Me which is associated with the form.

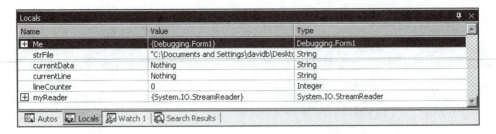

8. If you step through a couple of lines of code in the loop where the breakpoint has paused your program, you will see the values in the Locals window change. This is the same behavior that we saw in the Watch window.

You can continue to step through your code, or you can clear the breakpoint and click the Continue icon on the Debug toolbar to let your program run to completion.

Error Handling

Error handling is an essential part of any good code. In Visual Basic .NET, the error mechanism is based on the concept of exceptions that can be "thrown" to raise an error and "caught" when the error is handled. If you do not provide any type of error handling and an error occurs, your user will receive a message about an unhandled exception, which is provided by the CLR, and then the program will terminate. This is not a user-friendly message and really does not inform the user about the true nature of the error or how to resolve it. The unhandled error could also cause the user to lose the data that they were working with or leave the user and their data in an unknown state.

Visual Studio .NET provides **structured error-handling** statements that are common across all languages. In this section we will examine structured error handling and how it can be incorporated into your programs with very little effort.

> **Structured error handling is a way to organize error handling in a structured way, without the need for GoTo statements and the resulting spaghetti code.**

Try...Catch...Finally

Structured error handling in Visual Studio .NET is handled with the `Try...Catch...Finally` blocks. You execute the code that might throw an exception in the `Try` block and handle anticipated errors in the `Catch` block. The `Finally` block is always executed and allows you to place any cleanup code here regardless of whether an error has occurred or not. If an error occurs that was not handled in the `Catch` block, the CLR will display its standard error message and terminate your program. Therefore it is important to try to anticipate all possible errors for the code that is contained in the `Try` block.

Let's take a look at the syntax for the `Try...Catch...Finally` statement:

```
Try
    [ trystatements ]
Catch [ exception [ As type ] ] [ When expression ]
    [ catchstatements ]
[ Exit Try ]
...
[ Finally
    [ finallystatements ] ]
End Try
```

The *trystatements* argument in the syntax above is used to specify the statements to be executed that may cause an error.

The *exception* argument can be any variable name. It will be set to contain the value of the thrown error.

The optional *type* argument specifies the type of class filter that the exception belongs to. If this argument is not supplied, your Catch block will handle any exception defined in the System.Exception class. Using this argument allows you to specify the type of exception that you maybe looking for. An example of a specific exception is IOException, which is used when performing any type of IO (input/output) against a file.

The *expression* argument is any expression that describes a generic filter typically used to filter a specific error number. The expression used must return a Boolean value and the exception is handled only when the value evaluates to True. This is useful when you want to filter the exception handled to a specific error.

The *catchstatements* are the statements that handle the error that has occurred.

The Exit Try statement is used to break out of the error handling structure and execution of your code resumes after the End Try statement. This is optional and should only be used if you do not want the code following the Finally keyword to be executed.

The *finallystatements* are the statements to be executed after all other processing has occurred.

It should be noted that you can have multiple Catch blocks. That means you can test for multiple errors using multiple Catch blocks and *catchstatements* within the same Try block. When an error occurs in *trystatements*, control is passed to the appropriate *catchstatements* for processing.

Let's take a look at how the Catch block works. When you define a Catch block, you can specify a variable name for the exception and define the type of exception you want to catch, as shown in the following code fragment. In this code, we have defined an exception variable with a name of e and the type of the variable is defined as IOException. This example will trap any type of IO exception that may occur when processing files and store the error information in an object named e:

```
Catch e As IOException
    ...
    code to handle the exception goes here
    ...
```

When dealing with mathematical expressions, you can define and catch the various errors that you may encounter such as a divide-by-zero exception, where you divide a number by zero. You can also catch errors such as overflow errors that may occur when multiplying two numbers and trying to place the result in a variable that is too small for the result. However, in cases such as these it may be better to check for these sorts of problems in advance – we should only really use exceptions in exceptional circumstances.

In the next *Try It Out*, we want to add some structured error handling to the sample program that we have been working with. When we open a file for processing, it is possible that we could encounter an error. For example, the file could be deleted before we open it or it could be corrupt, causing the open statement to fail. This code is a prime candidate for structured error handling.

Another place where error handling can be incorporated is when we read the file. We can check for an end-of-file condition to ensure we do not try to read past the end of the file.

Try It Out – Structured Error Handling

1. Modify the code in the `ProcessFile` procedure as shown in the code below:

```
' Declare an object for the StreamReader class...
Dim myReader As StreamReader
```

```
Try
    ' Open the file...
    myReader = File.OpenText(fileName)
Catch e As IOException
    ' Display the messages...
    MessageBox.Show(e.ToString)
    MessageBox.Show(e.Message)
    ' Exit the procedure...
    Exit Sub
End Try
```

```
' Declare variables...
Dim lineCounter As Integer = 0
Dim currentLine As String, currentData As String
```

```
' Loop through the file counting the lines and loading the
' text box...
Do
    Try
        ' Read a line from the file...
        currentLine = myReader.ReadLine
        lineCounter = lineCounter + 1
    Catch e As EndOfStreamException
        ' Display the message...
        MessageBox.Show(e.Message)
        ' Exit the Do loop...
        Exit Do
    Finally
        ' Concatenate the data to the strData variable...
        currentData = currentData & currentLine & vbCrLf
    End Try
Loop While strLine <> Nothing
```

2. Save the project once more.

How It Works

The code we have entered contains two error handlers.

The first error handler that we have coded here only contains a `Try` block and a `Catch` block, both of which are required blocks of code in structured error handling. We have opted not to use the `Finally` block in this error handling routine:

```
Try
    ' Open the file...
    myReader = File.OpenText(fileName)
Catch e As IOException
    ' Display the messages...
    MessageBox.Show(e.ToString)
    MessageBox.Show(e.Message)
    ' Exit the procedure...
    Exit Sub
End Try
```

The error that we want to trap is any error that may occur when we open a file, so we have placed our open statement in the `Try` block as seen above. Using the `OpenText` method of the `File` class, we open the file that was returned in the **Open File** dialog and set it to our `StreamReader` object.

The `Catch` block in our structured error handler will trap any IO exception that may occur, such as if the file does not exist or the file is corrupt. We have defined the variable e for the exception argument, as is standard practice among most developers. We then define the type of exception that we want to test for and trap, which is an `IOException`.

We place our error handling code within the `Catch` block as we have done here. If an error should occur, we will display two message boxes using `MessageBox`. Our code only sets the message in the `MessageBox` dialogs; we will accept the default values for the other arguments for the `MessageBox` dialogs.

The first line of code will display all available information about the error. The `ToString` method of the `IOException` class is used here and will return the full details of the exception. This message contains a lot of detail, which is really not a lot of use to an end user. We will see this message when we test our code.

The second line of code here will display the `Message` property of the `IOException` class. This is a more meaningful message and one that the end user will understand.

The last line of code in the `Catch` block (`Exit Sub`) will exit the procedure. If any type of error occurs here, we cannot process the file so it only makes sense to exit the procedure, bypassing the rest of the code.

The next structured error handler that we have set up in this procedure is inside our `Do` loop, which processes the contents of the file. This time we have coded the `Finally` block of the structured error handler:

```
Try
    ' Read a line from the file...
    currentLine = myReader.ReadLine
    lineCounter = lineCounter + 1
Catch e As EndOfStreamException
    ' Display the message...
    MessageBox.Show(e.Message)
    ' Exit the Do loop...
    Exit Do
Finally
    ' Concatenate the data to the strData variable...
    currentData = currentData & currentLine & vbCrLf
End Try
```

The code in the `Try` block will read a line of text from the open text file and, if successful, increment the line count variable.

The `Catch` block will test for and trap an end-of-stream exception using the `EndOfStreamException` class. This class returns an exception when we attempt to read past the end of the stream in our text file. Again, we have specified the variable e as the exception argument. Within the `Catch` block, we display a message box using the `MessageBox` dialog and display the `Message` property of the `EndOfStreamException` class. We then exit the `Do` loop and process the rest of the code in this procedure.

The `Finally` block contains the code that will be executed regardless of whether an error occurred or not. In this case, the code simply concatenates the data read in the `strLine` variable to the `strData` variable, and places a carriage return line feed character at the end using the built-in `vbCrLf` constant.

At this point, we are ready to test our code.

Try It Out – Testing Our Error Handlers

1. Click the Start icon on the toolbar.

2. We want to set a breakpoint and also add a watch for the `fileName` variable in the `ProcessFile` procedure so we need to switch back to Visual Studio .NET.

Remember that the program must be in break mode before we can add a watch variable. Click on Break All on the Debug toolbar or select the Debug | Break All menu item. In the `ProcessFile` procedure, find and right-click the `fileName` variable. Then click on QuickWatch in the context menu to invoke the QuickWatch dialog.

3. In the QuickWatch dialog, the fileName variable should be shown in the Expression drop-down box as in the following figure. Click the Add Watch button to add this variable to the Watch window, and then click the Close button to close the QuickWatch dialog.

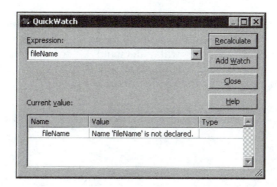

4. Next, we want to set a couple of breakpoints in our structured error handlers. In the first error handler, set a breakpoint on the following line of code by clicking in the gray margin to the left of this line:

```
myReader = File.OpenText(strFile)
```

5. Next, click on the Continue icon on the toolbar or click on the Debug | Continue menu item.

6. On the form, click the Open button to invoke the Open File dialog and choose a text file. Click the Open button in the dialog to open the file. Once your breakpoint has been encountered, click on the Watch window, to see the value of the `fileName` variable.

We now want to simulate the effects of the file not being found. The most 'realistic' way to do this would be to rename or delete the file that we selected. An easier way is simply to change the value of the `fileName` variable. To do this, click in the Value cell for `fileName` in the Watch window, and change the name of the file to something that does not exist by adding an extra letter or number in the file name. Click outside of the Value box in the Watch window to have the change take effect.

7. We now want to step through our code for a few lines, so click on the Step Into icon on the toolbar to step through the code.

8. An error is raised because the file does not exist and the first line of code in the `Catch` block is executed. Remember that this line uses the `ToString` method of the `IOException` class, which returns the full details of the error. This message, shown in the figure below, shows a lot of detail that is not really useful to the end user:

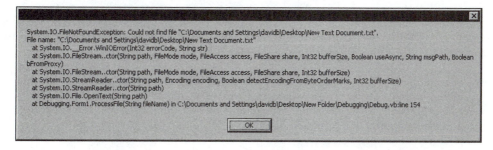

9. Click the OK button in the message box, to have the second message displayed. This next message is more user-friendly and gets to the point. This is the type of message that we want our users to see and one that they will understand. Of course, you would want to customize the message box to suit the error being displayed, such as displaying the appropriate caption and icon. Refer back to Chapter 8 for details on how to do this:

We have seen here that the ToString method can provide a lot of detail for the developer trying to debug a program, and that this type of message should be logged and not displayed to the user.

10. Click the OK button in the second message to let your code run. Once you do this the next line of code is executed, which is the Exit Sub statement. Since we could not successfully open a file we want to bypass the rest of the code in this procedure, which is what we have done by placing the Exit Sub statement in our Catch block.

As you become more familiar with the types of errors that can occur, you will be able to write more sophisticated structured error handlers. This only comes with experience and testing. You will discover more errors and will be able to handle them only by thoroughly testing your code.

The online documentation for most methods that you use in Visual Studio .NET will explain the errors that can arise when certain conditions occur. For example, the documentation for the **StreamReader.ReadLine** method explains that an **IOException** will occur on any I/O error.

Summary

This chapter has taken a look at some useful debugging tools that are built into the Visual Studio .NET development environment. We have seen how easy it is to debug our programs as we stepped through the various *Try It Out* sections.

Having thoroughly covered breakpoints, we saw how we could stop the execution of our program at any given point. As useful as this is, setting breakpoints with a hit counter in a loop is even more useful, as we are able to execute a loop several times before encountering a breakpoint in the loop.

We also examined the various windows available while debugging our program, such as the Locals window and the Watch window. These windows provide us with valuable information about the variables and expressions in our program. We are able to watch the values change and are even able to change the values to control the execution of our code.

You should know what types of major errors you may encounter while developing and debugging your code. You should be able to readily recognize syntax and execution errors and possibly correct them. While debugging a program for logic errors may be difficult at first, it does become easier with time and experience.

We have also covered structured error handling and you should incorporate this knowledge into your programs at every opportunity. Not only does it provide us with the opportunity to provide the user with a friendlier message when things do go wrong but it also helps you when debugging your code, because you will have some basis to go on (for example, a message of the actual error and the precise location of the line of code that caused the error).

In summary, you should know:

❑   How to recognize and correct major types of errors

❑   How to successfully use breakpoints to debug your program

❑   How to use the Locals and Watch windows to see, and change variables and expressions

❑   How to use the Command window to query and set variables

❑   How to use structured error handling

Questions

1.   How do you know when you have a syntax error in your code?

2.   We know that we can set a breakpoint with a hit counter, but can we set a conditional breakpoint?

3.   What information does the Locals window show?

4.   If you are stepping through your code line by line, how can you bypass stepping through the code of a called procedure?

5.   Can you define multiple Catch blocks in structured error handling?

6.   When we use our program to open a file with a blank line, like this:

```
Line 1
Line 2

Line 4
```

We do not get the hoped for result – only the first two lines get displayed.

Is this a syntax, execution, or logic error?

How might we identify the problem? And what could we do to fix it?

Building Class Libraries

In this chapter, we're going to look at building libraries of classes. This will gather together many of the concepts we've learned in this book, so let's have a quick review. So far we've learned a lot about developing Windows Applications by dragging controls onto forms, editing their properties, and adding code. When we edit a form in the Form Designer, we are actually designing a new class that inherits from the System.Windows.Forms.Form class. The first two lines of code in a VB.NET form will look something like this:

```
Public Class Form1
    Inherits System.Windows.Forms.Form
```

When we make changes to the form in the designer, the designer works out what code needs to be added to the class. We can view this code by opening up the Windows Form Designer generated code region. Then, when we run the program, an instance of this class is created – an object. Like most objects, the form has state and behavior – we can have variables and controls on the form (state), and we can perform actions when, for example, the user clicks a button on the form (behavior). In theory, we could write our forms without using the designer at all – but there are very few programmers who work this way when creating Windows forms.

Right from the start, then, we've been creating classes. We've also looked at creating our own classes from scratch. Think back to Chapter 4 *Building Objects*, where we created a project called Objects, which contained the classes Car and SportsCar. These classes were used in a Console Application because it made the objects easier to test, but they would have worked just as well in a Windows Application. We could even have used them in a Web Application or Web Service. In fact one of the key benefits of using classes is that, once we've designed a good one, we can use it over and over again in different applications.

In Chapter 10 we did use the same classes in two different applications. We built a favorites viewer application, and a task bar application using the same underlying classes. We did this by creating the class in one application, and then adding a copy of that code to the second. This was a quick and easy way of reusing code, but there were problems with it:

❑   To use the class, you need to have access to the source code file. One of the advantages of classes and objects is that they can be a 'black box'. Developers shouldn't need to know what goes on inside the classes they use. It's often a good thing if they don't. Also, we might want to keep our source secret – if we've developed a class, we might be happy to let people use it, but not let them copy how it works or improve it, or even claim it as their own work.

❑   Every time the program that uses the class is compiled, the class needs to be compiled too. This is not really a problem if the application uses a few simple classes, but if it's using lots of complex ones it will make compilation very slow. It will also make the resulting program very big because the one EXE will include all of the classes.

❑   If you realize that there is a bug in the class, or that there is a way to make it faster or more efficient, you need to make the change in lots of different places – in every application that uses the class.

The solution is **class libraries**. A class library is a collection of classes that compile to a file. You cannot run a class library, but you can use the classes in it from your applications. You can use a class library without the source code, it does not need to be recompiled when the application is compiled, and if the library changes then the applications using it will automatically get the advantage of the improved code.

In this chapter, we'll be looking at class libraries. We'll look at how to create our own class libraries, and how to get information about existing libraries that are not part of the Framework. We'll also look at how to strong-name assemblies (compiled files) to ensure that all assemblies have a unique identity, and finally how to register assemblies in a repository called the GAC so that they can be shared between applications on the same computer.

Creating a Class Library

Visual Studio .NET Professional and above possess built-in support for creating class libraries. Visual Basic .NET Standard does not – there needs to be some reason for saving all that money! Class libraries are considered a 'professional' requirement – as we saw in Chapter 10 it is perfectly possible to reuse classes on a small scale without using libraries.

However, in the current release of Visual Basic .NET Standard it is possible with a bit of fiddling to create a class library. This method comes with no guarantees, however. If you want to experiment with class libraries then the fiddle should work fine. If you want to create commercial-grade class libraries, then you should really use the right tool.

Anyway, here are instructions for creating a class library in Visual Studio .NET Professional or above. After them come the instructions for Visual Basic .NET Standard. These instructions are only for creating the new class library project. We're dealing with this simple item on its own because the process is different depending on what IDE you are using.

Try It Out – Creating a Class Library in Visual Studio .NET Professional or Above

1.   In Visual Studio .NET, select File | New | Project.

2.   Select Visual Basic Projects from the Project Types list, and then choose the Class Library icon from the Templates list. Enter the name MyClassLibrary:

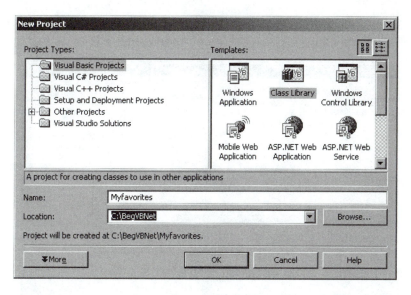

3. Click OK. A new Class Library project will be created, with a default class called `Class1.vb`. Right click on `Class1.vb` in the Solution Explorer and choose Delete. Then confirm the choice by clicking OK.

How It Works – Creating a Class Library in Visual Studio .NET Professional or Above

That was really easy. Let's just think about what Visual Studio .NET is doing during these two steps. Firstly, we chose a Class Library project. The Template that we choose controls how Visual Studio .NET sets up the project. The most obvious difference is that when we start a Windows Application we get a blank form and a designer. The blank form is called `Form1.vb`. When we start a class library, we get no designer, and a blank class called `Class1.vb`.

There are also more subtle differences. When we create a Windows Application, Visual Studio .NET knows that we will be compiling it into a program that can run. When we choose a Class Library, Visual Studio .NET knows that the resulting library will not be run on its own – so the choices we make here affect what Visual Studio .NET does when we build the project. We select a Class Library, meaning that Visual Studio .NET will build the project to a DLL file (dynamic link library).

After clicking OK, we delete the blank class that Visual Studio .NET generates. Having classes with the name `Class1` is not very helpful – it's much better to start from scratch with meaningful file and class names.

Now let's look at how to create a Class Library in Visual Basic .NET Standard. This is a bit more complicated, because we need to force Visual Basic .NET Standard to do some of the things that the full Visual Studio .NET does automatically.

Try It Out – Creating a Class Library in Visual Basic .NET Standard

1. In Visual Studio .NET, select File | New | Project.

2. Select **Visual Basic Projects** from the **Project Types** list, and then choose the **Console Application** icon from the **Templates** list. Enter the name `MyClassLibrary`:

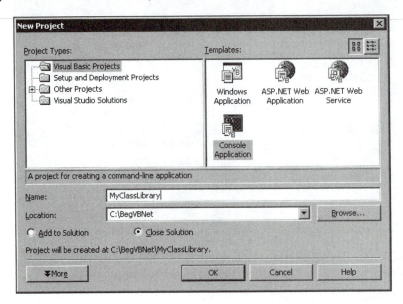

Select the whole content of the **Location** box and then press *Ctrl+C*. This will copy the location name to the Windows Clipboard, which we will use later. This example uses the location `C:\BegVBNet`, but of course you can locate it anywhere you like. Then click **OK**.

3. A new Console Application project will be created, with a default module called `Module1.vb`. Right click on `Module1.vb` in the Solution Explorer and choose **Delete**. Then confirm the choice by clicking **OK**.

4. Now close the solution. Do this by selecting **File | Close Solution**. Select **Yes** to save changes.

5. Now, go to the Windows Start menu and select **Programs | Accessories | Notepad**. Then in the Notepad window select **File | Open**. Paste the Location from Step 1 into the **File name** box by selecting the textbox and pressing *Ctrl+V*. If this doesn't work, then just type the location in. Then click **Open**. This will take you to the folder that contains the project:

Go into the `MyClassLibrary` folder, and then from the Files of type dropdown select All Files. The Open dialog should now look like this:

Select `MyClassLibrary.vbproj` and click Open. If you're computer does not display file extensions, then you can identify the right file by its icon:

Then click Open to open the file in Notepad.

6. The VBPROJ file is an XML file that keeps track of all the files in the project, as well as settings that apply to the whole project. We are going to edit it. The line we are interested in is this one – about 19 lines down the file:

```
DelaySign = "false"
OutputType = "Exe"
OptionCompare = "Binary"
```

Change the highlighted line to:

```
OutputType = "Library"
```

Take care not to change anything else. Now save the file, close Notepad, and return to Visual Basic .NET.

7. Select File | Recent Projects. `MyClassLibrary.sln` should be first on the list. Select it. If it does not appear on the list then open it in the usual way.

How It Works – Creating a Class Library in Visual Basic .NET Standard

This process was far more complicated than when using a full version of Visual Studio .NET. Behind the scenes, however, things are very similar. We want to create a Class Library, so there is no template available. The closest one that does exist is a Console Application (because it does not bring up a designer, for example) so we create one. This creates a default module – `Module1`. We do not want this, so we delete it. A Console Application is a program – it can run on its own. We need to change it so that instead of it building to something runnable, it builds to a library. Visual Basic .NET Standard offers no way for us to do this, but the information that makes the decision is in the VBPROJ file that Visual Basic .NET Standard creates. So, to get around the problem, we change the file ourselves.

> *The VBPROJ file stores information about the structure of the project (for example what source code files are part of the project, and what assemblies are referenced) as well as information needed to compile the project (for example compiler switches).*

We close the solution to avoid sharing problems when the file is open in Notepad, and then load up Notepad. Of course, any text editor would work here – most are better than Notepad.

> *Text editors enable us to edit unformatted text files such as source code files, HTML files, and XML files. Having a good text editor is very useful, and an important part of a programmer's toolbox. Textpad is a great text editor, so if you don't already have a favorite then give it a try – www.textpad.com.*

The line that tells Visual Basic .NET to build this project into a program is the one that we edited:

```
OutputType = "Exe"
```

Here, `Exe` is short for executable. It is also the file extension for most programs that run under Windows. We changed it to `Library`. This tells Visual Basic .NET Standard that, when we build this project, it should be built into a class library instead of a program.

Building a Class Library for Favorites Viewer

We've briefly mentioned that in Chapter 10 we created classes, and used the same VB.NET class in two projects – Favorites Viewer and Favorites Tray. In the following sections, we will see how to convert these applications so that they both use a copy of the same compiled class library. Of course, this is a somewhat unrealistic situation. Usually we would build a class library and application, rather than creating an application and then splitting it up into a smaller application and a class library. However, this will give us a good idea of how we would create a class library from scratch – and it will be much faster. First of all, open the Favorites Viewer project. Remember that this consists of the following files:

- ❑   `Favorites.vb` – contains the `Favorites` class

- ❑   `WebFavorite.vb` – contains the `WebFavorite` class

- ❑˙ `WebFavoriteCollection.vb` – contains the `WebFavoriteCollection` class

- ❑   `WebFavoriteListViewItem.vb` – contains the `WebFavoriteListViewItem` class

- ❑   `Form1.vb` – contains the `Form1` class, which represents the application's main form

- ❑   `AssemblyInfo.vb` – contains information about the assembly, which we don't need to worry about – yet!

Of these, the first three listed are also used in Favorites Tray. The remaining three are specific to this particular application. We want to build a class library that contains `Favorites`, `WebFavorite`, and `WebFavoriteCollection`.

When we're writing Visual Basic .NET applications, a **solution** can contain multiple projects. At the moment we have one project in the solution – the Favorites Viewer application. We need to add a Class Library project to this solution, and then move the classes from the Windows Application project to the Class Library project.

Try It Out – Adding a Class Library to an Existing Solution in Visual Studio .NET

1. Open the Favorites Viewer project.

2. Right-click the Solution 'Favorites Viewer' line in the Solution Explorer, and select Add | New Project...

3. Follow Steps 2 and 3 from the *Creating a Class Library in Visual Studio .NET Professional or Above* section, but give the project the name `FavoritesLib`.

Try It Out – Adding a Class Library to an Existing Solution in Visual Basic .NET Standard

1. Open the Favorites Viewer project.

2. Right-click the Solution 'Favorites Viewer' line in the Solution Explorer, and select Add | New Project...

3. Follow the same steps as for Steps 2 and 3 in the *Try It Out – Creating a Class Library in Visual Basic .NET Standard* section, but give the project the name `FavoritesLib`.

4. Right-click on the `FavoritesLib` project in the Solution Explorer and select **Remove**. Answer **OK** to the first prompt, and **Yes** to the second.

5. Follow the same steps as for Steps 5 and 6 in the *Try It Out – Creating a Class Library in Visual Basic .NET Standard* section, but of course edit `FavoritesLib.vbproj` this time.

6. Right-click the Solution 'Favorites Viewer' line in the Solution Explorer again, and this time select Add | Existing Project…

7. Find the VBPROJ file that you just edited, and select it.

How It Works – Adding a Class Library to an Existing Solution

This works in pretty much the same way as creating a new class library on its own in a solution – it is just a little easier to do it this way if we are adding a new class library to an existing solution.

We now have two projects within our solution. We have a Windows Application and a Class Library. Currently, the class library is empty – and all the classes that we want to add to the class library are in the Windows Application project.

We have already seen how to add a new class to a Windows Application, and we can add new classes to a Class Library in exactly the same way. We just right-click on the `FavoritesLib` project and select Add | **Add Class**. We don't want to do that though – the classes already exist. The quickest way to move a class between two projects in the same solution is to drag and drop them. Let's do that now.

Try It Out – Moving Classes Between Projects

1. Select the `Favorites.vb` file in the Solution Explorer, and drag it onto the `FavoritesLib` project:

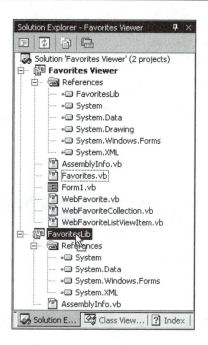

You may need to wait a second or two, but the Favorites.vb class file will be moved from the Favorites Viewer project to the FavoritesLib project. As well as changing projects, the file is physically moved from the folder containing the Favorites Viewer project to the folder containing the FavoritesLib folder.

2. Follow the same procedure for WebFavorite.vb and WebFavoriteCollection.vb.

So, we now have a Class Library and a Windows Application. However, even though they are both contained in the same project they cannot see each other. If you try running the application now, you will see a series of errors:

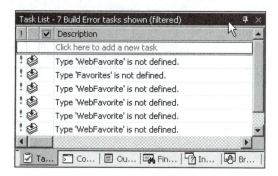

These errors are all caused by the same thing: the classes in Form1.vb and WebFavoriteListView.vb cannot see the classes in the class library. There are two stages to solving this problem:

❏ Add a reference to the Class Library project, so that the Windows Application knows to look for the compiled `FavoritesLib.dll` file that contains the classes. Previously all code was compiled into one file, so we didn't need to do this.

❏ Add an `Imports` statement to the `Form1` and `WebFavoriteListView` classes, so that they can use classes from the `FavoritesLib` namespace without giving a fully qualified name (that is, including the namespace as well as the class name). Previously all classes were in the same namespace so we didn't need to do this. As we saw in Chapter 4, classes are by default given the project name as their namespace.

If this doesn't seem very clear – don't worry! Both of these things are easy to do – let's see how to do each in turn.

Try It Out – Adding a Reference to Another Project

1. Right-click on the Favorites Viewer project in the Solution Explorer and select **Add Reference**.

2. Select the **Projects** tab, and then double-click `FavoritesLib` in the list. `FavoritesLib` will be added to the **Selected Components** list at the bottom of the dialog box:

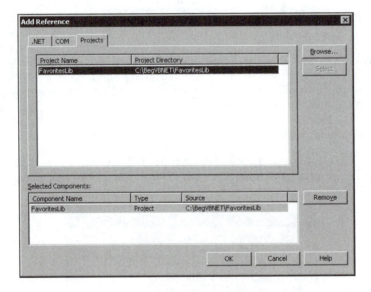

3. Now click OK. A reference to **FavoritesLib** will now appear in the Solution Explorer – under the **References** section for the Favorites Viewer project:

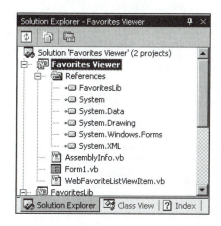

How It Works – Adding a Reference to Another Project

By adding a reference, you tell Visual Studio .NET that the `Favorites Viewer.exe` file will require the `FavoritesLib.dll` file in order to run. Visual Studio .NET can use the classes exposed from `FavoritesLib` in order to check the syntax of the code, so the automatic underlining of errors and so on will work correctly.

> **Whenever you want to use a class library, you must add a reference to it. You can add references to projects within the solution, or to compiled DLLs if you wish.**

However if you try to run the application now, you will still get lots of errors. This is because the classes in the Favorites Viewer application are trying to use classes in the `FavoritesLib` class library without giving a fully qualified name. Unless we specify otherwise, classes are given the same namespace name as the name of the project they are in. This means that the classes we moved from `Favorites Viewer` to `FavoritesLib` changed namespace too.

The easiest way to cope with this problem is to add an `Imports` statement to the top of the classes that rely on the class library. This is what we'll do in a minute, but remember that we did have two other choices:

❏ Use fully qualified names every time we want to access a class in the class library from a class in the application. This would have required quite a few changes.

❏ Change the namespace of either the classes in the application or the classes in the class library. If the namespace was the same for both projects, we would not need to use fully qualified names or have an `Imports` statement. However because the two projects are quite different, it would not really be sensible to give them both the same namespace.

Try It Out – Adding an Imports Statement

1. Right-click on `Form1.vb` in the Solution Explorer and select **View Code**. Notice that when the code refers to a class in `FavoritesLib`, the word is underlined in blue – because the class is unavailable:

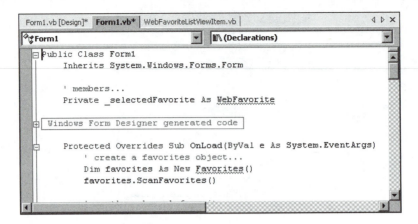

2. Add the following line right at the top of the code file:

```
Imports FavoritesLib
```

3. Do the same thing for `WebFavoritesListViewItem.cs`.

How It Works – Adding an Imports Clause

The imports clause means that any time there is a reference to a class that is not qualified with a namespace, the Visual Basic .NET compiler will check the `FavoritesLib` namespace to see if a matching class exists there. Visual Studio .NET knows this, so no longer has any problem with classes in the `FavoritesLib` namespace.

That's it! We have converted our Windows Application into a small 'client' application, and a class library. Run the application, and it will work perfectly:

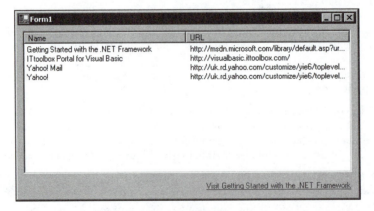

Note that when we ran this application, Visual Studio .NET compiled the class library to a DLL, then compiled the application to an EXE, and then ran the EXE. It needed to compile the DLL first because the compiler depends upon it when compiling the EXE.

Tiered Applications

Here we have split our application into two **tiers** or **layers**. The class library is a tier that handles the concept of a favorite, and obtains a list of my favorites from my computer. The other tier presents the favorites to the user and enables the user to perform actions on them. Class libraries are a really powerful tool for creating tiered applications, because they enable us to completely separate the code that exists in different tiers. You may often here the term **n-tier** design. What this means is that an application has at least three separate tiers. Usually these three tiers are:

❑   A **data tier** concerned with obtaining raw data from a data source such as a database, text file, or our favorites folder, and then writing data back. It generally doesn't worry about what the data means – it just enables read and write operations.

❑   A **business tier** concerned with applying certain business rules to the data retrieved from the data source, or ensuring that data being written to the data source obeys these rules. For example there may be certain sites that we would not want to list in our favorites viewer, or we may want to ensure that URLs are valid before displaying them. The business tier may also contain code to manipulate or work with data – for example the code needed to open a particular favorite.

❑   A **presentation tier** that displays the data to the user and lets them interact with it in some way. For example we have a Windows Form that displays a list of favorites and a link button that lets users view them.

Our application is so small that there's no practical need to separate the data tier and the business tier. However, in a big application it can make the project far more manageable – even if it does mean spending a bit more time on design before the coding starts.

One of the great things about tiers is that we can mix and match tiers quite easily. For example, if a new browser became popular then we could change the data tier to read a different data format but still use the same presentation tier and business tier. This would be much easier if the data tier and business tiers were separate.

Soon, we are going to use our class library – which is really a combined business and data tier – in conjunction with a different presentation tier – namely the Favorites Tray application.

> **In this chapter we are working with existing projects so that we can concentrate specifically on class libraries rather than writing code. In most cases we would develop the class library first and then develop applications to use that library. Of course, as we were building the application we might decide to modify the library slightly. Using Visual Studio .NET we can do this very easily. When working in Visual Studio .NET we can make any changes we like to the code in the library, and the change will instantly be available in the application.**

Strong Names

Let's take another quick recap. Our complete solution now compiles to two files – a DLL and an EXE. We have written both. Nobody else is writing applications that rely on the DLL, and nobody else is going to change the DLL. In real life, this is often not the case. Often we use off-the-shelf DLLs, or two separate developers are working on the DLL and the EXE.

Lets say that Kevin is working on `FavoritesLib.dll`, and Simone is working on `Favorites Viewer.exe`. Kevin decides that `ScanFavorites` is not a very good name for a method, and changes it to `LoadFavorites`. He then recompiles the DLL. Later, Simone runs `Favorites Viewer.exe`. `Favorites Viewer.exe` tries to call `ScanFavorites` in the DLL, but the method no longer exists. This generates an error, and the program won't work.

Of course, Kevin shouldn't really have made the change to the DLL. He should have known that applications existed that required the `ScanFavorites` method. All too often, however, developers of libraries don't realize this. They make changes to DLLs that render existing software unusable.

Another possible scenario is that David is working on a system to manage favorites, and creates a file called `FavoritesLib` that is different from the one Kevin's developed. There is a danger that the two different DLLs will become confused, and once again Favorites Viewer will stop working.

These DLL management problems have been a nightmare for Windows developers, and spawned the expression 'DLL Hell'. However, .NET goes a long way towards solving the problem. As we've seen in the scenarios above, the problem is connected with two things:

❑ There can be several versions of a DLL, and these can all work in different ways. It is not possible to tell the version from the file name alone.

❑ Different people can write DLLs with the same file name.

Strong named assemblies store information about their version and their author within the assembly itself. Because of this, it would be possible to tell the difference between the DLL used when Favorites Viewer compiled, and the changed version. It would also be possible to tell the difference between Kevin's `FavoritesLib.dll` and David's `FavoritesLib.dll`. Strong naming can also store information about other properties that will help to uniquely identify an assembly, for example the culture for which it was written, but we will concentrate on version and author.

Signing Assemblies

One way to certify who wrote an assembly is to **sign** it. To do this, we generate a key pair and sign the assembly with it. A key-pair is unique and therefore can identify the person or company that wrote an assembly. The principles behind assembly signing are quite advanced, but the actual practice is quite simple.

> **A strong-named assembly cannot reference a simple named assembly, as it would lose the versioning control that it enjoys.**

There are two steps involved in creating a strong-named, or signed, assembly:

❑ Create a key pair that we can use to sign our assembly

❑ Apply this key pair to our assembly, so that it will be used to sign the assembly at compile time

Try It Out – Creating a Key Pair

First, let's create a new key pair.

1. From the Windows Start menu select Programs | Microsoft Visual Studio .NET | Visual Studio .NET Tools | Visual Studio .NET Command Prompt.

2. Type the following into the Command Prompt that appears:

```
sn -k Testkey.snk
```

This will generate a key pair in the folder where the command is run (in this case, c:\).

How It Works

Running the Visual Studio .NET Command Prompt opens a DOS-style command window with the environment set up so that we can use the .NET command-line tools. We use this environment to run the .NET strong naming command. The `-k` switch means that the command will generate a new key pair and write it to the specified file.

We now have a key pair in the file c:\Testkey.snk. If you wish, you can move this to a more convenient location. After this, the next step is to use it to sign our assembly.

Try It Out – Signing the FavoritesLib Assembly

1. Open the AssemblyInfo.vb file in the FavoritesLib project, and add the following line:

```
<assembly:AssemblyKeyFileAttribute("c:\TestKey.snk")>
```

2. Build this project. The DLL will now be strong named.

How It Works

When we compile an assembly with an `AssemblyKeyFileAttribute`, it adds a copy of our public key to the assembly. It also adds a hash of the whole assembly, encrypted using the private key.

With public-private key cryptography, a message encrypted with one key can *only* be decrypted with the other key. We can't use the same key to encrypt and decrypt. We can give out a public key to lots of people, and they can encrypt messages with it. If we keep the private key secret, then nobody else will be able to read the encrypted messages – even if they have a copy of the public key.

We can also work this the other way around. If we encrypt a message with the private key, people can use the public key to decrypt it. If the decryption works, and we haven't let somebody else get their hands on our private key, this *proves* that we wrote the message.

493

Part of the purpose of signing an assembly is to prove who wrote it, and to prove that it has not been tampered with. This could be done by encrypting the whole assembly using the private key – and then decrypting the whole assembly using the public key when it needs to be used. However, this would end up being very slow. Instead, the Visual Basic .NET compiler takes a hash of the assembly, and encrypts that using the private key. If anybody tries to tamper with the assembly now, the hash will cease to be valid.

Assembly Versions

Visual Basic .NET automatically keeps track of versions for us. When we build an assembly, a number signifying the version is automatically updated. There are three elements to this number: major version, minor version, build, and revision. If you look again at the `AssemblyInfo.vb` file, you will see the following near the bottom:

```
<Assembly: AssemblyVersion("1.0.*")>
```

This means that when we compile this assembly the major version will be 1, the minor version will be 0, and the build and revision number will be generated by Visual Studio .NET. Every time we recompile the assembly, Visual Basic .NET will adjust these numbers to ensure that every compilation has a unique version number. We could choose to replace the star with our own hard-coded numbers, and increment them ourselves, but if we're happy with Visual Basic .NET's decision then we can just leave it. If we were changing an assembly significantly, we may want to change the major or minor version – and of course we are free to do that.

Registering Assemblies

We've seen how an assembly can contain information to prove who wrote it, and information to prove its own version. This is really useful, because it means that executables using these assemblies know what assembly author and version to look for, as well as just a file name. However, this doesn't prevent Kevin from overwriting an existing DLL with a new version – it just means that applications using the DLL will be able to tell that it's changed.

This is where the **GAC**, or **Global Assembly Cache**, comes in. The GAC can ensure that several versions of the same assembly are always available. If our application requires the `FavoritesLib` assembly version 1, and Kevin's application requires the assembly version 2, then both can go in the GAC and both can be available. Also, assemblies with the same name but written by different people can go in the GAC. Provided the required assembly is in the GAC, we can *guarantee* that our applications will use the same assembly when running as they did when they were compiled.

To register an assembly into the GAC, you simply need to drag the relevant DLL file into the GAC (located in the `c:\winnt\assembly` directory). In the following screenshot, a `FavoritesLib.dll` assembly has been registered in the GAC:

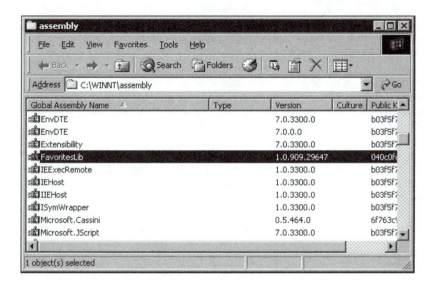

Designing Class Libraries

By now you should be aware of how useful class libraries are, and we have looked at the nature of classes, objects, and class libraries.

When designing an application it is best to understand what you are dealing with. Much like an architect designing a home, you will need to understand how things work (the rules, the regulations, the recommendations) in order for you to best know how to draw a plan.

When software architects plan, draw out and generate template code for components and applications, they may well use pen and paper, or a drawing tool such as Microsoft Visio that integrates with Visual Studio .NET. Visio contains various types of symbol libraries that can be used for creating schematics, flowcharts, and other diagrams. A very well known set of descriptive symbols and diagram types is **UML** (**Unified Modeling Language**), which has its own symbols and rules for drawing software and architecture models. UML has various types of symbol libraries containing symbols that have different meaning and functions. These symbols have been derived from previous modeling symbols to form something of a fusion of styles. UML also has many types of diagrams. These diagrams range from deployment type diagrams to component definition diagrams.

> *If you wish to learn more about UML then take a look at* Instant UML*, (Wrox Press, ISBN 1-86100-087-1).*

Let's look briefly at some of the issues to consider when designing classes to put in a class library.

Object Design

If the questions of, "how many parameters and methods should an object expose?" and "should an object have properties rather than methods?" are not answered correctly, your object would not be rendered completely useless, although it may be ineffective. There are though, some things to consider.

Imagine a class library that contains over forty methods and properties on each of its twenty or so classes. Also imagine that each class's methods contain at least fifteen parameters. This component might be a little daunting – in fact, a component should *never* be this way.

Instead, when designing your objects, try to follow the golden rule – *simplicity*. Simplicity is probably the most crucial element that you can have in your classes. While creating an extremely large class library is not necessarily a bad thing, using a small number of classes, aided by a few other class libraries, is by far a better solution.

When we're dealing with a large, complex set of business rules for a large system, the code within the library can be extremely complicated, often leading to debugging and maintenance nightmares. In many situations getting around the fact that many objects need to be created is a difficult task, but the point that needs to come across is that there are many situations that lend themselves to reuse. The more reusable class are, the smaller the end-product will be and the easier it will be to create new applications that need the same functionality provided by the components.

Every developer who uses your class library should be able to do so successfully, without the need for major effort, or a tremendous amount of reading on their part. You can achieve this in many ways:

❑ Try to keep your methods to a five or six parameters *maximum,* unless completely necessary. This will make for easier coding.

❑ Make sure that all of those parameters and your methods have meaningful names. Try to spell the function out rather than keeping it short. As an example, it is not easy to identify the meaning of StdNo as it is to identify the meaning of StudentNumber.

❑ Do not over-exert yourself by adding every conceivable method and functional enhancement that an object can have; rather, think ahead, but code later. You can easily complicate matters for your developers by granting them too much choice, and at the same time may be adding functionality that will never be used.

❑ Try to keep classes within your library down to a minimum, since better reuse comes from keeping your libraries smaller.

❑ Properties are extremely useful in a class and enable it to be used more easily.

Using Third-Party Class Libraries

As we've said before, as class library compiles to a DLL file. In order to use the class library we only need the DLL – we don't need the source code. This means that we can give our DLL to other people to use, and we can use other people's DLLs in our own applications. To demonstrate how to use a DLL, we're going to use the FavoritesLib.dll file that we created.

We've already seen how to create references to other projects in a Solution. This is a really good way to develop class libraries and applications at the same time. In this example we're going to pretend that we didn't create FavoritesLib.dll ourselves. We're going to modify the Favorites Tray so that it uses FavoritesLib.dll. This is a very quick way to demonstrate the use of DLLs, but remember that in real life we would add a reference to the DLL early on in developing the application, and then write code to use the DLL.

Try It Out – Using FavoritesLib.dll in the Favorites Tray Application

1. Open the Favorites Tray project.

2. Delete the following files from the project: `Favorites.vb`, `WebFavorite.vb`, `WebFavoriteCollection.vb`.

3. Now we need to add a reference to `FavoritesLib.dll`. Right-click on the Favorites Tray project and select **Add Reference**. Click the **Browse** button.

4. Find the folder where the `FavoritesLib` project resides. `FavoritesLib.dll` will be inside the `Bin` folder that is inside the `FavoritesLib` project folder. When you have found `FavoritesLib.dll`, double-click it. It will be added to the **Selected Components** list at the bottom of the **Add Reference** dialog:

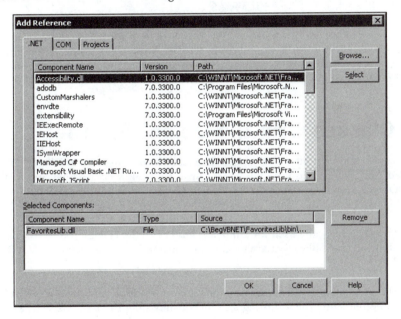

5. Click **OK** to add the reference to the project.

6. Remember that the classes in the class library are in the `FavoritesLib` namespace, so we need to tell our code to look in that namespace for class names we use. Add the following line to the top of `Form1.vb` and `WebFavoriteMenuItem.vb`:

```
Imports FavoritesLib
```

We do not need to add it to `ExitMenuItem.vb` because `ExitMenuItem` does not use any of the classes in the library.

7. Run the program. It will work as normal, but will be using the class library now instead of classes within the application's EXE file.

How It Works – Using FavoritesLib.dll in the Favorites Tray Application

This works in a very similar way to adding a reference to another project. We can use the classes in the class library in exactly the same way regardless of whether we reference the Class Library project or the compiled DLL. The main difference is that we cannot see or edit the class library's source code.

However, the Visual Studio .NET environment can still tell a lot about the classes, even without the source code. For example, IntelliSense still works. We can see available methods on an object:

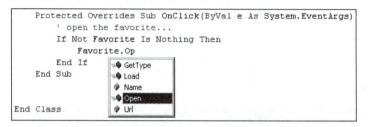

This is because Visual Studio .NET can tell from the DLL itself what methods and properties are available on each class. We can investigate a class without using IntelliSense using the Object Browser. Let's look at how to use it now.

Viewing Classes with the Object Browser

To view classes that can be used within Visual Basic .NET you can use a quick and easy tool known as the **Object Browser**. You can also use the Object Browser to view class names and method names on objects. The Object Browser window can be viewed inside Visual Studio .NET by pressing *Ctrl+Alt+J*. It is also available by clicking the View | Other Windows | Object Browser menu.

The Object Browser is basically used for a quick reference to the classes you need to see. The Object Browser will show all assemblies that are used in the current Solution, including VB Projects and pre-compiled DLLs.

The browser shows all members including methods, enumerations, and constants. Each member type is shown with a different icon. The following screenshot shows the `FavoritesLib.Favorite` class. We select this class by choosing the `FavoritesLib` assembly, and then within that the `FavortiesLib` namespace, and then within that the `Favorites` class:

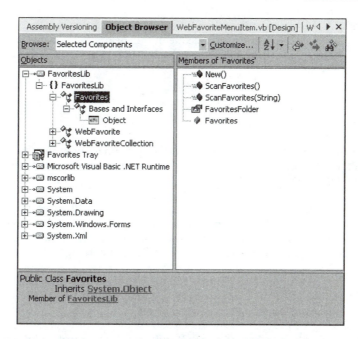

Remember that an assembly can contain several namespaces, and that the same namespace can be spread across several assemblies. It just happens that in Visual Basic .NET you normally have a singe namespace inside a single assembly of the same name.

Note that in order for the Object Browser to display anything, we need an open project. The Object Browser icon representations can be summarized as follows:

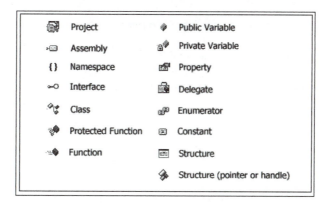

The MSDN documentation contains plenty of information about classes in the .NET Framework, so we don't often need to use the Object Browser when we're only using .NET Framework classes. It is really useful, however, when we are using a DLL from a third party that does not come with documentation. Often the method and property names can give us a clue of what's happening. Of course this underlines why it is necessary to choose good names for your classes and their members.

At other times the DLL will provide short descriptions of each of its classes and members. This is done using **attributes**, which is a subject outside the scope of this Beginning book. *Professional VB.NET* (Wrox Press, ISBN 1-86100-716-7) covers the subject, although using them is not essential in Visual Basic .NET development.

Summary

Class libraries are an integral part of Visual Basic .NET, and in fact important to all of the languages in the .NET Framework. They encompass what we use and what we need to know in terms of the CLR and within our developments.

In the course of this chapter, we have considered the nature of class libraries, and how to view the properties and methods contained within them using the Object Browser. We have seen how the .NET Framework allows developers to avoid DLL Hell through the use of keys and signatures, and looked at some of the broad issues regarding designing your own components.

This chapter is not the final word on class libraries and there is a wealth of information on the Internet, and in books such as *Visual Basic .NET Class Design Handbook: Coding Effective Classes* (Wrox Press, ISBN 1-86100-708-6), that will give you more insight into creating advanced components.

In the next chapter, you will learn how to create Windows forms controls, which are components with a user interface, as opposed to class library projects, which are purely code-based. There too you will see the importance of reusable and stable code.

Questions

1. What are the advantages of using Class Libraries?

2. What is the purpose of signing an assembly?

3. What is the purpose of the GAC (Global Assembly Cache)?

Creating Your Own Custom Controls

In this book we have used many of the controls that come with Visual Basic .NET in order to design applications. We've also seen how we can use object-oriented inheritance to add functionality to an existing class. In this chapter we're going to see how we can create our own controls, by adding custom functionality to existing control classes, and then use them in our Windows applications.

There are two variations of controls used with .NET. The first is the **Windows Form control** (often referred to as a **user control**) and these, obviously, are supposed to be used with Windows forms. They are the type that we will be examining in this chapter. The other kind is the **Web Form control**. As the name implies, these controls are supposed to be used with Web Applications. Creating Web Form controls is beyond the scope of this book but is covered in *Professional VB.NET 2nd Edition* (Wrox Press, ISBN 1-86100-497-4). When you're working through this chapter, bear in mind that the general principles you learn here can be migrated to Web Applications, should you feel the need.

There are several good reasons for wanting to create custom controls, including:

❑   We can use the same custom control throughout an application, or in lots of different applications, thus saving on code.

❑   We can keep code relating to a control within the control's class, making the code cleaner and easier to understand. For example, we could write a button that handled its own click event – meaning we don't need to handle the event in our form's code.

In terms of reusing controls between applications, there are two main ways to do this. The first is to add the control's source file to every project where we need to control. Then, when we build the application, the control will be compiled into the main executable. This is the approach we will take in this chapter.

The second way is to build a **control library**. Control libraries are very similar to class libraries. In fact, they *are* class libraries that happen to contain controls as classes. We saw how to create class libraries in the previous chapter, and the techniques for creating control libraries are very similar. Visual Studio .NET Professional and above has a Windows Control Library item in the New Project dialog. In Visual Basic .NET Standard we can just create a class library using the method presented in Chapter 12. Like a class library, a control library will compile to its own DLL, which we can use in our applications. This method is attractive because it means we can distribute the DLL to other developers without giving away our source code. We can also make changes to the DLL, and these will be reflected in the applications that use it – even without the applications being recompiled. The techniques for building the controls are the same regardless of whether we are using a control library, or just using a control within our application project.

Creating a User Control

Creating a user control from scratch is not difficult. From one perspective, it's very similar to building the kinds of forms that you're already used to building.

We are going to create a Windows application that uses User Controls. To start with, create a new Windows Application called `Controls`:

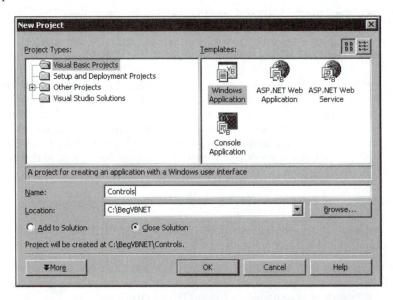

Once the project has been created, we'll have a blank form open and ready for us. We are not going to use this for the time being, though. Instead right-click on the `Controls` project in the Solution Explorer and choose Add | Add User Control. In the dialog box that appears, name the control `MyControl` and click OK. You'll be presented with something that looks very much like a form's designer, but which doesn't have the title bar or borders that a standard form does. Usually, when building a control, we paint on other controls and define a way in which those controls interact. It's this extra behavior that defines a control's purpose and makes it useful.

You might find, in the applications that you build, that you have a common need for a control that goes to a database to retrieve certain information, like employee or customer records. If you want to build this control well, you'll need to make it as useful as possible to developers using it down the line, while requiring the minimum amount of labor to get it working. You'll probably want to encapsulate the functionality of connecting to the database, querying the results, and populating the control with information, so that subsequent developers using your control don't have to know how to do this. This is a key precept of **encapsulation** – make life easier for the next developer. In this way you can also benefit from the more tangible advantage of reducing costs through quality application of code reuse.

For our first example, we're going to create a really simple control that has three basic button controls. This creates an **aggregate control**. When each button is pressed, a different message will be displayed. We'll then see how this control can be used in a standard Windows forms application.

Try It Out – Building the Control

1. Building the control is actually very simple indeed. All we have to do is grab three buttons off the Toolbox and place them onto the form, like this:

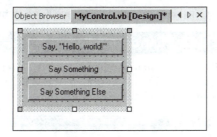

2. You'll notice that I've put text on each of the buttons, by changing their Text properties to the captions that you see above. I've also named the buttons btnSayHello, btnSaySomething, and btnSaySomethingElse (via their Name properties in the Properties window).

3. At the moment, this control won't do anything when the buttons are pressed – we need to wire up event code behind the Click event for each button in order for it to work. Double-click btnSayHello and add this code:

```
Private Sub btnSayHello_Click(ByVal sender As System.Object, _
            ByVal e As System.EventArgs) Handles btnSayHello.Click
    MsgBox("Hello, world!")
End Sub
```

4. There's nothing there that you haven't already seen before. When the button is pressed, the Click event is fired and so we display a message box. Now go back to the design view (either click on the UserControl1.vb[Design]* tab or the View Designer button in the Solution Explorer's toolbar), double-click btnSaySomething, and add this code:

```
Private Sub btnSaySomething_Click(ByVal sender As System.Object, _
            ByVal e As System.EventArgs) Handles btnSaySomething.Click
```

```
    MsgBox("Something!")
End Sub
```

5. Finally, double-click btnSaySomethingElse in the designer and add this code:

```
Private Sub btnSaySomethingElse_Click(ByVal sender As Object, _
        ByVal e As System.EventArgs) Handles btnSaySomethingElse.Click
    MsgBox("Something else!")
End Sub
```

6. The next thing we need to do is to build the project. Select Build | Build Solution.

Now we can test out the control!

Testing the Control

To test the control, we can't just run the project. Instead, we have to put the control onto a form.

Try It Out – Adding Our New User Control to a Form

1. Open the designer for Form1, which Visual Studio .NET created when we created the Windows Application, and scroll to the bottom of the Windows Forms tab of the Toolbox. MyControl should have appeared at the bottom:

2. Drag and drop a new `MyControl` control onto the form and you'll see something like this:

3. As well as having the same visual design, all of the functionality of the `UserControl1` control has been made available to `Control Test`. Try running the project and clicking on the buttons. You'll see that the encapsulated functionality of displaying the message boxes is now available to the developer.

Exposing Properties from User Controls

A user control is implemented in a class. Therefore, anything that we can do with a class we can also do with a user control. This means that we can add properties, methods, and events to the user control that can be manipulated by whoever's consuming it. First, we'll look at adding a new property to the control.

Your control can have two sorts of properties: ones that can be manipulated from the Properties window at design time and ones that have to be programmatically manipulated at run time. For example, at design time you might want to change properties pertaining to the color or the font used to draw the control. But, at run time you might want to change properties that depend on the contents of a file that the user selected and so on. Usually, if the property is a fairly simple type such as string, integer, or Boolean and doesn't have parameters, it can be manipulated at design time. If the property is a complex object, such as a database or file connection, or if it has parameters, you'll have to manipulate the property at run time.

Let's take a look at adding a property to our control. The property we're going to add is called `MessageText`. This will contain the text that we'd like to display instead of "Hello, world!" When this property is changed, we'll also want to change the text on the first of the three buttons that we have on the control.

Try It Out – Adding a New Property to UserControl1

1. To add a new property, we need a member variable that will store the value. Add this code to the top of `MyControl.vb`:

```
Public Class MyControl
    Inherits System.Windows.Forms.UserControl

    ' members...
    Private _messageText As String
```

2. As we said, when this property changes, we need to change the text on the first button. We'll also store the property value in the `_messageText` member that we just defined. Add this code directly after the lines you added in Step 1:

```
Public Property MessageText() As String
    Get
        Return _messageText
    End Get
    Set(ByVal Value As String)

        ' set the text...
        _messageText = Value

        ' update the button...
        btnSayHello.Text = "Say """ & _messageText & """"

    End Set
End Property
```

The reason why we need so many quotes when the Text *property is set is because, when we want to add a quotation mark to a string, we need to supply two – otherwise Visual Basic .NET believes we're marking the end of the string. The text we've entered here will resolve to:* Say "Whatever _messageText is set to"

3. By default, we want the button value of `_messageText` to be `"Hello, world!"` The best way to do this is to explicitly set the `MessageText` property when the object is created. That way, both `_messageText` and `btnSayHello.Text` will be appropriately configured from a single call. You'll need to open up the `Windows Form Designer generated code` region to find the `New` method. Add this code to the `New` method:

```
Public Sub New()
    MyBase.New()

    'This call is required by the Windows Form Designer.
    InitializeComponent()

    'Add any initialization after the InitializeComponent() call
    MessageText = "Hello, world!"

End Sub
```

Now, if we want to change the default text to something else, we only have to make the change in one place.

4. Of course, this new property will have no effect unless we alter the handler for `btnSayHello.Click`. Find the handler and change this code:

```
Private Sub btnSayHello_Click(ByVal sender As System.Object, _
    ByVal e As System.EventArgs) Handles btnSayHello.Click
    MsgBox(_messageText)
End Sub
```

5. To expose the new property, we need to build the project. Right-click on the **MyControl** project in the Solution Explorer and select **Build**.

6. If no build errors were found, the new property should be exposed.

7. Select the user control on `Form1` and scroll to the bottom of the Properties window. The new **MessageText** property will appear under the **Misc** category (or in the usual place if you have the properties arranged alphabetically):

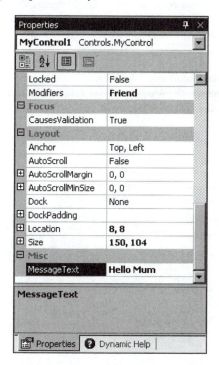

How It Works

You'll notice that the default value has passed through to the designer. If you change the property in the Properties window, the value on the first button on the control will change. Also, if you run the project and press the button, the text on the message box will change.

When the designer needs to update the Properties window, it will call into the object and request the `MessageText` property. Likewise, when you change the value, it will call into the object and set the property. This also happens when the form is loaded from disk when you start up the designer.

Exposing Methods from User Controls

As you've probably guessed, if you can expose new properties for your control, you can also expose new methods. All that we need to do to make this happen is to add a public function or sub to the control and then we'll be able to call it from the form that's hosting the control.

Try It Out – Adding a Method to MyControl.vb

1. Add this method to `MyControl.vb`:

```
Public Sub ResetMessageText()
   MessageText = "Hello, world!"
End Sub
```

This method uses the `MessageText` property to change the text of the top button back to the default setting. When this method is executed, both the text on the button, and the internal member `_messageText` will be changed to reflect the new value.

2. Go back to `Form1` on the `Control Test` project. To make things a little easier to follow, using the Properties window change the `Name` property of the user control from UserControl1 to MyControl. Also, change the MessageText value to Nothing. (That's the actual word "nothing", rather than the Visual Basic keyword.)

3. Now, add a new button to the form. Call it btnReset and set the Text to Reset. When you've finished, you should see something like this:

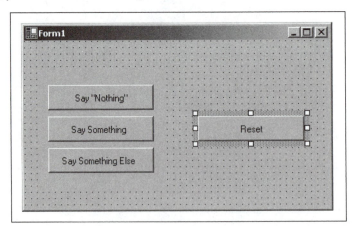

4. Double-click on `btnReset`. This will create a default event handler for its `Click` event. Add this code:

```
Private Sub btnReset_Click(ByVal sender As System.Object, _
        ByVal e As System.EventArgs) Handles btnReset.Click
    MyControl.ResetMessageText()
End Sub
```

5. Start the project and try clicking the Reset button. Notice how the text on our control changes back to Say "Hello, world!" as designed.

Exposing Events from User Controls

Now that we've seen how to expose new properties and new methods from our control, we need to take a look at how to expose events from the control. When you add events to one of your own controls, the person writing the form that uses your control can take action when the event is raised.

In this part of the exercise, we'll add an event called `HelloWorld` and we'll raise this event whenever the "Hello, world" button is clicked.

Try It Out – Defining Events

1. Defining an event is simply a matter of adding a statement to the class. Add this code to the top of `MyControl.vb`:

```
' members...
Private _text As String = "Hello, world!"

' events...
Event HelloWorld(ByVal sender As Object, ByVal e As System.EventArgs)
```

How It Works

In this case, we've defined an event called `HelloWorld` that takes two parameters: an `Object` representing the object that raised the event, and a `System.EventArgs` object.

Although an event can have any number of parameters, all events related to Windows forms follow this model: one parameter for the object that fired it and another object containing the event data. When building your events, you should follow this model too. That way, developers using your control won't be surprised by some weird approach that only you use.

Raising Events

To fire, or **raise** an event, we have to use the `RaiseEvent` keyword. This looks after the tricky aspect of actually telling the control's owner what event has been raised, and passes through the appropriate parameters.

We have to give some thought as to at what point in the control's behavior the event should be fired. In this example, do we want HelloWorld to be fired before or after the message box has been displayed? Well, it depends. If our motivation is to provide an opportunity for the owner to change the text before it's displayed, clearly RaiseEvent has to be called before MsgBox. If, on the other hand, we only want to tell the user that the message box has been displayed, we'll call RaiseEvent after MsgBox.

In the next *Try It Out*, we will add code to fire the event before showing the message box, giving the owner the freedom to change the MessageText property.

Try It Out – Raising the HelloWorld Event

1. To raise the event, we need to provide the name of the event and the parameters. Add this code to MyControl.vb:

```
Private Sub btnSayHello_Click(ByVal sender As System.Object, _
        ByVal e As System.EventArgs) Handles btnSayHello.Click

    ' raise the event...
    RaiseEvent HelloWorld(Me, New System.EventArgs)

    ' display the box...
    MsgBox(_messageText)

End Sub
```

How It Works

Notice how we pass Me as the value for sender through to the event. We might expect that we were supposed to pass the value of sender that was passed into btnSayHello_Click, but remember that the sender we were given corresponds to the button control that originated the event. This button control is not visible to forms using our control – as far as they are concerned it is the user control that raises events, so we pass Me – representing the current user control instance.

Consuming Events

All that remains now is to detect when the event has fired and do something. This is known as **consuming** an event. When a control that we own fires an event, we can **hook** into the event handler. By doing this, we receive notification that the event has fired and can do something. This is one of the core concepts of the control/event methodology that we've been using throughout this book.

Try It Out – Consuming the HelloWorld Event

1. If we go back to Form1 on MyControl, we can use the drop downs at the top of the window to locate and add the event handler. Remember, although we've specifically only defined a single event for this control, we still get all of the other events that were defined on the various base classes that our control class inherits from:

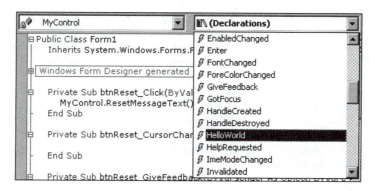

2. Of course, if we select the control and an event, we'll automatically be given a handler "stub" into which we can add our event-handling code. In this instance, we'll call the `ResetMessageText` method that we built earlier from within our event handler to make sure that the text changes back to "Hello, world!" before `MsgBox` is called. Add this code to `Form1`:

```
Private Sub MyControl_HelloWorld(ByVal sender As System.Object, _
        ByVal e As System.EventArgs) Handles MyControl.HelloWorld
    MyControl.ResetMessageText()
End Sub
```

3. Try running the project now and you'll notice that, whenever you click the button on the control, the text Hello, world! is always displayed. This is because we're responding to the `HelloWorld` event and using `ResetMessageText` to change the message text back to the default before the message box is ever displayed.

If you need further proof that this event handler is indeed being called, try setting a breakpoint on the `ResetMessageText` line. When the event is fired, Visual Studio .NET will suspend the program and show that the program does indeed get inside the event handler.

Inheriting Control Behavior

In early versions of Visual Basic, Visual Basic controls called VBXs became a very popular technology and this drove the adoption of Visual Basic. One of the reasons for this was that, when VBXs were introduced, Microsoft hadn't yet launched Windows 95. Windows 95 included a greatly enhanced control library offering things like progress bars, tracker bars, and the rich text edit box. Today, the control library included in Windows 2000 and Windows XP is extremely rich, meaning that the kinds of controls that we want to build are going to fall into three camps: they're either going to be a complex aggregate of many controls (like the control we just built), or they're going to somehow extend the behavior of an existing control, or they are going to cause us to start completely from scratch.

The topic of creating aggregate controls is now quite straightforward, thanks to the .NET Framework. Determining the need for controls in your applications often involves looking at previous applications and finding commonality, or intuiting the advantages of making a control reusable across later projects.

For example, you might find that all of your desktop applications feature the same login box that authenticates the user. This is a great candidate for reuse, but what's the best way to reuse it. Before .NET, by far the easiest way to achieve this in Visual Basic was to build a COM control that contained the requisite labels, textboxes, and buttons, and encapsulated the functionality of authenticating the user. This COM control could then be painted onto a form in the project.

However, with .NET, we can create a class in a completely separate project that contains the *entire form*. (This was possible before .NET, but it's much easier now!) The user could then create an instance of the class and call the `AuthenticateUser` method, say. This method would display the form, capture the details, and perform the authentication. This approach is a lot easier for the consumer to use, as they don't have to build a separate form.

Now imagine that the way that authentication is performed changes. A classic example here is that the application's authentication method is integrated into the Windows Authentication scheme. Now the class that implements `AuthenticateUser` can do without the dialog box altogether. This gives even greater advantage to the consumer, as they don't have to change their code in any way to adopt the new authentication approach.

What you need to do is look at the way that the functionality may be used and, if need be, implement it in a **form library** rather than control library. Basically, if the functionality needs to be painted on a form, so that you can put other controls on that form alongside it, the best method is as a user control, as we've just seen. If the functionality is designed to stand alone – in other words, you don't need to put other controls alongside it – implement it in a form library. We'll see how to build a form library in the next section.

The point of this discussion is to illustrate that, most of the time, if you're implementing controls there's a good chance that you'll be doing so by inheriting from an existing control and enhancing its functionality.

Enhancing Controls

So why might you want to enhance the functionality of a control? Well, common uses for enhancing functionality include adding new properties, new methods, and encapsulating event handling code. For example, you might create a button that is linked to a textbox control. The textbox contains the name of a file on the disk, and clicking the button automatically opens up the file and returns the contents of the file to the form or control that owns the button through an event. Another example would be creating a progress bar that was able to monitor some environmental information, for example disk space.

In this example, we'll look at how to enhance the functionality of the button control in such a way that it has a "buddy" textbox control and it is able to return the contents of a file through an enhanced version of the button `Click` event.

Try It Out – Creating an Enhanced Button Control

1. To get started, add a new User Control to the `Controls` project. Call it `FileButton`.

> It's very important that you create a new User Control at this point. Creating a User Control puts all of the appropriate designer information in place, meaning that the new control will appear properly in the Toolbox in **Controls**. If you create a class and then change its base class, the control won't appear in the Toolbox and you won't be able to use it with the designer.

2. By default, this class will be derived from `System.Windows.Forms.UserControl`. We need to derive it from `System.Windows.Forms.Button` in order to get the basic button functionality that we want. We'll also eventually need access to a couple of namespaces, so edit `FileButton.vb` so that it reads like this:

```
Imports System.IO
Imports System.ComponentModel

Public Class FileButton
    Inherits System.Windows.Forms.Button

    Windows Form Designer generated code

End Class
```

How It Works

To implement our control, we're going to need to add a property that lets the control know what textbox it's associated with, a method to get an actual `TextBox` object from the name of a control, and we'll also need to respond to the `Click` event and fire our own event.

Adding the BuddyBoxName Property

The `BuddyBoxName` property will be a string containing the name of a control also contained within the form. Any class derived from `System.Windows.Forms.Control` has a `Controls` property, which contains a list of controls that the control contains. The same class also has a `Parent` property that returns the container. Therefore, we'll need to look in our user control's `Parent.Controls` property for the associated textbox.

However, rather than storing a direct reference to the control through a `BuddyBox` property, it's more useful for us to store the name. This way, we can actually set the name from within the Properties window in Visual Studio .NET, rather than having to do so programmatically.

Try It Out – Adding the BuddyBoxName Property

1. Add this code to `FileButton.vb`:

```
Public Class FileButton

    Inherits System.Windows.Forms.Button
```

```
    ' members...
    Private _buddyBoxName As String


    ' BuddyBoxName property
    Property BuddyBoxName() As String
        Get
            Return _buddyBoxName
        End Get
        Set(ByVal Value As String)
            ' Perhaps add validation code here
            _buddyBoxName = Value
        End Set
    End Property
```

How It Works

Our original control was derived from UserControl and this class supports automatic discovery of properties for placing on the Properties window. This new control is derived from Button, and so we have to specifically declare the properties.

Try It Out – Testing the Property

1. We can now try adding this new control to our form. First, select Build | Build Solution. This will add the control to the Toolbox.

2. Now open up Form1 and add a new TextBox control and one of our new FileButton controls. Change the name of the textbox to txtFilename.

3. Use Notepad to create a new file and save it somewhere on your computer, then set the Text property of txtFilename to the path of the new file.

4. Also, change the name of our FileButton control to btnOpenFile and set its Text property to Open.

5. You'll see something like this:

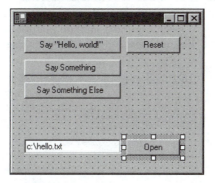

Remember, what's really smart here is the fact that our new FileButton control looks and behaves exactly like a button. We don't have to go through the hassle of trying to create a new control that looks like a button. The power of inheritance makes life very easy for us here!

6. Now, select btnOpenFile and take a look at the Properties window. You'll find a property called BuddyBoxName. Set this to txtFilename (in this view, the Properties window has been set to show properties alphabetically):

Now that we've created the property and added a new control to the form, we can wire in the code that opens the file and returns the contents through the event.

Responding to the Click Event

To respond to the Click event, we need to create a new event that will pass the data down to the owner. As we've already mentioned, we want to make sure that this event follows the standard format, which is that it has one Object parameter containing a reference to the object that fired the event, followed by a System.EventArgs parameter containing information about the event.

Try It Out – Responding to the Click Event

1. We're going to be writing a method into `FileButton` that responds to its own `Click` event. Before we can do that, we need to build a method that looks through the `Controls` collection of the parent, looking for a control with the name we gave to `BuddyBoxName`. Add this code to `FileButton.vb`:

```
' GetBuddyBox - return the actual TextBox control by looking through
' the parent's Controls property...
Public Function GetBuddyBox() As TextBox
    ' search name...
    Dim searchFor As String = BuddyBoxName.ToLower

    ' look through each control...
    Dim control As Control
    For Each control In Parent.Controls

        ' does the name match?
        If control.Name.ToLower = searchFor Then

            ' we have a match...  now, cast the control
            ' to a text box and return...
            Return CType(control, TextBox)

        End If

    Next
End Function
```

The trick is to use the `ToLower` method, so that we're always comparing lowercase strings. Otherwise, we'd run into problems with case sensitivity. Notice how we prepare a lowercase version of `BuddyBoxName` right at the top of the method, so that we're not inefficiently doing the conversion on each iteration of the loop. If we do find a control with the same name, we **cast** it to a `System.Windows.Forms.TextBox` control and return it. If the control can't be cast, an exception will be thrown, which we'll need to handle somewhere.

2. Drop down the object selector in the top left corner of the editor window for `FileButton.vb` and select **Base Class Events**. Then select **Click** from the other drop-down list:

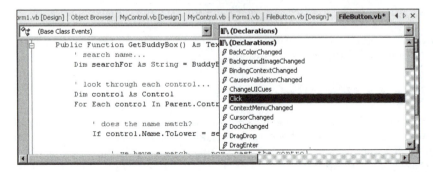

3. Now, inside the `Click` handler, we call our `GetBuddyBox` method and, provided we get a control back, we retrieve its `Text` property. We can then open the file and get all of the contents back. After we have the file contents, we will create a new `OpenFileEventArgs` object and package the data. Add this code:

```
Private Sub FileButton_Click(ByVal sender As Object, _
        ByVal e As System.EventArgs) Handles MyBase.Click

        ' try and get the buddy box...
        Dim buddyBox As TextBox = GetBuddyBox()
        If buddyBox Is Nothing Then
            MsgBox("The buddy box could not be found.")
        Else
            ' open the file and return the results...
            Dim stream As Stream = File.Open(buddyBox.Text, FileMode.Open)
            Dim reader As New StreamReader(stream)

            ' load the entire file...
            Dim contents As String = reader.ReadToEnd
            ' close the stream and the reader...
            stream.Close()
            reader.Close()

            ' do something with the contents
        End If

End Sub
```

Let's just pause for a moment and consider what we've achieved. We are opening the specified file when the user clicks a `FileButton`, and loading its contents into a `String`. We now need to find a way to send the text back to the application that's using the control. We are going to do this by adding a public event to the `FileButton` control called `OpenFile`. The arguments for this event will include the contents of the file.

We've already seen, however, that Windows forms events should only have two arguments. First, the object that raised the event. Second, an object that inherits from the `System.EventArgs` class and contains any other relevant information about the event. We are going to create a new class that derives from `System.EventArgs`, and includes public fields for the file name and file content.

4. We want to create a new class derived from `System.EventArgs` that we can package the name of the file and the text of the file into. This is very easy to do. Create a new class in `Controls` called `OpenFileEventArgs` (by right-clicking the `Controls` project and selecting **Add | Add Class**). Then add this code:

```
Public Class OpenFileEventArgs
    Inherits System.EventArgs

    ' extend the properties of EventArgs...
    Public FileName As String
    Public FileText As String

End Class
```

5. Now we need to declare the event in the `FileButton` control. Open the code editor for `FileButton` and add this code:

```
Public Class FileButton
    Inherits System.Windows.Forms.Button

        ' event...
        Public Event OpenFile(ByVal sender As Object, _
                    ByVal e As OpenFileEventArgs)

    ' members...
    Private _buddyBoxName As String
```

6. Finally we need to raise the event from the `FileButton` control's `Click` event handler. Add the indicated code:

```
Private Sub FileButton_Click(ByVal sender As Object, _
        ByVal e As System.EventArgs) Handles MyBase.Click

    ' try and get the buddy box...
    Dim buddyBox As TextBox = GetBuddyBox()
    If buddyBox Is Nothing Then
        MsgBox("The buddy box could not be found.")
    Else
        ' open the file and return the results...
        Dim stream As Stream = File.Open(buddyBox.Text, FileMode.Open)
        Dim reader As New StreamReader(stream)

        ' load the entire file...
        Dim contents As String = reader.ReadToEnd
        ' close the stream and the reader...
        stream.Close()
        reader.Close()

        ' raise the OpenFile event
        Dim args As New OpenFileEventArgs()
        args.FileName = buddyBox.Text
        args.FileText = contents
        RaiseEvent OpenFile(Me, args)
    End If

End Sub
```

Now, when a user clicks a `FileButton` control, and a file opens successfully, `FileButton` will raise an `OpenFile` event.

Try It Out – Testing the Control

1. To test the control, we need to make sure that we do receive the `OpenFile` event from the control. To do this, edit `Form1.vb` and use the dropdowns to create an event handler for `btnOpenFile.OpenFile`. Then add this code:

```
Private Sub btnOpenFile_OpenFile(ByVal sender As System.Object, _
    ByVal e As My_First_Control.OpenFileEventArgs) Handles _
    btnOpenFile.OpenFile
    MsgBox(e.FileText)
End Sub
```

As we defined this event as taking an `OpenFileEventArgs` object as its second parameter, this is what we'll be given. We can then gain direct access to the additional `FileText` and `FileName` properties that this class has.

2. Now, if you run the project and click the **Open** button, your file should be opened and your event handler will display the file contents in a message box.

Design Time or Run Time

Over the course of this discussion, we've mentioned the difference between design time and run time. In certain circumstances, it's useful to know if your control is in design mode or run mode. For example, imagine that you have a control that establishes a database connection when a certain property is set. It might not be appropriate for that control to establish the connection when the form is being designed, but we will want it to when the project is finally run.

Usefully, a control itself has a Boolean property called `DesignMode` that returns `True` if the control is in design mode, or `False` if it isn't.

We're going to create a new control derived from `Button` that contains a `Timer`. This timer updates the text on the button with the current date and time, but only when the program is running. If the control is in design mode, we're going to display the words "Design Mode".

Try It Out – Creating a Control that Understands "DesignMode"

1. Add a new User Control to the project. Call it `TickButton`.

2. Change this code in `TickButton.vb`:

```
Imports System.Windows.Forms

Public Class TickButton
    Inherits System.Windows.Forms.Button
```

3. Now open the design view for `TickButton`. Drag and drop a `Timer` control from the Toolbox onto the new control. Set the name of the timer to `ticker`. Make sure that `Enabled` is set to `False` and that `Interval` is set to `100`.

4. We can detect when our control has been added to a form through the `InitLayout` method that's defined on `System.Windows.Forms.Control`. This happens both at design time and run time. This is the best point to determine what mode we're in and, if appropriate, start the timer. Add this code:

```
Protected Overrides Sub InitLayout()

    ' are we in design mode?
    If DesignMode = True Then
        Text = "Design Mode"
    Else
        ticker.Enabled = True
    End If

End Sub
```

One important thing to note here: in the constructor of the form, `DesignMode` doesn't work. As the constructor is called the instant that the object is created, the `DesignMode` property will not have been set by the .NET Framework, so the property will always return `False`, even if, later in the control's lifetime, it will return `True`. `InitLayout` is the best place to check.

5. Go back to the design view of `TickButton` and double-click on the `Timer` control. Add the following code:

```
Private Sub ticker_Tick(ByVal sender As Object, ByVal e As System.EventArgs)
Handles ticker.Tick

    ' update the text...
    Text = Now.ToString

End Sub
```

6. Build the project.

7. Now, if you open the design view for `Form1` on `Control Test`, the new button should appear at the bottom of the Toolbox. Draw on a new `TickButton`. You'll see this:

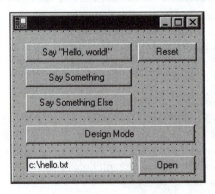

8. Now, try running the project. You'll see this:

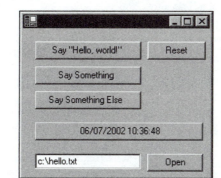

Of course, there are many other occasions when we might want our code to behave differently at run time or design time. An example could be that validation rules for a property will be different. In these cases, we would check the control's `DesignMode` property in exactly the same way.

Creating a Form Library

As we mentioned previously, we don't always have to encapsulate this kind of functionality as a control. We could encapsulate the entire form and display it on demand. This is, in fact, what happens whenever an application wants to display the Open File or Print dialogs, or any other standard dialog control. You may well discover common functionality in your applications that it would be useful to add to a reusable library. For example, you might want to have a "Customer Lookup" tool available to all of your applications, or a common login window like the one we discussed earlier.

Luckily, building form libraries is incredibly easy in .NET. In fact, it's no different from creating the kinds of forms that you've built so far. You just need to provide some kind of interface that allows the caller to quickly start up the form and get values back.

In this section, we'll build a simple login form. We won't bother adding any functionality behind it to actually authenticate the user. Instead, we'll concentrate on getting the form to display itself to the user.

Try It Out – Creating the Form Library Project

1. For this exercise, we're going to create a new project. Create a new Class Library project and call it Forms Library:

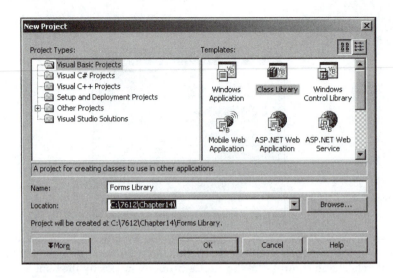

> Note that creating a Class Library in this way will only work in Visual Studio .NET
> Professional and above. See the previous chapter for instructions to use with Visual
> Basic .NET Standard.

2. The Class Library project type doesn't contain a reference to the Windows Forms library that
we need to use to build the form. To fix this, right-click on References in the Solution
Explorer and select Add Reference. Select System.Windows.Forms.dll from the available
.NET components, click Select, and then click OK:

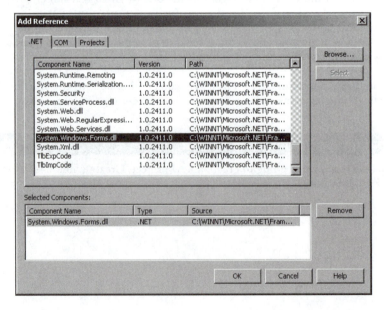

3. Now, create a new form by right-clicking on the project within the Solution Explorer and selecting **Add | Add Windows Form**. Call the new form `LoginUser` and click **Open**.

4. To build the form, we need to change quite a few of the properties. Change these properties:

Property	Value
Text	Login User
StartPosition	CenterScreen
FormBorderStyle	FixedDialog
MinimizeBox	False
MaximizeBox	False

5. Then, add two textboxes called `txtUsername` and `txtPassword`. Set the `PasswordChar` property of `txtPassword` to `*`, so that entered passwords are not displayed on the screen. Empty the `Text` properties of both textboxes. Next, add some labels to illustrate which is the username field and which is the password field.

6. Finally, add two buttons – `btnOk` and `btnCancel` – and change their `Text` properties until you end up with something like this:

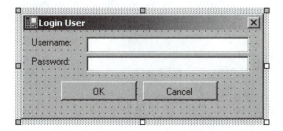

Now that we have the basic form in place, we can wire in the logic behind the **OK** and **Cancel** buttons.

Try It Out – Add Logic to the OK and Cancel Buttons

1. Add this code to `LoginUser.vb`:

```
Imports System.Windows.Forms

Public Class LoginUser
    Inherits Form

    ' members...
    Public Tries As Integer
    Public MaxTries As Integer = 3
    Public UserId As Integer
```

```vb
        ' events...
     Event LoginFailed(ByVal sender As Object, ByVal e As EventArgs)
     Event LoginSucceeded(ByVal sender As Object, _
                   ByVal e As LoginSucceededEventArgs)
     Event LoginCancelled(ByVal sender As Object, ByVal e As EventArgs)

  ' Go - authenticate the user...
  Public Function Go(ByVal owner As Form) As Integer

        ' reset ourselves...
        UserId = 0
        Tries = 0

        ' show ourselves...
        Me.ShowDialog(owner)

        ' return the user id back...
        Return UserId

  End Function

  Private Sub btnCancel_Click(ByVal sender As System.Object, _
         ByVal e As System.EventArgs) Handles btnCancel.Click
      RaiseEvent LoginCancelled(Me, New EventArgs())
      Me.DialogResult = DialogResult.Cancel
  End Sub

  Private Sub btnOk_Click(ByVal sender As System.Object, _
         ByVal e As System.EventArgs) Handles btnOk.Click

        ' did we get a username?
        If txtUsername.Text <> "" Then

            ' what password did we get?
            If txtPassword.Text = "secret" Then

                ' this is a successful login!
                UserId = 27

                ' create a new event...
                Dim newEventArgs As New LoginSucceededEventArgs()
                newEventArgs.UserId = UserId
                RaiseEvent LoginSucceeded(Me, newEventArgs)

                ' hide the dialog and return...
                Me.DialogResult = DialogResult.OK

            Else

                ' tell the username that the password was invalid...
                MsgBox("The password you entered was invalid.")
```

```
                              ' tell the caller that we failed...
                              RaiseEvent LoginCancelled(Me, New EventArgs())

                              ' add one to the number of tries...
                              Tries += 1
                              If Tries = MaxTries Then
                                  Me.DialogResult = DialogResult.OK
                              End If

                          End If

                  Else
                      MsgBox("You must supply a username.")
                  End If

          End Sub
```

Windows Form Designer generated code

```
End Class
```

2. Using the Solution Explorer, create a new class called `LoginSucceededEventArgs` and add this code:

```
Public Class LoginSucceededEventArgs
    Inherits EventArgs

    ' new member...
    Public UserId As Integer

End Class
```

3. Delete the existing `Class1.vb` file, if you haven't already.

How It Works

The first part of the class declaration includes the entire `System.Windows.Forms` namespace and then sets up the `LoginUser` class to derive from `System.Windows.Forms.Form`:

```
Imports System.Windows.Forms

Public Class LoginUser
    Inherits Form
```

The next part of the form defines several fields. We want one field that holds the number of attempts that the user has made to log in. We need another field to hold the maximum number of times that they are allowed to try. The last field holds the user ID that was authenticated. If the user cancels the dialog, or exceeds their maximum number of tries, the `UserId` will be `0`.

```
' members...
Public Tries As Integer
Public MaxTries As Integer = 3
Public UserId As Integer
```

We've gone ahead and defined three events for the form – one for when the user fails to authenticate themselves, one for when they succeed, and one for when they cancel. In order to receive these events, we need to manually wire up event handlers, as Visual Studio .NET can't handle events raised by a form itself. It can only handle events raised by controls on a form.

```
' events...
Event LoginFailed(ByVal sender As Object, ByVal e As EventArgs)
Event LoginSucceeded(ByVal sender As Object, _
                ByVal e As LoginSucceededEventArgs)
Event LoginCancelled(ByVal sender As Object, ByVal e As EventArgs)
```

The Go method will be called by the developer, who will pass in an object derived from Form. We'll reset our properties, display the form and, when the form has been closed, we'll return the user ID that we found (if any):

```
' Go - authenticate the user...
Public Function Go(ByVal owner As Form) As Integer

    ' reset ourselves...
    UserId = 0
    Tries = 0

    ' show ourselves...
    Me.ShowDialog(owner)

    ' return the user id back...
    Return UserId

End Function
```

If the user presses the Cancel button, we want to raise the LoginCancelled event and hide the dialog:

```
Private Sub btnCancel_Click(ByVal sender As System.Object, _
        ByVal e As System.EventArgs) Handles btnCancel.Click
    RaiseEvent LoginCancelled(Me, New EventArgs())
    Me.DialogResult = DialogResult.Cancel
End Sub
```

Using the DialogResult property of the form is the proper way to close a form displayed with ShowDialog. In this case, we're indicating that the dialog was canceled.

If the user clicks OK, the first thing we want to do is make sure that they actually supplied a username:

```
Private Sub btnOk_Click(ByVal sender As System.Object, _
        ByVal e As System.EventArgs) Handles btnOk.Click
```

```
' did we get a username?
If txtUsername.Text <> "" Then
```

For our logic, if the user enters any username with the password `"secret"`, we're going to authenticate them. We'll always give them a user ID of 27.

```
' what password did we get?
If txtPassword.Text = "secret" Then

    ' this is a successful login!
    UserId = 27

    ' create a new event...
    Dim newEventArgs As New LoginSucceededEventArgs()
    newEventArgs.UserId = UserId
    RaiseEvent LoginSucceeded(Me, newEventArgs)

    ' hide the dialog and return...
    Me.DialogResult = DialogResult.OK

Else
```

`LoginSucceededEventArgs` is derived from `System.EventArgs` and will contain an extra property called `UserId`. If the user has successfully logged in using the `"secret"` password then a value of `UserId` will be passed to `LoginSuccededEventArgs` and the `LoginSucceeded` event fired.

If the password supplied was not `"secret"`, we need to increment `Tries` and, if necessary, close the dialog:

```
' tell the username that the password was invalid...
MsgBox("The password you entered was invalid.")

' tell the caller that we failed...
RaiseEvent LoginCancelled(Me, New EventArgs())

' add one to the number of tries...
Tries += 1
If Tries = MaxTries Then
    Me.DialogResult = DialogResult.OK
End If
```

Finally, we round off the method definition, including the message box that tells the user that they need to supply a username:

```
    End If

Else
    MsgBox("You must supply a username.")
End If

End Sub
```

Testing the Form

To test the form, we need to jump through the same hoops we did when we first needed to test out our user control.

Try It Out – Testing the Login Form in an Application

1. Right-click on Solution 'Forms Library' (1 project) in the Solution Explorer and select Add | New Project. Create a new Visual Basic .NET Windows Application project and call it My Application.

2. As before, we need to set this new test application up as the startup project, so right-click My Application in the Solution Explorer and select Set as StartUp Project. You'll end up with something like this:

3. One last step. We need to add a reference to the `Forms Library` project to `My Application`. Right-click on the References entry underneath My Application and select Add Reference. Change to the Projects tab, select Forms Library, click Select, and then click OK.

4. Now we're free to create an instance of the `LoginUser` class from our application and ask it to log in the user.

Open up `Form1.vb` in the designer and draw on a button. Rename the button `btnLogin` and set its `Text` to `Login`:

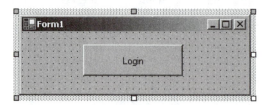

5. Now, double-click on `btnLogin` to create an event handler for its `Click` event. Add this code:

```
Private Sub btnLogin_Click(ByVal sender As System.Object, _
            ByVal e As System.EventArgs) Handles btnLogin.Click

        ' create a new instance of the form...
        Dim login As New Forms_Library.LoginUser()

        ' get the user id back...
        Dim userId As Integer = login.Go(Me)

        ' did we get a user?
        If userId <> 0 Then
            MsgBox("The logged in user has ID " & userId.ToString)
        Else
            MsgBox("No user ID was returned.")
        End If

End Sub
```

6. Now run the project and click the Login button. You'll be given three chances to login. Remember, to do this successfully, enter any username along with the password `"secret"`.

How It Works

The first thing we do is create an instance of our `LoginUser` class:

```
        ' create a new instance of the form...
        Dim login As New Forms_Library.LoginUser()
```

After we've done this, we ask the new object to display the form through the `Go` method:

```
        ' get the user id back...
        Dim userId As Integer = login.Go(Me)
```

By passing a reference to `Me` through, we're actually passing a reference to a `Form` object, which is then instantly passed through to the `ShowDialog` method of the `Form` object implemented by the `LoginUser` class. From this point, we're at the mercy of the encapsulated functionality.

When the dialog goes away, which can be because the user canceled the dialog, got the right password, or got the wrong password, we'll be given back the user ID as a return value from `Go`. If this value is 0, something went wrong and the user couldn't be logged in. Otherwise, the user could be logged in.

```
        ' did we get a user?
        If userId <> 0 Then
            MsgBox("The logged in user has ID " & userId.ToString)
        Else
            MsgBox("No user ID was returned.")
        End If
```

It's pretty unlikely that we'd implement this functionality by placing a button on a blank form that the user would click before being shown the dialog box. Rather, the application is more likely to do this automatically after its initialization routines have been completed.

Hooking up the Events

You'll recall that we built `LoginUser` so that it raises events at certain times. To round off this section, let's take a look at how we'd consume those events from within our form.

Try It Out – Receiving Events from LoginForm

1. Before we start, delete the `btnLogin` button that we created before, and dip into the code for `Form1.vb` and remove the `btnLogin_Click` method.

2. We can tell .NET that we want to automatically capture any events that an object raises by using the `WithEvents` keyword. The problem with this keyword is that it can't be used in conjunction with `New`. In other words, we need to define a member to contain an instance of `LoginForm` and create one when we need it. Add this code to the top of `Form1.vb`:

```
Public Class Form1
    Inherits System.Windows.Forms.Form

    ' members...
    Private _userId As Integer
    Private WithEvents _login As Forms_Library.LoginUser
```

We've also created another member that will hold the user ID, if logging in is successful.

3. At this point, Visual Studio .NET will pick up that we have a member that raises events and add that member to the two drop-down lists at the top of the code window. We can select **_login** from the left one, and then select **LoginSucceeded** from the right one.

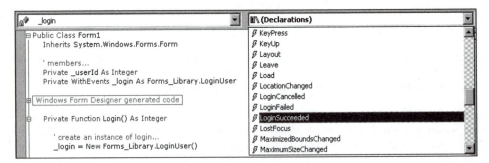

4. Simply, when we receive this event, we need to store the ID of the new user in our `_userId` member:

```
Private Sub _login_LoginSucceeded(ByVal sender As System.Object, _
        ByVal e As Forms_Library.LoginSucceededEventArgs) _
        Handles _login.LoginSucceeded
```

```
' store the user id...
_userId = e.UserId

' update our caption...
Me.Text &= " - User ID: " & _userId.ToString
```

End Sub

So that we can see what happens at design time, we also append the ID of the new user to the caption of the form.

5. Of course, nothing's going to happen until we create an instance of `LoginUser` and call `Go`. We're going to break this up into a separate function so that, if we want, we could call it from another point in the application. (Although it's not strictly necessary here, it's good practice to break functions out in this way, as it makes the code easier to maintain.) Add this method to `Form1.vb`:

```
Private Function Login() As Boolean

    ' create an instance of login...
    _login = New Forms_Library.LoginUser()

    ' login the user...
    Dim userId As Integer = _login.Go(Me)

    ' reset our login object...
    _login = Nothing

    ' return true or false...
    If userId <> 0 Then
        Return True
    Else
        Return False
    End If

End Function
```

As we mentioned before, we need to physically create an instance of `LoginUser` before we can use it and, in order to make sure that the event handling works, we *must* add this instance to a member variable defined using the `WithEvents` keyword, otherwise Visual Basic .NET will not be able to wire up the methods. For neatness, we also get rid of the object instance once we're finished. Finally, we return `True` or `False` to indicate whether the user properly logged in or not.

6. Use the drop-down lists to create an event handler for the form's `Load` event. Then, add this code:

```
Private Sub Form1_Load(ByVal sender As System.Object, _
        ByVal e As System.EventArgs) Handles MyBase.Load

....' try and login...
    If Login() = False Then
```

```
                    ' quit the application if we failed...
                    MsgBox("Login failed.  Quitting.")
                    Application.Exit()

            End If

    End Sub
```

7. Now try running the application. If the login process works, you'll see something like this:

How It Works

By virtue of the fact that the caption has been changed, we know that the user successfully managed to authenticate themselves and, moreover, that the user ID has indeed been properly passed through the event handler.

If the user failed to authenticate properly, we won't see the application window. Either way, the developer has been successfully able to reuse the code that provides a login dialog, which is the point of the exercise.

Although we've presented two methods for using the form here, there's no real advantage over using either as far as the developer is concerned. They still need to create an instance of `LoginUser`, still need to call it, and still need to examine the results and determine the next step that the application should make when the user can log in and when they can't.

Summary

In this chapter, we looked at two ways of packaging a user interface together with some encapsulated functionality. We looked at building user controls that aggregated a number of existing controls usefully, and how to build user controls that inherited the behavior of an existing control. In both cases, we extended the new controls with properties, methods, and events.

We then went on to look at the `DesignMode` property of a control, and how to use it to manage our control's behavior in a design-time environment.

Questions

1. How do we define an event called `SomethingHappened` in a user control?

2. What keyword is used to fire (or raise) an event?

3. How does a control know if it's design time or run time?

Programming Custom Graphics

So far in this book, we have built user interfaces entirely from existing controls. When we're writing programs with Visual Basic .NET, we also have the freedom to "draw" our own user interface. This gives us absolute freedom over the look and feel of our program, and makes certain programming tasks possible.

In this chapter, we're going to take a look at the graphics and drawing functionality available in Visual Basic .NET. We'll introduce the concepts by building a fairly complex drawing program, just to illustrate how simple drawing our own user interface actually is. Towards the end of the chapter, we'll examine some of the multimedia features of Visual Basic .NET and show how we can display common Internet file formats such as GIF, JPG, and PNG.

A Simple Paint Program

Without further ado, let's kick off our paint program. The way we're going to do this is to create a new Windows Application project and build some user controls that we'll wire up in order to provide the whole application.

Our motivation for building user controls for this application is simple: it's good practice to break our application down into components. By following this technique, if we want to pull our paint functionality out of this application and into another, we can do it relatively easily.

> **What we're doing here with our controls is taking over the responsibility for painting them. Whenever we do this, we say that we're owner drawing. Therefore, the controls we build are known as owner-draw user controls.**

Try It Out – Creating the Project

1. Create a new Visual Basic Windows Application project in the usual way. Call it WroxPaint.

2. In the Solution Explorer, right-click the WroxPaint project and select Add | Add User Control. Change the name to PaintCanvas and click Open.

3. Make sure the Form Designer for `PaintCanvas` is showing, click on the background of the control and from the Properties window, change the `BackColor` property to white. (To do this, use the `BackColor` property's drop-down list, change to the **Custom** tab, and click the white box in the top left corner.)

4. Before we can use the control, we need to build the project. From the menu select **Build | Build Solution**. This will create the new `PaintCanvas` control and let us use it.

5. Now, go back to the Designer for `Form1`. Scroll down to the bottom of the Toolbox and select the new **PaintCanvas** control:

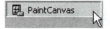

6. Add a **PaintCanvas** control so that it fills up the whole form. Set its `Anchor` property to **Top, Bottom, Left, Right** – this will ensure that the control always takes up the whole window. For the sake of neatness, change the **Text** property of the form to **WroxPaint**.

How Drawing Programs Work

Your computer screen is made up of **pixels** – hundreds of thousands of them. They're very small, but when working together they make the display on the screen. Since pixels on any given display are always a uniform size, they are the common unit of measurement used in computer graphics.

To find out how big your desktop is, minimize all your windows and right-click on your Windows desktop. Select **Properties** and change to the **Settings** tab. The slider in the bottom right corner controls the size of your desktop – or rather, it controls the density of pixels on your display. Here you can see that this screen is set to 1,280 pixels across and 1,024 pixels down:

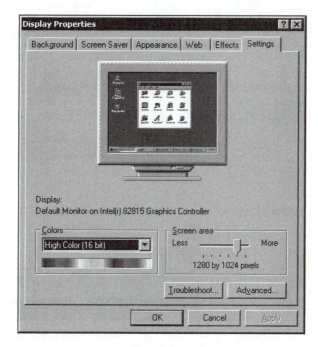

There are two very common computer graphics techniques: **raster** and **vector**. It is very useful to understand the difference between the two.

Raster Graphics

Raster graphics work a little like a physical canvas – you have this space and you fill it up with color using various tools like brushes and pens. In a raster graphics program, the space is divided up into pixels. Each pixel can be a color and it's the drawing program's responsibility to set the color of each square depending on what kind of drawing tool you're using and the position and movement of the mouse.

The graphics program stores the image that you've drawn as a **bitmap**, this being a description of the pixels that make up the image and the color of each. A bitmap is basically a two-dimensional array of pixels. Each element in the array, accessed through a pair of (x,y) coordinates, stores a color value. If you draw a rectangle in a raster graphics package, that rectangle is abstracted to a set of pixels on the bitmap. After it's been drawn, you can't change the rectangle at all, other than using other tools to draw over it and draw another one.

JPG, GIF, and PNG images use a variation of the bitmap format to save images. However, they are compressed in particular ways to save space and download time.

Vector Graphics

Vector graphics packages work in a different way. When you draw a rectangle onto the canvas, they physically record the fact that a rectangle exists at a given location. Vector graphics packages store a blueprint of how to draw the image, rather than storing the image that's been drawn. They do not abstract the rectangle down to a set of pixels. What this means is that you can pick it up again and move it, or change its shape or color later on because the package has an understanding of what it is.

539

> **A number of modern graphics packages offer a hybrid approach to this, combining raster graphics with vector graphics.**

Even in a vector graphics program, the screen itself works in pixels and is therefore a raster format. Therefore, in order for the program to be able to display the drawing, the picture that the package has recorded has to be converted into a raster format for the display. This process is known as **rendering**.

Our paint package is going to be a vector-based drawing package – for no other reason than it makes it easier to understand how drawing works in .NET. We're going to build a set of objects that represent certain shapes – namely circles and squares – and hold them in a list.

The GraphicsItem Class

In our application, we're going to have two basic drawing types: circle and square. Each drawing type will need to have an understanding of where it appears on the canvas (and ultimately, the screen), what its color is, and whether it is filled. We'll build a base class called `GraphicsItem`, from which we'll derive `GraphicsCircle`.

Try It Out – Building GraphicsItem and GraphicsCircle

1. Create a new class named `GraphicsItem` by right-clicking on **WroxPaint** in the Solution Explorer and selecting **Add | Add Class**. Name the class `GraphicsItem` and click **Open**.

2. Enter this code into `GraphicsItem`. Remember to add the `MustInherit` keyword to the first line. The `MustInherit` keyword tells Visual Basic .NET that we cannot create instances of `GraphicsItem` directly. Instead, we have to create classes that inherit from it. We also use the `MustOverride` keyword here. This has a similar meaning to `MustInherit` – we use it to force derived classes to add implementation for a particular method, without providing any implementation in the base class. It can only be used in `MustInherit` classes.

```
Public MustInherit Class GraphicsItem

    ' members...
    Public Color As Color
    Public IsFilled As Boolean
    Public Rectangle As Rectangle

    ' methods...
    Public MustOverride Sub Draw(ByVal graphics As Graphics)

    ' SetPoint - add an item at the given point...
    Public Sub SetPoint(ByVal x As Integer, ByVal y As Integer, _
        ByVal graphicSize As Integer, _
        ByVal graphicColor As Color, ByVal graphicIsFilled As Boolean)

        ' set the rectangle depending on the graphic and the size...
        Rectangle = New _
            Rectangle(x - (graphicSize / 2), y - (graphicSize / 2), _
            graphicSize, graphicSize)
```

```
                   ' set the color and isfilled...
                   Color = graphicColor
                   IsFilled = graphicIsFilled

           End Sub

   End Class
```

3. Create another class named `GraphicsCircle`. Add this code:

```
Public Class GraphicsCircle
       Inherits GraphicsItem

       Public Overrides Sub Draw(ByVal graphics As _
               System.Drawing.Graphics)

             ' create a new pen...
             Dim brush As New SolidBrush(Me.Color)

             ' draw the circle...
             graphics.FillEllipse(brush, Me.Rectangle)

       End Sub

   End Class
```

How It Works

We'll hold off discussing how this all works until after we can actually paint on `PaintCanvas` – it'll make the discussion easier to follow. For now, let's look at how we can 'paint' on the control.

Screen and Client Coordinates

When we get into the world of building our own painting code for our user interface, we usually have to work a lot with the mouse. We've already mentioned that in Windows and .NET, the base currency of drawing is the pixel. This means that when we ask the mouse for its position (for example when verifying that the user has moved the mouse across our control or clicked one of the buttons), we get a set of coordinates back given in pixels. If the user clicks the mouse in the very top-left pixel, we'll get back coordinates of (0,0). If we're using a 1,024x768 display and the user clicks in the very bottom-right pixel, we'll get back coordinates of (1024,768).

Although this seems straightforward, there is a wrinkle. When you click inside a window, the coordinates are adjusted depending on where the window itself is on the screen. Look at this screenshot:

In this screenshot, Notepad is shown in the bottom right corner. This display is configured at 1,024 pixels across by 786 pixels down, which means that the top-left corner of Notepad itself is at approximately (500,300).

Every window has a **client area**, which is the area the programmer can use to report the program's output. This client area is *exclusive* of the window border, the caption, menu, scrollbars, and the toolbar. When we're drawing onto the control or form, we're always dealing with this client area. The coordinates we use when drawing are adjusted so that the position of the window itself on the screen becomes irrelevant. These coordinates are known as **client coordinates**.

If we click in the top-left corner of the Notepad edit area (the white part), there are actually two different coordinates that we can get:

❑ The first one will be around (510, 330), a little in and down from the top-left hand corner of the window. These are the **screen coordinates**, also known as the **absolute position**.

❑ The second pair will be around (10,10) and these are the adjusted client coordinates. If we click the same graphic in the client, we'll get (10, 10) irrespective of where the window is positioned on the screen. This is sometimes known as the **relative position**.

Listening to the Mouse and Drawing GraphicsCircle Objects

For our graphics application to work, we'll monitor what the user is doing with the mouse, create new objects derived from GraphicsItem, and store them in a big list. When it is time for us to draw ourselves, we'll go through this list and ask each GraphicsItem in turn to render itself on the screen.

Try It Out – Drawing

1. In the Solution Explorer, right-click **PaintCanvas** and select **View Code**. Add these enumerations to the class. The first will be used to store the current graphics mode/tool, while the second stores the size of pen used to draw:

```
Public Class PaintCanvas
    Inherits System.Windows.Forms.UserControl

    ' enums...
    Public Enum GraphicTools As Integer
        CirclePen = 0
    End Enum

    Public Enum GraphicSizes As Integer
        Small = 4
        Medium = 10
        Large = 20
    End Enum
    ' Windows Forms Designer generated code
    ' ...
End Class
```

2. Next, add these members to the form:

```
Public Class PaintCanvas
    Inherits System.Windows.Forms.UserControl

    ' enums...
    Public Enum GraphicTools As Integer
        CirclePen = 0
    End Enum

    Public Enum GraphicSizes As Integer
        Small = 4
        Medium = 10
        Large = 20
    End Enum

    ' members...
    Public GraphicsItems As New ArrayList()
    Public GraphicTool As GraphicTools = GraphicTools.CirclePen
    Public GraphicSize As GraphicSizes = GraphicSizes.Medium
    Public GraphicColor As Color = Color.Black
```

Here's what each member will do. You'll notice that we define a default value for these members to make initialization of the application easier:

❑ GraphicItems – this will hold a list of the GraphicsItem objects that make up the drawing

❑ GraphicsTool – this will keep track of which graphic tool is currently being used

543

❏ GraphicsSize – this will keep track of how big we want each graphic to be

❏ GraphicsColor – this will keep track of the color of the item that we want to draw

Drawing the items on the page is a two-phase process. When the user moves the mouse around on the control, we want to create new GraphicsCircle objects and add them to the GraphicsItems list. At some point, Windows will ask us to paint the control, so we'll need to go through the GraphicsItems list and draw each one in turn.

3. Add this method to PaintCanvas:

```
' DoMousePaint - respond to a mouse movement...
Private Sub DoMousePaint(ByVal e As MouseEventArgs)

    ' store the new item somewhere...
    Dim newItem As GraphicsItem

    ' what tool are we using?
    Select Case GraphicTool

        ' circlepen?
        Case GraphicTools.CirclePen

            ' create a new graphics circle...
            Dim circle As New GraphicsCircle()
            circle.SetPoint(e.X, e.Y, GraphicSize, GraphicColor, True)

            ' store this for addition...
            newItem = circle

    End Select

    ' were we given an item?
    If Not newItem Is Nothing Then

        ' add it to the list...
        GraphicsItems.Add(newItem)

        ' invalidate...
        Invalidate()

    End If

End Sub
```

4. From the left drop-down list at the top of the code editor window, select (**Overrides**). From the right list, select **OnMouseDown**. Add this code to the new event handler:

```
Protected Overrides Sub OnMouseDown( _
                ByVal e As System.Windows.Forms.MouseEventArgs)
```

```
    ' is the button down?
    If e.Button = MouseButtons.Left Then
        DoMousePaint(e)
    End If

End Sub
```

5. Again from the left drop-down list, select (**Overrides**). Then select **OnMouseMove** from the right list. Add this code:

```
Protected Overrides Sub OnMouseMove( _
        ByVal e As System.Windows.Forms.MouseEventArgs)

    ' is the button down?
    If e.Button = MouseButtons.Left Then
        DoMousePaint(e)
    End If

End Sub
```

6. Finally, from the left drop-down list select (**Overrides**) once more. Then select **OnPaint** from the right list. Add this code:

```
Protected Overrides Sub OnPaint( _
        ByVal e As System.Windows.Forms.PaintEventArgs)

    ' go through the list...
    Dim item As GraphicsItem
    For Each item In GraphicsItems

        ' ask each item to draw itself...
        item.Draw(e.Graphics)

    Next

End Sub
```

7. Run the project and draw on the control by clicking and dragging the mouse over the surface. You'll see something like this:

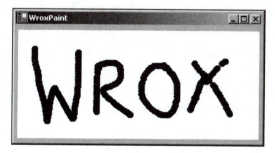

We now have a working paint program, but you'll notice that the more you paint, the more it flickers like crazy and the slower it gets. This illustrates an important aspect of drawing, as we'll see when we fix it. For now, let's look at what we've done.

How It Works

OK, we've done a lot, but let's look at what's actually happened.

When the user moves the mouse over the control, an event called MouseMove is fired. We've hooked into this event by overriding a method in the base System.Windows.Forms.UserControl class called OnMouseMove. When this happens, we check to see if the left mouse button is down and, if it is, we pass the System.Windows.Forms.MouseEventArgs object that we were given over to our private DoMousePaint method:

```
Protected Overrides Sub OnMouseMove( _
        ByVal e As System.Windows.Forms.MouseEventArgs)

    ' is the button down?
    If e.Button = MouseButtons.Left Then
        DoMousePaint(e)
    End If

End Sub
```

DoMousePaint is the method that we'll use to handle the drawing process. In this case, whenever MouseMove is received, we want to create a new GraphicsCircle item and add it to the list of vectors that make up our image.

As DoMousePaint will ultimately do more than add circles to the vector list, we need to do things in a (seemingly) counter-intuitive order. The first thing we need is somewhere to declare a variable to hold the new GraphicsItem that will be created – so we declare newItem:

```
' DoMousePaint - respond to a mouse movement...
Private Sub DoMousePaint(ByVal e As MouseEventArgs)

    ' store the new item somewhere...
    Dim newItem As GraphicsItem
```

Then, we look at our GraphicTool property to determine what we're supposed to be drawing. At this point, because we only have one tool defined, this will always be a circle:

```
' what tool are we using?
Select Case GraphicTool

    ' circlepen?
    Case GraphicTools.CirclePen

        ' create a new graphics circle...
        Dim circle As New GraphicsCircle()
```

546

After we have the circle, we call the `SetPoint` member, which if you recall was defined on `GraphicsItem`. This method is responsible for determining the point on the canvas that the item should appear. We give `SetPoint` the current drawing size and color, and tell it to draw a filled circle:

```
circle.SetPoint(e.X, e.Y, GraphicSize, GraphicColor, True)
```

We'll look at `SetPoint` itself in more detail in a moment.

After we have the item and have called `SetPoint`, we store it in `NewItem` and close the `Select...End Select`:

```
        ' store this for addition...
        newItem = circle

    End Select
```

If a new `GraphicsItem` was stored in `newItem`, we have to add it to the list:

```
    ' were we given an item?
    If Not newItem Is Nothing Then

        ' add it to the list...
        GraphicsItems.Add(newItem)
```

Finally, we have to **invalidate** the control. We have to do this to tell Windows that something about the appearance of the control has changed. .NET will not tell the control to paint itself unless something has told Windows that the control needs painting. Calling `Invalidate` in this way tells Windows that the appearance of the control is "invalid" and therefore needs updating:

```
        ' invalidate...
        Invalidate()

    End If

End Sub
```

> **Although we can invalidate the control with the `Invalidate` method, the control will be invalidated whenever Windows detects it needs redrawing. This may happen when the window is restored after being minimized, another window obscures an area that's been made visible, and so on.**

That covers everything from the user dragging the mouse over the control and adding a new `GraphicsCircle` item to the list. Now what?

With the control marked as requiring painting, it's down to Windows to choose a time for the window to be painted. In order to increase performance of the windowing subsystem, windows are only drawn when the system has enough "spare time" to do it. Painting is not considered to be a crucial task to the operating system and therefore may not happen immediately. You cannot rely on painting being done immediately, or within a given time-span of your marking something as invalid. At some point in the future, the control will be asked to paint itself. You may have noticed this effect when your computer is being used heavily – an image on the screen will appear to "freeze" for a period before the display is updated.

One point – don't try to force Windows to paint when it doesn't want to. There's a ton of optimization code in Windows to make sure that things are painted at absolutely the best time. Invalidate when you need to flag something as needing to be redrawn and let nature take its course.

When it is, the `Paint` event will be called. We tap into this event by overriding the `OnPaint` method on the base `UserControl` class. All that we have to do is loop through the entire array of `GraphicsItem` objects that we've collected in `GraphicsItems` and ask each one to draw itself:

```
Protected Overrides Sub OnPaint( _
        ByVal e As System.Windows.Forms.PaintEventArgs)

    ' go through the list...
    Dim item As GraphicsItem
    For Each item In GraphicsItems

        ' ask each item to draw itself...
        item.Draw(e.Graphics)

    Next

End Sub
```

The `Paint` event passes through its parameters as a `PaintEventArgs` object. This object, among other things, contains a property called `Graphics`. This property returns a `System.Drawing.Graphics` object.

When you have hold of a `Graphics` object, you are able to draw to the control, or the form, printer or whatever it is that's given you an object. This object contains a bundle of methods and properties that are actually used for painting. To keep in line with the principle of "only painting when needed", in typical day-to-day work you shouldn't try to create or otherwise obtain one of these objects. If you're given one then it's time to paint!

Painting is usually a matter of calling some simple methods on the `Graphics` object. In the case of `GraphicsCircle`, we call `FillEllipse`. This method draws and fills an ellipse (or circle, depending on which parameters you provide). Note that there's a similar method called `DrawEllipse`, which doesn't fill in the ellipse after it's drawn:

```
Public Overrides Sub Draw(ByVal graphics As _
        System.Drawing.Graphics)

    ' create a new pen...
    Dim brush As New SolidBrush(Me.Color)
```

```
' draw the circle...
graphics.FillEllipse(brush, Me.Rectangle)

End Sub
```

The `SetPoint` method is responsible for populating the `Color` and `Rectangle` properties on the `GraphicsCircle` object – and we'll see this in a minute. Painting in .NET is heavily dependent on this concept of a `Rectangle`, and this is a simple class that stores *x* and *y* coordinates for the top left of the rectangle, and the width and height. When we draw an ellipse, we provide a rectangle that describes the bounds of the ellipse.

You'll also notice that at the top of the method we created a new `SolidBrush`. We then pass this brush through to the `FillEllipse` method. This `SolidBrush` object, as you've probably guessed, describes the kind of brush we want to use.

Let's look at the `SetPoint` method now. You'll recall that we call this method from inside `DoMousePaint` whenever we create a new `GraphicsCircle` object:

```
' create a new graphics circle...
Dim circle As New GraphicsCircle()
circle.SetPoint(e.X, e.Y, GraphicSize, GraphicColor, True)
```

Basically, all we're using this method for is populating the object depending on the position of the mouse, and the current graphic size and color.

The first thing we need to do in `GraphicsItem.SetPoint` is set up the rectangle:

```
' SetPoint - add an item at the given point...
Public Sub SetPoint(ByVal x As Integer, ByVal y As Integer, _
   ByVal graphicSize As Integer, _
   ByVal graphicColor As Color, ByVal graphicIsFilled As Boolean)

   ' set the rectangle depending on the graphic and the size...
   Rectangle = New _
      Rectangle(x - (graphicSize / 2), y - (graphicSize / 2), _
      graphicSize, graphicSize)
```

When we want to draw a circle, we'll provide the mid-point. Therefore, the top left corner of the rectangle must be adjusted up and left depending on the size provided through `graphicSize`. We pass the top left corner through as the first and second parameters to `Rectangle`'s constructor. The third parameter supplied is the width and the fourth provides the height.

Once we have the parameter, we just need to store the color and also a flag that indicates if the circle is filled or not:

```
' set the color and isfilled...
Color = graphicColor
IsFilled = graphicIsFilled

End Sub
```

Now that you know how the painting works, let's see if we can get rid of the flickering!

Invalidation

This example is designed to flicker and slow down to illustrate an important consideration that you need to bear in mind when drawing controls: do the least amount of work possible! Drawing to the screen is slow. The less you draw, the faster the performance of your application should be and the better it should look on the screen.

The reason why the control flickers is because painting is a two-stage process. Before we're asked to paint, Windows automatically erases the region behind the area that needs to be painted. This means the whole control flashes white as everything is erased and then we fill in the details.

What we want to do is only invalidate the area that contains the new GraphicsItem. When we invalidate the control, we don't have to invalidate the whole thing. We can, if we want, just invalidate a small area. Let's do this now.

Try It Out – Invalidating a Small Area

1. In the PaintCanvas class, find the DoMousePaint method. Change the Invalidate method call at the end to this:

```
' were we given an item?
If Not newItem Is Nothing Then

        ' add it to the list...
        GraphicsItems.Add(newItem)

        ' invalidate...
        Invalidate(newItem.Rectangle)

End If
```

2. Run the project. You'll notice now that when you paint it doesn't flicker.

How It Works

After we call SetPoint on the new GraphicsCircle object, the Rectangle property is updated to contain the bounding rectangle of the circle.

This time when we call the Invalidate method, we pass in this rectangle. In this way, only a tiny area of the form is invalidated, therefore only that tiny area is erased and after it is erased we get the opportunity to draw our circle.

More Optimization

You'll notice that if you draw a lot on the control, after a while the edge of the line starts to become almost jagged. What we're experiencing here is that as the GraphicsItems list grows, the more calls to FillEllipse end up being made. As drawing to the screen is slow, the more times we have to do this, the longer the drawing process takes on aggregate. This lengthened drawing process prevents all of the MouseMove events from being fired and so the line appears to stutter. Let's see how we can avoid this problem.

Try It Out – Optimized Drawing

1. Find the `OnPaint` method on the `PaintCanvas` class. Add this code:

```
Protected Overrides Sub OnPaint( _
        ByVal e As System.Windows.Forms.PaintEventArgs)

    ' go through the list...
    Dim item As GraphicsItem
    For Each item In GraphicsItems

        ' do we need to be drawn?
        If e.ClipRectangle.IntersectsWith(item.Rectangle) = True Then

            ' ask each item to draw itself...
            item.Draw(e.Graphics)

        End If

    Next

End Sub
```

2. Run the project. You should now find that the drawing process is smoother.

How It Works

The `PaintEventArgs` object contains another property called `ClipRectangle`. This rectangle describes the area of the control that has been invalidated and is known as the **clipping rectangle**. The `Rectangle` class contains a method called `IntersectsWith` that can tell if two given rectangles overlap.

As we know the rectangle that describes the bounds of each of our `GraphicsItem` objects, we can use this rectangle with `IntersectsWith`. If the `GraphicsItem` overlaps, it needs drawing, which we duly do; otherwise we move on to the next control.

The two techniques we've seen here – only invalidating what changes and only drawing what falls into the invalidated region – are by far the two most important techniques you'll come across when painting. If you skip either of these, your control has a good chance of being sluggish and flickering.

Choosing Colors

Now that we can do some basic painting, we'll build a control that lets us choose the color that we're painting in. Like a lot of graphics programs, we'll build this so that we have a palette of different colors and we're able to choose two at a time – one for the left mouse button and one for the right.

There are a number of different ways to build this control, and perhaps the most logical is to create a control that contains a bundle of Button controls, each configured so that it displays the color that it represents. However, in this example I want to show you how to build a control completely from scratch. The techniques that you'll learn here will be really useful if you want to roll your own controls that display a picture of something and have **hot regions** on them. Hot regions are regions that fire an event when you click them. What we're doing might seem a little obscure, but it's a great example!

Creating the ColorPalette Control

To create the color palette control, we're going to need two classes. One, derived from `UserControl` and named `ColorPalette`, will provide the UI for the palette itself. The other, `ColorPaletteButton`, will be used to display the actual color box on the palette.

Try It Out – Creating the ColorPalette Control

1. In the Solution Explorer, add a new class to the `WroxPaint` project named `ColorPaletteButton` and add the following code to it:

```
Public Class ColorPaletteButton

    ' color...
    Public Color As Color = Color.Black
    Public Rectangle As Rectangle

    ' constructor...
    Public Sub New(ByVal newColor As Color)
        Color = newColor
    End Sub

    ' SetPosition - move the button to the given position...
    Public Sub SetPosition(ByVal x As Integer, ByVal y As Integer, _
                    ByVal buttonSize As Integer)

        ' update the members...
        Rectangle = New Rectangle(x, y, buttonSize, buttonSize)

    End Sub

    ' Draw - draw the button...
    Public Sub Draw(ByVal graphics As Graphics)

        ' draw the color block...
        Dim brush As New SolidBrush(Color)
        graphics.FillRectangle(brush, Rectangle)

        ' draw an "edge" around the control...
        Dim pen As New Pen(Color.Black)
        graphics.DrawRectangle(pen, Rectangle)

    End Sub

End Class
```

2. In a similar fashion, add a user control to the WroxPaint project named ColorPalette. Double-click on the background of the control to view the code editor. Add these members to the top of the class definition:

```
Public Class ColorPalette
    Inherits System.Windows.Forms.UserControl
```

```
' members...
Public Buttons As New ArrayList()
Public ButtonSize As Integer = 15
Public ButtonSpacing As Integer = 5
Public LeftColor As Color = Color.Black
Public RightColor As Color = Color.White
```

Here's what the members will do:

❑   Buttons – hold a list of the buttons on the palette

❑   ButtonSize – define the size of each of the buttons on the palette

❑   ButtonSpacing – define the gap between each button

❑   LeftColor – hold the current color that is assigned to the left mouse button

❑   RightColor – hold the current color that is assigned to the right mouse button

3.   Next, add this method to the class:

```
' AddColor - add a new color button to the control...
Public Function AddColor(ByVal newColor As Color) As _
        ColorPaletteButton

    ' create the button...
    Dim button As New ColorPaletteButton(newColor)

    ' add it to the list...
    Buttons.Add(button)

End Function
```

4.   When we create the control, we want a set of basic colors to be always available. Add this to the constructor of the class. This will create ten basic colors. To find the constructor, open the Windows Form Designer generated code region by clicking on its + sign:

```
Public Sub New()
    MyBase.New()

    'This call is required by the Windows Form Designer.
    InitializeComponent()

    ' add the colors...
    AddColor(Color.Black)
    AddColor(Color.White)
    AddColor(Color.Red)
    AddColor(Color.Blue)
    AddColor(Color.Green)
    AddColor(Color.Gray)
    AddColor(Color.DarkRed)
    AddColor(Color.DarkBlue)
    AddColor(Color.DarkGreen)
    AddColor(Color.DarkGray)

End Sub
```

How It Works

We'll talk about how all this works once we've managed to get it displayed on **Form1**!

Sizing the Control

Since we're handling the layout of the buttons on the control ourselves, we need to respond to the `Resize` event. This event is fired whenever the user changes the size of the control. We can hook into this event by overloading the `OnResize` method.

When `Resize` is fired, we need to alter the position of each of the buttons, starting in the top left corner and continuing in strips across the whole width of the control. When we've filled up one row, we need to start a new row.

Try It Out – Sizing and Painting the Control

1. In the code editor for the `ColorPalette` class, select **(Overrides)** from the left drop-down list and **OnResize** from the right one. Add this code to the `OnResize` method:

```vbnet
' OnResize - called when the control is resized...
Protected Overrides Sub OnResize(ByVal e As System.EventArgs)

    ' variables to hold the position...
    Dim x As Integer, y As Integer

    ' go through the array and position the buttons...
    Dim button As ColorPaletteButton
    For Each button In Buttons

        ' position the button...
        button.SetPosition(x, y, ButtonSize)

        ' move for the next one...
        x += (ButtonSize + ButtonSpacing)

        ' do we need to go down to the next row?
        If x + ButtonSize > Width Then

            ' move y...
            y += (ButtonSize + ButtonSpacing)

            ' reset x...
            x = 0

        End If

    Next

    ' redraw...
    Invalidate()

End Sub
```

2. We still need to paint the control. Select **(Overrides)** from the left drop-down list and **OnPaint** from the right one. Add this code:

```
' OnPaint - called when the control needs painting...
Protected Overrides Sub OnPaint( _
        ByVal e As System.Windows.Forms.PaintEventArgs)

        ' loop through...
        Dim button As ColorPaletteButton
        For Each button In Buttons

            ' do we need to draw?
            If e.ClipRectangle.IntersectsWith(button.Rectangle) Then
                button.Draw(e.Graphics)
            End If

        Next

End Sub
```

3. Before we can draw the control onto **Form1**, we need to build the project. Select **Build | Build Solution** from the menu.

4. After the project has been built, open the Designer for **Form1**. Resize the form and the `PaintCanvas` control, and add a new `ColorPalette` control. Rename the new control `paletteColor`, and set its `Anchor` property to **Bottom, Left, Right**. Your form should now look something like this:

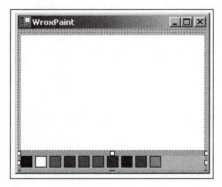

5. If you now try to rearrange the controls a little, you should see that our sizing code has proved successful.

How It Works

Hopefully, the behavior of `ColorPaletteButton` shouldn't be too much of a mystery. We have members on the class that hold the color and a rectangle, and also provide a constructor that automatically populates the color:

```
Public Class ColorPaletteButton

    ' color...
    Public Color As Color = Color.Black
    Public Rectangle As Rectangle

    ' constructor...
    Public Sub New(ByVal newColor As Color)
        Color = newColor
    End Sub
```

When the button is asked to paint itself, all we do is draw one filled rectangle of the color specified in the Color property using the FillRectangle method, and for neatness we surround it with a black border using the DrawRectangle method:

```
' Draw - draw the button...
Public Sub Draw(ByVal graphics As Graphics)

    ' draw the color block...
    Dim brush As New SolidBrush(Color)
    graphics.FillRectangle(brush, Rectangle)

    ' draw an "edge" around the control...
    Dim pen As New Pen(Color.Black)
    graphics.DrawRectangle(pen, Rectangle)

End Sub
```

When we resize the form (a subject we'll come onto in a moment), we pass the top left corner of the button through to SetPosition. All this method does is update the Rectangle property:

```
' SetPosition - move the button to the given position...
Public Sub SetPosition(ByVal x As Integer, ByVal y As Integer, _
                ByVal buttonSize As Integer)

    ' update the members...
    Rectangle = New Rectangle(x, y, buttonSize, buttonSize)

End Sub
```

The OnResize method is perhaps the most interesting method here. This is a fairly common algorithm to come across whenever we need to manage the position of controls or other graphic objects. Basically, we know the size of each object (in our case it's a combination of ButtonSize and ButtonSpacing) and we know the bounds of the control. All we do is start in the top left and keep moving right until we have no more space, in which case we flip down to the next row.

Here's how we start – we set up a loop that iterates through all of the buttons:

```
' OnResize - called when the control is resized...
Protected Overrides Sub OnResize(ByVal e As System.EventArgs)
```

```
' variables to hold the position...
Dim x As Integer, y As Integer

' go through the array and position the buttons...
Dim button As ColorPaletteButton
For Each button In Buttons
```

Throughout the loop, x and y hold the current coordinates of the top left corner of the control. When we start this is (0,0), or rather the very top left of the client area of the control. For each button, we call `SetPosition` passing in the current coordinates together with the size of the button:

```
' position the button...
button.SetPosition(x, y, ButtonSize)
```

After each button, we move x to the right. As well as adjusting by the size of the button, we also add a small gap to make the control more esthetically pleasing:

```
' move for the next one...
x += (ButtonSize + ButtonSpacing)
```

If we detect that we don't have enough space to fit the next control completely on the current row, we adjust y down to the next row and reset x back to the beginning:

```
' do we need to go down to the next row?
If x + ButtonSize > Width Then

    ' move y...
    y += (ButtonSize + ButtonSpacing)

    ' reset x...
    x = 0

End If

Next
```

Finally, after we've moved all of the buttons, we invalidate the control so that we can see the changes.

```
' redraw...
Invalidate()

End Sub
```

Responding to Clicks

Our control is going to fire an event whenever the left or right mouse button is clicked on a button.

Try It Out – Responding to Clicks

1. Go back to the code editor for `ColorPalette`. Add these event handlers to the top of the class definition:

```
Public Class ColorPalette
    Inherits System.Windows.Forms.UserControl

    ' members...
    Public Buttons As New ArrayList()
    Public ButtonSize As Integer = 15
    Public ButtonSpacing As Integer = 5
    Public LeftColor As Color = Color.Black
    Public RightColor As Color = Color.White

    ' events...
    Event LeftClick(ByVal sender As Object, ByVal e As EventArgs)
    Event RightClick(ByVal sender As Object, ByVal e As EventArgs)
```

2. We need a general-purpose method that will return the button that's positioned directly beneath the mouse. Add this method:

```
Public Function GetButtonAt(ByVal x As Integer, ByVal y As Integer) _
                As ColorPaletteButton

    ' go through each button in turn...
    Dim button As ColorPaletteButton
    For Each button In Buttons

        ' is this button in the rectangle...
        If button.Rectangle.Contains(x, y) = True Then Return button

    Next

End Function
```

3. Now, from the top left drop-down list select (**Overrides**) and then select **OnMouseUp** from the right list. (Our motivation for using `MouseUp` rather than `MouseDown` will become apparent.) Add this code:

```
Protected Overrides Sub OnMouseUp( _
        ByVal e As System.Windows.Forms.MouseEventArgs)

    ' find the button that we clicked on...
    Dim button As ColorPaletteButton = GetButtonAt(e.X, e.Y)
    If Not button Is Nothing Then

        ' select this color...
        If e.Button = MouseButtons.Left Then

            ' set the color...
            LeftColor = button.Color

            ' fire the event...
            RaiseEvent LeftClick(Me, New EventArgs())
```

```
            End If

            ' did we click with the right?
            If e.Button = MouseButtons.Right Then

                ' set right color...
                RightColor = button.Color

                ' fire the event...
                RaiseEvent RightClick(Me, New EventArgs())

            End If

        End If

    End Sub
```

4. To test the new method, open the Designer for **Form1**. Select the `PaintCanvas` control and set its **Name** property to **canvas**.

5. Open up the code editor for **Form1**. From the left drop-down menu, select `paletteColor`. From the right list select `LeftClick`. Add this code to the event handler:

```
Private Sub paletteColor_LeftClick(ByVal sender As System.Object, _
    ByVal e As System.EventArgs) Handles paletteColor.LeftClick
    canvas.GraphicColor = paletteColor.LeftColor
End Sub
```

6. Try running the project. You should be able to change the color using the control palette.

How It Works

Although we've called our buttons `ColorPaletteButton` they don't behave in the way we're used to seeing buttons behave. Button controls, like the ones we have been using up to now, have the intelligence to detect when they've been clicked and fire an event to tell us what happened. Until now, our 'buttons' have been just areas on the control painted in a pretty color – we actually need to write the logic to determine when a button is clicked.

The key to this is the `GetButtonAt` method. This method takes a set of client coordinates and returns the `ColorPaletteButton` object that contains the point we asked for. In this case, we use the `Contains` method of the `Rectangle` object to see if the coordinates are contained within the rectangle.

```
Public Function GetButtonAt(ByVal x As Integer, ByVal y As Integer) _
                As ColorPaletteButton

    ' go through each button in turn...
    Dim button As ColorPaletteButton
    For Each button In Buttons
```

```
        ' is this button in the rectangle...
        If button.Rectangle.Contains(x, y) = True Then Return button

    Next

End Function
```

Of course, it could be the case that there is no button under the coordinates if the user clicked the mouse on a blank area of the control. If this is the case, GetButtonAt will return Nothing:

```
Protected Overrides Sub OnMouseUp( _
        ByVal e As System.Windows.Forms.MouseEventArgs)

    ' find the button that we clicked on...
    Dim button As ColorPaletteButton = GetButtonAt(e.X, e.Y)
    If Not button Is Nothing Then
```

As we know, the Button property of MouseEventArgs tells us which button was used, or in this case released. If it's the left button, we update LeftColor and fire the LeftClick event:

```
        ' select this color...
        If e.Button = MouseButtons.Left Then

            ' set the color...
            LeftColor = button.Color

            ' fire the event...
            RaiseEvent LeftClick(Me, New EventArgs())

        End If
```

Alternatively, it could be the right mouse button:

```
        ' did we click with the right?
        If e.Button = MouseButtons.Right Then

            ' set right color...
            RightColor = button.Color

            ' fire the event...
            RaiseEvent RightClick(Me, New EventArgs())

        End If

    End If

End Sub
```

At the moment, PaintCanvas can only deal with one color, which is why we've only hooked up the LeftClick event. When we receive this event, we set the appropriate property on canvas and this new color will be used when creating new GraphicsCircle objects:

```
Private Sub paletteColor_LeftClick(ByVal sender As System.Object, _
        ByVal e As System.EventArgs) Handles paletteColor.LeftClick
    canvas.GraphicColor = paletteColor.LeftColor
End Sub
```

Dealing with Two Colors

Let's extend `PaintCanvas` so that it can deal with two colors.

Try It Out – Dealing with Two Colors

1. We need an additional property in `PaintCanvas` that will let us store the alternative color. For the sake of clarity, we'll also change the name of the existing `GraphicColor` property to `GraphicLeftColor`. Open the code editor for `PaintCanvas` and make these changes:

```
' members...
Public GraphicsItems As New ArrayList()
Public GraphicTool As GraphicTools = GraphicTools.CirclePen
Public GraphicSize As GraphicSizes = GraphicSizes.Medium
Public GraphicLeftColor As Color = Color.Black
Public GraphicRightColor As Color = Color.White
```

2. In `DoMousePaint`, we need to examine the `Button` property of `MouseEventArgs` to determine which color we want to use. Make these two changes to `DoMousePaint`:

```
' DoMousePaint - respond to a mouse movement...
Private Sub DoMousePaint(ByVal e As MouseEventArgs)

    ' store the new item somewhere...
    Dim newItem As GraphicsItem

        ' what color do we want to use?
        Dim useColor As Color = GraphicLeftColor
        If e.Button = MouseButtons.Right Then useColor = GraphicRightColor

    ' what tool are we using?
    Select Case GraphicTool

        ' circlepen?
    Case GraphicTools.CirclePen

            ' create a new graphics circle...
            Dim circle As New GraphicsCircle()
            circle.SetPoint(e.X, e.Y, GraphicSize, useColor, True)

            ' store this for addition...
            newItem = circle

    End Select
```

```
        ' did we get given an item?
        If Not newItem Is Nothing Then

                ' add it to the list...
                GraphicsItems.Add(newItem)

                ' invalidate...
                Invalidate(newItem.Rectangle)

        End If

End Sub
```

3. At the moment, `OnMouseDown` and `OnMouseMove` will only call `DoMousePaint` if the left button is pressed. We need to change this so that it will accept either the left or right button. Make these changes:

```
Protected Overrides Sub OnMouseDown( _
            ByVal e As System.Windows.Forms.MouseEventArgs)

        ' is the button down?
        If e.Button = MouseButtons.Left Or e.Button = MouseButtons.Right Then
            DoMousePaint(e)
        End If

End Sub

Protected Overrides Sub OnMouseMove( _
            ByVal e As System.Windows.Forms.MouseEventArgs)

        ' is the button down?
        If e.Button = MouseButtons.Left Or e.Button = MouseButtons.Right Then
            DoMousePaint(e)
        End If

End Sub
```

4. Next, we need to change the event handler in **Form1** to set the `GraphicLeftColor` property rather than the `GraphicColor` property. Open the code editor for **Form1** and make this change:

```
Private Sub paletteColor_LeftClick(ByVal sender As System.Object, _
    ByVal e As System.EventArgs) Handles paletteColor.LeftClick
    canvas.GraphicLeftColor = paletteColor.LeftColor
End Sub
```

5. Finally, we don't have an event handler for `RightClick`. Select **paletteColor** from the left drop-down list and then select **RightClick** from the right list. Add this code:

```
Private Sub paletteColor_RightClick(ByVal sender As System.Object, _
    ByVal e As System.EventArgs) Handles paletteColor.RightClick
    canvas.GraphicRightColor = paletteColor.RightColor
End Sub
```

Now if you run the project you should be able to assign different colors to the left and right mouse buttons and use both of the buttons to paint on the form.

Indicating the Assigned Buttons

I'm sure you've noticed that, at this point, using WroxPaint is a little confusing. There's no indication as to which color is assigned to which button. We need to resolve this issue, so what we'll do is display the letter L on a color assigned to the left button and the letter R on a color assigned to the right button.

Try It Out – Indicating the Assigned Buttons

1. First we'll make the ColorPaletteButton objects aware of which button they're assigned to, if any. Open the code editor for ColorPaletteButton and add this enumeration to the top of the class:

```
Public Class ColorPaletteButton

    ' enums...
    Public Enum ButtonAssignments As Integer
        None = 0
        LeftButton = 1
        RightButton = 2
    End Enum
```

2. Next, add this new member that will keep track of the button's assignment:

```
Public Class ColorPaletteButton

    ' enums...
    Public Enum ButtonAssignments As Integer
        None = 0
        LeftButton = 1
        RightButton = 2
    End Enum

    ' color...
    Public Color As Color = Color.Black
    Public Rectangle As Rectangle
    Public ButtonAssignment As ButtonAssignments = ButtonAssignments.None
```

3. Once the button has a way of storing what it's assigned to, we can change the Draw method to draw the L or R as appropriate. Add this code to Draw:

```
' Draw - draw the button...
Public Sub Draw(ByVal graphics As Graphics)
```

```
' draw the color block...
Dim brush As New SolidBrush(Color)
graphics.FillRectangle(brush, Rectangle)

' draw an "edge" around the control...
Dim pen As New Pen(Color.Black)
graphics.DrawRectangle(pen, Rectangle)

    ' are we selected?
    If ButtonAssignment <> ButtonAssignments.None Then

        ' create a font...
        Dim font As New Font("verdana", 8, FontStyle.Bold)

        ' what text do we use?
        Dim buttonText As String = "L"
        If ButtonAssignment = ButtonAssignments.RightButton Then _
                        buttonText = "R"

        ' what brush do we want...
        Dim fontBrush As SolidBrush
        If Color.R < 100 Or Color.B < 100 Or Color.G < 100 Then
            fontBrush = New SolidBrush(Color.White)
        Else
            fontBrush = New SolidBrush(Color.Black)
        End If

        ' draw some text...
        graphics.DrawString(buttonText, font, fontBrush, _
            Rectangle.Left, Rectangle.Top)

    End If

End Sub
```

4. To keep track of which button is selected, we need to add some private members to
`ColorPalette`. Open the code editor for this class and add this code:

```
Public Class ColorPalette
    Inherits System.Windows.Forms.UserControl

    ' members...
    Public Buttons As New ArrayList()
    Public ButtonSize As Integer = 15
    Public ButtonSpacing As Integer = 5
    Public LeftColor As Color = Color.Black
    Public RightColor As Color = Color.White
    Private leftButton As ColorPaletteButton
    Private rightButton As ColorPaletteButton
```

5. The next wrinkle we have to fix is quite verbose, but relatively straightforward. Basically, we have to make sure that a button cannot be assigned to both the left and right buttons – for no other reason than we just don't have a way of reporting that information to the user. Also, we have to mess around with the invalidation code, and we'll detail that once we have the example working. Make these changes to `OnMouseUp`:

```
Protected Overrides Sub OnMouseUp( _
    ByVal e As System.Windows.Forms.MouseEventArgs)

    ' find the button that we clicked on...
    Dim button As ColorPaletteButton = GetButtonAt(e.X, e.Y)
    If Not button Is Nothing Then

        ' select this color...
        If e.Button = MouseButtons.Left Then

            ' make sure that this button is not the current right...
            If Not button Is rightButton Then

                ' set the color...
                LeftColor = button.Color

                ' clear the existing selection...
                If Not leftButton Is Nothing Then
                    leftButton.ButtonAssignment = _
                        ColorPaletteButton.ButtonAssignments.None
                    Invalidate(leftButton.Rectangle)
                End If

                ' mark the button...
                button.ButtonAssignment = _
                    ColorPaletteButton.ButtonAssignments.LeftButton
                Invalidate(button.Rectangle)
                leftButton = button

                ' fire the event...
                RaiseEvent LeftClick(Me, New EventArgs())

            End If

        End If

        ' did we click with the right?
        If e.Button = MouseButtons.Right Then

            ' make sure this button is not the current left...
            If Not button Is leftButton Then

                ' set right color...
                RightColor = button.Color

                ' clear the existing selection...
```

```
              If Not rightButton Is Nothing Then
                  rightButton.ButtonAssignment = _
                      ColorPaletteButton.ButtonAssignments.None
                  Invalidate(rightButton.Rectangle)
              End If

              ' mark the button...
              button.ButtonAssignment = _
                  ColorPaletteButton.ButtonAssignments.RightButton
              Invalidate(button.Rectangle)
              rightButton = button

              ' fire the event...
              RaiseEvent RightClick(Me, New EventArgs())

          End If

      End If

  End If

End Sub
```

6. Finally, we have to set up the first two colors added to the control as being the selected buttons when the control is started. This involves updating our `leftButton` and `rightButton` members as well as setting the `ButtonAssignment` property on the button itself. Add this code to `AddColor`:

```
' AddColor - add a new color button to the control...
Public Function AddColor(ByVal newColor As Color) As ColorPaletteButton

    ' create the button...
    Dim button As New ColorPaletteButton(newColor)

    ' add it to the list...
    Buttons.Add(button)

    ' do we have a button assigned to the left button yet?
    If leftButton Is Nothing Then
        button.ButtonAssignment = _
            ColorPaletteButton.ButtonAssignments.LeftButton
        leftButton = button
    Else

        ' how about the right button?
        If rightButton Is Nothing Then
            button.ButtonAssignment = _
                ColorPaletteButton.ButtonAssignments.RightButton
            rightButton = button
        End If

    End If

End Function
```

7. Run the project now and you should see that when you change the color selection, an L and R appear on the buttons as appropriate:

How It Works

The first thing we did was to add an enumeration to `ControlPaletteButton` that could be used to set the state of the button:

```
' enums...
Public Enum ButtonAssignments As Integer
    None = 0
    LeftButton = 1
    RightButton = 2
End Enum
```

As you can see from the enumeration, a button can either be assigned to 'no buttons' or the left or the right button.

We also added members to the `ControlPalette` to keep track of which button was selected. This makes our life a little easier when it comes to changing the selection. When we select a new button, we have to set the `ButtonAssignment` property of the old button to `ButtonAssignments.None`. Just being able to look in the `_leftButton` or `_rightButton` members as appropriate saves us from having to look through the entire list of buttons to find the one we need to change.

The `OnMouseUp` method starts to look a little more complex when we add this new functionality. When we want to assign the left mouse button to a `button`, we have to make sure that the `button` is not already assigned to the right mouse button:

```
Protected Overrides Sub OnMouseUp( _
    ByVal e As System.Windows.Forms.MouseEventArgs)

    ' find the button that we clicked on...
    Dim button As ColorPaletteButton = GetButtonAt(e.X, e.Y)
    If Not button Is Nothing Then

        ' select this color...
        If e.Button = MouseButtons.Left Then

            ' make sure that this button is not the current right...
            If Not button Is rightButton Then
```

If we can set the color, we update the `LeftColor` property as we did before:

```
' set the color...
LeftColor = button.Color
```

If another button is already assigned to the left mouse button, we need to set its `ButtonAssignment` property back to `None`. We also have to invalidate this button so that the button is redrawn and the L is removed:

```
' clear the existing selection...
If Not leftButton Is Nothing Then
    leftButton.ButtonAssignment = _
        ColorPaletteButton.ButtonAssignments.None
    Invalidate(leftButton.Rectangle)
End If
```

Next, we set the new button's `ButtonAssignment` property to `Left`. We also invalidate the button (so that we can draw the L on this one instead) and update the `_leftButton` property to point at the new button:

```
' mark the button...
button.ButtonAssignment = _
    ColorPaletteButton.ButtonAssignments.LeftButton
Invalidate(button.Rectangle)
leftButton = button
```

Finally, we fire the `LeftClick` event as we did before:

```
' fire the event...
RaiseEvent LeftClick(Me, New EventArgs())
```

The remainder of `OnMouseUp` is the same as this, but obviously reversed to deal with the right-hand button.

When it's time to draw the button, we can check to see if a button assignment is set. If it is, we draw some text. (We've only fleetingly covered drawing text here, but we'll deal with it in more detail in a later section.) To draw the text, we need to create a new `System.Drawing.Font` object, and here we're creating a new 8-point Verdana font, in bold:

```
' Draw - draw the button...
Public Sub Draw(ByVal graphics As Graphics)

    ' draw the color block...
    Dim brush As New SolidBrush(Color)
    graphics.FillRectangle(brush, Rectangle)

    ' draw an "edge" around the control...
    Dim pen As New Pen(Color.Black)
    graphics.DrawRectangle(pen, Rectangle)
```

```
        ' are we selected?
        If ButtonAssignment <> ButtonAssignments.None Then

            ' create a font...
            Dim font As New Font("verdana", 8, FontStyle.Bold)
```

Next, we choose the text to draw:

```
            ' what text do we use?
            Dim buttonText As String = "L"
            If ButtonAssignment = ButtonAssignments.RightButton Then _
                        buttonText = "R"
```

Choosing the brush we want is quite tricky. We can't just choose a color because there's a chance it won't show up on the color that we're drawing. Instead, we have to examine the color to see whether it is a light color or a dark color. If it's dark, we choose to draw the letter in white; otherwise, we draw it in black:

```
            ' what brush do we want...
            Dim fontBrush As SolidBrush
            If Color.R < 100 Or Color.B < 100 Or Color.G < 100 Then
                fontBrush = New SolidBrush(Color.White)
            Else
                fontBrush = New SolidBrush(Color.Black)
            End If
```

Finally, we actually draw the text:

```
            ' draw some text...
            graphics.DrawString(buttonText, font, fontBrush, _
                    Rectangle.Left, Rectangle.Top)

        End If

    End Sub
```

Advanced Colors

So far, the only colors we've used are ones defined by the .NET Framework, such as `Color.Black` and `Color.Blue`. The list of colors available to us on the `Color` structure is considerable, but we can define our own colors if we want to.

> **To find a list of predefined colors, use the MSDN documentation to display "all members" of the "Color structure". Alternatively, you can use IntelliSense from within the code editor to display a list of possibilities.**

Windows defines a color as a 24-bit number, with the three bytes of the 24-bit representing a **red** value, a **green** value, and a **blue** value – this is commonly known as **RGB**. In effect, each component represents one of a possible 256 shades of red, green, and blue. By combining these shades together, we can get any color from a possible set of 16.7 million. For example, setting "red" to 255 and setting "blue" and "green" to 0 would result in "bright red". Setting all components to 255 would give "white". Setting all to 0 would give "black", and so on.

If you're used to mixing paints, these color combinations may seem strange. This is because we are working with colored lights instead of colored paints – and they combine in different ways.

To illustrate this, let's see how we can choose a color and then we'll manually add that color as a button to the control palette.

Try It Out – Custom Colors

1. Open the Form Designer for the `ColorPalette` control. In the Properties window, find the BackColor property.

2. Drop down the list and change to the **Custom** tab. Right-click in one of the bottom sixteen blank squares:

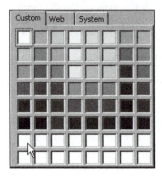

3. This will bring up the Color dialog. Use the two controls at the top to find a color you like. In the bottom right hand corner, you'll see three textboxes marked **Red**, **Green**, and **Blue**. Note down the values in these boxes:

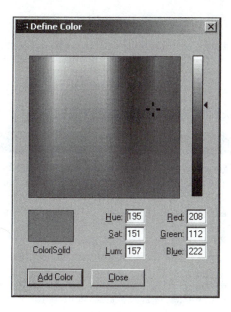

4. Close down the Define Color dialog.

5. Open up the code editor for `ColorPalette`. In the constructor, define a new button, but replace the three values I've used here with the three values you noted down. (Do this in order – the first value is the red component, the second is green, and the third is blue.)

```
Public Sub New()
    MyBase.New()

    'This call is required by the Windows Form Designer.
    InitializeComponent()

    ' add the colors...
    AddColor(Color.Black)
    AddColor(Color.White)
    AddColor(Color.Red)
    AddColor(Color.Blue)
    AddColor(Color.Green)
    AddColor(Color.Gray)
    AddColor(Color.DarkRed)
    AddColor(Color.DarkBlue)
    AddColor(Color.DarkGreen)
    AddColor(Color.DarkGray)
    AddColor(Color.FromArgb(208, 112, 222))

End Sub
```

Now run the project and the color you selected should appear in the palette.

How It Works

The `FromArgb` method is a shared method on the `Color` class. We can use this to define any color that we like, so long as we follow the "red, green, blue" convention Windows itself uses.

The Color Dialog

If we like, we can use the Color dialog that's built into Windows to let the user add colors to the palette.

Try It Out – Using the Color Dialog

1. Open the Form Designer for `ColorPalette`. From the toolbar, select a new `ColorDialog` control and paint it onto the form. Change the name of the control to `dlgColor`.

2. Now, open the code editor for `ColorPalette`. Find the `OnMouseUp` method. What we'll do is say that whenever the user clicks on the background to the control (in other words doesn't click on a button), we'll display the dialog. Go to the bottom of the method and add an `Else` clause along with this code. (I've omitted some of the existing code for brevity.)

```
Protected Overrides Sub OnMouseUp( _
    ByVal e As System.Windows.Forms.MouseEventArgs)

    ' find the button that we clicked on...
    Dim button As ColorPaletteButton = GetButtonAt(e.X, e.Y)
    If Not button Is Nothing Then

        ...

        Else

            ' display the color dialog...
            If dlgColor.ShowDialog = DialogResult.OK Then

                ' add the new color...
                AddColor(dlgColor.Color)

                ' resize the palette to show the dialog...
                OnResize(New EventArgs())

            End If

        End If

End Sub
```

After we've added the color, we need to "fake" a `Resize` event so that the new button is actually displayed.

3. Run the project. Now if you click on the background to the palette you should have the opportunity to add your own colors:

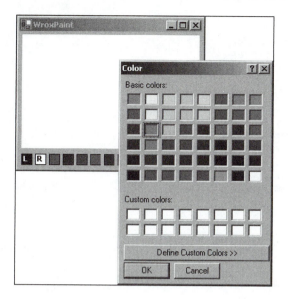

System Colors

Now we know that we can choose colors from a list of possibilities as well as defining our own. The final thing we need to talk about when it comes to colors is the idea of **system colors**.

When using Windows, the user has the ability to define all of the colors that are used for things like buttons, menus, captions, and so on. If we're building the UI for our own controls, it's reasonable to assume that from time to time we'll need to know what these colors are so that our controls have the same look and feel as the existing controls on the system.

System colors aren't exposed directly, but the Framework does give us a set of brushes and pens that can be used when we're drawing. Of course, we can dig into these objects to get the color out, and that's what we'll do.

If you want to find a list of all the brushes and pens, look in the MSDN documentation under `System.Drawing.Brushes` class and `SystemPens` class. Alternatively, use IntelliSense when in the code editor.

In this *Try It Out*, we'll add a button to the control palette that is the same as the currently selected active caption color.

Try It Out – Adding System Colors

1. Open the code editor for `ColorPalette`. Find the constructor and add this code:

```
Public Sub New()
    MyBase.New()

    'This call is required by the Windows Form Designer.
    InitializeComponent()
```

```
' add the colors...
AddColor(Color.Black)
AddColor(Color.White)
AddColor(Color.Red)
AddColor(Color.Blue)
AddColor(Color.Green)
AddColor(Color.Gray)
AddColor(Color.DarkRed)
AddColor(Color.DarkBlue)
AddColor(Color.DarkGreen)
AddColor(Color.DarkGray)
AddColor(Color.FromArgb(208, 112, 222))
AddColor(CType(SystemBrushes.ActiveCaption, SolidBrush).Color)

End Sub
```

2. Run the project. You should see a new color that matches the active caption color:

How It Works

When we ask `SystemBrushes` to return a brush that could be used to paint the active caption (and remember, with Windows 2000 the caption can be graduated, so what we're actually getting is the color that appears at the far left of the caption), it will return a `Brush` object. The `Brush` object doesn't contain a `Color` property, so we use `CType` to cast it to a `SolidBrush`.

`SolidBrush` does have a `Color` property, and we simply pass the value returned from this back to `AddColor` whereupon it's added to the palette.

Different Tools

Now that we've successfully cracked the nut of drawing filled circles on the page, let's turn our attention to building the other tools that we can use to put our applications together. The first thing we should do is to add a menu that lets us select the tool we want.

> **If you need a refresher on how use the Visual Basic .NET Menu Designer, refer back to Chapter 9.**

Try It Out – Adding a Tools Menu

1. Open the Designer for **Form1**. Draw a new `MainMenu` control onto the form and rename it as `mnuMain`.

2. With the `mnuMain` control selected, click in the white **Type Here** box that appears under the caption on `Form1`. Enter **&Tools** and press **Return**. Using the Properties window, change the **Name** property to `mnuTools`.

3. In the new **Type Here** box, enter **&Circle**. Using the Properties window, change the `Name` property to `mnuToolsCircle` and set the `Checked` property to `True`.

4. Again in the new **Type Here** box, enter **&Hollow Circle**. Using the Properties window, change the **Name** to `mnuToolsHollowCircle`:

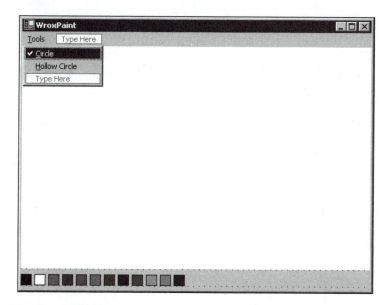

Implementing Hollow Circle

To implement the hollow circle tool, follow these steps:

Try It Out – Implementing Hollow Circle

1. The first thing we need to do is change the `GraphicTools` enumeration defined in `PaintCanvas` to include the hollow circle tool. Open the code editor for `PaintCanvas` and add this code to the enumeration:

```
Public Class PaintCanvas
    Inherits System.Windows.Forms.UserControl

    ' enums...
```

```
Public Enum GraphicTools As Integer
    CirclePen = 0
    HollowCirclePen = 1
End Enum
```

2. Go back to the Designer for `Form1` and on the menu editor double-click the **Circle** option. This will create a `Click` handler for `mnuToolsCircle`. Add this code:

```
Private Sub mnuToolsCircle_Click(ByVal sender As System.Object, _
        ByVal e As System.EventArgs) Handles mnuToolsCircle.Click

    ' set the tool...
    canvas.GraphicTool = PaintCanvas.GraphicTools.CirclePen

    ' update the menu...
    UpdateMenu()

End Sub
```

We've yet to build the `UpdateMenu` method, so ignore the blue wavy line that Visual Studio .NET will display.

3. Flip back to the Designer again and this time double-click the **Hollow Circle** option. Add this code:

```
Private Sub mnuToolsHollowCircle_Click(ByVal sender As System.Object, _
        ByVal e As System.EventArgs) Handles mnuToolsHollowCircle.Click

    ' set the tool...
    canvas.GraphicTool = PaintCanvas.GraphicTools.HollowCirclePen

    ' update the menu...
    UpdateMenu()

End Sub
```

4. Next, we need to implement the `UpdateMenu` method. Add this method below the `mnuToolsHollowCircle_Click` method:

```
' UpdateMenu - update the menu...
Private Function UpdateMenu()

    ' go through the menu items updating the check...
    If canvas.GraphicTool = PaintCanvas.GraphicTools.CirclePen Then
        mnuToolsCircle.Checked = True
    Else
        mnuToolsCircle.Checked = False
    End If
    If canvas.GraphicTool = PaintCanvas.GraphicTools.HollowCirclePen Then
        mnuToolsHollowCircle.Checked = True
    Else
```

```
                mnuToolsHollowCircle.Checked = False
        End If

End Function
```

5. Open the code editor for **PaintCanvas** by right-clicking on it in the Solution Explorer and selecting **View Code**. Find the `DoMousePaint` method and change this code:

```
' DoMousePaint - respond to a mouse movement...
Private Sub DoMousePaint(ByVal e As MouseEventArgs)

    ' store the new item somewhere...
    Dim newItem As GraphicsItem

    ' what color do we want to use?
    Dim useColor As Color = GraphicLeftColor
    If e.Button = MouseButtons.Right Then useColor = GraphicRightColor

    ' what tool are we using?
    Select Case GraphicTool

        ' circlepen?
        Case GraphicTools.CirclePen, GraphicTools.HollowCirclePen

            ' are we filled?
            Dim filled As Boolean = True
            If GraphicTool = GraphicTools.HollowCirclePen Then _
                filled = False

            ' create a new graphics circle...
            Dim circle As New GraphicsCircle()
            circle.SetPoint(e.X, e.Y, GraphicSize, useColor, filled)

            ' store this for addition...
            newItem = circle

    End Select

    ' were we given an item?
    If Not newItem Is Nothing Then

        ' add it to the list...
        GraphicsItems.Add(newItem)

        ' invalidate...
        Invalidate(newItem.Rectangle)

    End If

End Sub
```

6. Finally, we need to change the `GraphicsCircle` object itself so that it knows when to draw a filled circle and when to draw a hollow circle. Open the code editor for `GraphicsCircle` and add this code to the `Draw` method:

```
Public Overrides Sub Draw(ByVal graphics As System.Drawing.Graphics)

    If IsFilled = True Then

        ' create a new brush...
        Dim brush As New SolidBrush(Me.Color)

        ' draw the circle...
        graphics.FillEllipse(brush, Me.Rectangle)

    Else

    'create a pen
    Dim pen As New Pen(Me.Color)

        ' use DrawEllipse instead...
        Dim drawRectangle As Rectangle = Me.Rectangle
        drawRectangle.Inflate(-1, -1)
        graphics.DrawEllipse(pen, drawRectangle)

    End If

End Sub
```

7. Run the program. You should be able to select a new graphic tool from the menu and draw both filled and hollow circles:

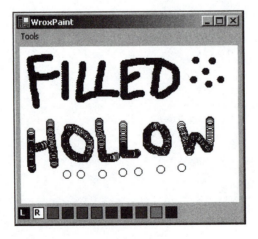

How It Works

When the menu options are selected, `Click` events get fired. We can respond to these messages and set the `GraphicsTool` property on the `PaintCanvas` control to a new mode:

```
Private Sub mnuToolsHollowCircle_Click(ByVal sender As System.Object, _
    ByVal e As System.EventArgs) Handles mnuToolsHollowCircle.Click

    ' set the tool...
    canvas.GraphicTool = PaintCanvas.GraphicTools.HollowCirclePen

    ' update the menu...
    UpdateMenu()

End Sub
```

When we do change the mode, we also need to change the check on the menu. UpdateMenu goes through each of the menu items in turn, switching on or off the check as appropriate:

```
' UpdateMenu - update the menu...
Private Function UpdateMenu()

    ' go through the menu items updating the check...
    If canvas.GraphicTool = PaintCanvas.GraphicTools.CirclePen Then
        mnuToolsCircle.Checked = True
    Else
        mnuToolsCircle.Checked = False
    End If
    If canvas.GraphicTool = PaintCanvas.GraphicTools.HollowCirclePen Then
        mnuToolsHollowCircle.Checked = True
    Else
        mnuToolsHollowCircle.Checked = False
    End If

End Function
```

Irrespective of the mode used, PaintCanvas.DoMousePaint still gets called whenever the mouse draws on the control. However, we do need to accommodate the new tool by changing the Select...End Select block to look for HollowCirclePen as well as CirclePen. Depending on which is selected, we pass True ("filled") or False ("not filled") through to SetPoint:

```
    ' what tool are we using?
    Select Case GraphicTool

        ' circlepen?
        Case GraphicTools.CirclePen, GraphicTools.HollowCirclePen

            ' are we filled?
            Dim filled As Boolean = True
            If GraphicTool = GraphicTools.HollowCirclePen Then _
                filled = False

            ' create a new graphics circle...
            Dim circle As New GraphicsCircle()
            circle.SetPoint(e.X, e.Y, GraphicSize, useColor, filled)
```

```
                    ' store this for addition...
                    newItem = circle

        End Select
```

In `GraphicsCircle` itself, choosing whether to use `FillEllipse` to draw a filled circle or use `DrawEllipse` for a hollow one is a simple determination. The only wrinkle we have to contend with is that with `DrawEllipse`, the width and height of the bounding rectangle have to be one pixel smaller than those used for `FillEllipse`. This is due to an idiosyncrasy in the way the Windows graphics subsystem works. You'll often find when working with graphics features you have to experiment a little!

```
    Public Overrides Sub Draw(ByVal graphics As System.Drawing.Graphics)

        If IsFilled = True Then

            ' create a new brush...
            Dim brush As New SolidBrush(Me.Color)

            ' draw the circle...
            graphics.FillEllipse(brush, Me.Rectangle)

        Else

            ' create a pen...
            Dim pen As New Pen(Me.Color)

            ' use DrawEllipse instead...
            Dim drawRectangle As Rectangle = Me.Rectangle
            drawRectangle.Inflate(-1, -1)
            graphics.DrawEllipse(pen, drawRectangle)

        End If

    End Sub
```

Now that we've learned the basics of building user controls that support their own user interface, let's take a look at the image handling capabilities in .NET.

Images

The Framework has very good support for loading and saving common image formats. In particular, we're able to load images of these types:

❑   BMP – the standard Windows bitmap format

❑   GIF – the standard, "loss-less" common Internet file format for graphic files and small images

❑   JPEG – the standard, "lossy" common Internet file format for photo-quality images

❑   PNG – the competitor to GIF that doesn't have the tricky licensing implications

❑   TIFF – the standard file format for storing and manipulated scanned documents

❑   WMF/EMF – the standard file formats for saving Windows Metafiles

❑   Icon – the standard file format for program icons

❑   EXIF – the preferred file format for storage used internally with digital cameras

Prior to .NET, developers wanting to work with the most common Internet file formats (namely GIF and JPEG) had to buy in third-party libraries. Now, support is built directly into the Framework so from day one you can start building applications that can handle these formats. What's more surprising is that the Framework also supports the saving of these files. This allows us to load a GIF file and save it as, say, a BMP or PNG file.

There are two ways that we can use images with .NET. Firstly, we can use the `PictureBox` control that we can find in the Visual Studio .NET Toolbox. This is a control that you place on a form, give a reference to an image to either at design time or run time, and it deals with painting itself. This is a quick way of getting a fixed image on a form.

The second way that we can use images is inside our owner-draw controls ourselves. In the following exercise we'll see how we can tweak `WroxPaint` so that rather than drawing on a dull, white background we're actually drawing on an image we load ourselves.

Drawing Images

The `Image` property on the `PictureBox` control takes a `System.Drawing.Image` object. As well as using the `Image` class with `PictureBox` and a few other controls in the Framework, we can use it with our own owner-draw controls.

Let's start by providing a way for our owner drawn controls to display an image loaded from one of the supported image formats.

Try It Out – Setting the BackgroundImage

1.   Open the Designer for `Form1`. Using the Toolbox, draw a new `OpenFileDialog` control onto the form. Rename the control `dlgFileOpenBackground`.

2.   Using the menu designer, add a new menu item called **&File**. Change its `Name` property to `mnuFile`. Reposition the menu at the left side of the menu bar by dragging it to its new location.

3.   Under the **File** menu, add a new menu item called **Open &Background Image…**. Rename the item as `mnuFileOpenBackground`.

4.   Double-click on the **Open Background Image** option. Add this code to the handler, and remember to add the new `OpenBackgroundImage` method:

```
Private Sub mnuFileOpenBackground_Click(ByVal sender As System.Object, _
        ByVal e As System.EventArgs) Handles mnuFileOpenBackground.Click
    OpenBackgroundImage()
End Sub
```

```
Public Sub OpenBackgroundImage()

    ' open the dialog...
    If dlgOpenBackground.ShowDialog() = DialogResult.OK Then

        ' create a new image that references the file...
        Dim backgroundImage As Image = _
            Image.FromFile(dlgFileOpenBackground.FileName)

        ' set the background...
        canvas.BackgroundImage = backgroundImage

    End If

End Sub
```

5. Run the project. Select File | Open Background Image from the menu and find a BMP, JPEG, or GIF file somewhere on your computer. (If you try to open a file from the network you may get a security exception.) The image will be displayed:

How It Works

"But we didn't do anything!" You're quite right – we didn't have to write any code to support the background image. By default, the `Control` class that `UserControl` is ultimately derived from already supports a `BackgroundImage` property and we've set this to the image we loaded. Therefore, the base class is dealing with drawing the image.

The loading is actually done with the shared `FromFile` method on the `Image` class. This method is the easiest way of loading a file from disk:

```
Public Sub ShowOpenBackgroundDialog()

    ' open the dialog...
    If dlgFileOpenBackground.ShowDialog() = DialogResult.OK Then

        ' create a new image that references the file...
        Dim backgroundImage As Image = _
```

```
                Image.FromFile(dlgFileOpenBackground.FileName)

            ' set the background...
            canvas.BackgroundImage = backgroundImage

        End If

    End Sub
```

Finally, when you're actually drawing on the image, you may find the paint process sluggish. This is because the control is spending a lot of time drawing the image onto the control and this slows everything down. Try using a smaller image or consider this *Try It Out* an illustration of how to manipulate images rather than providing a neat paint package!

Scaling Images

If you resize the form, you'll notice that the image is actually tiled. More importantly, if we make the control too small to accommodate the whole image, the sides of the image are clipped. What we want is for the image to be scaled so that it fits the control exactly. This will involve taking over control of drawing the background image from the base `Control` class and providing a new implementation of the `BackgroundImage` property.

Try It Out – Drawing the Image Ourselves

1. Open the code editor for **PaintCanvas**.

2. Rather than adding our code to draw the image to `OnPaint`, we're going to work with a different event called `PaintBackground`. This is called before `Paint` gets called. From the left dropdown select (**Overrides**) and from the right drop-down select **OnPaintBackground**. Add this code:

```
Protected Overrides Sub OnPaintBackground( _
        ByVal pevent As System.Windows.Forms.PaintEventArgs)

        ' paint the invalid region with the background brush...
        Dim backgroundBrush As New SolidBrush(BackColor)
        pevent.Graphics.FillRectangle(backgroundBrush, pevent.ClipRectangle)

        ' paint the image...
        If Not BackgroundImage Is Nothing Then

            ' find our client rectangle...
            Dim clientRectangle As New Rectangle(0, 0, Width, Height)

            ' draw the image...
            pevent.Graphics.DrawImage(BackgroundImage, clientRectangle)

        End If

    End Sub
```

3. At the end of the `OnPaintBackground` event, add the following code in order to enable the `Resize` event:

```
Protected Overrides Sub OnResize(ByVal e As System.EventArgs)
    Invalidate()
End Sub
```

4. Now run the project again. This time, the image will appear stretched to fit the whole screen and will adjust itself as you resize the form.

How It Works

All we're trying to do is take over the action of drawing the background image. As we mentioned before, painting is a two-phase process: first the background is erased (the `PaintBackground` event), and second the control is given the opportunity to paint its user interface (the `Paint` event).

With the `BackgroundImage` property set, when the base class needs to draw the background, it will automatically draw the image. We want it to stop doing this, otherwise we'll effectively be drawing the image twice – in other words, it'll draw the image, and then we'll draw our own image on top of it.

However, we do need to mimic the functionality that erases the background, otherwise things will not work properly. To do this, we create a new `SolidBrush` that uses the current background color (`BackColor`) and paint it on the area that's marked as invalid (`ClipRectangle`):

```
Protected Overrides Sub OnPaintBackground( _
        ByVal pevent As System.Windows.Forms.PaintEventArgs)

    ' paint the invalid region with the background brush...
    Dim backgroundBrush As New SolidBrush(BackColor)
    pevent.Graphics.FillRectangle(backgroundBrush, pevent.ClipRectangle)
```

After we've painted the background, we then need to draw the image. We can do this really easily by using the `DrawImage` method of the `Graphics` object. But, in order to stretch the image we need to provide a rectangle that describes the bounds of the image. Once we have that, we give `DrawImage` both the image and the rectangle and the image is drawn.

```
        ' paint the image...
    If Not BackgroundImage Is Nothing Then

            ' find our client rectangle...
            Dim clientRectangle As New Rectangle(0, 0, Width, Height)

            ' draw the image...
            pevent.Graphics.DrawImage(BackgroundImage, clientRectangle)

        End If

    End Sub
```

Preserving the Aspect Ratio

The problem we have now is that the image is all stretched out of shape. Ideally, we want to make the image bigger or smaller, but preserve the **aspect ratio** of the image. The aspect ratio describes the ratio between the width and height of the image.

The Framework doesn't have any support for preserving the aspect ratio when it stretches an image. However, with a little work we can do this ourselves.

Try It Out – Preserving the Aspect Ratio

1. Open the code editor for `PaintCanvas` again. Add this code to `OnPaintBackground`.

```
Protected Overrides Sub OnPaintBackground( _
    ByVal pevent As System.Windows.Forms.PaintEventArgs)

    ' paint the invalid region with the background brush...
    Dim backgroundBrush As New SolidBrush(BackColor)
    pevent.Graphics.FillRectangle(backgroundBrush, pevent.ClipRectangle)

    ' paint the image...
    If Not BackgroundImage Is Nothing Then

        ' find our client rectangle...
        Dim clientRectangle As New Rectangle(0, 0, Width, Height)

        ' how big is the image?
        Dim imageWidth As Integer = BackgroundImage.Width
        Dim imageHeight As Integer = BackgroundImage.Height

        ' what's the aspect ratio?
        Dim ratio As Double = _
            CType(imageHeight, Double) / CType(imageWidth, Double)
```

```
      ' scale the image...
      If imageWidth > clientRectangle.Width Then
          imageWidth = clientRectangle.Width
          imageHeight = CType(CType(imageWidth, Double) * ratio, Integer)
      End If
      If imageHeight > clientRectangle.Height Then
          imageHeight = clientRectangle.Height
          imageWidth = CType(CType(imageHeight, Double) / ratio, Integer)
      End If

      ' we just need to center the image... easy!
      Dim imageLocation As New Point( _
        (clientRectangle.Width / 2) - (imageWidth / 2), _
        (clientRectangle.Height / 2) - (imageHeight / 2))
      Dim imageSize As New Size(imageWidth, imageHeight)
      Dim imageRectangle As New Rectangle(imageLocation, imageSize)

      ' draw the image...
      pevent.Graphics.DrawImage(BackgroundImage, imageRectangle)

  End If

End Sub
```

2. Remove the `OnResize` method from `PaintCanvas`.

3. Run the project. Now if you load an image it should scale and preserve the aspect ratio:

How It Works

Preserving the aspect ratio is bit of rudimentary math coupled with throwing a few rectangles together. The first thing we need to know is how big the area that we have to fit the image into actually is. We call this `clientRectangle`.

```
Protected Overrides Sub OnPaintBackground( _
        ByVal pevent As System.Windows.Forms.PaintEventArgs)

    ' paint the invalid region with the background brush...
```

```
Dim backgroundBrush As New SolidBrush(BackColor)
pevent.Graphics.FillRectangle(backgroundBrush, pevent.ClipRectangle)

' paint the image...
If Not BackgroundImage Is Nothing Then

    ' find our client rectangle...
    Dim clientRectangle As New Rectangle(0, 0, Width, Height)
```

Next, we need to look at the image itself to see how big that is. We then need to know the aspect ratio, which is the ratio between the width and the height. If, for example, we had an aspect ratio of 2:1 (width:height), and we had an image that was 200 pixels wide, we'd know that the height had to be 100 pixels. Alternatively, if it were 25 pixels tall, it would be 50 pixels wide.

```
    ' how big is the image?
    Dim imageWidth As Integer = BackgroundImage.Width
    Dim imageHeight As Integer = BackgroundImage.Height

    ' what's the aspect ratio?
    Dim ratio As Double = _
        CType(imageHeight, Double) / CType(imageWidth, Double)
```

When we calculate the aspect ratio, we want a floating-point number so we have to convert the integer width and height values to `Doubles`.

Next, we look at the shape of the client area compared to the shape of the image. If the native width of the image (in other words the size before it's scaled) is wider than the width of the window, we fix the width of the image as being equal to the width of the client area. Once we've done that, we use the aspect ratio to work out how tall the image should be. (Again, we've used conversions to `Doubles` to make sure that the calculations work properly.)

```
    ' scale the image...
    If imageWidth > clientRectangle.Width Then
        imageWidth = clientRectangle.Width
        imageHeight = CType(CType(imageWidth, Double) * ratio, Integer)
```

Alternatively, if the height of the client area is taller than the height of the image, we need to do the opposite – in other words fix the height of the image and then work out the width:

```
    Else
        imageHeight = clientRectangle.Height
        imageWidth = CType(CType(imageHeight, Double) / ratio, Integer)
    End If
```

At this point, we now have an adjusted width and height of the image. When we have that, we need to work out the upper-left corner to start drawing at. To do this, we divide the width of the client area by two to get the exact middle and subtract half of the width of the image from it. This gives us the x coordinate at which drawing should start. Then, we do the same for the height:

```
' we just need to center the image... easy!
Dim imageLocation As New Point( _
     (clientRectangle.Width / 2) - (imageWidth / 2), _
     (clientRectangle.Height / 2) - (imageHeight / 2))
```

Once we have the location, we build a rectangle using the adjusted width and height:

```
Dim imageSize As New Size(imageWidth, imageHeight)
Dim imageRectangle As New Rectangle(imageLocation, imageSize)
```

Finally, we use `DrawImage` to actually draw the image on the screen:

```
' draw the image...
pevent.Graphics.DrawImage(BackgroundImage, imageRectangle)

  End If

End Sub
```

This brings us to the end of our discussion on functionality to add to `WroxPaint`.

More Graphics Methods

In this chapter, we've used a few of the graphics features available with .NET. There are some commonly used methods on the `Graphics` object that we haven't touched on.

Whenever you have a `Graphics` object, either when you're building owner-draw controls or forms, try using these methods:

❑   `DrawLine` – draws a single line between two points

❑   `DrawCurve` and `DrawClosedCurve` – draws a curve between a set of points

❑   `DrawArc` – draws a portion of a circle

❑   `DrawBezier` – draws a cubic Bezier curve defined by four points

❑   `DrawPie` – draws a slice of a circle (like a pie chart)

❑   `DrawPolygon` – draws regular and irregular polygons from an array of points

❑   `DrawIcon` – draws Windows icons

All of these methods use the `Brush`, `Pen`, `Point`, and `Rectangle` objects that we've seen used throughout this chapter. Each of these methods has an associated `Fill` method that fills in the shape after it's drawn it.

Summary

In this chapter, we looked at how we could build our own user interface on our controls and forms. Previously, we'd only been able to build our user interface by plugging other people's controls together. We focused on building controls derived from `System.Windows.Forms.UserControl` because we're interested in building component-based software.

After discussing the difference between vector and raster graphics, we proceeded to build a simple application that allowed the user to draw dots on the screen using the mouse. We then took a look at building a separate control that provided the user with a set of colors that they could choose from when drawing. We saw how to use the Color dialog to add new colors and how to create new colors using the Windows RGB (red, green, blue) color scheme.

Finally, we took a look at the `Image` class and saw how this could load a variety of file formats, include Windows Bitmap, JPEG, and GIF. We also saw how to scale images and preserve their aspect ratio.

Questions

1. What is a pixel?

2. What object do we need in order to draw on a control, form, or other object?

3. Describe the two-phases of painting in Windows.

4. What is the difference between client coordinates and screen coordinates?

5. How can we create `Color` objects with .NET?

Accessing Databases

Most applications manipulate data in some way. Visual Basic .NET applications often manipulate data that comes from relational databases. To do this, our application needs to interface with relational database software such as Microsoft Access, Microsoft SQL Server, Oracle, or Sybase.

Visual Studio .NET provides the data access tools and wizards to connect to these databases, and retrieve and update their data. In this chapter, we will look at these tools and wizards, and use them to retrieve data from a database.

In the next chapter we will concentrate more on writing code directly, which gives us more flexibility and control than relying on Visual Studio .NET to create it for us. With practice, writing code will also take less time than working through a wizard.

So, in this chapter we will:

- ❑ Discuss what a database really is
- ❑ Examine the SQL SELECT statement
- ❑ Examine data access components
- ❑ Discuss data binding in Windows Forms
- ❑ Use the data access wizards in Visual Studio .NET

> **Note that in order to work through the exercises in this chapter, you will need Microsoft Access 2000 or higher as well as Visual Studio .NET with the Crystal Reports option installed.**

What Is a Database?

Basically a **database** consists of one or more large complex files that store data in a structured format. The **database engine**, in our case Microsoft Access, manages the file or files and the data within those files.

Microsoft Access Objects

The Microsoft Access database file, which has an extension of mdb, contains tables, queries, forms, reports, pages, macros, and modules, which are referred to as **database objects**. That's a lot of information in one large file but Microsoft Access manages this data quite nicely. Forms, reports, pages, macros, and modules are generally concerned with letting users work with and display data. We will be writing Visual Basic .NET applications to do this, so the only database objects we're really concerned about at the moment are **tables** and **queries**.

Tables

A **table** contains a collection of data, which is represented by one or more columns, and one or more rows of data. Columns are typically referred to as **fields** in Microsoft Access and the rows are referred to as **records**. Each field in a table represents an attribute of the data stored in that table. For example, a field named First Name would represent the first name of an employee or customer. This field is an attribute of an employee or customer. Records in a table contain a collection of fields that form a complete record of information about the data stored in that table. For example, suppose a table contains two fields, First Name and Last Name. These two fields in a single record describe the name of a single person. This is illustrated in the screenshot below:

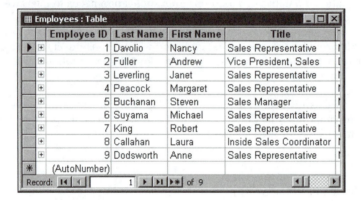

Queries

A **query** in a database is a group of SQL (Structured Query Language) statements that allow us to retrieve and update data in our tables. Queries can be used to select or update all of the data in one or more tables or to select or update specific data in one or more tables.

Query objects in Microsoft Access are a hybrid of two types of object in SQL Server – views and stored procedures. Using database query objects can make our Visual Basic .NET code simpler, because we have fewer complex SQL queries included in our code. They can also make our programs faster, because database engines can compile queries when we create them – whereas the SQL code in a Visual Basic .NET program needs to be reinterpreted every time it's used.

To really understand the implications of queries, we need to learn some SQL. Fortunately, compared to *real* programming languages, SQL is really simple. Let's quickly learn how to use SQL to retrieve data from a database.

SQL SELECT Statement

SQL is an acronym for **Structured Query Language**. The American National Standards Institute (ANSI) defines the standards for ANSI SQL. Most database engines implement ANSI SQL to some extent, and often add some features specific to the given database engine.

The benefits of ANSI SQL are that, once you learn the basic syntax for SQL, you have a solid grounding from which you can code the SQL language in almost any database. All you need to learn is a new interface for the database that you are working in. Many database vendors extended SQL to use advanced features or optimizations for the particular database. It is best to stick with the ANSI standards whenever possible in case you want to change databases at some point.

The SQL SELECT statement selects data from one or more fields in one or more records and from one or more tables in our database. Note that the SELECT statement only selects data – it does not modify the data in any way.

The simplest allowable SELECT statement is like this:

```
SELECT * FROM Employees;
```

This simply means 'retrieve every field for every record in the Employees table'. The * indicates 'every field'. Employees indicates the table name. Officially, SQL statements should end in a semi-colon. It usually doesn't matter if we forget it, though.

If we only wanted to retrieve first and last names, we can give a list of field names instead of a *:

```
SELECT [First Name], [Last Name] FROM Employees;
```

We need to enclose these field names in square brackets because these field names contain spaces. The square brackets indicate to the SQL interpreter that, even though there is a space in the name, it should treat 'First Name' as one object name, and 'Last Name' as one object name. Otherwise the interpreter would be unable to follow the syntax.

So far, this is pretty easy! In fact, SQL is a lot like plain English – even a non programmer could probably understand what it means. Now let's say we only wanted to retrieve the employees whose last name begins with D. To do this, we add a WHERE clause to our SELECT statement:

```
SELECT [First Name], [Last Name] FROM Employees WHERE [Last Name] LIKE 'D*';
```

Last of all, let's say we wanted to retrieve these items in a particular order. We can, for example, order the results by first name. We just need to add an ORDER BY clause to the end:

```
SELECT [First Name], [Last Name] FROM Employees
                    WHERE [Last Name] LIKE 'D*' ORDER BY [First Name];
```

This means that if we have employees called Angela Dunn, Zebedee Dean, and David Dustan we will get the following result:

```
Angela      Dunn
David       Dunstan
Zebedee     Dean
```

We're specifying quite a specific command here, but the syntax is pretty simple – and very similar to how an English speaker would describe what they want. Usually, when ordering by a name, we want to order in an ascending order – A comes first, Z comes last. If we were ordering by a number, though, we might want to have the bigger number at the top – for example so that a product with the highest price appears first. Doing this is really simple – just add DESC to the ORDER BY clause:

```
SELECT [First Name], [Last Name] FROM Employees
                    WHERE [Last Name] LIKE 'D*' ORDER BY [First Name] DESC;
```

The D* means 'has a D followed by anything'. If we'd said *D* it would mean 'anything followed by D followed by anything', basically, 'contains D'. This would return the following:

```
Zebedee     Dean
David       Dunstan
Angela      Dunn
```

If you want to make it very clear that you want the results in an ascending order, you can add ASC to the ORDER BY clause instead of DESC. But you don't really need to, since this is the default anyway.

We can summarize this syntax in the following way:

```
SELECT select-list
    FROM table-name
    [WHERE search-condition]
    [ORDER BY order-by-expression [ASC | DESC]]
```

This means that we must provide a list of fields to include, or use a * to select them all. We must provide a table name. We can choose to provide a search condition. We can choose to provide an order-by expression, and if we do we can make it either ascending or descending.

SQL gets considerably more complicated when we start working with several tables in the same query. But, for various reasons, we don't need to do this all that much when working with Visual Basic .NET.

Anyway, the best way to get SQL into your head is to practice. Before moving on, please try to answer these questions in your head:

How would you write a query to retrieve the Name, Description, and Price fields from a table called Product?

What would you add to the query retrieve only items with DVD in their description?

How would you order the results so that the most expensive item came first?

Queries in Access

SQL is really a basic programming skill, and if you are a programmer there's no real reason not to use it. However, Microsoft Access provides wizards and visual tools that enable non-programmers to write queries without knowing SQL. Even for SQL programmers, these can sometimes prove useful – so let's try them out. These tools end up producing SQL statements that we can view and modify if we wish, so they can be a good way to learn more about SQL.

For more information about Access programming, see *Professional Access 2000 Programming* (Wrox Press, ISBN 1-86100-408-7). If you want to learn more about SQL then take a look at *Beginning SQL Programming* (Wrox Press, ISBN 1-86100-180-0) or *Instant SQL Programming* (Wrox Press, ISBN 1-87441-650-8).

Let's use Access to create a simple query that will select customer information from the Customer table in the Xtreme.mdb database that gets installed with Visual Studio .NET. We'll create this query and then view the SQL SELECT statement that gets generated by Access.

Try It Out – Customer Query

1. Open Microsoft Access and in the Microsoft Access dialog select the Open an existing file option. If Northwind.mdb is in the list, select it. Otherwise, click More Files... from the list:

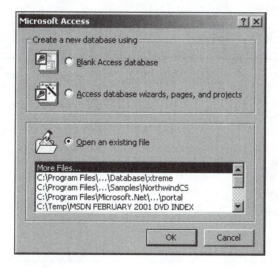

Then click the OK button. If you need to navigate to the Northwind database, its default location is:

```
C:\Program Files\Microsoft Office\Office\Samples\Northwind.mdb
```

2. When the database opens, you will see two sections in the bar on the left: Objects and Groups. The Objects section lists all of our database object types, which we discussed in the section on databases. We can also use Groups to gather together related objects of any type, in any way we want:

595

3. Since we want to take a look at how a SQL SELECT statement is built by Access, we need to click on the Queries icon under the Objects tab.

4. We are going to build a new query ourselves so double-click on **Create query in Design view** in the results window:

5. The Show Table dialog appears and allows you to select one or more tables to be used in your query. We only want to select one table, Customers. Click on the Customers table and then click the Add button to have this table added to the Query Designer and then click the Close button to close the Show Table dialog.

6. The Customers table is displayed with all available fields plus an asterisk (*). You can select the fields that you want to be added to your query or you can select the asterisk, which will select all fields from the table. Let's just select a few fields for our query.

Double-click on `CompanyName` in the `Customers` table, to add it to the first column in the grid below the table. The **Field** and **Table** cells are automatically filled in. We also want to sort the data by this field so click in the **Sort** cell and choose **Ascending** to have the results of our query sorted by this field:

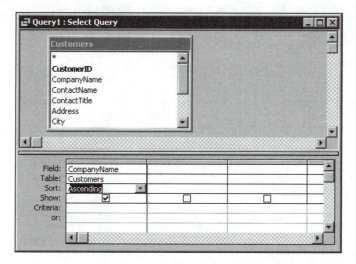

7. We now want to add the `ContactName` field to our grid. Double-click on this field in the `Customers` table and it will automatically be added to the next available column in the grid. Then add `ContactTitle` in the same way.

Your completed query should now look like the one shown below:

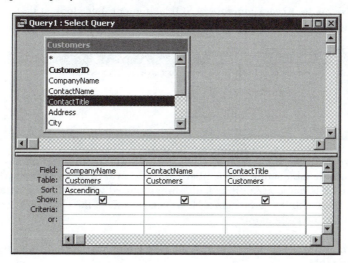

8. Click on the **Save** icon on the toolbar, enter the name **CustomerQuery** in the **Save As** dialog and click **OK**.

9. On the toolbar click on the run icon, indicated by !, and you should see results similar to the ones shown in the figure below. Notice that the results are sorted on the `CompanyName` field in ascending order:

Company Name	Contact Name	Contact Title
Alfreds Futterkiste	Maria Anders	Sales Representative
Ana Trujillo Emparedados y helados	Ana Trujillo	Owner
Antonio Moreno Taquería	Antonio Moreno	Owner
Around the Horn	Thomas Hardy	Sales Representative
Berglunds snabbköp	Christina Berglund	Order Administrator
Blauer See Delikatessen	Hanna Moos	Sales Representative
Blondel père et fils	Frédérique Citeaux	Marketing Manager
Bólido Comidas preparadas	Martín Sommer	Owner
Bon app'	Laurence Lebihan	Owner
Bottom-Dollar Markets	Elizabeth Lincoln	Accounting Manager
B's Beverages	Victoria Ashworth	Sales Representative
Cactus Comidas para llevar	Patricio Simpson	Sales Agent
Centro comercial Moctezuma	Francisco Chang	Marketing Manager
Chop-suey Chinese	Yang Wang	Owner
Comércio Mineiro	Pedro Afonso	Sales Associate
Consolidated Holdings	Elizabeth Brown	Sales Representative
Die Wandernde Kuh	Rita Müller	Sales Representative
Drachenblut Delikatessen	Sven Ottlieb	Order Administrator
Du monde entier	Janine Labrune	Owner
Eastern Connection	Ann Devon	Sales Agent
Ernst Handel	Roland Mendel	Sales Manager

CustomerQuery : Select Query — Record: 1 of 91

How It Works

From the choices we made, Access generates a SQL statement. Let's look at that now. Click on the View menu and select the SQL View menu item. This will display the SQL statements for us as shown below:

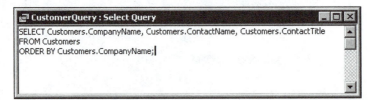

```
SELECT Customers.CompanyName, Customers.ContactName, Customers.ContactTitle
FROM Customers
ORDER BY Customers.CompanyName;
```

Notice that we have the basic SQL SELECT statement followed by the field names. Access has prefixed each field name with the table name. Remember that brackets are only required when the field names contain spaces. The table name prefix is actually only required when selecting data from multiple tables where both have a field with the same name. However, to reduce the chance of errors, Access has prefixed all fields with the table name.

The FROM clause in our SELECT statement specifies the table that data is being selected from, in this case the Customer table.

The ORDER BY clause specifies which fields should be used to sort the data, and in this case, the CompanyName field has been specified:

So how does this SQL statement actually get built for us? Well, when we first started creating this query we added a table name. Before any fields were added to the grid, Access generated the following SQL statement:

```
SELECT
FROM Customers;
```

Of course this on its own is not a valid SQL statement. Once we added the first field and set the sort order for that field, the following SQL statement was generated – which is valid:

```
SELECT Customer.CompanyName
FROM Customer
ORDER BY Customers.CompanyName;
```

As we continued to add fields, the rest of the field names were added to the SQL statement until the complete SQL statement shown earlier was generated.

Let's move on now and discuss the basic data access components that are needed in Windows Forms to display data. Since we have been using Microsoft Access in our examples here, we will discuss the data access components provided in Visual Studio .NET that assist us in accessing the data in an Access database.

Data Access Components

There are three main data access components in Visual Basic .NET that we need in order to retrieve and store data from the database: `OleDbConnection`, `OleDbDataAdapter`, and `DataSet`. Each of these components is located in the Toolbox under the **Data** tab as shown in the figure below. Let's take a brief look at each one of these components in turn.

These components are known as ADO.NET classes. In this chapter, we will simply see how to use them in a Windows application. We will discuss ADO.NET as a whole in the next chapter.

599

OleDbConnection

The `OleDbConnection` component represents an active connection to the database and provides some basic information such as the database name, location of the database, and the database driver to use to connect to the database.

In fact, the `OleDbConnection` connects to OLE DB, which is a database access platform that forms part of Windows. When we connect to OLE DB, we specify a database and database **provider** to use. When we try setting up a connection, we will specify `Northwind.mdb` and the Microsoft Access **provider**.

Note that there is also a `SqlConnection` component in the Toolbox. This works in a very similar way to the `OleDbConnection`. The main difference is that instead of connection to OLE DB, and then using OLE DB to connect to a database, it connects *directly* to Microsoft SQL Server databases. Because of this `SqlConnection` is much faster – but can only be used to access SQL Server or the Microsoft Data Engine (MSDE). `SqlDataAdapter` and `SqlCommand` are also very similar to `OleDbDataAdapter` and `OleDbCommand` – but are for use with `SqlConnection`.

We can add an `OleDbConnection` component to our form and set its properties. However, we can also simply add an `OleDbDataAdapter` to our form and it will automatically add the `OleDbConnection` and prompt us to set its properties – which is what we'll be doing in the next *Try It Out*.

DataSet

The `DataSet` component is a cache of data that is stored in memory. It's a lot like a mini database engine, but its data exists in memory. We can use it to store data in tables, and using the `DataView` component we can query the data in various ways.

The `DataSet` is very powerful. As well as storing data in tables, it also stores a rich amount of **meta-data** – or 'data about the data'. This includes things like table and column names, data types, and the information needed to manage and undo changes to the data. All of this data is represented in-memory as XML. A `DataSet` can be saved to an XML file, and then loaded back into memory very easily. It can also be passed in XML form over networks including the Internet.

Since the `DataSet` component stores all of the data in memory, we can scroll through the data both forwards and backwards, and can also make updates to the data in memory. The `DataSet` component is very powerful and we will be exploring this component in more detail in the next chapter. In this chapter, we will simply be using it to store data and bind it to a control on our form.

OleDbDataAdapter

The `OleDbDataAdapter` serves as a data bridge between the database and our `DataSet` object. It retrieves data from a database using an `OleDbConnection`, and adds it to a `DataSet` component. We can also use it to update the database with changes made in the `DataSet`. For our purposes, we will be using this component to simply retrieve data from a database.

The `OleDbDataAdapter` connects to a database using an `OleDbConnection`. When we use it, we specify SQL statements for selecting, deleting, inserting, and updating the database. The `OleDbDataAdapter` is able to work out which command to use in order to reflect the changes made to the `DataSet`.

The three components just mentioned are the three basic components that we will be working with in this chapter. However, just so you'll know, let's briefly cover the rest of the components listed here.

OleDbCommand

The `OleDbCommand` component is used to execute SQL statements against the database. These SQL statements can be statements to select, insert, update, or delete data. The `OleDbDataAdapter` internally uses an `OleDbCommand` for each of its main functions – insert, update, and delete. However, for this chapter we do not need to be aware of them.

An `OleDbCommand` can also be used directly on an `OleDbConnection`, without requiring an `OleDbDataAdapter`.

DataView

The last component to be covered here is the `DataView` component. This component is used to create a customized view of the data in a `DataSet`. A `DataView` can do many of the things that a query can do, such as displaying only selected columns or rows, and sorting data. We can also use it to view different states of data – for example we could choose to view the *original* data in rows that have been changed.

> *These components are derived from classes of the same name. In the next couple of chapters, we will be exploring these components in more detail by creating objects that are derived from their respective classes.*

Data Binding

Data binding means taking data contained in memory and binding it to a control. In other words, the control will receive its data from our data access components or objects and the data will automatically be displayed in the control for the user to see and manipulate. In VB.NET, most controls support some kind of data binding. Some are specifically designed for it, such as the `DataGrid`. In our next *Try It Out*, we will be binding data from a `DataSet` component to a `DataGrid` control so this is where we want to focus our attention.

The DataGrid Control

A **DataGrid** control is a control that is used to display data tables much like what we saw when we executed the results of our query in Access. This control displays all of the data contained in the data access component that it is bound to and allows the user to edit the data if the appropriate properties are set. This section explores how data is bound to `DataGrid` control by setting its properties. The next chapter discusses data binding to other Windows controls in more detail.

There are two main properties in the `DataGrid` control that must be set in order to bind the `DataSet` component to it. These are the `DataSource` and `DataMember` properties.

The DataSource Property

The DataSource property is used to set the source of the data that will be used to supply the DataGrid control with data. The data source can be one of several components or objects such as a DataSet, DataView, DataTable, or an array. In our exercise, we will be using a DataSet component to supply the DataGrid control with data.

The DataMember Property

The other property that should be set in the DataGrid control is the DataMember property. Like a database, a DataSet can contain several tables. The DataMember specifies which table in the DataSet will be used for the binding, if more than one is available. For example, suppose a DataSet contains the results of two queries listing data from the Customer and Orders tables. We must specify the table that contains the data that we want to see in our DataGrid control.

In fact, the DataGrid can display data from two tables simultaneously, and we can establish a parent-child relationship between the two tables. We won't be looking at this in this chapter.

> *For further details on the use of the DataGrid see* Professional VB.NET 2nd Edition *(Wrox Press, ISBN 1-86100-716-7).*

That's basically all we need to do to bind data to our DataGrid control so let's move on and put this newfound knowledge to use in a practical exercise.

In this *Try It Out*, we will be using the data access wizards in Visual Studio .NET to create the OleDbDataAdapter, OleDbConnection, and DataSet components. We will be using the Northwind.mdb sample database again as our data source.

Once we have populated the DataSet component, we will bind that data to our DataGrid control by setting the DataSource and DataMember properties of the DataGrid control. So let's get started!

Try It Out – Binding Data

1. Create a new Windows Application project called AccessDataBinding.

2. The first thing that we need to do in our project is to create the OleDbDataAdapter component. Click on the Toolbox and select the **Data** tab. Locate the OleDbDataAdapter component, and drag and drop it on to your form. This invokes the **Data Adapter Configuration Wizard** as shown in the next figure.

> *For those readers who are unfamiliar with the wizards in Visual Studio .NET, all wizards start with a Welcome screen. This Welcome screen describes what actions the wizard will perform and what information may be required on your part.*

> *You then have the option to continue with the wizard or to cancel the wizard by clicking on the appropriate button.*

Click the Next button to continue to the first step.

3. Our `OleDbDataAdapter` requires a connection to the database and uses an `OleDbConnection` component for this. The next step of the wizard prompts us for this information by allowing us to choose an existing data connection if there is one or to create a new one. A **data connection** is the information used by the `OleDbConnection` component to connect to the database. It specifies such information as where the database is located and what OLE DB provider it should use to connect to the database:

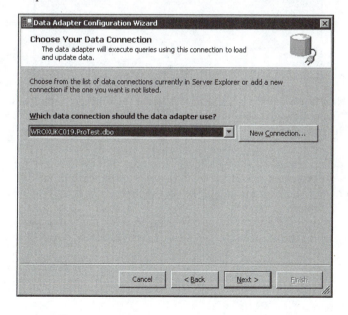

Since we do not have a data connection defined for the `Northwind.mdb` database we need to create a new one, so click on the **New Connection** button to invoke the Data Link Properties dialog.

4. By default, the Data Link Properties dialog displays the **Connection** tab. We need to move back a step, because we are not using the default **Provider**. Click on the **Provider** tab and choose **Microsoft Jet 4.0 OLE DB Provider**. This is the provider that we need to connect to the `Northwind.mdb` Microsoft Access database:

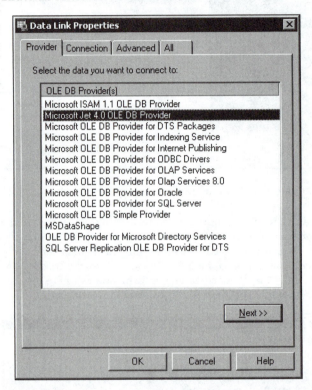

Click the **Next** button at the bottom of the dialog to continue to the next step. This will return us to the **Connection** tab, which will have changed slightly to reflect the settings for the Microsoft Jet provider.

5. The **Connection** tab in this dialog allows us to browse for and select the Access database that we want to use. Click on the **Browse** button next to the textbox for **Select or enter a database name**, and then locate and select the `Northwind.mdb` database. By default, this will be in the folder:

```
C:\Program Files\Microsoft Office\Office\Samples\Northwind.mdb
```

Select the `Northwind.mdb` database in the **Open** dialog and click the **Open** button to have this information applied to the **Data Link Properties** dialog:

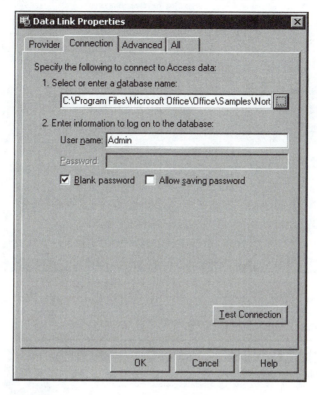

Since this database does not require a password we will accept the default information for username and password, as shown above.

Finally, to ensure that we have a good connection to the database, click on the **Test Connection** button to verify the connection. Once the connection test succeeds, you will receive a message box indicating this.

If you failed to connect to the database, check to ensure you selected the `Microsoft Jet 4.0 OLE DB Provider` *in the* **Provider** *tab and that you selected the correct database in the* **Connection** *tab.*

6. That's all the information we need to connect to our database. Click the **OK** button to have the `OleDbConnection` component created and populated in the Data Adapter Configuration Wizard:

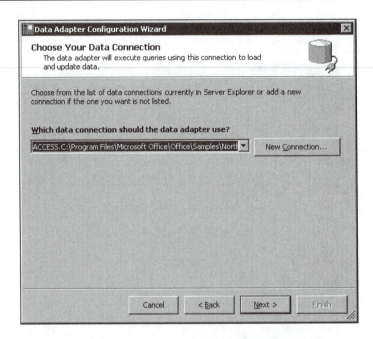

7. Click the Next button to proceed to the next step in this wizard. We now need to specify how we want to query the database for our data. Since we are using an Access database, we only have one option available to us: Use SQL statements:

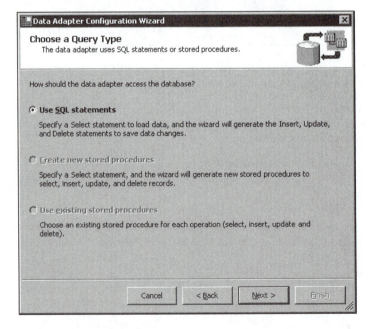

Just click the Next button to move on.

8. The next step of the Data Adapter Configuration Wizard provides several options. We can manually enter our SQL statement or we can use the Query Builder dialog.

The **Advanced Options** button allows us to specify what additional SQL statements should be generated to insert, update, and delete data in our database.

We will use the next several steps to complete this screen of the wizard:

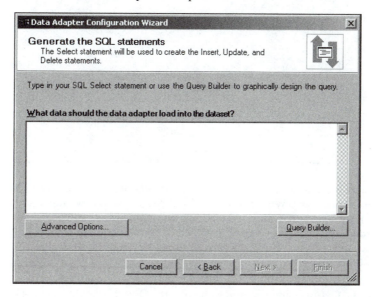

9. Click on the **Advanced Options** button to display the Advanced SQL Generation Options dialog as shown in the next figure. This dialog allows us to specify that insert, update, and delete statements be generated automatically to match the SELECT statement that we will create.

Along with this is the option to specify how the data updates should be handled as indicated by the **Use optimistic concurrency** option. Having this switched on helps our applications to cope with multiple users working with the same database at the same time.

The last option here specifies how the DataSet component should be refreshed when data in the database has been updated. When this option is checked, it will automatically add the necessary SQL statements to retrieve any changed data in the database after an insert or update.

By default, all options are selected. Since we only want to display data in our DataGrid control, we do not need to generate SQL statements that will insert, update, and delete data in our database.

Uncheck the first option and the second two options will be disabled and unchecked. Then click the **OK** button to close this dialog:

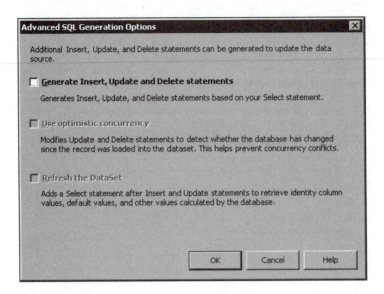

10. We are now back at the **Generate the SQL statements** step of the Data Adapter Configuration Wizard. We want to retrieve the same data as we did when we created our Access query: `CompanyName`, `ContactName`, and `ContactTitle` from the `Customers` table, ordered by `CompanyName`. If you are confident enough with SQL, you can just type the query into the textbox. If not, we can use the Query Builder to generate the SQL for us – let's see how to do that now.

11. Click on the **Query Builder** button to invoke the **Query Builder** dialog. The first step here is very similar to what we saw in Access. We need to choose the table that we want in our SQL `SELECT` statement. Click on the `Customers` table in the **Add Table** dialog and then click the **Add** button to have this table added:

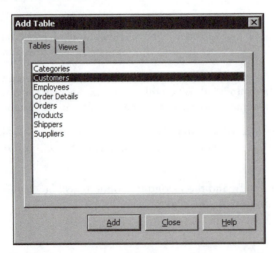

12. Click **Close** to bring the **Query Builder** to the foreground. The **Query Builder** dialog is now shown with the `Customers` table added. Note that the fields in the `Customers` table are listed alphabetically here. In the **Query Builder** in Access, the fields were listed in the order that they were defined.

We want to select the fields in the order that we want them in our query, so locate and select the fields in the `Customers` table in the following order:

❑ `CompanyName`

❑ `ContactName`

❑ `ContactTitle`

We want to sort the data by `CompanyName` so click on the **Sort Type** column in the grid and select **Ascending** from the drop-down list.

Your completed Query Builder dialog should now look like the one shown in the next figure:

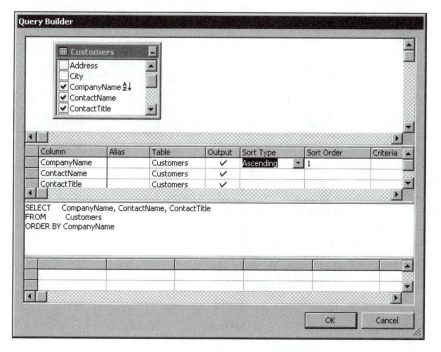

13. Notice the SQL statement that was generated. It looks a little different from the one that Access generated in our previous *Try It Out* in that it does not have the field names prefixed with the table name. The reason for this is simply that the Query Builder in Visual Studio .NET implements ANSI SQL a little differently from the Query Builder in Access. Both SQL statements are equally valid, though – and if we were to type the SQL that Access generated, it would work fine here too.

Click the OK button to have this SQL statement added to the Generate the SQL statements step of the Data Adapter Configuration Wizard as shown in the next figure:

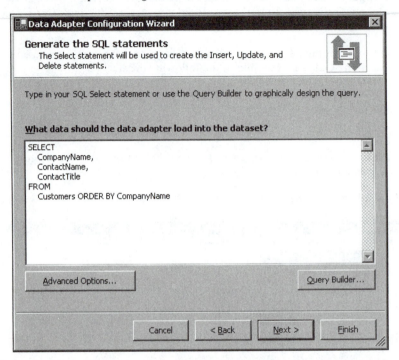

Notice that the SQL SELECT statement has been formatted a little differently from the way it was shown in the Query Builder. Each of the field names in the SELECT statement has been placed on a separate line. Also the ORDER BY clause has been combined with the table name that we are selecting data from. Since SQL is a declarative language, all parts of the SQL statement can be on the same line or multiple lines. However, it can help to separate the parts of the SQL statement onto separate lines for readability purposes.

Click the Next button to proceed to the next step of the wizard.

14. This next screen is the last step of the wizard and displays a list of tasks that the wizard has performed for you based on the information that you have supplied.

Click the Finish button to have the OleDbDataAdapter and OleDbConnection components added to your project:

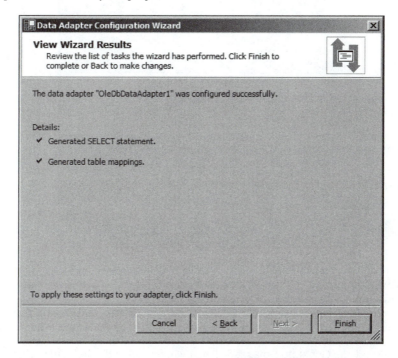

> Now that we have a means to connect to the database and a means to retrieve the data from the database, the next step is to create a component to hold the data that is retrieved.
>
> There are several options that are available to us here. We could create a **DataSet** component by dragging the **DataSet** component from the **Data** tab in the Toolbox and then set the various properties. Or we can have a **DataSet** component generated for us by the Generate DataSet wizard. Let's opt to go this second route, which is much easier and faster.

15. Click on the Data menu and then select the Generate DataSet menu item to display the Generate Dataset dialog:

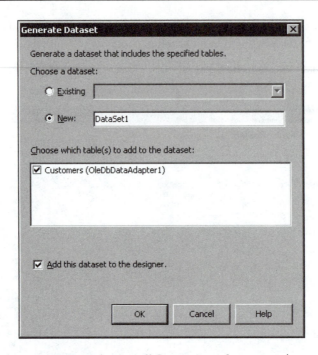

This dialog does some pretty clever stuff. In previous chapters, we've seen how in Visual Basic .NET we can base new classes on existing classes. This dialog actually creates a new class, which derives from the DataSet class, and adds features specifically for handling data from the selected tables. This makes the DataSet easier to work with, and ensures that it contains the data we expect it to. A class that derives from DataSet in this way is called a **typed dataset**.

When we use the **Generate Dataset** dialog, it will find all of the tables that will be returned from available data adapters. It then enables us to select which ones we want this DataSet to contain.

Let's look at the fields in this dialog. The first section of this dialog presents us with the option of using an existing DataSet class in our project or creating a new one. Our project does not contain any other typed dataset classes, so we can't use this option. The **New** option has been selected and a default name provided. Please change the name to CustomerDataSet.

This dialog has read the information from the data adapter in our project and has listed the table that it will return. Again this is what we want and we will accept the default values here. If we had several data adapters in our project we would see several tables listed here.

The last section of this dialog has a checkbox that specifies whether or not we want an instance of the CustomerDataSet class that will be created added to the designer. Having this checkbox checked will generate the code in our form to have the DataSet declared and initialized. This reduces the amount of code that we have to add so we also want to accept this default value.

Click the **OK** button to have the DataSet component generated and added to the project:

16. The `CustomerDataSet` component has been added to our project. We can see an instance of it – called `CustomerDataSet1` – in the component tray, underneath the form:

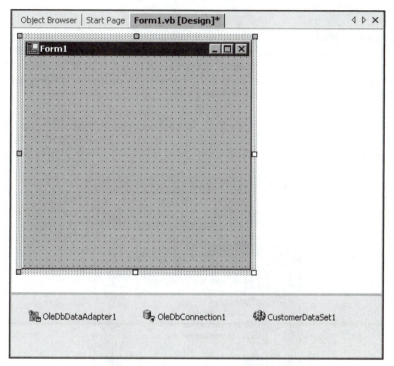

There is also a new item called `CustomerDataSet.xsd` in the Solution Explorer:

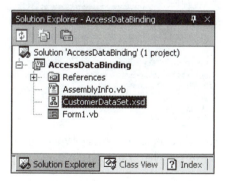

This is an XML schema that stores the information the data the `CustomerDataSet` can contain – for example, the table and column names.

We now need to add code in order to have the `CustomerDataSet` filled with data. Double-click on the form to have the `Form1_Load` procedure added to the code and then add the following line of code to this procedure in order to populate the `DataSet` component with data:

```
Private Sub Form1_Load(ByVal sender As System.Object, _
          ByVal e As System.EventArgs) Handles MyBase.Load
    OleDbDataAdapter1.Fill(CustomerDataSet1)
End Sub
```

17. We now need to add a DataGrid control to our form, so that we can see the data in CustomerDataSet1. Return to the form's designer, and select the **Windows Forms** tab on the Toolbox. Find the DataGrid control, and add it to the form. Resize the form and the DataGrid to a reasonable size, so that the DataGrid fills most of the form. Set its CaptionText property to **Customers**.

18. The DataGrid gives as quite a few ways to control its appearance. For this example, we will set the AlternatingBackColor property. Select this property, and pull down the drop-down menu:

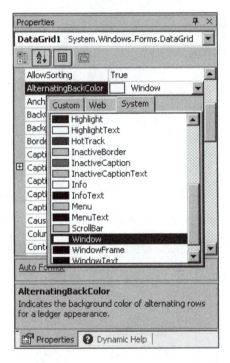

Now select the Web tab, and choose the **NavajoWhite** color (or whatever color takes your fancy – a light one will work out best though)

19. The last thing that we need to do here is to bind the DataSet component to our DataGrid by setting its DataSource and DataMember properties.

Display the form in design view and click on the DataGrid control. Then in the **Properties** window, locate its DataSource property and click on it. In the drop-down list, select CustomerDataSet1.

Next, click on the `DataMember` property and in the drop-down list select `Customers`. Note that we could have achieved the same effect by setting the `DataSource` property to `CustomerDataSet1.Customers`, but using this method is a little clearer for people looking at the code later on.

Your `DataGrid` should now look like this:

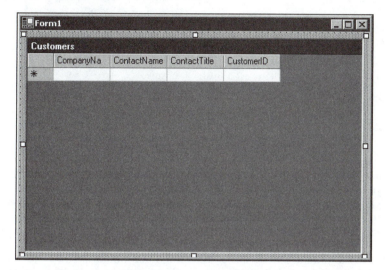

Notice the extra column that has been added to the end of our `DataGrid` control. We did not specify the `CustomerID` field in our SQL `SELECT` statement. The `OleDbDataAdapter` has added it because it is the **primary key field** for the `Customers` table.

> **A primary key is a field or fields whose value uniquely identifies a record in a table. In this case `CustomerID` field is the primary key that uniquely identifies a customer record in the `Customer` table.**

20. Now let's run this project to see what the final results look like. Click on the Start icon on the toolbar to run the project.

Your final results should look similar to those shown in the next figure. I have expanded the width of the form and the columns in the results so you can see the full column names and the data in the columns:

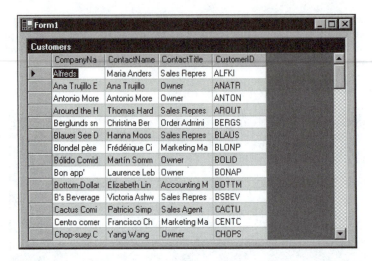

Note how setting the `AlternatingRowColor` property has affected the grid's appearance. This can be used as a purely decorative feature, but it can also prove very useful as rows start getting longer because it helps the user to look across a row without accidentally looking at a different row.

A further built-in feature that is worth mentioning is the ability to expand the width of the columns at run time. Users do this by hovering their mouse over the column boundary-lines in the header, and dragging across. Users can also double-click the boundary line to make the column width fit the data.

Another `DataGrid` feature is the ability to sort the data in the `DataGrid` simply by clicking on the column header. You can sort the data in ascending or descending order, and a little arrow pointing up or down in the right-hand of the column indicates the order that the data has been sorted in.

Finally, the `DataGrid` has built-in features for editing data. Changes to data in the `DataGrid` are automatically reflected back to the `DataSet`. In this application, however, we have not written the code needed to write the changes to the `DataSet` back to the database.

How It Works

We've discussed this application as we've gone along, so we don't need to look at how it works again in detail. Let's just take a brief overview of how the application works.

We added an `OleDbDataAdapter` component to the project, which automatically started the **Data Adapter Configuration Wizard**. Because we did not already have an `OleDbConnection` component in our project, we provided the information needed to build one using the **Data Link Properties** dialog.

We then specified the SQL `SELECT` statement in our `OleDbDataAdapter` component using the Query Builder dialog. Once we had provided this information, the `OleDbDataAdpater` was configured. The wizard automatically added an `OleDbConnection` component, based on the specifications we'd given in the **Data Link Properties** dialog.

The next stage was to create a typed dataset that would contain the data returned by the `OleDbDataAdapter`. We did using the **Generate Dataset** dialog. This dialog gathered the information provided in the `OleDbConnection` component and `OleDbDataAdapter` component in our project. We accepted the default values provided, except for the name, and then had this dialog generate the `DataSet` component.

Next, we needed a means to populate the `DataSet` component with data. We double-clicked the form's surface, to generate a handler for the form's `Load` event, and added this line of code:

```
Private Sub Form1_Load(ByVal sender As System.Object, _
        ByVal e As System.EventArgs) Handles MyBase.Load
    OleDbDataAdapter1.Fill(CustomerDataSet1)
End Sub
```

This procedure gets executed when the form loads and this line of code populates the `DataSet` with data. The `Fill` method of the `OleDbDataAdapter` uses the SQL `SELECT` statement that we generated to query the database and adds the rows of data that get returned to the specified `DataSet`.

We then added a `DataGrid` control to the form and set its `DataSource` property to the `DataSet` component. The `DataSet` component is the source of our data for the `DataGrid`.

We then set the `DataMember` property to `Customer`, which is the table in the `DataSet` that contains the data that we want displayed. Remember that a `DataSet` can contain more than one table, so we must specify which table in the `DataSet` we want displayed in the `DataGrid`.

When the project was run the connection was made to the database, and data was retrieved and then displayed in our form with only a single line of code. This is the power of the data components and data binding at work. With one additional line, and a few different steps when configuring the data adapter, we could have added the facility to save changes back to the database. We'll learn more about that in the next chapter.

Summary

We started this chapter by exploring what a database actually is and then looked at the SQL `SELECT` statement. We put this knowledge to use by creating a query in the `Northwind.mdb` database to see the SQL statements that Access generated for us.

We then took a look at the basics of binding data to controls on a form, specifically the `DataGrid` control. We have examined the necessary basic data access components required to retrieve and store the data from an Access database. We used the components provided in the **Data** tab of the Toolbox for our data access, and used the wizards to generate the necessary code to connect to the database and retrieve the data. We also added the necessary code to populate a `DataSet` component with the data retrieved by the `OleDbDataAdapter` component.

After working through this chapter, you should know:

❑ What a database is and the basic objects that make up a database

❑ How to use the SQL SELECT statement to select data from a database

❑ How to use the **Data Adapter Configuration Wizard** to create an OleDbDataAdapter component and OleDbConnection component

❑ How to create a DataSet component and fill it with data

❑ How to bind data to a DataGrid

While we have seen that the wizards provided in Visual Studio .NET make it simple to quickly bind data to the controls on a form, we sometimes need more control on how we interact with the data in a database and how we bind the data to the controls on a form. The next chapter takes a different approach to data binding by programmatically binding data to controls on a form. We will also be exploring the data access components in more detail and will learn how to set their properties and to execute their methods from our code.

Questions

1. Do you have to prefix the field name with the table name as shown in the following SQL SELECT statement?

```
SELECT Customer.[Customer Name]
FROM Customer
```

2. How do you sort the data in a DataGrid control?

3. How do you populate the DataSet component with data?

4. What two items does the OleDbDataAdapter need before it can retrieve data from a database?

Database Programming with SQL Server and ADO.NET

In the last chapter, we introduced database programming by obtaining data from a single table in an Access database, and displaying it on a grid. We managed to give the user some cool features while writing virtually no code.

We used wizards to write most of the code for us – including setting up the connection, configuring the data adapter, and generating a typed dataset. This works great for simple database access using one or two tables, but coding ourselves can give us a lot more control.

This chapter dives much deeper into the topic of database access. The database access technologies we used in the previous chapter – including components for retrieving data, storing data in memory, and binding data to controls – are collectively called **ADO.NET**. We will explore how we can use the built-in capabilities of ADO.NET to retrieve and update data from databases. We will also learn to manipulate, filter, and edit data held in memory by the `DataSet`.

The data we extract will be bound to controls on our form so we will also need to explore binding more thoroughly. We will see how we can use controls to view one record at a time, for example using textboxes, and how to navigate between records the `CurrencyManager` object.

So, in this chapter, we will cover the following topics:

- ❑ ADO.NET objects
- ❑ Binding data to controls
- ❑ Searching for and sorting in-memory data using ADO.NET `DataView` objects
- ❑ Selecting, inserting, updating, and deleting data in a database using ADO.NET

We will also use this chapter to see how to access SQL Server databases using the `SqlClient` data provider. As we mentioned in the previous chapter, `SqlClient` is significantly faster than `OleDb`, but will only work with SQL Server-compatible databases. In order to complete the exercises in this chapter, you will need to have access to MSDE, SQL Server 7, or SQL Server 2000 and have full access to the `pubs` database. MSDE is a SQL Server-compatible database engine that comes with Visual Studio .NET and Visual Basic .NET, and Microsoft plans for it to take over from Jet and Microsoft Access for desktop database applications. When this chapter uses the term SQL Server, the term covers SQL Server 7 and SQL Server 2000, as well as MSDE. The database can reside in SQL Server on your local machine or in SQL Server on a network.

ADO.NET

ADO.NET is designed to provide a **disconnected architecture**. This means that applications connect to the database to retrieve a load of data and store it in memory. They then disconnect from the database, and manipulate the in-memory copy of the data. If the database needs to be updated with changes made to the in-memory copy, then a new connection is made and the database is updated. The main in-memory data store is the `DataSet`, which contains other in-memory data stores such as `DataTable` objects. We can filter and sort data in a `DataSet` using `DataView` objects, as we will see later in the chapter.

Using a disconnected architecture provides many benefits, of which the most important to you is that it allows your application to scale up. This means that your database will perform just as well supporting hundreds of users as it does supporting ten users. This is made possible since the application only connects to the database long enough to retrieve or update data, thereby freeing up available database connections for other instances of your application or other applications using the same database.

ADO.NET Data Namespaces

The core ADO.NET classes exist in the `System.Data` namespace. This namespace, in turn, contains some child namespaces. The most important of these are `System.Data.SqlClient` and `System.Data.OleDb`. These provide classes for accessing SQL Server databases and OLE DB-compliant databases, respectively. We've already used classes from the `System.Data.OleDb` namespace in the previous chapter, where we used `OleDbConnection` and `OleDbDataAdapter`. In this chapter we will be using `System.Data.SqlClient` with its equivalent classes, including `SqlConnection` and `SqlDataAdapter`.

The `System.Data.SqlClient` and `System.Data.OleDb` namespaces are known as **data providers** in ADO.NET. There are other data providers available, for example for ODBC and Oracle. In this book we concentrate only on the standard two.

In this chapter we will be accessing SQL Server databases using the `SqlClient` namespace. However in ADO.NET, the different data providers work in a very similar way. So the techniques we use here can be easily transferred to the `OleDb` classes. Also, the techniques we learned in the previous chapter using `OleDb` apply to `SqlClient` too. With ADO.NET, we just use the data provider that best fits our data source – we do not need to learn a whole new interface, since all data providers work in a very similar way.

As you start working with ADO.NET you will soon come to realize how the pieces fit together and this chapter will help you in that direction. For a complete guide to ADO.NET, see *Professional ADO.NET* (Wrox Press, ISBN 1-86100-527-X).

Since the space here is limited, we will focus our attention on the specific classes that are relevant to our example programs in this chapter. The list below contains the data provider classes that we will be discussing:

- `SqlConnection`
- `SqlDataAdapter`
- `SqlCommand`
- `SqlParameter`

Remember that these are specifically `SqlClient` classes, but that the `OleDb` namespace has very close equivalents. Whenever we want to use these classes we must import the `System.Data.SqlClient` namespace as shown in the code fragment below:

```
Imports System.Data.SqlClient
```

If we want to use the core ADO.NET classes such as `DataSet` and `DataView` then we must import the `System.Data` namespace as shown in the next code fragment:

```
Imports System.Data
```

You should already be familiar with importing different namespaces in your project. However, to be thorough we will also cover this when we go through our hands-on exercises. Now let's take a look at the main classes that exist in the `System.Data.SqlClient` namespace.

SqlConnection

The `SqlConnection` class is at the heart of the classes that we will be discussing in this section as it provides a connection to a SQL Server database. When we construct a `SqlConnection` object, we can choose to specify a **connection string** as a parameter. If we don't specify one in the constructor, we can set it using the `SqlConnection.ConnectionString` property. The connection string contains all of the information required to open a connection to our database. In the previous chapter, Visual Studio .NET built a connection string for us from the details we specified in the Data Link Properties dialog box. However, it is often more useful or quicker to manually write a connection string – so let's take a look at how they work.

The Connection String

The way that the connection string is constructed will depend on what data provider we are using. We are using the SQL Server provider. When accessing SQL Server, we will usually provide a `Server` and `Database` parameter:

Parameter	Description
Server	The name of the SQL Server that we wish to access. This is usually the name of the computer that is running SQL Server. We can use (local) or localhost if SQL Server is on the same machine as the one running the application.
Database	The name of the database that we want to connect to.

As well as this, we also need some form of authentication information. There are two ways that this can be done: either by providing a username and password in the connection string, or by connection to SQL Server using the NT account that the application is running under. If we want to connect to the server by specifying a username and password, we need to include the following parameters in our connection string:

Parameter	Description
Uid	The username to use to connect to the database. An account with this user ID will need to exist in SQL Server, and have permission to access the specified database.
Pwd	The password for the specified user.

However, SQL Server can be set up to use the Windows NT account of the user who is running the program to open the connection. In this case, we don't need to specify a username and password. We just need to specify that we are using **integrated security**. (The method is called integrated security because SQL Server is integrating with Windows NT's security system). We do this using the Integrated Security parameter:

Parameter	Description
Integrated Security	Set to True when we want the application to connect to SQL Server using the current user's NT account.

Of course, for this to work the user of the application must have permission to use the SQL Server database. This is granted using the SQL Server Enterprise Manager.

Let's take a look at how we use the parameters above in a connection string to initialize a connection object. The code fragment below uses the SqlConnection class to initialize a connection object that uses a specific user ID and password in the connection string:

```
Dim myConnection As SqlConnection = New _
    SqlConnection("Server=localhost;Database=pubs;Uid=sa;Pwd=vbdotnet;")
```

The connection string shown above accesses a SQL Server database. The Server parameter specifies that the database resides on the local machine. The Database parameter specifies the database that we want to access – in this case it is the pubs database. Finally, the User ID and Password parameters specify the user ID and password of the user defined in the database. As you can see, each parameter has a value assigned to it using =, and each parameter-value pair is separated by a semi-colon.

Opening and Closing the Connection

Once we have initialized a connection object with a connection string as shown above, we can invoke the methods of the `SqlConnection` object such as `Open` and `Close`, which actually open and close a connection to the database specified in the connection string. An example of this is shown in the code fragment below:

```
' Open the database connection...
myConnection.Open()
' ... Use the connection
' Close the database connection...
myConnection.Close()
```

Although there are many more properties and methods available in the `SqlConnection` class, the ones mentioned above are all we are really interested in to complete our hands-on exercises and they should be enough to get you started.

> *If you would like to learn more about ADO.NET and programmatically accessing databases with Visual Basic .NET, you might like to read* Beginning Visual Basic .NET Database Programming *(Wrox Press, 1-86100-555-5).*

SqlCommand

The `SqlCommand` class represents a SQL command to execute against a data store. The command will usually be a select, insert, update, or delete query, and can be a SQL string or a call to a stored procedure. The query being executed may contain parameters or it may not.

In our example in the previous chapter, the **Data Adapter Configuration Wizard** generated a command object for us (although in that case it was an `OleDbCommand`). In that case, a data adapter was using the command to fill a dataset. We will look at how to write code to do this later in the chapter. For the moment, let's look at command objects alone. We will look at how they relate to data adapters in the next section.

The constructor for the `SqlCommand` class has several variations, but the simplest method is to initialize an `SqlCommand` object with no parameters. Then, once the object has been initialized, we can set the properties that we need to perform the task at hand. The code fragment below shows how to initialize a `SqlCommand` object:

```
Dim myCommand As SqlCommand = New SqlCommand()
```

When using data adapters and datasets, there isn't much call for using command objects on their own. They will mainly be used for executing a particular delete, insert, or update, so that is what we will cover in this chapter. We can also use command objects with a SELECT statement to return a **data reader**. A data reader is an alternative to a `DataSet` that uses fewer system resources, but gives us far less flexibility. In this book we will concentrate on using the `DataSet` because it is the most common and useful of the two.

The Connection Property

There are certain properties that must be set on the `SqlCommand` before we can execute the query. The first of these properties is the `Connection` property. This property is set to a `SqlConnection` object, as shown in the next code fragment.

```
myCommand.Connection = myConnection
```

In order for the command to execute successfully, the connection must be open at the time of execution.

The CommandText Property

The next property that must be set is the `CommandText` property. This property specifies the SQL string or stored procedure to be executed. Most databases requires that we place all *string* values in single quote marks as we have done here:

```
Dim myConnection As SqlConnection = New _
                        SqlConnection("server=(local);database=pubs;uid=sa;pwd=")
Dim myCommand As SqlCommand = New SqlCommand()
myCommand.Connection = myConnection
myCommand.CommandText = "INSERT INTO authors " & _
                    "(au_id, au_lname, au_fname, contract) " & _
                    "VALUES('123-45-6789', 'Barnes', 'David', true)"
```

The `INSERT` statement shown above is a very simple one that means: "Insert a new row into the `authors` table. In the au_id column put '123-45-6789', in the `au_lname` column put 'Barnes', in the au_fname column put 'David', and in the `contract` column put '1'."

This is the basic way that `INSERT` statements work in SQL. We have `INSERT INTO` followed by a table name. We then have a series of column names, in brackets. We then have the `VALUES` keyword followed by a set of values, to be inserted into the columns that we've just named and in the same order.

This assumes that we know the values to insert when we are writing the program. This is very unlikely in most cases. Fortunately we can create commands with parameters, and then set the values of these parameters separately. Let's have a look at how to use parameters.

The Parameters Collection

Placeholders are question marks in the SQL statement that get filled in by **parameters**. So if we wanted to update the authors table in the same way as above, but didn't know the values at write time, we would do this:

```
Dim myConnection As SqlConnection = New _
                        SqlConnection("server=(local);database=pubs;uid=sa;pwd=")
Dim myCommand As SqlCommand = New SqlCommand()
myCommand.Connection = myConnection
myCommand.CommandText = "INSERT INTO authors " & _
                    "(au_id, au_lname, au_fname, contract) " & _
                    "VALUES(@au_id,@au_lname,@au_fname,@au_contract)"
```

Here instead of providing values, we have provided placeholders. Placeholders always start with an @ symbol. They do not need to be named after the database column that they represent, but it is often easier if they are.

What we need to do next is to create parameters that will be used to insert the values into the placeholders when the SQL statement is executed. We need to create and add parameters to the `Parameters` collection of the `SqlCommand` object. When we talk about *parameters* here, we are talking about the parameters required to provide data to our SQL statement or stored procedure, and *not* the parameters that are required to be passed to a method.

We can access the `Parameters` collection of the `SqlCommand` object by specifying the `Parameters` property. Once we access the `Parameters` collection, we can use its properties and methods to create one or more parameters in the collection. The easiest way to add a parameter to a command is demonstrated in the following example:

```
Dim myConnection As SqlConnection = New _
                    SqlConnection("server=(local);database=pubs;uid=sa;pwd=")
Dim myCommand As SqlCommand = New SqlCommand()
myCommand.Connection = myConnection
myCommand.CommandText = "INSERT INTO authors " & _
                "(au_id, au_lname, au_fname, contract) " & _
                "VALUES(@au_id,@au_lname,@au_fname,@au_contract)"
myCommand.Parameters.Add("@au_id", txtAuId.Text)
myCommand.Parameters.Add("@au_lname", txtLastName.Text)
myCommand.Parameters.Add("@au_fname", txtFirstName.Text)
myCommand.Parameters.Add("@contract", chkContract.Checked)
```

The `Add` method here accepts the name of the parameter, and the object that we wish to add. In this case, we are using the `Text` property of various `TextBox` objects on a (fictitious) form for most of the columns. For the `Contract` column we use the `Checked` property of a `CheckBox` on the same form.

The ExecuteNonQuery Method

Finally we can execute the command. To do this, the connection needs to be opened. We can invoke the `ExecuteNonQuery` method of the `SqlCommand` object. This method will execute the SQL statement and cause the data to be inserted into the database. It will then return the number of rows that were affected by the query – which can be a useful way to check that the command worked as expected. To complete our code fragment, we need to open the connection, execute the query, and close the connection again:

```
Dim myConnection As SqlConnection = New _
                    SqlConnection("server=(local);database=pubs;uid=sa;pwd=")
Dim myCommand As SqlCommand = New SqlCommand()
myCommand.Connection = myConnection
myCommand.CommandText = "INSERT INTO authors " & _
                "(au_id, au_lname, au_fname, contract) " & _
                "VALUES(@au_id,@au_lname,@au_fname,@au_contract)"
myCommand.Parameters.Add("@au_id", txtAuId.Text)
myCommand.Parameters.Add("@au_lname", txtLastName.Text)
myCommand.Parameters.Add("@au_fname", txtFirstName.Text)
```

```
myCommand.Parameters.Add("@contract", chkContract.Checked)
myConnection.Open()
myCommand.ExecuteNonQuery())
myConnection.Close()
```

SqlDataAdapter

The `SqlDataAdapter` class is very similar to the `OleDbDataAdapter` that we configured with wizards in the previous chapter. The main difference is that the `OleDbDataAdapter` can access any data source that supports OLE DB, while the `SqlDataAdapter` only supports SQL Server databases. We can use them in a very similar way though – we can configure a `SqlDataAdapter` using wizards, just as we configured a `OleDbDataAdapter` in the previous chapter (provided we are accessing a SQL Server data source). In this chapter we will look at how to configure and use a `SqlDataAdapter` in code – but these guidelines also apply to the `OleDbDataAdapter`.

Data adapters act as a bridge between our data source and in-memory data objects such as the `DataSet`. In order to access the data source, they use the command objects we've just looked at. These command objects are associated with connections, so the data adapter relies on command and connection objects in order to access and manipulate the data source.

The `SqlDataAdapter` class's `SelectCommand` property is used to hold a `SqlCommand` that retrieves data from the data source. The data adapter then places the result of the query into a `DataSet` or `DataTable`. The `SqlDataAdapter` also has `UpdateCommand`, `DeleteCommand`, and `InsertCommand` properties. These are also `SqlCommand` objects, used to write changes made to a `DataSet` or `DataTable` back to the data source. This may all seem complicated, but in fact the tools are really easy to use. We learned enough SQL in the previous chapter to write a `SelectCommand`, and there are tools called **command builders** that we can use to automatically create the other commands based on this.

Let's start by taking a look at the `SelectCommand` property, and then look at how we can create commands for updating, deleting, and inserting records.

The SelectCommand Property

The `SqlDataAdapter` class's `SelectCommand` property is used to fill a `DataSet` with data from a SQL Server database, as shown in the following diagram:

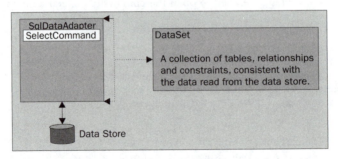

When we want to read data from the data store, we must set the `SelectCommand` property of the `SqlDataAdapter` class first. This property is a `SqlCommand` object and is used to specify what data to select and how to select that data. Therefore the `SelectCommand` property has properties of its own, and we need to set them just as we would set properties on a normal command. We've already seen the following properties of the `SqlCommand` object:

Property	Description
Connection	Sets the `OleDbConnection` object to be used to access the data store
CommandText	Sets the SQL statements or stored procedure name to be used to select the data

In the previous examples of `SqlCommand` objects, we've used straight SQL statements. If we want to use stored procedures, we need to be aware of an additional property – `CommandType`:

Property	Description
CommandType	Sets a value that determines how the `CommandText` property is interpreted

In this chapter we are going to concentrate on SQL statements, but stored procedures are often useful too – particularly if they already exist in the database. If you want to use one, then set the `CommandText` property to the name of the stored procedure (remember to enclose it in quote marks because the compiler treats this as a string), and set the `CommandType` property to `CommandType.StoredProcedure`. Here we are setting the `CommandType` property to a value from the `CommandType` enumeration so we do not need quote marks.

Setting SelectCommand to a SQL String

Let's take a look at how we set these properties in code. The code fragment below shows the typical settings for these properties when executing a SQL string:

```
' Declare a SqlDataAdapter object...
Dim myDataAdapter As New SqlDataAdapter()

' Assign a new SqlCommand to the SelectCommand property
myDataAdapter.SelectCommand = New SqlCommand()

' Set the SelectCommand properties...
myDataAdapter.SelectCommand.Connection = myConnection
myDataAdapter.SelectCommand.CommandText = _
    "SELECT au_lname, au_fname FROM authors " & _
    "ORDER BY au_lname, au_fname"
```

The first thing that this code fragment does is to declare a `SqlDataAdapter` object. This object has a `SelectCommand` property that is already set to a `SqlCommand` – we just need to set that command's properties. We set the properties by first setting the `Connection` property to a valid connection object – one that will already have been created before the code that we see here. Next, we set the `CommandText` property to our SQL `SELECT` statement.

Setting SelectCommand to a Stored Procedure

This next code fragment shows how we could set these properties when we want to execute a **stored procedure**. A stored procedure is a group of SQL statements that are stored in the database under a unique name and are executed as a unit. The stored procedure in this example (usp_select_author_titles) uses the same SQL statement that we used in the previous code fragment:

```
' Declare a SqlDataAdapter object...
Dim myDataAdapter As New SqlDataAdapter()

' Assign a new SqlCommand to the SelectCommand property
myDataAdapter.SelectCommand = New SqlCommand()

' Set the SelectCommand properties...
myDataAdapter.SelectCommand.Connection = myConnection
myDataAdapter.SelectCommand.CommandText = "usp_select_author_titles"
myDataAdapter.SelectCommand.CommandType = CommandType.StoredProcedure
```

The CommandText property now specifies the name of the stored procedure that we want to execute instead of the SQL string that was specified in the last example. Also notice the CommandType property. In the first example we did not change this property, because its default value is CommandType.Text – which is what we need to execute SQL statements. In this example, it is set to a value of CommandType.StoredProcedure, which indicates that the CommandText property contains the name of a stored procedure to be executed.

Using Command Builders to Create the Other Commands

The SelectCommand is all we need to transfer data from the database into our DataSet. Once we've let our users make changes to the DataSet, though, we will want to write the changes back to the database. We can do this by setting up command objects with the SQL for inserting, deleting, and updating. Alternatively we can use stored procedures. Both of these solutions require knowledge of SQL outside the scope of this book. Fortunately, there is an easier way – we can use command builders to create these commands for us. It only takes one more line:

```
' Declare a SqlDataAdapter object...
Dim myDataAdapter As New SqlDataAdapter()

' Assign a new SqlCommand to the SelectCommand property
myDataAdapter.SelectCommand = New SqlCommand()

' Set the SelectCommand properties...
myDataAdapter.SelectCommand.Connection = myConnection
myDataAdapter.SelectCommand.CommandText = "usp_select_author_titles"
myDataAdapter.SelectCommand.CommandType = CommandType.StoredProcedure
' automatically create update/delete/insert commands
Dim myBuilder As SqlCommandBuilder = New SqlCommandBuilder(myDataAdapter)
```

Now we can use this SqlDataAdapter to write changes back to a database. We will look more at this later in the chapter. For know, let's look at the method that gets data from the database to the DataSet in the first place – the Fill method.

The Fill Method

We use the `Fill` method to populate a `DataSet` object with the data that the `SqlDataAdapter` object retrieves from the data store using its `SelectCommand`. However, before we do this we must first initialize a `DataSet` object. Let's carry on with our previous example, although we don't need to use the command builder for this so we will leave it out:

```
' Declare a SqlDataAdapter object...
Dim myDataAdapter As New SqlDataAdapter()

' Assign a new SqlCommand to the SelectCommand property
myDataAdapter.SelectCommand = New SqlCommand()

' Set the SelectCommand properties...
myDataAdapter.SelectCommand.Connection = myConnection
myDataAdapter.SelectCommand.CommandText = "usp_select_author_titles"
myDataAdapter.SelectCommand.CommandType = CommandType.StoredProcedure
Dim myDataSet as DataSet = New DataSet()
```

Now we have a `DataSet` and a `SqlDataAdapter`, we can fill our `DataSet` with data. The `Fill` method has several overloaded versions, but we will be discussing the one most commonly used. The syntax for the `Fill` method is shown below:

```
SqlDataAdapter.Fill(DataSet, string)
```

The *DataSet* argument specifies a valid `DataSet` object that will be populated with data. The *string* argument gives the name we want the table to have in the `DataSet` – remember that one `DataSet` can contain many tables. We can use any name we like, but usually it's best to use the name of the table that the data has come from in the database.

The code fragment below shows how we invoke the `Fill` method. The string `"authors"` is specified as the *string* argument. This is the name of the table in the data source. It is also the name we want to use when playing with the in-memory version of the table:

```
' Declare a SqlDataAdapter object...
Dim myDataAdapter As New SqlDataAdapter()

' Set the SelectCommand properties...
myDataAdapter.SelectCommand.Connection = myConnection
myDataAdapter.SelectCommand.CommandText = "usp_select_author_titles"
myDataAdapter.SelectCommand.CommandType = CommandType.StoredProcedure
Dim myDataSet as DataSet = New DataSet()
' Fill the DataSet object with data...
myDataAdapter.Fill(myDataSet, "authors")
```

The `Fill` method uses the `SelectCommand.Connection` property to access the database. If the connection is already open, then the data adapter will use it to execute the `SelectCommand` and leave it open after it's finished. If the connection is closed then the data adapter will open it, execute the `SelectCommand`, and then close it again.

We now have data in memory, and can start manipulating it independently of the data source. Notice that the `DataSet` class does not have `Sql` at the start of its class name. This is because we can use a `DataSet` to contain just about any data – regardless of what data source it came from. The `DataSet` is not in the `System.Data.SqlClient` namespace, it is in the parent `System.Data` namespace. The classes in this namespace are primarily concerned with manipulating data in memory, rather than obtaining data from any particular data source. Let's have a look at two of the classes in this namespace – the `DataSet` and the `DataView`.

The DataSet Class

The `DataSet` class is used to store data retrieved from a data store, and stores that data in memory on the client. The `DataSet` object contains a collection of tables, relationships, and constraints that are consistent with the data read from the data store. It acts as a lightweight database engine, enabling us to store tables, edit data and run queries using a `DataView`.

The data in a `DataSet` is actually disconnected from the data store and you can operate on the data independently from the data store. You can manipulate the data in a `DataSet` object by adding, updating, and deleting the records. You can then apply these changes back to the data store using a data adapter.

The data in a `DataSet` object is persisted as **XML** (which we will discuss in detail in Chapter 18), meaning that we can save a `DataSet` as a file or easily pass it over a network. The XML is shielded from you as a developer and you should never need to edit the XML directly. All editing of the XML is done through the properties and methods of the `DataSet` class. Many developers like using XML and will sometimes choose to manipulate the XML representation of a `DataSet` directly, but this is not essential.

Like any XML document, a `DataSet` can have a **schema**. When we generated a typed dataset in the previous chapter, an XSD file was added to the solution explorer:

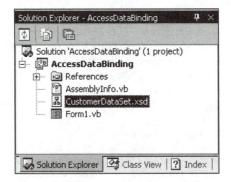

This file is an XML schema that describes the structure of the data that the `CustomerDataSet` would hold. From this, Visual Studio .NET was able to create a class that inherited from `DataSet` and that used this particular schema. A `DataSet` schema contains information about the tables, relationships, and constraints stored in the `DataSet`. Again, this is shielded from you and you do not need to know XML to work with a `DataSet`. For more information on the `DataSet` object and the XML contained in it, see *Beginning Visual Basic .NET Database Programming* (Wrox Press, ISBN 1-86100-555-5).

Since the `DataSet` contains the actual data retrieved from a data store, we can bind the `DataSet` to a control or controls to have them display (and allow editing of) the data in the `DataSet`. We did this a bit in the previous chapter, and we will see more later on in this chapter.

DataView

The `DataView` class is typically used for sorting, filtering, searching, editing, and navigating the data from a `DataSet`. A `DataView` is **bindable**, meaning that it can be bound to controls in the same way that the `DataSet` can be bound to controls. Again, we will cover data binding in code later in this chapter.

A `DataSet` can contain a number of `DataTable` objects – when we use the `SqlDataAdapter` class's `Fill` method to add data to a `DataSet`, we are actually creating a `DataTable` object inside the `DataSet`. The `DataView` provides a custom view of a `DataTable` – we can sort or filter the rows, for example, as we can in a SQL query.

You can create a `DataView` from the data contained in a `DataTable` that contains only the data that you want to display. For example, if the data in a `DataTable` contains all authors sorted by last name and first name, you can create a `DataView` that contains all authors sorted by first name and then last name. Or if you wanted, you could create a `DataView` that only contained last names or certain names.

Although we can view the data in a `DataView` in ways different from the underlying `DataTable`, it is still the same data. Changes made to a `DataView` affect the underlying `DataTable` automatically, and changes made to the underlying `DataTable` will automatically affect any `DataView` objects that are viewing that `DataTable`.

The constructor for the `DataView` class initializes a new instance of the `DataView` class and accepts the `DataTable` as an argument. The code fragment below declares a `DataView` object and initializes it using the `authors` table from the `DataSet` named `myDataSet`. Notice that we have accessed the `Tables` collection of the `DataSet` object, by specifying the `Tables` property and the table name:

```
' Set the DataView object to the DataSet object...
Dim myDataView = New DataView(objDataSet.Tables("authors"))
```

The Sort Property

Once a `DataView` has been initialized and is viewing data, you can alter our view of that data. For example, suppose we want to sort the data in a different order than in the `DataSet`. In order to sort the data in a `DataView`, we set the `Sort` property and specify the column or columns that we want sorted. The code fragment below sorts the data in a `DataView` by author's first name and then last name:

```
myDataView.Sort = "au_fname, au_lname"
```

Notice that this is the same syntax as the ORDER BY clause in a SQL SELECT statement. Like SQL SELECT statements, sorting operations on a `DataView` are always performed in an ascending order by default. If we wanted to perform the sort in descending order, we would need to specify the DESC keyword as shown in the next code fragment:

```
myDataView.Sort = "au_fname, au_lname DESC"
```

633

The RowFilter Property

When we have an initialized DataView, we can filter the rows of data that it will contain. This is very similar to specifying a WHERE clause in a SQL SELECT statement – only rows that match the criteria will remian in the view. The underlying data is not affected, though. The RowFilter property specifies the criteria that should be applied on the DataView. The syntax is very similar to the SQL WHERE clause. It contains at least a column name followed by an operator and the value. If the value is a string it must be enclosed in single quote marks as shown in the code fragment below.

This code fragment will only retrieve the authors whose last name is Green:

```
' Set the DataView object to the DataSet object...
myDataView = New DataView(myDataSet.Tables("authors"))
myDataView.RowFilter = "au_lname = 'Green'"
```

If we want to retrieve all rows of authors except those whose last name is Green, we would specify the "not equal to" operator as shown in the example below:

```
' Set the DataView object to the DataSet object...
myDataView = New DataView(myDataSet.Tables("authors"))
myDataView.RowFilter = "au_lname <> 'Green'"
```

We can also specify more complex filters, as we could in SQL. For example we can combine several criteria together using an AND operator:

```
myDataView.RowFilter = "au_lname <> 'Green' AND au_fname LIKE 'D*'"
```

This will return authors whose last name is Green and whose first name begins with D.

The Find Method

If we want to search for a specific row of data in a DataView, we invoke the Find method. The Find method searches for data in the sort key column of the DataView. Therefore, before invoking the Find method, we first need to sort the DataView on the column that contains the data that we want to find. The column that the DataView is sorted on becomes the sort key column in a DataView object.

For example, suppose we want to find the author who has a first name of Ann. We would need to sort the DataView by first name to set this column as the sort key column in the DataView, and then invoke the Find method as shown in the code fragment below:

```
Dim inPosition as Integer
myDataView.Sort = "au_fname"
intPosition = objDataView.Find("Ann")
```

If it finds a match, the Find method returns the position of the record within the DataView. Otherwise, the DataView returns a –1, indicating that no match was found. If the Find method finds a match, it stops looking and only returns the position of the first match. If you know there is more than one match in your data store, you could **filter** the data in the DataView – something that we'll discuss shortly.

The `Find` method is not case sensitive, meaning that in order to find the author who has a first name of Ann, you could enter either the text Ann or ann.

The `Find` method looks for an exact case-insensitive match, so this means that you must enter the whole word or words of the text that you are looking for. For example, suppose you are looking for the author who has the last name of Del Castillo. You cannot enter Del and expect to find a match – you must enter all of the words that make up the author's name. So in order to find this author, you would need to enter Del Castillo as shown in the code fragment below. Notice that in this example we have specified all lower case letters, which is perfectly fine and we will find a match:

```
objDataView.Sort = "au_lname"
intPosition = objDataView.Find("del castillo")
```

We have seen that a `DataView` can be sorted on more than one column at a time. If we want to sort on more than one column, we need to supply an array of values to the `Find` method instead of just a single value. Let's say we want to find where 'Simon Watts' appears in the `DataView`, if at all:

```
Dim intPosition As Integer
Dim vals(1) As Object
myDataView.Sort = "au_fname, au_lname"

' Find the author named "Simon Watts".
vals(0)= "Simon"
vals(1) = "Watts"
intPosition = myDataView.Find(vals)
```

The ADO.NET Classes in Action

We've now looked at the basics of the ADO.NET classes and how they allow us to retrieve and insert data into SQL Server. No doubt your head is spinning from information overload at this point, so the best way to ensure that you understand how to use all of the objects, methods, and properties that we have been looking at is to actually use them. In the next two *Try It Outs*, you'll see how to exploit the power of the `DataSet` object to expose data to your users. You may find that you'll want to come back and re-read the previous section after you've completed the *Try It Outs* – this will help to clarify ADO.NET in your mind.

The first *Try It Out* will implement the `SqlConnection`, `SqlDataAdapter`, and `DataSet` classes. We will see at first hand how to use these classes in a simple example where we need read-only data and we will be displaying this data in a data grid. In fact, what we do here will be very similar to the example in the previous chapter – but we will be doing it in code instead of using wizards.

> When writing your programs, you will often use a combination of wizards and coding. The components created in the previous chapter by drag and drop can be manipulated in code in exactly the same way as objects created in code. In the previous chapter we used wizards almost all the time. In this chapter we will concentrate on code. You will often want to combine these techniques in your own programs, though, to create powerful programs quickly and easily.

Before we dive into the details of creating the program, let's take a look at the data and the relationships of the data that we want to display. The data that we want comes from the pubs database in SQL Server 2000. However, if you are using SQL Server 7.0 or MSDE you should be seeing the exact same data.

We want to display a list of authors, their book titles, and the price of their books. The diagram below shows the tables that this data resides in and also the relationship of the tables:

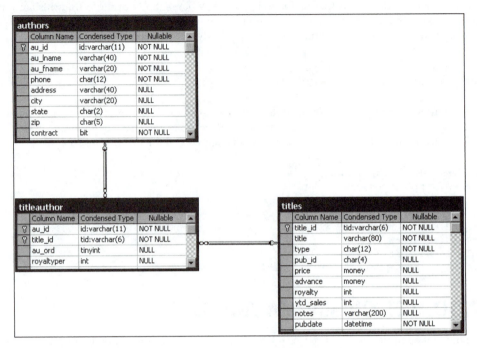

We want to display the author's first and last names, which reside in the authors table, and the book title and price of the book, which reside in the titles table. Because an author can have one or more books and a book can have one or more authors, the titles table is joined to the authors table via a **relationship table** called titleauthor. This table contains the many-to-many relationship of authors to books.

Having looked at the relationship of the tables and knowing what data we want, let's take a look at the SQL SELECT statement that we need to create to get this data:

```
SELECT au_lname, au_fname, title, price
FROM authors
JOIN titleauthor ON authors.au_id = titleauthor.au_id
JOIN titles ON titleauthor.title_id = titles.title_id
ORDER BY au_lname, au_fname
```

The first line of the SELECT statement shows the columns that we want to select.

The second line shows the main table that we are selecting data from, which is authors.

The third line joins the `titleauthor` table to the `authors` table using the `au_id` column. Therefore, when we select a row of data from the `authors` table, we will get every row in the `titleauthor` table that matches the `au_id` in the `authors` table.

The fourth line joins the `titles` table on the `titleauthor` table using the `title_id` column. Hence, for every row of data that is selected from the `titleauthor` table, we will select the corresponding row of data from the `titles` table.

The last line of the `SELECT` statement sorts the data by the author's last name and first name using the `ORDER BY` clause.

Now, let's create the project:

Try It Out – DataSet Example

1. Create a new Windows Application called **Dataset Example**.

2. Set the following properties of the form:

Property	Value
Size	600, 230
StartPosition	CenterScreen
Text	Bound DataSet

3. From the Toolbox, locate the **DataGrid** control under the **Windows Forms** tab and drag it onto your form. Set the properties of the **DataGrid** as shown in the table below:

Property	Value
Name	grdAuthorTitles
Location	5, 5
Size	584, 192
Anchor	Top, Bottom, Left, Right

4. First, we need to import the required namespaces. Open up the code window for your form and add these namespaces at the very top of your code:

```
' Import Data and SqlClient namespaces...
Imports System.Data
Imports System.Data.SqlClient

Public Class Form1
    Inherits System.Windows.Forms.Form
```

5. Next, we need to declare the objects necessary to retrieve the data from the database, so add the following code. Ensure you use a user ID and password that have been defined in your installation of SQL Server:

```
Public Class Form1
    Inherits System.Windows.Forms.Form

    Dim myConnection As SqlConnection = New _
        SqlConnection("server=(local);database=pubs;uid=sa;pwd=")

    Dim myDataAdapter As New SqlDataAdapter()
    Dim myDataSet As DataSet = New DataSet()
```

> **Notice our connection string in the constructor for this object. You will need to change the `server` parameter to point to the machine where SQL Server is running if it is not running on your local machine. You will also need to change the `uid` and `pwd` parameters to use a valid login that has been provided or that you set up yourself. If the `uid` that you use has no password assigned, then specify the `pwd` argument but do not enter anything for the actual password. For example, `pwd=;`.**

6. Return to the form designer and double-click a blank area of the form. This will add a handler for the form's `Load` event. Insert the following code:

```
Private Sub Form1_Load(ByVal sender As System.Object, _
                        ByVal e As System.EventArgs) Handles MyBase.Load
    ' Set the SelectCommand properties...
    myDataAdapter.SelectCommand = New SqlCommand()
    myDataAdapter.SelectCommand.Connection = myConnection
    myDataAdapter.SelectCommand.CommandText = _
        "SELECT au_lname, au_fname, title, price " & _
        "FROM authors " & _
        "JOIN titleauthor ON authors.au_id = titleauthor.au_id " & _
        "JOIN titles ON titleauthor.title_id = titles.title_id " & _
        "ORDER BY au_lname, au_fname"
    myDataAdapter.SelectCommand.CommandType = CommandType.Text

    ' Open the database connection...
    myConnection.Open()
    ' Now execute the command...
    'myDataAdapter.SelectCommand.ExecuteNonQuery()

    ' Fill the DataSet object with data...
    myDataAdapter.Fill(myDataSet, "authors")

    ' Close the database connection...
    myConnection.Close()

    ' Set the DataGrid properties to bind it to our data...
    grdAuthorTitles.DataSource = myDataSet
```

```
        grdAuthorTitles.DataMember = "authors"
End Sub
```

7. Let's run our project to see what we get. You should see results similar to this:

8. Note that the `DataGrid` control has built-in sorting capabilities. If you click on a column header, the data in the grid will be sorted by that column in ascending order. If you click on the same column again, the data will be sorted in descending order.

> It should be noted that error handling has been omitted from the exercise to preserve space. You should always add the appropriate error handling to your code. Please review Chapter 11 for error-handling techniques.

How It Works

To begin with, we imported the following namespaces:

```
' Import Data and OleDb namespaces...
Imports System.Data
Imports System.Data.SqlClient
```

Remember that the `System.Data` namespace is required for the `DataSet` and `DataView` classes, and that the `System.Data.SqlClient` namespace is required for the `SqlConnection`, `SqlDataAdapter`, `SqlCommand`, and `SqlParameter` classes. We will only be using a subset of the classes just mentioned in this example but we do require both namespaces.

Then we declared the objects that were necessary to retrieve the data from the database. These objects were declared with class-level scope so we placed those declarations just inside the class:

```
Public Class Form1
    Inherits System.Windows.Forms.Form

    Dim myConnection As SqlConnection = New _
        SqlConnection("server=(local);database=pubs;uid=sa;pwd=")

    Dim myDataAdapter As New SqlDataAdapter()
    Dim myDataSet As DataSet = New DataSet()
```

The first object that we declared was a `SqlConnection` object. Remember that this object establishes a connection to our data store, which in this case is SQL Server.

The next object that we have declared here is a `SqlDataAdapter` object. This object is used to read data from the database and to populate the `DataSet` object.

Then, of course, the last object in our declarations is the `DataSet` object, which serves as the container for our data. Remember that this object stores all data in memory and is not connected to the data store.

> **In this particular example, there was no need to give these objects class-level scope. We only use them in one method, and they could have been declared there. However, if our application enabled users to write changes back to the database then we would want to use the same connection and data adapter objects for both reading and writing to the database. In that case, having class-level scope would be really useful.**

With our objects defined, we placed some code to populate the `DataSet` in the initialization section of the form. Our `SqlDataAdapter` object is responsible for retrieving the data from the database. Therefore, we set the `SelectCommand` property of this object. This property is a `SqlCommand` object, so the `SelectCommand` has all the properties of an independent `SqlCommand` object:

```
' Set the SelectCommand properties...
myDataAdapter.SelectCommand = New SqlCommand()
myDataAdapter.SelectCommand.Connection = myConnection
myDataAdapter.SelectCommand.CommandText = _
    "SELECT au_lname, au_fname, title, price " & _
    "FROM authors " & _
    "JOIN titleauthor ON authors.au_id = titleauthor.au_id " & _
    "JOIN titles ON titleauthor.title_id = titles.title_id " & _
    "ORDER BY au_lname, au_fname"
```

The first thing that we do here is to initialize the `SelectCommand` by initializing an instance of the `SqlCommand` class, and assigning it to the `SelectCommand` property.

Then we set the `Connection` property to our connection object. This property sets the connection to be used to communicate with our data store.

The `CommandText` property is then set to the SQL string that we want to execute. This property contains the SQL string or stored procedure to be executed to retrieve our data. In this case we are using a SQL string, which was explained in detail earlier.

Once all of the properties have been set, we can open our connection, fill the dataset, and then close the connection again. We open the connection by executing the `Open` method of our `SqlConnection` object:

```
' Open the database connection...
myConnection.Open()
```

We then invoke the Fill method of the SqlDataAdapter object to fill our DataSet object. In the parameters for the Fill method, we specify the DataSet object to use and the table name – we will use authors, even though we are actually retrieving data from several tables:

```
' Fill the DataSet object with data...
myDataAdapter.Fill(myDataSet, "authors")
```

Once we have filled our DataSet object with data, we need to close the database connection and we do this by invoking the Close method of the SqlConnection object:

```
' Close the database connection...
myConnection.Close()
```

Then we set some properties of the DataGrid in order to bind our data to it. The first of these properties is the DataSource property. This property sets the data source for the DataGrid telling it where to get its data:

```
' Set the DataGrid properties to bind it to our data...
grdAuthorTitles.DataSource = objDataSet
grdAuthorTitles.DataMember = "authors"
```

The DataMember property sets the table in the DataSource and here we have set it to authors, which is the table used in our DataSet object.

What happened when we ran the example was that the DataGrid control read the schema information from the DataSet object and created the correct number of columns for our data in the DataGrid control. It has also used the column names in the schema as the column names for the grid, and each column has the same default width. The DataGrid has also read the entire DataSet object and has placed the contents into the grid.

Let's take a look at some of the DataGrid properties that we can use to make this a more user-friendly display of data.

Try It Out – Changing the DataGrid Properties

1. To make our DataGrid more user-friendly we want to:

❑ Add our own column header names

❑ Adjust the width of the column that contains the book titles so that we can easily see the full title

❑ Change the color of every other row so that the data in each one stands out

❑ Make the last column in the grid (which contains the price of the books) right-aligned

We can do all this by making the following modifications to our code in the Form_Load method:

```
' Set the DataGrid properties to bind it to our data...
grdAuthorTitles.DataSource = objDataSet
grdAuthorTitles.DataMember = "authors"
```

```
' Declare objects for the DataGrid...
Dim objDataGridTableStyle As New DataGridTableStyle()
Dim objTextCol As New DataGridTextBoxColumn()

' Set the AlternatingBackColor property...
objDataGridTableStyle.AlternatingBackColor = Color.WhiteSmoke

' Set the MappingName for the DataGridTableStyle...
objDataGridTableStyle.MappingName = "authors"

' Set the MappingName for the first column...
objTextCol.MappingName = "au_lname"
' Set the new HeaderText...
objTextCol.HeaderText = "Last Name"
' Add the column to the DataGridTableStyle...
objDataGridTableStyle.GridColumnStyles.Add(objTextCol)

' Get a new reference to the DataGridTextBoxColumn...
objTextCol = New DataGridTextBoxColumn()
' Set the MappingName for the second column...
objTextCol.MappingName = "au_fname"
' Set the new HeaderText...
objTextCol.HeaderText = "First Name"
' Add the column to the DataGridTableStyle...
objDataGridTableStyle.GridColumnStyles.Add(objTextCol)

' Get a new reference to the DataGridTextBoxColumn...
objTextCol = New DataGridTextBoxColumn()
' Set the MappingName for the third column...
objTextCol.MappingName = "title"
' Set the new HeaderText...
objTextCol.HeaderText = "Book Title"
' Set the Width of the column...
objTextCol.Width = 304
' Add the column to the DataGridTableStyle...
objDataGridTableStyle.GridColumnStyles.Add(objTextCol)

' Get a new reference to the DataGridTextBoxColumn...
objTextCol = New DataGridTextBoxColumn()
' Set the MappingName for the fourth column...
objTextCol.MappingName = "price"
' Set the new HeaderText...
objTextCol.HeaderText = "Retail Price"
' Set the Alignment within the column...
objTextCol.Alignment = HorizontalAlignment.Right
' Add the column to the DataGridTableStyle...
objDataGridTableStyle.GridColumnStyles.Add(objTextCol)

' Add the DataGridTableStyle to the DataGrid...
grdAuthorTitles.TableStyles.Add(objDataGridTableStyle)

End Sub
```

2. Run your project again. You should now see results similar to the figure below. You can compare this figure to the one shown earlier and see a world of difference. It's amazing what setting a few properties will do and how it makes this a more user-friendly display:

How It Works

Since the `DataGrid` control is already populated with data at this point, we can access the table that it has drawn through the `DataGridTableStyle` class.

To start, we declare some objects that will allow us to access the table styles for the `DataGrid`. The `DataGridTableStyle` class represents the table drawn by the `DataGrid` control and allows us to customize the columns in the `DataGrid`:

```
' Declare objects for the DataGrid...
Dim objDataGridTableStyle As New DataGridTableStyle()
Dim objTextCol As New DataGridTextBoxColumn()
```

The first thing that we do here is to alternate the background color of each row of data. This helps each row of data stand out and makes it easier to see the data in each column for a single row. The `Color` structure provides a large list of color constants, as well as a few methods that can be called to generate colors:

```
' Set the AlternatingBackColor property...
objDataGridTableStyle.AlternatingBackColor = Color.WhiteSmoke
```

We now need to specify the **mapping name** that is used to map this table to a data source. This is the table name contained in our `DataSet` object:

```
' Set the MappingName for the DataGridTableStyle...
objDataGridTableStyle.MappingName = "authors"
```

Now we can set the properties for a particular column using the `DataGridTextBoxColumn` class. This class hosts a textbox control in a cell of the `DataGrid`, but it can also be used to set the column names in a `DataGrid` control, which is how we are using it here.

The first thing that we do is map the column name in our `DataSet` object to the column name in our `DataGrid` by setting the `MappingName` property. Then we set the `HeaderText` property to give the column header a more meaningful name. Finally, we apply this class to the `DataGridTableStyle` object by adding it to the `GridColumnStyles` property:

```
' Set the MappingName for the first column...
objTextCol.MappingName = "au_lname"
' Set the new HeaderText...
objTextCol.HeaderText = "Last Name"
' Add the column to the DataGridTableStyle...
objDataGridTableStyle.GridColumnStyles.Add(objTextCol)
```

We repeat the same process above for the next column but we must first reinitialize our
`DataGridTextBoxColumn` object as shown in the first line of code:

```
' Get a new reference to the DataGridTextBoxColumn...
objTextCol = New DataGridTextBoxColumn()
' Set the MappingName for the second column...
objTextCol.MappingName = "au_fname"
' Set the new HeaderText...
objTextCol.HeaderText = "First Name"
' Add the column to the DataGridTableStyle...
objDataGridTableStyle.GridColumnStyles.Add(objTextCol)
```

We repeat the same process for the third column. Here, however, we have an additional line of code.
This column contains the title of the book so we want to expand the default width of the column and
setting the `Width` property can do this. We have specified a column width of 304 here. There is no
magic process for determining the width of a column; you simply need to set it, then test your code, and
make adjustments as necessary:

```
' Get a new reference to the DataGridTextBoxColumn...
objTextCol = New DataGridTextBoxColumn()
' Set the MappingName for the third column...
objTextCol.MappingName = "title"
' Set the new HeaderText...
objTextCol.HeaderText = "Book Title"
' Set the Width of the column...
objTextCol.Width = 304
' Add the column to the DataGridTableStyle...
objDataGridTableStyle.GridColumnStyles.Add(objTextCol)
```

The last column that we set here is the column for the price of a book. Since this column contains a
money value we want to align the data in this column to the right and do so by setting the `Alignment`
property. The `HorizontalAlignment` enumeration has three values for aligning text: `Left`, `Center`,
and `Right`. We have chosen `Right` since we want our text aligned to the right of the column:

```
' Get a new reference to the DataGridTextBoxColumn...
objTextCol = New DataGridTextBoxColumn()
' Set the MappingName for the fourth column...
objTextCol.MappingName = "price"
' Set the new HeaderText...
objTextCol.HeaderText = "Retail Price"
' Set the Alignment within the column...
objTextCol.Alignment = HorizontalAlignment.Right
' Add the column to the DataGridTableStyle...
objDataGridTableStyle.GridColumnStyles.Add(objTextCol)
```

The last thing that we need to do here is to apply the style changes made in the `DataGridTableStyle` object to the actual `DataGrid` control itself. We do this by adding this object to the `TableStyles` property of the `DataGrid`:

```
' Add the DataGridTableStyle to the DataGrid...
grdAuthorTitles.TableStyles.Add(objDataGridTableStyle)
```

We have now seen how to bind the `DataSet` object to a control, in this case a `DataGrid` control. In the next *Try It Out*, we will be expanding on this knowledge by binding several controls to a `DataView` object and using the `CurrencyManager` object to navigate the data in the `DataView` object. However, before we get to that let's have a discussion on data binding and how we can bind data to simple controls such as a textbox and how to navigate the records.

Data Binding

The `DataGrid` control is a great tool for displaying all your data at one time. We can also use it for editing, deleting, and inserting rows, provided we have the logic to write changes back to the data source. However, we often want to use a control to display a single column value from one record at a time. In cases like these, we need to bind individual pieces of data to simple controls, such as a textbox, and only display a single row of data at a time. This type of data binding gives us more control over the data, but also increases the complexities of our programs, as we must write the code to bind the data to the controls and also write the code to navigate between records.

This section takes a look at what is involved in binding data to simple controls and also how to manage the data bindings.

When we talk about *simple controls* we are talking about controls that can only display one item of data at a time such as a textbox, a button, a checkbox, or a radio button. Controls such as combo boxes, listboxes, and `DataGrid` controls can contain more than one item of data and are not considered simple controls when it comes to data binding. Generally speaking non-simple controls have particular properties intended for binding to a data object, such as a `DataTable` or `Array`. When binding to simple controls, we are actually binding a particular item of data to a particular property. This is usually the `Text` property, but it does not need to be.

BindingContext and CurrencyManager

Each form has a built-in `BindingContext` object that manages the bindings of the controls on the form. Since the `BindingContext` object is already built into each form, we don't need to do anything to set it up. The `BindingContext` object manages a collection of `CurrencyManager` objects. Whenever you add a data source to a form, a new `CurrencyManager` is automatically created. This makes working with data-bound controls very convenient and simple.

The `CurrencyManager` is responsible for keeping the data bound controls in sync with their data source and with other data bound controls that use the same data source. This ensures that all controls on the form are showing data from the same record. The `CurrencyManager` manages data from a variety of objects such as the `DataSet`, `DataView`, `DataTable`, and `DataSetView` objects.

If you have multiple data sources in your form, you can create a `CurrencyManager` object and set a reference to the appropriate `CurrencyManager` object in the collection managed by the `BindingContext` object. You then have the capability to manage the data in the data bound controls.

Let's take a look at how we can do this. Using the `DataSet` object that we used in the previous example we can define and set a reference to the `CurrencyManager` that manages the data source that contains the `authors` table. The code fragment below first declares an object using the `CurrencyManager` class.

Then we set our `CurrencyManager` object to our `DataSet` object (`objDataSet`) contained in the `BindingContext` object. We use the `CType` function to return an object that is explicitly converted. The `CType` function accepts two arguments: the expression to be converted and the type to which you want to convert the expression. Since we want to convert the expression to a `CurrencyManager` object, we have specified `CurrencyManager` for the type argument:

```
Dim objCurrencyManager As CurrencyManager
objCurrencyManager = _
    CType(Me.BindingContext(objDataSet), CurrencyManager)
```

Once we have a reference to the data-source object, we can manage the position of the records using the `Position` property as shown in the example below. This example will advance the current record position in the `objDataSet` object by one record:

```
objCurrencyManager.Position += 1
```

If we wanted to move backwards one record, we would use the following code:

```
objCurrencyManager.Position -= 1
```

To move to the first record contained in the `DataSet` object, we would use the following code:

```
objCurrencyManager.Position = 0
```

The `Count` property of the `CurrencyManager` contains the number of records in the `DataSet` object managed by the `CurrencyManager`. Therefore, in order to move to the very last record, we would use the following code:

```
objCurrencyManager.Position = objCurrencyManager.Count - 1
```

Notice that we have specified the `Count` property minus one. Since the `Count` property contains the actual number of records and the `DataSet` object has a base index of zero we must subtract one from the `Count` property to get to the last record.

Binding Controls

When we want to bind a data source to a control, we set the `DataBindings` property for that control. This property accesses the `ControlBindingsCollection` class. This class manages the bindings for each control and it has many properties and methods. The method that we are really interested in here is the `Add` method.

The Add method creates a binding for the control and adds it to the ControlBindingsCollection. The Add method has three arguments and its syntax is shown below:

object.DataBindings.Add(*propertyname, datasource, datamember*)

In the syntax above, *object* represents a valid control on your form.

The *propertyname* argument represents the property of the control to be bound.

The *datasource* argument represents the data source to be bound and can be any valid object that contains data such as a DataSet, DataView, or DataTable.

The *datamember* argument represents the data field in the data source to be bound to this control.

An example of how the Add method works is shown below. In this example we are binding the column name au_fname in the objDataView object to the Text property of a textbox named txtFirstName:

```
txtFirstName.DataBindings.Add("Text", objDataView, "au_fname")
```

Sometimes, after a control has been bound, you may want to clear the bindings for that control. To do this you can use the Clear method of the ControlBindingsCollection. The Clear method clears the collection of all bindings for this control. An example of this method is shown in the code fragment below:

```
txtFirstName.DataBindings.Clear()
```

Now that we have had a look at the BindingContext, CurrencyManager, and ControlBindingsCollection objects, let's see how all of these pieces fit and work together in a practical hands-on exercise.

Binding Example

The following *Try It Out* will demonstrate not only how to use the BindingContext, CurrencyManager, and ControlBindingsCollection objects, but also how to use the DataView, SqlCommand, and SqlParameter classes.

We will be using the query from the last example as the base for our new query and will display all authors' first and last names, as well as their book titles and the prices of their books. However, where this example differs from the last one is that this will only display one record at a time.

We will use the CurrencyManager object to navigate the records in the DataView object and provide the functionality to move forwards and backwards, as well as to the first and last records.

Try It Out – Binding Simple Controls

1. Create a new Windows Application project called BindingExample.

2. Set the various form properties using the following table:

Property	Value
FormBorderStyle	FixedDialog
MaximizeBox	False
MinimizeBox	False
Size	430, 376
StartPosition	CenterScreen
Text	Binding Controls

3. We are going to add objects to the form, so that the form ends up looking like this:

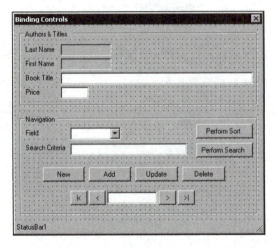

The steps that follow provide property settings to produce an exact replica of this form. However, the 'cosmetic' properties are not important – if you wish you can approximate the layout visually. It is crucial, however, to use the same control names as are used here in your own application.

4. Add a GroupBox control to the form. Set the GroupBox1 properties according to the following table:

Property	Value
Location	8, 8
Size	408, 128
Text	Authors && Titles

Note that to have an ampersand (&) displayed in the GroupBox title we have to write &&; this is because a single & causes the character following it to be underlined.

5. Using the table below, add the required controls to `GroupBox1` and set their properties:

Control	Name	Property
Label	Label1	Location = 8, 26; Size = 64, 16; Text = Last Name
Label	Label2	Location = 8, 50; Size = 64, 16; Text = First Name
Label	Label3	Location = 8, 74; Size = 56, 16; Text = Book Title
Label	Label4	Location = 8, 98; Size = 64, 16; Text = Price
TextBox	txtLastName	Location = 72, 24; Size = 88, 20; Text = *nothing*; ReadOnly = True
TextBox	txtFirstName	Location = 72, 48; Size = 88, 20; Text = *nothing*; ReadOnly = True
TextBox	txtBookTitle	Location = 72, 72; Size = 328, 20; Text = *nothing*
TextBox	txtPrice	Location = 72, 96; Size = 48, 20; Text = *nothing*

6. Now add a second `GroupBox` and set its properties according to this table:

Property	Value
Location	8, 152
Size	408, 168
Text	Navigation

7. In GroupBox2, add the following controls:

Control	Name	Property
Label	Label5	Location = 8, 23; Size = 64, 16; Text = Field
Label	Label6	Location = 8, 48; Size = 80, 16; Text = Search Criteria
ComboBox	cboField	Location = 88, 21; Size = 88, 21; DropDownStyle = DropDownList
TextBox	txtSearchCriteria	Location = 88, 48; Size = 200, 20; Text = *nothing*
TextBox	txtRecordPosition	Location = 152, 130; Size = 85, 20; Text = *nothing*; TabStop = False; TextAlign = Center
Button	btnPerformSort	Location = 304, 16; Size = 96, 24; Text = Perform Sort

Table continued on following page

Control	Name	Property
Button	btnPerformSearch	Location = 304, 48; Size = 96, 24; Text = Perform Search
Button	btnNew	Location = 40, 88; Size = 72, 24; Text = New
Button	btnAdd	Location = 120, 88; Size = 72, 24; Text = Add
Button	btnUpdate	Location = 200, 88; Size = 72, 24; Text = Update
Button	btnDelete	Location = 280, 88; Size = 72, 24; Text = Delete
Button	btnMoveFirst	Location = 88, 128; Size = 29, 24; Text = I<
Button	btnMovePrevious	Location = 120, 128; Size = 29, 24; Text = <
Button	btnMoveNext	Location = 240, 128; Size = 29, 24; Text = >
Button	btnMoveLast	Location = 272, 128; Size = 29, 24; Text = >I

8. Finally, add a StatusBar control. Leave its name as the default StatusBar1, and its default location and size.

9. When you are done, your completed form should look like the one shown in Step 30.

10. Again, we need to add references to the namespaces needed. To do this, switch to the code view and then insert the following lines of code at the very top:

```
' Import Data, OleDb, and DBNull namespaces...
Imports System.Data
Imports System.Data.SqlClient
```

11. Next we need to declare the objects that are global in scope to this form, so add the following code:

```
Public Class Form1
    Inherits System.Windows.Forms.Form

    ' Declare objects...
    Dim myConnection As SqlConnection = New _
        SqlConnection("server=(local);database=pubs;" & _
        "uid=sa;pwd=vbdotnet;")
    Dim myAdapter As SqlDataAdapter = New SqlDataAdapter( _
        "SELECT authors.au_id, au_lname, au_fname, " & _
        "titles.title_id, title, price " & _
        "FROM authors " & _
        "JOIN titleauthor ON authors.au_id = titleauthor.au_id " & _
        "JOIN titles ON titleauthor.title_id = titles.title_id " & _
        "ORDER BY au_lname, au_fname", myConnection)
    Dim myDS As DataSet
    Dim myDV As DataView
    Dim myCurrencyManager As CurrencyManager
```

> Be sure to update the connection string to match your settings for the **Uid** and **Pwd**, and also set the **Server** to the machine where SQL Server is running if it is not your local machine.

12. The first procedure that we need to create is the `FillDataSetAndView` procedure. This procedure, along with the following ones, will be called in our initialization code. Add the following code to the form's class, just below our object declarations:

```
Private Sub FillDataSetAndView()
    ' Initialize a new instance of the DataSet object...
    myDS = New DataSet()

    ' Fill the DataSet object with data...
    myAdapter.Fill(myDS, "authors")

    ' Set the DataView object to the DataSet object...
    myDV = New DataView(myDS.Tables("authors"))

    ' Set our CurrencyManager object to the DataView object...
    myCurrencyManager = CType(Me.BindingContext(myDV), CurrencyManager)
End Sub
```

13. The next procedure that we need to create is one that will actually bind the controls on our form to our `DataView` object:

```
Private Sub BindFields()
    ' Clear any previous bindings...
    txtLastName.DataBindings.Clear()
    txtFirstName.DataBindings.Clear()
    txtBookTitle.DataBindings.Clear()
    txtPrice.DataBindings.Clear()

    ' Add new bindings to the DataView object...
    txtLastName.DataBindings.Add("Text", myDV, "au_lname")
    txtFirstName.DataBindings.Add("Text", myDV, "au_fname")
    txtBookTitle.DataBindings.Add("Text", myDV, "title")
    txtPrice.DataBindings.Add("Text", myDV, "price")

    ' Display a ready status...
    StatusBar1.Text = "Ready"
End Sub
```

14. Now we need a procedure that will display the current record position on our form:

```
Private Sub ShowPosition()
    'Always format the number in the txtPrice field to include cents
    Try
        txtPrice.Text = FormatNumber(txtPrice.Text, 2, TriState.True)
        Catch e As System.Exception
```

```
        txtPrice.Text = "0"
        txtPrice.Text = FormatNumber(txtPrice.Text, 2, TriState.True)
    End Try
    ' Display the current position and the number of records
    txtRecordPosition.Text = myCurrencyManager.Position + 1 & _
    " of " & myCurrencyManager.Count()
End Sub
```

15. We've added some powerful procedures to our form. But at the moment there is no code to call them. We want these procedures, as well as some other code, to execute every time the form loads. So return to the form designer, double-click the form designer, and add the following to the `Form_Load` method (note that you must click on an area outside of the `GroupBox` controls):

```
Private Sub Form1_Load(ByVal sender As System.Object, _
                             ByVal e As System.EventArgs) Handles MyBase.Load
    ' Add items to the combo box...
    cboField.Items.Add("Last Name")
    cboField.Items.Add("First Name")
    cboField.Items.Add("Book Title")
    cboField.Items.Add("Price")

    ' Make the first item selected...
    cboField.SelectedIndex = 0

    ' Fill the DataSet and bind the fields...
    FillDataSetAndView()
    BindFields()

    ' Show the current record position...
    ShowPosition()
End Sub
```

16. Next, we'll add the code for our navigation buttons. You will need to switch back and forth between the design and code views, double-clicking each button and then adding the code. Let's add the code to the procedure for the `btnMoveFirst` button first:

```
Private Sub btnMoveFirst_Click(ByVal sender As Object, _
            ByVal e As System.EventArgs) Handles btnMoveFirst.Click
    ' Set the record position to the first record...
    myCurrencyManager.Position = 0

    ' Show the current record position...
    ShowPosition()
End Sub
```

17. Let's add code to the `btnMovePrevious` button next:

```
Private Sub btnMovePrevious_Click(ByVal sender As Object, _
            ByVal e As System.EventArgs) Handles btnMovePrevious.Click
```

```
      ' Move to the previous record...
      myCurrencyManager.Position -= 1

      ' Show the current record position...
      ShowPosition()
End Sub
```

18. The next procedure that we want to add code to is the `btnMoveNext` procedure:

```
Private Sub btnMoveNext_Click(ByVal sender As Object, _
          ByVal e As System.EventArgs) Handles btnMoveNext.Click
      ' Move to the next record...
      myCurrencyManager.Position += 1

      ' Show the current record position...
      ShowPosition()
End Sub
```

19. The final navigation procedure that we need to code is the `btnMoveLast` procedure:

```
Private Sub btnMoveLast_Click(ByVal sender As Object, _
          ByVal e As System.EventArgs) Handles btnMoveLast.Click
      ' Set the record position to the last record...
      myCurrencyManager.Position = myCurrencyManager.Count - 1

      ' Show the current record position...
      ShowPosition()
End Sub
```

20. At this point, you have entered a lot of code and are probably anxious to see the results of your work. Let's run the project to see how our `DataView` object gets bound to the controls on the form and to see the `CurrencyManager` object at work as we navigate through the records.

Once your form displays you should see results similar to the following figure. The only buttons that work are the navigation buttons, which change the current record position. Test your form by navigating to the next and previous records, and moving to the last record and the first record. Each time you move to a new record, the textbox between the navigation buttons will be updated to display the current record.

Once on the first record you can try to move to the previous record but nothing will happen because you are already on the first record. Likewise, you can move to the last record and try to navigate to the next record and nothing will happen because you are already on the last record.

If you hover your mouse pointer over the navigation buttons, you will see a tool tip indicating what each button is for. This just provides a nice user interface for your users.

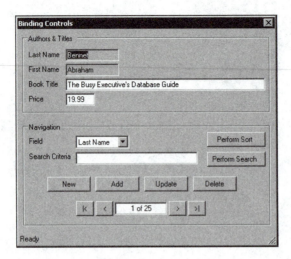

> It should be noted that error handling has been omitted from the exercise to preserve
> space. You should always add the appropriate error handling to your code. Please
> review Chapter 11 for error-handling techniques.

How It Works – Namespaces and Object Declaration

As usual we imported the `System.Data` and `System.Data.SqlClient` namespaces. Next, we
declared the objects on our form. The first three objects should be familiar to you as we used them in
our last project.

Let's just take a closer look at the initialization of the `SqlDataAdapter` object. We use a constructor
that initializes this object with a string value for the `SelectCommand` property and an object that
represents a connection to the database. This constructor saves us from writing code to manipulate the
`SqlDataAdapter` properties – it's already set up.

The `SELECT` statement that we are using here is basically the same as in the previous project, except
that we have added a couple more columns in the **select list** (the list of columns directly following the
word `SELECT`).

The `au_id` column in the select list has been prefixed with the table name `authors`, because this
column also exists in the `titleauthor` table. Therefore, we must tell the database which table to get
the data from for this column. This is the same for the `title_id` column, except that this column exists
in the `titles` and `titleauthor` tables:

```
' Initialize a new instance of the OleDbDataAdapter object...
myAdapter = New OleDbDataAdapter( _
    "SELECT authors.au_id, au_lname, au_fname, " & _
    "titles.title_id, title, price " & _
    "FROM authors " & _
    "JOIN titleauthor ON authors.au_id = titleauthor.au_id " & _
    "JOIN titles ON titleauthor.title_id = titles.title_id " & _
    "ORDER BY au_lname, au_fname", myConnection)
```

The last two objects are new but we discussed them in the section on binding. We will use the DataView to customize our view of the records returned from the database, and stored in the DataSet. The CurrencyManager object will be used to control the movement of our bound data as we saw in the previous section.

How It Works – FillDataSetAndView

The first procedure we created was the FillDataSetAndView procedure. This procedure will be called several times throughout our code and will get the latest data from the database and populate our DataView object.

The first thing we need to do is initialize a new instance of the DataSet object. We do this here because this procedure might be called more than once during the lifetime of the form. If it is, we do not want to add new records to the records already in the DataSet – we always want to start afresh:

```
Private Sub FillDataSetAndView()
    ' Initialize a new instance of the DataSet object...
    myDS = New DataSet()
```

Next we execute the Fill method on myAdapter to populate the myDS object. Then we specify that our DataView object will be viewing data from the authors table in the DataSet object. Remember that the DataView object allows us to sort, search, and navigate through the records in the DataSet:

```
    ' Fill the DataSet object with data...
    myAdapter.Fill(myDS, "authors")

    ' Set the DataView object to the DataSet object...
    myDV = New DataView(myDS.Tables("authors"))
```

Once we have initialized our DataView object, we want to initialize our CurrencyManager object. Remember that the BindingContext object is built into every Windows form and contains a collection of CurrencyManagers. The collection contains the available data sources, and we choose the DataView object:

```
    ' Set our CurrencyManager object to the DataView object...
    myCurrencyManager = _
        CType(Me.BindingContext(myDV), CurrencyManager)
```

How It Works – BindFields

The next procedure that we created (BindFields) actually bound the controls on our form to our DataView object. This procedure first cleared any previous bindings for the controls and then set them to our DataView object.

> It is important to clear the bindings first as, once we modify the **DataView** object by adding, updating, or deleting a row of data, the **DataView** object will only show the changed data. Therefore, after we update the database with our changes, we must repopulate our **DataView** object and rebind our controls. If we didn't do this then what data is actually in the database and what data is in the **DataView** may not be the same.

Using the `DataBindings` property of the controls on our form, we executed the `Clear` method of the `ControlBindingsCollection` class to remove the bindings from them. Notice that the controls that we have bound are all the textboxes on our form that will contain data from the `DataView` object:

```
Private Sub BindFields()
    ' Clear any previous bindings to the DataView object...
    txtLastName.DataBindings.Clear()
    txtFirstName.DataBindings.Clear()
    txtBookTitle.DataBindings.Clear()
    txtPrice.DataBindings.Clear()
```

Once we have cleared the previous bindings, we can set the new bindings back to the same data source, our `DataView` object. We do this by executing the `Add` method of the `ControlBindingsCollection` object returned by the `DataBindings` property. The `Add` method has three arguments as can be seen in the code below.

The first argument is the *propertyname* and specifies the property of the control to be bound. Since we want to bind our data to the `Text` property of the textboxes, we have specified `"Text"` for this argument.

The next argument is the *datasource* argument and specifies the data source to be bound. Remember that this can be any valid object that contains data such as a `DataSet`, `DataView`, or `DataTable` object. In our case we are using a `DataView` object.

The last argument specifies the *datamember*. This is the data field in the data source that contains the data to be bound to this control. Notice that we have specified the various column names from our `SELECT` statement that we executed in the previous procedure:

```
    ' Add new bindings to the DataView object...
    txtLastName.DataBindings.Add("Text", myDV, "au_lname")
    txtFirstName.DataBindings.Add("Text", myDV, "au_fname")
    txtBookTitle.DataBindings.Add("Text", myDV, "title")
    txtPrice.DataBindings.Add("Text", myDV, "price")
```

The last thing that we want to do in this procedure is to set a message in the status bar using the `Text` property of `StatusBar1`:

```
    ' Display a ready status...
    StatusBar1.Text = "Ready"
End Sub
```

How It Works – ShowPosition

The next procedure that we need to code will display the current record position on our form. The `CurrencyManager` object keeps track of the current record position within the `DataView` object.

The `price` column in the `titles` table in pubs is defined as a `Currency` data type. Therefore, if a book is priced at 40.00 dollars the number that we get is `40` – the decimal portion is dropped. The `ShowPosition` procedure seems like a good place to format the data in the `txtPrice` textbox, as this procedure is called whenever we move to a new record:

```
Private Sub ShowPosition()
'Always format the number in the txtPrice field to include cents
    Try
        txtPrice.Text = FormatNumber(txtPrice.Text, 2, TriState.True)
    Catch e As System.Exception
        txtPrice.Text = "0"
        txtPrice.Text = FormatNumber(txtPrice.Text, 2, TriState.True)
    End Try

    ' Display the current position and the number of records
    txtRecordPosition.Text = myCurrencyManager.Position + 1 & _
                                    " of " & myCurrencyManager.Count()
End Sub
```

This part of the function is enclosed in a `Try...Catch` block in case the `txtPrice` is empty. If `txtPrice` is empty the `FormatNumber` function will throw an exception and defaults the price to 0. The second line of code in this procedure uses the `FormatNumber` function to format the price in the `txtPrice` textbox. This function accepts the numeric data to be formatted as the first argument and the number of decimal places that should be included as the second argument. The third argument specifies whether or not a leading zero should be included if the price is zero – we've specified that we want a leading zero.

The last line of code displays the current record position and the total number of records that we have. Using the `Position` property of the `CurrencyManager` object, we can determine which record we are on. The `Position` property uses a zero-based index so the first record is always 0. Therefore, we have specified the `Position` property plus 1, in order to display the true number.

The `CurrencyManager` class's `Count` property returns the actual number of items in the list and we are using this property to display the total number of records in the `DataView` object.

How It Works – Form_Load

Now that we've looked at the code for the main procedures, we need to go back and look at our initialization code.

We have a combo box on our form that will be used when sorting or searching for data (as we'll see later). This combo box needs be populated with data representing the columns in the `DataView` object. We specify the `Add` method of the `Items` property of the combo box to add items to it. Here we are specifying text that represents the columns in the `DataView` object in the same order that they appear in the `DataView` object:

```
'Add any initialization after the InitializeComponent() call

' Add items to the combo box...
cboField.Items.Add("Last Name")
cboField.Items.Add("First Name")
cboField.Items.Add("Book Title")
cboField.Items.Add("Price")
```

Once we have loaded all of the items into our combo box, we want to select the first item. We do this by setting the `SelectedIndex` property to 0. The `SelectedIndex` property is zero-based so the first item in the list is item 0.

```
' Make the first item selected...
cboField.SelectedIndex = 0
```

Next, we call the `FillDataSetAndView` procedure to retrieve the data, and then call the `BindFields` procedure to bind the controls on our form to our `DataView` object. Finally, we call the `ShowPosition` procedure to display the current record position and the total number of records contained in our `DataView` object:

```
' Fill the DataSet and bind the fields...
FillDataSetAndView()
BindFields()

' Show the current record position...
ShowPosition()
```

How It Works – btnMoveFirst_Click

The procedure for the `btnMoveFirst` button causes the first record in the `DataView` object to be displayed. This is accomplished using the `Position` property of the `CurrencyManager` object. Here we set the `Position` property to 0 indicating that the `CurrencyManager` should move to the first record:

```
' Set the record position to the first record...
myCurrencyManager.Position = 0
```

Because our controls are bound to the `DataView` object they will always stay in sync with the current record in the `DataView` object and display the appropriate data.

Once we have repositioned the current record, we need to call the `ShowPosition` procedure to update the display of the current record on our form:

```
' Show the current record position...
ShowPosition()
```

How It Works – btnMovePrevious_Click

Next, we added the code for the `btnMovePrevious` button. We move to the prior record by subtracting 1 from the `Position` property. The `CurrencyManager` object will automatically detect and handle the beginning position of the `DataView` object. It will not let us move to a position prior to the first record – it will just quietly keep its position at 0:

```
' Move to the previous record...
myCurrencyManager.Position -= 1
```

Again, after we have repositioned the current record being displayed, we need to call the `ShowPosition` procedure to display the current position on the form.

How It Works – btnMoveNext_Click

In the btnMoveNext procedure, we want to increment the Position property by 1. Again, the CurrencyManager will automatically detect the last record in the DataView object and will not let us move past it:

```
' Move to the next record...
myCurrencyManager.Position += 1
```

We call the ShowPosition procedure to display the current record position.

How It Works – btnMoveLast_Click

When the btnMoveLast procedure is called, we want to move to the last record in the DataView object. We do this by setting the Position property equal to the Count property minus one. Then we call the ShowPosition procedure to display the current record:

```
' Set the record position to the last record...
myCurrencyManager.Position = myCurrencyManager.Count - 1

' Show the current record position...
ShowPosition()
```

Now that we have built the navigation, let's move on to add sorting functionality to this project.

Try It Out – Including Sorting Functionality

1. Double-click on the **Perform Sort** button on the form in design mode to have the empty procedure added to the form class. Insert the following code in the btnPerformSort_Click event procedure:

```
Private Sub btnPerformSort_Click(ByVal sender As Object, _
        ByVal e As System.EventArgs) Handles btnPerformSort.Click
    ' Determine the appropriate item selected and set the
    ' Sort property of the DataView object...
    Select Case cboField.SelectedIndex
        Case 0   'Last Name
            myDV.Sort = "au_lname"
        Case 1   'First Name
            myDV.Sort = "au_fname"
        Case 2   'Book Title
            myDV.Sort = "title"
        Case 3   'Price
            myDV.Sort = "price"
    End Select

    ' Call the click event for the MoveFirst button...
    btnMoveFirst_Click(Nothing, Nothing)

    ' Display a message that the records have been sorted...
    StatusBar1.Text = "Records Sorted"
End Sub
```

2. Let's test out this newest functionality that we have added to our project by running it – click the start button to compile and run it. Select a column to sort on and then click the **Perform Sort** button. You should see the data sorted by the column that you have chosen. The figure below shows the data sorted by book price:

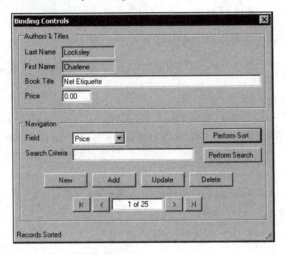

How It Works

The first thing that we want to do in this procedure is to determine which field we should sort on. This information is contained in the `cboField` combo box.

```
' Determine the appropriate item selected and set the
' Sort property of the DataView object...
Select Case cboField.SelectedIndex
    Case 0  'Last Name
        myDV.Sort = "au_lname"
    Case 1  'First Name
        myDV.Sort = "au_fname"
    Case 2  'Book Title
        myDV.Sort = "title"
    Case 3  'Price
        myDV.Sort = "price"
End Select
```

Using a `Select Case` statement to examine the `SelectedIndex` property of the combo box, we can determine which field the user has chosen. Once we have determined the correct entry in the combo box, we can set the `Sort` property of the `DataView` object using the column name of the column that we want sorted. Once the `Sort` property has been set, the data will be sorted.

Once the data has been sorted we want to move to the first record and there are a couple of ways we can do this. We could set the `Position` property of the `CurrencyManager` object and then call the `ShowPosition` procedure, or we can simply call the `btnMoveFirst_Click` procedure, passing it `Nothing` for both arguments. This is the procedure that would be executed had we actually clicked the **Move First** button on the form.

The btnMoveFirst_Click procedure has two arguments, ByVal sender As Object and ByVal e As System.EventArgs. Since these arguments are required we need to pass something to them, so we pass the Nothing keyword. The Nothing keyword is used to disassociate an object variable from an object. Thus by using the Nothing keyword we satisfy the requirement of passing an argument to the procedure, but have not passed any actual value:

```
' Call the click event for the MoveFirst button...
btnMoveFirst_Click(Nothing, Nothing)
```

After the first record has been displayed, we want to display a message in the status bar indicating that the records have been sorted. We do this by setting the Text property of the status bar as we have done before.

Note that another way would have been to have had a procedure called MoveFirst, and called that from here *and* from the btnMoveFirst_Click procedure. Some developers would opt for this because passing Nothing to a procedure is a bit messy. We have chosen to accept this messiness in order to avoid having lots of procedures.

Now let's take a look at what's involved in searching for a record.

Try It Out – Including Searching Functionality

1. Double-click the **Perform Search** button and add the following to the btnPerformSearch_Click event procedure:

```
Private Sub btnPerformSearch_Click(ByVal sender As Object, _
        ByVal e As System.EventArgs) Handles btnPerformSearch.Click
    ' Declare local variables...
    Dim intPosition As Integer

    ' Determine the appropriate item selected and set the
    ' Sort property of the DataView object...
    Select Case cboField.SelectedIndex
        Case 0  'Last Name
            myDV.Sort = "au_lname"
        Case 1  'First Name
            myDV.Sort = "au_fname"
        Case 2  'Book Title
            myDV.Sort = "title"
        Case 3  'Price
            myDV.Sort = "price"
    End Select

    ' If the search field is not price then...
    If cboField.SelectedIndex < 3 Then
        ' Find the last name, first name, or title...
        intPosition = myDV.Find(txtSearchCriteria.Text)
    Else
        ' otherwise find the price...
        intPosition = myDV.Find(CDec(txtSearchCriteria.Text))
    End If
```

```
    If intPosition = -1 Then
        ' Display a message that the record was not found...
        StatusBar1.Text = "Record Not Found"
    Else
        ' Otherwise display a message that the record was
        ' found and reposition the CurrencyManager to that
        ' record...
        StatusBar1.Text = "Record Found"
        myCurrencyManager.Position = intPosition
    End If

    ' Show the current record position...
    ShowPosition()
End Sub
```

2. Now let's test the searching functionality that we have added. Run the project and select a field in the Field combo box that you want to search on and then enter the search criteria in the Search Criteria textbox. Finally, click the Perform Search button.

If a match is found you will see the first matched record displayed along with a message in the status bar indicating that the record was found. If no record was found you will see a message in the status bar indicating the record was not found.

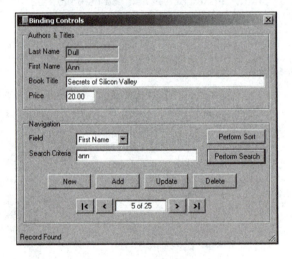

How It Works

This is a little more involved as there are multiple conditions that we must test for and handle such as a record that was not found.

The first thing that we do in this procedure is to declare a variable that will receive the record position of the record that has been found or not found.

```
    ' Declare local variables...
    Dim intPosition As Integer
```

Next, we sort the data based on the column that is used in the search. The `Find` method will search for data in the sort key. Therefore, by setting the `Sort` property, the column that is sorted on thereby becomes the sort key in the `DataView` object. We use a `Select Case` statement just as we did in the previous procedure:

```
' Determine the appropriate item selected and set the
' Sort property of the DataView object...
Select Case cboField.SelectedIndex
    Case 0   'Last Name
        myDV.Sort = "au_lname"
    Case 1   'First Name
        myDV.Sort = "au_fname"
    Case 2   'Book Title
        myDV.Sort = "title"
    Case 3   'Price
        myDV.Sort = "price"
End Select
```

The columns for the authors' first and last names as well as the column for the book titles all contain text data. However, the column for the book price contains data that is in a currency format. Therefore, we need to determine which column we are searching on, and if that column is the price column, we need to format the data in the `txtSearchCriteria` textbox to a decimal value.

Again, we use the `SelectedIndex` property of the `cboField` combo box to determine which item has been selected. If the `SelectedIndex` property is less than 3 then we know that we want to search on a column that contains text data.

We then set the `intPosition` variable to the results returned by the `Find` method of the `DataView` object. The `Find` method accepts the data to search for as the only argument. Here we are passing it the data contained in the `Text` property of the `txtSearchCriteria` textbox.

If the `SelectedIndex` equals 3 we are searching for a book with a specific price and this requires us to convert the value contained in the `txtSearchCriteria` textbox to a decimal value. The `CDec` function accepts a string value that contains numbers and returns a decimal value. This value is then used as the search criteria by the `Find` method.

```
' If the search field is not price then...
If cboField.SelectedIndex < 3 Then
    ' Find the last name, first name or title...
    intPosition = myDV.Find(txtSearchCriteria.Text)
Else
    ' otherwise find the price...
    intPosition = myDV.Find(CDec(txtSearchCriteria.Text))
End If
```

Once we have executed the `Find` method of the `DataView` object, we need to check the value contained in the `intPosition` variable. If this variable contains a value of -1 then no match was found. Any value other than -1 points to the record position of the record that contains the data.

So, if the value in this variable is −1 we want to display a message in the status bar that says that no record was found.

If the value is greater than −1 we want to display a message that the record was found and position the `DataView` object to that record using the `Position` property of the `CurrencyManager object`:

```
StatusBar1.Text = "Record Found"
myCurrencyManager.Position = intPosition
```

> It is worth noting that the **Find** method of the **DataView** object performs a search looking for an exact match of characters. There is no "wildcard" search method here so we must enter the entire text string that we want to search for. The case, however, does *not* matter, so the name 'Bennet' is the same as 'bennet' and we do not need to be concerned with entering proper case when we enter our search criteria.

The last thing that we want to do in this procedure is to show the current record position, which we do by calling the `ShowPosition` procedure.

Now all that is left is to add the functionality to add, update, and delete records. Let's take a look at what is required to add a record first.

Try It Out – Adding Records

1. First, we need to add just two lines of code to the procedure for the New button, as shown below:

```
Private Sub btnNew_Click(ByVal sender As Object, _
            ByVal e As System.EventArgs) Handles btnNew.Click
    ' Clear the book title and price fields...
    txtBookTitle.Text = ""
    txtPrice.Text = ""
End Sub
```

2. The next procedure that we want to add code to is the `btnAdd_Click` procedure. This procedure will be responsible for adding a new record. This procedure has the largest amount of code by far of any of the procedures we have coded or will code in this project. The reason for this is the relationship of book titles to authors and the primary key used for book titles:

```
Private Sub btnAdd_Click(ByVal sender As Object, _
            ByVal e As System.EventArgs) Handles btnAdd.Click
    ' Declare local variables and objects...
    Dim intPosition As Integer, intMaxID As Integer
    Dim strID As String
    Dim objCommand As SqlCommand = New SqlCommand()

    ' Save the current record position...
    intPosition = myCurrencyManager.Position
```

```vb
' Create a new SqlCommand object...
Dim maxIdCommand As SqlCommand = New SqlCommand _
    ("SELECT MAX(title_id) AS MaxID " & _
    "FROM titles WHERE title_id LIKE 'DM%'", myConnection)

' Open the connection, execute the command
myConnection.Open()
Dim maxId As Object = maxIdCommand.ExecuteScalar()

' If the MaxID column is null...
If maxId Is System.DBNull.Value Then
    ' Set a default value of 1000...
    intMaxID = 1000
Else
    ' otherwise set the strID variable to the value in MaxID...
    strID = CStr(maxId)
    ' Get the integer part of the string...
    intMaxID = CInt(strID.Remove(0, 2))
    ' Increment the value...
    intMaxID += 1
End If

' Finally, set the new ID...
strID = "DM" & intMaxID

' Set the SqlCommand object properties...
objCommand.Connection = myConnection
objCommand.CommandText = "INSERT INTO titles " & _
    "(title_id, title, type, price, pubdate) " & _
    "VALUES(@title_id,@title,@type,@price,@pubdate);" & _
    "INSERT INTO titleauthor (au_id, title_id) VALUES(@au_id,@title_id)"

' Add parameters for the placeholders in the SQL in the
' CommandText property...

' Parameter for the title_id column...
objCommand.Parameters.Add("@title_id", strID)

' Parameter for the title column...
objCommand.Parameters.Add("@title", txtBookTitle.Text)

' Parameter for the price column...
objCommand.Parameters.Add("@price", txtPrice.Text).DbType _
                        = DbType.Currency

' Parameter for the au_id column...
objCommand.Parameters.Add _
            ("@au_id", BindingContext(myDV).Current("au_id"))

' Parameter for the type column
objCommand.Parameters.Add("@type", "Demo")
```

```
' Parameter for the pubdate column
objCommand.Parameters.Add("@pubdate", Date.Now)

' Execute the SqlCommand object to insert the new data...
Try
    objCommand.ExecuteNonQuery()
Catch err As SqlException
    MessageBox.Show(err.Message)
End Try

' Close the connection...
myConnection.Close()

' Fill the dataset and bind the fields...
FillDataSetAndView()
BindFields()

' Set the record position to the one that we saved...
myCurrencyManager.Position = intPosition

' Show the current record position...
ShowPosition()

' Display a message that the record was added...
StatusBar1.Text = "Record Added"
End Sub
```

3. Run your project. Find an author that you want to add a new title for and then click the New button. The Book Title and Price fields will be cleared and you are ready to enter new data to be added. Take note of the number of records that are in the DataView (25).

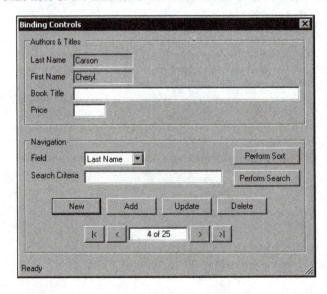

4. Now enter a title and price for the new book and click on the **Add** button. You will see a message in the status bar that the record has been added and you will also see that the number of records has changed (to 26):

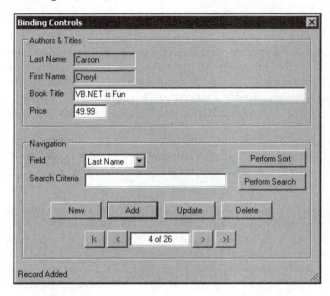

Now that you have added a record, let's examine what we actually did.

How It Works

Remember that the only data that we can add is a new book title and its price. So instead of selecting the data in each of these fields, deleting it, and then entering the new data, we want to be able to simply click the New button. The job of the New button is to clear the book title and price fields for us. All we need to do here is to set the Text properties of these textboxes to an empty string as we have done here:

```
' Clear the book title and price fields...
txtBookTitle.Text = ""
txtPrice.Text = ""
```

The primary key used in the titles table is not the database's Identity column. Identity columns use a sequential number and automatically increment the number for you when a new row is inserted. Instead of an Identity column, the primary key is made up of a category prefix and a sequential number. This means that we must first determine the maximum number used in a category and then increment that number by 1 and use the new number and category prefix for the new key. We'll see all of this in just a moment.

The first thing that we want to do in the btnAdd_Click event procedure is declare our local variables and objects that will be used here. The intPosition variable will be used to save the current record position and the intMaxID variable will be used to set and increment the maximum sequential number for a category. The strID will be used to store the primary key from the authors table and to set the new key for the authors table. Finally, the objCommand object will be used to build a query to insert a new record into the titleauthor and titles tables.

Before we do anything, we want to save the position of the current record that we are on. This will allow us to go back to this record once we reload the `DataView` object, which will contain the new record that we will add in this procedure:

```
intPosition = myCurrencyManager.Position
```

We need to execute a command on the database in order to work out what ID to give our new title. We use a `SqlCommand` object to do this. We pass in a SQL string and the connection that we use throughout our program. This SQL string will select the maximum value in the `title_id` column, where the `title_id` value begins with the prefix of `DM`.

> There is no category for demo so we will add all of the test records under this category and will use the category prefix of **DM**. This will allow you to quickly identify the records that you have inserted just in case you want to manually get rid of them later.

Because the function we are using in the `SELECT` statement, `MAX`, is an **aggregate function** (meaning that it is a function that works on groups of data), the data that is returned will be returned without a column name. Therefore, we use the `AS` keyword in the `SELECT` statement and tell SQL Server to assign a column name to the value, in this case `MaxID`. We use a `LIKE` clause in the `SELECT` statement to tell SQL Server to search for all values that begin with `DM`:

```
Dim maxIdCommand As SqlCommand = New SqlCommand( _
    "SELECT MAX(title_id) AS MaxID " & _
    "FROM titles WHERE title_id LIKE 'DM%'", myConnection)
```

This sets up our command object but doesn't execute it. To execute it we need to open the connection, and then call one of the `SqlCommand` execute methods. In this case we use `ExecuteScalar`:

```
' Open the connection, execute the command
myConnection.Open()
Dim maxId As Object = maxIdCommand.ExecuteScalar()
```

`ExecuteScalar` is a very useful method when we have a database command that returns a single value. Other commands we've used so far have returned a whole table of values (we have used these as the `SelectCommand` of a data adapter), or no values at all (we have executed these with `ExecuteNonQuery`). In this case we are only interested in one number, so we can use `ExecuteScalar`. This returns the first column of the first row in the result set. In this case there is only one column and one row, so that is what we get.

We want to check for a `Null` value returned from the command, so we compare the resulting `Object` against the `Value` property of the `DBNull` class:

```
' If the MaxID column is null...
If maxId Is System.DBNull.Value Then
```

If the expression evaluates to `True`, then we have no primary key in the `titles` table that begins with `DM` so we set the initial value of the `intMaxID` variable to a value of `1000`. We have chosen `1000` because all of the other primary keys contain a numeric value of less than `1000`:

```
' Set a default value of 1000...
intMaxID = 1000
```

If the column value evaluates to `False`, then we have at least one primary key in the `titles` table that begins with `DM`. In this case we need to obtain the integer portion of this ID, in order to work out what integer to use for our ID. To do this, we must convert our `maxId` Object to a `String`:

```
Else
    ' otherwise set the strID variable to the value in MaxID...
    strID = CStr(maxId)
```

Then we can extract the integer portion of the key by using the `Remove` method of the string variable, `strID`. The `Remove` method removes the specified number of characters from a string. You specify the offset at which to begin removing characters and the number of characters to be removed. This method returns a new string with the removed characters. In this line of code, we are removing the prefix of `DM` from the string so that all we end up with is the integer portion of the string. We then use the `CInt` function to convert the string value that contains a number to an `Integer` value, which we place in the `intMaxID` variable. Finally, we increment it by one to give us the integer portion of the ID that we will use:

```
    ' Get the integer part of the string...
    intMaxID = CInt(strID.Remove(0, 2))
    ' Increment the value...
    intMaxID += 1
End If
```

Now we've got the integer part, we build a new primary key in the `strID` variable by concatenating the numeric value contained in the `intMaxID` variable with the prefix `DM`:

```
    ' Finally, set the new ID...
    strID = "DM" & intMaxID
```

Next, we build the SQL statements to insert a new row of data into the `titles` and `titleauthor` tables. If you look closely, there are two separate `INSERT` statements in the `CommandText` property of our `objCommand` object. The two separate `INSERT` statements are separated by a semicolon, which allows us to concatenate multiple SQL statements. The SQL statements that we built use placeholders that will get filled in by the `SqlParameter` objects.

> Note that because of the relationship between the `titles` table and the `authors` table, we must first insert a new title for an author into the `titles` table and then insert the relationship between the title and the author in the `titleauthor` table. You'll notice that our **INSERT** statements are specifying the columns that we want to insert data into and then specify the values that are to be inserted, some of which are represented by placeholders.

We have seen the properties of the `SqlCommand` object before. This time, however, we are using properties rather than the constructor. We set the `Connection` property to a `SqlConnection` object and then set the `CommandText` property to the SQL string that we want executed, in this case, the two separate `INSERT` statements:

```
objCommand.Connection = myConnection
objCommand.CommandText = "INSERT INTO titles " & _
    "(title_id, title, type, price, pubdate) " & _
    "VALUES(@title_id,@title,@type,@price,@pubdate);" & _
    "INSERT INTO titleauthor (au_id, title_id) VALUES(@au_id,@title_id)"
```

We then add entries to the `Parameters` collection property for each of our placeholders in the SQL statements above. Where the same parameter name is used twice in the `CommandText` property – as `title_id` is here – we only need one `SqlParameter` object:

```
' Add parameters for the placeholders in the SQL in the
' CommandText property...

' Parameter for the title_id column...
objCommand.Parameters.Add("@title_id", strID)

' Parameter for the title column...
objCommand.Parameters.Add("@title", txtBookTitle.Text)

' Parameter for the price column...
objCommand.Parameters.Add _
                    ("@price", txtPrice.Text).DbType = DbType.Currency

' Parameter for the au_id column...
objCommand.Parameters.Add("@au_id", BindingContext(myDV).Current("au_id"))

' Parameter for the type column
objCommand.Parameters.Add("@type", "Demo")

' Parameter for the pubdate column
objCommand.Parameters.Add("@pubdate", Date.Now)
```

For the `@title_id` parameter, we use the `strID` variable that we created and set earlier in this method. For the `@title` parameter, we use the text in the **Book Title** textbox entered by the user. For the `@price` parameter we use the text in the **Price** textbox. However, the `Text` property is a `String`. SQL Server cannot automatically convert between a `String` and a `Currency` data type, so we particularly specify that the parameter is of the `DbType.Currency` data type.

For `@au_id` we need to use the ID of the currently selected author. There are no bound controls for the au_id column, so we need to use some code to obtain the value. Let's take a close look at that particular statement:

```
BindingContext(myDV).Current("au_id")
```

Here we are getting the form's `BindingContext` for the `myDV` data source, which is the one we're using for all of our bound controls. When we're accessing a `DataView` through `BindingContext`, the `Current` property returns a `DataRowView` object. This object represents the view of the particular row that the user is currently looking at. We are then able to select a particular column from that row, thus giving us a specific value. Here, of course, we are obtaining the `au_id` column.

The remaining parameters mark that the new record is a `Demo` record, and timestamp the record with the current date and time:

```
' Parameter for the type column
objCommand.Parameters.Add("@type", "Demo")

' Parameter for the pubdate column
objCommand.Parameters.Add("@pubdate", Date.Now)
```

Once we have added all of our parameters, we want to execute the command using the `ExecuteNonQuery` method. This will cause our SQL statements to be executed and the data inserted. Once our new data has been inserted we close the database connection.

This is the one spot in your code that is really subject to failure so we have included very basic error handling here. We execute our `INSERT` statement inside the `Try` block of our error handler and if an error is encountered, the code in the `Catch` block will be executed. The code there simply displays a message box that shows the error encountered:

```
' Execute the SqlCommand object to insert the new data...
Try
    objCommand.ExecuteNonQuery()
Catch err As SqlException
    MessageBox.Show(err.Message)
Finally
    ' Close the connection...
    myConnection.Close()
End Try
```

Then the `FillDataSetAndView` and `BindFields` procedures are called to reload the `DataView` object, and to clear and rebind our controls. This ensures that we get all new data added, updated, or deleted from the tables in SQL Server.

We then reposition the `DataView` object back to the record that was being displayed by setting the `Position` property of the `CurrencyManager` using the `intPosition` variable. This variable was set using the current record position at the beginning of this procedure.

The position that we set here is only approximate. It does not take into account any records that have been inserted or deleted by someone else or us. It is possible that the title we just inserted for a specific author could be returned prior to the title that was displayed before. If you need more detailed control over the actual record position you will need to add more code to handle finding and displaying the exact record that was displayed; however, this is beyond the scope of this book.

After we have repositioned the record that is being displayed, we call the `ShowPosition` procedure to show the current record position.

Finally, we display a message in the status bar indicating that the record has been added.

The next procedure that we want to code is the `btnUpdate_Click` procedure. This procedure is a little simpler because all we need to do here is to update the `titles` table. We do not have to select any data to build a primary key.

Try It Out – Updating Records

1. To the `btnUpdate_Click` event procedure, add the following code:

```
Private Sub btnUpdate_Click(ByVal sender As Object, _
            ByVal e As System.EventArgs) Handles btnUpdate.Click
    ' Declare local variables and objects...
    Dim intPosition As Integer
    Dim objCommand As SqlCommand = New SqlCommand()

    ' Save the current record position...
    intPosition = myCurrencyManager.Position

    ' Set the OleDbCommand object properties...
    objCommand.Connection = myConnection
    objCommand.CommandText = "UPDATE titles " & _
            "SET title = @title, price = @price WHERE title_id = @title_id"
    objCommand.CommandType = CommandType.Text

    ' Add parameters for the placeholders in the SQL in the
    ' CommandText property...

    ' Parameter for the title field...
    objCommand.Parameters.Add("@title", txtBookTitle.Text)

    ' Parameter for the price field...
    objCommand.Parameters.Add("@price", txtPrice.Text)

    ' Parameter for the title_id field...
    objCommand.Parameters.Add _
                        ("@title_id", BindingContext(myDV).Current("title_id"))

    ' Open the connection...
    myConnection.Open()

    ' Execute the OleDbCommand object to update the data...
    objCommand.ExecuteNonQuery()

    ' Close the connection...
    myConnection.Close()

    ' Fill the DataSet and bind the fields...
    FillDataSetAndView()
    BindFields()
```

```
' Set the record position to the one that we saved...
myCurrencyManager.Position = intPosition

' Show the current record position...
ShowPosition()

' Display a message that the record was updated...
StatusBar1.Text = "Record Updated"
End Sub
```

2. Run your project. You can update the price of the book that you have just added or you can update the price of another book. Choose a book, change the price in the Price field, and then click the Update button.

Once the record has been updated, you will see the appropriate message in the status bar and the record will still be the current record:

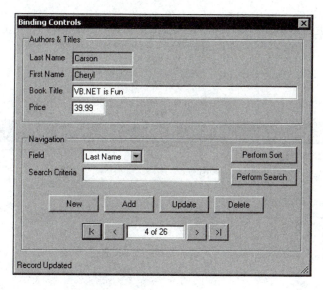

How It Works

As always, the first thing that we want to do is to declare our variables and objects. We need one variable to save the current record position and one object for the SqlCommand object. Next, we save the current record position just as we did in the last procedure.

By adding the following code, we set the Connection property of the SqlCommand object using our myConnection object. Then we set the CommandText property using a SQL string. The SQL string here contains an UPDATE statement to update the title and price columns in the titles table. Notice that there are three placeholders in this UPDATE statement. Two placeholders are for the title and price, and one is for the title_id in the WHERE clause:

```
' Set the OleDbCommand object properties...
objCommand.Connection = myConnection
```

```
objCommand.CommandText = "UPDATE titles " & _
    "SET title = ?, price = ? WHERE title_id = ?"
objCommand.CommandType = CommandType.Text
```

Again, once we have set the `CommandText` property, we set the `CommandType` property to indicate that this is a SQL string.

We now want to add the appropriate parameters to the `Parameters` collection. The first parameter that we needed to add was for the `title` column in our `UPDATE` statement. We have seen parameters several times before. The title of the book is coming from the `Text` property of the `txtBookTitle` text box on our form.

The second parameter was for the `price` in our `UPDATE` statement. This parameter will be used to update the price of a book and the data is coming from the `txtPrice` textbox on our form. Once again, we need to explicitly set the `DbType` for this parameter.

This last parameter was for our `WHERE` clause in the `UPDATE` statement. The data for the `Value` property is coming directly from the form's `BindingContext`, as the `au_id` did in the *Adding Records* example.

The rest of the procedure is similar to the `btnAdd_Click` event procedure.

The final procedure that we need to code is `btnDelete_Click`.

Try It Out – Deleting Records

1. To include delete functionality in your project, add the following code to the `btnDelete_Click` event procedure:

```
Private Sub btnDelete_Click(ByVal sender As Object, _
        ByVal e As System.EventArgs) Handles btnDelete.Click
    ' Declare local variables and objects...
    Dim intPosition As Integer
    Dim objCommand As SqlCommand = New SqlCommand()

    ' Save the current record position - 1 for the one to be
    ' deleted...
    intPosition = Me.BindingContext(myDV).Position - 1

    ' If the position is less than 0 set it to 0...
    If intPosition < 0 Then
        intPosition = 0
    End If

    ' Set the Command object properties...
    objCommand.Connection = myConnection
    objCommand.CommandText = "DELETE FROM titleauthor " & _
        "WHERE title_id = @title_id;" & _
        "DELETE FROM titles WHERE title_id = @title_id"
```

```
' Parameter for the title_id field...
objCommand.Parameters.Add _
                    ("@title_id", BindingContext(myDV).Current("title_id"))

' Open the database connection...
myConnection.Open()

' Execute the OleDbCommand object to update the data...
objCommand.ExecuteNonQuery()

' Close the connection...
myConnection.Close()

' Fill the DataSet and bind the fields...
FillDataSetAndView()
BindFields()

' Set the record position to the one that we saved...
Me.BindingContext(myDV).Position = intPosition

' Show the current record position...
ShowPosition()

' Display a message that the record was deleted...
StatusBar1.Text = "Record Deleted"
End Sub
```

2. That's it for this project so let's test this newest functionality. Run your project and choose any book that you want to delete and then click on the **Delete** button. Keep in mind though that the pubs database is a sample database for everyone to use and it's probably a good idea to delete a book that you have added. Before you delete a book, however, take note of the record count that is displayed on the form:

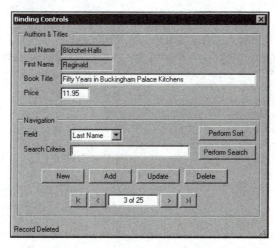

After the delete has been performed you will see one less record in the record count on the form.

How It Works

This procedure is a little more involved than the `btnUpdate_Click` procedure because of the relationship of titles to authors. Remember that there is a relationship table to join `authors` and `titles`. We must delete the row in the `titleauthor` relationship table, before we can delete the row of data in the `titles` table. Therefore we need two DELETE statements in our SQL string.

Notice that this time, after we have declared our variables, we have specified the `Position` property minus 1. This will allow for the user being on the last record and deleting it. We have also allowed for the user being on the first record as we check the value of the `intPosition` variable. If it is less than 0 we know that the user was on the first record and so we set it to 0; this means that when we restore the record position later it will once again be on the first record.

Notice also that we have not used the `CurrencyManager` object this time. Instead, we have used the `BindingContext` object and have specified the `myDV` object as the object to be manipulated. Remember that the `BindingContext` object is automatically part of the form and there is nothing you need to do to have it added. The reason for using the `BindingContext` object here is to demonstrate how to use it and so that you know that you do not have to use the `CurrencyManager` object to navigate the records contained in the `myDV`:

```
' Declare local variables and objects...
Dim intPosition As Integer
Dim objCommand As SqlCommand = New SqlCommand()

' Save the current record position - 1 for the one to be
' deleted...
intPosition = Me.BindingContext(myDV).Position - 1

' If the position is less than 0 set it to 0...
If intPosition < 0 Then
    intPosition = 0
End If
```

When we set the properties of our `SqlCommand` object, the SQL string specified in the `CommandText` property contained two DELETE statements separated by a semicolon. The first DELETE statement will delete the relationship between the `titles` and `authors` table for the book being deleted. The second DELETE statement will delete the book from the `titles` table:

```
' Set the Command object properties...
objCommand.Connection = myConnection
objCommand.CommandText = "DELETE FROM titleauthor " & _
    "WHERE title_id = @title_id;" & _
    "DELETE FROM titles WHERE title_id = @title_id"
```

Again, we have used placeholders for the primary keys in the WHERE clause our DELETE statements.

This statement only uses one parameter. The next line sets it up in the normal way:

```
' Parameter for the title_id field...
objCommand.Parameters.Add("@title_id", _
                                BindingContext(myDV).Current("title_id"))
```

The rest of the code is the same as the code for the previous two methods, and should be familiar by now. That wraps up this project and this chapter. Hopefully you will walk away with some valuable knowledge about data binding and how to perform inserts, updates, and deletes using SQL to access a database.

Before we leave, remember that error handling is a major part of any project. Except for one place in our code it has been omitted to preserve space. We have also omitted data validation, so trying to insert a new record with no values could cause unexpected results and errors.

Summary

This chapter has taken a look at a few very important ADO.NET classes, particularly the `SqlConnection`, `SqlDataAdapter`, `SqlCommand`, and `SqlParameter` classes. We have seen first hand how valuable these classes can be when selecting, inserting, updating, and deleting data. These particular classes are specifically for accessing SQL Server, but similar principles apply to the OLE DB counterparts.

We have also seen the `DataSet` and `DataView` classes from the `System.Data` namespace put to use and used both of these classes to create objects that were bound to the controls on our forms. Of particular interest to this discussion is the `DataView` object, as it provides the functionality to perform sorting and searching of data. The `DataView` class provides the most flexibility between the two classes as we can also present a subset of data from the `DataSet` in the `DataView`.

We have seen how easy it is to bind the controls on our form to the data contained in either the `DataSet` or `DataView`. We have also seen how to manage the navigation of the data in these objects with the `CurrencyManager` class. This class provides quick and easy control over the navigation.

This chapter has demonstrated using manual control over the navigation of data on the form and manual control over the insertion, update, and deletion of data in a data store. You should use the techniques that you have learned in this chapter when you need finer control of the data, especially when dealing with complex table relationships such as we have dealt with here.

To summarize, after reading this chapter you should:

- ❑ Feel comfortable using the ADO.NET classes discussed in this chapter

- ❑ Know when to use the `DataSet` class and when to use the `DataView` class

- ❑ Know how to manually bind controls on your form to either a `DataSet` or `DataView` object

- ❑ Know how to use the `CurrencyManager` class to navigate the data in a `DataSet` or `DataView` object

- ❑ Know how to sort and search for data in a `DataView` object

Questions

1. When is it better to bind to a `DataView` object instead of straight to a `DataSet` object?

2. When using the `SqlCommand` object, you set the `CommandText` property to a SQL string to be executed. How an you use a stored procedure instead of a SQL string?

3. What do the words beginning with @ mean in the following SQL string?

```
objCommand.CommandText = "INSERT INTO titles " & _
    "(title_id, title, type, price, pubdate) " & _
    "VALUES(@title_id,@title,@type,@price,@pubdate);" & _
    "INSERT INTO titleauthor (au_id, title_id) VALUES(@au_id,@title_id)"
```

4. When binding a control, when is it necessary to first clear the binding as shown in the following example?

```
txtLastName.DataBindings.Clear()
txtLastName.DataBindings.Add("Text", myDV, "au_lname")
```

Web Forms

No matter how hard you try, you can't escape the presence of the Web; it is becoming a vital part of many of the things we do. With Visual Basic .NET, we can write web applications in a way that's quite similar to writing Windows applications.

In the last chapter, we took a look at binding data to controls in Windows Forms. This chapter discusses programmatically binding data to controls in web forms. We will not only take a look at data binding, but will also take a look the major differences between Windows Forms and web forms, and how it affects data binding.

When we deal with web applications the term **thin client** is often used, as the client can be any browser such as Microsoft Internet Explorer or Netscape Navigator and requires very few resources as most of the processing is done on the server. We will explore how this type of client-server architecture affects you as a developer and explain what you need to know to ramp up on creating web forms.

In this chapter we will cover:

❑   A basic overview of thin client architecture

❑   Web forms architecture and how it differs from Windows Forms

❑   ADO.NET objects as they relate to the `System.Data.SqlClient` namespace and ASP.NET applications

❑   Data binding in web forms

❑   Sorting data

❑   Updating data

> Remember that in order to develop and run the code in this chapter, you will need to have IIS 5.x and the .NET Framework installed on the machine that you intend to run it on. In addition, error handling has been omitted from all of the *Try It Outs* in this chapter to save space. You should always add the appropriate error handling to your code. Please review Chapter 11 for error handling techniques.

Thin Client Architecture

When dealing with a Windows Forms application we have a compiled program that must be distributed to the user's desktop before they can use it. Depending on the application, there may also be one or more supporting DLLs or other executables.

In thin client architecture, there is typically no program or DLL to be distributed. A user merely needs to start their browser and enter the URL of the web site that they want to access. The server hosting the web site is responsible for maintaining all resources that are required by the web application. The resources are used at the server and provide functionality to the web site.

All code required in a thin client architecture is stored in one central location, the server hosting the web site. Any update that is made to the code is immediately available the next time a user requests a web page that was updated.

Thin client architecture provides several key benefits. First and foremost is the cost of initial distribution of the application; there is none. In a traditional client-server architecture, the program would have to be distributed to every client that wants to use it, which could be quite a time-consuming task if the application is used in offices throughout the world.

Another major benefit is the cost of distributing updates to the application; again there are none. All updates to the web site and its components are distributed to the web server. Once an update is made it is immediately available to every user the next time they access the updated web page. In traditional client-server architecture, the updated program would have to be distributed to every client and the updates could take days or weeks to roll out. This allows a new version of an application to be distributed instantly to all the users without having to touch a single desktop.

Another major benefit is that you can make changes to the back-end architecture and not have to worry about the client. Suppose for example that you want to change the location of the database from a low-end server to a new high-end server. The new server would typically have a new machine name. In a traditional client-server application, the machine name of the database server is stored in the code or registry setting. You would need to modify either the code or registry setting for every user who uses the application. In thin client architecture, you simply need to update the setting of the web server to point to the new database server and you are in business and so are all of the clients.

We can see that in a thin client architecture model, any client with a browser can access your web site and immediately have access to updates. In fact, if your changes were transparent to the user, the client wouldn't even know that changes have been made.

Now that we have a basic understanding of thin client architecture, let's move on to look at how web forms work.

Web Forms Versus Windows Forms

In this section, we want to take a high-level look at how both Windows Forms and web forms work so that you can compare the differences in architecture between the two. This will give you an idea of the challenges that you face when working with web forms. We will then proceed to point out some differences in the development environment when working with web forms. So let's get started!

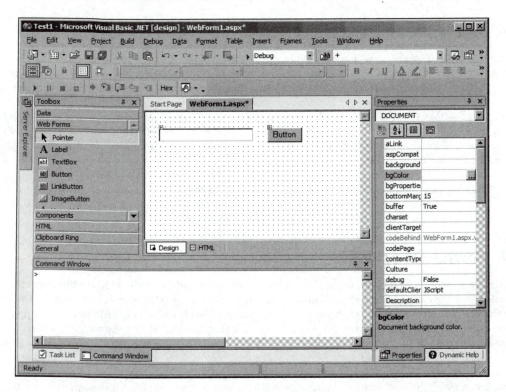

Notice at the bottom of the Web form that there are two tabs, one for Design mode and one for HTML mode. That's right, the source HTML behind the form can be viewed and manipulated. The next figure shows what the HTML looks like.

Windows Forms Overview

When you execute a program that uses Windows Forms, you click on a desktop icon or navigate to the appropriate `Programs` group folder and click on the icon that represents the program that you want to execute. The Windows operating system then loads the program, executes the code, and displays the form.

Let's suppose that you are working with data in the `authors` table in the sample `pubs` database. Your form displays a combo box listing all the states that authors live in. When you select a state in the combo box, the code in your form then sends a query to the database to retrieve all authors for that state and display them in a data grid.

All of this happens in a blink of the eye and happens right there in the code in the form on your local computer. The form not only contains the code to handle the events of the controls, but also the code to perform the data retrieval. This is not the case with web forms.

Web Forms Overview

When we execute a web form, we first must open a browser and enter the URL of the web site, which is usually on a web server somewhere. **Internet Information Server** (**IIS**) is invoked, looks at the page that we want displayed and executes the appropriate ASP.NET web page. The code in the web page is processed: retrieving the data for the combo box, building the HTML for the web form, and then sending this data to the browser.

Now that the web form is displayed in the browser, we can select a US state from the combo box. Wh
we select a state, the web form will post a request back to the web server for the appropriate data. IIS
turn loads the same web page again for our web form and determines that we now want to select all
authors who live in a particular state. It will send the query to the database to retrieve all the author
that state. IIS will then build the HTML for our web form and send the data to our browser.

As you can see, when dealing with resources that are not located on the client, there are a lot of r
trips back and forth between the browser and the web server. This is something that we must kee
mind when we write web applications. We want to reduce the number of trips to the server to as
possible because each trip requires the user to wait and requires resources on the server. That's
important to perform validation of input fields on the client side; we don't need to make a trip
server to validate fields.

Web Form Code

By now you are familiar with the Visual Studio .NET development environment and know
view a Windows Form in design mode or view the code behind the form. You know that y
double-click a control on the form and the appropriate event handler will be added to you

Design Mode

Web forms offer the same flexible functionality and more. When you open a new Web
project, you are presented with a web form in design mode. You can drag and drop co
toolbox onto the form as shown in the figure overleaf:

684

HTML View

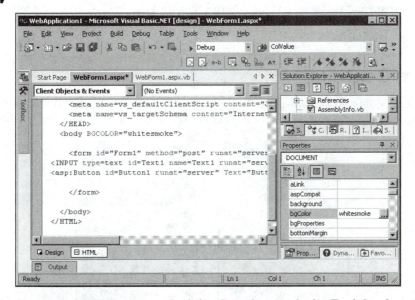

However, the Design and HTML views only define how the page looks. To define how it behaves, we need to write Visual Basic .NET code. The Visual Basic .NET code goes into a separate file called the code behind.

The Code Behind the Web Form

The code behind the web form looks very similar to what you have seen in your Visual Basic .NET projects. The next figure shows what the code looks like:

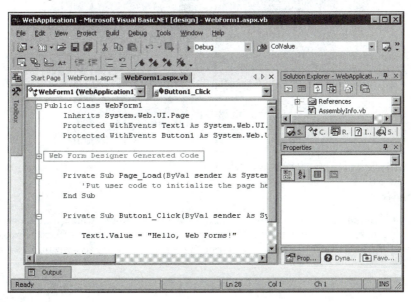

Now that we have seen how web forms look in the development environment and how we can view the code, let's move on and take a look at the controls that are available. While we'll progress fairly quickly here, keep in mind that you will be getting first hand experience building web forms and each step will be thoroughly explained.

Web Form Controls

Web form controls are broken down into two separate categories in the toolbox in the development environment: Web Forms and HTML – these are the tabs that you will see in the Toolbox:

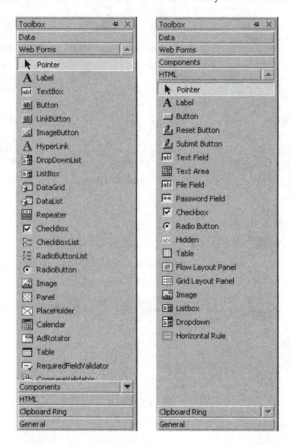

Let's take a look at the HTML Server controls first.

HTML Controls

HTML controls are the controls that you are used to seeing in today's web applications and include such controls as TextBox, Label, Button, and Table. These are the controls that are used in standard HTML pages. Of course there are many more but these are the most recognizable.

Under normal circumstances, we cannot manipulate these controls at run time from our Visual Basic .NET code. However, Visual Studio .NET puts a twist on these controls by allowing you to convert them into **HTML Server controls**. When you convert an HTML control to an HTML Server control, this control then becomes available in your server-side code and has properties and methods exposed that can be programmed against. However, as far as the web browser is concerned it's still plain HTML. The ASP.NET environment does the work of making it appear as normal HTML to the browser, and a proper codeable object to us.

> Note that although HTML controls are not accessible from our server-side VB.NET code, they *are* accessible from client-side JavaScript and VBScript code. We will be using client-side VBScript to demonstrate this in the following sections.

The conversion process can be performed in one of two ways and the difference between an HTML control and an HTML Server control is very distinguishable on the web form in design mode. You can convert an HTML control to an HTML Server control by right-clicking on the control in design mode and choosing the Run As Server Control menu item.

This will cause one or more attributes to be added to the control. At a minimum, the RUNAT=SERVER property will be added. In addition, depending on the control, the asp: prefix may be added to the control and an ID property may be assigned. This property allows you to access the control in code using this ID, which is basically the same as the Name property.

> *You could also perform the conversion from HTML control to HTML Server control manually, by viewing the HTML and modifying the controls in the HTML code. However, this is not a simple process and you should let the development environment do the work for you.*

The figure overleaf shows two sets of HTML controls, each a TextBox and a Button. The first sets of controls are HTML Server controls and the second sets are HTML controls. The little green arrow icon on the top left corner of the controls distinguishes them as HTML Server controls:

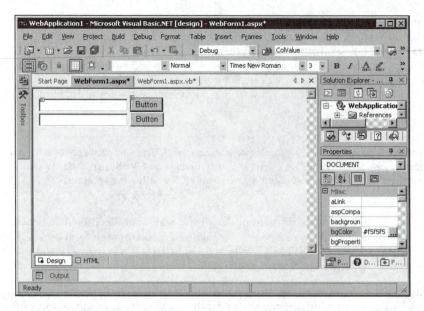

Now that we have seen the two controls in design mode, let's take a look at the HTML behind the scenes for these controls. The next figure shows how the HTML for these two sets of controls differs:

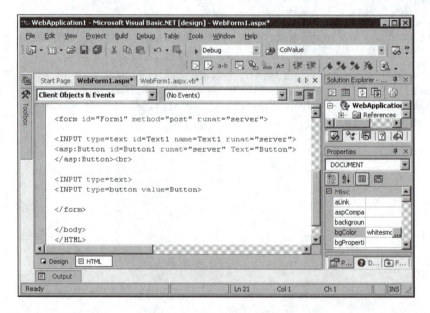

Notice that the first INPUT type=text control contains the id and runat properties, indicating that this control is an HTML Server control. The second INPUT type=text control has neither of these properties, indicating that it is a standard HTML control and cannot be manipulated from our Visual Basic .NET code.

The first button on our form has been transformed from a `INPUT type=button` HTML control to an `asp:Button` HTML Server control. The second button is a regular HTML control. The code difference between the two buttons is another good reason to let the development environment handle the transition from HTML control to HTML Server control.

Web Server Controls

Let's move on now and talk about Web Server controls. These are the rich controls that behave very much like the Windows controls we've used throughout the book. When we say these are *rich controls*, we mean that they have lots of properties that can be set to customize the look and feel of the control. They can be bound to data and they expose their events to you in the development environment so that you can insert event handlers and write code to run when these events occur (such as when a user clicks on a button).

While the number of controls under the **Web Forms** tab in the Toolbox is far less than the number of controls found in the Windows Forms tab of the Toolbox, they are in fact very important to you as a developer. As we just mentioned, they are capable of being bound to data, which is very important when writing web applications. They also can be programmed in the same familiar environment to which you have become accustomed as shown in the figure below:

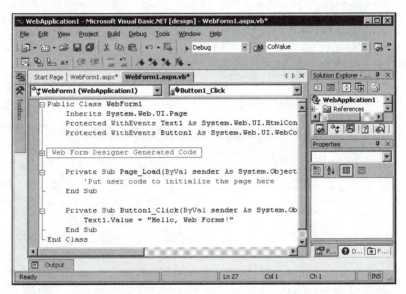

Notice that this figure shows the Visual Basic .NET code behind the web form and looks very similar to the code behind Windows Forms. This makes coding a web form very similar to coding a Windows Form.

There are controls in the **Web Forms** tab in the Toolbox that are not found in a Windows Forms project. These include such items as validator controls: for example **CheckBoxList** and **RadioButtonList**. **Validator controls** are typically used to perform client-side validation of data (although server-side validation can also be performed) and there are many validator controls that will do validation such as ensuring a field contains data, a field contains data in a certain range, a field contains data that compares to certain values, and so on. The `CheckBoxList` and `RadioButtonList` controls are particularly useful as, when bound to data, they can be used to automatically build a list of items from a `DataSet` object.

Creating a Web Application

In this section, we will walk through the basic steps required to create a web application. We will also be exploring the basic parts of a web form, the controls available, the code behind the form, and how the web form works.

The web form in this exercise will contain two sets of controls, one whose code executes at the server and one that executes at the client. We will see how to add these controls, write code for them, and explore the basic processing steps that are taking place.

Try It Out – Web Form Creation

1. Bring up the New Project dialog. As usual, select Visual Basic Projects from the Project Types list, but this time, select ASP.NET Web Application from the Templates list. Enter the name of Client-Server Processing after the server in the Location box.

2. The Location textbox contains the web server on your local machine by default and this is fine for our exercise. You can also replace your machine name with the text localhost, which basically refers to the local machine. This allows the application to be developed on any machine without any changes. However, you can use the Browse button and choose another web server. Keep in mind though, that the web server that you choose must be running IIS 5.x or later and it must have the .NET Framework installed on it. Be sure IIS is up and running at this point so the project can be created.

Click the OK button to have this application created:

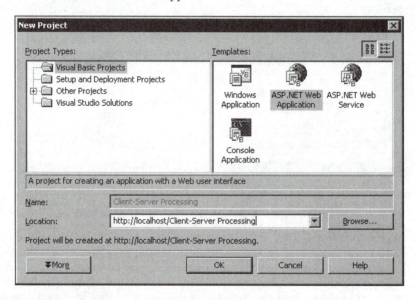

Visual Studio .NET will not only create the physical directory for this project, but also a **virtual directory** in IIS for this project and the files for this project.

The physical directory will be created in the default location where IIS was installed. For example, if IIS was installed using the default location, then your physical directory will be created as `C:\Inetpub\wwwroot\Client-Server Processing`. The virtual directory is used by IIS to specify your web site. This is the address that you enter in a browser to get to your web site.

3. By default, your web page uses a grid layout as shown in the next figure. As the message says on the page, you can change this layout mode by clicking on the pageLayout property in the Properties window and choosing FlowLayout. However, for our purposes, the GridLayout will do just fine:

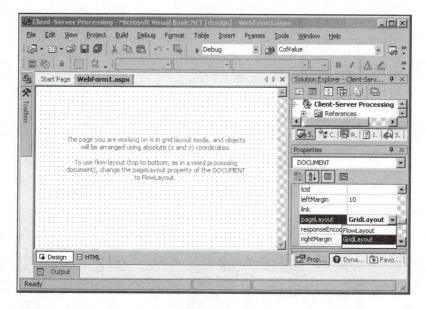

4. The default title that is displayed in the browser when you run your project is the URL for the page being displayed. We want something more meaningful here so click on the form and then in the Properties window set the title property to Client-Server Processing.

5. We want to add some HTML controls to this form so bring up the Toolbox. Then click on the HTML tab and add the controls listed in the table below to your web form:

Control	ID	Properties
Text Field	txtServerTextField	Size = 30; Style = Z-INDEX: 101; LEFT: 10px; POSITION: absolute; TOP: 15px
Button	btnServerButton	Style = Z-INDEX: 102; LEFT: 238px; WIDTH: 93px; POSITION: absolute; TOP: 14px; HEIGHT: 24px; Value = Server-Side

Table continued on following page

Control	ID	Properties
Text Field	txtClientTextField	Size = 30; Style = Z-INDEX: 103; LEFT: 10px; POSITION: absolute; TOP: 46px
Button	btnClientButton	Style = Z-INDEX: 104; LEFT: 238px; WIDTH: 93px; POSITION: absolute; TOP: 45px; HEIGHT: 24px; Value = Client-Side
Button	btnClearButton	Style = Z-INDEX: 105; LEFT: 238px; WIDTH: 93px; POSITION: absolute; TOP: 78px; HEIGHT: 24px; Value = Clear Fields

6. We now want to convert the first Text Field and Button controls from HTML controls to HTML Server controls. Right-click on the first Text Field and choose the Run As Server Control from the context menu.

Visual Studio .NET will convert this control to an HTML Server control and you will see a little green arrow icon in the upper left corner of the control. This is your indication that this is an HTML Server control.

7. Next, right-click on the first button and again choose Run As Server Control from the context menu. Again, you will see the icon in the upper left corner of the control once it has been converted.

Your completed web form should look similar to the one shown in the next figure:

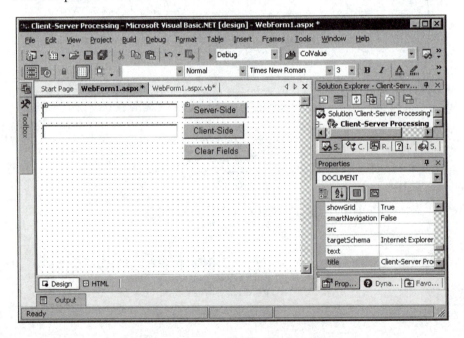

8. Before we begin, we want to run the project so you can get a feel for what the completed form will look like in a browser. Click on the Start icon on the toolbar or select the Debug | Start menu option.

9. You should see your web form displayed in a browser just like the one shown below. Of course, since we have not added any code yet, there will be no functionality and clicking the buttons will not perform any actions. Notice that there is no identifiable difference between the HTML Server controls and the HTML controls as displayed on the form. The difference comes in the code that generates these controls and how we program them:

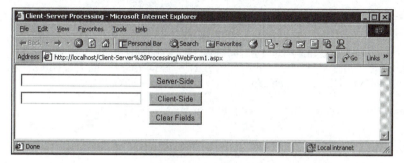

10. Shut down your browser so we can start looking at the code that has been generated thus far.

Try It Out – The HTML

1. Click on the HTML tab at the bottom of the web form. We can now view the HTML behind the form. The following HTML has been autogenerated and contains the necessary HTML to generate this web form:

```
<%@ Page Language="vb" AutoEventWireup="false" Codebehind="WebForm1.aspx.vb"
Inherits="Client_Server_Processing.WebForm1"%>
<!DOCTYPE HTML PUBLIC "-//W3C//DTD HTML 4.0 Transitional//EN">
<HTML>
  <HEAD>
    <title>Client-Server Processing</title>
    <meta name="GENERATOR" content="Microsoft Visual Studio.NET 7.0">
    <meta name="CODE_LANGUAGE" content="Visual Basic 7.0">
    <meta name=vs_defaultClientScript content="JavaScript">
    <meta name=vs_targetSchema
          content="http://schemas.microsoft.com/intellisense/ie5">
  </HEAD>
  <body MS_POSITIONING="GridLayout">

    <form id="Form1" method="post" runat="server">
      <INPUT id=txtServerTextField style="Z-INDEX: 101; LEFT: 10px;
            POSITION: absolute; TOP: 15px" type=text size=30
            runat="server">
      <INPUT id=btnServerButton style="Z-INDEX: 102; LEFT: 238px;
            WIDTH: 93px; POSITION: absolute; TOP: 14px; HEIGHT: 24px"
            type=button value=Server-Side runat="server">
```

```
      <INPUT id=btnClientButton style="Z-INDEX: 104; LEFT: 238px;
            WIDTH: 93px; POSITION: absolute; TOP: 45px; HEIGHT: 24px"
            type=button value=Client-Side>
      <INPUT id=txtClientTextField style="Z-INDEX: 103; LEFT: 10px;
            POSITION: absolute; TOP: 46px" type=text size=30>
      <INPUT id=btnClearButton style="Z-INDEX: 105; LEFT: 238px;
            WIDTH: 93px; POSITION: absolute; TOP: 78px; HEIGHT: 24px"
            type=button value="Clear Fields">
    </form>

  </body>
</HTML>
```

2. Since this book is about Visual Basic .NET, let's change the default client-side language that will be used from JavaScript to VBScript. Note that doing this will limit the browser that is supported to IE, since Netscape does not support VBScript.

In the editor, highlight the following line of HTML:

```
<meta name=vs_defaultClientScript content="JavaScript">
```

You will see the entire line highlighted and the various properties that can be set for this <META> element in the Properties window. Click in the box for the **defaultClientScript** property and you will see a list of available languages for the client script. Choose **VBScript** from the list. Your altered line of HTML should now look like the one shown below:

```
<meta name=vs_defaultClientScript content="VBScript">
```

3. We want to add some client-side code to execute when the page loads in the browser to set the Value property of our HTML Text Field. In order to do this we need to add a script block.

Insert a blank line between the </HEAD> element and the <BODY> element. Next, right-click on this blank line and choose **Insert Script Block | Client** from the context menu that appears. This will cause the blank script block to be inserted as shown below so that we may insert client-side script here:

```
  </HEAD>
<script language=vbscript>
<!--

-->
</script>
<body MS_POSITIONING="GridLayout">
```

Notice that the language property has been specified automatically and is vbscript. This is because we modified the <META> element for the default client script.

4. We want to place our code in the `OnLoad` event to set the `Value` property of our `Text Field`. Place the following procedure inside the script as shown below:

```
<script language=vbscript>
<!--
Sub Window_OnLoad()

End Sub
-->
</script>
```

5. Place the line of code shown below in the `Window_OnLoad` procedure. This will cause the Text Field to contain the value shown below when this page is loaded:

```
Sub Window_OnLoad()
    document.all.txtClientTextField.value = "Click the button ==>"
End Sub
```

6. We now want to add the appropriate client-side code for the two client-side buttons in our web form. Unlike server-side controls or in Visual Basic .NET, we cannot double-click the control in Design mode to have the procedure added. We must be in HTML mode, and select the control in the **Object** combo box and then select the appropriate event in the **Event** combo box. (These are the two combo boxes at the top of your code just below the tabs.)

In the **Object** combo box select **btnClientButton** and in the **Event** combo box select the **OnClick** event. The following code will be added to your project:

```
<script id=clientEventHandlersVBS language=vbscript>
<!--
Sub btnClientButton_onclick

End Sub
-->
</script>
```

We want to add some code in the `btnClientButton_onclick` procedure to change the text that is displayed in the client-side Text Field. When you click this button the text that is displayed in the client-side Text Field will change. Add the code below to this procedure:

```
Sub btnClientButton_onclick
    document.all.txtClientTextField.value = _
            "Client-side processing performed"
End Sub
```

7. Now let's add the procedure for `btnClearButton`. Select **btnClearButton** in the **Object** combo box and then select the **OnClick** event in the **Event** combo box. The procedure for this button will be added just below the previous procedure.

We want the code in `btnClearButton_onclick` to clear both Text Fields on the form. Add the following code to your project:

```
Sub btnClearButton_onclick
    document.all.txtServerTextField.value = ""
    document.all.txtClientTextField.value = ""
End Sub
```

How It Works

The first line of code that we see is the @ Page directive. This directive defines the **page-specific attributes** for the page such as the language used and the class name of the code behind the web form. This directive can be placed anywhere in the web page but it is common practice to place this directive at the top.

> Note that Visual Studio .NET has done most of this for us. If you are happy with what Visual Studio .NET has done automatically, you don't need to understand all of the following details.

The @ Page directive is enclosed in **server-side script tags**. The beginning server-side script tag is specified with the less than and percent symbol (<%). The ending server-side script tag is specified with the percent symbol and a greater than sign (%>). You place all server-side code between these symbols:

```
<%@ Page Language="vb" AutoEventWireup="false" Codebehind="WebForm1.aspx.vb"
Inherits="Client_Server_Processing.WebForm1"%>
```

There are many attributes that can be specified in the @ Page directive but let's focus our attention on the ones that are in our code:

❑ The first attribute is the Language attribute, which specifies the language to be used when compiling code contained in the server-side script blocks (<% %>).

❑ The AutoEventWireup attribute is used to specify whether the page events are automatically enabled. This value is True by default, but in this case, Visual Studio .NET has set this value to False.

❑ The Codebehind attribute specifies the name of the file that contains the Visual Basic .NET code for our web form. This file is a separate file from the web form and contains all of the Visual Basic .NET code for our form.

❑ The Inherits attribute specifies the **code-behind class** in the Codebehind file that this form inherits.

The next line of HTML is the <!DOCTYPE> element. We don't need to worry about this element, but it defines the document type definition for the page and the version of HTML that this document was written for:

```
<!DOCTYPE HTML PUBLIC "-//W3C//DTD HTML 4.0 Transitional//EN">
```

The next few lines of code are the HTML elements that start our web form. Every web form starts with the <HTML> element followed by the <HEAD> element that describes the header section of the web page.

Notice that the first line of HTML code in the <HEAD> section is the <TITLE> element. This is the text that is displayed in the title bar when our page is displayed in a browser:

```
<HTML>
  <HEAD>
    <title>Client-Server Processing</title>
```

Following the `<TITLE>` element are several `<META>` elements. These elements contain information about the page and can be used by some search engines to index the page. They are also used to convey information about the page to the server and to the client browser and are used by Visual Studio .NET as we write code for this web form.

The first `<META>` element specifies that this page is a Visual Studio .NET-generated page. The next `<META>` element specifies that the language that this page was generated with was Visual Basic .NET. The third `<META>` element specifies the default client-side language for the page (VBScript). The fourth `<META>` element is used to specify the target browser for this page (IE5):

```
<meta name="GENERATOR" content="Microsoft Visual Studio.NET 7.0">
<meta name="CODE_LANGUAGE" content="Visual Basic 7.0">
<meta name=vs_defaultClientScript content="VBScript">
<meta name=vs_targetSchema
      content="http://schemas.microsoft.com/intellisense/ie5">
```

> **`<META>` elements are normally optional but are used here by Visual Studio .NET for various tasks and documentation as we saw when we changed the client-side scripting language and then inserted our client-side script block.**

Notice in the code above that there is a **closing tag** for the `<HEAD>` element (`</HEAD>`). Most HTML elements have a closing tag which is the element name proceeded by a forward slash. The `<META>` elements just happen to be one of those HTML elements that do not require a closing element.

The next two lines of code are the starting elements for the `<BODY>` element and the `<FORM>` element:

```
<body MS_POSITIONING="GridLayout">
<form id=Form1 method=post runat="server">
```

The `<BODY>` element defines the start of the body of our page and the `<FORM>` element defines the start of our form.

Almost every HTML element has multiple properties that can be specified to further define how that element will render the HTML that you see.

If you click on the `<BODY>` element and look in the **Properties** window, you will see all of the available properties that can be set for the `<BODY>` element.

The `<FORM>` element has its ID property set, which allows us to access this element in our code. It also has the Method property set with a value of POST, which means that this form will post the values to the server when we submit this form. The other Method option is GET, which we do not use very often because it shows the values in the form in the URL address bar of the web browser. The RUNAT property distinguishes the code from client-side code, and ensures that the form is run on the server side and the resulting HTML is sent to the client.

The next two elements are <INPUT> elements. The <INPUT> element creates a variety of input controls on a page and uses the Type property to distinguish what type of control should be built. The first type of control being built here is the Text Field control as specified by the Type property of text and the second type of control being built is the button control:

```
<INPUT id=txtServerTextField style="Z-INDEX: 101; LEFT: 10px;
       POSITION: absolute; TOP: 15px" type=text size=30
       runat="server">
<INPUT id=btnServerButton style="Z-INDEX: 102; LEFT: 238px;
       WIDTH: 93px; POSITION: absolute; TOP: 14px; HEIGHT: 24px"
       type=button value=Server-Side runat="server">
```

Remember that these controls were modified to be HTML Server controls and can be distinguished as such by the RunAt property, which has been set to use a value of server.

The Style property is used to position these controls at absolute *x* and *y* coordinates on the page because we are using a MS_POSITIONING property value of GridLayout.

The Z-Index property indicates the stacking order of the elements and only applies to elements that specify the Position property.

The Size property in the first <INPUT> control is used to specify how wide the Text Field should be. The Value property in the second <INPUT> control is used to specify the text on the Button.

The next three <INPUT> controls are for the second Text Field and the last two Buttons. Notice the absence of the RunAt property indicating that these controls are strictly HTML controls:

```
<INPUT id=btnClientButton style="Z-INDEX: 104; LEFT: 238px;
       WIDTH: 93px; POSITION: absolute; TOP: 45px; HEIGHT: 24px"
       type=button value=Client-Side>
<INPUT id=txtClientTextField style="Z-INDEX: 103; LEFT: 10px;
       POSITION: absolute; TOP: 46px" type=text size=30>
<INPUT id=btnClearButton style="Z-INDEX: 105; LEFT: 238px;
       WIDTH: 93px; POSITION: absolute; TOP: 78px; HEIGHT: 24px"
       type=button value="Clear Fields">
```

Again, we see the Style property has been set for us to position these controls at absolute *x* and *y* coordinates. These were set when we positioned these controls on the web form.

The code in our page is wrapped up by specifying the closing elements for the <FORM>, <BODY>, and <HTML> elements.

```
      </FORM>
   </body>
</HTML>
```

There are several client-side events that happen when a web page loads in a browser and one of those events is the OnLoad event for the Window object. The Window object represents an open window in a browser. One Window object is created for each page that gets loaded into a browser. For example, our page will cause one Window object to be created. If our page contained frames, then one Window object for the page as a whole and one Window object for each frame in the page would be created.

Our Text Field is defined inside the <FORM> element, meaning that the form is the parent of this control. We cannot access this Text Field directly, we must access it though its parent. So what does this mean? When we access a control inside a form, we must first specify the form name followed by the control name as shown in the code fragment below:

```
form1.txtClientTextField.value = "Click the button ==>"
```

However, the form itself is a child of the Document object and the Text Field is considered a child of the Document object. We access the Document object by using the name document. All controls in your page are considered children of the Document object so we can actually access the Text Field as shown in the next code fragment.

Notice that in this example we have specified the All collection of the Document object. This will retrieve all elements that are contained in the Document object. We then follow this using the ID of our Text Field:

```
document.all.txtClientTextField.value = "Click the button ==>"
```

Which method should you use? This depends on the complexity of your web forms. If all controls are located inside your form then you can use the first method. However, I find it easier to use one method, which reduces confusion and keeps the code in your web page consistent, so I always use the second method.

Note that at the moment, we have no server-side code. Every time a user views this page, the server will send the same HTML and VBScript code to the browser and the browser will interprets it. In the next stage, we will write some code that executes on the server.

Try It Out – Client-Server Processing Using Visual Basic .NET

1. If you right-click on **WebForm1.aspx** in the Solution Explorer window and then select the **View Code** option, you will see the form class code for this form. Opening up all the plus signs will display the Visual Basic .NET code and allows you to write server-side code:

```
Public Class WebForm1
    Inherits System.Web.UI.Page
    Protected WithEvents txtServerTextField As _
            System.Web.UI.HtmlControls.HtmlInputText
    Protected WithEvents btnServerButton As _
            System.Web.UI.HtmlControls.HtmlInputButton


#Region " Web Form Designer Generated Code "

    'This call is required by the Web Form Designer.
    <System.Diagnostics.DebuggerStepThrough()> Private Sub _
            InitializeComponent()

    End Sub

    Private Sub Page_Init(ByVal sender As System.Object, _
            ByVal e As System.EventArgs) Handles MyBase.Init
        'CODEGEN: This method call is required by the Web Form Designer
```

699

```
            'Do not modify it using the code editor.
            InitializeComponent()
        End Sub

    #End Region

        Private Sub Page_Load(ByVal sender As Object, _
                ByVal e As System.EventArgs) Handles MyBase.Load
        'Put user code to initialize the page here

        End Sub

    End Class
```

2. Modify the Page_Load method as shown below. This will cause the Value property in the server-side Text Field control to be set here in code and the resulting HTML sent to the browser. Note that you can only manipulate server-side controls here; you cannot manipulate client-side (HTML) controls:

```
    Private Sub Page_Load(ByVal sender As Object, _
            ByVal e As System.EventArgs) Handles MyBase.Load
        'Put user code to initialize the page here
        txtServerTextField.Value = "Click the button ==>"
    End Sub
```

3. We also want to add some code to the HTML Server button. The easiest way to have the appropriate procedure added to our code is to switch to the web form in Design mode and double-click on the button. Once you do, the procedure below will be added to your class.

Add the following line of code to this procedure. This will change the text in the Value property of our Text Field when the server processes this procedure:

```
    Private Sub btnServerButton_ServerClick(ByVal sender As _
            System.Object, ByVal e As System.EventArgs) _
            Handles btnServerButton.ServerClick
        txtServerTextField.Value = "Server-side processing performed"
    End Sub
```

How It Works

As you can see, this is very similar to the code you are used to seeing when coding Windows Forms as we have a public class. Instead of the class inheriting from System.Windows.Forms.Form, this class inherits from System.Web.UI.Page, which renders a web form instead of a Windows form.

Since we converted two HTML controls to HTML Server controls, we see the code that has been added to our class so that we may access these controls in code:

```
    Public Class WebForm1
        Inherits System.Web.UI.Page
        Protected WithEvents txtServerTextField As _
                System.Web.UI.HtmlControls.HtmlInputText
        Protected WithEvents btnServerButton As _
                System.Web.UI.HtmlControls.HtmlInputButton
```

The next bit of code was also autogenerated and should not be modified. Like its counterpart in a Windows form, this code is used to initialize and build the resulting HTML that gets sent to the browser.

The Page_Load method (on the server) is where we place any code that we need to run before the page is sent from the server to the browser. Here we can set the various properties of the two HTML Server controls, before the HTML is sent to the browser.

We added code to display some initial text in the first Text Field on the form. We could do this by setting the Value property while viewing the web form in either Design mode or HTML mode, simply by clicking on the code and modifying the Value property in the Properties window. However, we modified the property by adding the following code:

```
txtServerTextField.Value = "Click the button -->"
```

That's all the code we need to add and now we are ready to test.

Try It Out – Testing Our Web Form

1. Click on the Start icon on the toolbar, or click on the Debug | Start menu option.

The form that is displayed should look similar to the one shown below. Before we begin testing, notice the title in the title bar. This is the text that we specified in the <TITLE> element. This is always followed by a dash and the text Microsoft Internet Explorer (when using Internet Explorer):

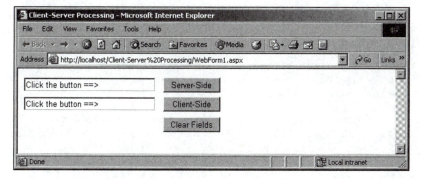

2. Click on the Server-Side button and you will see the text in the Text Field change from Click the button ==> to Server-side processing performed. The Web form was posted back to the server to process the request as indicated by a flicker of the browser and the text in the status bar showing it is processing the web page. This is because the Button and Text Field controls were defined as server-side controls, so the server must process the events for these controls and build the HTML to be sent back to the browser.

3. Now click on the Client-Side button. Notice that the text changed in this Text Field to Client-side processing performed and the form did not get posted back to the server to process the request because the status bar did not indicate that it was processing the web page. This change in the text was made at the client in our client-side script and your web page should now look like the one shown here:

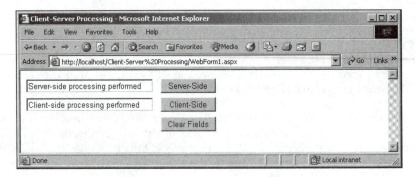

4. Click on the **Server-Side** button again. Your Web page should now look like the one shown here, again indicating that the form was posted back to the server for processing:

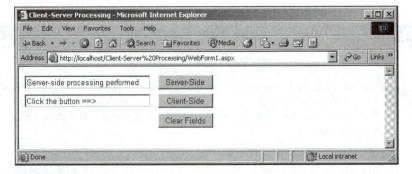

How It Works

If you view the source in the browser for this web page, you will see the client-side script that you coded. To view the source, right-click on an empty area of the page and choose **View Source** from the context menu, or select **View | Source** from the browser's menu.

You will see the scripts that we coded and the HTML that we saw in HTML mode when working with our web form. There is also some HTML and script that has been added by Visual Studio .NET, which allows this web form to be posted back to the server for processing.

> *Visual Studio .NET automatically generates this code when the web page is compiled and provides the appropriate event handlers to post the form back to the server.*

When you clicked on the **Server-Side** button, the web form was posted back to the server to process the request. This is because Button and Text Field were defined as server-side controls, and the server must process the events for these controls and build the HTML to be sent back to the browser.

In contrast, when the **Client-Side** button was clicked, the form did not get posted back to the server to process the request. This change in the text was made at the client in our client-side script and your web page should now look like the one shown above.

To further illustrate the point that the first button will post the form back to the server for processing, the **Server-Side** button was clicked again. You should have noticed that the text in the second Text Field had been changed back to its original state, but the text in the first Text Field looked the same.

The reason for this is that the form was posted back to the server for processing, which caused the text in the first Text Field to indicate that the **Server-Side** button was clicked. The server built a new page, with the new text, and then sent the resulting HTML back to the browser. Our script that executes on the `Window_OnLoad` event caused the text in the second Text Field to be set back to its original state.

You can further test this by clicking on the **Clear Fields** button, which will cause all Text Fields to be cleared and then clicking on the **Server-Side** button again. You will see the same results as you saw above.

This *Try It Out* has shown you how a web form is built, sent to the client for processing, and posted back to the server for processing. The next couple of *Try It Outs* that we go through will further demonstrate how a web form is posted back to the server for processing.

Data Binding in Web Forms

Having had a first hand look at how a web form is built and processed, we now want to move on and incorporate data access into our web forms. We will be using a `DataGrid` control in our web form to display authors' names, book titles, and the price of their books. The next two Try It Outs will use the `DataGrid` control, but each one will incorporate different functionality for it.

You can always use the Wizards to set up and perform data binding but we will be focusing on how to do this through code as we did in the last chapter. This allows us to see what is actually going on behind the scenes and provides us with greater control on how updates are applied. There are several different ways that you can perform data binding in a web form. One way is to place all of your code in the web form class, which is the code behind the web form. Another way is to place your code in a server-side script block within the HTML in the web form itself. We will be taking a look at both methods in the remaining *Try It Outs* in this chapter. You could also mix your code between the web form class and server-side script blocks but we will not be covering that method here.

Since data binding itself is basically the same for a web form as it is for a Windows Form we will forgo all of the details since we covered it in the last chapter. However, if you need to refresh your memory, peruse the *Data Binding* section in the last chapter.

The thing to keep in mind as we start to work with bound data in our web forms is the fact that each time you need to perform some sort of operation on the data (such as editing it), the web form gets posted back to the server for processing. For example, suppose you need to sort the data, the web form is posted back to the server for this operation to take place. Once the web form is posted back to the server, it is built from scratch, the appropriate logic executed, and the resulting HTML sent back to the browser.

All of these round trips take time to process and can be costly when dealing with large amounts of data. We did not have to worry about this round trip processing with Windows Forms as the form did not have to be rebuilt, only the fields refreshed with the new data.

There is a solution to this problem and it lies with XML. We can use XML on the client and perform all of this sorting there. However, this is a topic that is beyond the scope of this book. Further details on this can be found in *Professional VB.NET 2nd Edition* (Wrox Press, ISBN 1-86100-716-7).

When building web forms for a production application, keep in mind the processing that must take place and always try to reduce the amount of data that must be sent back and forth between the client and the server.

DataGrid Example

This *Try It Out* will use a `DataGrid` control in a web form and we will bind data to it through code. The functionality that we will incorporate in this `DataGrid` will allow the user to sort the data in it by clicking on the header for a specific column. The web form will then post the request back to the server for processing, and the web form will be rebuilt and then sent back to the client.

Once again, we will be using the `pubs` database in SQL Server for our data. We will be using the `System.Data.SqlClient` namespace to access SQL Server. Remember that this namespace has been optimized for use exclusively with SQL Server and will provide better performance than the `System.Data.OleDb` namespace.

The data binding that we will perform in this exercise will be written exclusively in the web form class, the code-behind the web form. This is the environment with which you are most familiar when coding Windows Forms and we will demonstrate how you can use this class. Let's get started!

Try It Out – DataGrid Sorting

1. Create a new **ASP.NET Web Application** project called **DataGrid Sorting**. Remember that the **Location** combo box specifies the web server that this project will use. The project folder will be placed on that web server under the `WWWRoot` folder:

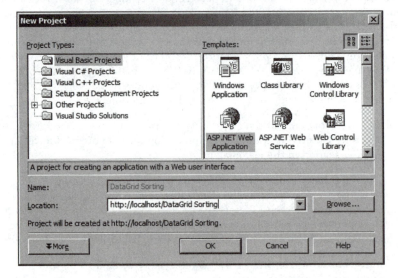

2. In the Toolbox, click on the **Web Forms** tab and drag the **DataGrid** control from the toolbox onto your form. Position the `DataGrid` near the upper left corner of the form. The exact position is not important here.

3. We have seen how to set the properties of a control while in Design mode, so let's explore how to set the properties while in HTML mode. At the bottom of the web form, click on the **HTML** tab to view the HTML behind our form.

4. Click on the line of code that defines the `DataGrid` control. The partial line of code that will be generated is shown below.

```
<asp:DataGrid id=DataGrid1
```

Notice that the Properties window reflects that your cursor is on the `DataGrid` control and displays its properties. This is another easy way to set the properties for this control.

5. Set the following properties of the `DataGrid` control in your project:

Property	Value
(ID)	grdAuthors
AllowSorting	True
AlternatingItemStyle-BackColor	Any light color you like
AutoGenerateColumns	True
BackColor	White, or any other light color you prefer
CellPadding	3
Font-Name	Verdana
Font-Size	8pt
GridLines	None
HeaderStyle-BackColor	Maroon, or any other dark color you prefer
HeaderStyle-Font-Bold	True
HeaderStyle-ForeColor	White

After setting these properties, you can switch to Design mode and see how these settings affect the look of the `DataGrid`:

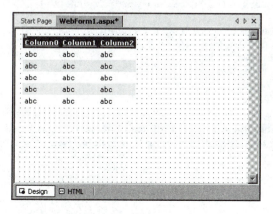

6. There is one last item that we want to change in the HTML. Switch back to HTML mode and set the <TITLE> element to DataGrid Sorting. This will be the title that is displayed in our browser:

```
<title>DataGrid Sorting</title>
```

7. In the Solution Explorer window, right-click on WebForm1.aspx and choose View Code from the context menu to view the code behind.

The first thing that we need to do here is to import the necessary namespaces to access SQL Server. Add the following namespaces to your code:

```
Imports System.Data
Imports System.Data.SqlClient

Public Class WebForm1
```

8. Next we need to declare a Connection object that is global in scope to this class, so add the following code:

```
Public Class WebForm1
    Inherits System.Web.UI.Page
    Protected WithEvents grdAuthors As _
            System.Web.UI.WebControls.DataGrid

    ' Declare a Connection object that is global in scope...
    Dim objConnection As SqlConnection
```

9. Add the following code to the Page_Load method as shown below:

```
'Put user code to initialize the page here

    ' Initialize the Connection object...
    objConnection = New SqlConnection("Server=localhost;" & _
        "Database=Pubs;User ID=sa;Password=vbdotnet;")

    ' Only bind the data the first time the page is built...
    ' Subsequent post backs will be to sort the data in the grid...
    If Not (IsPostBack) Then
        BindGrid("Last Name")
    End If
```

> **Don't forget to update the connection information (server, password, and user ID) so that it will connect to your SQL Server or MSDE database.**

10. The next method that we want to code is `BindGrid`, which we call from `Page_Load`:

```
Sub BindGrid(ByVal strSortField As String)
    ' Declare objects...
    Dim objDataSet As DataSet
    Dim objDataAdapter As SqlDataAdapter

    ' Set the SQL string...
    objDataAdapter = New SqlDataAdapter( _
     "SELECT au_lname AS 'Last Name', au_fname AS 'First Name', " & _
     "title AS 'Book Title', price AS 'Retail Price' " & _
     "FROM authors " & _
     "JOIN titleauthor ON authors.au_id = titleauthor.au_id " & _
     "JOIN titles ON titleauthor.title_id = titles.title_id " & _
     "ORDER BY au_lname, au_fname", objConnection)

    ' Initialize the DataSet object and fill it...
    objDataSet = New DataSet()
    objDataAdapter.Fill(objDataSet, "Authors")

    ' Declare a DataView object, populate it,
    ' and sort the data in it...
    Dim objDataView As DataView = _
        objDataSet.Tables("Authors").DefaultView
    objDataView.Sort = strSortField

    ' Bind the DataView object to the DataGrid control...
    grdAuthors.DataSource = objDataView
    grdAuthors.DataBind()

    ' Clean up...
End Sub
```

11. The next method will be called when we click on a column in the `DataGrid` to be sorted and will pass the column name on to `BindGrid`.

To have this procedure inserted into your code, click on the **Class Name** combo box and select **grdAuthors**. Then click on the **Method Name** combo box and select **SortCommand**.

```
Private Sub grdAuthors_SortCommand(ByVal source As Object, _
        ByVal e As _
        System.Web.UI.WebControls.DataGridSortCommandEventArgs) _
        Handles grdAuthors.SortCommand
    ' Bind the DataGrid using the sort column requested
    BindGrid(e.SortExpression)

End Sub
```

12. That's all the code we need to make this project functional. Let's test it out now! Click the **Run** button on the Visual Studio .NET toolbar. This will start up a web browser. When the browser loads your web page (and this might take a while), you should see results similar to this:

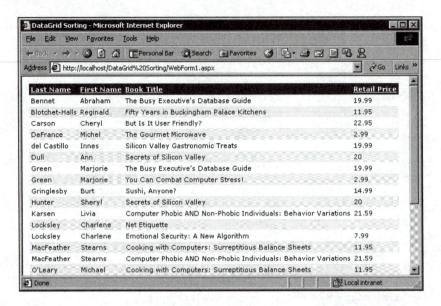

13. At this point, you can test the functionality of the `DataGrid` control by clicking on a column header. The web form is posted back to the server and the page will start executing from the top. The first procedure that is executed is the `Page_Load` procedure, followed by the `grdAuthors_SortCommand` procedure. `grdAuthors_SortCommand` calls the `BindGrid` procedure, passing it the column to be sorted on.

You will then see the `DataGrid` redisplayed, sorted by the column that you clicked on.

As you can see, we implemented some very useful functionality here and it did not take a lot of code. We also were able to do this by a method that we are already familiar with, writing code in a form class.

How It Works

To begin with, we added the necessary namespaces to utilize SQL Server functionality:

```
Imports System.Data
Imports System.Data.SqlClient
```

Then we declared a `SqlConnection` object that was global in scope to this class. This will allow us to access this object in multiple procedures in the class. As we've learned in previous chapters, we use `SqlConnection` when we are accessing SQL Server or MSDE.

```
' Declare a Connection object that is global in scope...
Dim objConnection As SqlConnection
```

One of the first procedures that executes when a web page loads is the `Page_Load` procedure. This is where we want to place the code to initialize our connection to the database. This procedure will be called every time this page is loaded and executed:

```
        ' Initialize the Connection object...
        objConnection = New SqlConnection("Server=localhost;" & _
            "Database=Pubs;User ID=sa;Password=vbdotnet;")
```

The `IsPostBack` property returns a `True` or `False` value indicating whether the page has been posted back from a client request or whether the page is being loaded for the first time. The value is returned as `True` when the client posts the page back to the server for processing.

If this is the initial load of the page then we want to call the `BindGrid` procedure and pass it a sort parameter of `"Last Name"`. This will cause the data to be sorted by the `Last Name` column before it is bound to the `DataGrid` if this is the first time that the screen has loaded.

If this is not the initial load of the page, `IsPostBack` will be `True` and the following code will not execute:

```
        If Not (IsPostBack) Then
            BindGrid("Last Name")
        End If
```

The `BindGrid` method will extract the data from SQL Server, sort it, and bind it to our `DataGrid` control. Notice that this procedure has one parameter defined (`strSortField`) and that is for the sort field.

> When you are working with ASP.NET, always consider whether code in **`Page_Load`** should only execute if the page is executing for the first time. Otherwise, your application will end up being far slower.

The first thing that we did in `BindGrid` was to declare some objects that will be needed. We covered the `DataSet` class and the `SqlDataAdapter` class's counterpart (`OleDbDataAdapter`) in Chapters 15 and 16. These two classes perform the exact same function and that is to act as a data bridge between your application and the database:

```
    Sub BindGrid(ByVal strSortField As String)
        ' Declare objects...
        Dim objDataSet As DataSet
        Dim objDataAdapter As SqlDataAdapter
```

We then initialized the `SqlDataAdapter` object and set the SQL string to be executed. In the last chapter, we saw how we could modify the `DataGrid` control by setting the column headers to text that was more meaningful. This time we are using the SQL statement to return more meaningful column names.

When we select a column from a table, we can assign what is known as a **column alias** to that column. We do this by specifying the `AS` keyword in our `SELECT` statement following the column that has been selected and assigning a new name to that column. Notice that our column names are enclosed in single quotes because there are spaces in the column names. If we did not include spaces in the alias column names then we would not have to enclose them in single quotes.

We are assigning a column alias to every column selected in this `SELECT` statement. Note that this `SELECT` statement is very similar to the one that we used in the beginning of the last chapter:

```
' Set the SQL string...
objDataAdapter = New SqlDataAdapter( _
  "SELECT au_lname AS 'Last Name', au_fname AS 'First Name', " & _
  "title AS 'Book Title', price AS 'Retail Price' " & _
  "FROM authors " & _
  "JOIN titleauthor ON authors.au_id = titleauthor.au_id " & _
  "JOIN titles ON titleauthor.title_id = titles.title_id " & _
  "ORDER BY au_lname, au_fname", objConnection)
```

Remember that, when the DataSet has been populated with data, it will contain not only the data, but the structure of the data also. This means that it will contain column names and the name of the table that the data was selected from. Hence, the new column names that we assigned in the SELECT statement will be propagated down to the DataSet object.

Once we have populated our DataSet, we declare a DataView object and populate it with the data contained in the DataSet. We need to do this because the DataSet object does not allow us to sort the data within the object.

```
Dim objDataView As DataView = _
    objDataSet.Tables("Authors").DefaultView
```

After we have populated the DataView object, we can sort the data in it using the Sort property. We do that here by using the strSortField parameter that was passed into this procedure:

```
objDataView.Sort = strSortField
```

The DataGrid control, like the Windows controls that you have worked with up to this point, has events that are fired and we can place code inside the procedures for these events.

When we click on a header column in the DataGrid, the web form will be posted back to the server and the grdAuthors_SortCommand procedure will be executed.

The e parameter in this procedure contains the SortExpression property, which returns the column name that the user clicked on and wants to sort by:

```
Private Sub grdAuthors_SortCommand(ByVal source As Object, _
        ByVal e As _
        System.Web.UI.WebControls.DataGridSortCommandEventArgs) _
        Handles grdAuthors.SortCommand
    ' Bind the DataGrid using the sort column requested
    BindGrid(e.SortExpression)

End Sub
```

Remember that the BindGrid procedure retrieves the data from SQL Server, populates the DataView object, sorts the data, and finally binds the DataGrid control with the sorted data. This procedure simply calls the BindGrid procedure to sort on the column that the user has selected.

When you ran the project, you should have noticed that the column headers matched the column names in our SQL statement and were underlined, indicating that they were hyperlinks that performed an action. In this case, they execute JavaScript that will post the form data back to the server for processing. This JavaScript was automatically built for us and will handle the steps necessary to post this web form back to the server.

Once the `DataGrid` is sent to the browser, it is nothing more than HTML – you can check by viewing the source code in your browser.

Updating Data with a DataGrid

In the first *Try It Out* that we did in this chapter, we wrote client-side script in our HTML that would load the initial contents and change the contents of a Text Field on our web form. We have seen how to write client-side script in our HTML and in the next *Try It Out* we will be taking this one step further by showing you how to write server-side script in your HTML.

Not only will we write server-side script to extract data and bind it to a `DataGrid`, but we will also be writing code to handle the various events from the `DataGrid`, such as editing and updating a row of data in it. This will give you an opportunity to explore an alternative method of handling the events of the controls on your form, and also show you how to bind data to your controls using script.

Writing a server-side VB.NET code that is embedded in HTML in order to bind data is not that much different from writing code in a form class to bind data. We still have to define our data objects, access the database, and bind our controls. We have the same procedures that we did in a form class and we will be using the same language, Visual Basic .NET. There are a few minor differences, because we are mixing server-side code in with our HTML and we will point out the differences as we go along.

In this *Try It Out*, we will build a web form that contains a `DataGrid` that allows us to update the rows of data within it. Once the updates are made, we will be able to apply the updates or cancel them by clicking on a hyperlink as we did when we sorted data.

All of the updates to SQL Server are made using server-side script with the updated data. Therefore, we will be using the classes in the `System.Data.SqlClient` namespace.

In addition to writing server-side script, we will be exploring more details about the `DataGrid` control as we provide the functionality to edit and update rows of data. This will involve manually defining the columns to be bound and also specifying templates for the data in a column. **Templates** allow us to provide labels and textboxes in a cell in the `DataGrid` to display and allow editing of the data. We can apply styles to the data so that it is displayed in different fonts and colors, and we can also apply special formatting of the data, such as formatting numeric values into currency values.

We will be displaying the same data that we saw in the last *Try It Out*. However, our SELECT statement will be slightly different, as we will see later.

Try It Out – DataGrid Updates

1. Create a new ASP.NET Web Application called DataGrid Updates.

2. In the Toolbox, click on the **Web Forms** tab and drag the `DataGrid` control onto your form. Position it near the upper left corner of the form. Again, the exact position is not important here.

3. Switch to HTML mode by clicking on the **HTML** tab. Find and click on the `DataGrid` control and then set its properties according to the table below (the important ones are highlighted here):

Property	Value
(ID)	**grdAuthors**
AlternatingItemStyle-BackColor	WhiteSmoke
AutoGenerateColumns	**False**
BackColor	White
CellPadding	3
DataKeyField	**title_id**
Font-Name	Verdana
Font-Size	8pt
GridLines	None
HeaderStyle-BackColor	Maroon
HeaderStyle-Font-Bold	True
HeaderStyle-ForeColor	White

4. Now add the following event handlers to the `DataGrid` control:

```
<asp:DataGrid id=grdAuthors
    style="Z-INDEX: 101; LEFT: 13px; POSITION: absolute; TOP: 12px"
    runat="server"
    AlternatingItemStyle-BackColor=WhiteSmoke
    AutoGenerateColumns=false
    BackColor=White
    CellPadding=3
    DataKeyField="title_id"
    Font-Name=Verdana
    Font-Size=8pt
    GridLines=None
    HeaderStyle-BackColor=Maroon
    HeaderStyle-Font-Bold=true
    HeaderStyle-ForeColor=White
    OnEditCommand="EditGridData"
    OnCancelCommand="CancelGridData"
    OnUpdateCommand="UpdateGridData">
</asp:DataGrid>
```

5. Place the following lines of HTML directly below those shown above (before the
`</asp:DataGrid>` close tag). This defines the start and end of the `Columns` collection for
the `DataGrid` control:

```
<Columns>

</Columns>
```

6. Next we need to add the columns between the `<Columns>` and `</Columns>` elements. The
first column that we need to add is a column for the edit commands:

```
<Columns>
    <asp:EditCommandColumn
        EditText="Edit Row"
        CancelText="Cancel Edit"
        UpdateText="Update Row"
        ItemStyle-Wrap="False"/>
</Columns>
```

7. The rest of the columns that we want to add are: the first column of bound data in the
`DataGrid` (the ID, which we will keep hidden), the author's last name, author's first name,
title of the book, and finally the price of the book:

```
    ItemStyle-Wrap="False"/>

  <asp:BoundColumn
    DataField="title_id"
    Visible="False"/>

  <asp:BoundColumn
    DataField="au_lname"
    HeaderText="Last Name"
    ReadOnly="True"
    ItemStyle-Wrap="False"/>

  <asp:BoundColumn
    DataField="au_fname"
    HeaderText="First Name"
    ReadOnly="True"
    ItemStyle-Wrap="False"/>

  <asp:TemplateColumn
    HeaderText="Title"
    ItemStyle-Wrap="False">
    <ItemTemplate>
      <asp:Label runat="server"
        Text='<%# DataBinder.Eval (Container.DataItem, "title") %>'/>
    </ItemTemplate>

    <EditItemTemplate>
```

```
      <asp:TextBox runat="server"
      ID="edit_title"
      Font-Name="Verdana"
      Font-Size="8pt"
      Width="400"
      Text='<%# DataBinder.Eval(Container.DataItem, "title") %>'/>
    </EditItemTemplate>
  </asp:TemplateColumn>

  <asp:TemplateColumn
    HeaderText="Price"
    HeaderStyle-Font-Bold="True"
    ItemStyle-HorizontalAlign=Right>
    <ItemTemplate>
      <asp:Label runat="server"
      Text='<%# DataBinder.Eval(Container.DataItem, "price", "{0:C2}")%>'/>
    </ItemTemplate>
    <EditItemTemplate>
      <asp:TextBox runat="server"
      ID="edit_price"
      Font-Name="Verdana"
      Font-Size="8pt"
      Width="50"
      Text='<%# DataBinder.Eval(Container.DataItem, "price", "{0:C2}") %>'/>
    </EditItemTemplate>
  </asp:TemplateColumn>
</Columns>
```

8. The last bit of HTML code that we want to add is the code to set the title in the page. Find the `<TITLE>` element at the beginning of the page and add a title of `DataGrid Updates`:

```
<title>DataGrid Updates</title>
```

9. Since we will not be using the form class for any code in this exercise we need to remove the `@ Page` directive. Remove this line of code from your project. Leaving it in will prevent the `Page_Load` and `Page_Unload` events from firing.

10. Next, we want to import the namespaces that are required when accessing data in a data store. These are the same namespaces that we used in the last *Try It Out*. Place them at the top of the page:

```
<%@ Import Namespace="System.Data.SqlClient" %>
<%@ Import Namespace="System.Data" %>
```

11. We need to add a server-side script block between the ending `</HEAD>` element and before the `<BODY>` element. Right-click between these two elements and select **Insert Script Block | Server**. The following code is inserted into your project:

```
<script runat=server>

</script>
```

12. We want to set the language for this script block so click on the first line of this script block and notice that the Properties window displays all available properties for this script block. Set the **language** property to **VB**. Your script block should now show the language property and it should be set to vb:

```
<script runat=server language=vb>

</script>
```

13. The first line of code that we need to place inside this script block is the declaration for our Connection object as shown below. This is the same Connection object that we used in the last *Try It Out* and, again, we are using the SqlConnection class for this object.

```
' Declare a Connection object that is global
' in scope to this script...
Dim objConnection As SqlConnection
```

14. The Page_Load procedure is one of the first procedures to be executed, so insert the following in the script block as well:

```
Sub Page_Load(Sender As Object, E As EventArgs)
    objConnection = New _
        SqlConnection("Server=localhost;Initial Catalog=Pubs;" & _
        "User ID=sa;Password=vbdotnet;")

    If Not (IsPostBack)
        BindGrid()
    End If
End Sub
```

Remember that you need to specify the **User ID** and **Password** parameters that are defined in your database.

---

15. Now we want to add the BindGrid procedure to the script block. As we mentioned above, this procedure will not perform any sorting this time so we have not specified any parameters in this procedure:

```
Sub BindGrid()
    Dim objDataSet As DataSet
    Dim objDataAdapter As SqlDataAdapter

    objDataAdapter = New SqlDataAdapter( _
        "SELECT au_lname, au_fname, titles.title_id, title, price " & _
        "FROM authors " & _
        "JOIN titleauthor ON authors.au_id = titleauthor.au_id " & _
        "JOIN titles ON titleauthor.title_id = titles.title_id " & _
        "ORDER BY au_lname, au_fname", _
        objConnection)
```

```
    objDataSet = New DataSet()
    objDataAdapter.Fill(objDataSet, "Authors")

    grdAuthors.DataSource = objDataSet
    grdAuthors.DataBind()

End Sub
```

16. Next, we want to add the `EditGridData` procedure to the script block. We defined this event handler in the `DataGrid` control:

```
Sub EditGridData(Sender As Object, E As DataGridCommandEventArgs)
    grdAuthors.EditItemIndex = CInt(E.Item.ItemIndex)
    BindGrid()
End Sub
```

17. `CancelGridData`, which should also be added to the script block, is necessary should the user choose to cancel the update:

```
Sub CancelGridData(Sender As Object, E As DataGridCommandEventArgs)
    grdAuthors.EditItemIndex = -1
    BindGrid()
End Sub
```

18. Finally, the `UpdateGridData` procedure will be called when the user clicks on the **Update Text** link for the row of data that they are editing. Both this and the event handler for `CancelGridData` were added to the `DataGrid` control at the start of this *Try It Out*:

```
Sub UpdateGridData(Sender As Object, E As DataGridCommandEventArgs)
    Dim objCommand As SqlCommand
    Dim objTextBox As TextBox

    Dim strSQL As String = "UPDATE titles " & _
        "SET title = @Title, price = @Price " & _
        "WHERE title_id = @ID"

    objCommand = New SqlCommand(strSQL, objConnection)

    objCommand.Parameters.Add(New SqlParameter("@ID", _
            SqlDbType.VarChar, 6))
    objCommand.Parameters.Add(New SqlParameter("@Title", _
            SqlDbType.VarChar, 80))
    objCommand.Parameters.Add(New SqlParameter("@Price", _
            SqlDbType.Money, 8))

    objCommand.Parameters("@Id").Value = _
            grdAuthors.DataKeys(CInt(E.Item.ItemIndex))

    objTextBox = E.Item.FindControl("edit_title")
    objCommand.Parameters("@Title").Value = objTextBox.Text
```

```
        objTextBox = E.Item.FindControl("edit_price")

        If Left(objTextBox.Text,1) = "$" Then
            objTextBox.Text = Right(objTextBox.Text,Len(objTextBox.Text)-1)
        End If
        objCommand.Parameters("@Price").Value = objTextBox.Text

        objCommand.Connection.Open()

        objCommand.ExecuteNonQuery()

        grdAuthors.EditItemIndex = -1

        objCommand.Connection.Close()

        BindGrid()

    End Sub
```

We are now ready to run this project and test it out, but before we do, we'll go through what we have actually done during the addition of the previous code.

How It Works

When we write server-side script while in HTML mode, we do not have access to the events for the DataGrid control as we did when we wrote code in the form class. Therefore, we need to add these events for the DataGrid to our code manually. These event handlers will post the form back to the server and instruct the server on which procedures to execute. We are specifying the event name, followed by the procedure in our script that it should execute:

```
OnEditCommand="EditGridData"
OnCancelCommand="CancelGridData"
OnUpdateCommand="UpdateGridData">
```

We needed to add some columns since we are not allowing the DataGrid to automatically generate the columns. We began by adding a column for the edit commands. This special column, defined by the HTML asp:EditCommandColumn, will automatically provide hyperlinks that will execute JavaScript when we click on the text. The JavaScript will be automatically generated for us.

```
<asp:EditCommandColumn
    EditText="Edit Row"
    CancelText="Cancel Edit"
    UpdateText="Update Row"
    ItemStyle-Wrap="False"/>
```

The first property in this column is EditText and defines the text that is displayed in the column. The next two properties, CancelText and UpdateText, will display the corresponding text in this column once you click the **Edit Row** hyperlink.

The ItemStyle-Wrap property indicates whether the text in this column can wrap over two or more lines. By setting this property to False, we prevent the text from wrapping and so the width of the column will expand to allow all of the text to be displayed on one line.

The next column is the first column of bound data in the `DataGrid`. This column is defined by the HTML `asp:BoundColumn` and will bind the column of data from our `DataSet` object as specified in the `DataField` property.

```
<asp:BoundColumn
    DataField="title_id"
    Visible="False"/>
```

The `DataField` property specifies the column of data in the `DataSet` object that should be bound to this column. The second property (`Visible`) specifies whether the column should be shown in the grid. We have set this property to `False` indicating that this column is hidden. The reason for this is that we need the data for this row as it provides the primary key for the row and will be posted back to the server when we perform updates.

Next, we added a column for the author's last name, followed by one for the author's first name. The `HeaderText` property is used to change the text that is displayed in the header. Remember that by default the text that is displayed in the header is the column name. Since the column name doesn't make much sense to the end user, we specify text that is meaningful. In the last *Try It Out*, we did this in the `SELECT` statement by assigning column aliases. The method you choose is entirely up to you and one method is not better than the other. However, this method provides better self-documentation within the code:

```
<asp:BoundColumn
    DataField="au_lname"
    HeaderText="Last Name"
    ReadOnly="True"
    ItemStyle-Wrap="False"/>

<asp:BoundColumn
    DataField="au_fname"
    HeaderText="First Name"
    ReadOnly="True"
    ItemStyle-Wrap="False"/>
```

The `ReadOnly` property will let the `DataGrid` control know that this column cannot be edited.

The fourth column we added was the one for the title of the book. We must specify a definition for our own edit fields, which is what we are doing here with the `asp:TemplateColumn`. This column type allows us to customize the controls in a column in the `DataGrid`:

```
<asp:TemplateColumn
    HeaderText="Title"
    ItemStyle-Wrap="False">
```

We specify the `HeaderText` and `ItemStyle` properties just as we did for the other columns.

Then we specify the `ItemTemplate` for the data that is displayed. This property sets the template to be used to display the data in a read-only format. This is how we will initially see the data in the `DataGrid`. We need to specify an `ItemTemplate` for when the data is in read-only mode, and an `EditItemTemplate` to control how the data is displayed when we edit a row of data:

```
<ItemTemplate>
<asp:Label runat="server"
   Text='<%# DataBinder.Eval (Container.DataItem, "title") %>'/>
</ItemTemplate>
```

Within the `ItemTemplate` property, we define a `Label` control as indicated by the `asp:Label` code. We set its `Text` property using the `DataBinder.Eval` method, which evaluates a binding expression against an object. The `Container.DataItem` method is used to extract the `title` column from the `DataSet` object and place the contents into this label.

Notice that we use the standard ASP.NET data binding tags (`<%#` and `%>`) to encapsulate our data binding expression. The `Eval` method of the `DataBinder` class is used to parse and evaluate a data binding expression at run time.

The `EditItemTemplate` is used to specify the control to display when a column is being edited. Within this template, we have defined a `TextBox` and have set the various properties of it, the first of which is the `ID` property. We assign an `ID` property to this control to make it easier to access in our server-side script:

```
<EditItemTemplate>
<asp:TextBox runat="server"
   ID="edit_title"
   Font-Name="Verdana"
   Font-Size="8pt"
   Width="400"
   Text='<%# DataBinder.Eval(Container.DataItem, "title") %>'/>
</EditItemTemplate>
</asp:TemplateColumn>
```

The other properties set the font name, font size, and the width of the textbox. The last property here sets the text in the textbox and again uses the `DataBinder.Eval` method.

Finally, we added a column for the price of the book. You may have noticed in the last *Try It Out* that we did not format the price of the books. However, we want to do it this time to demonstrate the formatting options when binding data. The `Text` property of the `Label` and `TextBox` controls has special formatting being applied to the data using an overloaded version of the `Eval` method:

```
Text='<%# DataBinder.Eval(Container.DataItem, "price", "{0:C2}")%>'/>
```

The `DataFormatString` of `{0:C2}`, indicates that the data should be formatted in the currency format and that it should contain two decimal places. This property has two parts separated by a colon. The part before the colon specifies the index of the data in a zero-based list. Since we have no list, we have specified a value of 0.

The second part contains the format character to be used, in our case C for currency and the number following the format character, which is specified when formatting currency or decimal values. We have specified a value of 2, indicating that two digits are required to present after the decimal. If a price has no cents then two zeros will be inserted.

719

When importing namespaces in an ASPX page we must use the @ Import directive. This directive imports the namespace that we specify. We added the code shown below to our project where the @ Page directive was defined:

```
<%@ Import Namespace="System.Data.SqlClient" %>
<%@ Import Namespace="System.Data" %>
```

Remember that the Page_Load procedure is one of the first procedures to be executed and this is where we placed our code in the last *Try It Out* to initialize our Connection object. Therefore, we must code this procedure in our script as shown below.

The first thing that we do in this procedure is to initialize our Connection object:

```
Sub Page_Load(Sender As Object, E As EventArgs)
    objConnection = New _
        SqlConnection("Server=localhost;Initial Catalog=Pubs;" & _
        "User ID=as;Password=vbdotnet;")
```

The last part of the procedure should also look familiar to you as we are using the IsPostBack property to determine if this is the first time this page has been loaded. Remember that this property only returns a value of False if this is the first time this page is loaded:

```
    If Not (IsPostBack)
        BindGrid()
    End If
End Sub
```

We are calling the same procedure as we did in our last *Try It Out*, which is the BindGrid procedure. Notice that this time, however, we have no parameters. This is because we are not performing any sorting in this *Try It Out*. When the data is displayed it will be sorted by the author's last name and first name because we used the ORDER BY clause in our SELECT statement.

As we mentioned above, the BindGrid procedure will not perform any sorting this time so we have not specified any parameters in this procedure. The first thing that we do in this procedure is to declare the objects that we need. Again, we are using the DataSet and SqlDataAdapter classes to declare our objects:

```
Sub BindGrid()
    Dim objDataSet As DataSet
    Dim objDataAdapter As SqlDataAdapter
```

Next, we initialize the SqlDataAdapter object setting the SQL string to be executed. Our SELECT statement looks a little different from the last *Try It Out*, as we are not using column aliases, we have an ORDER BY statement, and we are also selecting an extra column. This new column, title_id, is the primary key column in the titles table. When we update a book title and price we need this data to let us know which row of data to update:

```
objDataAdapter = New SqlDataAdapter( _
  "SELECT au_lname, au_fname, titles.title_id, title, price " & _
  "FROM authors " & _
  "JOIN titleauthor ON authors.au_id = titleauthor.au_id " & _
  "JOIN titles ON titleauthor.title_id = titles.title_id " & _
  "ORDER BY au_lname, au_fname", _
  objConnection)
```

Next, we initialize the `DataSet` object and then populate it by executing the `Fill` method of the `SqlDataAdapter` object:

```
objDataSet = New DataSet()
objDataAdapter.Fill(objDataSet, "Authors")
```

We then bind the `DataGrid` to the `DataSet` object by specifying the `DataSource` property and setting it to our `DataSet` object. Then we call the `DataBind` method of the `DataGrid` to actually perform the binding.

```
grdAuthors.DataSource = objDataSet
grdAuthors.DataBind()

End Sub
```

When we click on the **Edit Text** hyperlink in the `DataGrid` for a specific row, it will cause the web form to be posted back to the server for processing. This will allow the server to format the selected row in the `DataGrid` for editing, which causes the textboxes to be displayed with the current data in it. The `EditGridData` procedure below contains the necessary code to make this happen.

```
Sub EditGridData(Sender As Object, E As DataGridCommandEventArgs)
    grdAuthors.EditItemIndex = CInt(E.Item.ItemIndex)
    BindGrid()
End Sub
```

The `EditItemIndex` property determines which row in the `DataGrid` should be edited. When we set this property, the `DataGrid` will display textboxes in this row of data for editing.

We set this property using the `DataGridCommandEventArgs` that are passed to this procedure when the web form is posted back to the server. This class contains information about the events raised and lets us know on which row of data the event was raised. Using the `Item` property, we can determine which row of data the user wants to edit. We use the `CInt` function just to ensure the value in the `ItemIndex` property is converted to an `Integer` value since this is what the `EditItemIndex` property expects.

Finally, we call the `BindGrid` procedure to reload the `DataGrid` with data and to set it up for editing. The selected row will have the textboxes added because the `EditItemIndex` property is set.

Once a user has started editing a row of data, they have the option of either canceling the edit or updating the data. This next procedure (`CancelGridData`) will be executed if the user chooses to cancel the update. We do this simply by setting the `EditItemIndex` property to −1. This causes the textboxes for this row of data to be removed. Then we call the `BindGrid` procedure to reload the `DataGrid`:

```
Sub CancelGridData(Sender As Object, E As DataGridCommandEventArgs)
    grdAuthors.EditItemIndex = -1
    BindGrid()
End Sub
```

The `UpdateGridData` procedure will be executed if the user decides to update the data. The first thing that we do in this procedure is to declare the objects that we need. Here we are declaring a `SqlCommand` object that will be used to execute the `UPDATE` statement to update the row of data in the database and a `TextBox` object to retrieve the data that is being updated from the `DataGrid`:

```
Sub UpdateGridData(Sender As Object, E As DataGridCommandEventArgs)
    Dim objCommand As SqlCommand
    Dim objTextBox As TextBox
```

We then declare and set the SQL string that will be used to update the database. The `SqlCommand` class uses parameters in our SQL string as shown below, and as we saw in the previous chapter. These parameters are defined with an at (@) sign followed by the name of the parameter:

```
Dim strSQL As String = "UPDATE titles " & _
    "SET title = @Title, price = @Price " & _
    "WHERE title_id = @ID"
```

We initialize the `SqlCommand` object next, specifying the SQL string variable and the `SqlConnection` object:

```
objCommand = New SqlCommand(strSQL, objConnection)
```

We start adding parameters to the `SqlCommand` object next. This should look familiar as we added parameters to the `SqlCommand` object in the last chapter. Here we initialize and add a new parameter all in one step. We pass the parameter several arguments, the first of which is the parameter name. Then we specify the data type for the parameter followed by the size of the data type.

The first parameter is a SQL `VarChar` data type, which contains string data. We have specified that this parameter can contain a maximum of six characters:

```
objCommand.Parameters.Add(New SqlParameter("@ID", _
        SqlDbType.VarChar, 6))
```

The second parameter is also a SQL `VarChar` data type and we have specified that this parameter can contain a maximum of 80 characters:

```
objCommand.Parameters.Add(New SqlParameter("@Title", _
        SqlDbType.VarChar, 80))
```

The third and final parameter contains a SQL `Money` data type. Remember that instead of specifying the maximum value here, we must specify the storage size for this parameter in SQL Server, which is 8 bytes:

```
objCommand.Parameters.Add(New SqlParameter("@Price", _
        SqlDbType.Money, 8))
```

Now that our parameters have been defined, we populate these parameters with data. The `@ID` parameter is populated with the data in the `DataKeys` property of the `DataGrid`. We get the correct data by specifying the `Item` property, which contains the row of data that we are editing:

```
objCommand.Parameters("@Id").Value = _
        grdAuthors.DataKeys(CInt(E.Item.ItemIndex))
```

Next, we must find the control with the name of `edit_title`. We do this by using the `FindControl` method of the `Item` property of the `DataGridCommandEventArgs` class. Once we find the control, we assign it to the `TextBox` object that we defined earlier. This allows us to access the data that was placed in the textbox when the data was edited.

Using the `Text` property of the `TextBox` object, we assign the data in that control to the parameter `@Title`:

```
objTextBox = E.Item.FindControl("edit_title")
objCommand.Parameters("@Title").Value = objTextBox.Text
```

We perform the same process to find the `edit_price` textbox. However, before assigning the value in the `TextBox` object to the parameter, we first check for and remove the dollar sign if one is present. This is not a valid character for the `Money` data type and will cause an error if we try to assign it to the `@Price` parameter.

Using the `Left` function, we check for the presence of the dollar sign in the first position, and if present, remove it using the `Right` function. The `Left` function returns the specified number of characters in the left portion of a string, while the `Right` function returns the specified number of characters to the right of a string.

When we use the `Left` function in our code below, we are only returning the left-most character in the string because we have specified a value of 1 in the call to the function. When we use the `Right` function, we are returning all of the characters in the string except the first character. We determine the length of the string using the `Len` function, which returns the length of a string and then we substract 1 from it.

Once we have checked for and if necessary removed the dollar sign, we assign the value in this `TextBox` object to the `@Price` parameter:

```
objTextBox = E.Item.FindControl("edit_price")
If Left(objTextBox.Text,1) = "$" Then
    objTextBox.Text = _
        Right(objTextBox.Text,Len(objTextBox.Text)-1)
End If
objCommand.Parameters("@Price").Value = objTextBox.Text
```

At this point, we are ready to execute our SQL string to update the database so we open our `SqlConnection` object first. Then we execute the SQL string by executing the `ExecuteNonQuery` method of the `SqlCommand` object:

```
objCommand.Connection.Open()

objCommand.ExecuteNonQuery()
```

We then set the `EditItemIndex` of the `DataGrid` to −1, to indicate that no row is to be in edit mode and then call the `BindGrid` procedure to have the `DataGrid` repopulated with data. Once the `DataGrid` is repopulated with data, it will reflect the updated row of data.

```
grdAuthors.EditItemIndex = -1

objCommand.Connection.Close()

BindGrid()

End Sub
```

Now we can go on to test our project!

Try It Out – Testing the DataGrid Updates Project

1. Start the project. Once the web form has been loaded in the browser, you should see results similar to the figure:

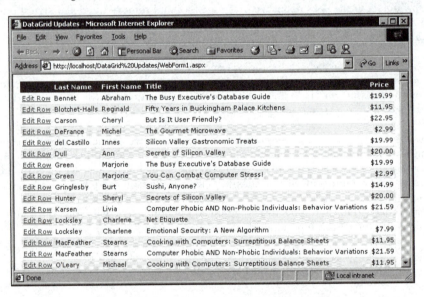

2. Choose a row of data to edit and click on the Edit Row hyperlink. This should result in a figure similar to the following:

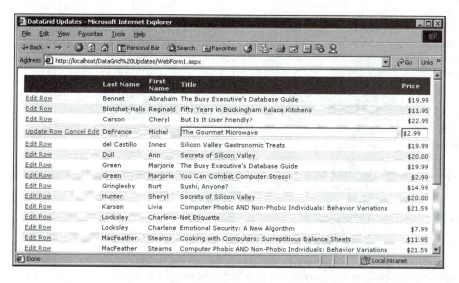

3. At this point, you have two choices: cancel the edit or update the row of data. If you chose to cancel it, you would click on the Cancel Edit hyperlink.

4. If you chose to edit the row of data, you would make your changes and then click on the Update Row hyperlink. The following figure reflects that the fourth row of data was updated by slightly changing the book title and changing the price:

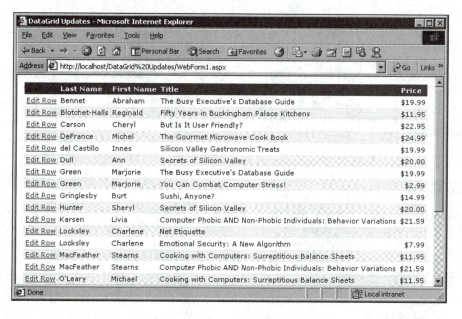

How It Works

Notice that the first column in the DataGrid contains the text **Edit Row**. This was the first column that we defined in our DataGrid and it has a hyperlink that will execute JavaScript to post this form back to the server.

When we click on the **Edit Row** hyperlink, the form gets posted back to the server and the EditGridData procedure is executed. This procedure sets the EditItemIndex property of the row to be edited. Once the BindGrid procedure is called, the DataGrid will be built and this row will be displayed with textboxes in columns that allow editing.

When we click on the **Cancel Edit** hyperlink, the JavaScript will be executed, which in turn will post the form back to the server for processing. The CancelGridData procedure will then be executed and the EditItemIndex property set to a value of −1, which will cause this row to be displayed normally when we call the BindGrid procedure.

Editing rows and choosing the **Update Row** hyperlink causes the appropriate JavaScript to be executed, which in turns submits this form back to the server for processing. Once at the server, the UpdateGridData procedure gets executed, which updates the database for this row of data. Once the updates are made, the EditItemIndex property is once again set to a value of −1, indicating that this row should no longer be edited. The BindGrid procedure is once again executed and the DataGrid is populated with data, reflecting the updates made.

While we did not provide sorting capability in this *Try It Out*, you could very easily do so by incorporating the code from the previous example.

This *Try It Out* has shown you how to provide update capabilities to a DataGrid. In the process, we have seen how to add template columns to it to control the size and look of the textboxes that are displayed when editing a row of data. We have also seen how to format the text in a column in the DataGrid.

Along with all of this, we have seen how easy it is to write server-side script in our HTML. While the differences are small, some of them are significant. For example, we do not have a means to insert the empty procedures for the events of the DataGrid control that we need, so we must code them all by hand. In this author's opinion it is best to use the Web Form class and not to mix the HTML code with the server script.

Summary

This chapter has introduced you to web forms and how they differ from Windows Forms. We can see that there is a lot of processing going on when working with web forms, as the form and its data is posted back to the server whenever we need to update data or change how it is displayed. One of the major benefits of this processing though, is that the JavaScript to handle posting the web form back to the server is automatically generated for us.

Having coded two projects that performed data binding, we have seen how to perform data binding through code in both a form class and server-side script. While there were not a whole lot of differences between the two, being exposed to these two methods can only benefit you in the long run. Knowing how to code both methods will better prepare you for the real world.

While we did not cover data binding using the wizards, they are also available when coding web forms. You should be able to apply the same principals to web forms as you did when using the wizards in Windows Forms back in Chapter 15.

To summarize, you should now know:

- How to bind data through code in a web form
- How to perform sorting and updating in a `DataGrid`
- The major differences between Windows Forms and web forms
- How to write code in a form class and in server-side script

Questions

1. How do Web Server controls differ from HTML controls?

2. Can HTML controls also be programmed at the server?

3. What does the `IsPostBack` property do?

4. Can we mix the code that we use? For example, can we write server-side code in a form class and also write server-side code in a script block in the HTML?

Visual Basic .NET and XML

Put simply, **Extensible Markup Language**, or **XML**, is a language used for exchanging data between applications. Although XML has been around for some time, it's now considered to be the *de facto* data exchange standard for Internet applications. XML is not only used on the Internet, but it is now being used to simply exchange data between different platforms and applications.

In this chapter, we are not going to get bogged down in the details regarding XML, for example, its validation and "well-formedness". Instead XML is going to be introduced generally and then we will look at its role with VB. After that we will focus on showing how XML can be used when building applications.

XML

The need for XML is simple: in commercial environments, applications need to exchange information in order to **integrate**. This integration is more applicable to the line-of-business software that a company may have rather than desktop productivity applications like Microsoft Office. For example, a company may have invested in a piece of software that allows it to track the stock in its warehouse – that piece of software would be an example of "line-of-business" software.

Integration has traditionally been very difficult to do, and XML together with web services (which we'll talk about in the next chapter) are both technologies designed to reduce the difficulty and cost involved in software integration. In reducing the difficulty of software integration there is, not unnaturally, a knock-on benefit in terms of the ease with which more general data/information exchange can occur.

Let's look at an example. Imagine you are a coffee retailer who wants to place an order with a supplier. The "old school" technique of doing this is to phone in or fax your order. However, this introduces a human element into the equation. It's likely that your own line-of-business applications (telling you what products you've sold) are suggesting that you buy more of a certain machine or certain blend of coffee. From that suggestion, you formulate an order and "transmit" it to your supplier. In the case of phone or fax, a human being at the supplier then has to transcribe the order into their own line-of-business system for processing.

An alternative way of carrying out this order would be to get the "suggestion" that's been raised by your line-of-business system to automatically create an order in the remote system of your supplier. This makes life easier and more efficient for both you and the management of your chosen supplier. However, getting to a point where the two systems are integrated in this way requires a lot of negotiation, coordination, and cost. Thus, it is only relevant for people doing so much business that economies of scale come into play and the whole deal becomes worthwhile.

Before the Internet, for two companies to integrate in this way, specific negotiations had to be undertaken to set up some sort of dedicated connection between the two companies. With the connection in place, data is exchanged not only in order to place the order with the supplier, but also for the supplier to report the status of the order back to the customer. With the Internet, this dedicated connection is no longer required – providing both parties are on the Internet, data exchange can take place.

However, without a common language for this data exchange to be based on, the problem is only half solved. XML is this common language. As the customer, you can create an **XML document** that contains the details of the order. You can use the Internet to somehow transmit that order written in XML over to the supplier, either over the Web, through e-mail, or by using web services. The supplier receives the XML document, decodes it and raises the order in their own system. Likewise, if the supplier needs to report anything back to the customer, they can construct a different document (again using XML), and use the Internet to transmit it back again.

The actual structure of the data contained within the XML document is up to the customer and supplier to decide. (Usually it's for the supplier to decide upon and the customer to adhere to.) This is where the "eXtensible" in XML comes in – any two parties who wish to exchange data using XML are completely free to decide exactly what the documents should look like.

XML is a text-based format. This means that it can easily be moved across platforms and moved around using Internet technologies like e-mail, the Web, and FTP. Traditional software integration was difficult when moving data between platforms, such as between Windows, UNIX, Mac, AS/400, OS 390, or any other platform and so the fact that it's text-based removes a lot of these cross-platform communication issues.

What Does XML Look Like?

If you have any experience of HTML, XML is going to look familiar to you. In fact, both have a common ancestor in **Standard General Markup Language** (**SGML**). In many ways, XML is not a language as the name suggests, but is rather a set of rules for defining your own markup languages that allow the exchange of data.

XML is **tag based**, meaning that the document is made up of tags that contain data. Here's how we might choose to describe this book in XML:

```
<Book>
    <Title>Beginning Visual Basic.NET</Title>
    <ISBN>1861007612</ISBN>
    <Publisher>Wrox Press</Publisher>
</Book>
```

In XML, we delimit **tags** using the < and > symbols. There are two sorts of tags: **start tags** and **end tags**, an example of a start tag being <Title> and an end tag being </Title>. Together, the tags and the content between them are known as an **element**. In our above example, the Title element is written like this:

```
<Title>Beginning Visual Basic.NET</Title>
```

while the ISBN element looks like this:

```
<ISBN>1861007612</ISBN>
```

and the Publisher element looks like this:

```
<Publisher>Wrox Press</Publisher>
```

Note that elements can contain other elements. In this case, for example, our Book element contains three sub-elements:

```
<Book>
    <Title>Beginning Visual Basic.NET</Title>
    <ISBN>1861007612</ISBN>
    <Publisher>Wrox Press</Publisher>
</Book>
```

If we were given this XML document, we'd need to have an understanding of its structure. Usually, the company that designed the structure of the document will tell us what it looks like. In this case, someone might tell us that if we first look for the Book element and then the Title element, we will determine the title of the book. The value between the <Title> start tag and the </Title> end tag is the title, in this case Beginning Visual Basic.NET.

XML is largely common sense, which is one of the things that makes it so simple. For example, I believe you can guess what this document represents, even though you've only just started thinking about XML:

```
<Books>
    <Book>
        <Title>Beginning Visual Basic.NET</Title>
        <ISBN>1861007612</ISBN>
        <Publisher>Wrox Press</Publisher>
    </Book>
    <Book>
        <Title>Beginning Visual Basic.NET Databases </Title>
        <ISBN>1861005555</ISBN>
        <Publisher>Wrox Press</Publisher>
    </Book>
</Books>
```

If you guessed that this document represents a list of two books, well done! You're well on the way to understanding what XML is.

XML for Visual Basic Newcomers

As a newcomer to programming and Visual Basic, it's unlikely that you'll be undertaking projects that involve complex integration work. If XML is so popular because it makes systems integration so much easier, how is it relevant to a newcomer?

The answer to this question is that, as well as being a great tool for integration; XML is also a great tool for storage and general data organization. Before XML, the two ways that an application could store its data were by using a separate database or by having its own proprietary file format with code that could save into and read from it.

In many cases, a database is absolutely the right tool for the job, because you need the fast access, shared storage, and advanced searching facilities that a database like Access or SQL Server gives you. In other cases, such as with a graphics package or word processor, building your own proprietary format is the right way to go. The reasons for this may be you want the application to be light and don't want to have the hassle of showing the user how to set up and maintain a database, or simply don't want to deal with the licensing implications of needing a separate application to support yours.

XML gives us a new way of storing application data, though it is still based on the concept of defining our own proprietary application storage format. The key difference, in contrast to formats such as `.doc` files for Word documents, however, is that the XML storage format is a universal standard.

The Address Book Project

We're going to build a demonstration application that allows us to create an XML file format for an address book. We'll be able to create a list of new addresses in our list and save the whole lot as an XML file on our local disk. We'll also be able to load the XML file and walk through the addresses one by one.

Creating the Project

As always, the first thing we have to do is create a new project.

Try It Out – Creating the Project

1. Open Visual Studio .NET and select File | New Project from the menu. Create a new Visual Basic .NET Windows Application project and call it Address Book.

2. The Form Designer for Form1 will open. Change its Text property to Address Book. Now add ten textboxes, twelve labels, and a button to the form so that it looks like this:

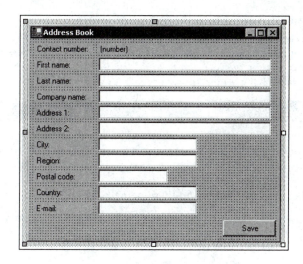

3. The textboxes should be named as follows, in the order given:

❑ txtFirstName

❑ txtLastName

❑ txtCompanyName

❑ txtAddress1

❑ txtAddress2

❑ txtCity

❑ txtRegion

❑ txtPostalCode

❑ txtCountry

❑ txtEmail

4. The button should be named **btnSave**. Finally, the label control marked (**number**) should be called **lblAddressNumber**.

That's all we need to do with respect to form design. Let's move on and write some code to save the data as an XML file.

The SerializableData Class

Our application is going to have two classes: `Address` and `AddressBook`. `Address` will be used to store a single instance of a contact in the address book. `AddressBook` will store our entire list of addresses and provide ways for us to navigate through the book.

Both of these classes will be inherited from another class called `SerializableData`. This base class will contain the logic needed for saving the addresses to disk and loading them back again. In XML parlance, the saving process is known as **serialization** and the loading process is known as **deserialization**. In this next section, we're going to build the `SerializableData` and `Address` classes so that we can demonstrate saving a new address record to disk.

Try It Out – Building SerializableData

1. The first class we need to build is the base `SerializableData` class. Using the Solution Explorer, right-click on the **Address Book** project and select **Add | Add Class**. Call the new class **SerializableData** and click **Open**.

2. At the top of the class definition, add these namespace import directives:

```
Imports System.IO
Imports System.Xml.Serialization

Public Class SerializableData

End Class
```

3. Next, add these two methods to the class:

```
' Save - serialize the object to disk...
Public Function Save(ByVal filename As String)

    ' make a temporary filename...
    Dim tempFilename As String
    tempFilename = filename & ".tmp"

    ' does the file exist?
    Dim tempFileInfo As New FileInfo(tempFilename)
    If tempFileInfo.Exists = True Then tempFileInfo.Delete()

    ' open the file...
    Dim stream As New FileStream(tempFilename, FileMode.Create)

    ' save the object...
    Save(stream)

    ' close the file...
    stream.Close()

    ' remove the existing data file and
    ' rename the temp file...
    tempFileInfo.CopyTo(filename, True)
    tempFileInfo.Delete()

End Function

' Save - actually perform the serialization...
```

```
Public Function Save(ByVal stream As Stream)

    ' create a serializer...
    Dim serializer As New XmlSerializer(Me.GetType)

    ' save the file...
    serializer.Serialize(stream, Me)

End Function
```

4. Create a new class called `Address`. Set the class to derive from `SerializableData`, like this:

```
Public Class Address
    Inherits SerializableData

End Class
```

5. Next, add the members to the class that will be used to store the address details:

```
Public Class Address
    Inherits SerializableData

    ' members...
    Public FirstName As String
    Public LastName As String
    Public CompanyName As String
    Public Address1 As String
    Public Address2 As String
    Public City As String
    Public Region As String
    Public PostalCode As String
    Public Country As String
    Public Email As String

End Class
```

6. Go back to the Form Designer for **Form1**. Double-click on the **Save** button to create a new `Click` event handler. Add this code to it:

```
Private Sub btnSave_Click(ByVal sender As System.Object, _
    ByVal e As System.EventArgs) Handles btnSave.Click

    ' create a new address object...
    Dim address As New Address()

    ' copy the values from the form into the address...
    PopulateAddressFromForm(address)

    ' save the address...
    Dim filename As String = DataFilename
    address.Save(filename)
```

```
' tell the user...
   MsgBox("The address was saved to " & filename)

End Sub
```

7. Visual Studio will highlight the fact that we haven't defined the `DataFilename` property or the `PopulateAddressFromForm` method by underlining these respective names. To remove these underlines, let's first add the `DataFileName` property to the `Form1` code:

```
' DataFilename - where should we store our data?
Public ReadOnly Property DataFilename() As String
    Get

        ' get our working folder...
        Dim folder As String
        folder = Environment.CurrentDirectory

        ' return the folder with the name "Addressbook.xml"...
        Return folder & "\AddressBook.xml"

    End Get
End Property
```

8. Now we need to add the `PopulateAddressFromForm` method to our `Form1` code:

```
' PopulateAddressFromForm - populates Address from the form fields...
Public Sub PopulateAddressFromForm(ByVal address As Address)

    ' copy the values...
    address.FirstName = txtFirstName.Text
    address.LastName = txtLastName.Text
    address.CompanyName = txtCompanyName.Text
    address.Address1 = txtAddress1.Text
    address.Address2 = txtAddress2.Text
    address.City = txtCity.Text
    address.Region = txtRegion.Text
    address.PostalCode = txtPostalCode.Text
    address.Country = txtCountry.Text
    address.Email = txtEmail.Text

End Sub
```

9. Run the project and fill in an address:

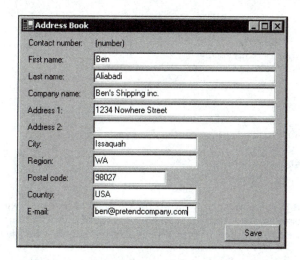

10. Click the Save button. You should be told where the file has been saved:

11. Go to the folder that this XML file has been saved into using Windows Explorer. Double-click on it, and Internet Explorer should open and list the contents:

```xml
<?xml version="1.0" ?>
<Address xmlns:xsi="http://www.w3.org/2001/XMLSchema-instance"
xmlns:xsd="http://www.w3.org/2001/XMLSchema">
  <FirstName>Ben</FirstName>
  <LastName>Aliabadi</LastName>
  <CompanyName>Ben's Shipping inc.</CompanyName>
  <Address1>1234 Nowhere Street</Address1>
  <Address2 />
  <City>Issaquah</City>
  <Region>WA</Region>
  <PostalCode>98027</PostalCode>
  <Country>USA</Country>
  <Email>ben@pretendcompany.com</Email>
</Address>
```

How It Works

First of all, let's look at the XML that's been returned. For this discussion, we can ignore the first line starting `<?xml` because all that's doing is saying, "Here is an XML version 1.0 document." We can also ignore the `xmlns` attributes on the second line as all this is doing is providing some extra information about the file, which at this level is something that we can let .NET worry about and we don't need to get involved with. With those two parts removed, this is what we get:

```
<Address>
  <FirstName>Ben</FirstName>
  <LastName>Aliabadi</LastName>
  <CompanyName>Ben's Shipping inc.</CompanyName>
  <Address1>1234 Nowhere Street</Address1>
  <Address2 />
  <City>Issaquah</City>
  <Region>WA</Region>
  <PostalCode>98027</PostalCode>
  <Country>USA</Country>
  <Email>ben@pretendcompany.com</Email>
</Address>
```

You can see how this is pretty similar to what we spoke about earlier on – we have start tags and end tags and when taken together these tags form an element. Each element contains data, and it's pretty obvious to see that, for example, the `CompanyName` element contains Ben's company name.

You'll notice as well that there is an `Address` tag at both the start and the bottom of the document. All of the other elements are enclosed by these tags, and this means that each of the elements in the middle *belongs* to the `Address` element. The `Address` element is the first element in the document and is therefore known as the **top-level** element or **root** element.

> It's worth noting that an XML document can only have one root element; all other elements in the document are child elements of this root.

Look at the `<Address2 />` line. By placing the slash at the end of the tag, what we're saying is that the element is empty. We could have written this as `<Address2></Address2>`, but this would have used up more storage space in the file.

The `XmlSerializer` class itself chooses the naming of the tags, although we'll talk about this a little later on.

So now that we know what was created, how did we get there? Let's follow the path of the application from the clicking of the **Save** button.

The first thing this method did was create a new `Address` object and call the `PopulateAddressFromForm` method. (This method just reads the `Text` property for every textbox on the form and populates the matching property on the `Address` object.)

```
Private Sub btnSave_Click(ByVal sender As System.Object, _
    ByVal e As System.EventArgs) Handles btnSave.Click

    ' create a new address object...
    Dim address As New Address()

    ' copy the values from the form into the address...
    PopulateAddressFromForm(address)
```

Then, we asked the `DataFilename` property (which we wrote in Step 7 of this *Try It Out*) to give us the name of a file that we can save the data to. We do this by using the `Environment.CurrentDirectory` property to return the folder that the address book is executing in and then tacking `"\AddressBook.xml"` to the end of this directory pathway. This is going to be the convention we use when saving and loading files with our application – we won't bother with giving the user the opportunity to save a specific file. Rather, we'll just assume that the file we want always has the same name and is always in the same place

```
        ' save the address...
        Dim filename As String = DataFilename
```

We then call the `Save` method on the `Address` object. This method is inherited from `SerializableData` and in a moment we'll take a look at what this method actually does. After we've saved the file, we tell the user where it is:

```
        address.Save(filename)

        ' tell the user...
        MsgBox ("The address was saved to " & filename)

    End Sub
```

It's the two `Save` methods on `SerializableData` that are the really interesting part of this project. The first version of the method takes a filename and opens the file. The second version of the method actually saves the data using the `System.Xml.Serialization.XmlSerializer` class, as we'll soon see.

When we save the file, we want to be quite careful. We have to save over the top of an existing file, but we also want to make sure that if the file cannot be saved for any reason we don't end up trashing the only good copy of the data the user has. This is a fairly common problem with a fairly common solution – we save the file to a different file, wait until we know that everything has been saved properly and then replace the existing file with the new one.

To get the name of the new file, we just tack `.tmp` onto the end. So, if we had the filename given as `C:\MyPrograms\AddressBook\AddressBook.xml`, we'd actually try and save to `C:\MyPrograms\AddressBook\AddressBook.xml.tmp`. If this file exists, we delete it by calling the `Delete` method:

```
    ' Save - serialize the object to disk...
    Public Function Save(ByVal filename As String)

        ' make a temporary filename...
        Dim tempFilename As String
        tempFilename = filename & ".tmp"

        ' does the file exist?
        Dim tempFileInfo As New FileInfo(tempFilename)
        If tempFileInfo.Exists = True Then tempFileInfo.Delete()
```

Once the existing file is gone, we can create a new file. This will return a `System.IO.FileStream` object:

```
' open the file...
Dim stream As New FileStream(tempFilename, FileMode.Create)
```

We then pass this stream to another overloaded `Save` method. We'll go through this method in a moment, but for now all you need to know is that this method will do the actual serialization of the data.

Then, we close the file:

```
' close the file...
stream.Close()
```

Finally, we replace the existing file with the new file. We have to do this with `CopyTo` (the `True` parameter we pass to this method means "overwrite any existing file") and finally delete the temporary file:

```
' remove the existing data file and
' rename the temp file...
tempFileInfo.CopyTo(filename, True)
tempFileInfo.Delete()

End Function
```

The other version of `Save` looks like this:

```
' Save - actually perform the serialization...
Public Function Save(ByVal stream As Stream)

    ' create a serializer...
    Dim serializer As New XmlSerializer(Me.GetType)

    ' save the file...
    serializer.Serialize(stream, Me)

End Function
```

The `System.Xml.Serialization.XmlSerializer` class is what we use to actually serialize the object to the stream that we specify. In this case, we're using a stream that points to a file, but later in the chapter we'll use a different kind of file.

`XmlSerializer` needs to know ahead of time what type of object it's saving. We use the `GetType` method to return a `System.Type` object that references the class that we actually are saving, which in this case is `Address`. The reason why `XmlSerializer` needs to know the type is because it works by iterating through all of the properties on the object looking for ones that are both readable and writable (in other words ones that are *not* flagged as read-only or write-only). Every time it finds one, it writes it to the stream, which in this case means it subsequently gets written to the `AddressBook.xml` file.

`XmlSerializer` bases the name of the element in the XML document on the name of the matching property. For example, the `FirstName` element in the document matches the `FirstName` property on `Address`. In addition, the top-level element of `Address` matches the name of the `Address` class, in other words, the root element name matches the class name.

`XmlSerializer` is a great way of using XML in your programs because you don't need to mess around creating and manually reading XML documents – it does all the work for you.

Loading the XML File

Let's now prove that we can load the address back from the XML file on the disk.

Try It Out – Loading the XML File

1. Using the Solution Explorer, open the code editor for `SerializableData`. Add these two methods:

```
' Load - deserialize from disk...
Public Shared Function Load(ByVal filename As String, _
                ByVal newType As Type) As Object

    ' does the file exist?
    Dim fileInfo As New FileInfo(filename)
    If fileInfo.Exists = False Then

        ' create a blank version of the object and return that...
        Return System.Activator.CreateInstance(newType)

    End If

    ' open the file...
    Dim stream As New FileStream(filename, FileMode.Open)

    ' load the object from the stream...
    Dim newObject As Object = Load(stream, newType)

    ' close the stream...
    stream.Close()

    ' return the object...
    Return newObject

End Function
```

```
Public Shared Function Load(ByVal stream As Stream, _
                ByVal newType As Type) As Object

    ' create a serializer and load the object....
    Dim serializer As New XmlSerializer(newType)
    Dim newObject As Object = serializer.Deserialize(stream)

    ' return the new object...
    Return newobject

End Function
```

2. Go back to the Form Designer for **Form1**. Delete the **Save** button (we don't need it anymore) and replace it with a new button. Set the **Text** property to **Load** and set the **Name** to **btnLoad**.

3. Double-click on the **Load** button and add this code to the event handler:

```
Private Sub btnLoad_Click(ByVal sender As System.Object, _
        ByVal e As System.EventArgs) Handles btnLoad.Click

    ' load the address using a shared method on SerializableData...
    Dim newAddress As Address = _
     SerializableData.Load(DataFilename, GetType(Address))

    ' update the display...
    PopulateFormFromAddress(newAddress)

End Sub
```

4. You'll also need to add this method to **Form1**:

```
' PopulateFormFromAddress - populates the form from an
' address object...
Public Sub PopulateFormFromAddress(ByVal address As Address)

    ' copy the values...
    txtFirstName.Text = address.FirstName
    txtLastName.Text = address.LastName
    txtCompanyName.Text = address.CompanyName
    txtAddress1.Text = address.Address1
    txtAddress2.Text = address.Address2
    txtCity.Text = address.City
    txtRegion.Text = address.Region
    txtPostalCode.Text = address.PostalCode
    txtCountry.Text = address.Country
    txtEmail.Text = address.Email

End Sub
```

5. Run the project and click the **Load** button. The address should be loaded from the XML file and displayed on the screen:

How It Works

De-serialization is the opposite process to serialization. It can be used to load the data from the file, whereas before we saved the data to the file. (Note that here I'm using the word *file* for simplification. In fact, we can serialize to and de-serialize from any kind of stream.)

Whenever we ask `XmlSerializer` to de-serialize an object for us, it will create a new object. We can use this functionality to get `XmlSerializer` to create a new object for us rather than having to create one ourselves. This is a good candidate for an overloaded method on the `SerializableData` object. We create an overloaded method called `Load`, the first version of which takes a filename and also a `System.Type` object. This `Type` object represents the type of object we ultimately want to end up with. Specifically, we'll need to pass in a `Type` object that tells `XmlSerializer` where to find a list of properties that exist on our `Address` object.

Since `XmlSerializer` doesn't save .NET class namespaces or assembly information into the XML file, it relies on an explicit statement saying what class the file contains, otherwise things get ambiguous. (Imagine – we might have a hundred assemblies on our machine, each containing a class called `Address`. How could `XmlSerializer` know which one we mean?)

Obviously, when the method is called the first thing we do is check to see if the file exists. If it doesn't, we'll return a blank version of the object that we asked for. (The motivation behind doing this will become apparent later.)

```
' Load - deserialize from disk...
Public Shared Function Load(ByVal filename As String, _
                ByVal newType As Type) As Object

    ' does the file exist?
    Dim fileInfo As New FileInfo(filename)
    If fileInfo.Exists = False Then

        ' create a blank version of the object and return that...
        Return System.Activator.CreateInstance(newType)

    End If
```

If the file does exist, we open it and pass it to the other version of `Load`, which we'll see in a moment. We then close the file and return the new object to the caller:

```
    ' open the file...
    Dim stream As New FileStream(filename, FileMode.Open)

    ' load the object from the stream...
    Dim newObject As Object = Load(stream, newType)

    ' close the stream...
    stream.Close()

    ' return the object...
    Return newObject

End Function
```

The other version of `Load` uses the `XmlSerializer` again and, as you can see, it's no more complicated than when we used it last time. Except, of course, that the `Deserialize` method returns a new object to us:

```
Public Shared Function Load(ByVal stream As Stream, _
              ByVal newType As Type) As Object

    ' create a serializer and load the object....
    Dim serializer As New XmlSerializer(newType)
    Dim newObject As Object = serializer.Deserialize(stream)

    ' return the new object...
    Return newobject

End Function
```

What `XmlSerializer` does when it's de-serializing is to go through each of the properties on the new object that it has created, again looking for ones that are both readable and writable. When it finds one, it takes the value stored against it in the XML document and sets the property. The result: we are given a new object, fully populated with the data from the XML document.

Once we've called `Load` and got a new `Address` object back, we pass the new object to `PopulateFormFromAddress`:

```
Private Sub btnLoad_Click(ByVal sender As System.Object, _
        ByVal e As System.EventArgs) Handles btnLoad.Click

    ' load the address using a shared method on SerializableData...
    Dim newAddress As Address = _
      SerializableData.Load(DataFilename, GetType(Address))

    ' update the display...
    PopulateFormFromAddress(newAddress)

End Sub
```

window will reappear.

...ent value of the `txtEmail` field and put `mailto:` at the beginning. This ...a URL. We then call the shared `Start` method on the ...rocess class, passing it this URL:

```
...mail_LinkClicked(ByVal sender As System.Object, _
...Windows.Forms.LinkLabelLinkClickedEventArgs) _
...ail.LinkClicked

    ...ail client...
    ...ics.Process.Start("mailto:" & txtEmail.Text)
```

...aves in exactly the same way as the Run dialog. Both tap into Windows' built-in ...lity. In this case, we've used this functionality to integrate our application with ...e'd specified a protocol of `http:` rather than `mailto:`, our application could ...ge, as we've already seen. Likewise, if we had supplied a path to a Word ...eadsheet, the application could open those too. Note that when we're working ...ed to supply a protocol – for example, we only need to do this:

```
...Budget.xls
```

...t of Addresses

...exercise is to build an application that allows us to store a list of addresses in XML. ...an successfully load and save just one address, so now we have to turn our attention ...f addresses.

...efore, the class we're going to build to do this is called `AddressBook`. We'll inherit ...zableData because ultimately we want to get to a point where we can tell the ...ject itself to load and save to the XML file without us having to do anything.

...ing AddressBook

...lution Explorer, create a new class called `AddressBook`.

...dd this namespace declaration:

```
...stem.Xml.Serialization
```

```
...ss AddressBook
```

...dly, set the class to inherit from `SerializableData`:

Changing the Data

To prove that nothing funny is going on, we'll change the XML file using Notepad and try clicking the Load button again.

Try It Out – Changing the Data

1. Open up Windows Notepad and load the XML file into it.

2. Inside the `FirstName` element, change `Ben` to `Gretchen`, save the file, and exit Notepad:

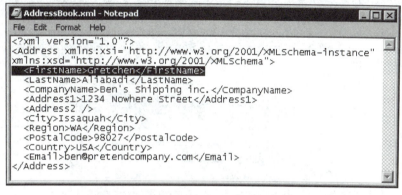

3. Go back to the Address Book program. Click the Load button again and Gretchen's name should appear rather than Ben's:

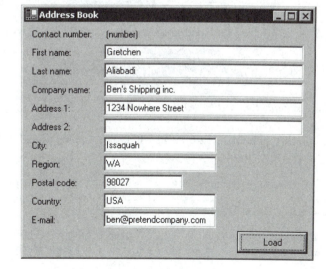

How It Works

What we've done here is to prove that XmlSerializer does indeed use the AddressBook.xml file as the source of its data. We changed the data, and when we loaded the Address object again, the FirstName property had indeed been changed to Gretchen.

Send E-mail

For this next *Try It Out*, we'll go quickly off-topic and I'll demonstrate how we can integrate this application with Outlook and Outlook Express.

Try It Out – Sending E-mail from the Client

1. Go back to the Form1 designer and, using the Toolbox, draw a LinkLabel control to the right of the e-mail field. Set its Text property to Send E-mail and change its Name property to lnkSendEmail.

Note that this will work with a normal button control, too.

2. Double-click on the LinkLabel control. This will create an event handler for the LinkClicked event. Add this code:

```
Private Sub lnkSendEmail_LinkClicked(ByVal sender As System.Object, _
    ByVal e As System.Windows.Forms.LinkLabelLinkClickedEventArgs) _
    Handles lnkSendEmail.LinkClicked

    ' start the e-mail client...
    System.Diagnostics.Process.Start("mailto:" & txtEmail.Text)


End Sub
```

---

3. Run the project and
your email applicati

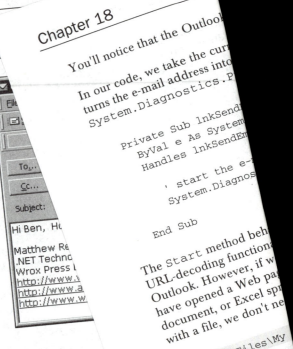

You'll notice that the Outloo

In our code, we take the cur
turns the e-mail address into
System.Diagnostics.P

```
Private Sub lnkSend
    ByVal e As System
    Handles lnkSendEm

    ' start the e-
    System.Diagnos


End Sub
```

The Start method beh
URL-decoding function
Outlook. However, if w
have opened a Web pa
document, or Excel spr
with a file, we don't ne

c:\My Files\My

How It Works

Windows has a built-in ability to decode In
with them.

When Outlook or Outlook Express is installe
When Internet Explorer is installed, it regist
http from when you've browsed the Web.

An Internet address is known as a **URL**, or **Unif**
protocol. The second part of the URL is a **protoc**
is mailto:ben@pretendcompany.com.

Close down the Outlook window, click the Start b
your screen, and select Run. Enter mailto:ben@pre

Creating a Lis

The purpose of this
At the moment we
to managing a list o

As we mentioned
this from Seriali
AddressBook ob

Try It Out – Creat

1. Using S

2. Firstly,

```
Imports S

Public Cl

End Class
```

3. Seco

```
Imports System.Xml.Serialization

Public Class AddressBook
    Inherits SerializableData

End Class
```

4. To store the addresses, we're going to use a `System.Collections.ArrayList` object. We also need a method that we can use to create new addresses in the list. Add the following member and method to the class:

```
Imports System.Xml.Serialization

Public Class AddressBook
    Inherits SerializableData

    ' members...
    Public Items As New ArrayList()

    ' AddAddress - add a new address to the book...
    Public Function AddAddress() As Address

        ' create one...
        Dim newAddress As New Address()

        ' add it to the list...
        Items.Add(newAddress)

        ' return the address...
        Return newAddress

    End Function

End Class
```

5. Open the code editor for Form1. Add these members to the top of the class:

```
Public Class Form1
    Inherits System.Windows.Forms.Form

    ' members...
    Public AddressBook As AddressBook
    Private _currentAddressIndex As Integer
```

6. Next, add this property:

```
' CurrentAddress - property for the current address...
ReadOnly Property CurrentAddress() As Address
    Get
        Return AddressBook.Items(CurrentAddressIndex - 1)
    End Get
End Property
```

7. Then, add this property:

```
' CurrentAddressIndex - property for the current address...
Property CurrentAddressIndex() As Integer
    Get
        Return _currentAddressIndex
    End Get
    Set(ByVal Value As Integer)

        ' set the address...
        _currentAddressIndex = Value

        ' update the display...
        PopulateFormFromAddress(CurrentAddress)

        ' set the label...
        lblAddressNumber.Text = _
        _currentAddressIndex & " of " & AddressBook.Items.Count

    End Set
End Property
```

8. Double-click on the form to create the `Load` event for `Form1` and add this code:

```
Private Sub Form1_Load(ByVal sender As System.Object, _
        ByVal e As System.EventArgs) Handles MyBase.Load

    ' load the address book...
    AddressBook = _
      SerializableData.Load(DataFilename, GetType(AddressBook))

    ' if the address book only contains one item, add a new one...
    If AddressBook.Items.Count = 0 Then AddressBook.AddAddress()

    ' select the first item in the list...
    CurrentAddressIndex = 1

End Sub
```

9. Now that we can load the address book, we need to be able to save the changes. From the left drop-down list, select (**Overrides**). From the right list, select **OnClosed**. Add this code to the event handler, and also add the `SaveChanges` and `UpdateCurrentAddress` methods:

```
Protected Overrides Sub OnClosed(ByVal e As System.EventArgs)

    ' save the changes...
    UpdateCurrentAddress()
    SaveChanges()

End Sub
```

```
' SaveChanges - save the address book to an XML file...
Public Sub SaveChanges()

    ' tell the address book to save itself...
    AddressBook.Save(DataFilename)

End Sub
```

```
' UpdateCurrentAddress - make sure the book has the current
' values currently entered into the form...
Private Sub UpdateCurrentAddress()
    PopulateAddressFromForm(CurrentAddress)
End Sub
```

Before running the project, it's *very* important that you delete the existing **AddressBook.xml** file.

If you don't, **XmlSerializer** will try to load an **AddressBook** object from a file containing an **Address** object and an exception will be thrown.

---

10. Run the project. Don't bother entering any information into the form because the save routine won't work – I've deliberately introduced a bug to illustrate an issue with XmlSerializer. Close the form and you should see this:

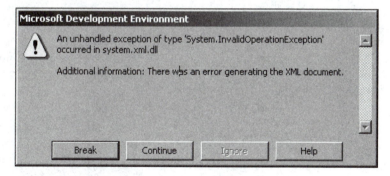

How It Works (or Why It Doesn't!)

When the form is loaded, the first thing we do is ask SerializableData to create a new AddressBook object for us from the AddressBook.xml file. As we deleted this before we ran the project, this file won't exist and as you recall we rigged the Load method so that if the file didn't exist it would just create an instance of whatever class we asked for. In this case, we get an AddressBook:

```
Private Sub Form1_Load(ByVal sender As System.Object, _
        ByVal e As System.EventArgs) Handles MyBase.Load

    ' load the address book...
    AddressBook = _
        SerializableData.Load(DataFilename, GetType(AddressBook))
```

However, the new address book won't have any addresses in it. We ask `AddressBook` to create a new address if the list is empty:

```
' if the address book only contains one item, add a new one...
If AddressBook.Items.Count = 0 Then AddressBook.AddAddress()
```

At this point, we'll either have an `AddressBook` object that's been loaded from the file and therefore contains a set of `Address` objects, or we'll have a new `AddressBook` object that contains one, blank address. We set the `CurrentAddressIndex` property to 1, meaning the first item in the list:

```
' select the first item in the list...
CurrentAddressIndex = 1

End Sub
```

The `CurrentAddressIndex` property does a number of things. Firstly, it updates the private `_currentAddressIndex` member:

```
' CurrentAddressIndex - property for the current address...
Property CurrentAddressIndex() As Integer
    Get
        Return _currentAddressIndex
    End Get
    Set(ByVal Value As Integer)

        ' set the address...
        _currentAddressIndex = Value
```

Then, it uses the `CurrentAddress` property to get the `Address` object that corresponds to whatever `_currentAddressIndex` is set to. This `Address` object is passed to `PopulateFormFromAddress` whose job it is to update the display:

```
' update the display...
PopulateFormFromAddress(CurrentAddress)
```

Finally, it changes the `lblAddressNumber` control so that it displays the current record number:

```
' set the label...
lblAddressNumber.Text = _
_currentAddressIndex & " of " & AddressBook.Items.Count

    End Set
End Property
```

We'll just quickly look at `CurrentAddress`. This property's job is to turn an integer index into the corresponding `Address` object stored in `AddressBook`. However, because `AddressBook` works on the basis of an `ArrayList` object that numbers items from 0, and our application starts numbering items at 1, we have to decrement our index value by one to get the matching value from `AddressBook`:

```
' CurrentAddress - property for the current address...
ReadOnly Property CurrentAddress() As Address
    Get
        Return AddressBook.Items(CurrentAddressIndex - 1)
    End Get
End Property
```

All good so far, but why is `XmlSerializer` throwing an exception? Well the problems occur when we close the application. This fires the `OnClosed` method, which ultimately calls the `Save` method of the `AddressBook`.

As we know, to save an object to disk, `XmlSerializer` walks through each of the properties looking for ones that are readable and writable. So far, we've only used `XmlSerializer` with `System.String`, but when the object comes across a property that uses a complex type, like `Address`, it uses the same principle – in other words, it looks through all of the properties that the complex type has. If properties on that that object return complex types, it will drill down again. What it's doing is looking for simple types that it knows how to turn into text and write to the XML document.

However, some types cannot be turned into text and at this point `XmlSerializer` chokes. The `ArrayList` object that we're using to store a list of addresses had some properties that cannot be converted to text, which is the reason why the exception is being thrown. What we need to do is provide an alternative property that `XmlSerializer` can hook into in order to get a list of addresses and tell it not to bother trying to serialize the `ArrayList`.

Ignoring Members

Although `XmlSerializer` cannot cope with certain data types, it has no problems with arrays. We've also seen that `XmlSerializer` has no problems with our `Address` class, simply because this object doesn't have any properties of a type that `XmlSerializer` cannot support. What we'll do is provide an alternative property that returns an array of `Address` objects and tell `XmlSerializer` to keep away from the `Items` property because `XmlSerializer` cannot deal with `ArrayList` objects.

Try It Out – Ignoring Members

1. Open the code editor for `AddressBook`. Find the `Items` property and prefix it with the `System.Xml.Serialization.XmlIgnore` attribute:

```
Public Class AddressBook
    Inherits SerializableData

    ' members...
    <XmlIgnore()>Public Items As New ArrayList()
```

2. Now, add this new property:

```
' Addresses - property that works with the items
' collection as an array...
Public Property Addresses() As Address()
    Get
```

```
            ' create a new array...
            Dim addressArray(Items.Count - 1) As Address
            Items.CopyTo(addressArray)
            Return addressArray

        End Get
        Set(ByVal Value As Address())

            ' reset the arraylist...
            Items.Clear()

            ' did we get anything?
            If Not Value Is Nothing Then

                ' go through the array and populate items...
                Dim address As Address
                For Each address In Value
                    Items.Add(address)
                Next

            End If

        End Set
    End Property
```

3. Run the project and then close the application; this time everything functions correctly. Run the project again and this time around, enter some data into the address fields. Close the application and you should now find that `AddressBook.xml` does contain data. (I've removed the `xmlns` and `?xml` values for clarity here.)

```xml
<AddressBook>
  <Addresses>
    <Address>
      <FirstName>Ben</FirstName>
      <LastName>Aliabadi</LastName>
      <CompanyName>Ben Shipping inc.</CompanyName>
      <Address1>1234 Nowhere Street</Address1>
      <Address2 />
      <City>Issaquah</City>
      <Region>WA</Region>
      <PostalCode>98027</PostalCode>
      <Country>USA</Country>
      <Email>ben@pretendcompany.com</Email>
    </Address>
  </Addresses>
</AddressBook>
```

How It Works

The XML that we've got saved into the file proves that our approach works, but why?

At this point, our `AddressBook` object has two properties: `Items` and `Addresses`. Both are read/write properties, so both are going to be examined as candidates for serialization by `XmlSerializer`. As we know, `Items` returns an `ArrayList` object and `Addresses` returns an array of `Address` objects.

However, we marked `Items` with the `XmlIgnore` attribute. This means, not surprisingly, that `XmlSerializer` will ignore the property, despite the fact that it is readable and writable. Instead, it will move on to the `Addresses` property.

The `Get` portion of the `Addresses` property is what interests us. All we do is create a new array of `Address` objects and use the `CopyTo` method on the `ArrayList` to populate it:

```
' Addresses - property that works with the items
' collection as an array...
Public Property Addresses() As Address()
    Get

        ' create a new array...
        Dim addressArray(Items.Count - 1) As Address
        Items.CopyTo(addressArray)
        Return addressArray

    End Get
    Set(ByVal Value As Address())
        …
    End Set
End Property
```

When `XmlSerializer` gets an array of objects that it can deal with, all it does is iterate through the array serializing each of these contained objects in turn. We can see this in the XML that we received – the structure of the XML contained within the `Addresses` element exactly matches the structure of the XML we saw when we tested out the process and wrote a single `Address` object to the file:

```
<AddressBook>
  <Addresses>
    <Address>
      <FirstName>Ben</FirstName>
      <LastName>Aliabadi</LastName>
      <CompanyName>Ben Shipping inc.</CompanyName>
      <Address1>1234 Nowhere Street</Address1>
      <Address2 />
      <City>Issaquah</City>
      <Region>WA</Region>
      <PostalCode>98027</PostalCode>
      <Country>USA</Country>
      <Email>ben@pretendcompany.com</Email>
    </Address>
  </Addresses>
</AddressBook>
```

Loading Addresses

If we're lucky, loading addresses should just work! Close the program and run the project again. You'll see this:

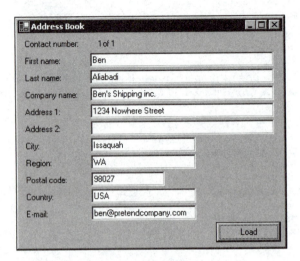

We already set up the project to load the `AddressBook` the first time we ran the project after creating the `AddressBook` class itself. This time, however, `AddressBook.Load` can find a file on the disk and so rather than creating a blank object, it's getting `XmlSerializer` to de-serialize the lot. As `XmlSerializer` has no problems writing arrays, we can assume it has no problem reading them.

It's the `Set` portion of the `Addresses` property that does the magic for us this time. One thing we have to be careful of with this property is that, if we are passed a blank array (in other words `Nothing`) we want to prevent exceptions being thrown:

```
' Addresses - property that works with the items
' collection as an array...
Public Property Addresses() As Address()
    Get
        ...
    End Get
    Set(ByVal Value As Address())

        ' reset the arraylist...
        Items.Clear()

        ' did we get anything?
        If Not Value Is Nothing Then

            ' go through the array and populate items...
            Dim address As Address
            For Each address In Value
                Items.Add(address)
            Next
```

```
            End If

        End Set
    End Property
```

For each of the values in the array, all we have to do is take each one in turn and add them to the list.

Adding New Addresses

Next, we'll look at how we can add new addresses to the list.

Try It Out – Adding New Addresses

1. Open the Form Designer for `Form1`, remove the **Load** button before adding these four buttons:

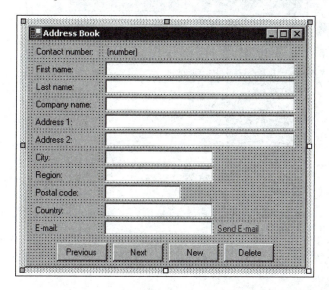

2. Name the buttons in turn as: **btnPrevious**, **btnNext**, **btnNew**, and **btnDelete**.

3. Double-click on the **New** button to create a `Click` handler. Add this code to the event handler and also add the `AddNewAddress` method:

```
Private Sub btnNew_Click(ByVal sender As System.Object, _
        ByVal e As System.EventArgs) Handles btnNew.Click
    AddNewAddress()
End Sub

Public Function AddNewAddress() As Address

    ' save the current address...
    UpdateCurrentAddress()
```

```
    ' create a new address...
    Dim newAddress As Address = AddressBook.AddAddress

    ' update the display...
    CurrentAddressIndex = AddressBook.Items.Count

    ' return the new address...
    Return newAddress

End Function
```

4. Run the project. Click New and a new address record will be created. Enter a new address:

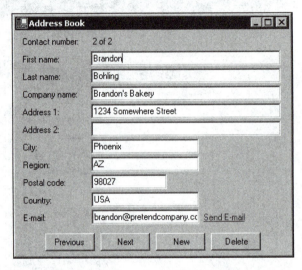

5. Close down the program and the changes will be saved. Open up AddressBook.xml and you should see the new address. (Again, I've removed the ?xml tag and the xmlns entries.)

```
<AddressBook>
  <Addresses>
    <Address>
      <FirstName>Ben</FirstName>
      <LastName>Aliabadi</LastName>
      <CompanyName>Ben Shipping inc.</CompanyName>
       <Address1>1234 Nowhere Street</Address1>
      <Address2 />
      <City>Issaquah</City>
      <Region>WA</Region>
      <PostalCode>98027</PostalCode>
      <Country>USA</Country>
      <Email>ben@pretendcompany.com</Email>
    </Address>
    <Address>
      <FirstName>Brandon</FirstName>
      <LastName>Bohling</LastName>
```

```
            <CompanyName>Brandon's Bakery</CompanyName>
            <Address1>1234 Somewhere Street</Address1>
            <Address2 />
            <City>Phoenix</City>
            <Region>AZ</Region>
            <PostalCode>98027</PostalCode>
            <Country>USA</Country>
            <Email>brandon@pretendcompany.com</Email>
        </Address>
    </Addresses>
</AddressBook>
```

How It Works

OK, so this time we have a new address object added to the XML document. It's contained within the `Addresses` element so we know that it's part of the same array.

The implementation was very simple – all we had to do was ask `AddressBook` to create a new address and then we updated the `CurrentAddressIndex` property so that it equaled the number of items in the `AddressBook`. This had the effect of changing the display so that it changed to record **2 of 2** ready for editing.

However, it's important that, before we actually do this, we save any changes that the user might have made. With this application, we're ensuring that any changes the user makes will always find themselves being persisted into the XML file. Whenever the user closes the application, creates a new record, or moves backwards or forwards in the list, we want to call `UpdateCurrentAddress` in order that any changes will be saved:

```
Public Function AddNewAddress() As Address

    ' save the current address...
    UpdateCurrentAddress()
```

After we've saved any changes, it's then safe to create the new record and show the new record to the user:

```
    ' create a new address...
    Dim newAddress As Address = AddressBook.AddAddress

    ' update the display...
    CurrentAddressIndex = AddressBook.Items.Count

    ' return the new address...
    Return newAddress

End Function
```

Navigating Addresses

Now that we can add new addresses to the address book, we need to wire up the Next and Previous buttons so that we can move through the list.

Try It Out – Navigating Addresses

1. Open the Form Designer for **Form1**. Double-click the **Next** button to create a new `Click` handler. Add this code and the associated `MoveNext` method:

```
Private Sub btnNext_Click(ByVal sender As System.Object, _
    ByVal e As System.EventArgs) Handles btnNext.Click
    MoveNext()
End Sub

Public Sub MoveNext()

    ' get the next index...
    Dim newIndex As Integer = CurrentAddressIndex + 1
    If newIndex > AddressBook.Items.Count Then
        newIndex = 1
    End If

    ' save any changes...
    UpdateCurrentAddress()

    ' move the record...
    CurrentAddressIndex = newIndex

End Sub
```

2. Next, flip back to the Form Designer and double-click the **Previous** button. Add this code:

```
Private Sub btnPrevious_Click(ByVal sender As System.Object, _
    ByVal e As System.EventArgs) Handles btnPrevious.Click
    MovePrevious()
End Sub

Public Sub MovePrevious()

    ' get the previous index...
    Dim newIndex As Integer = CurrentAddressIndex - 1
    If newIndex = 0 Then
        newIndex = AddressBook.Items.Count
    End If

    ' save changes...
    UpdateCurrentAddress()

    ' move the record...
    CurrentAddressIndex = newIndex

End Sub
```

3. Run the project. You should now be able to move between addresses.

How It Works

All we've done here is wire up the buttons so that each one changes the current index. By incrementing the current index, we move forward in the list. By decrementing it, we move backwards.

However, it's *very* important that we don't move outside the bounds of the list (in other words, try to move to a position before the first record or to a position after the last record), which is why we check the value and adjust it as appropriate. When we move forward (MoveNext) we flip to the beginning of the list if we go off the end. When we move backwards (MovePrevious) we flip to the end if we go off the start.

In both cases, we make sure that before we actually change the CurrentAddressIndex property, we call UpdateCurrentAddress to save any changes:

```
Public Sub MoveNext()

    ' get the next index...
    Dim newIndex As Integer = CurrentAddressIndex + 1
    If newIndex > AddressBook.Items.Count Then
        newIndex = 1
    End If

    ' save any changes...
    UpdateCurrentAddress()

    ' move the record...
    CurrentAddressIndex = newIndex

End Sub
```

Deleting Addresses

To finish off the functionality of our address book, we'll deal with deleting items.

Try It Out – Deleting Addresses

1. Go back to the Form Designer for **Form1** and double-click the **Delete** button. Add this code to the event handler, and also add the DeleteAddress method:

```
Private Sub btnDelete_Click(ByVal sender As System.Object, _
        ByVal e As System.EventArgs) Handles btnDelete.Click

    ' ask the user if they are ok with this?
    If MsgBox ("Are you sure you want to delete this address?", _
        MsgBoxStyle.Question Or MsgBoxStyle.YesNo) = _
        MsgBoxResult.Yes Then
        DeleteAddress(CurrentAddressIndex)
    End If

End Sub

' DeleteAddress - delete an address from the list...
```

761

```
Public Sub DeleteAddress(ByVal index As Integer)

    ' delete the item from the list...
    AddressBook.Items.RemoveAt(index - 1)

    ' was that the last address?
    If AddressBook.Items.Count = 0 Then

        ' add a new address?
        AddressBook.AddAddress()

    Else

        ' make sure we have something to show...
        If index > AddressBook.Items.Count Then
            index = AddressBook.Items.Count
        End If

    End If

    ' display the record...
    CurrentAddressIndex = index

End Sub
```

2. Run the project. You should be able to delete records from the address book. Note that if you delete the last record, a new record will automatically be created.

How It Works

The algorithm we've used here to delete the records is an example of how to solve another classic programming problem.

Our application is set up so that it always has to display a record. That's why, when the program is first run and there is no `AddressBook.xml`, we automatically create a new record. Likewise, when an item is deleted from the database we have to find something to present to the user.

To physically delete an address from the disk, we use the `RemoveAt` method on the `ArrayList` that holds the `Address` objects.

```
' DeleteAddress - delete an address from the list...
Public Sub DeleteAddress(ByVal index As Integer)

    ' delete the item from the list...
    AddressBook.Items.RemoveAt(index - 1)
```

Again, notice here that, because we're working with a zero-based array, when we ask to delete the address with an index of 3, we actually have to delete the address at position 2 in the array.

The problems start after we've done that. It could be that we've deleted the one remaining address in the book. In this case, because we always have to display an address, we create a new one:

```
' was that the last address?
If AddressBook.Items.Count = 0 Then

    ' add a new address?
    AddressBook.AddAddress()
```

Alternatively, if there are items in the address book, we have to change the display. In some cases, the value that's currently stored in CurrentAddressIndex will be valid. For example, if we had five records and are looking at the third one, _currentAddressIndex will be 3. If we delete that record, we have four records, but the third one as reported by _currentAddressIndex will still be 3 and will still be valid. However, as 4 has now shuffled into 3's place we need to update the display.

It could be the case that we've deleted the last item in the list. When this happens, the index isn't valid because the index would be positioned over the end of the list. (You have four items in the list, delete the fourth one, you only have three, but _currentAddressIndex would be 4, which isn't valid.) So, when the last item is deleted, the index will be over the end of the list, so we set it to be the last item in the list:

```
Else

    ' make sure we have something to show...
    If index > AddressBook.Items.Count Then
        index = AddressBook.Items.Count
    End If

End If
```

Whatever actually happens, we still need to update the display. As we know, the CurrentAddressIndex property can do this for us:

```
' display the record...
CurrentAddressIndex = index

End Sub
```

Sidenote – Test at the Edges

This brings me onto a programming technique that can greatly help you test your applications.

When writing software, things usually go wrong at the "edge". What I mean by this is, for example, you have a function that takes an integer value, but for the method to work properly, the value supplied must lie between 0 and 99.

Once you're satisfied that your algorithm works properly when you give it a valid value, test some values at the "edge" of the problem (in other words, at the boundaries of the valid data). For example: -1, 0, 99 and 100. In most cases, if your method works properly for one or two of the possible valid values, it will work properly for the entire set of valid values. Testing a few values at the edge will show you where potential problems with the method lie.

A classic example of this is with our `MoveNext` and `MovePrevious` methods. If we had a hundred addresses in our address book and only tested that `MoveNext` and `MovePrevious` worked between numbers `10` and `20`, it most likely would have worked between `1` and `100`. However, the moment we move past `100` (in other words "go over the edge"), problems can occur. If we hadn't handled this case properly by flipping back to `1`, our program would have crashed.

Integrating with the Address Book Application

So far we've built an application that is able to save and load its data as an XML document. We've also taken a look at the document as it's been changing over the course of the chapter, so by now you should have a pretty good idea of what an XML document looks like and how it works.

Right at the beginning of this chapter, we pitched XML as a technology for integrating software applications. We then went on to say that for newcomers to Visual Basic, using XML for integration is unlikely to be something that you would do on a day-to-day basis and so we've been using XML to store data. In the rest of this chapter, I'm going to try to demonstrate why XML is such a good technology for integration. What we'll do is build a separate application that, with very little work, is able to read in and understand the proprietary data format that we've used in `AddressBook.xml`.

Using XML is an advanced topic – so if you would like to learn more about the technology and its application, try the following Wrox titles:

❑ *Beginning XML, 2nd Edition* (ISBN 1-86100-559-8)

❑ *Professional XML, 2nd Edition* (ISBN 1-86100-505-9)

Demonstrating the Principle of Integration

Before we build the application that can integrate with our address book application, we should try and illustrate the principles involved. Basically, XML documents are good for integration because they can be easily read, understood, and changed by other people. Old-school file formats require detailed documentation to understand and often don't "evolve" well. (By that I mean when new versions of the format are released, software that worked with the old formats often breaks.)

XML documents are typically easily understood. Imagine you'd never seen or heard of our address book before and look at this XML document:

```xml
<Addresses>
  <Address>
    <FirstName>Ben</FirstName>
    <LastName>Aliabadi</LastName>
    <CompanyName>Ben's Shipping Corp</CompanyName>
    <Address1>1234 Nowhere Street</Address1>
    <Address2 />
    <City>Issaquah</City>
    <Region>WA</Region>
    <PostalCode>98027</PostalCode>
    <Country>USA</Country>
    <Email>ben@pretendcompany.com</Email>
  </Address>
</Addresses>
```

Common sense tells us what this document represents. We can also intuit how the program that generated it uses it. In addition, we can use the various tools in .NET to load, manipulate, and work with this document. To an extent, we still need to work with the people that designed the structure of the document, especially when more esoteric elements come into play, but we can use this document to some meaningful effect without too much stress.

Providing we know what structure the document takes, we can build our own document or add new things to it. For example, if we know that the Addresses element contains a list of Address elements, and that each Address element contains a bunch of elements that describe the address, we can add our own Address element using our own application.

To show this happening, open the AddressBook.xml file in Notepad now. Copy the last Address element (complete with the contents) to the bottom of the document, but make sure it remains inside the Addresses element. Change the address data to something else. Here's mine:

```xml
<?xml version="1.0"?>
<AddressBook xmlns:xsi="http://www.w3.org/2001/XMLSchema-instance"
xmlns:xsd="http://www.w3.org/2001/XMLSchema">
  <Addresses>
    <Address>
      <FirstName>Ben</FirstName>
      <LastName>Aliabadi</LastName>
      <CompanyName>Ben's Shipping Corp</CompanyName>
      <Address1>1234 Nowhere Street</Address1>
      <Address2 />
      <City>Issaquah</City>
      <Region>WA</Region>
      <PostalCode>98027</PostalCode>
      <Country>USA</Country>
      <Email>ben@pretendcompany.com</Email>
    </Address>
    <Address>
      <FirstName>Brandon</FirstName>
      <LastName>Bohling</LastName>
      <CompanyName>Brandon's Bakery</CompanyName>
      <Address1>1234 Somewhere Street</Address1>
      <Address2 />
      <City>Phoenix</City>
      <Region>AZ</Region>
      <PostalCode>98027</PostalCode>
      <Country>USA</Country>
      <Email>brandon@pretendcompany.com</Email>
    </Address>
    <Address>
      <FirstName>Darren</FirstName>
      <LastName>Clarke</LastName>
      <CompanyName>Madras inc</CompanyName>
      <Address1>1234 Nowhere Lane</Address1>
      <Address2 />
      <City>Watford</City>
      <Region>Hertfordshire</Region>
      <PostalCode>WD17 7DH</PostalCode>
```

```
            <Country>UK</Country>
            <Email>darren@pretendcompany.com</Email>
        </Address>
    </Addresses>
</AddressBook>
```

Save the file and run the address book application. You should now find that we have three addresses and that the last one is the new one that you added:

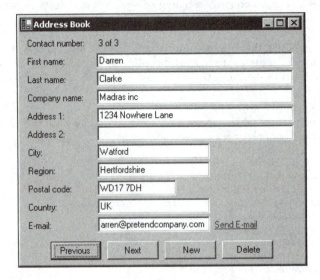

What this shows us is that, providing we understand the format of the XML that the application uses, we can manipulate the document and gain some level of integration.

Reading the Address Book from Another Application

To further the illustration, what we'll do now is build a completely separate application from Address Book that's able to load in the XML file that Address Book uses and do something useful with it. Specifically, we'll extract all of the addresses in the file and display a list of names together with their matching e-mail addresses.

Try It Out – Reading Address Book Data

1. Create a new Visual Basic .NET Windows Application project. Call it Address List.

2. On Form1, draw a ListBox control. Change its IntegralHeight property to False and its Name to lstEmails:

3. Remember to add this namespace declaration:

```
Imports System.Xml

Public Class Form1
    Inherits System.Windows.Forms.Form
```

4. Double-click on the form background. Add this code to the `Load` event handler:

```
Private Sub Form1_Load(ByVal sender As System.Object, _
        ByVal e As System.EventArgs) Handles MyBase.Load

    ' where do we want to get the XML from...
    Dim filename As String = _
        "c:\MyPrograms\AddressBook\AddressBook.xml"

    ' open the document...
    Dim reader As New XmlTextReader(filename)

    ' move to the start of the document...
    reader.MoveToContent()

    ' start working through the document...
    Dim addressData As Collection, elementName As String
    Do While reader.Read

        ' what kind of node to we have?
        Select Case reader.NodeType

            ' is it the start of an element?
            Case XmlNodeType.Element

                ' if it's an element start, is it "Address"?
                If reader.Name = "Address" Then

                    ' if so, create a new collection...
                    addressData = New Collection()
                Else
```

```
                                ' if not, record the name of the element...
                                elementName = reader.Name

                End If

            ' if we have some text, try storing it in the
            ' collection...
            Case XmlNodeType.Text

                ' do we have an address?
                If Not addressData Is Nothing Then
                    addressData.Add(reader.Value, elementName)
                End If

            ' is it the end of an element?
            Case XmlNodeType.EndElement

                ' if it is, we should have an entire address stored...
                If reader.Name = "Address" Then

                    ' try to create a new listview item...
                    Dim item As String
                    Try
                        item = addressData("firstname") & _
                            " " & addressData("lastname")
                        item &= " (" & addressData("email") & ")"
                    Catch
                    End Try

                    ' add the item to the list...
                    lstEmails.Items.Add(item)

                    ' reset...
                    addressData = Nothing

                End If

        End Select

    Loop

End Sub
```

I've assumed in this code listing that your **AddressBook.xml** will be in
c:\MyPrograms\AddressBook. If yours isn't, change the **filename** value
specified at the top of the code.

5. Run the project; you should see something like this:

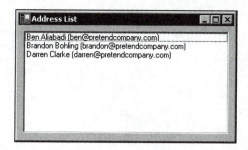

How It Works

To fully appreciate the benefit of this exercise (and therefore the benefit of XML), imagine that before writing the application you'd never seen the XML format used by the Address Book application. Since XML is a text-based format, you're able to open it in a normal text editor, read it, and make assumptions about how it works. You know that you want to get a list of names and e-mail addresses, and you understand that you have an array of Address elements, each one containing the three elements you need: FirstName, LastName, and Email. All that remains is to extract and present the information.

Since announcing .NET, Microsoft has a made a big play about how it is built on XML. This shows in the .NET Framework support for XML – there is a dazzling array of classes for reading and writing XML documents. The XmlSerializer object that we've been using up until now is by far the easiest one to use, but it relies on your having classes that exactly match the document structure. Therefore, if we are given a document from a business partner, we won't have a set of classes that matches the document. As a result, we need some other way to read the document and fit it into whatever classes we do have.

In our Address List project, we don't have applicable AddressBook or Address classes, so we had to use some classes to "walk" through a file. The one we're going to use is System.Xml.XmlTextReader. This class provides a "pointer" that starts at the top of the document and, on command, moves to the next part of the document. (Each of these parts is called a **node**.) The pointer will stop at anything, and this includes start tags, end tags, data values, and whitespace.

So, when we start walking, the first thing XmlTextReader will tell us about is this node:

```
<?xml version="1.0" ?>
```

When we ask it to move on, it will tell us about this node:

```
<AddressBook xmlns:xsi="http://www.w3.org/2001/XMLSchema-instance"
xmlns:xsd="http://www.w3.org/2001/XMLSchema">
```

Then, we ask it to move on again, it will tell us about this node:

```
<Addresses>
```

Then this node:

```
<Address>
```

Then this node:

```
<FirstName>
```

Then this node:

```
Ben
```

Then this node:

```
</FirstName>
```

Then this node:

```
<LastName>
```

...and so on until it gets to the end of the document. In between each one of these, we may or may not get told about whitespace nodes. By and large, we can ignore these.

What our algorithm has to do, then, is get hold of an `XmlTextReader` and start moving through the document one piece at a time. When we first start, the pointer will be set ahead of the first node in the document. Each call to `Read` moves the pointer along one node, so the first call to `Read` that we see at the start of the `Do While` loop actually sets the pointer to the first node:

```
Private Sub Form1_Load(ByVal sender As System.Object, _
        ByVal e As System.EventArgs) Handles MyBase.Load

    ' where do we want to get the XML from...
    Dim filename As String = _
        "c:\MyPrograms\AddressBook\AddressBook.xml"

    ' open the document...
    Dim reader As New XmlTextReader(filename)

    ' move to the start of the document...
    reader.MoveToContent()

    ' start working through the document...
    Dim addressData As Collection, elementName As String
    Do While reader.Read
```

We can use the `NodeType` property of `XmlTextReader` to find out what kind of node we're looking at. If we have an `Element` node, this maps directly onto a start tag in the document. We can use the `Name` property to get the name of the tag. When we find the `<Address>` start tag, we create a new collection called `addressData`. If the start tag that we're looking at isn't the `<Address>` tag, we store the name in `elementName` for later use:

```
        ' what kind of node to we have?
        Select Case reader.NodeType

            ' is it the start of an element?
```

```
Case XmlNodeType.Element

    ' if it's an element start, is it "Address"?
    If reader.Name = "Address" Then

        ' if so, create a new collection...
        addressData = New Collection()
    Else

        ' if not, record the name of the element...
        elementName = reader.Name

    End If
```

Alternatively, the node we get might be a lump of text. If this is the case, we check to see if `addressData` points to a `Collection` object. If it does, we know that we are inside an `Address` element. Remember, we've also stored the name of the element that we are looking at inside `elementName`. This means that if `elementName` is set to `FirstName`, we know we're in the `FirstName` element and therefore the text element we're looking at must be the first name in the address. We then add this element name and the value into the collection for later use:

```
    ' if we have some text, try storing it in the
    ' collection...
    Case XmlNodeType.Text

        ' do we have an address?
        If Not addressData Is Nothing Then
            addressData.Add(reader.Value, elementName)
        End If
```

As we work through the file, we'll get to this point for each of the elements stored in the `Address` element. Effectively, by the time we reach `</Address>`, `addressData` will contain entries for each value stored against the address in the document.

To detect when we get to the `</Address>` tag, we need to look for `EndElement` nodes:

```
    ' is it the end of an element?
    Case XmlNodeType.EndElement
```

When we get one of these, if `Name` is equal to `Address`, we know that we have reached `</Address>`, and this means that `addressData` should be fully populated. We form a string and add it to the list:

```
    ' if it is, we should have an entire address stored...
    If reader.Name = "Address" Then

        ' try to create a new listview item...
        Dim item As String
        Try
            item = addressData("firstname") & _
                " " & addressData("lastname")
```

```
                    item &= " (" & addressData("email") & ")"
              Catch
              End Try

              ' add the item to the list...
              lstEmails.Items.Add(item)

              ' reset...
              addressData = Nothing

          End If
```

You'll notice that in our `Try...Catch` we won't do anything if an exception does occur. To keep this example simple, we're going to ignore any problems that do occur. Specifically, we'll run into problems if the `Address` element we're looking through has sub-elements missing – for example, we might not always have an e-mail address for each address.

We then continue the loop. On each iteration of the loop, `XmlTextReader.Read` will be called, which advances the pointer to the next node. If there are no more nodes in the document, `Read` returns `False` and the loop stops:

```
          End Select

      Loop

  End Sub
```

I hope that this example has illustrated the power of XML from a software integration perspective. With very little work, we've managed to integrate the `Address Book` and `Address List` applications together.

If you want to experiment with this a little, try adding and deleting addresses from `Address Book`. You'll need to close the program to save the changes to `AddressBook.xml`, but each time you start `Address List` you should see the changes you made.

Summary

In this chapter, we introduced the concept of XML. XML is a language based on open standards that can be used as a tool for software integration. Within a single organization XML can be used to easily transport data across platforms. It allows two organizations to define a common format for data exchange and, because XML is text-based, it can easily be moved around using Internet technologies like e-mail, the Web, and FTP. XML is based on building up a document constructed of tags and data.

XML is primarily used for integration work to make the tasks of data transportation and exchange easier, and you, as a newcomer to Visual Basic and programming in general, are unlikely to do integration work (as it's typically done by developers with lots of experience). Nevertheless, this chapter has "dipped your toes in" so to speak, by focusing on using the `System.Xml.Serialization.XmlSerializer` class to save entire objects to disk (known as serialization). This same object was used to load objects from disk (known as de-serialization). We built a fully functional address book application that was able to use an XML file stored on the local computer as its primary source of data.

To round off the chapter and to demonstrate that XML is great for software integration work, we wrote a separate application that was able to load and make sense of the XML document used by the Address Book application.

Questions

1. What does XML stand for?

2. What is XML primarily used for?

3. What kinds of data can XmlSerializer work with?

4. How do you stop XmlSerializer working with a property that it might otherwise try and serialize?

5. Which class can be used to iterate through an XML document one node at a time?

Web Services

Industry watchers have been predicting for some time that **web services** are going to be the "next big thing" in Internet development. In this chapter, we'll introduce the concept of Web Services and show you how you can build your own.

What Is a Web Service?

When you use the Internet, the two things you'll most likely use it for are to send (and receive) e-mail and to surf the Web. These two applications are far and away the most popular uses of the Internet that we've seen so far.

However, from time to time as Internet usage grows, new technologies and applications are released, which have the potential to change the way we use the Internet forever. In recent times, Napster has been a commercial product that has grown from nothing to "ridiculously huge" in a very short space of time. (In fact, the rate of growth of Napster, until the various court decisions that clipped its wings took hold, was far in excess of the rate of growth of the Web itself!) Naturally, of course, its fall from grace was just as fast!

Building upon the success of the World Wide Web as we know it today and having the potential to be "the next big thing" is the Web service.

We all know that the Web is a great way to share information. However, the problem with the Web as it is today is that in order to use it you have to be a human. Web sites are built to be read with human eyes and interpreted with the human mind. Web services, on the other hand, are built to be read and interpreted by computer programs, not by humans. Web services are, in effect, web sites for computers to use. These web sites tend to be dynamic in nature, so they don't contain static unchanging content but can react and adapt to choices and selections. For example, I might want to use a web service that accepts a quantity in US Dollars and returns the number of equivalent Euros.

Why is this a good thing? Well, when building computer systems in a commercial information technology environment, the most costly factor involved is always integrating disparate computer systems. Imagine you have two pieces of software; one used to keep track of stock in your warehouse, the other used to capture customer orders. These two pieces of software were developed by different companies and bought at different times. However, when an order is placed using the second piece of software, that software has to be able to tell the warehousing software that a quantity of a particular product has been sold. This may trigger some autonomous action in the warehousing software, such as placing an order to replenish the stock, or asking someone to go and pick it off of the shelf.

When two pieces of software work together, we call it **integration**. But, integration is rarely easy and on large installations often involves hiring teams of consultants and spending thousands of dollars on custom-written integration software.

Without going into too much detail, web services make integration far, far easier. By making something far, far easier, you inevitably make it far, far cheaper and that's why it's predicted to be the next big thing. Not only will companies who are already integrating have a more cost-effective option than before, but also companies will be able to integrate their computer systems in previously unseen ways. Web services will also provide opportunities for new businesses wanting to introduce specialized services with relative ease.

The commercial pros and cons of web services together with a discussion of the movers and shakers in this particular space are beyond the scope of this book. However, if you'd like to learn more, take a look at http://www.webservicesarchitect.com/.

How Does a Web Service Work?

First of all, I should mention that web services are based upon completely open standards that are not tied to any particular platform or any particular company. Part of their attraction is that it doesn't matter whether you deploy your web service on Solaris, Unix, Mac, or Windows – anyone will be able to connect to and use the thing. This is the same with normal web sites – you don't care what platform the web sites you visit every day actually run on, so long as they work.

Secondly, the .NET implementation of web services are based entirely around a programming paradigm that developers have been falling in love with for years: object orientation. If you're used to using objects (and by Chapter 19 of this book, you should be!) you'll have absolutely no problems with web services.

The principle behind a web service is that you build a class that has methods in it. However, the traditional method of deployment and instantiation does not apply. Here's what happens traditionally:

- ❏   A developer builds an object
- ❏   That object is installed (copied onto a computer)
- ❏   A piece of software running on that *same* computer creates an instance of the class (the "object")
- ❏   The piece of software calls a method on the object
- ❏   The object does something and returns a value
- ❏   The piece of software receives the value and does something with it

But here's what happens with a web service:

- ❑ A developer builds an object

- ❑ That object is copied onto a server computer running a web server (like Microsoft IIS)

- ❑ A piece of software running on a *different, remote* computer (usually located somewhere on the Internet) asks the web server to run a particular method on the class

- ❑ The server creates an instance of the class and calls the method

- ❑ The server returns the results of the method to the calling computer

- ❑ The piece of software on the remote computer receives the value and does something with it

You can see that the technique is very similar, but there's a disconnection between the server that the object is actually installed on and the computer that wants to use the object. In fact, with a web service there is a huge process gulf (namely, the Internet) between the client of the object and the object itself. A solution to handle this disconnection is provided by the standards used by and specifically developed for web services, as we'll soon see.

SOAP – Simple Object Access Protocol

As web services are, in effect, "web sites for computers to use", they've been built on the same technology that's made the World Wide Web so popular. Specifically, we're talking about the **Hypertext Transfer Protocol** (**HTTP**) standard that powers all web servers.

When we're dealing with "web sites for people to read", the client ("browser") and server usually exchange a mixture of documents. HyperText Markup Language (HTML) documents, and their extension technologies like Dynamic HTML and JavaScript, describe the page layout and text on the page and common image formats like GIF and JPEG are used to exchange images.

However, when we we're dealing with "web sites for computers to use", we only exchange one kind of document. These documents are known as **SOAP** documents, where SOAP stands for **Simple Object Access Protocol**.

When a client application wants to ask the web service for some information, such as the current stock level for a product, or the status of an order, or to get the computer at the end of the connection to do something like convert currencies or place an order, the application constructs a SOAP **request document**. Using the HTTP protocol, this document is sent over the Internet to the web server that powers the web service. This document contains all of the information that the web service needs to determine what has been asked for. As web services work on the common object/method paradigm, the request document includes things like the name of the method and any data that should be passed through to the method as parameters.

At the server end, the web service receives the SOAP request, decodes it, and runs the appropriate piece of software. (We're going to build some of these "appropriate pieces of software" in this chapter.) During the call, the method generates a SOAP **response document** that contains the information to be passed back to the caller. Like the request document, this new document is transferred using HTTP through the web server.

SOAP documents are constructed with XML. This means that if you read a SOAP document it'll look very similar to the sort of document that we saw in the last chapter. However, at the level to Visual Basic we don't need to look too hard at the SOAP documents themselves. As we work through the chapter, I'll be showing you some of the SOAP response documents that come back from the server, but I won't be showing you any of the request documents.

We know that web service technology is not tied to a specific platform, so from a developer's perspective the value of choosing one platform over another is determined by how transparent this SOAP document construction and transfer work actually is or what is available at the site where development will take place. .NET is very good for both building and using Web services – you don't have to go within a hundred yards of a SOAP document. (This is why in this chapter we're not going to dwell on SOAP too much, even though without SOAP we wouldn't be able to do anything we can do in this chapter.) On the other hand, other platforms will be equally good for building web services but still more will require you to jump through a few more hoops to create powerful web services.

Obviously, in this book we're interested in how web services work with .NET, which is something we'll now cover. But first, here's a diagram that should tie everything together:

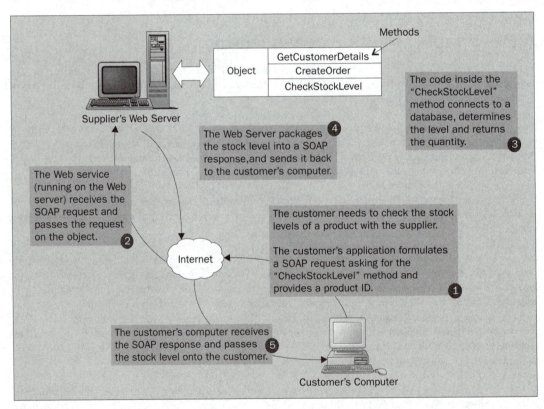

Building a Web Service

Building web services with Visual Studio .NET is a breeze! In this section, we'll build a sample web service and introduce some of the concepts involved.

A Demonstration

A web service is basically a class that sits on the server. Some of the methods on that class are marked in a special way, and it's by looking for these special marks that .NET knows which methods to publish on the service. You'll see how this works as we go through the first *Try it Out* in this chapter. Anyone wishing to use the web service can then call these methods on the remote web service, as if the method existed in a class installed on their local computer. We'll also see a method that allows us to test the web service from within Internet Explorer.

Try It Out – A Demonstration Web Service

1. Open Visual Studio and select File | New | Project from the menu.

2. Make sure Visual Basic Projects is selected in the left box and select ASP.NET Web Service from the right list. Enter the name as DemoService and click OK:

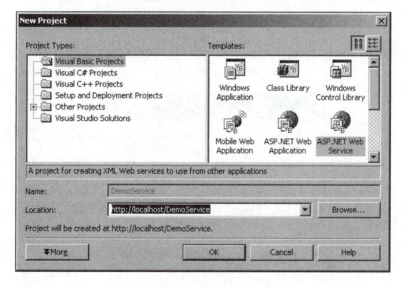

Web services are based on ASP.NET technology, so the project will be created in the same way as the Web applications we worked with in Chapter 17. If you have problems creating the project, look back at this chapter for troubleshooting information.

Visual Studio .NET will create a new web site and create a new page on the site called Service1.asmx, where .asmx stands for **Active Server Methods**. (The extra x comes from the original name of ASP.NET: ASP+. The x is the plus sign turned through 45 degrees.) This page represents one service, and a web service project (or site) can contain many different services.

3. Using the Solution Explorer, right-click Service1.asmx and select **View Code**.

4. When Visual Studio .NET created the page, it put an example method on the service called HelloWorld. This is commented out at the moment, so remove the comments such that it looks like this:

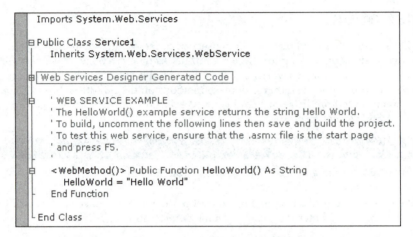

```
Imports System.Web.Services

Public Class Service1
    Inherits System.Web.Services.WebService

    Web Services Designer Generated Code

    ' WEB SERVICE EXAMPLE
    ' The HelloWorld() example service returns the string Hello World.
    ' To build, uncomment the following lines then save and build the project.
    ' To test this web service, ensure that the .asmx file is the start page
    ' and press F5.
    '
    <WebMethod()> Public Function HelloWorld() As String
        HelloWorld = "Hello World"
    End Function

End Class
```

5. Run the project by selecting **Debug | Start** from the menu. The project will be compiled and Internet Explorer will open and display the Service1.asmx page. This is the test interface, which is something we'll talk about later. On this initial page, all of the methods supported by the service appear in a list at the top of the page:

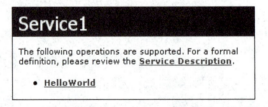

6. Click on the HelloWorld link. This will open another page that lets you run the method. At the top of the page you should see the following:

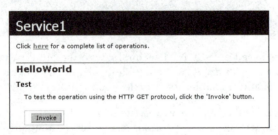

7. Click the Invoke button and another browser window will open. This window contains the SOAP response from the server:

How It Works

Just as in Web Forms where we have a class *behind* the .aspx page, we also have a class behind each .asmx page with web services. This class is the one that we enabled the HelloWorld method on. If you look at the definition for the class, you'll see that it's inherited from System.Web.Services.WebService:

```
Public Class Service1
    Inherits System.Web.Services.WebService
```

The WebService class is responsible for presenting the pages that we clicked through in Internet Explorer to invoke the HelloWorld method. (You can use another browser to test the service, but Visual Studio .NET chooses Internet Explorer by default.) These pages are known as the **test interface**. Methods on the class that we want exposed to the web service must be marked with the WebMethod attribute. You can see this attribute defined at the beginning of the method (note that it must be encased in a similar fashion to HTML tags):

```
<WebMethod()> Public Function HelloWorld() As String
    HelloWorld = "Hello World"
End Function
```

When the test interface starts, it displays the methods flagged to be exposed on the server. When we click through to the page tied to a specific method, the test interface presents a form that we can use to invoke it.

When the method is invoked, to the method it "feels" just like a normal call – in other words there's nothing special about writing aeb services, and everything that you've learned so far still applies.

We already know that web services are powered by SOAP. When we click the Invoke button, the SOAP message that's returned to the caller (in this case, that's us using Internet Explorer) contains the response. You can see that this is indeed the value we returned from the method buried within a block of XML:

```
<?xml version="1.0" encoding="utf-8" ?>
<string xmlns="http://tempuri.org/">Hello World</string>
```

The structure of the XML that makes up the SOAP message by and large isn't important. However, when we're working through more examples I'll point out where the actual results can be found.

Adding More Methods

Let's build some methods now that illustrate our web service actually doing something.

Try It Out – Adding a SquareRoot Method

1. Open the code editor for `Service1.asmx`. Add this new method to the `Service1` class, below the existing `HelloWorld` method:

```
Public Function GetSquareRoot(ByVal number As Double) As Double
    Return Math.Sqrt(number)
End Function
```

If you can't type into the code window, the instance of Internet Explorer that Visual Studio .NET opened is still running. Close down the test interface windows and any extra windows displaying the SOAP responses and the project should stop running. Alternatively, select **Debug | Stop Debugging** from the menu.

2. Run the project. You'll notice that the new method does not appear in the list at the top of the page:

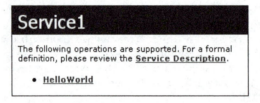

3. We didn't mark the method with the `WebMethod` attribute. I did this to show you that a class can contain methods that, although public, aren't exposed on the web service. Close the browser and add the `WebMethod` attribute:

```
<WebMethod()> Public Function GetSquareRoot(ByVal number As Double) _
            As Double
    Return Math.Sqrt(number)
End Function
```

4. Run the project again, and you should see this at the top of the page:

5. Click on the GetSquareRoot link. This time, the Invoke form should contain somewhere for you to enter a number. Don't enter a number and click Invoke.

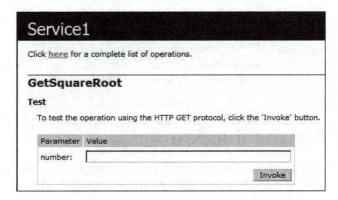

6. When the new browser appears, you won't see a SOAP response, but instead you'll see something that looks like this:

```
System.Exception: Cannot convert to System.Double.
Parameter name: type ---> System.FormatException: Input string was not in a correct format.
  at System.Number.ParseDouble(String s, NumberStyles style, NumberFormatInfo info)
  at System.Double.Parse(String s, NumberStyles style, IFormatProvider provider)
  at System.Convert.ToDouble(String value, IFormatProvider provider)
  at System.String.System.IConvertible.ToDouble(IFormatProvider provider)
  at System.Convert.ChangeType(Object value, Type conversionType, IFormatProvider provider)
  at System.Convert.ChangeType(Object value, Type conversionType)
  at System.Web.Services.Protocols.ScalarFormatter.FromString(String value, Type type)
  --- End of inner exception stack trace ---
  at System.Web.Services.Protocols.ScalarFormatter.FromString(String value, Type type)
  at System.Web.Services.Protocols.ValueCollectionParameterReader.Read(NameValueCollection
collection)
  at System.Web.Services.Protocols.UrlParameterReader.Read(HttpRequest request)
  at System.Web.Services.Protocols.HttpServerProtocol.ReadParameters()
  at System.Web.Services.Protocols.WebServiceHandler.Invoke()
  at System.Web.Services.Protocols.WebServiceHandler.CoreProcessRequest()
```

You'll see this kind of message whenever you enter invalid information into the Invoke form. In this case, it's telling us that it Cannot convert to System.Double, which should be a big giveaway that it can't convert an empty string to a floating-point value.

7. Close the browser window and enter 2 into the number field. Click Invoke and you'll get this:

```
<?xml version="1.0" encoding="utf-8" ?>
<double xmlns="http://tempuri.org/">1.4142135623730952</double>
```

How It Works

If we look in the SOAP message that was returned, we've been given a double value that's as close as we can get to the square root of 2.

```
<?xml version="1.0" encoding="utf-8" ?>
<double xmlns="http://tempuri.org/">1.4142135623730952</double>
```

So we know that the method works. You should have also seen by now that building simple web services is not hard. This was Microsoft's intent with the web services support in .NET – the plumbing to build a service is remarkably easy. Everything we've learned about creating classes, building methods with parameters, and returning values is paying dividends here because there's virtually no learning curve to climb. We can concentrate on building the logic behind the web service, which, after all, is the bit we get paid to do!

The Picture Server Service

As building simple web services is so straightforward, we'll move on relatively quickly to building a proper application that does something practical with a web service. We'll also look at building a desktop client application that uses the web service, because up to now all we've used is the test interface provided by the `WebService` class. The specific example we'll use is to build a web service that allows an application to view pictures placed on a remote server.

What'll we'll do is this:

❑   Set up a folder on our web service server (this could be your local machine or a remote machine where the web service will run) that contains pictures downloaded from a digital camera. We'll divide this folder into subfolders for different events, for example "Deborah's Graduation", "Trip to Boston", and so on.

❑   Build a web service that can interrogate the folder to return a list of subfolders. We'll also be able to return a list of the files in each subfolder.

❑   When we do return a file, we'll also return details on the file, such as graphic format, width, height, and so on.

❑   Set up the web site so that we can view the pictures we find using a web browser.

That doesn't sound like anything that we can't already do using an ASP.NET web site. However, what we can do with this web service that we can't do with a web site is build our own custom front-end Windows Forms application. With a web site, we're tied to using HTML and a web browser to present the information on the server to the user.

Creating the Project

Let's get going by building the web service project.

Try It Out – Creating the Project

1.   Select File | New | Project from the menu to create a new ASP.NET Web Service project and call it PictureService.

2.   When the project loads, we don't want to use the default `Service1.asmx` file. Using the Solution Explorer, right-click `Service1.asmx` and select Delete. Press OK when asked.

3. Using the Solution Explorer again, right-click the PictureService project. Select Add | Add Web Service. Enter the name of the service as Service and click Open. The Solution Explorer should now look like this:

4. Now that we've created this new .asmx page, when we run the project we want this to be the one that gets loaded into Internet Explorer. In the Solution Explorer right-click on Service.asmx and select Set as Start Page. In order to make the pictures available over the web site, we need to create a folder called Pictures, directly within the folder that the web service itself runs out of. There is a problem, however; thanks to the way Visual Studio .NET works with IIS, this folder will vary wildly from installation to installation. To ensure that we get the right folder, what we need to do is get the web service itself to tell us the folder it is running from.

Right-click on Service.asmx in the Solution Explorer and select View Code. Find the HelloWorld method again, remove the comments from the code, and alter the code so that it looks like this:

```
Public Class Service
    Inherits System.Web.Services.WebService

    ' WEB SERVICE EXAMPLE
    ' The HelloWorld() example service returns the string Hello World.
    ' To build, uncomment the following lines then save and build the
    ' project. To test this web service, ensure that the .asmx file is
    ' the start page and press F5.
    '
    <WebMethod()> Public Function HelloWorld() As String
        Return _
    Server.MapPath(Context.Request.ServerVariables.Item("script_name"))
    End Function

End Class
```

6. Run the project. As usual, when Internet Explorer starts, click the HelloWorld method link. Click the Invoke button when the page loads. The web service should now tell you the full path of Service.asmx:

```xml
<?xml version="1.0" encoding="utf-8" ?>
  <string xmlns="http://tempuri.org/">
    c:\inetpub\wwwroot\PictureService\Service.asmx
  </string>
```

7. You can see that, on my computer, the folder containing `Service.asmx` is `c:\inetpub\wwwroot\PictureService`. We'll refer to this folder as the **service root folder** from this point.

8. Open a copy of Windows Explorer (that's the normal file Explorer, not Internet Explorer). Go to the service root folder and create a new subfolder called `Pictures`:

9. Now you'll need to go and find some pictures that you want to use with the service. I'm going to use some that a friend of mine took with his digital camera, but you can use any pictures you like so long as they are in either GIF or JPEG format.

10. Divide the pictures into a set of subfolders, like I have done here:

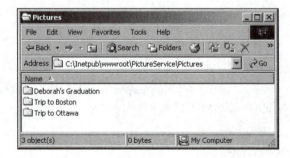

11. Within each folder, I've got a set of JPG files. In my case they don't have particularly useful names, however:

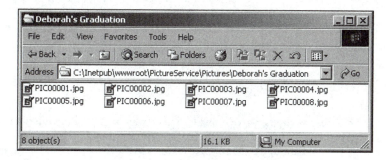

How It Works

At this point, you should have both a Web service and a load of pictures that you can use with the service. In a moment, we'll start building methods on the service that are able to return the folders to the user.

The only piece of code we wrote in this section was the code that returned the complete path of `Service.asmx`:

```
<WebMethod()> Public Function HelloWorld() As String
    Return _
  Server.MapPath(Context.Request.ServerVariables.Item("script_name"))
End Function
```

This is quite an advanced ASP.NET trick (web services are, after all, based on ASP.NET technology) and is beyond the scope of the book. However, what I can tell you is that all pages running on ASP.NET are able to make many determinations about their environment, including the physical path in which the server is located.

> For more information on building web sites with ASP.NET, check out *Beginning ASP.NET 1.0 with VB.NET* (Wrox Press, ISBN 1-86100-733-7). You'll also find a lot of articles on this subject on Wrox's ASPToday site – **http://www.asptoday.com/**.

Returning Arrays

In the first part of this chapter, we looked at a web service that returned single values from each method call, for example a string or a number.

In some cases, we want to return arrays of information. This is particularly true when we ask the web service for a list of the picture subfolders. We want to return an array of string values, each one containing the name of a folder.

Try It Out – Returning a List of Picture Subfolders

1. Open the code editor for `Service.asmx` again. Delete the `HelloWorld` method.

2. We need a reference to the `System.IO` namespace for this exercise, so go to the top of the code listing and add this new namespace reference:

```
Imports System.Web.Services
Imports System.IO
```

3. When we're building methods, we're going to need a way of getting the full path to our `Pictures` folder. This uses the work we did before to find the service root folder, but with an extra bit of code to actually get the full path to the `Pictures` folder. Add this property to `Service`:

```
' PictureFolderPath - readonly property to return the picture
' folder...
Public ReadOnly Property PictureFolderPath() As String
    Get

        ' get the full path of this asmx page...
        Dim asmxPath As String, picturePath As String
        asmxPath = _
    Server.MapPath(Context.Request.ServerVariables.Item("script_name"))

        ' step back through the string until the first "\"...
        Dim n As Integer
        For n = asmxPath.Length - 1 To n Step -1

            ' do we have a string?
            If asmxPath.Chars(n) = "\"c Then

                ' get the service path - everything up to the "\"
                Dim servicePath As String = asmxPath.Substring(0, n)

                ' append the word "Pictures" to the end of the path...
                picturePath = servicePath & "\Pictures"

                ' now, stop the loop...
                Exit For

            End If

        Next

        ' return the path...
        Return picturePath

    End Get
End Property
```

4. Having the name of the folder is just half the battle. In order to do anything useful, we need an object that lets us search through the folder looking for subfolders. `System.IO.DirectoryInfo` is the class for such an object, so add this property to `Service`:

```
' PictureFolder - property to the DirectoryInfo containing
' the pictures...
Public ReadOnly Property PictureFolder() As DirectoryInfo
    Get
        Return New DirectoryInfo(PictureFolderPath)
    End Get
End Property
```

5. Now we can actually build the `GetPictureFolders` web method:

```
' GetPictureFolders - return an array of the picture folders...
<WebMethod()> Public Function GetPictureFolders() As String()

    ' get hold of the picture folder...
    Dim pictureFolder As DirectoryInfo = Me.PictureFolder

    ' get the array of subfolders...
    Dim pictureSubFolders() As DirectoryInfo = _
        pictureFolder.GetDirectories()

    ' create a string array to accommodate the names...
    Dim folderNames(pictureSubFolders.Length - 1) As String

    ' now, loop through the folders...
    Dim pictureSubFolder As DirectoryInfo, index As Integer
    For Each pictureSubFolder In pictureSubFolders

        ' add the name...
        folderNames(index) = pictureSubFolder.Name

        ' next...
        index += 1

    Next

    ' finally, return the list of names...
    Return folderNames

End Function
```

6. Run the project and when Internet Explorer appears, click on the GetPictureFolders link. When prompted, click Invoke and you should see this:

```
<?xml version="1.0" encoding="utf-8" ?>
<ArrayOfString xmlns:xsi="http://www.w3.org/2001/XMLSchema-instance"
xmlns:xsd="http://www.w3.org/2001/XMLSchema" xmlns="http://tempuri.org/">
  <string>Deborah's Graduation</string>
```

```
<string>Trip to Boston</string>
        <string>Trip to Ottawa</string>
</ArrayOfString>
```

How It Works

We can see by the results that we do indeed have an array of strings returned. We know this because firstly we have the ArrayOfString tag appearing in the string and, secondly we actually have the three strings for our three folders.

```
<?xml version="1.0" encoding="utf-8" ?>
- <ArrayOfString xmlns:xsi="http://www.w3.org/2001/XMLSchema-instance"
xmlns:xsd="http://www.w3.org/2001/XMLSchema" xmlns="http://tempuri.org/">
    <string>Deborah's Graduation</string>
    <string>Trip to Boston</string>
    <string>Trip to Ottawa</string>
</ArrayOfString>
```

The PictureFolderPath property is quite important, since we'll frequently use this in our methods. The first thing we do is to get hold of the complete path to the Service.asmx file that's powering the service:

```
' PictureFolderPath - readonly property to return the picture
' folder...
Public ReadOnly Property PictureFolderPath() As String
    Get

        ' get the full path of this asmx page...
        Dim asmxPath As String, picturePath As String
        asmxPath = _
    Server.MapPath(Context.Request.ServerVariables.Item("script_name"))
```

However, this string will return something like:

c:\inetpub\wwwroot\PictureService\Service.asmx

and what we ultimately want is:

c:\inetpub\wwwroot\PictureService\Pictures

Therefore, we have to clip off the Service.asmx at the end and replace it with Pictures. To do this, we walk backwards through the string starting at the x and moving towards the c, checking each character in turn to see if it's a backslash:

```
' step back through the string until the first "\"...
        Dim n As Integer
        For n = asmxPath.Length - 1 To n Step -1

            ' do we have a string?
            If asmxPath.Chars(n) = "\"c Then
```

When we find the backslash, we create a string that lops off the `\Service.asmx`, so we'll have `c:\inetpub\wwwroot\PictureService`:

```
' get the service path - everything up to the "\"
Dim servicePath As String = asmxPath.Substring(0, n)
```

Then, we tack the text "`\Pictures`" on the end, quit looping through, and return what we found:

```
' append the word "Pictures" to the end of the path...
picturePath = servicePath & "\Pictures"

' now, stop the loop...
Exit For

    End If

Next

' return the path...
Return picturePath

    End Get
End Property
```

As we mentioned before, `System.IO.DirectoryInfo` is a class that can help us learn more about a folder on the computer or the network. We create a new property called `PictureFolder` that returns a `DirectoryInfo` object based on the value returned by the `PictureFolderPath` property:

```
' PictureFolder - property to the DirectoryInfo containing
' the pictures...
Public ReadOnly Property PictureFolder() As DirectoryInfo
    Get
        Return New DirectoryInfo(PictureFolderPath)
    End Get
End Property
```

Once we have that, we can create our `GetPictureFolders` method. The first thing this does is use the `PictureFolder` property to get hold of the `DirectoryInfo` object that points to `c:\inetpub\wwwroot\PictureService\Pictures`. We have to use the `Me` keyword because we have a local variable with the same name. This removes the ambiguity of the call and makes sure that when we ask for `PictureFolder` we actually go off to find the value of the property, rather than returning the current value of `pictureFolder`, which would be an empty string:

```
' GetPictureFolders - return an array of the picture folders...
<WebMethod()> Public Function GetPictureFolders() As String()

    ' get hold of the picture folder...
    Dim pictureFolder As DirectoryInfo = Me.PictureFolder
```

The `GetDirectories` method will return an array of `DirectoryInfo` objects, one for each of the subfolders:

```
' get the array of subfolders...
Dim pictureSubFolders() As DirectoryInfo = _
    pictureFolder.GetDirectories()
```

Once we have this array, we can use its `Length` property to determine how many subfolders the `Pictures` folder actually has. We can then use this folder to create an empty array of the correct length:

```
' create a string array to accommodate the names...
Dim folderNames(pictureSubFolders.Length - 1) As String
```

With the array in place, we can loop through the `pictureSubFolders` array and copy the name of each folder into the `folderNames` array:

```
' now, loop through the folders...
Dim pictureSubFolder As DirectoryInfo, index As Integer
For Each pictureSubFolder In pictureSubFolders

    ' add the name...
    folderNames(index) = pictureSubFolder.Name

    ' next...
    index += 1

Next
```

Finally, we can return the array back to the caller:

```
' finally, return the list of names...
Return folderNames

End Function
```

Here's a quick point – why do we appear to have some inconsistency of naming between directories and folders? Well, with the introduction of Windows 95, Microsoft decided that directories as they had been called for decades should actually be called folders. However, the group in charge of the `DirectoryInfo` class in the .NET team apparently believed that *directory* was a better name than *folder*. If you noticed, we've always called folders "folders" and the Framework has always called folders "directories". Providing that each party sticks to their own convention, things shouldn't get confusing.

Returning Complex Information

So far, whenever we've returned anything from a web service, we've only returned simple values, albeit that we now know how to return arrays of simple values. With a little work, however, we can return complex structures of information from the web service.

In this section, we want to return a list of the pictures that are contained within each folder. However, unlike with the picture subfolders where we only needed to know the name, for each picture we would like to return the following information:

❑   The filename of the picture (for example Pic1.jpg)

❑   The complete URL that points to the picture (for example,
http://chimaera/PictureService/Pictures/Trip+to+Boston/Pic1.jpg)

❑   The name of the folder that contains the picture (for example Trip to Boston)

❑   The size of the image (for example 58,308 bytes)

❑   The date the image was created (for example 4/4/2002)

❑   The format of the image (for example JPEG)

Try It Out – Returning Complex Information

1. To return a set of information, we need to create a structure that we can populate with the information we want. To do this, add a new class to the project by right-clicking on the **PictureService** project in the Solution Explorer and selecting **Add | Add Class**. Call it **PictureInfo**. We want to create a structure rather than a class (although in this particular case either will do), so change Class and End Class to Structure and End Structure, and add these members:

```
Public Structure PictureInfo

    ' members...
    Public Name As String
    Public Url As String
    Public FolderName As String
    Public FileSize As Integer
    Public FileDate As Date
    Public ImageFormat As String

End Structure
```

2. To get the pictures contained within a folder, we'll create a new web method that takes the name of the folder as a parameter. Open the code editor for Service.asmx and add this code:

```
' GetPicturesInFolder - return an array of pictures from the folder...
<WebMethod()> Public Function GetPicturesInFolder(ByVal folderName _
    As String) As PictureInfo()

    ' get hold of the folder that we want...
    Dim pictureSubFolder As DirectoryInfo
    pictureSubFolder = _
            New DirectoryInfo(PictureFolderPath & "\" & folderName)
```

```
' we need to get the URL of the picture folder...
Dim pictureFolderUrl As String, n As Integer
pictureFolderUrl = _
    Context.Request.ServerVariables.Item("script_name")
For n = pictureFolderUrl.Length - 1 To 0 Step -1

    ' do we have a slash?
    If pictureFolderUrl.Chars(n) = "/"c Then

        ' manipulate the URL...
        pictureFolderUrl = pictureFolderUrl.Substring(0, n) & _
         "/Pictures"

        ' this is great, but we need an absolute URL...
        pictureFolderUrl = _
         "http://" & _
         Context.Request.ServerVariables.Item("server_name") & _
         pictureFolderUrl

        ' quit the loop...
        Exit For

    End If

Next

' get the list of files in the subfolder...
Dim pictureFiles() As FileInfo = pictureSubFolder.GetFiles

' create somewhere to put the picture infos...
Dim pictureList(pictureFiles.Length - 1) As PictureInfo

' loop through each picture...
Dim pictureFile As FileInfo, index As Integer
For Each pictureFile In pictureFiles

    ' create a new pictureinfo object...
    Dim pictureInfo As New PictureInfo()
    pictureInfo.Name = pictureFile.Name
    pictureInfo.FolderName = folderName
    pictureInfo.Url = pictureFolderUrl & "/" & _
        folderName & "/" & pictureFile.Name
    pictureInfo.FileSize = pictureFile.Length
    pictureInfo.FileDate = pictureFile.LastWriteTime
    pictureInfo.ImageFormat = _
        pictureFile.Extension.Substring(1).ToUpper

    ' add it to the array...
    pictureList(index) = pictureInfo
    index += 1

Next
```

```
        ' return the list of pictures...
        Return pictureList

End Function
```

3. Run the service. When Internet Explorer loads, click on the **GetPicturesInFolder** link. When prompted, enter the name of the folder whose images you want to return:

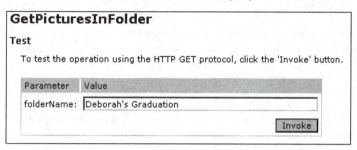

4. When you click **Invoke**, you'll get a list of files back. In my **Deborah's Graduation** folder, I have eight images, so the document I get back is relative to this. Here is an abbreviated version of the document containing information regarding two of the files:

```xml
<?xml version="1.0" encoding="utf-8" ?>
<ArrayOfPictureInfo xmlns:xsi="http://www.w3.org/2001/XMLSchema-instance"
xmlns:xsd="http://www.w3.org/2001/XMLSchema" xmlns="http://tempuri.org/">
  <PictureInfo>
    <Name>PIC00001.jpg</Name>
    <URL>http://localhost/PictureService/Pictures/Deborah's Graduation/PIC00001.jpg</URL>
    <FolderName>Deborah's Graduation</FolderName>
    <FileSize>2071</FileSize>
    <FileDate>2002-06-26T15:31:48.0330592+01:00</FileDate>
    <ImageFormat>JPG</ImageFormat>
  </PictureInfo>
  <PictureInfo>
    <Name>PIC00002.jpg</Name>
    <URL>http://localhost/PictureService/Pictures/Deborah's Graduation/PIC00002.jpg</URL>
    <FolderName>Deborah's Graduation</FolderName>
    <FileSize>2071</FileSize>
    <FileDate>2002-06-26T15:31:55.0330592+01:00</FileDate>
    <ImageFormat>JPG</ImageFormat>
  </PictureInfo>
</ArrayOfPictureInfo>
```

How It Works

Once we have a folder name, we can get a `DirectoryInfo` object from it and use a method called `GetFiles` to return an array of `System.IO.FileInfo` objects that describe each file. However, we have to mate the folder name with the value returned by `PictureFolderPath`. This way, if we ask for **Deborah's Graduation**, we'll get a folder name of
`c:\inetpub\wwwroot\PictureService\Pictures\Deborah's Graduation`:

795

```
' GetPicturesInFolder - return an array of pictures from the folder...
<WebMethod()> Public Function GetPicturesInFolder(ByVal folderName _
     As String) As PictureInfo()

    ' get hold of the folder that we want...
    Dim pictureSubFolder As DirectoryInfo
    pictureSubFolder = _
            New DirectoryInfo(PictureFolderPath & "\" & folderName)
```

When the user has used the service to learn what pictures are available on the server, we'll expect them to use a web browser to download them. That's why we put our `Pictures` folder within the `c:\inetpub\wwwroot\PictureService` folder itself – IIS will share the folders and files for us without us having to do any extra configuration work.

However, the URL that we need on the client has to be an absolute name that includes the name of the server and the http:// part. If we ask the web service to return the name of its own `.asmx` file, we get a relative URL, like this: `/PictureService/Service.asmx`.

```
    ' we need to get the URL of the picture folder...
    Dim pictureFolderUrl As String, n As Integer
    pictureFolderUrl = _
        Context.Request.ServerVariables.Item("script_name")
```

As before, we have to walk backwards through this string starting at the x looking for the first forward-slash. When we find it, we replace `/Service.asmx` with `/Pictures`:

```
    For n = pictureFolderUrl.Length - 1 To 0 Step -1

        ' do we have a slash?
        If pictureFolderUrl.Chars(n) = "/"c Then

            ' manipulate the URL...
            pictureFolderUrl = pictureFolderUrl.Substring(0, n) & _
             "/Pictures"
```

This is only half the problem, however. We need to add the name of the server and the http:// part to form a complete URL of http://localhost/PictureService/Pictures:

```
            ' this is great, but we need an absolute URL...
            pictureFolderUrl = _
             "http://" & _
             Context.Request.ServerVariables.Item("server_name") & _
             pictureFolderUrl
```

Once we've done that, we can stop walking through the string:

```
            ' quit the loop...
            Exit For
```

```
        End If

    Next
```

The next thing we need is a list of the files that the folder contains:

```
        ' get the list of files in the subfolder...
        Dim pictureFiles() As FileInfo = pictureSubFolder.GetFiles
```

For each file in the folder, we're going to create and populate a new `PictureInfo` structure. We'll be returning these in an array, so next we create that array:

```
        ' create somewhere to put the picture infos...
        Dim pictureList(pictureFiles.Length - 1) As PictureInfo
```

Now we can start looping through the files. For each one, we create a new `PictureInfo` and populate it. When we come to populate the `ImageFormat` member, we want to chop off the initial period (hence the need for `Substring`) and then convert the remaining characters to uppercase (hence `ToUpper`):

```
        ' loop through each picture...
        Dim pictureFile As FileInfo, index As Integer
        For Each pictureFile In pictureFiles

            ' create a new pictureinfo object...
            Dim pictureInfo As New PictureInfo()
            pictureInfo.Name = pictureFile.Name
            pictureInfo.FolderName = folderName
            pictureInfo.Url = pictureFolderUrl & "/" & _
                folderName & "/" & pictureFile.Name
            pictureInfo.FileSize = pictureFile.Length
            pictureInfo.FileDate = pictureFile.LastWriteTime
            pictureInfo.ImageFormat = _
                pictureFile.Extension.Substring(1).ToUpper
```

Once we have the image information, we can put it into its position in the array:

```
            ' add it to the array...
            pictureList(index) = pictureInfo
            index += 1

    Next
```

Finally, we return the results to the caller:

```
        ' return the list of pictures...
        Return pictureList

    End Function
```

That's it! Our service only needs those two methods so let's now look at how we can use this web service with our applications.

The Picture Server Client

So far in this chapter we've seen how to create web services and how to manipulate them using the browser interface that the .NET Framework creates for us. This browser interface is actually a test interface – it's not what we'd expect people using our web service to use.

The principle behind web services is that they enable software to integrate – therefore when we actually want to use a web service, we effectively want to build the functionality that the service offers into our own applications.

In this section, we're going to build a desktop Windows Application that can display a list of the picture subfolders on the remote server. The user can select one of these folders and see the list of files contained within. Clicking on one of the images will show the image in Internet Explorer.

(As a special treat, we're going to host Internet Explorer inside our own application!)

> **Using a web service is often known as consuming a web service.**

WSDL – Web Services Description Language

In order to consume a web service, we can use something called a **Web Services Description Language** (**WSDL**) **document**. This is an XML document that contains a list of all of the methods available on the web service. It details the parameters for each method and what each method is expected to return.

Our `WebService` class automatically creates a WSDL document for us, as we'll soon see, but because WSDL is an accepted industry standard, it's good practice for all web services on any platform to expose a WSDL document. Theoretically (web services are still too new to say that in practice this always works!), if we have the WSDL document for a web service running on .NET or on another platform, we'll be able to build a Visual Basic .NET application that can use the web service it belongs to.

Creating the Client

Firstly, we'll create the client. As we're going to want to use Internet Explorer inside our application, we'll also customize the Toolbox to include the Microsoft Web Browser control.

Try It Out – Creating the Client

1. In Visual Studio .NET, create a new Windows Application project called PictureClient.

2. When the Designer for the new Form1 loads, right-click on the open Toolbox and select Customize Toolbox.

The control we're going to add is Internet Explorer. This isn't a cut-down browser – the object we use is the same one that the standalone Internet Explorer itself uses to display web content. However, .NET is pretty new and Internet Explorer is an old product still based on old COM technology. There isn't a specific .NET version of Internet Explorer available, as this would involve a complete rewrite of it, and Internet Explorer is a pretty complicated application in its own right, although this rewrite may happen in the future. We can use old style COM controls as well as the new .NET controls in our Windows forms. However, we must go through the following steps to add them to a project.

3. When the Customize Toolbox dialog appears, make sure the **COM Components** tab is selected and scroll down until you find **Microsoft Web Browser**. Check this and click **OK**:

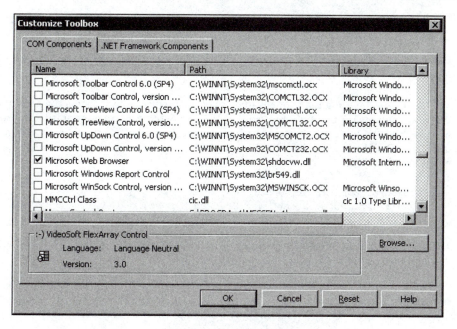

4. At the bottom of the Toolbox you'll now find an **Explorer** control:

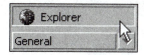

5. Select this and draw the control onto the form, like this:

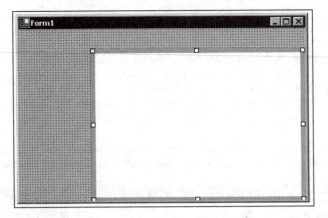

6. Using the Properties window, change the name of the control to **iePicture**. Also, set its **Anchor** property to **Top, Bottom, Left, Right**.

7. We're going to be using the browser to display the pictures, but it seems a shame not to prove that it actually works as a fully-functioning Web browser. So let's temporarily add some code to show how the full-blown features of Internet Explorer can be utilized within Windows forms in .NET. Double-click on the background of the form and add this code to the Load event handler:

```
Private Sub Form1_Load(ByVal sender As System.Object, _
        ByVal e As System.EventArgs) Handles MyBase.Load

    ' set the browser to a default page...
    iePicture.Navigate2("http://www.google.com/")

End Sub
```

Run the project, and you should see Google's home page. Try entering some search terms and you'll notice that this browser behaves in exactly the same way as the full Internet Explorer does

> If you try using the browser, you'll notice you don't have a toolbar, so if you want to
> go back a page, right-click on the page and select **Back**.

Adding a Web Reference

To use a web service, we need to add a **web reference** to the project. This will prompt Visual Studio
.NET to go away and create some classes for us that will let us call methods on the web service.

Try It Out – Adding a Web Reference

1. To add a web reference, we need the WSDL file that describes the web service. Open up your
web browser and point it at the `Service.asmx` file. If you've followed along the instructions
as given here, this should be http://localhost/PictureService/Service.asmx. However, if you
can't find the service, open the `PictureService` project and run it. You'll get the same
effect.

2. The problem we have here is that we've specified the server name as `localhost`. `localhost`
is a bit of Internet shorthand which means "this computer". This means that we're limited to
running the client on the same computer that the service is running on. This defeats the object of
the exercise a bit, because if you have more than one computer at your location it would be neat
to run the client on a different computer from that of the service. Replace `localhost` with the
network name of your computer (or wherever the service is running).

*If you don't know what this is, ask your systems administrator. Alternatively you can find the
network name of your own machine by opening the Control Panel and navigating to the
System / Network Identification menu.*

My computer is called `Chimaera`, so my URL would be:
http://Chimaera/PictureService/Service.asmx. Point the browser to the new URL and you
should see the same thing.

3. At the top of the page, you'll see a link to Service Description. This is a link to the WSDL file
that describes the web service.

Service

The following operations are supported. For a formal
definition, please review the **Service Description**.

4. Click Service Description. This will open a pretty lengthy XML document. Select everything in
the Address bar (which should be http://YourServer/PictureService/Service.asmx?WSDL), right-
click on the selection, and choose Copy. We'll need to paste this URL into Visual Studio .NET.

5. Go back to Visual Studio .NET. Using the Solution Explorer, right-click on the PictureClient
project and select Add Web Reference.

6. In the **Address** box of the new dialog, right-click and select **Paste**. Press the green arrow button to the right of the **Address** box. This will load the WSDL file and the right-hand side of the window will list a single Web service:

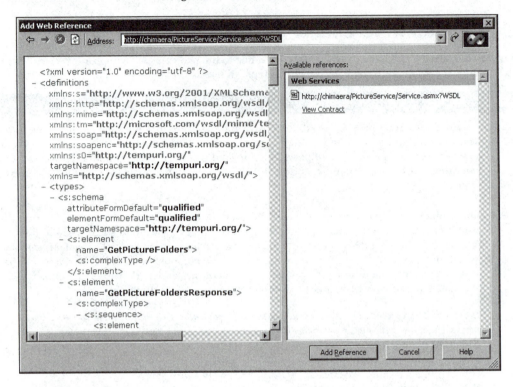

7. Click the **Add Reference** button.

8. A new web reference will be added to the Solution Explorer and this will match the name of the server (so either **localhost** or your computer name). Right-click the new reference and select **Rename**. Change the name to PictureService:

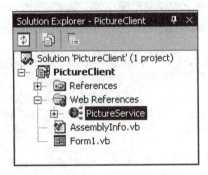

How It Works

At this point, Visual Studio .NET has successfully added a reference to the remote (or local) server. It's also created a new class for us called `PictureService.Service`. By creating instances of this object (as we're about to see) we can call methods on the web service.

The name that we choose when we rename the web service in Solution Explorer acts as the namespace for the new class.

In this case, we've used `PictureService`, *but if we hadn't renamed it from, say,* `localhost` *the new class that exposes the web service methods would be called* `localhost.Service`.

Displaying the Folder List

We can now call methods on the web service. Let's start off by adding a drop-down list to the project that will display a list of the remote picture subfolders by calling the `GetPictureFolders` method.

Try It Out – Displaying the Folder List

1. Open the Designer for Form1. Draw on a **ComboBox** control at the top of the form, like this:

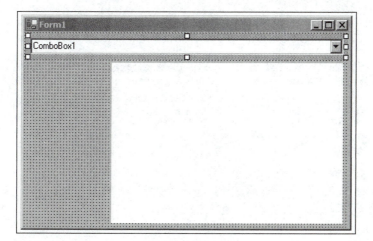

2. Using the Properties window, change the **Name** property to **cboFolders**. Clear the **Text** property. Change the **DropDownStyle** to **DropDownList** and the **AnchorProperty** to **Top, Left, Right**.

3. Double-click on the form background to open the `Load` event handler for the form. When we start the application, we'll want to run the remote `GetPictureFolders` method. Add this code:

```
Private Sub Form1_Load(ByVal sender As System.Object, _
        ByVal e As System.EventArgs) Handles MyBase.Load

    ' set the browser to a default page...
    iePicture.Navigate2("http://www.google.com/")
```

```
    ' get the pictures...
    Try

        ' create a connection to the service...
        Dim service As New PictureService.Service()

        ' get a list of the folders...
        Dim folderNames() As String
        folderNames = service.GetPictureFolders

        ' go through the list and add each name...
        Dim folderName As String
        For Each folderName In folderNames
            cboFolders.Items.Add(folderName)
        Next

    Catch ex As Exception
        HandleException(ex)
    End Try

End Sub
```

4. You'll notice a blue wavy line appear under `HandleException`. This is to indicate an error, since we haven't built this method yet, so let's add it now:

```
' HandleException - handle a Web service exception...
Private Function HandleException(ByVal e As Exception)

    ' loop through the inner exceptions...
    Do While Not e.InnerException Is Nothing
        e = e.InnerException
    Loop

    ' report the problem...
    MsgBox("An exception occured. " & e.Message)

End Function
```

> **Remember, if you need a refresher on how exceptions work, take a look at Chapter 11.**

5. Run the project. You'll notice the form takes a while to appear (the first connection to a Web service is often slower than the rest as it takes .NET a short time to get its "house in order" before establishing the connection), but when it does the folder names will be available if you drop down the list:

How It Works

OK, that wasn't complicated! Basically, .NET abstracts away a lot of the complexity involved in consuming a web service.

After pointing the web browser at Google, we start a `Try...Catch` block:

```
Private Sub Form1_Load(ByVal sender As System.Object, _
        ByVal e As System.EventArgs) Handles MyBase.Load

    ' set the browser to a default page...
    iePicture.Navigate2("http://www.google.com/")

    ' get the pictures...
    Try
```

It's very important that when consuming a web service you use exception handling around any code that could cause an exception. A lot of things can go wrong with connecting to a web service and passing data between service and client, and if anything does go wrong we'll get an exception. It's important that we handle them.

Next, we create an instance of the `PictureService.Service` class that Visual Studio created for us. At this point, we haven't connected to the web service – we've just prepared things for when we do:

```
        ' create a connection to the service...
        Dim service As New PictureService.Service()
```

The beauty of web services in .NET is that calling methods on a remote object is no different from calling methods on an object installed on your local machine. Here, we call `GetPictureFolders` and get back an array of strings:

```
        ' get a list of the folders...
        Dim folderNames() As String
        folderNames = service.GetPictureFolders
```

Once we have the array, we loop through each of the strings and add the folder name to the list:

```
' go through the list and add each name...
Dim folderName As String
For Each folderName In folderNames
    cboFolders.Items.Add(folderName)
Next
```

If an exception is thrown, we call `HandleException`:

```
Catch ex As Exception
    HandleException(ex)
End Try

End Sub
```

That's all we have to do to call the web service. But, before we go on let's take a look at `HandleException`.

The SOAP standard dictates that, whenever the service detects a problem, it must use an exception-handling model to tell the client about the problem.

> *Notice, we say, "model". Web services can be deployed on any platform, and that platform may well not have the great exception handling functionality that .NET has. But the principle is the same – shout about the problem and hope someone hears it.*

When .NET detects that an exception has been thrown on the server, it will wrap that exception in its own "problem on the server" exception. The actual exception that occurred on the server will be buried within the `InnerException` property, so `HandleException` has the logic to keep stepping down through the buried exceptions until it gets the one that the server actually threw:

```
' HandleException - handle a Web service exception...
Private Function HandleException(ByVal e As Exception)

    ' loop through the inner exceptions...
    Do While Not e.InnerException Is Nothing
        e = e.InnerException
    Loop

    ' report the problem...
    MsgBox("An exception occured. " & e.Message)

End Function
```

You can test out the exception handling by stopping the IIS service. To do this, click the **Start** button at the bottom of your screen and select **Run**. Enter this command:

```
net stop iisadmin
```

You'll see this and at some point you'll be prompted as to whether or not you want to continue. Enter *Y* and press *Return*:

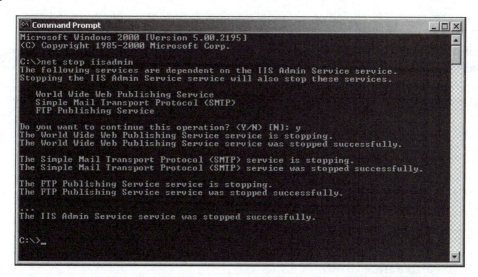

Now run the project and you'll see an exception.

To restart IIS, back at the command prompt enter:

```
iisreset
```

You'll see this:

Displaying the File List and Choosing Files

When we change the selected folder, we want to connect to the server once more and get a list of the files in the folder we request.

Try It Out – Displaying the File List

1. To display the file list, we need to create a new class that encapsulates the `PictureInfo` structures we're going to get back from the server. Create a new class using the Solution Explorer by right-clicking on the **PictureClient** project and selecting **Add | Class**. Call it **PictureItem**.

2. Add this code to `PictureItem`:

```
Public Class PictureItem

    Public PictureInfo As PictureService.PictureInfo

    ' Constructor...
    Public Sub New(ByVal info As PictureService.PictureInfo)
        PictureInfo = info
    End Sub

    ' ToString - provide a better representation of the object...
    Public Overrides Function ToString() As String
        Return PictureInfo.Name
    End Function

End Class
```

3. Go back to the Designer for **Form1**. Add a **ListBox** control to the form. Change its **Name** property to **lstFiles**. Set its **IntegralHeight** property to **False** and its **Anchor** property to **Top, Bottom, Left**:

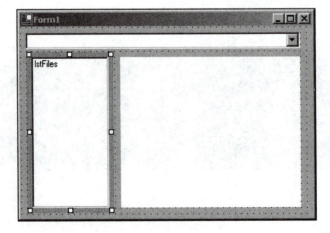

4. Double-click on the cboFolders drop-down list. This will create a new SelectedItemChanged handler. Add this code:

```
Private Sub cboFolders_SelectedIndexChanged(ByVal sender As _
        System.Object, ByVal e As System.EventArgs) _
        Handles cboFolders.SelectedIndexChanged

        ' what folder did we select?
        Dim folderName As String = _
            cboFolders.Items(cboFolders.SelectedIndex)

        ' clear the files list...
        lstFiles.Items.Clear()

        ' connect to the service again and get the files back...
        Try

            ' connect...
            Dim service As New PictureService.Service()

            ' get the files back...
            Dim pictureList() As PictureService.PictureInfo
            pictureList = service.GetPicturesInFolder(folderName)

            ' add the pictures to the list...
            Dim pictureInfo As PictureService.PictureInfo
            For Each pictureInfo In pictureList

                ' just add the name...
                lstFiles.Items.Add(New PictureItem(pictureInfo))

            Next

        Catch ex As Exception
            HandleException(ex)
        End Try

End Sub
```

5. After you've done that, go back to the Designer for **Form1** and double-click on the lstFiles list. Add this code to the new event handler:

```
Private Sub lstFiles_SelectedIndexChanged(ByVal sender As _
        System.Object, ByVal e As System.EventArgs) Handles _
        lstFiles.SelectedIndexChanged

        ' get the pictureitem...
        Dim item As PictureItem = lstFiles.Items(lstFiles.SelectedIndex)
        If Not item Is Nothing Then

            ' tell ie to show the picture...
```

```
        iePicture.Navigate2(item.PictureInfo.Url)

    End If

End Sub
```

6. Try running the project and selecting a picture from the list on the left. Internet Explorer should load the image:

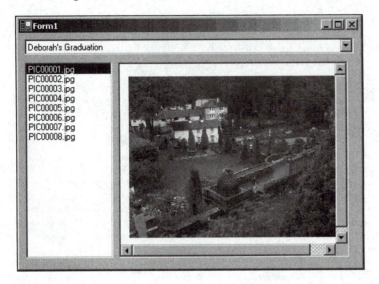

How It Works

The ListBox control in Windows forms works best if you can supply a custom-built object for each item. In our case, we built a separate object that contained an instance of a PictureInfo object and overloaded the ToString method available on all objects in .NET to return the Name property of PictureInfo:

```
Public Class PictureItem

    Public PictureInfo As PictureService.PictureInfo

    ' Constructor...
    Public Sub New(ByVal info As PictureService.PictureInfo)
        PictureInfo = info
    End Sub

    ' ToString - provide a better representation of the object...
    Public Overrides Function ToString() As String
        Return PictureInfo.Name
    End Function

End Class
```

When the item gets added to the list, the `ListBox` will call `ToString` on the object to get the value that should be displayed in the list. If we wanted, rather than returning `Name`, we could return the URL, in which case the list would appear as a list of URLs rather than a list of names.

One thing that's worth noting – the `PictureInfo` we have on the client is *not* the same object that we had on the server. Visual Studio .NET has also automatically created the `PictureInfo` class just like it did for the `Service` class. (This is why on the client `PictureInfo` is a **class**, whereas on the server it's actually a **structure**.)

When the drop-down list selection changes, we find the currently selected item, which is the folder name, and clear the file list:

```
Private Sub cboFolders_SelectedIndexChanged(ByVal sender As _
        System.Object, ByVal e As System.EventArgs) _
        Handles cboFolders.SelectedIndexChanged

    ' what folder did we select?
    Dim folderName As String = _
        cboFolders.Items(cboFolders.SelectedIndex)

    ' clear the files list...
    lstFiles.Items.Clear()
```

We then open up a `Try...Catch` so that we can manage any problems that occur:

```
    ' connect to the service again and get the files back...
    Try
```

Connecting the service is just a matter of creating a `Service` object again:

```
        ' connect...
        Dim service As New PictureService.Service()
```

Calling `GetPicturesInFolder` and providing the folder name retrieves the list of files contained in the folder as an array of `PictureInfo` objects. If the folder doesn't exist on the server, the service itself will throw an exception and this will find its way back and be "felt" as an exception in our own code that `HandleException` can deal with:

```
        ' get the files back...
        Dim pictureList() As PictureService.PictureInfo
        pictureList = service.GetPicturesInFolder(folderName)
```

When we have the array, we create new `PictureItem` objects and add them to the file list:

```
        ' add the pictures to the list...
        Dim pictureInfo As PictureService.PictureInfo
        For Each pictureInfo In pictureList
```

```
                    ' just add the name...
                    lstFiles.Items.Add(New PictureItem(pictureInfo))

            Next

        Catch ex As Exception
            HandleException(ex)
        End Try

    End Sub
```

When the selection on the file list itself changes, the currently selected item will be a `PictureItem` object. We can use the `PictureInfo` property of this object to get hold of the `PictureInfo` that was returned by the server, and then use the `Url` property of `PictureInfo` to find the URL that relates to the selected file, and tell Internet Explorer to go away and display that URL. We also check to make sure that `item` is not `Nothing` as this would cause an exception if the user clicked on the `lstFiles` control when no files were displayed:

```
    Private Sub lstFiles_SelectedIndexChanged(ByVal sender As _
            System.Object, ByVal e As System.EventArgs) _
            Handles lstFiles.SelectedIndexChanged

        ' get the pictureitem...
        Dim item As PictureItem = lstFiles.Items(lstFiles.SelectedIndex)
        If Not item Is Nothing Then

            ' tell ie to show the picture...
            iePicture.Navigate2(item.PictureInfo.Url)

        End If

    End Sub
```

This brings us to the end of our discussion of how to build and consume a Web service able to return arrays of simple and complex values back to the client. I hope you've seen just how easy building and consuming web services can be! To learn more about Web services please see *Beginning .NET Web Services with VB.NET* (ISBN 1-86100-725-6).

Summary

In this chapter, we introduced what's tipped to be the "next big thing" in Internet development: web services.

Web services work by allowing a developer to expose an object that's accessible through a web server. Web services are based on open standards like SOAP and WSDL and are underpinned by tried-and-tested technologies like HTTP and XML.

We started off this chapter by building a basic web service that could return some information, and also do something useful – namely return the square root of a number that we gave it. As a more practical example, we then built a web service (and web site, actually) that allowed the consumer to download a list of pictures from the service. With the service in place, we built a simple client application that connected to the web service and called methods on the remote object. We also briefly demonstrated how to utilize the COM interoperability layer on .NET in order to put Internet Explorer actually inside our application.

This concludes the final chapter of this book. You've come a long way over the course of these 19 chapters. You've learned about many things including: variables and constants, loops and branching structures, object-oriented programming, adding menus, dialog boxes, graphics, and controls to your applications, accessing databases and creating a web service.

We hope that you've found that this book has given you a thorough grounding in programming using Visual Basic .NET. If you want to pursue learning about Visual Basic .NET (and we hope that you will), you'll find a whole network of resources to help you. Appendix A, *Where to Now?* will give you some useful pointers on directions you might like to take next.

Happy programming!

Questions

1. What's the difference between a Web site and a Web service?

2. What is SOAP?

3. How do we mark a method as being available on a Web service?

4. What kinds of information can we return from a Web service method?

5. What's unusual about the way the Internet Explorer control is used in Windows forms?

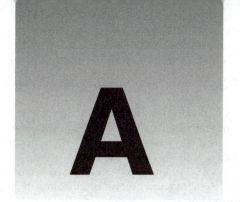

Where to Now?

Now that you've come to the end of this book, you should have a relatively good idea of how to put together an application using Visual Basic .NET. Although you have come a long way, there is still a lot further to go. Unfortunately, just learning the basic semantics of a language is often just not enough to turn you into a full-fledged programmer. This book is just one of the many steps you are going to take on your road to being a Visual Basic .NET programmer.

You should find that a great deal of information has been covered and even those of you with some experience of Visual Basic should have found a lot of it was new. Of course, this is only the beginning of the journey to becoming a Visual Basic .NET expert. Throughout this book, we have looked at a number of different subjects within Visual Basic .NET, some in more detail than others. What you should take away with you right now is a good firm foundation to continue your learning. The problem now is, "What next?"

Don't worry, in this appendix, we are going to offer you some advice on what your possible next step(s) could be. As you can imagine, there are a number of different routes open to any one person. The path you chose will probably depend on what your goal is or what you are being asked to do by your employer. Some of you will want to continue on at a more general level with some knowledge about all aspects of Visual Basic .NET, while others may want to drill down into more specific areas. Hopefully, we will give a possible answer for most of you to the question of "Where to now?"

We're not going to leave you high and dry to find your way blindly to the next level. This appendix is here to help you succeed in your quest for knowledge and experience. The most important piece of information you need now is where to look. For the rest of this appendix, we are going to look at available resources both on and offline to help you decide where you are going to go now.

Online Resources

Basically, there are thousands of places you can go online for help with any problems you may have. The good news is that many of them are free too. Whenever you come across a problem, and unfortunately, you will, there are always loads of people out there who are willing to help. These unknown souls range from others who are at the same stage as you and may have had a similar problem, to experts with a great deal of knowledge. The key is to not be intimidated and to use these resources as much as you like. Remember everyone was a complete beginner at some point and has had many of the same experiences as you.

In this section, we are going to begin by examining the P2P site provided by Wrox and then follow on with some of the more general sites around. If you can't find what you want through any of the sites listed here or if you have some time and want to explore, just search for Visual Basic .NET and you will be on your way!

P2P.Wrox.com

P2P provides programmer-to-programmer support on mailing lists, forums, and newsgroups in addition to a one-to-one e-mail system. You can join any of the mailing lists for author and peer support in Visual Basic .NET (plus any others you may be interested in).

You can choose to join the mailing lists and you can receive a weekly digest of the list. If you don't have the time or facilities to receive mailing lists, you can search the online archives using subject areas or keywords.

Should you wish to use P2P for online support, it can be done in a few simple steps:

1. Go to p2p.wrox.com where you'll find announcements about new lists, any removals, etc.

2. Click on the Visual Basic link in the list on the left side.

3. Choose which list you would be interested in, for example vb_dotnet, and click on the link on the screen.

4. At this point, you can either view the list without joining it or you can create an account in the list. If you wish to join, navigate through the buttons and screens, selecting a password and how you would like to receive the messages from the list, ending with Save.

That's all there is to using or becoming a member of P2P. These lists are moderated so you can be confident of the information presented by these lists. Also, junk and spam mail are deleted and your e-mail is protected by the unique Lyris system from web-bots that can automatically hoover up newsgroup mailing list addresses.

Microsoft Resources

Probably one of the first sites you'll intuitively turn to is the Microsoft site (www.microsoft.com). It only makes sense as it's full of information, including support, tips, hints, downloads, and newsgroups (news://msnews.microsoft.com/microsoft.public.dotnet.languages.vb).

There are also a number of sites on MSDN that you may find to be very helpful, including:

❑ Microsoft Developer Network site – http://msdn.microsoft.com

❑ Microsoft Visual Basic site – http://msdn.microsoft.com/vbasic/

❑ Microsoft Visual Studio site – http://msdn.microsoft.com/vstudio/

❑ .NET download site – http://msdn.microsoft.com/net

Other Resources

As said earlier, there are hundreds of sites online that discuss both Visual Basic and Visual Basic .NET. These sites give everything from news on moving from Visual Basic 6 to Visual Basic .NET, to listings of up and coming conferences worldwide. Although you can do a search for Visual Basic .NET, the number of sites returned can be extremely overwhelming. We are going to quickly look at two of these possible sites, one for the UK and one for the US.

In the UK, www.vbug.co.uk offers a wealth of information on Visual Basic .NET. This is the website for the **Visual Basic Users Group** (**VBUG**), which you can join. Besides the web site, this group holds meetings and an annual conference plus provides a magazine. On the web site, of course, there is a listing of further links and you may want to use this to start your search over the Internet.

In the US, you can get a journal, **The Visual Basic Programmers Journal**, from a similar user group. Again, this journal is backed by meetings and four yearly conferences along with a web site, http://www.devx.com/vsm/, which can give e-mail updates. On the web site, you have access to a number of different areas both in Visual Basic and other related and non-related .NET areas.

Of course, these are just two of the many out there to try to get you started. Some of you may decide to use these two and many of you may choose others as your favored sites, it's all up to you! What you need to remember though, is that the Internet is not the only place to find information so we'll go on to look at some resources not found on the Web.

Offline Resources (Books)

Wrox Press is committed to providing books that will help you develop your programming skills in the direction that you want. We have a selection of tutorial-style books that build on the VB.NET knowledge gained here. These will help you to specialize in particular areas. Here are details of a few of the key titles.

Beginning Visual Basic .NET Databases

(Wrox Press, ISBN 1-86100-555-5)

In Chapters 15 and 16, we began investigating how Visual Basic .NET can be used to access and program with databases. Databases are ubiquitous and all programmers need to know how to build programs to interact with them, so you'll probably want to develop your skills in this area. This book will provide a comprehensive beginner-level guide to this topic.

This book is for people with some basic experience of Visual Basic .NET and Access, who want to begin programming database applications with Visual Basic .NET.

The book covers:

❑ Database design and construction principles

❑ Building functional user interfaces for database access with Visual Basic .NET and MSDE

❑ Basic SQL

❑ ADO.NET and XML

❑ Basic Internet database applications using Web Forms and Web Services

Beginning VB.NET Web Programming in Visual Studio

(Wrox Press, ISBN 1-86100-736-1)

We saw in Chapter 17 that developing Web applications in ASP.NET and Visual Studio .NET is very similar to creating Windows applications. However, we only really scratched the surface of what's possible. *Beginning VB.NET Web Programming in Visual Studio* will teach you to transfer your existing VB.NET development skills to the Web, showing how to build powerful web-based solutions.

Beginning .NET Web Services with VB.NET

(Wrox Press, ISBN 1-86100-725-6)

Web Services are an exciting new technology that lets you expose functionality over the Web. Web Services provide an easy and powerful way to create networked applications, where different tiers exist on completely different machines – not just different assemblies on the same machine. This paves the way for powerful, distributed applications. *Beginning .NET Web Services with VB.NET* will show how to create and use these Web Services in Visual Basic .NET, opening the doors to a whole new way of building and distributing software.

One the other hand, if you are confident with the Visual Basic .NET skills, *Professional VB.NET 2nd Edition* (Wrox Press, ISBN 1-86100-716-7), provides a strong professional-level guide to the Visual Basic .NET language.

Professional VB.NET, 2nd Edition

(Wrox Press, ISBN 1-86100-716-7)

This book takes a deeper look at all aspects of Visual Basic .NET. It will establish you as an all-round Visual Basic .NET expert. However, it does assume a reasonable level of programming experience – so it's worth getting some practice at programming before trying to move on to this title.

Topics include:

- ❑ Introducing the Common Language Runtime
- ❑ Changes to data types, variables, error handling, and window creation in Visual Basic .NET
- ❑ Object inheritance
- ❑ Threading (having different methods executing at the same time)
- ❑ Integration with COM
- ❑ Using XML
- ❑ ADO.NET
- ❑ Web forms
- ❑ Web services
- ❑ Remoting
- ❑ Creating Windows services

Exercise Answers

Chapter 1 – Welcome to Visual Basic .NET

1. *Question:*
What Modified-Hungarian prefix should you use for a combo box? A label? A textbox?

Answer:
Combo boxes are given the prefix cbo. Labels are prefixed with lbl. Textboxes are prefixed with txt.

2. *Question:*
(*This assumes you set the Help Filter to Visual Basic and Related.*) Open the Help System and search for MessageBox. Notice how many topics are returned. Change the Help Filter option on the My Profile screen, to No Filter. Repeat the search for MessageBox. Did the Help System return more or fewer topics?

Answer:
If you search for the word MessageBox with the Help Filter setting at No Filter, you'll return many more topics than if you searched with it set to Visual Basic and Related. The drawback is that you get topics that are only relevant if you're working in C# or C++ as well. Be sure to select the right Help Filter setting for your needs.

3. *Question:*
When creating a button, how would you make the button respond to a keyboard hot key?

Answer:
You can create a keyboard hot key by using an ampersand (&) in the Text property before the correct letter. To create a hot key for Cancel button, you would enter &Cancel as the Text property.

Chapter 2 – Writing Software

1. *Question:*
What is camel casing?

Answer:
Code written in camel casing has a hump, for example `camelCasing`.

2. *Question:*
What are we more likely to use – variables that store integer values or variables that store decimal values?

Answer:
In day-to-day programming, we're more likely to use integer variables than decimal variables. Integers are usually used to keep track of the state of the program, whereas you'll probably find that you rarely want to perform calculations.

3. *Question:*
How do you define a variable that contains character data?

Answer:
We use `As String`, like this:

```
Dim s As String
```

4. *Question:*
Write a line of code that multiplies n by 64, using the shorthand operator.

Answer:
Here's the answer:

```
n *= 64
```

5. *Question:*
What is an algorithm?

Answer:
An algorithm is a step-by-step description of *how* the problem that can be solved in software is going to be solved. It's the base currency of all software and good algorithm skills are essential if you want to become a good programmer.

Chapter 3 – Controlling the Flow

1. *Question:*
What are the six possible arithmetic operators that can be used with an `If` statement?

Answer:
Equal to (=), not equal to (<>), less than (<), less than or equal to (<=), greater than (>), and greater than or equal to (>=).

2. *Question:*
How do we do case-insensitive string comparisons?

Answer:
The `String.Compare` method can be used to perform case insensitive string comparisons in an `If` statement. In a `Select Case` statement, we use `ToLower` or `ToUpper`.

3. *Question:*
What kind of loop is appropriate for iterating through items in an array?

Answer:
If we have a set of objects provided in an array, we can use a `For Each...Next` loop to automatically loop through each item in the array.

4. *Question:*
How can we exit a loop early?

Answer:
In the case of a `For` loop, we can use the `Exit For` statement. For `Do` loops, we can use `Exit Do`.

5. *Question:*
Why is a `Select Case` statement useful?

Answer:
A `Select Case` statement is useful for making decisions based on a set of possible values. It is more efficient and easier to read than using combinations of `If...End If` statements.

Chapter 4 – Building Objects

1. *Question:*
What's the difference between a public and private member?

Answer:
A private member can only be accessed by functions, methods, and properties defined on the same class. A public member is accessible to anyone consuming the class.

2. *Question:*
How do you decide if something should be a property or a method? Give an example.

Answer:

A property describes something about the object, whereas a method does something to the object. On a class representing a TV, the current channel should be described as a property because it's a fact about the state of the TV, whereas if you wanted to turn the TV on you'd use a method because that's something you're doing to the object.

3. *Question:*

What is a constructor? Why are they useful?

Answer:

A constructor is a block of code that gets called whenever the object is created. They are useful whenever you need the object to be in a certain state before the consumer starts using it.

4. *Question:*

What class do all other classes in .NET inherit from?

Answer:

All classes in .NET inherit from `System.Object`.

5. *Question:*

What is overriding?

Answer:

Overriding is providing a new implementation for a method or a property that already exists on the base class (the class that the new class inherits from).

Chapter 5 – The Microsoft .NET Framework

1. *Question:*

What's the general premise behind .NET?

Answer:

The premise behind .NET is to create an abstraction away from the underlying operating system and processor. Microsoft's motivation for doing this is to relieve the dependence on the Windows platform itself.

2. *Question:*

What's the similarity between .NET and Java?

Answer:

.NET is very similar to Java, but whereas Java from day one has said "write once, run on many platforms", .NET is saying "write in many languages, run on one platform... for now".

3. *Question:*

What is the Framework Class Library?

Answer:
The Framework Class Library is a vast set of classes that abstracts the various subsystems of the operating system away in to a set of easy-to-use classes that we can use in our programs.

4. *Question:*
What is interoperation?

Answer:
Interoperation (or interop) is the principle of accessing software not built in .NET.

5. *Question:*
How is application code compiled in .NET?

Answer:
Code is compiled from the source language into Microsoft Intermediate Language, or MSIL. When the code is executed, it is further compiled from MSIL into the native language understood by the processor.

Chapter 6 – Working with Data Structures

1. *Question:*
What is an array?

Answer:
An array is a set of similar data that is held in a list. Providing an index can access individual items in this list.

2. *Question:*
What's the difference between a structure and a class?

Answer:
The differences are subtle, but the two main differences are that you don't have to use the New keyword with a structure before you can use it and you cannot inherit from a structure. It's also relatively tricky to convert from one to the other once you've chosen and started using the structure/class, so it's worth choosing wisely before you write a lot of code based on it.

3. *Question:*
What's the best way to build a collection?

Answer:
The best way to build a collection is to inherit a new class from System.Collections.CollectionBase and provide implementations for Add and Remove methods and provide an Item property. This approach makes working with lists of classes or structures that you build very easy for both yourself and other developers.

4. *Question:*
What is an enumeration?

Answer:
An enumeration is a list, based on a simple data type such as an integer or a string, that limits the values that can be stored in a specific variable.

5. *Question:*
What is a `Hashtable`?

Answer:
A Hashtable is a way of associating a key with a value. You can build a Hashtable up by adding items and giving each item a specific key. Coming back to the Hashtable later on with a specific key will unlock the item and make it available to you again.

Chapter 7 – Building Windows Applications

1. *Question:*
What event is fired when the mouse pointer crosses over a button's boundary to hover over it? What event is fired as it moves the other direction, away from the button?

Answer:
The button's `MouseEnter` event is fired when the mouse pointer "enters" a control. As the mouse pointer leaves the `MouseLeave` event is fired.

2. *Question:*
How can we prevent our controls from being accidentally deleted or resized?

Answer:
We can lock our controls to the form by using the Format | Lock Controls menu option.

3. *Question:*
What should we consider when choosing names for controls?

Answer:
Controls should be named whenever you need to refer to them from code. You should choose a convention for naming, and in this chapter, we've made the control names descriptive of what the control itself does. We also prefix the name with the type of control (`btnOK` for example) and make sure we follow camel casing.

4. *Question:*
What's special about the toolbar and status bar controls?

Answer:
The toolbar and status bar controls automatically dock themselves to an edge of the form. When the form is resized, these docked controls stay in their relative positions glued to whatever edge they're attached to.

5. *Question:*
How can you add a separator to your toolbar?

Answer:
Separators are created by setting the Style property of a toolbar button to Separator.

Chapter 8 – Dialogs

1. *Question:*
Write the code to display a message box with a message and caption of your choice, no icon, and OK and Cancel buttons. The Cancel button should be the default button.

Answer:
The answer to this question is shown in the code fragment below. Since we did not want to display an icon in the message box, we specified Nothing where we would have normally have specified a constant from the MessageBoxIcon enumeration:

```
MessageBox.Show("This is your message.", "caption goes here", _
    MessageBoxButtons.OKCancel, Nothing, MessageBoxDefaultButton.Button2)
```

To display the same message using MsgBox, write this:

```
MsgBox("This is your message.", _
    MsgBoxStyle.OKCancel + MsgBoxStyle.DefaultButton2, _
    "caption goes here")
```

2. *Question:*
How can you display the Open dialog with a default file name already displayed?

Answer:
Set the FileName property to the file name that should be displayed in the Name drop-down box before calling the ShowDialog method.

3. *Question:*
How can you change the color of the text displayed in a textbox using the Color dialog?

Answer:
Set the ForeColor property of the textbox to the Color property of the ColorDialog.

4. *Question:*
When you save a file using the SaveFileDialog control and the file already exists, you are prompted to replace it. If you choose Yes, does the file actually get overwritten?

Answer:

Yes and no. Remember that the SaveFileDialog is merely a means to specify where the file should be saved. It does not actually save the file; we use the StreamWriter class for this. However, clicking on the **Save** button in the dialog when a file already exists will cause a prompt to be displayed. Clicking on the **Yes** button in this prompt will cause the SaveFileDialog control to return a DialogResult of OK. Then your code would overwrite the existing file.

5. *Question:*

The Font dialog has been displayed and you have chosen a font, clicked the **OK** button, and applied the font. When you display the Font dialog again, do you need to set the Font property to have the same font displayed as was previously selected?

Answer:

No, the FontDialog control is smart enough to display the same font again. The reason for this is that the FontDialog control never goes out of scope until you end the program. However, if you created your own object and displayed the Font dialog as shown in the code fragment below, the same font that was previously selected would not be displayed:

```
' Declare and set a font object...
Dim objFont As FontDialog = New FontDialog()

' Show the dialog...
If objFont.ShowDialog() = DialogResult.OK Then
    ' If OK then set the font in the text box...
    txtFile.Font = objFont.Font
End If

' Clean up...
objFont = Nothing
```

You would need to set the Font property to the font that was previously selected before calling the ShowDialog method. The reason for this is that the Font object that we declared goes out of scope as soon as we are done with it because we set it to Nothing:

```
' Declare and set a font object...
Dim objFont As FontDialog = New FontDialog()

' Set the Font property before calling the ShowDialog method...
objFont.Font() = txtFile.Font

' Show the dialog...
If objFont.ShowDialog() = DialogResult.OK Then
    ' If OK then set the font in the text box...
    txtFile.Font = objFont.Font
End If

' Clean up...
objFont = Nothing
```

Chapter 9 – Creating Menus

1. *Question:*
How do you specify an access key for a menu item?

Answer:
Use an ampersand in the text. For example, to specify an access key of *F* for the File menu, you specify the text &File. If a menu or menu item contains an ampersand in the name you need to specify two consecutive ampersands in order to not have it interpreted as an access key. For example, suppose you had the menu item Tools & Tips. In order to have the first T as the access key and the ampersand in the text displayed correctly, you would need to specify the text &Tools && Tips.

2. *Question:*
Can you specify any shortcut key that you want?

Answer:
Absolutely! As long as it is in the list of shortcuts in the drop-down list in the ShortCut property. The shortcut that you assign here will be the shortcut executed for this menu item.

3. *Question:*
Can you specify checkmarks and radiochecks in a context menu?

Answer:
Yes. You use the same properties as you did when you did this in the menu.

4. *Question:*
Can you create submenu items in a context menu?

Answer:
Yes. When creating a context menu item, a text area appears to the right and to the bottom of the context menu item that you are working on.

5. *Question:*
Can you create as many menu items as you want?

Answer:
Yes, however, keep in mind that menus should be short and to the point. If you have too many menu items, it will be hard to locate the correct menu item. You should consider splitting a long menu into two or more separate menus.

Chapter 10 – Advanced Object-Oriented Techniques

1. *Question:*
What's the advantage of using a class library?

Answer:

The advantage of a class library is that objects, and therefore the functionality encapsulated within them, can easily be reused in other applications. All we have to do is build the classes in a separate library (or move them from existing projects into new class libraries) and include references between library and application.

2. *Question:*

In our `Favorites Tray` application, why did we create a new class that inherited from `System.Windows.Forms.MenuItem`?

Answer:

The menu items we added had to know which `WebFavorite` instance they related to in order that Internet Explorer could be told to open the proper URL. Creating a new class inherited from `MenuItem` means that we can add a new property for storing the `WebFavorite` instance.

3. *Question:*

Why do we create our own collections?

Answer:

When a developer wants to work with our classes, it's useful to have a separate class optimized for moving around lists. Creating a new class inherited from `System.Collections.CollectionBase` and adding a few properties makes this very easy for them.

4. *Question:*

How much time usually elapses between an object no longer having references and the Garbage Collector cleaning it up?

Answer:

Trick question! There is no way to determine the time that will elapse between the final reference to an object being released and the object being cleaned up by the Garbage Collector.

5. *Question:*

What is the difference between `Dispose` and `Finalize`?

Answer:

The `Dispose` method should be called by the consumer as soon as the resources used by the object are no longer required. The Garbage Collector automatically calls the `Finalize` method.

Chapter 11 – Debugging and Error Handling

1. *Question:*

How do you know when you have a syntax error in your code?

Answer:
The Visual Studio.NET development environment will underline syntax errors caused by improper use of methods and properties of objects and for variables not declared when the Option Explicit option or statement is turned on, which is turned on by default.

2. *Question:*
We know that we can set a breakpoint with a hit counter, but can we set a conditional breakpoint?

Answer:
Yes. To set a conditional breakpoint, click on the line of code where you want the breakpoint such as a variable and then click on the **Debug | New Breakpoint** menu item to invoke the New Breakpoint dialog. In the New Breakpoint dialog, click on the **Condition** button to invoke the Breakpoint Condition dialog and enter the condition in which you want the breakpoint activated. For example, to break when the intLineCount variable is equal to 5, enter intLineCount = 5 in the Breakpoint Condition dialog.

3. *Question:*
What information does the Locals window show?

Answer:
It shows all variables and objects "visible" to the current function or procedure executing, and allows you to change these values.

4. *Question:*
If you are stepping through your code line by line, how can you bypass stepping through the code of a called procedure?

Answer:
Click on the **Step Over** icon on the **Debug** toolbar or click on the **Debug | Step Over** menu item.

5. *Question:*
Can you define multiple Catch blocks in structured error handling?

Answer:
Yes. You can test for specific errors as shown in the code below:

```
Try
    intX = 1
    intY = 0
    intResult = intX / intY
Catch e As DivideByZeroException
    ...
    error handling code here
    ...
Catch e As OverflowException
    ...
    error handling code here
    ...
```

```
Finally
    ...
    code here always executes
    ...
End Try
```

6. *Question:*
When we use our program to open a file with a blank line, like this:

```
Line 1
Line 2

Line 4
```

we do not get the hoped for result – only the first two lines get displayed.

Is this a syntax, execution, or logic error? What could we do to fix it?

Answer:
This is a logic error. The code compiles (so it is not a syntax error), and runs without raising any complaints (so it is not an execution error). However, there is something in our code that means the program doesn't do what we want it to (our *logic* is flawed).

The reason for this problem is the following line:

```
Loop While currentLine <> Nothing
```

which assumes that if there are no characters in a line, we have reached the end of the file. We could have found this line by stepping through the program, and finding that this was the line where the program made the wrong decision to stop reading the file. The way to fix it is to change the condition so that it uses a more reliable test:

```
Loop While myReader.Peek <> -1
```

This condition now peeks ahead at the file, and checks if there is any more data to read. If there is not, the Peek method returns –1 – so we go around the loop *until* the Peek method returns –1. Then we stop looping and carry on with the rest of the program.

Chapter 12 – Building Class Libraries

1. *Question:*
What are the advantages of using Class Libraries?

Answer:
Class Libraries enable us to reuse code without having access to the original source, or recompiling the reused code into every program that uses it. There are lots of other advantages of course, but these are the main ones.

2. *Question:*
What is the purpose of signing an assembly?
Answer:
To prove that it was written by a specific person or organization.

3. *Question:*
What is the purpose of the GAC (Global Assembly Cache)?

Answer:
To store copies of a given version of an assembly, to prevent conflicts with assemblies that have the same name but for some reason do different things. It's also a useful way of sharing assemblies between applications.

Chapter 13 – Creating Your Own Custom Controls

1. *Question:*
How do we define an event called `SomethingHappened` in a user control?

Answer:
At a minimum, an event should be defined by:

```
Event SomethingHappened(ByVal sender As Object, _
    ByVal e As System.EventArgs)
```

However, an event can have any number of additional parameters.

2. *Question:*
What keyword is used to fire (or raise) an event?

Answer:
To raise an event, you use the `RaiseEvent` keyword, and supply the event that you want to raise along with values for the event parameters. For example, to raise the `SomethingHappened` event, we'd write something like this:

```
RaiseEvent SomethingHappened(Me, New System.EventArgs)
```

3. *Question:*
How does a control know if it's design time or run time?

Answer:
A control has a property called `DesignMode`, which is `True` if the control is in design mode and `False` if it is in run mode.

Chapter 14 – Graphics

1. *Question:*
   What is a pixel?

   Answer:
   A pixel (or picture element) is a tiny square. Pixels are grouped together into bitmaps whereupon a programmer can set the color of each pixel individually in order to build up a picture.

2. *Question:*
   What object do we need in order to draw on a control, form, or other object?

   Answer:
   Whenever we want to draw with .NET, we need to be given a System.Drawing.Graphics object. This object exposes most of the methods we need in order to draw shapes and images.

3. *Question:*
   Describe the two-phases of painting in Windows.

   Answer:
   Whenever a "thing" in Windows (control, form, menu, whatever) needs painting, it is invalidated. Windows knows which windows are invalidated and which ones need drawing. In the first phase, the invalid area is erased. In the second phase, we get the opportunity to paint our user interface.

4. *Question:*
   What is the difference between client coordinates and screen coordinates?

   Answer:
   Client coordinates do not change when the user moves the form around on the desktop. Our client area always starts at (0,0) irrespective of where the form is on the screen. Screen coordinates on the other hand describe any point on the screen, starting at (0,0) in the top-left.

5. *Question:*
   How can we create Color objects with .NET?

   Answer:
   System.Drawing.Color objects come from a number of sources. We can either use shared properties on the Color object to get hold of common system colors, for example Color.Blue or Color.Red. Alternatively, we can use Color.FromArgb and provide a red component, a blue component, and a green component to make up any color that we wish. Finally, we can use the SystemBrushes and SystemPens classes to get hold of brushes and pens used for painting in the user-defined Windows user interface object colors.

Chapter 15 – Accessing Databases

1. *Question:*
Do you have to prefix the field name with the table name as shown in the following SQL SELECT statement?

```
SELECT Customer.[Customer Name]
FROM Customer
```

Answer:
No. You only need to prefix the field name with the table name when you are selecting data from multiple tables and the tables contain the same field names.

2. *Question:*
How do you sort the data in a DataGrid control?

Answer:
Once the DataGrid is displayed, simply click on the column header of the column that you want sorted to have the data sorted in ascending order. Clicking on the same again will sort the data in that column in descending order.

3. *Question:*
How do you populate the DataSet component with data?

Answer:
Use the Fill method of the OleDbDataAdapter as shown in the following code fragment.

```
OleDbDataAdapter1.Fill(DataSet1)
```

4. *Question:*
What two items does the OleDbDataAdapter need before it can retrieve data from a database?

Answer:
An SqlCommand component and a SQL SELECT statement.

Chapter 16 – Database Programming with SQL Server and ADO.NET

1. *Question:*
When is it better to bind to a DataView object instead of straight to a DataSet object?

Answer:
When you need just a subset of data from the DataSet object or you need the ability to sort or search for data.

2. *Question:*

When using the `OleDbCommand` object, you set the `CommandText` property to a SQL string to be executed. How do you use a stored procedure instead of a SQL string?

Answer:

You simply need to specify the stored procedure name and set the `CommandType` property to indicate that the `CommandText` property contains a stored procedure, as shown in the following code fragment:

```
objCommand.CommandText = "usp_sel_authortitles"
objCommand.CommandType = CommandType.StoredProcedure
```

3. *Question:*

What do the words beginning with @ mean in the following SQL string?

```
objCommand.CommandText = "INSERT INTO titles " & _
    "(title_id, title, type, price, pubdate) " & _
    "VALUES(@title_id,@title,@type,@price,@pubdate);" & _
    "INSERT INTO titleauthor (au_id, title_id) VALUES(@au_id,@title_id)"
```

Answer:

They represent placeholders for data that will be inserted by the `SqlParameter` objects in the `Parameters` collection.

4. *Question:*

When binding a control, when is it necessary to first clear the binding as shown in the following example?

```
txtLastName.DataBindings.Clear()
txtLastName.DataBindings.Add("Text", objDataView, "au_lname")
```

Answer:

If the control has been previously bound as was done in the `Binding Example` program.

Chapter 17 – Web Forms

1. *Question:*

How do Web Server controls differ from HTML controls?

Answer:

Web Form controls provide a more feature-rich object model and can be programmed at the server. This allows us to bind data to these controls and to also use VB code, which we are most familiar with.

2. *Question:*

Can HTML controls also be programmed at the server?

Answer:

Yes and no. HTML controls cannot be programmed at the server. However, HTML controls can be converted to HTML Server controls by right-clicking on the control while in Design mode and choosing the Run As Server Control from the context menu. This will convert the "pure" HTML control to a server-side control, which can be programmed against at the server.

3. *Question:*

What does the `IsPostBack` property do?

Answer:

The `IsPostBack` property returns a `True/False` value indicating whether the page has been posted back from a client request or whether the page is being loaded for the first time.

4. *Question:*

Can we mix the code that we use? For example, can we write server-side code in a form class and also write server-side code in a script block in the HTML?

Answer:

Yes. However, remember that if you want to write code in a server-side script block that is for an event for a control, that you must specify the event in the control and then specify the procedure name that should be executed.

The example control below specifies the procedure to be executed when the `OnClick` event is fired. When you click on the button in a form, the form will be posted back to the server and the procedure `Button1_Click` in server-side script will be executed:

```
<asp:Button id=Button1 runat="server" Text="Server-Side" OnClick=Button1_Click>
```

Chapter 18 – Visual Basic.NET and XML

1. *Question:*
What does XML stand for?

Answer:
eXtensible Markup Language.

2. *Question:*
What is XML primarily used for?

Answer:
XML is an open standard that's primarily used in software integration. It allows an application vendor to define its own text-based format for data that can be transferred around the network and Internet and, with a little cooperation, be easily understood by third parties.

3. *Question:*
What kinds of data can `XmlSerializer` work with?

Answer:

XmlSerializer ultimately wants to work with simple data types, like strings, integers, Booleans, and doubles. It can work with complex structures and classes, providing that each of the properties it tries to work with ultimately ends up as a simple type.

4. *Question:*

How do you stop XmlSerializer working with a property that it might otherwise try to serialize?

Answer:

By putting the System.Xml.Serialization.XmlIgnore attribute before a property or public member variable, you can tell XmlSerializer not to bother trying to work with the property.

5. *Question:*

Which class can be used to iterate through an XML document one node at a time?

Answer:

System.Xml.XmlTextReader is the object that we used to work through an XML document node-by-node.

Chapter 19 – Web Services

1. *Question:*

What's the difference between a web site and a web service?

Answer:

A web *site* is designed to be used by a human being. A web *service* is designed to be used by a piece of computer software.

2. *Question:*

What is SOAP?

Answer:

SOAP, or Simple Object Access Protocol, is the open standard that defines how web services and client applications exchange information. Requests are made of the web service through a SOAP request document, which is an XML document transferred over a web server like Microsoft IIS. When the service wants to return a value, it's packaged in another XML document called a SOAP response document.

3. *Question:*

How do we mark a method as being available on a web service?

Answer:

To mark a method as being available on a web service, we use the WebMethod attribute at the beginning of the method definition.

4. *Question:*
What kinds of information can we return from a web service method?

Answer:
We can return all kinds of information from a web service, including simple values and arrays of simple values. If we want to return a set of information (such as customer record, or information about a picture), we can package the results as a separate structure or class.

5. *Question:*
What's unusual about the way the Internet Explorer control is used in Windows forms?

Answer:
There is no .NET version of Internet Explorer because Microsoft hasn't got round to porting it from COM to .NET technologies. When we want to use the Internet Explorer control in our applications, we have to use the COM interoperability layer. Luckily, Visual Studio does this for us, so if we want to use any old COM controls in our project we just have to add them to the Toolbox.

Index

X

Z

Register your book on Wrox.com!

When you download this book's code from wrox.com, you will have the option to register.

What are the benefits of registering?

- You will receive updates about your book
- You will be informed of new editions, and will be able to benefit from special offers
- You became a member of the "Wrox Developer Community", giving you exclusive access to free documents from Wrox Press
- You can select from various newsletters you may want to receive

Registration is easy and only needs to be done once. After that, when you download code books after logging in, you will be registered automatically.

Just go to www.wrox.com

wrox

Programmer to Programmer™

Registration Code: 76123EZJS0G2BP04

Wrox writes books for you. Any suggestions, or ideas about how you want
information given in your ideal book will be studied by our team.
Your comments are always valued at Wrox.

Free phone in USA 800-USE-WROX
Fax (312) 893 8001

UK Tel.: (0121) 687 4100   Fax: (0121) 687 4101

Beginning VB.NET 2nd Edition – Registration Card

Name _____

Address _____

_____

_____

City _____ State/Region _____

Country _____ Postcode/Zip _____

E-Mail _____

Occupation _____

How did you hear about this book?

☐ Book review (name) _____

☐ Advertisement (name) _____

☐ Recommendation _____

☐ Catalog _____

☐ Other _____

Where did you buy this book?

☐ Bookstore (name) _____ City_____

☐ Computer store (name) _____

☐ Mail order_____

☐ Other _____

What influenced you in the purchase of this book?

☐ Cover Design ☐ Contents ☐ Other (please specify):

_____

How did you rate the overall content of this book?

☐ Excellent   ☐ Good   ☐ Average   ☐ Poor

What did you find most useful about this book? _____

_____

What did you find least useful about this book? _____

_____

Please add any additional comments. _____

_____

What other subjects will you buy a computer book on soon?

_____

What is the best computer book you have used this year?

_____

Note: This information will only be used to keep you updated
about new Wrox Press titles and will not be used for
any other purpose or passed to any other third party.

Programmer to Programmer™

Note: If you post the bounce back card below in the UK, please send it to:

Wrox Press Limited, Arden House, 1102 Warwick Road,
Acocks Green, Birmingham B27 6HB. UK.

Computer Book Publishers